The Guide to the
PROFESSIONAL
CONDUCT
OF SOLICITORS

Eighth Edition
1999

The Guide to the
PROFESSIONAL CONDUCT OF SOLICITORS

Eighth Edition
1999

Editorial Board

Sam Wilson, M.A., *Solicitor, Birketts, Law Society Council Member,*
Robert Venables, *Solicitor, Bircham & Co, Law Society Council Member,*
Christopher Heaps LL.B., F.C.I.T., *Solicitor and Traffic Commissioner, former Law Society Council Member and former Chairman of the Adjudication and Appeals Committee*
Andrew Hopper, *Solicitor, Jay, Benning & Peltz*

General Editor

Nicola Taylor, B.A.(Hons.), *Solicitor, the Law Society's Professional Ethics Division*

REF 344·1
GUI

law society publishing

2 8045 00016 9428

© The Law Society 1999

ISBN 1 85328 645 1

First published as
A Guide to the Professional Conduct and Etiquette of Solicitors,
Sir Thomas Lund CBE, 1960
A Guide to the Professional Conduct of Solicitors, 1974
The Professional Conduct of Solicitors, 1986
The Professional Conduct of Solicitors (updated), 1987
The Guide to the Professional Conduct of Solicitors, 1990
The Guide to the Professional Conduct of Solicitors, 1993
The Guide to the Professional Conduct of Solicitors, 1996

The material in Annexes 2A, 3A, 3B, 10A, 14A, 14B,
14C, 14D, 27A, 28A and 30A is Crown copyright.

This 8th edition published by The Law Society
113 Chancery Lane
London WC2A 1PL

Typeset and printed by Thanet Press Limited, Margate

Contents

PART II – INTERNATIONAL ASPECTS OF PRACTICE

PART III – RELATIONSHIP WITH THE CLIENT

Page

Page

PART VII – COMPLAINTS AND DISCIPLINE

Foreword

As we enter the new millennium, the rules and principles which govern solicitors' professional conduct continue to evolve to reflect changes in society and the role of solicitors in society. This edition of the Guide reflects the developments which have taken place over the last three years; there are no major shifts in approach from earlier editions.

The Society has, however, set up a working party to re-examine the principles which underlie its rule making function, and to enhance consistency in rule making in line with those principles. As part of this process we intend to listen to the profession and input from members will be crucial. I hope the result will be a rule book which reflects both the realities of running a solicitor's practice in the twenty-first century and the importance of protecting the public interest. The next edition may well, therefore, be a very different type of rule book.

Whatever changes take place, one thing remains certain: a proper standard of conduct is an essential hallmark of our profession and vital to the administration of justice. This Guide is intended to help solicitors maintain that standard.

I thank the Editorial Board and the staff in Professional Ethics for their hard work in producing this edition of the Guide.

Michael Mathews
President
The Law Society

1998–1999

Introduction

This eighth edition of the Guide replaces the 1996 edition. The text has been updated to reflect changes to the practice rules, guidance and legislation.

New to this edition

There are no new chapters, but new material includes the following:

- ▶ new practice rule 11 (name of a solicitor's firm) – see **3.04** (p.69);

- ▶ new practice rule 13 (supervision and management of a practice) – see Annex 3C (p.113);

- ▶ immigration guidelines – see **12.05** (p.246) and Annex 12C (p.262);

- ▶ 'yellow card' warning on banking instrument fraud – see Annex 12B, p.258;

- ▶ new practice rule 15 and the Solicitors' Costs Information and Client Care Code – see Chapter 13 (p.265);

- ▶ guidance on disclosure of conveyancing files to lenders – see Annex 16C (p.341);

- ▶ attending advocates at court; amendments to conduct requirements – see **20.04** (p.365);

- ▶ new mediation codes – see Annexes 22A and 22B (pp.419 and 428);

- ▶ amendments to practice rule 6 (avoiding conflicts of interest in conveyancing, property selling and mortgage related matters) – see **25.01** (p.455);

- ▶ amendments to practice rule 12 (investment business) – see **27.21** (p.533);

- ▶ Solicitors' Accounts Rules 1998 – see Chapter 28 and Annex 28B (pp.677 and 684);

- ▶ Solicitors' Indemnity Rules 1998 (see Annex 29A, p.793) – later indemnity rules are published separately.

This Guide was prepared during the implementation of the civil justice reforms. Where possible, references have been changed in the light of the reforms. For information on the reforms, see Annex 21I (p.409).

The structure of the Guide

The Editorial Board have drawn on the results of independent research into readers' reactions to the seventh edition. Readers' comments have been used to enhance the content, structure and presentation of this edition.

For example, in the seventh edition, the practice rules were integrated into the relevant chapters. In this edition the relevant practice rules remain in each chapter, but as a result of readers' comments, are also set out in full in Annex 1A (p.9).

Chapter 3 has been reorganised so that the information appears in a more logical order.

As an experiment, the Editorial Board thought it would be helpful to illustrate, with an introductory note, the core values of Chapter 15 (conflict of interests) and Chapter 16 (confidentiality).

Chapter 28 is much shorter than in earlier editions because the accounts rules have been consolidated, and now include all the guidance which previously appeared in the chapter. The 1998 accounts rules appear in Annex 28B, p.684.

Presentation

This new edition of the Guide has retained all the useful features that were introduced in the last edition:

▶ a 'thumb mark' appears in the right-hand margin to help locate each chapter;

▶ a 'mini contents box' appears at the start of each chapter and lists the topics covered in the chapter and its annexes;

▶ extensive cross-referencing, including page numbers;

▶ the contact details for organisations referred to in the text have been moved to the front of the Guide, as have the tables of cases and statutes;

▶ the index has been enhanced to make this new edition easier to use.

The cover reflects the new style of publications produced by the Law Society.

The future

In the past, changes have been published, from time to time, in the Professional Standards Bulletin. The Society, however, is reviewing how solicitors are to be regulated. The outcome of this debate may well affect how regulation is presented to the profession – in particular, electronic publication may be used more in the future.

Readers are invited to give their views on this edition, and suggestions for any future changes, to the Editorial Board, Professional Ethics (see p.xv for contact details).

August 1999

Useful addresses

Set out below is a list of names, addresses and telephone numbers of Law Society departments and external bodies whose functions are mentioned in the Guide.

Law Society

Website: www.lawsociety.org.uk
Central switchboard: 0870 606 2500

113 Chancery Lane
London WC2A 1PL
DX 56 London/Chancery Lane

International Directorate	0870 606 2500 (central switchboard)
Multi-party actions co-ordinator	0870 606 2522
Practice Advice Service	0870 606 2522
Professional Adviser	020 7320 5712 Fax: 020 7320 5673

Ipsley Court
Berrington Close
Redditch, Worcestershire B98 0TD
DX 19114 Redditch

Legal Education	0870 606 2500 (central switchboard)
Professional Ethics Division	0870 606 2577 Fax: 020 7320 5897
Professional Indemnity Section	0870 606 2577 Fax: 020 7320 5897

Regulation and Information Services   0870 606 2555
Fax: 020 7320 5862
(accountants' reports, PCs and s.12 matters)
020 7320 5964
(all other matters)

Solicitors' Assistance Scheme   020 7320 5795
Fax: 020 7320 5897

Office for the Supervision of Solicitors
Victoria Court
8 Dormer Place
Leamington Spa
Warwickshire CV32 5AE
DX 292320 Leamington Spa 4   0870 606 6565

Client Care Workshops   01926 822001

Fraud Intelligence Unit   020 7320 5703

Monitoring and Investigation Unit   01926 822114

Red Alert   01926 431671

Remuneration Certificates   01926 822007/8/9

Solicitors Practice Unit   01926 820082

External bodies

Association of British Insurers
51 Gresham Street
London EC2V 7HQ
Tel: 020 7600 3333
Fax: 020 7696 8999

British Records Association
c/o London Metropolitan Archives
40 Northampton Road
London EC1R 0HB
Tel: 020 7833 0428
Fax: 020 7833 0416

British Recovered Paper Association
Alexander House
Station Road
Aldershot
Hants GU11 1BG
Tel: 01793 889624
Fax: 01793 886182 (marked 'BRPA')

Council for Licensed Conveyancers
16 Glebe Road
Chelmsford
Essex CM1 1QG
DX: 121925 Chelmsford 6
Tel: 01245 349599
Fax: 01245 341300

Council of Mortgage Lenders
3 Savile Row
London W1X 1AF
DX: 81551 Savile Row, London
Tel: 020 7437 0655
Fax: 020 734 6416

Financial Services Authority
25 The North Colonnade
Canary Wharf
London E14 5HS
Tel: 020 7676 1000
Fax: 020 7676 1099

General Council of the Bar
3 Bedford Row
London WC1R 4DB
DX: 240 London/Chancery Lane
Tel: 020 7242 0082
Fax: 020 7831 9217

Institute of Legal Executives
Kempston Manor
Kempston
Bedford MK42 7AB
DX: 124780 Kempston 2
Tel: 01234 841000
Fax: 01234 840373

Joint Money Laundering Steering Group
Pinners Hall
105–108 Old Broad Street
London EC2N 1EX
Tel: 020 7216 8863
Fax: 020 7216 8907

Lawyers' Support Group
Barry Pritchard
Tel: 01766 514277

Legal Aid Board Head Office
85 Gray's Inn Road
London WC1X 8AA
DX: 450 London
Tel: 020 7813 1000
Fax: 020 7813 8631
  (Legal Department)

Legal Services Ombudsman
22 Oxford Court
Oxford Street
Manchester M2 3WQ
DX: 18569 Manchester 7
Tel: 0161 236 9532
Fax: 0161 236 2651

Lord Chancellor's Department
Selborne House
54–60 Victoria Street
London SW1E 6QW
DX: 117000 Victoria
Tel: 020 7210 8500
  (Enquiry Line)

Marston Book Services
P.O. Box 312
Abingdon
Oxon OX14 4YH
DX: 130431 Didcot 2
Tel: 01235 465656
Fax: 01235 465660

Master of the Rolls
Royal Courts of Justice
Strand
London WC2A 2LL
DX: 44450 Strand
Tel: 020 7936 6000
Fax: 020 7936 7475

National Criminal Intelligence
 Service
Duty Officer
Economic Crime Unit
P.O. Box 8000
London SE11 5EN
Tel: 020 7238 8271
 (office hours)
020 7238 8607
 (outside office hours)
Fax: 020 7238 8286

Official Receiver
21 Bloomsbury Street
London WC1B 3SS
DX: 120875 Bloomsbury 6
Tel: 020 7637 1110
Fax: 020 7636 4709

Official Solicitor
81 Chancery Lane
London WC2A 1DD
DX: 0012 London/Chancery Lane
WC2
Tel: 020 7911 7127
Fax: 020 7911 7105

Personal Investment Authority
25 The North Colonnade
Canary Wharf
London E14 5HS
Tel: 020 7676 1000
Investors Helpline: 020 7417 7001
Fax: 020 7676 10999

Public Trust Office
(Court of Protection)
Stewart House
24 Kingsway
London WC2B 6JX
DX: 37965 Kingsway
Tel: 020 7664 7000
Fax: 020 7664 7705

SolCare
P.O. Box 6
Porthmadog
Gwynedd LL49 9ZE
Tel: 01766 512222
Fax: 01766 514761

Solicitors Benevolent Association
1 Jaggard Way
Wandsworth Common
London SW12 8SG
DX: 41608 Balham
Tel: 020 8675 6440
Fax: 020 8675 6441

Solicitors Disciplinary Tribunal
113 Chancery Lane
London WC2A 1PL
DX: 56 London/Chancery Lane
Tel: 020 7242 0219
Fax: 020 7320 5967

Solicitors Indemnity Fund Ltd
100 St John Street
London EC1M 4LR
DX: 46601 Barbican
Tel: 020 7566 6000
Fax: 020 7566 6006
 (General)
020 7566 6003
 (Claims)

List of abbreviations

ABI   Association of British Insurers
ADR   Alternative dispute resolution
AJA   Administration of Justice Act
CAT   Cost, Access and Term
CCBE   Council of the Bars and Law Societies of the European Union
CHAPS   Clearing House Automated Payments System
CML   Council of Mortgage Lenders
CPD   Continuing professional development
DIB   Discrete investment business
DIE   Designated investment exchange
EC   European Community
EEA   European Economic Area
EIS   Enterprise investment scheme
EU   European Union
FIMBRA   Financial Intermediaries, Managers and Brokers Regulatory Association
FSA   Financial Services Act/Financial Services Authority
IBA   International Bar Association
ISA   Individual Savings Account
IMRO   Investment Management Regulatory Organisation
IPS   Inadequate professional services
ISD   Investment Services Directive
IVA   Individual voluntary arrangement
LSO   Legal Services Ombudsman
LAUTRO   Life Assurance and Unit Trust Regulatory Organisation
LCD   Lord Chancellor's Department
MNP   Multi-national practice
NVQ   National vocational qualification
OEIC   United Kingdom open-ended investment company
OSS   Office for the Supervision of Solicitors
PACE   Police and Criminal Evidence Act 1984
PDC   Property display centre
PEP   Personal equity plan
PIA   Personal Investment Authority
PTP   Permitted third party
PVA   Partnership voluntary arrangement
RFL   Registered foreign lawyer
RPB   Recognised professional body
SAS   Solicitors' Assistance Scheme
SEAL   Solicitors' Estate Agency Limited
SERPS   State Earnings Related Pension Scheme

SFA	Securities and Futures Authority
SIB	Securities and Investments Board
SIBR	Solicitors' Investment Business Rules
SIF	Solicitors' Indemnity Fund/Solicitors Indemnity Fund Limited
SIPR	Solicitors' Incorporated Practice Rules
SIP	Solicitor insolvency practitioner
SOPR	Solicitors' Overseas Practice Rules
SRO	Self-regulatory organisation

Table of cases

All references are to pages, not paragraphs.

Table of statutes

All references are to pages, not paragraphs.

Table of statutory instruments, EU directives, rules, codes, etc.

All references are to pages, not paragraphs.

    THE GUIDE TO THE PROFESSIONAL CONDUCT OF SOLICITORS 1999

PART I – SOLICITORS IN PRACTICE

Chapter 1

Rules and principles of professional conduct

1.01 Practice rule 1 (basic principles)

'A solicitor shall not do anything in the course of practising as a solicitor, or permit another person to do anything on his or her behalf, which compromises or impairs or is likely to compromise or impair any of the following:

(a) the solicitor's independence or integrity;

(b) a person's freedom to instruct a solicitor of his or her choice;

(c) the solicitor's duty to act in the best interests of the client;

(d) the good repute of the solicitor or of the solicitors' profession;

(e) the solicitor's proper standard of work;

(f) the solicitor's duty to the Court.'

Solicitors' Practice Rules 1990, rule 1

1.02   Basic principles – additional guidance

1.   'Solicitors' in the Guide means solicitors of the Supreme Court of England and Wales.

2.   A rule identical to rule 1 of the Solicitors' Practice Rules appears as rule 3 of the Solicitors' Overseas Practice Rules 1990, making it clear that the basic principles apply to English and Welsh solicitors wherever they practise.

3.   For the application and interpretation of the Solicitors' Practice Rules 1990, see rule 18 (Annex 1A at p.28).

4.   Practice rule 1 sums up the basic principles of conduct governing the professional practice of solicitors. These principles stem from the ethical duties imposed on solicitors by the common law and it is arguable that no further rules or guidance are required. However, to assist both the public and the profession, further practice rules have been made by the Council and this Guide has been prepared.

5.   The Guide comprises, in addition to the practice rules and other statutory material, the Council's interpretation of the basic principles summarised in rule 1, as applied to the various circumstances arising in the course of a solicitor's practice.

6.   Where two or more of the principles in practice rule 1 come into conflict, the determining factor in deciding which principle should take precedence must be the public interest, and especially the public interest in the administration of justice. For examples see Annex 21F (Guidance – citation of criminal convictions – misleading the court, p.403) and **16.02** (circumstances which override confidentiality, p.325).

7.   The following are instances where acting in accordance with rule 1(c) (client's best interests) would bring the solicitor into conflict with rule 1(b) (freedom of choice of solicitor), and where the public interest demands that the latter take precedence:

(a)   A solicitor would breach rule 1 (and be guilty of unprofessional conduct) if he or she were to pass on to another person any requirement of the solicitor's client that that person instruct a solicitor other than the solicitor of that person's choice. A solicitor should cease to act for any client whom he or she knows to have made such a requirement direct to the other side, unless the client agrees to retract the requirement.

It would, for example, be wrong for solicitor X, acting for a landlord, to require that a prospective tenant use a solicitor other than solicitor Y because solicitor X (or the landlord) knew that solicitor Y had already advised another prospective tenant that a lease contained unfavourable terms.

(b)   A solicitor would breach rule 1 if he or she were to pass on to another person any requirement by the solicitor's client that the other person's solicitor must agree not to act for other parties in other matters.

It would, for example, be wrong for solicitor X, acting for a defendant in litigation, to offer a settlement which included a provision that the claimant's solicitor Y refrain from acting for other claimants against the defendant in other, future matters. Equally, it would be wrong for solicitor Y to accept any such restriction.

However, a solicitor may nevertheless be unable to act for other potential claimants where information has been disclosed under compulsion, and the information has not been referred to in open court. The solicitor would be unable to use the information for other purposes. In such a case the solicitor's duty to the Court (rule 1(f)) would take precedence over the principle of freedom of choice of solicitor (rule 1(b)).

8.   The civil justice reforms (see Annex 21I, p.409 for summary) impose new requirements on solicitors. The duties owed under rule 1(c) (client's best interests) are tempered by the new requirements (e.g. cases should be pursued only in a way which is proportionate to the likely benefit; the court will not allow every point to be pursued; some procedural tactics will no longer be permitted).

1.03   Sources

The requirements of solicitors' professional conduct derive from both statutory and non-statutory sources. The latter include Law Society guidance on conduct, which is treated as authoritative by the Compliance and Supervision Committee, the Solicitors Disciplinary Tribunal and the Court.

1.   Statutory provisions which regulate solicitors' professional conduct are:

(a)   the Solicitors Act 1974, the Administration of Justice Act 1985 and the Courts and Legal Services Act 1990;

(b)   other statutes, such as the Financial Services Act 1986;

(c)   rules, orders and regulations made under statute, such as the Solicitors' Practice Rules 1990 (see Annex 1A, p.9);

(d)   codes and guidance made under statutory rules, such as the Solicitors' Publicity Code 1990 (see Annex 11A, p.229);

(e)   principles, rules and codes applied under statutory rules, such as the Statement of Principle of the Securities and Investments Board (now the Financial Services Authority) (see Annex 27C, p.610).

2.   Non-statutory sources are:

    (a)   the common law, which has developed and elaborated the basic principles of conduct;

    (b)   Law Society guidance on conduct, including:

        ▶   the principles and other guidance contained in the chapters and annexes of the Guide;

        ▶   the Solicitors' Anti-Discrimination Code (see **7.02**, p.167);

        ▶   the International Code of Ethics of the International Bar Association (see Annex 9B, p.192);

    (c)   decisions of the Compliance and Supervision Committee and its predecessors, the Solicitors Disciplinary Tribunal, the Master of the Rolls and the Court on matters of complaint, regulation and discipline.

3.   The statutory and non-statutory bases of conduct are closely intertwined:

    (a)   A statutory rule may be based on a common law ethical requirement, such as practice rule 10 on receipt of commissions from third parties (see **14.13**, p.283).

    (b)   Non-statutory guidance may be based on an interpretation of statutory rules, such as the guidance on claims to specialisation and particular expertise (see **11.03** note 4, p.223).

    (c)   Practice rule 1 (see **1.01**, p.1) sums up, in the form of a statutory rule, the basic principles of conduct derived from the common law.

    (d)   If a change in non-statutory guidance amounts to an alteration in the rules as to the conduct required of solicitors in exercising a right of audience or right to conduct litigation, the change requires to be approved by the Lord Chancellor and the four designated judges under section 29 and Schedule 4 to the Courts and Legal Services Act 1990.

4.   The requirements of professional conduct should not be confused with the requirements of the general law of contract or tort, or the requirements of the criminal law, even though the requirements of conduct may in some cases follow or closely parallel the general legal requirements. For the general law on solicitors, reference should be made to the appropriate authorities, including *Cordery on Solicitors* (currently the 9th edition, Butterworths).

5.   Some items appearing in the annexes, whilst closely connected with conduct requirements, are reproduced in the Guide for information rather than as requirements of conduct. These are designated as 'practice information'.

1.04   Practice rules

Under section 31 of the Solicitors Act 1974 the Council of the Law Society makes rules governing the professional practice, conduct and discipline of solicitors.

1.   The Solicitors' Practice Rules 1990 (see Annex 1A, p.9) summarise the basic principles of professional conduct and make specific provision for a number of aspects of solicitors' practice.

2.   Various detailed codes have been made under provisions in the practice rules:

   (a)   the Solicitors' Publicity Code 1990 (see Annex 11A, p.229);

   (b)   the Solicitors' Introduction and Referral Code 1990 (see Annex 11B, p.238);

   (c)   the Employed Solicitors Code 1990 (see Annex 4A, p.152);

   (d)   the Solicitors' Separate Business Code 1994 (see Annex 3E, p.129);

   (e)   the Law Society's Code for Advocacy (see Annex 21A, p.385).

3.   The Solicitors' Anti-Discrimination Rule 1995 (see Annex 1B, p.31) prohibits discrimination on grounds of race, sex, sexual orientation and disability.

4.   The Solicitors' Investment Business Rules 1995 regulate the investment business activities of firms which have been issued with an investment business certificate by the Society (see Annex 27B, p.562).

5.   The Solicitors' Overseas Practice Rules 1990 regulate the professional conduct of English and Welsh solicitors practising as such outside England and Wales (see Annex 9A, p.180).

6.   The Solicitors' Incorporated Practice Rules 1988 regulate recognised bodies (incorporated practices) – see Annex 3D, p.118. The Solicitors' Practice Rules, Anti-Discrimination Rule, Investment Business Rules and Overseas Practice Rules, as well as non-statutory guidance, apply to recognised bodies as they apply to solicitors.

7.   The Solicitors' Practice Rules, Anti-Discrimination Rule and Investment Business Rules, as well as non-statutory guidance, apply to registered foreign lawyers practising with solicitors in a multi-national partnership – see rule 18(1A)(b) of the Solicitors' Practice Rules 1990 (Annex 1A at p.29). An incorporated practice of solicitors and registered foreign lawyers is regulated in the same way as an incorporated practice of solicitors.

1.05 Accounts rules

Solicitors are required to comply with accounts rules made under section 32 of the Solicitors Act 1974, and to submit an annual accountant's report under section 34 of the Act.

1. The Solicitors' Accounts Rules 1998 regulate the handling of clients' money and controlled trust money, the payment of deposit interest and the accounting records which must be maintained (see Annex 28B, p.684).

2. Rule 26 of the Solicitors' Investment Business Rules 1995 deals with bills relating to discrete investment business (see Annex 27B at p.582).

3. Section 34 of the Solicitors Act 1974 (accountants' reports) appears in Annex 28A, p.681.

4. Part F of the Solicitors' Accounts Rules 1998 regulates the submission and content of accountants' reports (see Annex 28B, at p.720).

5. Rules 12–16 of the Solicitors' Overseas Practice Rules 1990 (see Annex 9A at p.185) regulate the handling of clients' money and trust money, the payment of deposit interest, the accounting records which must be maintained, and the submission and content of accountants' reports. Rule 9(3) of the Overseas Practice Rules (at p.184) applies rules 12–16 to certain solicitors practising through overseas corporations.

1.06 Indemnity rules

Under section 37 of the Solicitors Act 1974 the Council has made rules which establish the Solicitors' Indemnity Fund to provide professional indemnity cover for solicitors in private practice.

1. The Solicitors' Indemnity (Enactment) Rules 1998 and the Solicitors' Indemnity Rules 1998 (see Annex 29A, p.793) require principals in private practice to contribute to the Indemnity Fund, to provide information to Solicitors Indemnity Fund Limited, and to co-operate in claims handling. For details of the indemnity scheme see Chapter 29, p.782.

2. The Solicitors' Indemnity Rules apply to recognised bodies (incorporated practices) as they apply to firms of solicitors. For details see **29.07**, p.790. Rule 13 of the Solicitors' Incorporated Practice Rules 1988 (see Annex 3D at p.122) provides for compulsory top-up cover for certain recognised bodies.

3. The Solicitors' Indemnity Rules apply to multi-national partnerships and to registered foreign lawyers in partnership with solicitors as they apply to solicitors' practices and to solicitor principals. For details, see **29.01**, p.782.

4. The Employed Solicitors Code 1990 (see Annex 4A, p.152) governs in-house solicitors who in the course of employment act for clients other than

the employer. The code contains requirements on professional indemnity cover:

(a) paragraphs 1(d) and (f) are of general application and contain provisions about indemnity cover when acting for a client other than the employer;

(b) paragraph 7(a)(v) prescribes the indemnity cover required for law centres, charities and other non-commercial advice services;

(c) paragraph 8(b) prescribes the indemnity cover required for commercial legal advice services.

5. Rule 17 of the Solicitors' Overseas Practice Rules 1990 prescribes the indemnity cover required by solicitors practising outside England and Wales (see Annex 9A at p.189).

1.07   Waivers and other dispensations

Most of the rules affecting the conduct of solicitors, as well as the Training Regulations, contain power for the Council of the Law Society to grant waivers.

1. Waivers must be in writing, and may be revoked by the Society. See, for example, rule 17 of the Solicitors' Practice Rules 1990 (Annex 1A at p.28).

2. Other dispensations which the Council is empowered to grant under the primary legislation or under the rules include:

(a) dispensation under section 34(1) of the Solicitors Act 1974 (see Annex 28A, p.681) and a waiver of rule 35 of the Solicitors' Accounts Rules 1998 from the obligation to submit an accountant's report;

(b) approval under the Solicitors' Accounts Rules 1998 (rule 22(1)(h) or rule 22(2)(h) – see Annex 28B at p.705) to draw money from a client account.

3. Where previous rules have been repealed, waivers of those rules have now expired. This applies to waivers of the Solicitors' Practice Rules 1936/72, 1975, 1987 and 1988 and the Solicitors' Overseas Practice Rules 1987, and to waivers of the previous versions of rules 5 and 6 of the Solicitors' Practice Rules 1990. For the Council statement on waivers of the previous version of rule 13 (supervision and management of an office) see Annex 3C at p.117.

4. The Council's powers are delegated to a number of senior Law Society staff. Applications for waivers and other dispensations should be addressed to Professional Ethics, the Professional Indemnity Section, Regulation and Information Services or Legal Education, as appropriate (see p.xv for contact details).

5.   Apart from the provisions in respect of granting dispensations from the requirement to deliver an accountant's report, there is no power to waive the Solicitors' Accounts Rules 1998 or the Solicitors' Anti-Discrimination Rule 1995.

1.08   Behaviour outside legal practice

Solicitors are officers of the Court, and must conduct themselves so as not to bring the profession into disrepute.

1.   Solicitors, whether practising or not, are officers of the Supreme Court. Certain standards of behaviour are required of solicitors, as officers of the Court and as members of the profession, in their business activities outside legal practice and even in their private lives. Disciplinary sanctions may be imposed if, for instance, a solicitor's behaviour tends to bring the profession into disrepute.

2.   When solicitors are acting on their own behalf, whether in conveyancing, litigation or any other legal matter, they are expected to observe the same standards of conduct as are required in the course of practice.

1.09   Advice and help

Confidential advice and help are available on matters relating to professional conduct.

1.   Professional Ethics are almost always able to advise in confidence, and can always give telephone advice on a 'no names' basis.

2.   The Solicitors' Assistance Scheme is administered by Professional Ethics with the assistance of local law societies. The members of the Scheme are independent, experienced and sympathetic solicitors. They provide confidential advice to solicitors who are experiencing problems of a financial or personal nature, or who are having difficulty in coping with the pressures of practice, or who are facing Tribunal proceedings or action by the Office for the Supervision of Solicitors. No charge is made for an initial interview. Details of Scheme members in or near a solicitor's home town, or in a different part of the country, may be obtained from Professional Ethics (see p.xv for contact details).

3.   The Lawyers' Support Group is a self-help group offering confidential help to lawyers who need assistance with an alcohol or drugs problem – see p.xv for contact details. The Group is independent of the Law Society.

4.   SolCare is a registered charity independent of the Law Society. It helps solicitors and their staff who need assistance with alcohol and drugs related problems, stress and depression. It provides a confidential service. See p.xv for contact details.

Annex 1A

Solicitors' Practice Rules 1990

(with consolidated amendments to 1st October 1999)

Rules dated 18th July 1990 made by the Council of the Law Society with the concurrence of the Master of the Rolls under section 31 of the Solicitors Act 1974 and section 9 of the Administration of Justice Act 1985, regulating the English and Welsh practices of solicitors, registered foreign lawyers and recognised bodies and, in respect of Rule 12 only, regulating the English and Welsh and overseas practices of such persons in the conduct of investment business in or into any part of the United Kingdom.

Rule 1 (Basic principles)

A solicitor shall not do anything in the course of practising as a solicitor, or permit another person to do anything on his or her behalf, which compromises or impairs or is likely to compromise or impair any of the following:

    (a)   the solicitor's independence or integrity;

    (b)   a person's freedom to instruct a solicitor of his or her choice;

    (c)   the solicitor's duty to act in the best interests of the client;

    (d)   the good repute of the solicitor or of the solicitors' profession;

    (e)   the solicitor's proper standard of work;

    (f)   the solicitor's duty to the Court.

Rule 2 (Publicity)

Solicitors may at their discretion publicise their practices, or permit other persons to do so, or publicise the businesses or activities of other persons, provided there is no breach of these rules and provided there is compliance with a Solicitors' Publicity Code promulgated from time to time by the Council of the Law Society with the concurrence of the Master of the Rolls.

Rule 3 (Introductions and referrals)

Solicitors may accept introductions and referrals of business from other persons and may make introductions and refer business to other persons, provided there is no breach of these rules and provided there is compliance with a Solicitors' Introduction and Referral Code promulgated from time to time by the Council of the Law Society with the concurrence of the Master of the Rolls.

Rule 4 (Employed solicitors)

(1) Solicitors who are employees of non-solicitors shall not:

    (a) choose an advocate; nor

    (b) exercise any extended right of audience under one of the Law Society's higher courts qualifications; nor

    (c) as part of their employment do for any person other than their employer work which is or could be done by a solicitor acting as such;

in any way which breaches the Employed Solicitors Code promulgated from time to time by the Council of the Law Society with the concurrence of the Master of the Rolls.

(2) Solicitors who are employees of multi-national partnerships shall not be regarded as "employees of non-solicitors" for the purpose of this rule.

Rule 5 (Providing services other than as a solicitor)

Solicitors must comply with the Solicitors' Separate Business Code in controlling, actively participating in or operating (in each case alone, or by or with others) a business which:

    (a) provides any service which may properly be provided by a solicitor's practice, and

    (b) is not itself a solicitor's practice or a multi-national partnership.

Rule 6 (Avoiding conflicts of interest in conveyancing, property selling and mortgage related services)

(1) (General)

This rule sets out circumstances in which a solicitor may act for more than one party in conveyancing, property selling or mortgage related services, in connection with:

    (i) the transfer of land for value at arm's length;

    (ii) the grant or assignment of a lease, or some other interest in land, for value at arm's length; or

    (iii) the grant of a mortgage of land.

The rule must be read in the light of the notes.

    Notes

    (i) "Solicitor" (except where the notes specify otherwise) means a solicitor, his or her practice, and any associated practice, and includes a SEAL; and

    "associated practices" are practices with at least one principal in common;

    a "principal" is a sole practitioner, a partner in a practice (including a registered foreign lawyer partner), a director of a recognised body, a member of or beneficial owner of a share in a recognised body, or a recognised body; and

    a "SEAL" (Solicitors' Estate Agency Limited) means a recognised body which:

    (a) does not undertake conveyancing;

(b) is owned jointly by at least four participating practices which do not have any principals in common and none of which own a controlling majority of the shares; and

(c) is conducted from accommodation physically divided from, and clearly differentiated from that of any participating practice; and

a "participating practice" means a practice one or more of whose principals is a member of, or a beneficial owner of a share in, the SEAL.

(ii) "Property selling" means negotiating the sale for the seller.

(iii) "Mortgage related services" means advising on or arranging a mortgage, or providing mortgage related financial services, for a buyer; and

"seller" and "buyer" include lessor and lessee.

(iv) Whether a transaction is "at arm's length" will depend on the relationship between the parties and the context of the transaction, and will not necessarily follow from the fact that a transaction is at market value, or is stated to be on arm's length terms.

A transaction would not usually be at arm's length, for example, if the parties are:

related by blood, adoption or marriage;

the settlor of a trust and the trustees;

the trustees of a trust and its beneficiary or the beneficiary's relative;

personal representatives and a beneficiary;

the trustees of separate trusts for the same family;

a sole trader or partners and a limited company set up to enable the business to be incorporated;

associated companies (i.e. where one is a holding company and the other is its subsidiary within the meaning of the Companies Act 1985, or both are subsidiaries of the same holding company); or

a local authority and a related body within the meaning of paragraph 6(b) of the Employed Solicitors Code 1990.

(v) "Mortgage" includes a remortgage.

(vi) Nothing in the rule allows a solicitor to act in breach of rule 6A(5) (acting for seller and one of two prospective buyers), or any other rule or principle of professional conduct.

(2) *(Solicitor acting for seller and buyer)*

(a) A solicitor must not act for seller and buyer:

(i) without the written consent of both parties;

(ii) if a conflict of interest exists or arises; or

(iii) if the seller is selling or leasing as a builder or developer.

(b) Otherwise, a solicitor may act for seller and buyer, but only if:

(i) both parties are established clients; or

(ii) the consideration is £10,000 or less and the transaction is not the grant of a lease; or

(iii) there is no other qualified conveyancer in the area whom either the seller or the buyer could reasonably be expected to consult; or

(iv) seller and buyer are represented by two separate offices in different localities, and:

    (A) different solicitors, who normally work at each office, conduct or supervise the transaction for seller and buyer; and

    (B) no office of the practice (or an associated practice) referred either client to the office conducting his or her transaction; or

(v) the only way in which the solicitor is acting for the buyer is in providing mortgage related services; or

(vi) the only way in which the solicitor is acting for the seller is in providing property selling services through a SEAL.

(c) When a solicitor's practice (including a SEAL) acts in the property selling for the seller and acts for the buyer, the following additional conditions must be met:

    (i) different persons must conduct the work for the seller and the work for the buyer; and if the persons conducting the work need supervision, they must be supervised by different solicitors; and

    (ii) the solicitor must inform the seller in writing, before accepting instructions to deal with the property selling, of any services which might be offered to a buyer, whether through the same practice or any practice associated with it; and

    (iii) the solicitor must explain to the buyer, before the buyer gives consent to the arrangement:

        (A) the implications of a conflict of interest arising; and

        (B) the solicitor's financial interest in the sale going through; and

        (C) if the solicitor proposes to provide mortgage related services to the buyer through a SEAL which is also acting for the seller, that the solicitor cannot advise the buyer on the merits of the purchase.

Notes

(i) If a builder or developer acquires a property in part exchange, and sells it on without development, he or she is not, for the purpose of this rule, selling "as a builder or developer".

(ii) The test of whether a person is an "established client" is an objective one; that is, whether a reasonable solicitor would regard the person as an established client.

A seller or buyer who is instructing the solicitor for the first time is not an established client.

A person related by blood, adoption or marriage to an established client counts as an established client.

A person counts as an established client if selling or buying jointly with an established client.

(iii) The consideration will only count as £10,000 or less if the value of any property given in exchange or part exchange is taken into account.

(iv) Even where none of the other exceptions apply, a SEAL may act for the seller, and provide mortgage related services to the buyer; one of the participating practices may do the buyer's conveyancing, and another participating practice may do the seller's conveyancing.

(v)   *"Solicitor"*

in paragraph (2)(b)(iv)(A), means any individual solicitor conducting or supervising the matter; and

in paragraph (2)(c)(i), means the individual solicitor supervising the transaction.

(3)   *(Solicitor acting for lender and borrower)*

[Note: Paragraph 3 of rule 6 comes into force on 1st October 1999. For the version of rule 6(3) which is in force prior to 1st October 1999, see Professional Standards Bulletin No. 18.]

(a)   A solicitor must not act for both lender and borrower on the grant of a mortgage of land:

    (i)   if a conflict of interest exists or arises;

    (ii)   on the grant of a private mortgage of land at arm's length;

    (iii)   if, in the case of an institutional mortgage of property to be used as a private residence only, the lender's mortgage instructions extend beyond the limitations contained in paragraphs (3)(c) and (3)(e), or do not permit the use of the certificate of title required by paragraph (3)(d); or

    (iv)   if, in the case of any other institutional mortgage, the lender's mortgage instructions extend beyond the limitations contained in paragraphs (3)(c) and (3)(e).

(b)   A solicitor who proposes to act for both lender and borrower on the grant of an institutional mortgage of land, must first inform the lender in writing of the circumstances if:

    (i)   the solicitor or a member of his or her immediate family is a borrower; or

    (ii)   the solicitor proposes to act for seller, buyer and lender in the same transaction.

(c)   A solicitor acting for both lender and borrower in an institutional mortgage may only accept or act upon instructions from the lender which are limited to the following matters:

    (i)   taking reasonable steps to check the identity of the borrower (and anyone else required to sign the mortgage deed or other document connected with the mortgage) by reference to a document or documents, such as a passport, precisely specified in writing by the lender;

           following the guidance in the Law Society's "green card" warning on property fraud and "blue card" warning on money laundering;

           checking that the seller's solicitors or licensed conveyancers (if unknown to the solicitor) appear in a current legal directory or hold practising certificates issued by their professional body;

           and, in the case of a lender with no branch office within reasonable proximity of the borrower, carrying out the money laundering checks precisely specified in writing by the lender;

    (ii)   making appropriate searches relating to the property in public registers (for example, local searches, commons registration searches, mining searches), and reporting any results specified by the lender or which the solicitor considers may adversely affect the lender; or effecting search insurance;

(iii)   making enquiries on legal matters relating to the property reasonably specified by the lender, and reporting the replies;

(iv)   reporting the purchase price stated in the transfer and on how the borrower says that the purchase money (other than the mortgage advance) is to be provided; and reporting if the solicitor will not have control over the payment of all the purchase money (other than a deposit paid to an estate agent or a reservation fee paid to a builder or developer);

(v)   reporting if the seller or the borrower (if the property is already owned by the borrower) has not owned or been the registered owner of the property for at least six months;

(vi)   if the lender does not arrange insurance, confirming receipt of satisfactory evidence that the buildings insurance is in place for at least the sum required by the lender and covers the risks specified by the lender; giving notice to the insurer of the lender's interest and requesting confirmation that the insurer will notify the lender if the policy is not renewed or is cancelled; and supplying particulars of the insurance and the last premium receipt to the lender;

(vii)   investigating title to the property and appurtenant rights; reporting any defects revealed, advising on the need for any consequential statutory declarations or indemnity insurance, and approving and effecting indemnity cover if required by the lender; and reporting if the solicitor is aware of any rights needed for the use or enjoyment of the property over other land;

(viii)   reporting on any financial charges (for example, improvement or repair grants or Housing Act discounts) secured on the property revealed by the solicitor's searches and enquiries which will affect the property after completion of the mortgage;

(ix)   in the case of a leasehold property, confirming that the lease contains the terms stipulated by the lender and does not include any terms specified by the lender as unacceptable; obtaining a suitable deed of variation or indemnity insurance if the terms of the lease are unsatisfactory; enquiring of the seller or the borrower (if the property is already owned by the borrower) as to any known breaches of covenant by the landlord or any superior landlord and reporting any such breaches to the lender; reporting if the solicitor becomes aware of the landlord's absence or insolvency; making a company search and checking the last three years' published accounts of any management company with responsibilities under the lease; if the borrower is required to be a shareholder in the management company, obtaining the share certificate, a blank stock transfer form signed by the borrower and a copy of the memorandum and articles of association; obtaining any necessary consent to or prior approval of the assignment and mortgage; obtaining a clear receipt for the last payment of rent and service charge; and serving notice of the assignment and mortgage on the landlord;

(x)   if the property is subject to a letting, checking that the type of letting and its terms comply with the lender's requirements;

(xi) making appropriate pre-completion searches, including a bankruptcy search against the borrower, any other person in whom the legal estate is vested and any guarantor;

(xii) receiving, releasing and transmitting the mortgage advance, including asking for any final inspection needed and dealing with any retentions and cashbacks;

(xiii) procuring execution of the mortgage deed and form of guarantee as appropriate by the persons whose identities have been checked in accordance with any requirements of the lender under paragraph (3)(c)(i) as those of the borrower, any other person in whom the legal estate is vested and any guarantor; obtaining their signatures to the forms of undertaking required by the lender in relation to the use, occupation or physical state of the property; and complying with the lender's requirements if any document is to be executed under a power of attorney;

(xiv) asking the borrower for confirmation that the information about occupants given in the mortgage instructions or offer is correct; obtaining consents in the form required by the lender from existing or prospective occupiers of the property aged 17 or over specified by the lender, or of whom the solicitor is aware;

(xv) advising the borrower on the terms of any document required by the lender to be signed by the borrower;

(xvi) advising any other person required to sign any document on the terms of that document or, if there is a conflict of interest between that person and the borrower or the lender, advising that person on the need for separate legal advice and arranging for him or her to see an independent conveyancer;

(xvii) obtaining the legal transfer of the property to the mortgagor;

(xviii) procuring the redemption of (A) existing mortgages on property the subject of any associated sale of which the solicitor is aware, and (B) any other mortgages secured against a property located in England or Wales made by an identified lender where an identified account number or numbers or a property address has been given by the lender;

(xix) ensuring the redemption or postponement of existing mortgages on the property, and registering the mortgage with the priority required by the lender;

(xx) making administrative arrangements in relation to any collateral security, such as an endowment policy, or in relation to any collateral warranty or guarantee relating to the physical condition of the property, such as NHBC documentation;

(xxi) registering the transfer and mortgage;

(xxii) giving legal advice on any matters reported on under this paragraph (3)(c), suggesting courses of action open to the lender, and complying with the lender's instructions on the action to be taken;

(xxiii) disclosing any relationship specified by the lender between the solicitor and borrower;

(xxiv) storing safely the title deeds and documents pending registration and delivery to or as directed by the lender;

(xxv) retaining the information contained in the solicitor's conveyancing file for at least six years from the date of the mortgage.

(d) In addition, a solicitor acting for both lender and borrower in an institutional mortgage of property to be used as a private residence only:

(i) must use the certificate of title set out in the Appendix, or as substituted from time to time by the Council with the concurrence of the Master of the Rolls ("the approved certificate"); and

(ii) unless the lender has certified that its mortgage instructions are subject to the limitations contained in paragraphs (3)(c) and (3)(e), must notify the lender on receipt of instructions that the approved certificate will be used, and that the solicitor's duties to the lender are limited to the matters contained in the approved certificate.

(See also note (iii) below.)

(e) The terms of this rule will prevail in the event of any ambiguity in the lender's instructions, or discrepancy between the instructions and paragraph (3)(c) or the approved certificate.

Anti-avoidance

(f) A solicitor who is acting only for the borrower in an institutional mortgage of property must not accept or act upon any requirements by way of undertaking, warranty, guarantee or otherwise of the lender, the lender's solicitor or other agent which extend beyond the limitations contained in paragraph (3)(c).

Notes

(i) An "institutional mortgage" is a mortgage on standard terms, provided by an institutional lender in the normal course of its activities; and

▶ *a "private mortgage" is any other mortgage.*

(ii) A solicitor will not be in breach of paragraphs (3)(a)(iii)–(iv) or (c) if the lender has certified that its mortgage instructions and documents sent pursuant to those instructions are subject to the limitations set out in paragraphs (3)(c) and (e), and certifies any subsequent instructions and documents in the same way. If there is no certification, a solicitor acting in an exclusively residential transaction must notify the lender that the approved certificate of title will be used and that the solicitor's duties to the lender will be limited accordingly (see paragraph (3)(d)(ii)). In other types of transaction, the solicitor should draw the lender's attention to the provisions of paragraphs (3)(c) and (e) and state that he or she cannot act on any instructions which extend beyond the matters contained in paragraph (3)(c).

(iii) As an alternative to printing the approved certificate for each transaction, it is acceptable for a lender to use a short form certificate of title which incorporates the approved certificate by reference. The form must include in the following order:

▶ *the title "Certificate of Title";*

▶ *the contents of the details box in the order set out in the approved certificate (use of two columns is acceptable) but with details not required shaded out or stated not to be required; and*

▶ *the wording "We, the conveyancers named above, give the Certificate of Title set out in the Appendix to Rule 6(3) of the Solicitors' Practice Rules 1990 as if the same were set out in full, subject to the limitations contained in it".*

Administrative details, such as a request for cheque, may follow the Certificate of Title.

(iv) *The approved certificate of title is only required for a transaction where the property is to be used as a private residence by the owner. The certificate need not, therefore, be used for "buy to let mortgages" on properties which are not intended for owner-occupation.*

(v) *"Solicitor" in paragraph (3)(b)(i) means any principal in the practice (or an associated practice), and any solicitor conducting or supervising the transaction, whether or not that solicitor is a principal; and*

▶ *"immediate family" means spouse, children, parents, brothers and sisters.*

"Solicitor" in sub-paragraphs (i)–(xxv) of paragraph (3)(c) means the practice instructed and any solicitor conducting or supervising the transaction.

(vi) *The lender must be informed of the circumstances, in accordance with paragraph (3)(b) so that the lender can decide whether or not to instruct the solicitor.*

(vii) *A lender's instructions (see paragraph (3)(c)(xxiii)) may require a wider disclosure of a solicitor's circumstances than paragraph (3)(b) requires; and a solicitor must assess whether the circumstances give rise to a conflict. For example, there will be a conflict between lender and borrower if the solicitor becomes involved in negotiations relating to the terms of the loan. A conflict might arise from the relationship a solicitor has with the borrower – for example, if the solicitor is the borrower's creditor or debtor or the borrower's business associate or co-habitant.*

APPENDIX

CERTIFICATE OF TITLE

Details Box

TO: (Lender)
Lender's Reference or Account No:
The Borrower:
Property:
Title Number:
Mortgage Advance:
Price stated in transfer:
Completion Date:
Conveyancer's Name & Address:
Conveyancer's Reference:
Conveyancer's bank, sort code and account number:
Date of instructions:

WE THE CONVEYANCERS NAMED ABOVE CERTIFY as follows:

(1) If so instructed, we have checked the identity of the Borrower (and anyone else required to sign the mortgage deed or other document connected wth the mortgage) by reference to the document or documents precisely specified in writing by you.

(2) Except as otherwise disclosed to you in writing:

(i)   we have investigated the title to the Property, we are not aware of any other financial charges secured on the Property which will affect the Property after completion of the mortgage and, upon completion of the mortgage, both you and the mortgagor (whose identity has been checked in accordance with paragraph (1) above) will have a good and marketable title to the Property and to appurtenant rights free from prior mortgages or charges and from onerous encumbrances which title will be registered with absolute title;

(ii)   we have compared the extent of the Property shown on any plan provided by you against relevant plans in the title deeds and/or the description of the Property in any valuation which you have supplied to us, and in our opinion there are no material discrepancies;

(iii)   the assumptions stated by the valuer about the title (its tenure, easements, boundaries and restrictions on use) in any valuation which you have supplied to us are correct;

(iv)   if the Property is leasehold the terms of the lease accord with your instructions, including any requirements you have for covenants by the Landlord and/or a management company and/or by a deed of mutual covenant for the insurance, repair and maintenance of the structure, exterior and common parts of any building of which the Property forms part, and we have or will obtain on or before completion a clear receipt for the last payment of rent and service charge;

(v)   we have received satisfactory evidence that the buildings insurance is in place, or will be on completion, for the sum and in the terms required by you;

(vi)   if the Property is to be purchased by the Borrower:

     (a)   the contract for sale provides for vacant possession on completion;

     (b)   the seller has owned or been the registered owner of the Property for not less than six months;

     (c)   we are not acting on behalf of the seller;

(vii)   we are in possession of: (A) either a local search or local search insurance and (B) such other searches or search insurance as are appropriate to the Property, the mortgagor and any guarantor, in each case in accordance with your instructions;

(viii)   nothing has been revealed by our searches and enquiries which would prevent the Property being used by any occupant for residential purposes;

(ix)   neither any principal nor any other solicitor in the practice giving this certificate nor any spouse, child, parent, brother or sister of such a person is interested in the Property (whether alone or jointly with any other) as mortgagor.

WE :

(a)   undertake, prior to use of the mortgage advance, to obtain in the form required by you the execution of a mortgage and a guarantee as appropriate by the persons whose identities have been checked in accordance with paragraph (1) above as those of the Borrower, any other person in whom the legal estate is vested and any guarantor; and, if required by you:

> to obtain their signatures to the forms of undertaking required by you in relation to the use, occupation or physical state of the Property;
>
> to ask the Borrower for confirmation that the information about occupants given in your mortgage instructions or offer is correct; and
>
> to obtain consents in the form required by you from any existing or prospective occupier(s) aged 17 or over of the Property specified by you or of whom we are aware;

(b) have made or will make such Bankruptcy, Land Registry or Land Charges Searches as may be necessary to justify certificate no. (2)(i) above;

(c) will within the period of protection afforded by the searches referred to in paragraph (b) above:

    (i) complete the mortgage;

    (ii) arrange for stamping of the transfer if appropriate;

    (iii) deliver to the Land Registry the documents necessary to register the mortgage in your favour and any relevant prior dealings;

    (iv) effect any other registrations necessary to protect your interests as mortgagee;

(d) will despatch to you such deeds and documents relating to the Property as you require with a list of them in the form prescribed by you within ten working days of receipt by us of the Charge Certificate from the Land Registry;

(e) will not part with the mortgage advance (and will return it to you if required) if it shall come to our notice prior to completion that the Property will at completion be occupied in whole or in part otherwise than in accordance with your instructions;

(f) will not accept instructions, except with your consent in writing, to prepare any lease or tenancy agreement relating to the Property or any part of it prior to despatch of the Charge Certificate to you;

(g) will not use the mortgage advance until satisfied that, prior to or contemporaneously with the transfer of the Property to the mortgagor, there will be discharged (A) any existing mortgage on property the subject of an associated sale of which we are aware and (B) any other mortgages made by a lender identified by you secured against a property located in England or Wales where you have given either an account number or numbers or a property address;

(h) will notify you in writing if any matter comes to our attention before completion which would render the certificate given above untrue or inaccurate and, in those circumstances, will defer completion pending your authority to proceed and will return the mortgage advance to you if required;

(i) we confirm that we have complied, or will comply, with your instructions in all other respects to the extent that they do not extend beyond the limitations contained in paragraph (3)(c) of rule 6 of the Solicitors' Practice Rules 1990.

OUR duties to you are limited to the matters set out in this certificate and we accept no further liability or responsibility whatsoever. The payment by you to us (by whatever means) of the mortgage advance or any part of it constitutes acceptance of this limitation and any assignment to you by the Borrower of any rights of action against us to which the Borrower may be entitled shall take effect subject to this limitation.

Signature Box

SIGNED on behalf of THE CONVEYANCERS   ....
NAME of Authorised Signatory   ....
QUALIFICATION of Authorised Signatory   ....
DATE of Signature   ....

Rule 6A (Seller's solicitor dealing with more than one prospective buyer)

(1)   This rule applies to the conveyancing of freehold and leasehold property. The rule is to be interpreted in the light of the notes.

Notes

(i)   *Rule 6A replaces the Council Direction of 6th October 1977 and Principle and Commentary 24.04 in the 1993 edition of "The Guide to the Professional Conduct of Solicitors" with effect from 1st March 1995. As was the case with the Council Direction, it applies to all conveyancing of land, whether the transaction is of a "commercial" or "domestic" nature.*

(ii)   *The Council Direction did not and Rule 6A does not set terms for a contract race. It lays down requirements which must be met when a solicitor is instructed to deal with more than one prospective buyer. The rule imposes no obligation on the seller's solicitor to exchange contracts with the first buyer to deliver a signed contract and deposit. It will be a matter of law whether or not the seller has entered into a contractual obligation to exchange with the buyer "first past the post", or whether the whole matter remains "subject to contract".*

(iii) *References to "solicitor" throughout the rule include a firm of solicitors, a multi-national partnership or a recognised body.*

(2)   Where a seller instructs a solicitor to deal with more than one prospective buyer, the solicitor (with the client's consent) shall immediately disclose the seller's decision, if possible by telephone or fax, to the solicitor or other conveyancer acting for each prospective buyer or direct to the prospective buyer if acting in person. Such disclosure, if made by telephone, shall at once be confirmed by letter or fax. If the seller refuses to authorise disclosure, the solicitor shall immediately cease to act. Each prospective buyer must be notified each time a decision is taken to deal with any further prospective buyer.

Notes

(i)   *It is the seller's decision to deal with more than one prospective buyer which must be notified. The seller's solicitor must not wait until contracts are actually submitted but must notify the appropriate parties immediately upon receiving instructions to deal with a prospective buyer (other than the first).*

(ii) *A solicitor will have been instructed to deal with a prospective buyer where the solicitor is asked to submit a draft contract or to provide any other documentation or information (e.g. a plan or a note of the Land Registry title number) in order to facilitate the conveyancing of the premises to the prospective buyer. The rule does not, however, cover activities normally performed by an estate agent, such as issuing particulars of sale, showing prospective buyers round the property, and negotiating the price.*

(iii) *The rule will apply where the contracts are to contain non-identical terms (e.g. where one contract is to include additional land). It will also apply where the contracts are to relate to different interests in the same property where the sale of one such interest would affect the sale of the other. For example, a party negotiating to take a lease of premises will be affected by another party negotiating to buy the freehold with vacant possession, since the sale of one precludes the sale of the other. On the other hand, the rule would not apply where the seller is proposing to grant a lease and to effect a simultaneous sale of the freehold reversion subject to that lease, since neither transaction precludes the other.*

(iv) *Where a prospective buyer has retained an unqualified conveyancer, solicitors are reminded to consult the Council guidance on dealing with unqualified conveyancers [see Annex 25A, p.482 in this edition of the Guide]. However, so far as rule 6A is concerned, the obligations in paragraph (2) will be met by disclosure either to the prospective buyer direct or to the unqualified conveyancer.*

(3)   The obligations in paragraph (2) of this rule apply where a seller client, to the solicitor's knowledge, deals (whether directly or through another solicitor or other conveyancer) with another prospective buyer (or with that buyer's solicitor or other conveyancer).

Note

"Deals with another prospective buyer" should be interpreted in the light of note (ii) to paragraph (2).

(4)   A solicitor shall not act for more than one of the prospective buyers.

Notes

(i) *"Prospective buyers" should be interpreted in the light of note (ii) to paragraph (2).*

(ii) *This part of the rule recognises the inevitable conflict of interest which makes it impossible for a solicitor to act for more than one of the prospective buyers.*

(5)   A solicitor shall not act for both the seller and one of the prospective buyers, even in a case which would fall within rule 6(2) of these rules.

Notes

(i) *"Prospective buyers" should be interpreted in the light of note (ii) to paragraph (2).*

(ii) *Clearly a solicitor must not act for both where it is known at the time of taking instructions on behalf of the buyer that there is more than one prospective buyer. In addition, this part of the rule does not permit a solicitor to continue to act for both in a case falling within rule 6(2), where another prospective buyer is introduced during the course of the transaction because of the significant inherent conflict; the solicitor would find it impossible to reconcile the interests of both clients if, for example, it was in the seller's best interests to exchange with the other prospective buyer.*

(6)   For the purposes of this rule a prospective buyer shall continue to be treated as such until either the prospective buyer or the seller gives written notice (either by letter or by fax) of withdrawal from the transaction, such notice to be between solicitors or other conveyancers save where such notice is given by or to a prospective buyer acting in person.

Notes

(i) *Solicitors should take particular care where a contract has been submitted but nothing has been heard from the prospective buyer's solicitor for some time. If the seller decides to deal with another buyer, the rule must still be complied with unless the seller's solicitor has already given notice of withdrawal.*

(ii) *Where a prospective buyer has retained an unqualified conveyancer, the provisions of paragraph (6) should be interpreted in the light of note (iv) to paragraph (2).*

(7)   This rule does not apply to a proposed sale by auction or tender. The rule does, however, apply to require disclosure to a prospective buyer by private treaty of instructions to offer the property by auction or tender.

Rule 7 (Fee sharing)

(1)   A solicitor shall not share or agree to share his or her professional fees with any person except:

(a)   a practising solicitor;

(b)   a practising foreign lawyer (other than a foreign lawyer whose registration in the register of foreign lawyers is suspended or whose name has been struck off the register);

(c)   the solicitor's *bona fide* employee, which provision shall not permit under the cloak of employment a partnership prohibited by paragraph (6) of this rule; or

(d)   a retired partner or predecessor of the solicitor or the dependants or personal representatives of a deceased partner or predecessor.

(2)   Notwithstanding paragraph (1) of this rule a solicitor who instructs an estate agent as sub-agent for the sale of properties may remunerate the estate agent on the basis of a proportion of the solicitor's professional fee.

(3)   The exceptions set out in paragraphs 2 to 9 of the Employed Solicitors Code shall where necessary also operate as exceptions to this rule but only to permit fee sharing with the solicitor's employer.

(4)   A solicitor who works as a volunteer in a law centre or advice service operated by a charitable or similar non-commercial organisation may pay to the organisation any fees or costs that he or she receives under the legal aid scheme.

(5)   For the purposes of sub-paragraph (1)(d) above, the references to a retired or deceased partner shall be construed, in relation to a recognised body, as meaning a retired or deceased director or member of that body, or a retired or deceased beneficial owner of any share in that body held by a member as nominee.

(6)   (a)   A solicitor shall not enter into partnership with any person other than a solicitor, a registered foreign lawyer or a recognised body.

(b)   A recognised body shall not enter into partnership with any person other than a solicitor or a recognised body.

(c)   In this paragraph, "solicitor" means a solicitor of the Supreme Court of England and Wales.

(7)   A solicitor shall not practise through any body corporate except a recognised body, or save as permitted under rule 4 of these rules.

Rule 8 (Contingency fees)

(1)   A solicitor who is retained or employed to prosecute or defend any action, suit or other contentious proceeding shall not enter into any arrangement to receive a contingency fee in respect of that proceeding, save one permitted under statute or by the common law.

(2)   Paragraph (1) of this rule shall not apply to an arrangement in respect of an action, suit or other contentious proceeding in any country other than England and Wales to the extent that a local lawyer would be permitted to receive a contingency fee in respect of that proceeding.

Rule 9 (Claims assessors)

(1)   A solicitor shall not, in respect of any claim or claims arising as a result of death or personal injury, either enter into an arrangement for the introduction of clients with or act in association with any person (not being a solicitor) whose business or any part of whose business is to make, support or prosecute (whether by action or otherwise, and whether by a solicitor or agent or otherwise) claims arising as a result of death or personal injury and who in the course of such business solicits or receives contingency fees in respect of such claims.

(2)   The prohibition in paragraph (1) of this rule shall not apply to an arrangement or association with a person who solicits or receives contingency fees only in respect of proceedings in a country outside England and Wales, to the extent that a local lawyer would be permitted to receive a contingency fee in respect of such proceedings.

Rule 10 (Receipt of commissions from third parties)

(1)   Solicitors shall account to their clients for any commission received of more than £20 unless, having disclosed to the client in writing the amount or basis of calculation of the commission or (if the precise amount or basis cannot be ascertained) an approximation thereof, they have the client's agreement to retain it.

(2)   Where the commission actually received is materially in excess of the amount or basis or approximation disclosed to the client the solicitor shall account to the client for the excess.

(3)   This rule does not apply where a member of the public deposits money with a solicitor who is acting as agent for a building society or other financial institution and the solicitor has not advised that person as a client as to the disposition of the money.

Rule 11 (Names used by a firm)

(1)   A firm must not use a name which:

    (a)   is misleading; or

    (b)   brings the profession into disrepute.

(2)   A firm name appearing on any letterhead (or fax heading, or heading used for bills), if the name does not itself include the word "solicitor(s)", must be accompanied by either:

    (a)   the word "solicitor(s)"; or

    (b)   the words "regulated by the Law Society".

(3)   This rule must be interpreted in the light of the notes.

Notes

(i)   *The rule applies to any name used by a firm (which includes a sole practitioner or a recognised body – see rule 18(2)(d)) for its practice or part of its practice.*

(ii)   *The rule would allow, for example:*

    (a)   *a non-conventional name, such as "The Legal Clinic", "XYZ Solicitors" or "Briefcase Legal Services";*

    (b)   *a name with a geographical reference, such as "Browne and Son (Chancery Lane)" or "Guildford Solicitors" – but not a name that would breach note (iii)(e);*

    (c)   *a name including a field of practice, such as "Smith & Co. Conveyancers" or "Redditch Conveyancing Service";*

    (d)   *a firm name consisting of the names of solicitors or foreign lawyers who are or were principals in the firm or a predecessor firm, such as "Lewis & Smith", even though Lewis and Smith have died and Browne is now the sole principal;*

    (e)   *a firm name which includes the name of an historical character unconnected with the practice, or the name of a fictional character, or an invented name, or a name selected at will – but not a name that would breach note (iii)(c);*

    (f)   *the use of "& Co." or "Solicitors", even for a sole practitioner.*

(iii) *The rule would not allow:*

    (a)   *a name which uses the words "Law Centre";*

    (b)   *a name which implies a connection with a business other than a legal practice, for example "Safeway Solicitors Group";*

    (c)   *a firm name which includes the name of, or refers to, any actual person unless that person is either:*

        (A)   *a solicitor or foreign lawyer who is or was a principal in the firm or a predecessor firm; or*

        (B)   *an historical character unconnected with the practice;*

    for example, "Jones and Co." or "JMJ Financial and Legal Services", where J. M. Jones is a financial adviser employed in the firm;

    (d)   *a name which implies that a firm is bigger than it is (for example "French & Partners", if French is a sole practitioner), unless the name is permitted by note (ii)(d);*

    (e)   *a name which uses the definite article together with a geographical reference, for example "The Chancery Lane Solicitors" or "The Redditch Property Centre".*

(iv)   *If the name of a multi-national practice includes the word "Solicitor(s)", the name must also include:*

    (a)   *words denoting the countries or jurisdictions of qualification of the foreign lawyer principals and their professional qualifications; or*

    (b)   *the words "Registered Foreign Lawyer(s)";*

    and the categories of lawyer must appear in order, with the largest group of principals first.

(v)   *Compliance with rule 11(2)(a) in the case of a solicitors' practice will be satisfied by, for example:*

    (a)   *adding after the name a description of the firm which comprises or includes the word "solicitor(s)"; or*

(b) the appearance of the word "solicitor(s)" against a list of the partners (or directors); or

(c) a statement that the partners (or directors) are solicitors.

(vi) A firm which wishes to comply with rule 11(2)(b), and which uses a statement of authorisation under rule 21 of the Solicitors' Investment Business Rules, may adopt the formula "regulated by the Law Society; authorised by the Society to conduct investment business".

(vii) The notepaper of a multi-national practice has to comply with paragraph 7(b) of the Publicity Code (naming and describing partners and staff), which will ensure compliance with rule 11(2). (The notepaper could, in addition, bear the words "regulated by the Law Society".)

(viii) "Principal" in the case of a recognised body means a director, registered member or beneficial shareowner.

(ix) Rule 11 applies to private practice only.

Rule 12 (Investment business)

(1)   Without prejudice to the generality of the principles embodied in rule 1 of these rules, solicitors shall not in connection with investment business:

(a)   be appointed representatives; or

(b)   have any arrangements with other persons under which the solicitors could be constrained to recommend to clients or effect for them (or refrain from doing so) transactions in some investments but not others, with some persons but not others, or through the agency of some persons but not others; or to introduce or refer clients or other persons with whom the solicitors deal to some persons but not others.

(2)   Solicitors shall not alone, or by or with others, control, actively participate in or operate any separate business which is an appointed representative, unless it is the appointed representative of an independent financial adviser.

(3)   Where a solicitor, authorised to conduct investment business, is required by the rules of the relevant regulatory body to use a particular form of terms of business letter, the solicitor shall use a terms of business letter in a form which has been approved by the Council of the Law Society.

(4)   This rule shall have effect in relation to the conduct of investment business within or into any part of the United Kingdom.

(5)   In this rule "appointed representative", "investment" and "investment business" have the meanings assigned to them by the Financial Services Act 1986.

Rule 13 (Supervision and management of an office)

[Note: This rule will be replaced on 23rd December 1999 – see Annex 3C, p.113.]

(1)   Solicitors shall ensure that every office where they or their firms practise is and can reasonably be seen to be properly supervised in accordance with the following minimum standards:

(a)   Every such office shall be attended on each day when it is open to the public or open to telephone calls from the public by:

(i)   a solicitor who holds a practising certificate and has been admitted for at least three years; or

(ii)   in the case of an office from which no right of audience or right to conduct litigation is exercised and from which no exercise of any such right is supervised, a registered foreign lawyer who is a principal of the firm and who has been qualified in his or her own jurisdiction for at least three years;

who shall spend sufficient time at such office to ensure adequate control of the staff employed there and afford requisite facilities for consultation with clients. In the case of a firm in private practice such solicitor may be a principal, employee or consultant of the firm, provided that the firm must have at least one principal who is a solicitor who has been admitted for at least three years, or alternatively, in the case of a firm none of whose principals exercise any right of audience or right to conduct litigation or supervise or assume responsibility for the exercise of any such right, a foreign lawyer who has been qualified in his or her own jurisdiction for at least three years.

(b)   Every such office shall be managed by one of the persons listed below who shall normally be in attendance at that office during all the hours when it is open to the public or open to telephone calls from the public:

(i)   a solicitor holding a current practising certificate;

(ii)   a Fellow of the Institute of Legal Executives confirmed by the Institute as being of good standing and having been admitted as a Fellow for not less than three years;

(iia) in the case of an office from which no right of audience or right to conduct litigation is exercised and from which no exercise of any such right is supervised, a registered foreign lawyer who is a principal of the firm;

(iii) in the case of an office dealing solely with conveyancing, a licensed conveyancer; or

(iv)   in the case of an office dealing solely with property selling and surveying, a chartered surveyor or person holding another professional qualification approved by the Council under Rule 14 of these rules.

(2)   In determining whether or not there has been compliance with the requirement as to supervision in paragraph (1) of this rule, account shall be taken of, *inter alia*, the arrangements for principals to see incoming mail.

(3)   Where daily attendance or normal attendance in accordance with sub-paragraphs (1)(a) or (1)(b) of this rule is prevented by illness, accident or other sufficient or unforeseen cause for a prolonged period, suitable alternative arrangements shall be made without delay to ensure compliance.

(4)   [Transitional provision now expired.]

(5)   In this rule:

(a)   references to a principal shall be construed, in relation to a recognised body, as references to a director of that body;

(b)   in paragraph (2) of this rule, "principals" shall be construed, except in relation to a firm none of whose principals exercise any right of audience or right to conduct litigation or supervise or assume responsibility for the exercise of any such right, as referring to principals who are solicitors; and

(c)   "right of audience" and "right to conduct litigation" shall be construed in accordance with Part II and section 119 of the Courts and Legal Services Act 1990.

Rule 14 (Structural surveys and formal valuations)

Solicitors may not provide structural surveys or formal valuations of property unless:

(a)   the work is carried out by a principal or employee who is a chartered surveyor or who holds another professional qualification approved by the Council; and

(b)   the appropriate contribution has been paid to the Solicitors' Indemnity Fund.

Rule 15 (Costs information and client care)

Solicitors shall:

(a)   give information about costs and other matters, and

(b)   operate a complaints handling procedure,

in accordance with a Solicitors' Costs Information and Client Care Code made from time to time by the Council of the Law Society with the concurrence of the Master of the Rolls, but subject to the notes.

Notes

(i)   *A serious breach of the code, or persistent breaches of a material nature, will be a breach of the rule, and may also be evidence of inadequate professional services under section 37A of the Solicitors Act 1974.*

(ii)   *Material breaches of the code which are not serious or persistent will not be a breach of the rule, but may be evidence of inadequate professional services under section 37A.*

(iii)   *The powers of the Office for the Supervision of Solicitors on a finding of inadequate professional services include:*

     (a)   *disallowing all or part of the solicitor's costs; and*

     (b)   *directing the solicitor to pay compensation to the client up to a limit of £1,000.*

(iv)   *Non-material breaches of the code will not be a breach of the rule, and will not be evidence of inadequate professional services under section 37A.*

(v)   *Registered foreign lawyers, although subject to rule 15 as a matter of professional conduct, are not subject to section 37A. However, solicitor partners in a multi-national partnership are subject to section 37A for professional services provided by the firm.*

Rule 16 (Cross-border activities within the European Community)

(1)   In relation to cross-border activities within the European Community, solicitors shall, without prejudice to their other obligations under these rules or any other rules, principles or requirements of conduct, observe the rules codified in articles 2 to 5 of the CCBE Code of Conduct for Lawyers in the European Community adopted on 28th October 1988, as interpreted by article 1 (the preamble) thereof and the Explanatory

Memorandum and Commentary thereon prepared by the CCBE's Deontology Working Party and dated May 1989.

(2)   In this rule:

    (a)   "cross-border activities" means:

        (i)   all professional contacts with lawyers of member states of the European Community other than the United Kingdom; and

        (ii)   the professional activities of the solicitor in a member state other than the United Kingdom, whether or not the solicitor is physically present in that member state; and

    (b)   "lawyers" means lawyers as defined in Directive 77/249 of the Council of the European Communities dated 22nd March 1977 as amended from time to time.

Rule 16A (Solicitors acting as advocates)

Any solicitor acting as advocate shall at all times comply with the Law Society's Code for Advocacy.

Rule 16B (Choice of advocate)

(1)   A solicitor shall not make it a condition of providing litigation services that advocacy services shall also be provided by that solicitor or by the solicitor's firm or the solicitor's agent.

(2)   A solicitor who provides both litigation and advocacy services shall as soon as practicable after receiving instructions and from time to time consider and advise the client whether having regard to the circumstances including:

    (i)   the gravity, complexity and likely cost of the case;

    (ii)   the nature of the solicitor's practice;

    (iii)   the solicitor's ability and experience;

    (iv)   the solicitor's relationship with the client;

the best interests of the client would be served by the solicitor, another advocate from the solicitor's firm, or some other advocate providing the advocacy services.

Rule 17 (Waivers)

In any particular case or cases the Council of the Law Society shall have power to waive in writing any of the provisions of these rules for a particular purpose or purposes expressed in such waiver, and to revoke such waiver.

Rule 18 (Application and interpretation)

(1)   *(Application to solicitors)*

These rules shall have effect in relation to the practice of solicitors whether as a principal in private practice, or in the employment of a solicitor or of a non-solicitor employer, or in any other form of practice, and whether on a regular or on an occasional basis.

(1A) *(Application to registered foreign lawyers)*

(a) For the avoidance of doubt, neither registration in the register of foreign lawyers, nor anything in these rules or in any other rules made under Part II of the Solicitors Act 1974 or section 9 of the Administration of Justice Act 1985, shall entitle any registered foreign lawyer to be granted any right of audience or any right to conduct litigation within the meaning of Part II and section 119 of the Courts and Legal Services Act 1990, or any right to supervise or assume responsibility for the exercise of any such right.

(b) A registered foreign lawyer shall do nothing in the course of practising in partnership with a solicitor which, if done by a solicitor, would put the solicitor in breach of any of these rules, or any other rules, principles or requirements of conduct applicable to solicitors.

(c) A registered foreign lawyer shall do nothing in the course of practising as the director of a recognised body which puts the recognised body in breach of any of these rules, or any other rules, principles or requirements of conduct applicable to recognised bodies.

(2) *(Interpretation)*

In these rules, except where the context otherwise requires:

(a) "arrangement" means any express or tacit agreement between a solicitor and another person whether contractually binding or not;

(b) "contentious proceeding" is to be construed in accordance with the definition of "contentious business" in section 87 of the Solicitors Act 1974;

(c) "contingency fee" means any sum (whether fixed, or calculated either as a percentage of the proceeds or otherwise howsoever) payable only in the event of success in the prosecution or defence of any action, suit or other contentious proceeding;

(d) "firm" includes a sole practitioner or a recognised body;

(da) "foreign lawyer" means a person who is a member, and entitled to practise as such, of a legal profession regulated within a jurisdiction outside England and Wales;

(db) "multi-national partnership" has the meaning given in section 89 of the Courts and Legal Services Act 1990;

(e) "person" includes a body corporate or unincorporated association or group of persons;

(ea) "principal in private practice" includes a recognised body;

(f) "recognised body" means a body corporate for the time being recognised by the Council under the Solicitors' Incorporated Practice Rules from time to time in force;

(fa) "registered foreign lawyer" means a person registered in accordance with section 89 of the Courts and Legal Services Act 1990; and "register" and "registration" are to be construed accordingly;

(g) "solicitor" means a solicitor of the Supreme Court of England and Wales and, except in rule 7(6) of these rules, also includes a firm of solicitors or a recognised body; and

(h)   words in the singular include the plural, words in the plural include the singular, and words importing the masculine or feminine gender include the neuter.

Rule 19 (Repeal and commencement)

(1)   The Solicitors' Practice Rules 1988 are hereby repealed.

(2)   These rules shall come into force on 1st September 1990.

Annex 1B

Solicitors' Anti-Discrimination Rule 1995

Rule dated 18th January 1995 made by the Council of the Law Society with the concurrence of the Master of the Rolls under section 31 of the Solicitors Act 1974 and section 9 of the Administration of Justice Act 1985, regulating the professional conduct of solicitors and recognised bodies in England and Wales.

(1)　Solicitors must not discriminate on grounds of race, sex or sexual orientation, and must not discriminate unfairly or unreasonably on grounds of disability, in their professional dealings with clients, staff, other solicitors, barristers or other persons.

(2)　Principal solicitors in private practice must operate a policy dealing with the avoidance of such discrimination, and solicitors with management responsibilities in employed practice must use reasonable endeavours to secure the operation of such a policy.

(3)　Principal solicitors in private practice who have not developed and adopted their own policy dealing with the avoidance of such discrimination will be deemed to have adopted the model anti-discrimination policy for the time being promoted for such purposes by the Law Society.

(4)　Paragraph (1) applies to a recognised body as it applies to a solicitor, and paragraphs (2) and (3) apply to a recognised body as they apply to a principal solicitor in private practice.

(5)　This rule comes into force on 18th July 1995.

Chapter 2

Regulatory requirements

2.01   The Law Society

The Law Society, established under Royal Charter, is a voluntary body representing English and Welsh solicitors, as well as exercising statutory functions in the regulation of solicitors.

1. The Society's Royal Charter (1845) recites the purposes of the Society as 'promoting professional improvement, and facilitating the acquisition of legal knowledge'.

2. Important functions in the regulation of solicitors' practices are given to the Society and its Council by the Solicitors Act 1974, the Administration of Justice Act 1985 and the Courts and Legal Services Act 1990.

2.02 The roll of solicitors

The roll of solicitors of the Supreme Court is kept by the Law Society.

1. Arrangements for the keeping of the roll of solicitors are governed by sections 6–8 of the Solicitors Act 1974, and by the Solicitors (Keeping of the Roll) Regulations 1999 (see Annex 2C, p.52).

2. Solicitors who do not hold practising certificates are required to confirm annually if they wish to remain on the roll. The regulations provide for a notice to be sent to such solicitors, who must pay a fee determined by the Council of the Law Society if they wish to remain on the roll. If such solicitors do not indicate within a given period their wish to remain on the roll, the Society may remove their names from the roll after publishing a notice of intention.

2.03 Requirement to hold a practising certificate

'No person shall be qualified to act as a solicitor unless –

    (a) he has been admitted as a solicitor, and

    (b) his name is on the roll, and

    (c) he has in force a certificate issued by the Society in accordance with the provisions of this Part authorising him to practise as a solicitor (in this Act referred to as a "practising certificate").'

Solicitors Act 1974, section 1

1. A solicitor is acting as a solicitor, and therefore needs a practising certificate (see also sections 20–22 and 23–24 of the Solicitors Act 1974 in Annex 2A at p.45) if he or she:

    (a) is a principal in private practice;

    (b) works in private practice as an employee, consultant or locum in connection with the provision of any legal services (see also section 1A of the Solicitors Act 1974 in Annex 2A, p.42);

    (c) is held out (whether by use of the term 'solicitor' or otherwise) as a solicitor qualified to act as such by a non-solicitor employer;

    (d) conducts litigation as a solicitor (see also section 28 of the Courts and Legal Services Act 1990);

    (e) appears as an advocate in reliance on his or her qualification as a solicitor before a court or tribunal (see also section 27 of the Courts and Legal Services Act 1990);

(f)   for or in expectation of any fee, gain or reward:

    (i)   draws or prepares certain legal documents (i.e. instruments relating to any legal proceeding, contracts for the sale of land, certain instruments of conveyance or transfer relating to real or personal estate, papers upon which to found or oppose a grant of probate or letters of administration); or

    (ii) makes an application or lodges a document for registration at the Land Registry;

(g)   administers an oath (see section 81 of the Solicitors Act 1974);

(h)   instructs counsel.

2.   The requirement in note 1(f) above will not apply to an in-house solicitor who is not held out as a solicitor qualified to act as such, and who is supervised by a qualified person – see **4.01** note 3, p.145.

Newly admitted solicitors

3.   A person who, during employment in private practice, applies to be admitted as a solicitor needs to apply simultaneously for a practising certificate if that employment is to continue – see section 1A of the Solicitors Act 1974 (solicitor employed in private practice must hold a practising certificate) in Annex 2A, p.42.

Suspension from practising

4.   The Master of the Rolls has held that section 1A of the Solicitors Act 1974 does not prevent the Society from giving permission under section 41 of the Act (see Annex 3A, p.92) for the employment in private practice of a person who is suspended from practising as a solicitor. Such a person must not be held out as a solicitor, and can only do work which may be done by a solicitor's clerk.

Supervision of an office and operation of client accounts

5.   Law Society rules provide that certain functions can only be carried out by a solicitor if he or she has a practising certificate. These functions are:

(a)   supervising or managing an office which is open to the public or open to telephone calls from the public (see practice rule 13(1)(a)–(b) at **3.08**, p.73); and

(b)   authorising the withdrawal of money from a client account (see rule 23(1)(a) of the Solicitors' Accounts Rules 1998, Annex 28B at p.708).

In private practice, such a solicitor would in any case need to have a practising certificate by virtue of section 1A of the Solicitors Act 1974. However, solicitors in in-house practice need to be aware of these provisions in the rules.

Overseas practice

6. By rule 2 of the Solicitors' Overseas Practice Rules 1990 (see Annex 9A at p.181), a solicitor practising as such outside England and Wales must hold a practising certificate.

Solicitors employed by public departments

7. By section 88 of the Solicitors Act 1974 solicitors in certain public departments are exempted from the need to hold a practising certificate; and see also section 22(2)(b) of the Act (Annex 2A at p.46).

No costs payable for work done by uncertificated solicitor

8. Costs in respect of work done by an uncertificated solicitor are not recoverable by the solicitor or any other person – see section 25 of the Solicitors Act 1974 (Annex 2A at p.48).

9. Where work is billed in the name of a partnership, and at least one of the partners held a practising certificate at the time the work was done, the fact that a partner who did not do any of the work was uncertificated would not prevent the firm from recovering the costs (see *Hudgell Yeates & Co.* v. *Watson* [1978] Q.B. 451).

Non-practising solicitors

10. A solicitor who does not hold a practising certificate but wishes to use the description 'solicitor', should qualify it by adding words such as 'not practising' in any case where such a description might otherwise mislead people into thinking that he or she is qualified to act as a solicitor, e.g. in the context of carrying out the type of services which might be provided by a solicitor.

11. An uncertificated solicitor may describe himself or herself as 'solicitor' in situations where there is no implication that he or she is entitled to practise as a solicitor, e.g. in the context of the authorship of a book. When witnessing documents, an uncertificated solicitor may use the description 'solicitor' (provided, of course, that the document is not required to be witnessed by a practising solicitor).

12. A completely retired consultant who plays no part in the provision of any legal services can appear on the notepaper of a practice as 'consultant', but only with the addition of such explanatory words as 'retired solicitor' – see section 1A of the Solicitors Act 1974 (Annex 2A, p.42) and paragraph 7(a)(i) and (iv) of the Solicitors' Publicity Code (Annex 11A at p.233).

2.04   Issue of practising certificates

Practising certificates are issued by the Society under Part I of the Solicitors Act 1974 and are renewable annually.

Application procedure

1.   Applications for and the issue of practising certificates are regulated by sections 10–13 and 14 of the Solicitors Act 1974 and the Practising Certificate Regulations 1995 (see Annex 2B, p.49).

2.   Applications for a practising certificate must be made by the solicitor either on form RF3 for an individual application, or on the bulk form RF1 for applications on behalf of all the solicitors in a practice. In either case it is the solicitor's responsibility to ensure that statements made on the form are correct. The application forms are available from Regulation and Information Services (see p.xv for contact details).

Fees and contributions

3.   The appropriate fee must accompany every application for a practising certificate. The fees are fixed annually under section 11(1) of the Solicitors Act 1974.

4.   An additional fee, currently £50, is payable under section 12A of the Solicitors Act 1974 by any solicitor subject to section 12(1)(ee) of the Act (late accountant's report) – see Annex 2A at p.44.

5.   In addition to the practising certificate fee, a solicitor must pay the appropriate annual contribution to the Solicitors' Compensation Fund (see Schedule 2 to the Solicitors Act 1974).

6.   A solicitor is exempt from payment of the annual contribution to the Compensation Fund in respect of his or her first three practising certificates (see paragraph 2(2)(a) of Schedule 2). Crown prosecutors are also exempted from payment (see paragraph 2(2A) of Schedule 2).

Compliance with Indemnity Rules

7.   Before the Society is required to issue a practising certificate under section 10 of the Solicitors Act, it must be satisfied *inter alia* that the applicant either:

   (a)   has complied with the Solicitors' Indemnity Rules (whether by payment of the required contributions or by submission of a valid direct debit mandate); or

   (b)   is not subject to the indemnity rules (e.g. because he or she is not a principal in private practice); or

   (c)   is exempt from the indemnity rules by virtue of rule 29 (see Annex 29A at p.817); or

2

    (d)   is exempt from the Indemnity Rules by virtue of a waiver, details of which must be supplied to the Society with the practising certificate application.

8.   A solicitor who is a director of a recognised body which is a limited company has to provide evidence of the company's compulsory top-up cover under rule 13 of the Solicitors' Incorporated Practice Rules, or of the company's exemption from the rule (see Annex 3D at p.122).

Annual renewal or withdrawal of certificates

9.   The practising certificate year runs from 1st November to 31st October.

10.   Every practising certificate bears the 'replacement date' of the 31st October next after it is issued. By that date, application must be made for a new certificate if required. If the replacement date has passed, and a solicitor has made no application for a new certificate, the Society may withdraw the solicitor's existing certificate (see section 14 of the Solicitors Act 1974).

2.05   Refusal of a practising certificate or imposition of a condition

In certain cases the Society has discretion to refuse a practising certificate or to issue a conditional certificate.

1.   In most cases, a solicitor who applies for a practising certificate is entitled to receive one as of right, provided the application is in order. However, in certain circumstances, the Society has a discretion under sections 10 or 12 of the Solicitors Act 1974 to refuse to issue a certificate, or to issue a conditional certificate. Some of the situations where section 12 applies are:

▶   application after a lapse of twelve months or more;

▶   application after a solicitor has failed to give the Office for the Supervision of Solicitors a satisfactory explanation of his or her conduct;

▶   application after a solicitor has entered into a composition with his or her creditors;

▶   application when a solicitor has been late in delivering an accountant's report.

The full text of section 12 appears in Annex 2A at p.42.

2.   Where section 12 applies, an applicant must give six weeks' notice to the Society of his or her intention to apply for a practising certificate, unless the Master of the Rolls orders otherwise. This notice must be given on form RFS12, which includes a certificate of fitness signed by two practising solicitors (unless this requirement is waived – see note 3 below).

3.   Applications under section 12(1)(a) (first application) or 12(1)(c) (application after a lapse of twelve months or more) do not normally require a certificate of fitness. Solicitors subject to section 12(1)(ee) (late accountant's report) may in certain cases apply for a waiver of the requirement to submit form RFS12.

4.   If the Society refuses to issue a new certificate, an existing certificate will expire as soon as the replacement date has passed (see **2.04** note 10, p.37). If the replacement date has already passed, the existing certificate will expire immediately upon the Society taking the decision not to issue a new certificate.

5.   An appeal against refusal of a practising certificate, or against the imposition of a condition, lies to the Master of the Rolls or to the High Court – see section 13 of the Solicitors Act 1974, and the Master of the Rolls (Appeals and Applications) Regulations 1991 (Annex 2D, p.55).

6.   In certain cases, the Society may impose conditions on a practising certificate during the currency of the certificate (see section 13A of the Solicitors Act 1974).

2.06   Limitation on practice for newly qualified solicitors

A solicitor cannot normally practise as a sole principal until he or she has been admitted for three years. At least one of the partners in a firm must normally have been admitted for at least three years.

1.   A solicitor who has been admitted for less than three years does not qualify to supervise an office open to the public or open to telephone calls from the public, under rule 13(1)(a) of the Solicitors' Practice Rules 1990 (see **3.08**, p.73). The duty of supervision in private practice can be fulfilled by an assistant solicitor or consultant rather than a principal, but at least one principal in the practice must be a solicitor who has been admitted for at least three years.

2.   Rule 13 makes specific provision for multi-national partnerships and for recognised bodies (incorporated practices).

3.   A new version of rule 13 (see Annex 3C, p.113) will come into force on 23rd December 1999. It contains important transitional provisions.

2.07   Special qualifications for particular types of work

For investment business, surveys and valuations, insolvency practice or extended rights of advocacy in the higher courts, it is not sufficient only to hold a practising certificate – further qualification is also required.

Investment business

1. For a solicitor to carry on investment business within the meaning of the Financial Services Act 1986, the solicitor's firm must either hold an investment business certificate from the Society, or have authorisation from another appropriate regulator such as the Personal Investment Authority. Sole practitioners, recognised bodies (incorporated practices), multi-national partnerships and, in restricted circumstances, in-house solicitors may apply for an investment business certificate, as well as firms of solicitors (see also Chapter 27, p.522).

2. If discrete investment business (DIB) is to be conducted by a firm holding an investment business certificate from the Society, that has to be a 'category 2 certificate' (see rule 4(4)(b) of the Solicitors' Investment Business Rules 1995 – Annex 27B at p.566). All DIB must be conducted by or under the direct supervision of a principal, director or employee who is recognised by the Society as a 'qualified person' for the category of DIB concerned (see rule 7(1)(a) at p.568). The categories are:

    (a) retail branded/packaged products (including life policies and unit trusts);

    (b) securities/portfolio management;

    (c) corporate pensions and advanced schemes.

3. In the case of a firm holding an investment business certificate from the Law Society, the following types of business must not be transacted unless the Council has given permission under rule 7(1)(b) of the Solicitors' Investment Business Rules 1995 (see Annex 27B at p.568):

    (a) advising on or effecting contingent liability transactions;

    (b) advising on or effecting pension transfers or opt outs;

    (c) managing ISAs.

Surveys and valuations

4. Structural surveys and formal valuations of property may be provided only if the work is carried out by a principal or employee who is a chartered surveyor (see practice rule 14 at **26.11**, p.517).

Insolvency practice

5. To act as an insolvency practitioner within the meaning of the Insolvency Act 1986 a solicitor must, as an individual, hold a certificate of authorisation from the Society, unless he or she is directly authorised by the Department of Trade and Industry (see also Chapter 23, p.439).

Advocacy in the higher courts

6. To exercise rights of audience in the higher courts, other than those rights already enjoyed by solicitors before the coming into force of the Courts and

Legal Services Act 1990, a solicitor must obtain the appropriate qualification from the Society (see **21.06**, p.375):

(a)   the higher courts (all proceedings) qualification;

(b)   the higher courts (criminal proceedings) qualification; or

(c)   the higher courts (civil proceedings) qualification.

2.08   Continuing professional development

Solicitors are subject to a scheme of compulsory continuing professional development.

1.   The requirements of the scheme are set out in the Training Regulations 1990, relevant extracts from which appear in Annex 2E, p.61.

2.   The ways in which the requirements can be satisfied are set out in guidance on continuing professional development obligations (see Annex 2F, p.63).

3.   The requirements of the scheme apply to solicitors who are in legal practice or employment, whether or not they hold a practising certificate.

2.09   Notification requirements

'For the purpose of facilitating the service of notices and other documents, every solicitor who has in force, or has applied for, a practising certificate shall give notice to the Society of any change in his place or places of business before the expiration of 14 days from the date on which the change takes effect.'

Solicitors Act 1974, section 84(1)

1.   Notification under section 84(1) should be to Regulation and Information Services (see p.xv for contact details).

2.   Firms in private practice must notify Solicitors Indemnity Fund Limited of all partnership changes (see **29.04**, p.788 – and p.xv for contact details).

3.   Firms holding an investment business certificate from the Society must inform Regulation and Information Services of all partnership changes. For further details see rule 8 of the Solicitors' Investment Business Rules 1995 (Annex 27B at p.570).

2.10   Indemnity Fund

Under section 37 of the Solicitors Act 1974 the Council has established the Solicitors' Indemnity Fund, which provides professional indemnity cover for solicitors in private practice.

For details of the indemnity scheme see Chapter 29, p.782. For the Solicitors' Indemnity Rules see Annex 29A, p.793.

2.11 Compensation Fund

Section 36 of the Solicitors Act 1974 establishes the Solicitors' Compensation Fund, which provides compensation to those who suffer loss resulting from a solicitor's dishonesty.

For the requirement to contribute to the Fund see **2.04** notes 5–6, p.36. For claims on the Compensation Fund see **30.08**, p.847.

2.12 Accountants' reports

Under section 34 of the Solicitors Act 1974, and rule 35 of the Solicitors' Accounts Rules 1998, solicitors must deliver to the Society each year an accountant's report on the handling of clients' money and controlled trust money and operation of clients' own accounts (e.g. operated under a power of attorney).

1. Section 34 appears in Annex 28A, p.681. Detailed provisions on accountants' reports appear in the Solicitors' Accounts Rules 1998 (see Annex 28B, p.684). See also rule 16 of the Solicitors' Overseas Practice Rules (Annex 9A at p.187).

2. Solicitors who do not hold or receive clients' money or controlled trust money or operate clients' own accounts are exempted by the rules from the requirement to deliver a report. However, consultants and assistant solicitors should be aware that endorsing a cheque over to another party is receiving clients' money (see **4.02** note 1, p.147).

2.13 Monitoring by the Society

The Society has powers to monitor investment business, insolvency practice and compliance with the accounts rules.

1. Investment business within the meaning of the Financial Services Act 1986 is monitored under rule 28 of the Solicitors' Investment Business Rules 1995 (see Annex 27B at p.583).

2. Isle of Man investment business is monitored under rule 28 as applied to firms in the Isle of Man by the Mutual Assistance Agreement and regulation agreements made under it.

3. Insolvency practice is monitored by virtue of powers derived from the Insolvency Act 1986.

4. Compliance with the accounts rules is monitored under Part E of the Solicitors' Accounts Rules 1998 (see Annex 28B at p.719) and rule 15 of the Solicitors' Overseas Practice Rules 1990 (see Annex 9A at p.187).

5. Monitoring is the responsibility of the Monitoring and Investigation Unit of the Office for the Supervision of Solicitors (see p.xv for contact details).

Annex 2A

Solicitors Act 1974

sections 1–1A, 12–12A, 20–22 and 23–25 (right to practise as solicitor)

(with consolidated amendments to May 1995)

---

1. Qualifications for practising as solicitor

No person shall be qualified to act as a solicitor unless –

(a)   he has been admitted as a solicitor, and

(b)   his name is on the roll, and

(c)   he has in force a certificate issued by the Society in accordance with the provisions of this Part authorising him to practise as a solicitor (in this Act referred to as a "practising certificate").

1A. Practising certificates: employed solicitors

A person who has been admitted as a solicitor and whose name is on the roll shall, if he would not otherwise be taken to be acting as a solicitor, be taken for the purposes of this Act to be so acting if he is employed in connection with the provision of any legal services –

(a)   by any person who is qualified to act as a solicitor;

(b)   by any partnership at least one member of which is so qualified; or

(c)   by a body recognised by the Council of the Law Society under section 9 of the Administration of Justice Act 1985 (incorporated practices).

12. Discretion of Society with respect to issue of practising certificates in special cases

(1)   Subject to subsections (2) and (3), this section shall have effect in any case where a solicitor applies for a practising certificate –

(a)   for the first time; or

(b)   not having held a practising certificate free of conditions since the date of his admission; or

(c)   when, on what would be the commencement date for the certificate, if it were granted, a period of twelve months or more will have elapsed since he held a practising certificate in force; or

(d)   after the Tribunal has ordered a penalty or costs to be paid by him or that he be reprimanded; or

(e)   after he has been invited by the Society to give an explanation in respect of any matter relating to his conduct and has failed to give an explanation in respect of that matter which the Council regard as sufficient and satisfactory, and has been notified in writing by the Society that he has so failed; or

(ee)   when, having been required by section 34(1) to deliver an accountant's report to the Society, he has not delivered that report within the period allowed by section 34(2); or

(f)   when, having been suspended from practice, the period of his suspension has expired; or

(g)   when, having had his name removed from or struck off the roll, his name has been restored to the roll; or

(h)   while he is an undischarged bankrupt; or

(i)   after having been adjudged bankrupt and discharged or after having entered into a composition with his creditors or a deed of arrangement for the benefit of his creditors; or

(j)   while he is a patient as defined by section 94 of the Mental Health Act 1983 (which relates to the judge's functions in relation to the patient), or while he is a person as to whom powers have been exercised under section 104 of the Mental Health Act 1959 or section 98 of the said Act of 1983 (which relates to the judge's powers in cases of emergency); or

(k)   after having been committed to prison in civil or criminal proceedings; or

(l)   after having had given against him any judgment which involves the payment of money, not being a judgment –

    (i)   limited to the payment of costs; or

    (ii)   as to the whole effect of which upon him he is entitled to indemnity or relief from some other person; or

    (iii)   evidence of the satisfaction of which has been produced to the Society.

(2)   Where a practising certificate free of conditions is issued by the Society under subsection (4) to a solicitor in relation to whom this section has effect by reason of any such circumstances as are mentioned in paragraph (d), (e), (ee), (f), (g), (i), (k) or (l) of subsection (1) then, except in the case of any circumstances of whose existence the Society is unaware at the time the certificate is issued, this section shall not thereafter have effect in relation to that solicitor by reason of those circumstances.

(3)   Where a solicitor's practising certificate is suspended by virtue of section 15(1) by reason of his suspension from practice and the suspension of his practising certificate is terminated unconditionally under section 16(4) or (5), then, notwithstanding subsection (1)(f), this section shall not thereafter have effect in relation to that solicitor by reason of that suspension from practice and the expiry of the period of that suspension.

(4)   In any case where this section has effect, the applicant shall, unless the Society or the Master of the Rolls otherwise orders, give to the Society not less than six weeks before he applies for a practising certificate notice of his intention so to apply; and, subject to subsections (6) and (7), the Society may in its discretion –

(a)   grant or refuse the application, or

(b)   decide to issue a certificate to the applicant subject to such conditions as the Society may think fit.

(4A)   Without prejudice to the generality of subsection (4)(b) –

(a)   conditions may be imposed under that provision for requiring the applicant to take any specified steps that will, in the opinion of the Society, be conducive to his carrying on an efficient practice as a solicitor; and

(b)   conditions may be so imposed (whether for the purpose mentioned in paragraph (a) or otherwise) notwithstanding that they may result in expenditure being incurred by the applicant.

(5)   Where the Society decides to issue a certificate subject to conditions, it may, if it thinks fit, postpone the issue of the certificate pending the hearing and determination of any appeal under section 13(2)(b).

(6)   The Society shall not refuse an application by a solicitor for a practising certificate in a case where this section has effect by reason only –

(a)   that he is applying for the first time; or

(b)   that he has not held a practising certificate free from conditions since the date of his admission;

and, in a case falling within paragraph (b), the certificate shall not be made subject to any conditions binding on the applicant in respect of any period more than three years after the date on which the first practising certificate issued to him had effect.

(7)   Where a solicitor applies for a practising certificate in a case where this section has effect by reason only of any such circumstances as are mentioned in paragraph (h), (k) or (l) of subsection (1) and an appeal has been made to the appropriate court against the order or judgment in question, the Society shall not refuse the application before the determination of that appeal, unless in the opinion of the Society the proceedings on that appeal have been unduly protracted by the appellant or are unlikely to be successful.

12A. Additional fee payable by certain solicitors on applying for practising certificates

(1)   Where a solicitor applies for a practising certificate at a time when section 12 has effect in relation to him by reason of the circumstances mentioned in section 12(1)(ee), he shall pay an additional fee to the Society when making his application.

(2)   The amount of that additional fee –

(a)   shall be fixed by order of the Master of the Rolls made with the concurrence of the Lord Chancellor and the Lord Chief Justice; and

(b)   shall be designed to provide reasonable compensation to the Society for the additional cost of dealing with such applications.

2

20. Unqualified person not to act as solicitor

(1)   No unqualified person shall –

   (a)   act as a solicitor, or as such issue any writ or process, or commence, prosecute or defend any action, suit or other proceeding, in his own name or in the name of any other person, in any court of civil or criminal jurisdiction; or

   (b)   act as a solicitor in any cause or matter, civil or criminal, to be heard or determined before any justice or justices or any commissioners of Her Majesty's revenue.

(2)   Any person who contravenes the provisions of subsection (1) –

   (a)   shall be guilty of an offence and liable on conviction on indictment to imprisonment for not more than two years or to a fine or to both; and

   (b)   shall be guilty of contempt of the court in which the action, suit, cause, matter or proceeding in relation to which he so acts is brought or taken and may be punished accordingly;

   (c)   [repealed]

[NOTES

1.   Section 27(10) of the Courts and Legal Services Act 1990 provides that section 20 shall not apply in relation to any act done in the exercise of a right of audience, and section 28(6) of that Act provides that section 20 shall not apply in relation to any act done in the exercise of a right to conduct litigation.

2.   Section 9(3) of the Administration of Justice Act 1985 provides that, notwithstanding section 24(2) of the Solicitors Act 1974, section 20 shall not apply to a recognised body (i.e. an incorporated practice recognised under section 9 of the 1985 Act).

3.   Further amendment of section 20 by Schedule 18 paragraph 11 of the Courts and Legal Services Act 1990 (containing further exemptions from section 20) not yet in force as at 31st March 1999.]

21. Unqualified person not to pretend to be a solicitor

Any unqualified person who wilfully pretends to be, or takes or uses any name, title, addition or description implying that he is, qualified or recognised by law as qualified to act as a solicitor shall be guilty of an offence and liable on summary conviction to a fine not exceeding the fourth level on the standard scale.

22. Unqualified person not to prepare certain instruments

(1)   Subject to subsections (2) and (2A), any unqualified person who directly or indirectly –

   (a)   draws or prepares any instrument of transfer or charge for the purposes of the Land Registration Act 1925, or makes any application or lodges any document for registration under that Act at the registry, or

   (b)   draws or prepares any other instrument relating to real or personal estate, or any legal proceeding,

shall, unless he proves that the act was not done for or in expectation of any fee, gain or reward, be guilty of an offence and liable on summary conviction to a fine not exceeding level 3 on the standard scale.

(2)   Subsection (1) does not apply to –

(a)   a barrister or duly certificated notary public;

(aa)   a registered trade mark agent drawing or preparing any instrument relating to any design or trade mark;

(ab)   a registered patent agent drawing or preparing any instrument relating to any invention, design, technical information or trade mark;

(ac)   any accredited person drawing or preparing any instrument –

(i)   which creates, or which he believes on reasonable grounds will create, a farm business tenancy (within the meaning of the Agricultural Tenancies Act 1995), or

(ii)   which relates to an existing tenancy which is, or which he believes on reasonable grounds to be, such a tenancy;

(b)   any public officer drawing or preparing instruments or applications in the course of his duty;

(c)   any person employed merely to engross any instrument, application or proceeding;

and paragraph (b) of that subsection does not apply to a duly certificated solicitor in Scotland.

(2A)   Subsection (1) also does not apply to any act done by a person at the direction and under the supervision of another person if –

(a)   that other person was at the time his employer, a partner of his employer or a fellow employee; and

(b)   the act could have been done by that other person for or in expectation of any fee, gain or reward without committing an offence under this section.

(3)   For the purposes of subsection (1)(b), "instrument" includes a contract for the sale or other disposition of land (except a contract to grant such a lease as is referred to in section 54(2) of the Law of Property Act 1925 (short leases)), but does not include –

(a)   a will or other testamentary instrument;

(b)   an agreement not intended to be executed as a deed other than a contract that is included by virtue of the preceding provisions of this subsection;

(c)   a letter or power of attorney; or

(d)   a transfer of stock containing no trust or limitation thereof.

(3A)   In subsection (2) –

"accredited person" means any person who is –

(a)   a Full Member of the Central Association of Agricultural Valuers,

(b)   an Associate or Fellow of the Incorporated Society of Valuers and Auctioneers, or

(c)   an Associate or Fellow of the Royal Institution of Chartered Surveyors;

"registered trade mark agent" has the same meaning as in the Trade Marks Act 1994; and "registered patent agent" has the same meaning as in section 275(1) of the Copyright, Designs and Patents Act 1988.

(4)   A local weights and measures authority may institute proceedings for an offence under this section.

[NOTES

1.   Section 11(4) of the Administration of Justice Act 1985 provides that section 22(1) shall not apply to any act done by a licensed conveyancer in the course of the provision of any conveyancing services if he or she is not precluded from providing those services as a licensed conveyancer by any conditions imposed as mentioned in section 16(3)(a) of the 1985 Act.

2.   Section 27(10) of the Courts and Legal Services Act 1990 provides that section 22 shall not apply in relation to any act done in the exercise of a right of audience, and section 28(6) of that Act provides that section 22 shall not apply in relation to any act done in the exercise of a right to conduct litigation.

3.   Section 9(3) of the Administration of Justice Act 1985 provides that, notwithstanding section 24(2) of the Solicitors Act 1974, section 22(1) shall not apply to a recognised body (i.e. an incorporated practice recognised under section 9 of the 1985 Act).

4.   Section 9(4) of the Administration of Justice Act 1985 provides that section 22(1) shall not apply to any act done by an officer or employee of a recognised body if:

'(a) it was done by him at the direction and under the supervision of another person who was at the time an officer or employee of the body; and

(b) it could have been done by that other person for or in expectation of any fee, gain or reward without committing an offence under the said section 22'.

5.   For the exemption, in certain circumstances, from section 22(1) of a licensed conveyancers' incorporated practice and its officers and employees see section 32(4)–(5) of the Administration of Justice Act 1985.]

23. Unqualified person not to prepare papers for probate, etc.

(1)   Subject to subsections (2) and (3), any unqualified person who, directly or indirectly, draws or prepares any papers on which to found or oppose –

(a)   a grant of probate, or

(b)   a grant of letters of administration,

shall, unless he proves that the act was not done for or in expectation of any fee, gain or reward, be guilty of an offence and liable on summary conviction to a fine not exceeding the first level on the standard scale.

(2)   Subsection (1) does not apply to a barrister or duly certificated notary public.

(3)   Subsection (1) also does not apply to any act done by a person at the direction and under the supervision of another person if –

(a)   that other person was at the time his employer, a partner of his employer or a fellow employee; and

(b)   the act could have been done by that other person for or in expectation of any fee, gain or reward without committing an offence under this section.

[NOTES

1.   Section 9(3) of the Administration of Justice Act 1985 provides that, notwithstanding section 24(2) of the Solicitors Act 1974, section 23(1) shall not apply to a recognised body (i.e. an incorporated practice recognised under section 9 of the 1985 Act).

2.   Section 9(4) of the Administration of Justice Act 1985 provides that section 23(1) shall not apply to any act done by an officer or employee of a recognised body if:

'(a) it was done by him at the direction and under the supervision of another person who was at the time an officer or employee of the body; and

(b) it could have been done by that other person for or in expectation of any fee, gain or reward without committing an offence under the said . . . section 23.'

3.   Further amendment of section 23 by section 54(1) of the Courts and Legal Services Act 1990 and Schedule 21 paragraph 5 of the Friendly Societies Act 1992 (containing further exemptions from section 23) not yet in force as at 31st March 1999.

4.   Section 55 of the Courts and Legal Services Act 1990 (containing a further exemption from section 23) not yet in force as at 31st March 1999.]

24. Application of penal provisions to body corporate

(1)   If any act is done by a body corporate, or by any director, officer or servant of a body corporate, and is of such a nature or is done in such a manner as to be calculated to imply that the body corporate is qualified or recognised by law as qualified to act as a solicitor –

(a)   the body corporate shall be guilty of **an** offence and liable on summary conviction to a fine not exceeding the fourth level on the standard scale, and

(b)   in the case of an act done by a director, officer or servant of the body corporate, he also shall be guilty of an offence and liable on summary conviction to a fine not exceeding the fourth level on the standard scale.

(2)   For the avoidance of doubt it is hereby declared that in sections 20, 22 and 23 references to unqualified persons and to persons include references to bodies corporate.

[NOTE

Section 9(3) of the Administration of Justice Act 1985 provides that nothing in section 24(1) shall apply in relation to a recognised body (i.e. an incorporated practice recognised under section 9 of the 1985 Act).]

25. Costs where unqualified person acts as solicitor

(1)   No costs in respect of anything done by an unqualified person acting as a solicitor shall be recoverable by him, or by any other person, in any action, suit or matter.

(2)   Nothing in subsection (1) shall prevent the recovery of money paid or to be paid by a solicitor on behalf of a client in respect of anything done by the solicitor while acting for the client without holding a practising certificate in force if that money would have been recoverable if he had held such a certificate when so acting.

[NOTES

1.   Section 27(10) of the Courts and Legal Services Act 1990 provides that section 25 shall not apply in relation to any act done in the exercise of a right of audience, and section 28(6) of that Act provides that section 25 shall not apply in relation to any act done in the exercise of a right to conduct litigation.

2.   Amendment of section 25 by Schedule 18 paragraph 12 of the Courts and Legal Services Act 1990 (containing further exemptions from section 25) not yet in force as at 31st March 1999.]

Practising Certificate Regulations 1995

Made on 24th January 1995 by the Master of the Rolls with the concurrence of the Lord Chancellor and the Lord Chief Justice under sections 14(2) and 28 of the Solicitors Act 1974, regulating solicitors' practising certificates and applications for them.

Commencement

1. These regulations replace the Practising Certificate Regulations 1976 in relation to all practising certificates, and applications for practising certificates, for any period commencing on or after 1st November 1995.

Requests for information

2. In addition to information supplied on any prescribed form under these regulations, solicitors must supply to the Law Society such information as to their practice as solicitors as the Society shall from time to time reasonably require for the purpose of processing applications.

Replacement date and conditions

3. The replacement date for every practising certificate shall be the 31st October following the issue of the applicant's current practising certificate.

4. Every practising certificate shall specify its commencement date, its replacement date, and any conditions imposed by the Law Society.

Applications for practising certificates

5. Any application made or certificate or notice given to the Law Society under these regulations must be on the prescribed form, correctly completed, and accompanied by such additional information, documents and references as the Society shall specify.

6. Every application for a practising certificate must be accompanied by:

    (a) the fee payable in respect of the certificate under section 11 of the Solicitors Act 1974;

    (b) if appropriate, any fee payable under section 12A of the Solicitors Act 1974; and

(c) any annual contribution to the Solicitors' Compensation Fund, and any special levy payable by the applicant, under Schedule 2 to the Solicitors Act 1974.

7. (1) Every application for a practising certificate which is to follow on immediately from the applicant's current practising certificate must reach the Law Society on or before the replacement date.

(2) If no application is received from a solicitor with a current practising certificate by the replacement date the Law Society may terminate that solicitor's current practising certificate.

Advance notice of application

8. (1) Unless the Law Society or the Master of the Rolls otherwise orders, a solicitor to whom section 12 of the Solicitors Act 1974 applies must give at least six weeks' notice of his or her intention to apply for a practising certificate.

(2) Any notice under this regulation must, unless the Law Society in writing dispenses with this requirement, be accompanied by a certificate of fitness completed by two practising solicitors to whom the applicant is personally known. The certificate may not be completed by a solicitor who is the applicant's relative, employee, fellow employee junior in rank or a person to whom section 12 of the Solicitors Act 1974 applies, or by two solicitors who are the applicant's partner, former partner, employer or fellow employee.

(3) Any such notice must also be accompanied by such additional information, documents and references as the Law Society shall specify.

Obligations on completing prescribed form

9. Every applicant must ensure that all details relating to him or her given on any form prescribed under these regulations are correct and complete.

10. Every form submitted under these regulations must be personally signed by the applicant unless:

(a) another solicitor has been given written permission by the Law Society, in exceptional circumstances, to sign on the applicant's behalf; or

(b) the form used is completed on behalf of a number of applicants in one practice, and the person signing the form is a solicitor authorised by the practice, and has the consent of all the persons named in the form, to sign on their behalf.

11. If any form submitted under these regulations is signed by a person other than the applicant, the person signing the form must take reasonable steps to ensure that all details given on the form are correct and complete.

Delivery of practising certificate

12. Every practising certificate shall be sent by post to the applicant at the applicant's principal practising address or to such other address as may be specified by or on behalf of the applicant in writing, to the Society's Controller of Administration [*now Regulation and Information Services, see p.xv for contact details*].

Interpretation

13. The Interpretation Act 1978 shall apply to the interpretation of these regulations as it applies to the interpretation of an Act of Parliament.

14. In these regulations:

"practice" means a solicitor's practice, and includes a multi-national partnership, a recognised body, the in-house legal department of a non-solicitor and an overseas partnership or corporate practice of solicitors and other lawyers; and

"prescribed form" means a form or forms prescribed from time to time by the Law Society with the concurrence of the Master of the Rolls.

Solicitors (Keeping of the Roll) Regulations 1999

1. Authority and date

These regulations, dated 22nd January 1999, are made under section 28 of the Solicitors Act 1974 by the Master of the Rolls with the concurrence of the Lord Chancellor and the Lord Chief Justice.

2. Commencement and repeal

As from 1st February 1999 these regulations replace the Solicitors (Keeping of the Roll) Regulations 1989.

3. Address for correspondence

When the Society writes to any person under these regulations it shall write to the solicitor's last notified address.

4. Annual enquiry

The Society shall once a year ask every solicitor without a practising certificate whether the solicitor wishes his or her name to remain on the roll.

5. Removal from the roll

The Society may remove from the roll the name of any solicitor who:

(a) replies, following an enquiry under regulation 4, that he or she does not wish to remain on the roll; or

(b) fails to reply within eight weeks to an enquiry under regulation 4; or

(c) fails, within eight weeks of an enquiry under regulation 4, to pay the fee prescribed by regulation 13(a) for remaining on the roll; or

(d) applies to have his or her name removed from the roll; or

(e) has died.

6. Application for restoration to the roll

(a) A person whose name has been removed from the roll may apply to the Society for his or her name to be restored to the roll.

(b)   This regulation does not apply if:

   (i)   the Solicitors Disciplinary Tribunal has made an order prohibiting the restoration of the person's name to the roll except by order of the Tribunal; or

   (ii)   the person's name has been struck off the roll.

7. Application for change of name on the roll

A solicitor whose name has changed may apply to the Society to change his or her name on the roll.

8. Outstanding complaints

The Society may refuse to remove from or restore to the roll the name of a solicitor or former solicitor against whom there is an outstanding complaint.

9. Disciplinary proceedings

The Society shall not remove from or restore to the roll the name of any solicitor or former solicitor against whom disciplinary proceedings are pending before the Supreme Court or Tribunal.

10. Notice of intention to remove name

Where regulation 5(b) or (c) applies, the Society shall not remove a solicitor's name from the roll until it has notified the solicitor in writing that it intends to remove his or her name.

11. Letter of confirmation or notice of refusal

The Society shall write to a solicitor or former solicitor:

(a)   confirming that his or her name on the roll has been removed from, restored to or changed on the roll; or

(b)   giving notice that the Society has refused to remove from, restore to or change his or her name on the roll.

12. Forms

The Society may prescribe forms for replies or applications to the Society and in the case of an application under regulation 7 may require such evidence as it sees fit.

13. Fees

(a)   Subject to paragraph (b) any reply, following an enquiry under regulation 4, that a solicitor wishes to remain on the roll must be accompanied by a fee of £15.

(b)   No fee is payable under regulation 4 by any solicitor whose name has been on the roll for 50 years or more or for such shorter period as the Society may from time to time prescribe.

(c)   Any application under regulation 6 for restoration of a person's name to the roll shall be accompanied by such fee as the Society may from time to time prescribe.

14. Appeals

(a) Any person who is aggrieved because:

    (i)   the Society has removed his or her name from the roll; or

    (ii)   the Society refused to remove his or her name from the roll; or

    (iii)   the Society refused to change his or her name on the roll

    may appeal to the Master of the Rolls under this regulation.

(b) Any person aggrieved by the Society's refusal to restore his or her name to the roll under regulation 6 may appeal to the Master of the Rolls under section 8(4) of the Solicitors Act 1974.

(c) The procedure for any appeal is governed by the Master of the Rolls (Appeals and Applications) Regulations 1991, which state that an appeal must be made within four weeks of the Society writing to confirm the removal or to give notice of the refusal.

Annex 2D

Master of the Rolls (Appeals and Applications) Regulations 1991

relevant extracts

(with consolidated amendments to 20th December 1995)

Part I – Preliminary

2. (i) The Interpretation Act 1978 applies to these regulations in the same manner as it applies to an Act of Parliament.

(ii) In these regulations, unless the context otherwise requires:

(a) "the Act" means the Solicitors Act 1974;

(b) "the Council" means the Council of the Law Society;

(c) "Master of the Rolls" includes any judge of the Supreme Court appointed to exercise the relevant functions of the Master of the Rolls under section 73 of the Courts and Legal Services Act 1990;

(d) "the Society" means the Law Society;

(e) "the Tribunal" means the Solicitors Disciplinary Tribunal.

Part II – Scope of the regulations and powers of the Master of the Rolls

3. These regulations apply to appeals and applications made to the Master of the Rolls in the following circumstances:

(ix) **an appeal under section 13(1) of the Act** in respect of the refusal or neglect of the Society to issue a practising certificate on application duly made otherwise than in a case where section 12 of the Act has effect;

in respect of which appeal the Master of the Rolls is empowered by section 13(1) of the Act to make such order, including an order for the payment of costs by the Society to the applicant or by the applicant to the Society, as may be just;

(ixA) **an appeal under section 13(2)(a) of the Act** in respect of a decision of the Society made in the exercise of its powers under section 10 of the Act to issue a practising certificate subject to a training condition or an indemnity condition, such appeal to be made within one month of the appellant being notified of the Society's decision;

in respect of which appeal the Master of the Rolls is empowered by section 13(3) of the Act to:

    (a)   affirm the decision of the Society;

    (b)   direct the Society to issue a certificate to the applicant free from conditions; or

    (c)   if regulations under section 28 of the Act specify a number of training conditions or indemnity conditions, direct the Society to issue a certificate to the applicant subject to a training condition, or, as the case may be, an indemnity condition, different from that subject to which it was originally issued;

(x)   **an appeal under section 13(2)(b) of the Act** in respect of a decision of the Society made in the exercise of its powers under section 12 of the Act to refuse to issue a practising certificate or to issue a certificate subject to conditions, such appeal to be made within one month of the appellant being notified of the Society's decision;

in respect of which appeal the Master of the Rolls is empowered by section 13(4) of the Act to:

    (a)   affirm the decision of the Society;

    (b)   direct the Society to issue a certificate to the applicant free from conditions or subject to such conditions other than training conditions or indemnity conditions as the Master of the Rolls may think fit;

    (c)   direct the Society not to issue a certificate;

    (d)   order the suspension of a certificate which has been issued; or

    (e)   make such other order as the Master of the Rolls thinks fit;

(xi)   **an application under section 12(4) of the Act** for an order that the applicant may be at liberty to give less than six weeks' notice of his or her intention to apply for a practising certificate;

in respect of which appeal the Master of the Rolls may make such order as the Master of the Rolls thinks fit;

(xii)   **an appeal under section 16(5) of the Act** in respect of an order of the Society, on an application under section 16(3) for the termination of the suspension of the appellant's practising certificate, that the suspension be terminated subject to conditions, or the refusal of any such application;

in respect of which appeal the Master of the Rolls is empowered by section 16(5) of the Act to:

    (a)   affirm the decision; or

    (b)   terminate the suspension either unconditionally or subject to such conditions as the Master of the Rolls may think fit;

(xiii)   **an appeal under section 13A(6) of the Act** in respect of a direction of the Society made in exercise of its powers under section 13A of the Act that the appellant's current practising certificate shall have effect subject to a condition or conditions, such appeal to be made within one month of the appellant being notified of the Society's decision;

in respect of which appeal the Master of the Rolls is empowered by section 13(7) of the Act to:

(a)   affirm the decision of the Society;

(b)   direct that the appellant's current certificate shall have effect subject to such conditions as the Master of the Rolls thinks fit;

(c)   revoke the direction by order; or

(d)   make such other order as the Master of the Rolls thinks fit;

(xiv)   **an appeal under section 13B(7) of the Act** in respect of a direction by the Society made in exercise of its powers under section 13B(1) or (4) of the Act that the appellant's practising certificate be suspended or that the suspension of the appellant's practising certificate be continued, such appeal to be made within one month of the appellant being notified of the direction;

in respect of which appeal the Master of the Rolls is empowered by section 13B(8) of the Act to:

(a)   affirm the suspension;

(b)   direct that the appellant's certificate shall not be suspended but shall have effect subject to such conditions as the Master of the Rolls thinks fit;

(c)   by order revoke the direction; or

(d)   make such other order as the Master of the Rolls thinks fit;

(xv)   **an appeal under section 41(3) of the Act** in respect of a decision of the Society upon an application to employ or remunerate a person disqualified from practising as a solicitor by reason of the fact that:

(a)   his or her name has been struck off the roll;

(b)   he or she is suspended from practising as a solicitor;

(c)   his or her practising certificate is suspended whilst he or she is an undischarged bankrupt; or

(d)   there is a direction in force under section 47(2)(g) of the Act prohibiting the restoration of his or her name to the roll except by order of the Tribunal;

in respect of which appeal the Master of the Rolls is empowered by section 41(3) of the Act to:

(a)   confirm the refusal or the conditions, as the case may be; or

(b)   grant a permission under section 41 of the Act for such period and subject to such conditions as the Master of the Rolls thinks fit;

(xvi)   **an appeal under section 49(1)(a) of the Act** in respect of a decision of the Tribunal upon an application made under section 43(3) of the Act for the revocation of an order made by the Tribunal in respect of the employment of a clerk; such appeal to be made within 28 days from the pronouncement of the findings and order;

in respect of which appeal the Master of the Rolls is empowered by section 49(4) of the Act to make such order as the Master of the Rolls may think fit;

(xvii)   **an appeal under section 49(1)(a) of the Act** in respect of a decision of the Tribunal on an application under section 47(1)(d), (e) or (f) of the Act:

    (a)   by a solicitor who has been suspended from practice for an unspecified period, by order of the Tribunal, for the termination of that suspension;

    (b)   by a former solicitor whose name has been struck off the roll to have his or her name restored to the roll; or

    (c)   by a former solicitor in respect of whom a direction has been given under section 47(2)(g) prohibiting the restoration of his or her name to the roll except by order of the Tribunal, to have his or her name restored to the roll; such appeal to be made within 28 days of the pronouncement of the findings and order;

in respect of which appeal the Master of the Rolls is empowered by section 49(4) of the Act to make such order as the Master of the Rolls may think fit;

(xviii)   **an appeal under section 8(4) of the Act** in respect of a decision of the Society on the application of a former solicitor whose name is not on the roll because it has been removed from it, to have his or her name entered on the roll;

in respect of which appeal the Master of the Rolls may make such order as the Master of the Rolls thinks fit;

(xix)   **an appeal under regulation 15 of the Solicitors (Keeping of the Roll) Regulations 1989** *[now regulation 14 of the 1999 regulations]* in respect of the removal of a person's name from the roll, or the refusal by the Society to grant an application for the removal of a solicitor's name from the roll, or restoration of a solicitor's name to the roll or change of a solicitor's name on the roll in accordance with the said regulations; such appeal to be made within 28 days of the applicant being notified of the Society's decision;

in respect of which appeal the Master of the Rolls may make such order as the Master of the Rolls may think fit;

(xx)   **an appeal under paragraph 2 of Schedule 2 to the Administration of Justice Act 1985** in respect of the refusal of the Council to grant recognition to a body corporate under section 9 of the said Act, such appeal to be made within one month of the applicant being notified of the Society's decision;

in respect of which appeal the Master of the Rolls is empowered by paragraph 2 of Schedule 2 to the said Act to:

    (a)   direct the Council to grant recognition of the body in question under section 9 of the said Act; or

    (b)   affirm the refusal of the Council;

and to make such order as to the payment of costs by the Council or by that body as the Master of the Rolls thinks fit;

(xxi)   **an appeal under paragraph 2 of Schedule 2 to the Administration of Justice Act 1985** by virtue of rule 17(2) of the Solicitors' Incorporated Practice Rules 1988 where recognition of a body corporate under section 9 of the said Act has been neither granted nor refused by the Council within three months of the date on which the application for recognition was received;

in respect of which appeal the Master of the Rolls may make such order as the Master of the Rolls thinks fit;

(xxii)   **an appeal by a foreign lawyer under paragraph 14 of Schedule 14 to the Courts and Legal Services Act 1990** in respect of:

(a)   the refusal of the Society to register or to renew the registration of a foreign lawyer;

(b)   the refusal of the Society to terminate the suspension of the registration of a foreign lawyer on an application made by the foreign lawyer under paragraph 12 of the said schedule;

(c)   the failure of the Society to deal with any application by a foreign lawyer for registration, renewal of registration or the termination (under paragraph 12(2) of the said schedule) of a suspension within a reasonable time; or

(d)   any condition imposed by the Society under paragraph 2(3), 12(2) or 13 of the said schedule;

appeals set out in (a), (b) or (d) above to be brought within the period of one month beginning with the date on which the Society notifies the applicant of its decision on his or her application;

in respect of which appeal the Master of the Rolls is empowered by paragraph 14(3) of the said schedule to make such order as the Master of the Rolls thinks fit;

(xxiii)   **an appeal under paragraph 17(1)(a) of Schedule 14 to the Courts and Legal Services Act 1990** in respect of:

(a)   an order of the Tribunal on an application under paragraph 15(2)(d) of the said schedule by a foreign lawyer whose name has been struck off the register by order of the Tribunal to have his or her name restored to the register, or the refusal of any such application; or

(b)   an order of the Tribunal on an application under paragraph 15(2)(e) of the said schedule by a foreign lawyer whose registration has been suspended for an indefinite period by order of the Tribunal for the termination of that suspension, or the refusal of any such application;

in respect of which appeal the Master of the Rolls may make such order as the Master of the Rolls thinks fit;

(xxiv)   **an appeal under regulation 7(ii) of the Higher Courts Qualification Regulations 1992** in respect of a decision of the Society upon an application for review under regulation 7(i) of a decision under the said regulations;

such appeal to be made within three months of the appellant receiving notification of the Society's decision upon the application for review;

in respect of which appeal the Master of the Rolls is empowered by regulation 7(ii) of the said regulations to:

(a)   affirm the decision of the Society; or

(b)   give a direction as to how the Society should exercise its functions under the said regulations, including a direction that the Society grant to the appellant a Higher Courts Qualification;

(xxv)   **an appeal under rule 6 of the Solicitors' Investment Business Rules 1995** in respect of:

(a)   the refusal of the Council to issue a certificate or a certificate of the category sought; or

(b)   a decision of the Council to issue a certificate subject to conditions; or

(c)   a decision of the Council to impose conditions on a certificate; or

(d)   a decision of the Council to suspend or withdraw a certificate;

such appeal to be made, after exhausting any internal appeal procedure, within one month of the appellant being notified of the Council's final decision;

in respect of which appeal the Master of the Rolls may make such order as the Master of the Rolls thinks fit.

Part III – Procedure for appeals and applications

5.   The appellant or applicant shall lodge with the Clerk to the Master of the Rolls:

(a)   a petition signed by the appellant or applicant asking for the appropriate relief and setting out the circumstances in which the appeal or application is made and the matters of fact upon which the appellant or applicant relies in support of the appeal or application; and

(b)   a statutory declaration verifying the facts stated in the petition; and

(c)   in the case of an appeal against a decision of the Tribunal, copies of all documents referred to at the hearing before the Tribunal;

and shall within two days of lodging the said documents with the Clerk to the Master of the Rolls lodge copies at the Society's offices.

5A.   The Society may make written submissions to the Master of the Rolls on the substance of the appeal or application, or on the jurisdiction of the Master of the Rolls to deal with the appeal or application, within six weeks of receipt of copies of the documents lodged by the appellant or applicant. The Society shall at the same time send copies of any such submissions to the appellant or applicant.

6.   The Master of the Rolls may appoint a time for hearing any appeal or application made to the Master of the Rolls, allowing normally six weeks from the date of the filing of the petition before the appeal or application is heard, but an earlier date may be appointed on request.

7.   On the hearing of the appeal or application the appellant or applicant and the Society may appear in person, or by solicitor or counsel or, in the case of a body corporate, by a director.

8.   On the hearing of the appeal or application the strict rules of evidence shall not apply.

8A.   Nothing in these regulations shall affect the inherent jurisdiction of the Master of the Rolls to make such order as to costs as the Master of the Rolls thinks fit.

9.   Any order made by the Master of the Rolls shall be signed by the Master of the Rolls and shall be filed with the Society by the Secretary to the Master of the Rolls. The Society shall take such action as is necessary to give effect to the order.

Annex 2E

Training Regulations 1990

extracts relating to continuing professional development

(with consolidated amendments to 19th December 1994)

PART I – INTRODUCTORY

2. Interpretation and definitions

(3)   In these Regulations:

"continuing professional development" means a course, lecture, seminar or other programme or method of study (whether requiring attendance or not) that is relevant to the needs and professional standards of solicitors and complies with guidance issued from time to time by the Society.

PART VI – CONTINUING PROFESSIONAL DEVELOPMENT (CPD)

34. Application of Part VI

This Part shall apply:

(a)   on 1st November 1992 to solicitors admitted after 1st August 1987;

(b)   on 1st November 1994 to solicitors admitted on or after 1st November 1982;

(c)   on 1st November 1998 to all solicitors.

35. CPD requirement during the first three years of admission

A solicitor must in the first three years following admission attend such continuing professional development courses as the Society may prescribe.

36. CPD requirement during the first months after admission

A solicitor who has been admitted after this Part has come into force must undertake one hour of continuing professional development for each whole month in legal practice or employment between admission and the next 1st day of November.

37. CPD requirement in first three complete years of legal practice or employment and subsequent years

(1)   A solicitor must in each of the first three complete years in legal practice or employment commencing with the 1st day of November immediately following admission undertake 16 hours of continuing professional development.

(2)   A solicitor must in each subsequent three year period undertake 48 hours of continuing professional development.

38. CPD requirement for solicitors admitted on or before 2nd November 1989

Solicitors admitted on or before 2nd November 1989 must undertake 48 hours of continuing professional development in each successive three year period the first of which commences as follows:

> (a)   on 1st November 1992 for solicitors admitted on or after 2nd August 1987 and on or before 2nd November 1989;
>
> (b)   on 1st November 1994 for solicitors admitted on or after 1st November 1982 and on or before 1st August 1987;
>
> (c)   on 1st November 1998 for solicitors admitted on or before 31st October 1982.

39. Obligation to keep record

A solicitor must keep a record of such continuing professional development undertaken to comply with these regulations and produce the record to the Society on demand.

40. CPD undertaken pre-admission

A solicitor who has undertaken continuing professional development between the expiry of articles or a training contract and the date of admission shall be credited with the relevant number of hours for the purpose of Regulations 36 and 37 provided that at the time of undertaking the continuing professional development an application for admission in accordance with admission regulations current at that time had been lodged with the Society and a record kept in accordance with Regulation 39.

41. Suspension

If a solicitor does not work for any period in legal practice or employment in England and Wales the application of this Part is suspended for that period.

42. Part-time working

If a solicitor works part-time in legal practice or employment the requirements under this Part are reduced on the basis that in each year one hour of continuing professional development must be undertaken for every two hours per week worked.

PART VII – GENERAL

43. Waiver of Regulations

In any particular case the Society has power to waive in writing any of the provisions of these Regulations and to revoke such waiver.

Annex 2F

Guidance – continuing professional development

issued under regulation 2(3) of the Training Regulations 1990

A. Lifelong learning is vital to the competitiveness of solicitors. This guidance sets out the ways by which continuing professional development can be undertaken to meet the Training Regulations.

B. Solicitors are reminded of their responsibility under practice rule 1. Failure to keep up-to-date with developments in law and practice relating to their work could compromise their proper standard of work contrary to paragraph (e) of that rule. The importance of maintaining the highest standards of client care is emphasised.

C. Over and above the general professional responsibility mentioned above there are compulsory requirements for CPD which are set out in the Training Regulations 1990. These requirements are modest and details of how they may be met are set out below:

1. At least 25% of the requirement to undertake CPD will be undertaken by participation in courses offered by providers authorised by the Law Society and which require attendance for one hour or more. "Attendance" means attendance at the complete course. "Course" includes face-to-face sessions forming part of a course otherwise delivered by an authorised distance learning provider.

2. The remaining 75% of the requirements may be met by any combination of the following:

   ▶ participation in courses offered by providers authorised by the Law Society;

   ▶ participation in courses offered by providers which are not authorised by the Law Society;

   ▶ writing law books or articles in legal journals;

   ▶ legal research which is of use beyond the particular case and results in the production of a precedent, practice note or other form of written guidance;

   ▶ study for or production of a dissertation counting towards a qualification recognised by the Law Society;

   ▶ undertaking courses offered by an authorised provider delivered by audio/visual means;

▶ distance learning courses where there is provision for the answering of enquiries or for discussion. (Distance learning courses may be delivered by correspondence, video and audio cassettes, television or radio broadcasts and computer based learning programmes);

▶ preparation and delivery of training courses forming part of the process of qualification or post admission training;

▶ work towards the Training and Development Lead Body Units D32, D33 and D34 relating to assessing and verifying the achievement of National Vocational Qualifications;

▶ participating in the development of specialist areas of law and practice by attending meetings of specialist committees and/or working parties of relevant professional or other competent bodies charged with such work;

▶ work towards the achievement of an NVQ in any business-related area and at any level including time spent building a portfolio of evidence;

▶ study towards the following professional examinations:

(i)   Joint Insolvency Examination

(ii)   Royal Town Planning Institute Examinations

(iii)   Financial Planning Certificate

(iv)   Advanced Financial Planning Certificate

(v)   Institute of Taxation Examination

(vi)   Pensions Management Institute Examination

(vii)   Associate Membership of the Chartered Insurance Institute Examination

(viii)   Institute of Chartered Secretaries and Administrators Examination

(ix)   Law Society Test in Evidence and Procedure leading to Rights of Audience

(x)   Other professional examinations approved by the Society.

NOTE   To count towards meeting CPD requirements the activity should be at an appropriate level and contribute to a solicitor's general professional skill and knowledge and not merely advance a particular fee-earning matter.

Suspension of the requirements

Under Regulation 41 of the Training Regulations 1990 the CPD requirement is suspended for the length of time a solicitor is not in legal practice or employment. The dates of and reasons for the suspension should be noted on the training record.

On return to legal employment the solicitor will be required to undertake two hours of CPD for every complete month from the date of return to the following 31st October up to a total of 16 hours for that CPD year. Where a solicitor has been admitted for three or more complete years a new three year period will start from the 1st November following his/her return to legal practice or employment.

2

Part-time work

The requirement to undertake CPD is automatically adjusted pro-rata where a solicitor is working part-time on the basis that one hour per annum of CPD should be undertaken for every two hours per week worked. No specific application to the Society is required but the dates of and reasons for the variations should be noted on the training record.

Exemptions

In limited circumstances individuals may be exempt from the provisions of paragraph C above. These relate primarily to solicitors working in firms accredited to certain national standards. Details will be published from time to time by the Society.

Effective from 1st November 1998

Chapter 3

Private practice

3.01   Setting up in practice

A firm must normally have at least one principal who has been admitted for three years. In addition, every solicitor who is a principal in private practice or who is employed in private practice in connection with the provision of any legal services must hold a practising certificate.

1.   All firms must be covered by the Solicitors' Indemnity Fund, before the commencement of the practice (see Chapter 29, p.782).

2.   If a solicitor sets up a new practice, Regulation and Information Services (see p.xv for contact details) must be advised, in writing, of the name of the firm, the date the practice commenced, details of members of the firm (i.e. fee-earners) and the practising address (see section 84 of the Solicitors Act 1974, p.40 for details of notifying new practising address). There is no special form to complete for this but a detailed booklet on setting up in practice is available from Professional Ethics (see p.xv for contact details).

3.   The requirement to hold a practising certificate applies to assistants, associates, consultants and locums (see **2.03**, p.33).

4.   Where a partner fails to hold a practising certificate, not only will he or she commit serious breaches of the Solicitors Act 1974 and the Solicitors' Practice Rules, but also the partnership will be rendered illegal. This has the effect of dissolving the partnership under section 34 of the Partnership Act 1890 (see *Hudgell Yeates & Co.* v. *Watson* [1978] Q.B. 451; and the appropriate authorities on partnership law).

5.   See **3.07** note 7 (p.72) for restrictions on employing certain staff.

6.   Under rule 2 of the Solicitors' Overseas Practice Rules, solicitors who practise as such outside England and Wales are required to hold practising certificates (see Annex 9A at p.181).

3.02   Partnerships

A solicitor shall not enter into partnership with any person other than a solicitor, a registered foreign lawyer or a recognised body.

1.   See rule 7(6) of the Solicitors' Practice Rules 1990, **3.03**, p.68.

2.   A recognised body shall not enter into partnership with any person other than a solicitor or a recognised body.

3.   Solicitors practising outside England and Wales must comply with the Solicitors' Overseas Practice Rules 1990. Under rule 8(2) of those rules it is possible for such solicitors, subject to any relevant overseas law or local rules, to enter into a partnership with a lawyer of another jurisdiction or an English barrister (see Annex 9A at p.183).

3.03 Practice rule 7 (fee sharing)

'(1) A solicitor shall not share or agree to share his or her professional fees with any person except:

(a) a practising solicitor;

(b) a practising foreign lawyer (other than a foreign lawyer whose registration in the register of foreign lawyers is suspended or whose name has been struck off the register);

(c) the solicitor's *bona fide* employee, which provision shall not permit under the cloak of employment a partnership prohibited by paragraph (6) of this rule; or

(d) a retired partner or predecessor of the solicitor or the dependants or personal representatives of a deceased partner or predecessor.

(2) Notwithstanding paragraph (1) of this rule a solicitor who instructs an estate agent as sub-agent for the sale of properties may remunerate the estate agent on the basis of a proportion of the solicitor's professional fee.

(3) The exceptions set out in paragraphs 2 to 9 of the Employed Solicitors Code shall where necessary also operate as exceptions to this rule but only to permit fee sharing with the solicitor's employer.

(4) A solicitor who works as a volunteer in a law centre or advice service operated by a charitable or similar non-commercial organisation may pay to the organisation any fees or costs that he or she receives under the legal aid scheme.

(5) For the purposes of sub-paragraph (1)(d) above, the references to a retired or deceased partner shall be construed, in relation to a recognised body, as meaning a retired or deceased director or member of that body, or a retired or deceased beneficial owner of any share in that body held by a member as nominee.

(6) (a) A solicitor shall not enter into partnership with any person other than a solicitor, a registered foreign lawyer or a recognised body.

(b) A recognised body shall not enter into partnership with any person other than a solicitor or a recognised body.

(c) In this paragraph, "solicitor" means a solicitor of the Supreme Court of England and Wales.

(7) A solicitor shall not practise through any body corporate except a recognised body, or save as permitted under rule 4 of these rules.'

Solicitors' Practice Rules 1990, rule 7

For additional guidance on commissions and payment by credit card see **14.02**, p.277.

3.04　Practice rule 11 (names used by a firm)

'(1)　A firm must not use a name which:

(a)　is misleading; or

(b)　brings the profession into disrepute.

(2)　A firm name appearing on any letterhead (or fax heading, or heading used for bills), if the name does not itself include the word "solicitor(s)", must be accompanied by either:

(a)　the word "solicitor(s)"; or

(b)　the words "regulated by the Law Society".

(3)　This rule must be interpreted in the light of the notes.

Notes

(i)　*The rule applies to any name used by a firm (which includes a sole practitioner or a recognised body – see rule 18(2)(d)) for its practice or part of its practice.*

(ii)　*The rule would allow, for example:*

(a)　*a non-conventional name, such as "The Legal Clinic", "XYZ Solicitors" or "Briefcase Legal Services";*

(b)　*a name with a geographical reference, such as "Browne and Son (Chancery Lane)" or "Guildford Solicitors" – but not a name that would breach note (iii)(e);*

(c)　*a name including a field of practice, such as "Smith & Co. Conveyancers" or "Redditch Conveyancing Service";*

(d)　*a firm name consisting of the names of solicitors or foreign lawyers who are or were principals in the firm or a predecessor firm, such as "Lewis & Smith", even though Lewis and Smith have died and Browne is now the sole principal;*

(e)　*a firm name which includes the name of an historical character unconnected with the practice, or the name of a fictional character, or an invented name, or a name selected at will – but not a name that would breach note (iii)(c);*

(f)　*the use of "& Co." or "Solicitors", even for a sole practitioner.*

(iii)　*The rule would not allow:*

(a)　*a name which uses the words "Law Centre";*

(b)　*a name which implies a connection with a business other than a legal practice, for example "Safeway Solicitors Group";*

(c)　*a firm name which includes the name of, or refers to, any actual person unless that person is either:*

(A)　*a solicitor or foreign lawyer who is or was a principal in the firm or a predecessor firm; or*

(B)　*an historical character unconnected with the practice;*

*for example, "Jones and Co." or "JMJ Financial and Legal Services",
where J. M. Jones is a financial adviser employed in the firm;*

(d) *a name which implies that a firm is bigger than it is (for example
"French & Partners", if French is a sole practitioner), unless the name
is permitted by note (ii)(d);*

(e) *a name which uses the definite article together with a geographical
reference, for example "The Chancery Lane Solicitors" or "The
Redditch Property Centre".*

(iv) *If the name of a multi-national practice includes the word "Solicitor(s)", the
name must also include:*

(a) *words denoting the countries or jurisdictions of qualification of the
foreign lawyer principals and their professional qualifications; or*

(b) *the words "Registered Foreign Lawyer(s)";*

*and the categories of lawyer must appear in order, with the largest group of
principals first.*

(v) *Compliance with rule 11(2)(a) in the case of a solicitors' practice will be
satisfied by, for example:*

(a) *adding after the name a description of the firm which comprises or
includes the word "solicitor(s)"; or*

(b) *the appearance of the word "solicitor(s)" against a list of the partners
(or directors); or*

(c) *a statement that the partners (or directors) are solicitors.*

(vi) *A firm which wishes to comply with rule 11(2)(b), and which uses a statement
of authorisation under rule 21 of the Solicitors' Investment Business Rules,
may adopt the formula "regulated by the Law Society; authorised by the
Society to conduct investment business".*

(vii) *The notepaper of a multi-national practice has to comply with paragraph 7(b)
of the Publicity Code (naming and describing partners and staff), which will
ensure compliance with Rule 11(2). (The notepaper could, in addition, bear
the words "regulated by the Law Society".)*

(viii) *"Principal" in the case of a recognised body means a director, registered
member or beneficial shareowner.*

(ix) *Rule 11 applies to private practice only.'*

Solicitors' Practice Rules 1990, rule 11

3.05   Individual's name on firm's stationery

**Solicitors must comply with the provisions of the Solicitors' Publicity Code
1990 when naming partners and staff on the firm's stationery and in other
publicity.**

Naming of solicitor staff on stationery

1.   The code is contained in Annex 11A, p.229. See in particular paragraph 7
(naming partners and staff).

Naming of non-solicitor staff on stationery

2.   For the description on notepaper of a former partner who has completely retired from practice, see **2.03** note 12, p.35.

3.   If non-partners are named on notepaper, their status should be made clear (see paragraph 7(a)(iii) of the code at p.233). In the opinion of the Council a printed line is not in itself sufficient to distinguish partners from non-partners in a list.

Salaried partners

4.   If a salaried partner's name appears on headed notepaper of a firm in the list of partners, he or she will be treated by the Society as a full partner and as holding or receiving clients' money irrespective of whether that partner can operate the client account. This is so even if the partner's name appears on the notepaper under a separate heading of 'salaried partners'. Thus he or she will be required to deliver an annual accountant's report. The salaried partner must accept responsibility for the books of the firm and for any breach of the Solicitors' Accounts Rules 1998 (see Annex 28B, p.684), even if he or she is not permitted access to the books.

5.   A salaried partner whose name appears on headed notepaper of a firm in the list of partners, whether or not separately designated as a salaried partner, is thereby held out as a principal. Thus he or she must comply with the Solicitors' Indemnity Rules 1998 (see Annex 29A, p.793).

Misleading publicity

6.   The publicity code states at paragraph 1(c) that publicity must not be inaccurate or misleading in any way. The Solicitors Disciplinary Tribunal have held that it is improper for two sole principals to hold themselves out as being in partnership when that was not in fact the case.

3.06   Responsibility of principals in conduct

As a matter of conduct a principal is *prima facie* responsible for the acts or omissions of the firm and this extends to the acts or omissions of staff.

1.   Where a partner or an employee of the firm has committed acts of dishonesty entitling clients to make claims against the other partners, Solicitors Indemnity Fund Limited should be notified as well as the Office for the Supervision of Solicitors (see p.xv for contact details).

2.   Every partner is personally responsible for complying with the rules relating to solicitors' accounts and the delivery of an annual accountant's report. Therefore, if the book-keeping is left to one partner or to an

employee, all the partners will be liable to disciplinary action if there is a failure to comply with the rules. The nature of the disciplinary action will depend upon the seriousness of the breach and the extent to which the partner concerned knew or should have known of the breach.

3. See **3.07** below for responsibility for supervision of staff.

3.07 General duty of supervision of staff

A solicitor is responsible for exercising proper supervision over both admitted and unadmitted staff.

1. The duty to supervise staff covers not only employees but also independent contractors engaged to carry out work on behalf of the firm, e.g. consultants, locums, solicitors' clerks.

2. A principal cannot escape responsibility for work carried out by the firm by leaving it entirely to staff, however well qualified.

3. For the specific duties of managing and supervising an office see also rule 13 of the Solicitors' Practice Rules 1990 at **3.08**, p.73.

4. For guidance on the supervision of clerks exercising rights of audience under section 27 of the Courts and Legal Services Act 1990, see Annex 21G, p.407.

5. Good practice guidelines on the recruitment and supervision of employees undertaking investment business are in Annex 27O, p.673.

6. See **24.01** note 3, p.449 for the duty of supervision where a solicitor's clerk is appointed executor of a client's will.

7. Sections 41–44 of the Solicitors Act 1974 (see Annex 3A, p.92) impose restrictions on the employment of certain persons by a solicitor. Under section 41, permission must be obtained from the Society by the solicitor if he or she wishes to employ or remunerate any person who, to the solicitor's knowledge, is disqualified from practising as a solicitor by reason of having been struck off the roll, suspended from practice, or by reason of being an undischarged bankrupt. Further, under section 43, the Solicitors Disciplinary Tribunal have the power to order that no solicitor shall employ a named clerk without permission from the Society. Solicitors can check with Regulation and Information Services (see p.xv for contact details) whether an order restricting the employment of a clerk is in existence, or whether a solicitor has been struck off or suspended.

3.08 Practice rule 13 (supervision and management of an office)

[Note: This rule will be replaced on 23rd December 1999 – see Annex 3C, p.113. Advice on the new rule is available from Professional Ethics, see p.xv for contact details.]

'(1) Solicitors shall ensure that every office where they or their firms practise is and can reasonably be seen to be properly supervised in accordance with the following minimum standards:

(a) Every such office shall be attended on each day when it is open to the public or open to telephone calls from the public by:

    (i) a solicitor who holds a practising certificate and has been admitted for at least three years; or

    (ii) in the case of an office from which no right of audience or right to conduct litigation is exercised and from which no exercise of any such right is supervised, a registered foreign lawyer who is a principal of the firm and who has been qualified in his or her own jurisdiction for at least three years;

who shall spend sufficient time at such office to ensure adequate control of the staff employed there and afford requisite facilities for consultation with clients. In the case of a firm in private practice such solicitor may be a principal, employee or consultant of the firm, provided that the firm must have at least one principal who is a solicitor who has been admitted for at least three years, or alternatively, in the case of a firm none of whose principals exercise any right of audience or right to conduct litigation or supervise or assume responsibility for the exercise of any such right, a foreign lawyer who has been qualified in his or her own jurisdiction for at least three years.

(b) Every such office shall be managed by one of the persons listed below who shall normally be in attendance at that office during all the hours when it is open to the public or open to telephone calls from the public:

    (i) a solicitor holding a current practising certificate;

    (ii) a Fellow of the Institute of Legal Executives confirmed by the Institute as being of good standing and having been admitted as a Fellow for not less than three years;

    (iia) in the case of an office from which no right of audience or right to conduct litigation is exercised and from which no exercise of any such right is supervised, a registered foreign lawyer who is a principal of the firm;

> (iii) in the case of an office dealing solely with conveyancing, a licensed conveyancer; or
>
> (iv) in the case of an office dealing solely with property selling and surveying, a chartered surveyor or person holding another professional qualification approved by the Council under rule 14 of these rules.

(2) In determining whether or not there has been compliance with the requirement as to supervision in paragraph (1) of this rule, account shall be taken of, *inter alia*, the arrangements for principals to see incoming mail.

(3) Where daily attendance or normal attendance in accordance with sub-paragraphs (1)(a) or (1)(b) of this rule is prevented by illness, accident or other sufficient or unforeseen cause for a prolonged period, suitable alternative arrangements shall be made without delay to ensure compliance.

(4) [Transitional provision now expired.]

(5) In this rule:

> (a) references to a principal shall be construed, in relation to a recognised body, as references to a director of that body;
>
> (b) in paragraph (2) of this rule, "principals" shall be construed, except in relation to a firm none of whose principals exercise any right of audience or right to conduct litigation or supervise or assume responsibility for the exercise of any such right, as referring to principals who are solicitors; and
>
> (c) "right of audience" and "right to conduct litigation" shall be construed in accordance with Part II and section 119 of the Courts and Legal Services Act 1990.'

Solicitors' Practice Rules 1990, rule 13

3.09 Supervision and management – additional guidance

1. Practice rule 13 sets out the minimum standards of supervision and management in relation to a solicitor's office when it is open to the public or open to telephone calls from the public. The rule requires daily supervision of an office by a solicitor who has been admitted for at least three years. An office must be managed on a full-time basis by a solicitor or other suitably qualified person as defined in the rules.

2. Examples of offices which are normally considered to be open to the public include building society agencies, consulting rooms, annexes, property selling or financial services departments where those offices are separate

from the main office, as well as any office through which appointments with clients are made. However, an office used purely for administrative purposes and through which there is no contact with clients is not open to the public. Nor would an office dealing exclusively with the affairs of a single client normally be subject to the requirements of the rule. In determining whether or not an office is open to the public, no distinction should be drawn between existing and potential clients.

3. A breach of rule 13(1)(b) (management provisions) will not necessarily occur merely by virtue of the manager of an office being on holiday. However, steps must be taken to ensure that adequate supervision of the office under rule 13(1)(a) is maintained throughout the manager's absence.

4. Rule 17 of the Solicitors' Practice Rules 1990 (see Annex 1A at p.28) gives the Council a power to grant waivers. A solicitor seeking a waiver must satisfy the Council that the circumstances of his or her application are sufficiently exceptional to justify a departure from the requirements of rule 13. In addition, it is the Council's practice to seek the views of the appropriate local law society when considering applications for waivers.

5. In some circumstances the Council may grant waivers limited as to time. These circumstances could include, for example, the death or unexpected absence of a manager or supervisor. Save in exceptional cases, these waivers will not be renewed on expiry; consequently solicitors to whom such waivers are granted will be required to bring their arrangements into compliance with the rules on or before the expiry of the waiver.

6. If a sole principal wishes to practise from more than one office (including a consulting room) and does not propose to employ a person qualified to manage each office in accordance with rule 13(1)(b), he or she should consult Professional Ethics as to the possibility of a waiver being granted (see p.xv for contact details). The Council are not prepared to grant waivers in this category to sole principals practising from more than two offices, save in very exceptional circumstances.

7. A solicitor who practises from a conventional office and also from home must include both addresses in his or her application for a practising certificate and must comply with rule 13 in respect of both addresses. The rule also applies where a solicitor practises exclusively from his or her home. However, a solicitor who uses his or her home for an occasional interview cannot be said to be practising from home and consequently need not comply with the rule in relation to his or her home address.

8. A solicitor must normally have been admitted for three years or more before he or she is entitled to practise as a sole principal for an office which is open to the public. See also **3.01**, p.67.

3.10   Absence of sole principal

A sole principal should make suitable arrangements for the running of the practice during a period of absence.

1. There is a continuing duty to ensure that the practice will be carried on with the minimum interruption to clients' business. Adequate arrangements must therefore be made for the practice to be administered during the period of absence. See also rule 13(1) of the Solicitors' Practice Rules 1990 (**3.08**, p.73). Because it is reasonable to plan for holiday periods a waiver of rule 13(1)(a) would not normally be available. Rule 23 of the accounts rules requires that a withdrawal from a client account cannot be made without a specific authority. This rule cannot be complied with if a sole principal leaves blank cheques for completion by staff at a later date, as signing a blank cheque is not giving a specific authority (see Annex 28B at p.708).

2. If a solicitor has not made adequate arrangements in advance to meet unforeseen circumstances, difficulties will arise in the conduct of clients' affairs and in the administration of the solicitor's own business. For example, an accountant's report must be submitted, a practising certificate must be applied for and indemnity cover must be obtained notwithstanding a solicitor's absence. Consequently, a sole principal should have an arrangement with another solicitor (who is of sufficient seniority and who holds a practising certificate) to supervise the sole principal's practice until such time as the sole principal returns. Further, the sole principal should notify his or her bankers in advance of these arrangements so that the incoming solicitor can operate the client and office accounts of the principal.

3. If the absence of the principal lasts beyond the period covered by his or her practising certificate, the principal may be able to obtain permission, through Regulation and Information Services (see p.xv for contact details), for another solicitor to complete the application for a practising certificate; only if the principal continues to hold a practising certificate can his or her name remain on the professional stationery.

4. If a sole principal is struck off or suspended, any incoming solicitor will take full professional responsibility for the practice. The incoming solicitor must inform clients of the practice, Solicitors' Indemnity Fund, any top-up insurer and Regulation and Information Services (see **3.11**, p.77).

5. If a sole principal decides to stop practising, he or she must inform clients of the fact so that they may instruct other solicitors. Failure to inform clients could amount not only to an act of negligence but also to unbefitting conduct leading to disciplinary action. Guidance for solicitors considering retirement is contained in Annex 3G, p.136.

3.11   Change in composition of the firm

Where there has been a material alteration to the composition of the firm, all clients of the firm who may be affected must be informed promptly.

Obligations to clients

1. Whether a change in the composition of a firm amounts to a material change will depend on the circumstances. A partner leaving a small firm (for example a four partner firm) would almost always amount to a material change, but a partner leaving a large firm (for example 20 partners or more) would not normally do so.

2. The departure of a partner will affect all the clients for whom that partner was acting as fee-earner and all the clients whose matters he or she was responsible for supervising. The departure of a partner who was in charge of a branch office might be material for all the clients using that office. Clients whose wills or deeds are held by the firm are likely to be affected if those documents are moved. If provisions in a will or deed are affected – for example, where unnamed partners of the firm or its successor are appointed executors or trustees and there is no clear successor firm – it is likely to be appropriate to seek instructions to vary the appointment.

3. Where a firm amalgamates with another firm, **3.11** requires that clients affected should be notified of the amalgamation. Where two or more firms amalgamate and have previously been acting for clients who have conflicting interests, the new firm must cease to act for both clients unless it is able to continue to act for one with the consent of the other (see **15.03**, p.316 and guidance on amalgamations in Annex 15A, p.322).

Free choice of solicitor

4. A solicitor who acquires or retains the 'goodwill' of a firm does not thereby acquire or retain any automatic right to continue to act for its clients, who are always free to instruct other solicitors. However, a sale or transfer of goodwill may, as a matter of law, restrict what the transferor may do in the way of competition. This may mean that he or she has entered voluntarily into legal obligations which affect the method by which clients can be notified. Whilst nothing in **3.11** should be taken to override any contractual obligation of any partner, contractual obligations between partners will not absolve the partners from their obligation to fulfil the duties they owe to clients as a matter of professional conduct. Care should be taken to ensure that partnership deeds and other agreements do not put obstacles in the way of the proper discharge of duties to clients.

5. The principle, set out in rule 1(b) of the Solicitors' Practice Rules 1990, **1.01**, p.1, that a client is free to instruct a solicitor of his or her own choice,

applies equally where the firm, in effect, ceases to exist, e.g. when a new firm takes over from a firm which has ceased to practise or an existing firm is dissolved and the partners divide into two new firms. It would not be proper for the new firm to take over clients' business, including papers or money previously held, without the clients being notified as soon as possible. Prompt notification by a letter is therefore essential, as is an agreement between the solicitors concerned as to the contents of such a letter. It is a useful practice for the letter to state the amount standing to the credit of that particular client's account. The letter may add that, unless instructions are received to the contrary within a specified time, the writer will continue to deal with the client's affairs in accordance with instructions given to the previous firm. It is a matter for the new firm to decide whether to notify clients for whom no current work is in progress and for whom no money or original documents of value are held. For a specimen letter see Annex 3F, p.135.

Partners' disagreements

6. Where the partners disagree about the arrangements for notifying clients of a material change in the composition of the firm, there is no rule of conduct which prevents one or more partners separately notifying all the clients of the firm. This notification should be a short factual statement informing the clients of the change as the result of a dissolution of the partnership, and may give the new practising addresses of each partner. The letter could include an invitation to contact that solicitor if he or she could be of assistance to the client, but solicitors should have regard to note 3 above. If the client is invited to instruct a particular firm, there should also be a statement that the client is free to instruct a solicitor of his or her choice.

Client care

7. Quite apart from the requirements of **3.11**, the Solicitors' Costs Information and Client Care Code (**13.02**, p.266) requires that solicitors ensure that clients know the name and status of the person dealing with the matter in which they have instructed the practice, and the principal responsible for its overall supervision. Therefore, where a fee-earner having conduct of a matter leaves a firm, the client in question must be informed, preferably in advance, and told the name and status of the person who is to take over his or her matter. If the client enquires where the fee-earner can be found the information should not be withheld from the client unless there are good reasons for withholding the information, or at the request of the fee-earner.

Notifying the Law Society

8. Solicitors who are authorised by the Society to conduct investment business must, under rule 8 of the Solicitors' Investment Business Rules 1995 (Annex 27B at p.570), notify Regulation and Information Services (see p.xv for contact details) of any change in the composition of the firm.

9. Regulation and Information Services should also be notified if an alteration to the composition of a firm results in a change in any solicitor's practising address (see **2.09**, p.40).

Notifying other organisations

10. Some other organisations who may need to be notified are listed in Annex 3I, p.144.

3.12 Fee-earner leaving a firm

It is not in itself misconduct for a solicitor, whether partner or employee, to write to clients of a firm after leaving that firm, inviting their instructions. However, nothing in this principle can absolve the solicitor from any legal obligations arising out of his or her former contract of employment or partnership agreement.

Restrictive covenants

1. Sometimes a solicitor leaving a firm will have entered into restrictive covenants in a partnership deed or contract of employment, which could have the effect of preventing him or her from approaching the firm's clients or former clients. Where there is a breach of such a contractual term, enforcement is a matter for the courts, and not for the Office for the Supervision of Solicitors, which cannot adjudicate on contractual obligations between partners, or between employers and employees.

2. Where a solicitor is subject to restrictive covenants which might prevent him or her from acting for clients of the firm, there may be rare cases where to enforce such a covenant in particular circumstances would act against the best interests of the client. If a solicitor having conduct of a matter of some complexity leaves the firm at a crucial stage in the proceedings, and it is necessary for the proper conduct of the client's case that he or she should continue to act, an agreement to a transfer should be sought as early as possible and should not be withheld against the client's interests. For transfer of papers see **12.13**, p.251.

Advertising

3. A solicitor who ceases to be a partner or employee in a firm is entitled to advertise his or her new firm provided there is no breach of the Solicitors' Practice Rules or the Solicitors' Publicity Code (see Annex 11A, p.229). An example of a breach of the Publicity Code would be where a solicitor makes a direct comparison between the services provided by his or her new firm and those of the firm he or she has left. A solicitor may inform clients that he or she is shortly to leave a firm.

Legal obligations

4.   Solicitors employing a former partner or employee of another firm may need to bear in mind that acts done in breach of legal obligations with the authority of the new employer may give rise to a right of action by the employee's previous firm. This applies whether an employee is a solicitor or a non-solicitor.

Breach of practice rule 1

5.   Care should be taken to ensure that there is no breach of rule 1 of the Solicitors' Practice Rules (see **1.01**, p.1) on the part of either a solicitor leaving a firm or its remaining principals, as might happen where any pressure is placed on clients to transfer instructions or remain with the firm, or where there is an unseemly and public dispute about the right to accept a client's instructions or where a firm refuses without justification to transfer papers at the client's request.

3.13   Solicitors who retire from full-time practice

Solicitors who retire from full-time practice but continue to practise on a part-time or *ad hoc* basis, or act as consultant with a firm, must continue to comply with all relevant provisions of the Solicitors Act 1974, the Solicitors' Practice Rules 1990 and all the requirements of professional conduct generally.

1.   For detailed guidance see Annex 3G, p.136, which also contains guidance for retired solicitors who continue to hold money as professional trustees.

2.   The Solicitors (Keeping of the Roll) Regulations 1999 (Annex 2C, p.52) require solicitors who do not hold practising certificates to confirm annually that they wish to remain on the roll and pay the appropriate fee.

3.14   Arrangements on death of sole principal

A sole principal should make a will containing adequate provision for the running of the practice, after his or her death, by a solicitor who is admitted for at least three years and holds a current practising certificate.

Making arrangements

1.   Clear instructions should be left by the sole principal to ensure that the executors are able to make arrangements immediately after his or her death to appoint a solicitor of sufficient seniority to run the practice, pending its disposal.

2.   Although it is not essential to appoint a solicitor as executor, this would greatly facilitate the running of the practice. The will could include an authority for the solicitor-executor to purchase the practice if he or she desires.

3.   An executor who is not a solicitor may not, as a sole signatory, sign cheques on the client account of the deceased's practice. For guidance on who can authorise withdrawals from client account see rule 23 of the Solicitors' Accounts Rules 1998 (Annex 28B at p.708).

4.   In view of the provisions of rule 9 of the Solicitors' Incorporated Practice Rules 1988 (Annex 3D at p.122) it is advisable for a solicitor shareholder in a recognised body to appoint a solicitor as executor in respect of his or her shares.

Intervention

5.   If no appointment of a suitable solicitor-manager is made, the Society may intervene in the practice in accordance with the provisions of Schedule 1 to the Solicitors Act 1974 (Annex 30A, p.850). The powers of intervention are available where the Council have reason to suspect dishonesty on the part of the personal representatives, where there has been undue delay on the part of the personal representatives, or where the Schedule applied to the sole principal before his or her death. To avoid difficulties to clients following intervention, every effort should be made by the personal representatives to find a solicitor-manager. In cases of difficulty, the honorary secretary of the local law society may be able to help.

Intestacy

6.   If a sole principal dies intestate, those entitled to apply for letters of administration strictly have no right to take active steps in administering the estate until so authorised. However, in these circumstances the prospective administrators are encouraged to nominate a manager for the practice before the grant is obtained.

7.   Where there is a failure, within a reasonable time of death, to apply for a grant of representation in respect of the estate of a deceased sole principal (whether under a will or on intestacy), the court has power to protect the interests of the clients. In exercise of the discretion conferred by section 116 of the Supreme Court Act 1981, the court can make an order for a grant in respect of the deceased solicitor's estate in favour of a nominee or nominees of the Society. The grant may be general or limited depending on the circumstances and the power is in addition to that conferred on the Society by paragraph 11 of Schedule 1 to the Solicitors Act 1974 (see Annex 30A at p.854).

Appointment of a solicitor-manager

8. Where a solicitor-manager is appointed in respect of a deceased solicitor's practice, he or she becomes the sole principal and must comply personally with all professional obligations in relation to the practice.

Solicitor-manager's responsibilities

9. The solicitor-manager should take care to ensure that confidential information relating to the clients of the deceased sole principal is kept confidential and that any conflict of interest is avoided. (For conflict of interests see Chapter 15, p.313.)

10. The manager must personally exercise control over staff and must supervise or arrange for the supervision of the office(s) in accordance with rule 13 of the Solicitors' Practice Rules 1990 (see **3.08**, p.73). The manager will conduct the practice for the personal representatives and pay the profits, less any remuneration agreed to be paid to him or her, to the estate. Arrangements for remuneration of the manager are a matter between the manager and the personal representatives. The personal representatives are entitled to the professional profits earned during this period. Only in exceptional circumstances should these arrangements continue beyond the executor's year.

11. The manager must arrange for the stationery of the practice to be changed so that his or her name appears on the letterhead as the sole principal. He or she may be described as the manager of the firm.

12. The manager must inform the clients of the practice of the arrangements made – see **3.11**, p.77 for details of the information that should be given to the clients. Further, Solicitors Indemnity Fund Limited and any insurers concerned (e.g. those providing top-up cover) should be advised so that cover will be in force for the solicitor-manager. Regulation and Information Services must also be notified of the arrangements (see p.xv for contact details).

13. The manager must comply with practice rule 15, and the Solicitors' Costs Information and Client Care Code (see Chapter 13, p.265).

Operation of client account

14. The sole principal's client account will be frozen on death. Fresh books must be opened immediately. They should be kept as the solicitor-manager's books until the practice is disposed of or closed. The solicitor-manager will normally arrange with the sole principal's bank to open a new client account with an overdraft matching that of the existing client account. (See rule 22(8)(b) of the Solicitors' Accounts Rules 1998, Annex 28B at p.707.) The solicitor-manager must make arrangements for the

former client account balances to be transferred to the new (overdrawn) client account as soon as the grant of representation is registered with the bank or building society. The solicitor-manager must not draw money from the new account in any circumstances where it would be improper to draw the same amount from the old account.

15. A similar arrangement can be made for office account purposes.

16. No further monies should be paid into the deceased principal's client account. Client's money received by the practice must be placed in the new account operated by the solicitor-manager. The solicitor-manager should encourage the personal representatives to supply an accountant's report up to the date of death. The solicitor-manager must deliver a separate report in respect of any other client monies which he or she has held in any other practice.

Investment business

17. The solicitor-manager should consider his or her position in relation to the Financial Services Act 1986. An investment business certificate which has been issued to a sole principal lapses on death. Therefore the solicitor-manager must apply for an investment business certificate in his or her own name if he or she intends to conduct investment business. This is so even when the solicitor-manager holds separate authorisation in relation to another practice. Applications for an investment business certificate should be made to Regulation and Information Services. (See also Chapter 27, p.522.)

Sale of the practice

18. If the solicitor-manager purchases the practice from the personal representatives, he or she must not act for the personal representatives and must insist that they be independently advised in this transaction. Regulation and Information Services must be informed of the arrangements for the disposal or sale of the practice (see p.xv for contact details).

3.15   Bankruptcy

Bankruptcy automatically suspends a practising certificate.

Guidance for practitioners who become bankrupt or enter into voluntary arrangements with creditors is contained in Annex 3H, p.141. For the effect of a solicitor's bankruptcy on the retainer, see also **12.12** note 4, p.251 and **30.06**, p.846.

3.16   Money laundering

Principals in private practice should consider what procedures should be instituted, given the nature of their practice, to ensure compliance with the Money Laundering Regulations 1993.

1.   The Money Laundering Regulations 1993 (see Annex 3B, p.95) apply to solicitors who conduct investment business within the meaning of the Financial Services Act 1986, and may apply to solicitors who undertake any of the activities listed in the Annex to the Banking Co-ordination (Second Council Directive) Regulations 1992 (S.I. 1992 no. 3218) ('Annex activities'), including money transmission services, and mergers and acquisitions. The Annex appears as a schedule to the Money Laundering Regulations at p.112.

2.   Chapter 27, p.522, deals with investment business. Note that the definition of investment business in Schedule 1 to the Financial Services Act 1986 (Annex 27A, p.535) is wider than the definition of 'discrete investment business' in the Solicitors' Investment Business Rules. If it is doubtful whether an activity constitutes investment business, solicitors are advised to comply with the regulations. See also **27.17** note 2, p.530.

3.   As well as those who conduct investment business, it is recommended that all solicitors who are authorised to conduct investment business, or who undertake Annex activities, meet the following requirements:

   ▶   appointment of a compliance officer to ensure compliance with internal money laundering procedures;

   ▶   initial and continuing training for staff in the requirements of the money laundering legislation and in the recognition and handling of suspicious transactions;

   ▶   establishment of internal reporting procedures, including the appointment of a reporting officer (who could be the same person as the compliance officer);

   ▶   establishment of procedures for obtaining and keeping for a minimum period satisfactory evidence of clients' identity when appropriate;

   ▶   establishment of procedures for keeping records of transactions for a minimum period when appropriate.

   Solicitors might also consider applying these procedures to other areas of work involving the handling of money or other securities, e.g. conveyancing.

4.   In addition to the regulations, solicitors may be affected by the substantive law relating to money laundering – see Annex 16B, p.337. See also **16.07** and notes, p.333, for a summary of the effect on a solicitor's duties of confidentiality and disclosure.

5.   Further guidance and information on money laundering can be obtained from Professional Ethics (see p.xv for contact details).

3.17   Incorporated practices

Solicitors may practise in corporate form, subject to compliance with the Solicitors' Incorporated Practice Rules 1988 and other rules and principles of conduct applying to solicitors' incorporated practices and to individual solicitors.

3

Setting up a recognised body

1. Solicitors may practise in corporate form, provided the incorporated practice is recognised by the Society under section 9 of the Administration of Justice Act 1985 (AJA). Such an incorporated practice is known as a recognised body. For the Solicitors' Incorporated Practice Rules 1988 (SIPR), see Annex 3D, p.118. An information pack on incorporated practices is available from Professional Ethics (see p.xv for contact details).

2. Schedule 2 to the AJA applies provisions in the Solicitors Act 1974 to recognised bodies, and the Solicitors' Incorporated Practices Order 1991 (S.I. 1991 no. 2684) applies provisions in other statutes applying to solicitors, to recognised bodies, sometimes with modifications. The combined effect of the Schedule and the statutory instrument is to place a recognised body, for practical purposes, in the same position as a solicitor or partnership of solicitors, and to impose on it similar legal requirements.

3. A recognised body's registered office must be in England and Wales and at its place of business or one of its places of business (see rule 8 of the SIPR at p.121). A recognised body could practise overseas as well as in England and Wales, subject to local law and compliance with the Solicitors' Overseas Practice Rules (see Annex 9A, p.180).

4. The SIPR do not apply to a corporate practice conducted entirely outside England and Wales. For corporate practice overseas see **9.01** note 4, p.176, and rule 9 of the Solicitors' Overseas Practice Rules 1990, Annex 9A at p.183.

Control and ownership

5. A recognised body must be managed and controlled by solicitors or by solicitors together with one or more registered foreign lawyers (RFLs) – see rule 3 of the SIPR at p.119.

6. Only solicitors with practising certificates and RFLs may be directors of a recognised body. At all times at least one of the directors must be a solicitor. A recognised body cannot be a director. The company secretary need not be a solicitor or an RFL. See rule 4 of the SIPR at p.119.

7. Only solicitors with practising certificates, RFLs and other recognised bodies may be shareholders of a recognised body (see rule 5 of the SIPR at p.119).

8. A shareholder in a recognised body may not hold shares as a nominee for anyone except a solicitor, an RFL or a recognised body. A shareholder may not create any charge or other third party interest over his or her shares.

9. At least one share in a recognised body must be owned by a solicitor or another recognised body; thus no recognised body can be owned only by RFLs (see rule 5(2)(a)(ii) of the SIPR at p.120).

Application of the conduct rules

10. Rules governing the conduct of solicitors apply to recognised bodies (see rule 12 of the SIPR at p.122).

11. The Solicitors' Indemnity Rules (see Annex 29A, p.793) apply to recognised bodies. A company will not obtain recognition unless the Society is satisfied that it complies or will comply with the indemnity rules; which in effect means that the company is or will be covered by the indemnity provided by the Solicitors' Indemnity Fund. A recognised body will be treated, for indemnity purposes, as one practice with the partnership which owns it if:

    (a) the beneficial owners of shares in the company are the same in number and identity as the partners in the partnership, including salaried partners; or

    (b) the beneficial owners of shares in the company comprise only some of the partners in the partnership, provided that any income from the recognised body accrues to the benefit of the partnership.

    (See rules 12.19 and 12.21 of the indemnity rules at pp.799 and 800.)

12. Under rule 13 of the SIPR at p.122, a recognised body which is a limited company and not exempt from the requirement, must obtain top-up insurance to a specified level over and above that provided by the Solicitors' Indemnity Fund. A company will not obtain recognition unless it can supply evidence of compliance with, or exemption from, the rule. To be exempt from the requirement to have top-up insurance a company must be able to show that it is treated as one practice with a partnership for indemnity purposes, and has no power to act except as agent for the partners in their capacity as such.

Renewing recognition

13. Recognition as a recognised body is renewable every three years.

Compensation Fund payments

14. Recognised bodies must, on initially obtaining recognition and on renewing recognition, pay a contribution to the Compensation Fund. Solicitors and RFLs who are directors or shareowners of a recognised body must pay the individual annual contributions to the Compensation Fund payable by solicitors or RFLs. If the recognised body (or another recognised body in which it owns shares) has held or received clients' money, such solicitors and RFLs will have to pay the annual contribution at the full rate for solicitors or RFLs.

3.18 Executor, trustee and nominee companies

A solicitor or a registered foreign lawyer practising in partnership with a solicitor may not control, actively participate in or operate an executor, trustee or nominee company in England and Wales, unless the company is a recognised body.

1. Practice rule 5 and the Solicitors' Separate Business Code 1994 (see **3.20**, p.89 and Annex 3E, p.129) prohibit solicitors from being involved in providing, other than through a solicitor's practice, services as trustee, executor or nominee in England and Wales.

2. A company which is owned by a partnership of solicitors and operated as part of the commercial practice of that partnership is a 'business' for the purpose of practice rule 5. This is the case whether or not it was dormant for Companies Act purposes and whether or not a charge was made for the service provided to the clients of the partnership.

3. Where a company is executor, trustee or nominee, that company is providing the executor, trustee or nominee service for the purpose of practice rule 5.

4. A company which is not a recognised body cannot provide services in England and Wales as a solicitors' practice – see practice rule 7(7) (**3.03**, p.68) and section 24 of the Solicitors Act 1974 (Annex 2A at p.48). For recognised bodies see **3.17**, p.85.

5. Some firms may wish to operate their executor, trustee and nominee companies as if there were no distinction between the company and the partnership. The following matters should be borne in mind:

    (a) A recognised body will be treated, for indemnity purposes, as one practice with the partnership which owns it if:

        (i) the beneficial owners of shares in the company are the same in number and identity as the partners in the partnership; or

        (ii) the beneficial owners of shares in the company comprise only some of the partners in the partnership, provided that any income from the recognised body accrues to the benefit of the partnership.

(See rules 12.19 and 12.21 of the indemnity rules at pp.799 and 800.)

(b) A recognised body and a partnership which are treated, for indemnity purposes, as one practice, may submit a single accountant's report in respect of both, subject to bringing the relevant accounting periods into line.

(c) A solicitors' wholly owned recognised body must, under the Solicitors' Accounts Rules 1998 (see Annex 28B, p.684), have its own client account, in its own name. However a single set of accounting records may be used for the partnership and the recognised body.

(d) A recognised body, when holding money, or receiving dividends on shares held, *as nominee* for another person, acts as a controlled trustee. (See rule 31(2) of the Solicitors' Accounts Rules 1998 at p.714.)

6. To be exempt from the requirement to have top-up insurance (see **3.17** note 12, p.86) a company must be able to show that it is treated as one practice with a partnership for indemnity purposes, and has no power to act except as agent for the partners in their capacity as such. Alternatively, the firm may consider it simpler to ask the top-up insurer to extend cover to the recognised body.

7. Solicitors' overseas executor, trustee and nominee companies cannot be recognised bodies. They may be operated either as corporate practices under rule 9 of the Solicitors' Overseas Practice Rules (see Annex 9A at p.183) or as 'separate businesses' (see **3.21** note 10(c), p.90) and the Solicitors' Separate Business Code, section 5(4) (Annex 3E at p.133).

3.19   Service companies

Solicitors may, subject to conditions, form service companies.

1. The formation of a service company to carry out necessary administrative functions concerned with the running of the practice, e.g. the employment of staff, qualified and non-qualified, hiring premises, furniture and equipment and general maintenance, is permitted, provided membership of the company is limited to members or partners of the firm, solicitors holding practising certificates, retired partners of the firm and dependants of retired or deceased partners.

2. The books of the company must be made available where the Council require an inspection of accounts under rule 34 of the Solicitors' Accounts Rules 1998 (Annex 28B at p.719) or rule 15 of the Solicitors' Overseas Practice Rules 1990 (Annex 9A at p.187).

3.20 Practice rule 5 (providing services other than as a solicitor)

'Solicitors must comply with the Solicitors' Separate Business Code in controlling, actively participating in or operating (in each case alone, or by or with others) a business which:

(a) **provides any service which may properly be provided by a solicitor's practice, and**

(b) **is not itself a solicitor's practice or a multi-national partnership.'**

Solicitors' Practice Rules 1990, rule 5

3.21 Separate businesses – additional guidance

1. The Solicitors' Separate Business Code 1994 is at Annex 3E, p.129. The following notes should be read in conjunction with the code.

2. When considering the code solicitors need to distinguish between:

   ▶ 'specified' services

   ▶ 'either way' services

   ▶ non-solicitor services.

3. A list of 'specified' services appears in section 3 of the code at p.130. A solicitor may provide these services only through a solicitor's practice which is fully regulated by the Society.

4. 'Either way' services are those which a solicitor may provide *either* through a fully regulated practice *or* through a separate business entity which is not regulated by the Society. The code is intended to ensure that it is always clear to clients and customers whether services are being provided through a solicitors' practice or through a separate business.

5. Non-solicitor services are those which cannot be provided through a solicitors' practice; they are without the regulation of the Society (but see **1.08**, p.8, for the behaviour of solicitors outside legal practice).

Separate business activities

6. Sections 4–5 of the code (at p.130) set out safeguards for the public which apply when either way services are offered through a separate business.

7. Section 5 deals with the specific safeguards for the following business activities (section 4 deals with all others):

   ▶ estate agency

   ▶ investment business

    ►   parliamentary agent, trade mark agent, patent agent or European patent attorney and (for dually qualified solicitors) practice as a foreign lawyer (see note 9 below)

    ►   overseas executor, trustee and nominee companies and other overseas businesses.

8.   A solicitors' executor, trustee or nominee company in England and Wales cannot be run as a separate business (see section 3(d) of the code at p.130 and **3.18**, p.87) and therefore must be a recognised body.

Parliamentary agents, trade mark agents, patent agents, European patent attorneys and foreign lawyers

9.   Despite the prohibitions in section 3 of the code, section 5(3), at p.133, permits solicitors to have a separate business as:

    ►   a parliamentary agent

    ►   a trade mark agent, a patent agent or a European patent attorney

    ►   a lawyer of a jurisdiction outside England and Wales.

Limited requirements are imposed on these separate businesses, with the aim of making it clear to their customers that the businesses are governed by a different legal and regulatory regime from the solicitors' practice. The section also prohibits the practice's client account from being used for the separate business.

Overseas connections

10. (a) If a solicitor practises in England and Wales and has a separate business either in England and Wales or overseas, practice rule 5 and the code will apply.

   (b) If a solicitor practises only overseas and has a separate business either in England and Wales or overseas, rule 18A of the overseas practice rules (see Annex 9A at p.189) will apply. Rule 18A is intended to ensure that it is always clear to clients and customers whether services are being provided through a solicitor's overseas practice or through a separate business.

   (c) If a solicitor has an executor, trustee or nominee company outside England and Wales, it may be run as a separate business (unlike one based in England and Wales), but the solicitor will be subject either to section 5(4) of the code or to rule 18A of the overseas practice rules.

   (d) Rule 9 of the overseas practice rules at p.183 allows solicitors to run an overseas company as a solicitors' practice provided all the directors and shareowners are lawyers.

(e) If a solicitor has a separate business overseas which has no link with his or her solicitor's practice it is not affected by practice rule 5, the code or rule 18A of the overseas practice rules (see section 5(5)(b) of the code at p.134).

Exceptions

11. (a) The prohibitions in sections 3(f) and (h) of the code (on providing legal advice and drafting certain documents through separate businesses) do not apply if these activities are, merely, necessary but subsidiary parts of another service which is not included in section 3.

    (b) The code does not apply to a solicitor as:

    ▶   a non-executive company director

    ▶   an employed solicitor acting in accordance with the Employed Solicitors Code (see Annex 4A, p.152)

    ▶   a notary public operating a notarial practice in conjunction with a practice as a solicitor.

Annex 3A

Solicitors Act 1974

sections 41–44 (restrictions on employment of certain persons)

(with consolidated amendments to May 1995)

---

41. Employment by solicitor of person struck off or suspended

(1) No solicitor shall, except in accordance with a written permission granted under this section, employ or remunerate in connection with his practice as a solicitor any person who to his knowledge is disqualified from practising as a solicitor by reason of the fact that –

    (a)   his name has been struck off the roll, or

    (b)   he is suspended from practising as a solicitor, or

    (c)   his practising certificate is suspended while he is an undischarged bankrupt.

(1A) No solicitor shall, except in accordance with a written permission granted under this section, employ or remunerate in connection with his practice as a solicitor any person if, to his knowledge, there is a direction in force under section 47(2)(g) in relation to that person.

(2) The Society may grant a permission under this section for such period and subject to such conditions as the Society thinks fit.

(3) A solicitor aggrieved by the refusal of the Society to grant a permission under subsection (2), or by any conditions attached by the Society to the grant of any such permission, may appeal to the Master of the Rolls who may –

    (a)   confirm the refusal or the conditions, as the case may be; or

    (b)   grant a permission under this section for such period and subject to such conditions as he thinks fit.

(4) If any solicitor acts in contravention of this section or of any conditions subject to which a permission has been granted under it, the Tribunal or, as the case may be, the High Court shall order –

    (a)   that his name be struck off the roll; or

    (b)   that he be suspended from practice for such period as the Tribunal or the court thinks fit.

(5) The Master of the Rolls may make regulations about appeals to him under subsection (3).

42. Failure to disclose fact of having been struck off or suspended

(1) Any person who, while he is disqualified from practising as a solicitor by reason of the fact that –

(a) his name has been struck off the roll, or

(b) he is suspended from practising as a solicitor, or

(c) his practising certificate is suspended while he is an undischarged bankrupt,

seeks or accepts employment by a solicitor in connection with that solicitor's practice without previously informing him that he is so disqualified shall be guilty of an offence and liable on summary conviction to a fine not exceeding level 3 on the standard scale.

(1A) Any person –

(a) with respect to whom a direction is in force under section 47(2)(g); and

(b) who seeks or accepts employment by a solicitor in connection with that solicitor's practice without previously informing him of the direction,

shall be guilty of an offence and liable on summary conviction to a fine not exceeding level three on the standard scale.

(2) Notwithstanding anything in the Magistrates' Courts Act 1980, proceedings under this section may be commenced at any time before the expiration of six months from the first discovery of the offence by the prosecutor, but no such proceedings shall be commenced except by, or with the consent of, the Attorney General.

43. Control of employment of certain clerks

(1) Where a person who is or was a clerk to a solicitor but is not himself a solicitor –

(a) has been convicted of a criminal offence which discloses such dishonesty that in the opinion of the Society it would be undesirable for him to be employed by a solicitor in connection with his practice; or

(b) has, in the opinion of the Society, occasioned or been a party to, with or without the connivance of the solicitor to whom he is or was clerk, an act or default in relation to that solicitor's practice which involved conduct on his part of such a nature that in the opinion of the Society it would be undesirable for him to be employed by a solicitor in connection with his practice,

an application may be made to the Tribunal with respect to that person by or on behalf of the Society.

(2) The Tribunal, on the hearing of any application under subsection (1), may make an order that as from such date as may be specified in the order no solicitor shall, except in accordance with permission in writing granted by the Society for such period and subject to such conditions as the Society may think fit to specify in the permission, employ or remunerate, in connection with his practice as a solicitor, the person with respect to whom the application is made.

(3) An order made by the Tribunal under subsection (2) may, on the application of the Society or of the person with respect to whom the application for the order was made, be revoked by a subsequent order of the Tribunal; and where in the opinion of the Tribunal no prima facie case is shown in favour of an application for revocation, the Tribunal may refuse the application without hearing the applicant.

(4)   The Tribunal, on the hearing of any application under this section, may make an order as to the payment of costs by any party to the application.

(5)   Orders made under this section and filed with the Society may be inspected by any solicitor during office hours without payment but shall not be open to the inspection of any person other than a solicitor.

(6)   [repealed]

(7)   For the purposes of this section an order under Part I of the Powers of Criminal Courts Act 1973 discharging a person absolutely or conditionally shall, notwithstanding anything in section 1C of that Act, be deemed to be a conviction of the offence for which the order was made.

44. Offences in connection with orders under section 43(2)

(1)   Any person who, while there is in force in respect of him an order under section 43(2), seeks or accepts any employment by or remuneration from a solicitor in connection with that solicitor's practice without previously informing him of that order shall be guilty of an offence and liable on summary conviction to a fine not exceeding level 3 on the standard scale.

(2)   Where an order is made under section 43(2) in respect of any person and that order is one –

  (a)   against which no appeal has been made or which has been confirmed on appeal; and

  (b)   which has not been revoked under section 43(3),

then, if any solicitor knowingly acts in contravention of that order or of any conditions subject to which permission for the employment of that person has been granted under it, a complaint in respect of that contravention may be made to the Tribunal by or on behalf of the Society.

(3)   Any document purporting to be an order under section 43(2) and to be duly signed in accordance with section 48(1) shall be received in evidence in any proceedings under this section and be deemed to be such an order without further proof unless the contrary is shown.

(4)   Notwithstanding anything in the Magistrates' Courts Act 1980, proceedings under subsection (1) may be commenced at any time before the expiration of six months from the first discovery of the offence by the prosecutor, but no such proceedings shall be commenced, except with the consent of the Director of Public Prosecutions, by any person other than the Society or a person acting on behalf of the Society.

[NOTE

For the application of section 44 to a recognised body (i.e. an incorporated practice recognised under section 9 of the Administration of Justice Act 1985) see paragraphs 12 and 16(1)(d) of Schedule 2 to the Administration of Justice Act 1985.]

Annex 3B

Money Laundering Regulations 1993

3

(S.I. 1993 no. 1933)

The Treasury being a government department designated [S.I. 1992/1711] for the purposes of section 2(2) of the European Communities Act 1972 [1972 c.68] in relation to measures relating to preventing the use of the financial system for the purpose of money laundering, in exercise of the powers conferred by that section hereby make the following regulations:

GENERAL

Citation and commencement

1. (1) These Regulations may be cited as the Money Laundering Regulations 1993.

   (2) These Regulations shall come into force on 1st April 1994.

Interpretation

2. (1) In these Regulations –

   "applicant for business" means a person seeking to form a business relationship, or carry out a one-off transaction, with a person who is carrying out relevant financial business in the United Kingdom;

   "business relationship" has the meaning given by regulation 3 below;

   "Case 1", "Case 2", "Case 3" and "Case 4" have the meanings given in regulation 7 below;

   "constable" includes a person commissioned by the Commissioners of Customs and Excise;

   "European institution" has the same meaning as in the Banking Coordination (Second Council Directive) Regulations 1992 [S.I. 1992/3218];

   "insurance business" means long term business within the meaning of the Insurance Companies Act 1982 [1982 c.50];

   "the Money Laundering Directive" means the Council Directive on prevention of the use of the financial system for the purpose of money laundering (No. 91/308/ EEC) [OJ No. L166, 28.6.91, p.77];

"one-off transaction" means any transaction other than a transaction carried out in the course of an established business relationship formed by a person acting in the course of relevant financial business;

"relevant financial business" has the meaning given by regulation 4 below; and

"supervisory authority" has the meaning given by regulation 15 below.

(2)   In these Regulations "ecu" means the European currency unit as defined in article I of Council Regulation No. 3180/78/EEC [OJ No. L379, 30.12.78, p.1: the relevant amending instrument is Council Regulation (EEC) No. 1971/89, OJ No. L189, 4.7.89, p.1]; and the exchange rates as between the ecu and the currencies of the member States to be applied for each year beginning on 31st December shall be the rates applicable on the last day of the preceding October for which rates for the currencies of all the member States were published in the Official Journal of the Communities.

(3)   In these Regulations, except in so far as the context otherwise requires, "money laundering" means doing any act which constitutes an offence under –

(a)   section 23A or 24 of the Drug Trafficking Offences Act 1986 [1986 c.32; section 23A was inserted by section 16 of the Criminal Justice Act 1993 (c.36); section 24 was amended by section 103(1) of, and paragraphs 1 and 13 of Schedule 5 to, the Criminal Justice Act 1988 (c.33)] (which relate to the handling etc of proceeds of drug trafficking);

(b)   section 42A or 43 of the Criminal Justice (Scotland) Act 1987 [1987 c.41; section 42A was inserted by section 17 of the Criminal Justice Act 1993 (c. 36)] (which relate to the handling etc of proceeds of drug trafficking);

(c)   section 93A, 93B or 93C of the Criminal Justice Act 1988 [1988 c.33; sections 93A, 93B and 93C were inserted by section 29 of the Criminal Justice Act 1993 (c.36); section 93E of the 1988 Act (which was inserted by section 33 of the 1993 Act) makes provision as to the application in Scotland of sections 93A to 93C] (which relate to the handling etc of proceeds of certain other criminal conduct);

(d)   section 11 of the Prevention of Terrorism (Temporary Provisions) Act 1989 [1989 c.4] (which relates to financial assistance for terrorism);

(e)   section 14 of the Criminal Justice (International Co-operation) Act 1990 [1990 c.5] (concealing or transferring proceeds of drug trafficking);

(f)   Article 29 or 30 of the Criminal Justice (Confiscation) (Northern Ireland) Order 1990 [S.I. 1990/2588 (N.I.17)] (which relate to the handling etc of proceeds of drug trafficking);

(g)   section 53 or 54 of the Northern Ireland (Emergency Provisions) Act 1991 [1991 c.24; sections 53 and 54 were amended by section 47 of the Criminal Justice Act 1993 (c.36)] (which relate to the handling etc of proceeds of terrorist-related activities); or

(h)   any provision, whenever made, which has effect in Northern Ireland and corresponds to any of the provisions mentioned in sub-paragraph (a) or (c) above;

or, in the case of an act done otherwise than in England and Wales, Scotland or, as the case may be, Northern Ireland would constitute such an offence if done in England and Wales, Scotland or Northern Ireland.

(4)   The reference in paragraph (3) above to doing any act which would constitute an offence under the provisions mentioned in sub-paragraph (c) of that paragraph shall, for the purposes of these Regulations, be construed as a reference to doing any act which would constitute an offence under those provisions if, for the definition of "criminal conduct" in section 93A(7) of the Criminal Justice Act 1988, there were substituted –

"(7)   In this Part of this Act 'criminal conduct' means –

(a)   conduct which constitutes an offence to which this Part of this Act applies; or

(b)   conduct which –

(i)   would constitute such an offence if it had occurred in England and Wales or (as the case may be) Scotland; and

(ii)   contravenes the law of the country in which it occurred.".

(5)   For the purposes of these Regulations, any provision having effect in Northern Ireland which corresponds to the provisions referred to in paragraph (3)(c) above shall be construed as if it had been amended by a provision which corresponds to paragraph (4) above, with appropriate modifications.

(6)   For the purposes of this regulation, a business relationship formed by any person acting in the course of relevant financial business is an established business relationship where that person has obtained, under procedures maintained by him in accordance with regulation 7 below, satisfactory evidence of the identity of the person who, in relation to the formation of that business relationship, was the applicant for business.

Business relationships

3. (1)   Any reference in this regulation to an arrangement between two or more persons is a reference to an arrangement in which at least one person is acting in the course of a business.

(2)   For the purposes of these Regulations, "business relationship" means any arrangement between two or more persons where –

(a)   the purpose of the arrangement is to facilitate the carrying out of transactions between the persons concerned on a frequent, habitual or regular basis; and

(b)   the total amount of any payment or payments to be made by any person to any other in the course of that arrangement is not known or capable of being ascertained at the time the arrangement is made.

Relevant financial business

4. (1)   For the purposes of these Regulations, "relevant financial business" means, subject to paragraph (2) below, the business of engaging in one or more of the following –

(a)   deposit-taking business carried on by a person who is for the time being authorised under the Banking Act 1987 [1987 c.22];

(b)   acceptance by a building society of deposits made by any person (including the raising of money from members of the society by the issue of shares);

(c)   business of the National Savings Bank;

(d)   business carried on by a credit union within the meaning of the Credit Unions Act 1979 [1979 c.34] or the Credit Unions (Northern Ireland) Order 1985 [S.I. 1985/1205 (N.I.12)];

(e)   any home regulated activity carried on by a European institution in respect of which the requirements of paragraph 1 of Schedule 2 to the Banking Coordination (Second Council Directive) Regulations 1992 [S.I. 1992/3218] have been complied with;

(f)   investment business within the meaning of the Financial Services Act 1986 [1986 c.60];

(g)   any activity carried on for the purpose of raising money authorised to be raised under the National Loans Act 1968 [1968 c.13] under the auspices of the Director of National Savings;

(h)   any of the activities in points 1 to 12, or 14, of the Annex to the Second Banking Coordination Directive (the text of which is, for convenience of reference, set out in the Schedule to these Regulations), other than an activity falling within sub-paragraphs (a) to (g) above;

(i)   insurance business carried on by a person who has received official authorisation pursuant to Article 6 or 27 of the First Life Directive.

(2)   A business is not relevant financial business in so far as it consists of –

(a)   any of the following activities carried on by a society registered under the Industrial and Provident Societies Act 1965 [1965 c.12] –

(i)   the issue of withdrawable share capital within the limit set by section 6 of that Act [Section 6 has been amended by the Industrial and Provident Societies (Increase in Shareholding Limit) Order 1981 (S.I. 1981/395) and by section 4 of, and paragraph 8 of Schedule 2 to, the Housing (Consequential Provisions) Act 1985 (c.71)]; or

(ii)   the acceptance of deposits from the public within the limit set by section 7(3) of that Act [Section 7(3) has been amended by the Industrial and Provident Societies (Increase in Deposit-taking Limits) Order 1981 (S.I. 1981/394)];

(b)   the issue of withdrawable share capital within the limit set by section 6 of the Industrial and Provident Societies Act (Northern Ireland) 1969 [1969 c.24; section 6 has been amended by the Industrial and Provident Societies (Increase in Shareholding Limit) Regulations (Northern Ireland) 1991 (S.R. 1991 No. 375)] by a society registered under that Act;

(c)   activities carried on by the Bank of England;

(d)   in relation to any person who is an exempted person for the purposes of section 45 of the Financial Services Act 1986 [1986 c.60; section 45 has been amended by section 78(1) of, and paragraph 14 of Schedule 6 to the Charities Act 1992 (c.41) and by regulation 55 of, and paragraph 8 of Schedule 9 to, the Banking Coordination (Second Council Directive) Regulations 1992 (S.I. 1992/3218)] (miscellaneous exemptions for holders of certain judicial and other offices), such of the activities as are specified in that section in relation to that person; or

(e)   in relation to any person who is an exempted person for the purposes of any order made under section 46 of the Financial Services Act 1986 [at the date on which these Regulations were laid, the following orders had been made under section 46 of the Financial Services Act 1986: S.I.s 1988/350, 1988/723, 1989/431, 1990/696, 1990/1492, 1990/2235, 1991/493 and 1991/1516] which was made before the date on which these Regulations come into force, any activities carried on by him or, as the case may be, such of the activities as are specified in such an order in relation to him.

(3)   For the purposes of paragraph (1)(f) above, any reference in these Regulations to the carrying on of relevant financial business in the United Kingdom shall be construed in accordance with section 1(3) of the Financial Services Act 1986.

(4)   In this regulation –

"building society" has the same meaning as in the Building Societies Act 1986;

"deposit-taking business" has the same meaning as in the Banking Act 1987;

"the First Life Directive" means the First Council Directive on the co-ordination of laws, regulations and administrative provisions relating to the taking up and pursuit of the business of direct life assurance (No. 79/267/EEC) [OJ No. L63, 13.3.79, p.l, as amended by the 1979 Act of Accession (Greece) (OJ No. L291, 19.11.79, p.17), the 1985 Act of Accession (Portugal and Spain) (OJ No. L302, 15.11.85, p.23) and Council Directive 90/619/EEC]; and

"the Second Banking Coordination Directive" means the Second Council Directive on the co-ordination of laws, regulations and administrative provisions relating to the taking up and pursuit of the business of credit institutions (No. 89/646/EEC)[OJ No. L386, 30.12.89, p.l].

SYSTEMS AND TRAINING TO PREVENT MONEY LAUNDERING

Systems and training to prevent money laundering

5. (1)   No person shall, in the course of relevant financial business carried on by him in the United Kingdom, form a business relationship, or carry out a one-off transaction, with or for another unless that person –

(a)   maintains the following procedures established in relation to that business –

(i)   identification procedures in accordance with regulations 7 and 9 below;

(ii)   record-keeping procedures in accordance with regulation 12 below;

(iii)   except where the person concerned is an individual who in the course of relevant financial business does not employ or act in association with any other person, internal reporting procedures in accordance with regulation 14 below; and

(iv)   such other procedures of internal control and communication as may be appropriate for the purposes of forestalling and preventing money laundering;

(b)   takes appropriate measures from time to time for the purposes of making employees whose duties include the handling of relevant financial business aware of –

      (i)   the procedures under sub-paragraph (a) above which are maintained by him and which relate to the relevant financial business in question, and

      (ii) the enactments relating to money laundering; and

  (c) provides such employees from time to time with training in the recognition and handling of transactions carried out by, or on behalf of, any person who is, or appears to be, engaged in money laundering.

(2) Any person who contravenes this regulation shall be guilty of an offence and liable –

  (a) on conviction on indictment, to imprisonment not exceeding a term of two years or a fine or both;

  (b) on summary conviction, to a fine not exceeding the statutory maximum.

(3) In determining whether a person has complied with any of the requirements of paragraph (1) above, a court may take account of –

  (a) any relevant supervisory or regulatory guidance which applies to that person;

  (b) in a case where no guidance falling within sub-paragraph (a) above applies, any other relevant guidance issued by a body that regulates, or is representative of, any trade, profession, business or employment carried on by that person.

(4) In proceedings against any person for an offence under this regulation, it shall be a defence for that person to show that he took all reasonable steps and exercised all due diligence to avoid committing the offence.

(5) In this regulation –

"enactments relating to money laundering" means the enactments referred to in regulation 2(3) above and the provisions of these Regulations; and

"supervisory or regulatory guidance" means guidance issued, adopted or approved by a supervisory authority.

Offences by bodies corporate, partnerships and unincorporated associations

6. (1) Where an offence under regulation 5 above committed by a body corporate is proved to have been committed with the consent or connivance of, or to be attributable to any neglect on the part of, any director, manager, secretary or other similar officer of the body corporate or any person who was purporting to act in any such capacity he, as well as the body corporate, shall be guilty of that offence and shall be liable to be proceeded against and punished accordingly.

(2) Where the affairs of a body corporate are managed by the members, paragraph (1) above shall apply in relation to the acts and defaults of a member in connection with his functions of management as if he were a director of a body corporate.

(3) Where an offence under regulation 5 above committed by a partnership, or by an unincorporated association other than a partnership, is proved to have been committed with the consent or connivance of, or is attributable to any neglect on

the part of, a partner in the partnership or (as the case may be) a person concerned in the management or control of the association, he, as well as the partnership or association, shall be guilty of that offence and shall be liable to be proceeded against and punished accordingly.

IDENTIFICATION PROCEDURES

Identification procedures; business relationships and transactions

7. (1)   Subject to regulations 8 and 10 below identification procedures maintained by a person are in accordance with this regulation if in Cases 1 to 4 set out below they require, as soon as is reasonably practicable after contact is first made between that person and an applicant for business concerning any particular business relationship or one-off transaction –

    (a)   the production by the applicant for business of satisfactory evidence of his identity; or

    (b)   the taking of such measures specified in the procedures as will produce satisfactory evidence of his identity;

    and the procedures are, subject to paragraph 6 below, in accordance with this regulation if they require that where that evidence is not obtained the business relationship or one-off transaction in question shall not proceed any further.

    (2)   Case 1 is any case where the parties form or resolve to form a business relationship between them.

    (3)   Case 2 is any case where, in respect of any one-off transaction, any person handling the transaction knows or suspects that the applicant for business is engaged in money laundering, or that the transaction is carried out on behalf of another person engaged in money laundering.

    (4)   Case 3 is any case where, in respect of any one-off transaction, payment is to be made by or to the applicant for business of the amount of ecu 15,000 or more.

    (5)   Case 4 is any case where, in respect of two or more one-off transactions –

    (a)   it appears at the outset to a person handling any of the transactions –

        (i)   that the transactions are linked, and

        (ii)   that the total amount, in respect of all of the transactions, which is payable by or to the applicant for business is ecu 15,000 or more; or

    (b)   at any later stage, it comes to the attention of such a person that paragraphs (i) and (ii) of sub-paragraph (a) above are satisfied.

    (6)   The procedures referred to in paragraph (1) above are in accordance with this regulation if, when a report is made in circumstances falling within Case 2 (whether in accordance with regulation 14 or directly to a constable), they provided for steps to be taken in relation to the one-off transaction in question in accordance with any directions that may be given by a constable.

    (7)   In these Regulations references to satisfactory evidence of a person's identity shall be construed in accordance with regulation 11(1) below.

Payment by post, etc.

8. (1) Where satisfactory evidence of the identity of an applicant for business would, apart from this paragraph, be required under identification procedures in accordance with regulation 7 above but –

    (a) the circumstances are such that a payment is to be made by the applicant for business; and

    (b) it is reasonable in all the circumstances –

        (i) for the payment to be sent by post or by any electronic means which is effective to transfer funds; or

        (ii) for the details of the payment to be sent by post, to be given on the telephone or to be given by any other electronic means;

then, subject to paragraph (2) below, the fact that the payment is debited from an account held in the applicant's name at an institution mentioned in paragraph (4) below (whether the account is held by the applicant alone or jointly with one or more other persons) shall be capable of constituting the required evidence of identity.

(2) Paragraph (1) above shall not have effect to the extent that –

    (a) the circumstances of the payment fall within Case 2; or

    (b) the payment is made by any person for the purpose of opening a relevant account with an institution falling within paragraph (4) (a) or (b) below.

(3) For the purposes of paragraph (1) (b) above, it shall be immaterial whether the payment or its details are sent or given to a person who is bound by regulation 5(1) above or to some other person acting on his behalf.

(4) The institutions referred to in paragraph (1) above are –

    (a) an institution which is for the time being authorised by the Bank of England under the Banking Act 1987 [1987 c.22] or by the Building Societies Commission under the Building Societies Act 1986 [1986 c.53];

    (b) a European authorised institution within the meaning of the Banking Co-ordination (Second Council Directive) Regulations 1992 [S.I. 1992/3218]; or

    (c) any other institution which is an authorised credit institution.

(5) For the purposes of this regulation –

"authorised credit institution" means a credit institution, as defined in Article 1 of the First Council Directive on the co-ordination of laws, regulations and administrative provisions relating to the taking up and pursuit of the business of credit institutions (77/780/EEC) [OJ No. L322, 17.12.77, p.30, as amended by Council Directive No. 86/524/EEC (OJ No. L309, 4.11.86, p.15) and by Council Directive No. 89/646/EEC (OJ No. L386, 30.12.89, p.1.)], which is authorised to carry on the business of a credit institution by a competent authority of a member state; and

"relevant account" means an account from which a payment may be made by any means to a person other than the applicant for business, whether such a payment –

(a)   may be made directly to such a person from the account by or on behalf of the applicant for business; or

(b)   may be made to such a person indirectly as a result of –

(i)   a direct transfer of funds from an account from which no such direct payment may be made to another account, or

(ii)   a change in any of the characteristics of the account.

Identification procedures; transactions on behalf of another

9. (1)   This regulation applies where, in relation to a person who is bound by regulation 5(1) above, an applicant for business is or appears to be acting otherwise than as principal.

(2)   Subject to regulation 10 below, identification procedures maintained by a person are in accordance with this regulation if, in a case to which this regulation applies, they require reasonable measures to be taken for the purpose of establishing the identity of any person on whose behalf the applicant for business is acting.

(3)   In determining, for the purposes of paragraph (2) above, what constitutes reasonable measures in any particular case regard shall be had to all the circumstances of the case and, in particular, to best practice which, for the time being, is followed in the relevant field of business and which is applicable to those circumstances.

(4)   Without prejudice to the generality of paragraph (3) above, if the conditions mentioned in paragraph (5) below are fulfilled in relation to an applicant for business who is, or appears to be, acting as an agent for a principal (whether undisclosed or disclosed for reference purposes only) it shall be reasonable for a person bound by regulation 5(1) above to accept a written assurance from the applicant for business to the effect that evidence of the identity of any principal on whose behalf the applicant for business may act in relation to that person will have been obtained and recorded under procedures maintained by the applicant for business.

(5)   The conditions referred to in paragraph (4) above are that, in relation to the business relationship or transaction in question, there are reasonable grounds for believing that the applicant for business –

(a)   acts in the course of a business in relation to which an overseas regulatory authority exercises regulatory functions; and

(b)   is based or incorporated in, or formed under the law of, a country other than a member State in which there are in force provisions at least equivalent to those required by the Money Laundering Directive.

(6)   In paragraph (5) above, "overseas regulatory authority" and "regulatory functions" have the same meaning as in section 82 of the Companies Act 1989 [1989 c.40; section 82 was amended by section 79 of, and paragraph 16 of Schedule 5 to, the Criminal Justice Act 1993 (c.36); there are no other relevant amendments].

Identification procedures; exemptions

10.(1) Subject to paragraph (2) below, identification procedures under regulations 7 and 9 above shall not require any steps to be taken to obtain evidence of any person's identity –

(a) where there are reasonable grounds for believing that the applicant for business is a person who is bound by the provisions of regulation 5(1) above;

(b) where there are reasonable grounds for believing that the applicant for business is otherwise a person who is covered by the Money Laundering Directive;

(c) where any one-off transaction is carried out with or for a third party pursuant to an introduction effected by a person who has provided an assurance that evidence of the identity of all third parties introduced by him will have been obtained and recorded under procedures maintained by him, where that person identifies the third party and where –

(i) that person falls within sub-paragraph (a) or (b) above; or

(ii) there are reasonable grounds for believing that the conditions mentioned in regulation 9(5)(a) and (b) above are fulfilled in relation to him;

(d) where the person who would otherwise be required to be identified, in relation to a one-off transaction, is the person to whom the proceeds of that transaction are payable but to whom no payment is made because all of those proceeds are directly reinvested on his behalf in another transaction –

(i) of which a record is kept, and

(ii) which can result only in another reinvestment made on that person's behalf or in a payment made directly to that person;

(e) in relation to insurance business consisting of a policy of insurance in connection with a pension scheme taken out by virtue of a person's contract of employment or occupation where the policy –

(i) contains no surrender clause, and

(ii) may not be used as collateral for a loan;

(f) in relation to insurance business in respect of which a premium is payable in one instalment of an amount not exceeding ecu 2,500; or

(g) in relation to insurance business in respect of which a periodic premium is payable and where the total payable in respect of any calendar year does not exceed ecu 1,000.

(2) Nothing in this regulation shall apply in circumstances falling within Case 2.

(3) In this regulation "calendar year" means a period of twelve months beginning on 31st December.

Identification procedures; supplementary provisions

11.(1) For the purposes of these Regulations, evidence of identity is satisfactory if –

(a) it is reasonably capable of establishing that the applicant is the person he claims to be; and

(b)   the person who obtains the evidence is satisfied, in accordance with the procedures maintained under these Regulations in relation to the relevant financial business concerned, that it does establish that fact.

(2)   In determining for the purposes of regulation 7(1) above the time span in which satisfactory evidence of a person's identity has to be obtained, in relation to any particular business relationship or one-off transaction, all the circumstances shall be taken into account including, in particular –

(a)   the nature of the business relationship or one-off transaction concerned;

(b)   the geographical locations of the parties;

(c)   whether it is practical to obtain the evidence before commitments are entered into between the parties or before money passes;

(d)   in relation to Case 3 or 4, the earliest stage at which there are reasonable grounds for believing that the total amount payable by an applicant for business is ecu 15,000 or more.

RECORD-KEEPING PROCEDURES

Record-keeping procedures

12.(1)   Record-keeping procedures maintained by a person are in accordance with this regulation if they require the keeping, for the prescribed period, of the following records –

(a)   in any case where, in relation to any business relationship that is formed or one-off transaction that is carried out, evidence of a person's identity is obtained under procedures maintained in accordance with regulation 7 or 9 above, a record that indicates the nature of the evidence and –

(i)   comprises a copy of the evidence;

(ii)   provides such information as would enable a copy of it to be obtained; or

(iii)   in a case where it is not reasonably practicable to comply with paragraph (i) or (ii) above, provides sufficient information to enable the details as to a person's identity contained in the relevant evidence to be re-obtained; and

(b)   a record containing details relating to all transactions carried out by that person in the course of relevant financial business.

(2)   For the purposes of paragraph (1) above, the prescribed period is, subject to paragraph (3) below, the period of at least five years commencing with –

(a)   in relation to such records as are described in sub-paragraph (a), the date on which the relevant business was completed within the meaning of paragraph (4) below; and

(b)   in relation to such records as are described in sub-paragraph (b), the date on which all activities taking place in the course of the transaction in question were completed.

(3)   Where a person who is bound by the provisions of regulation 5(1) above –

   (a)   forms a business relationship or carries out a one-off transaction with another person;

   (b)   has reasonable grounds for believing that that person has become insolvent; and

   (c)   after forming that belief, takes any step for the purpose of recovering all or part of the amount of any debt payable to him by that person which has fallen due;

   the prescribed period for the purposes of paragraph (1) above is the period of at least five years commencing with the date on which the first such step is taken.

(4)   For the purposes of paragraph (2)(a) above, the date on which relevant business is completed is, as the case may be –

   (a)   in circumstances falling within Case 1, the date of the ending of the business relationship in respect of whose formation the record under paragraph (1) (a) above was compiled;

   (b)   in circumstances falling within Case 2 or 3, the date of the completion of all activities taking place in the course of the one-off transaction in respect of which the record under paragraph (1)(a) above was compiled;

   (c)   in circumstances falling within Case 4, the date of the completion of all activities taking place in the course of the last one-off transaction in respect of which the record under paragraph (1)(a) above was compiled;

   and where the formalities necessary to end a business relationship have not been observed, but a period of five years has elapsed since the date on which the last transaction was carried out in the course of that relationship, then the date of the completion of all activities taking place in the course of that last transaction shall be treated as the date on which the relevant business was completed.

Record-keeping procedures; supplementary provisions

13.(1)   For the purposes of regulation 12(3)(b) above, a person shall be taken to be insolvent if, but only if, in England and Wales –

   (a)   he has been adjudged bankrupt or has made a composition or arrangement with his creditors;

   (b)   an order has been made with respect to him under section 112, 112A or 112B of the County Courts Act 1984 [1984 c.28; section 112 was amended by section 220(2) of the Insolvency Act 1985 (c.65); and section 112 was amended, and sections 112A and 112B were inserted, by section 13 of the Courts and Legal Services Act 1990 (c.41)] (administration orders, orders restricting enforcement and administration orders with composition provisions);

   (c)   he has died and his estate falls to be administered in accordance with an order under section 421 of the Insolvency Act 1986 [1986 c.45] (insolvent estates of deceased persons); or

   (d)   where that person is a company, a winding up order or an administration order has been made or a resolution for voluntary winding up has been passed with respect to it, or a receiver or manager of its undertaking has been duly appointed, or possession has been taken, by or on behalf of the holders of any debentures secured by a floating charge, of any property of the company comprised in or subject to the charge, or a voluntary arrangement proposed for the purpose of Part I of the Insolvency Act 1986 has been approved under that Part, or a compromise or arrangement in accordance with section 425 of the Companies Act 1985 [1985 c.6; section 425 was amended by section 109(1) of, and paragraph 11 of Schedule 6 to, the Insolvency Act 1986 (c.45)] has taken effect.

(2) For the purposes of regulation 12(3)(b) above, a person shall be taken to be insolvent if, but only if, in Scotland –

(a) his estate has been sequestrated, he has granted a trust deed for the benefit of his creditors or he has made a composition or arrangement for the benefit of his creditors; or

(b) where that person is a company, a winding up order or an administration order has been made or a resolution for voluntary winding up has been passed with respect to it, or a receiver has been appointed under a floating charge over any property of the company, or a voluntary arrangement proposed for the purpose of Part I of the Insolvency Act 1986 has been approved under that Part, or a compromise or arrangement in accordance with section 425 of the Companies Act 1985 has taken effect.

(3) For the purposes of regulation 12(3)(b) above, a person shall be taken to be insolvent if, but only if, in Northern Ireland –

(a) he has been adjudged bankrupt or has made a composition or arrangement with his creditors;

(b) an administration order has been made with respect to him under Article 80 of the Judgements Enforcement (Northern Ireland) Order 1981 [S.I. 1981/226 (N.I.6)] (power to make administration order on application of debtor);

(c) he has died and his estate falls to be administered in accordance with an order under Article 365 of the Insolvency (Northern Ireland) Order 1989 [S.I. 1989/2405 (N.I.19)] (insolvent estates of deceased persons); or

(d) where that person is a company, a winding up order or an administration order has been made or a resolution for voluntary winding up has been passed with respect to it, or a receiver or manager of its undertaking has been duly appointed, or possession has been taken, by or on behalf of the holders of any debentures secured by a floating charge, of any property of the company comprised in or subject to the charge, or a voluntary arrangement proposed for the purpose of Part II of the Insolvency (Northern Ireland) Order 1988 has been approved under that Part, or a compromise or arrangement in accordance with Article 418 of the Companies (Northern Ireland) Order 1986 [S.I. 1986/1032 (N.I.6)] has taken effect.

(4) Where a person bound by regulation 5(1) above –

(a) is an appointed representative; and

(b) is not –

(i) an authorised person within the meaning of the Financial Services Act 1986 [1986 c.60],

      (ii) authorised under the Building Societies Act 1986 [1986 c.53] or the Banking Act 1987 [1987 c.22], or

      (iii) a European institution;

it shall be the responsibility of the appointed representative's principal to ensure that record-keeping procedures in accordance with regulation 12 above are maintained in respect of any relevant financial business carried out by the appointed representative which is investment business carried on by him for which the principal has accepted responsibility in writing under section 44 of the Financial Services Act 1986.

(5)   Where record-keeping procedures in accordance with regulation 12 above are not maintained in respect of business relationships formed, and one-off transactions carried out, in the course of such relevant financial business as is referred to in paragraph (4) above, an appointed representative's principal shall be regarded as having contravened regulation 5 in respect of those procedures and he, as well as the appointed representative, shall be guilty of an offence and shall be liable to be proceeded against and punished accordingly.

(6)   Section 44(2) of the Financial Services Act 1986 (construction of references to appointed representative, his principal and investment business carried out by an appointed representative) shall apply for the purposes of paragraphs (4) and (5) above as it applies for the purposes of that Act.

INTERNAL REPORTING PROCEDURES

Internal reporting procedures

14.   Internal reporting procedures maintained by a person are in accordance with this regulation if they include provision –

(a)   identifying a person ('the appropriate person') to whom a report is to be made of any information or other matter which comes to the attention of a person handling relevant financial business and which, in the opinion of the person handling that business, gives rise to a knowledge or suspicion that another person is engaged in money laundering;

(b)   requiring that any such report be considered in the light of all other relevant information by the appropriate person, or by another designated person, for the purpose of determining whether or not the information or other matter contained in the report does give rise to such a knowledge or suspicion;

(c)   for any person charged with considering a report in accordance with sub-paragraph (b) above to have reasonable access to other information which may be of assistance to him and which is available to the person responsible for maintaining the internal reporting procedures concerned; and

(d)   for securing that the information or other matter contained in a report is disclosed to a constable where the person who has considered the report under the procedures maintained in accordance with the preceding provisions of this regulation knows or suspects that another person is engaged in money laundering.

DUTY OF SUPERVISORY AUTHORITIES TO REPORT EVIDENCE OF MONEY LAUNDERING

Supervisory authorities

15.(1)   References in these Regulations to supervisory authorities shall be construed in accordance with the following provisions.

(2)   For the purposes of these Regulations, each of the following is a supervisory authority –

(a)   the Bank of England;

(b)   the Building Societies Commission;

(c)   a designated agency within the meaning of the Financial Services Act 1986 [1986 c.60];

(d)   a recognised self-regulating organisation within the meaning of the Financial Services Act 1986;

(e)   a recognised professional body within the meaning of the Financial Services Act 1986;

(f)   a transferee body within the meaning of the Financial Services Act 1986;

(g)   a recognised self-regulating organisation for friendly societies within the meaning of the Financial Services Act 1986;

(h)   the Secretary of State;

(i)   the Treasury;

(j)   the Council of Lloyd's;

(k)   the Director General of Fair Trading;

(l)   the Friendly Societies Commission;

(m)   the Chief Registrar of Friendly Societies;

(n)   the Central Office of the Registry of Friendly Societies;

(o)   the Registrar of Friendly Societies for Northern Ireland;

(p)   the Assistant Registrar of Friendly Societies for Scotland.

(3)   These Regulations apply to the Secretary of State in the exercise, in relation to any person carrying on relevant financial business, of his functions under the enactments relating to insurance companies, companies or insolvency or under the Financial Services Act 1986.

Supervisors etc. to report evidence of money laundering

16.(1)   Subject to paragraph (2) below, where a supervisory authority –

(a)   obtains any information; and

(b)   is of the opinion that the information indicates that any person has or may have been engaged in money laundering,

the authority shall, as soon as is reasonably practicable, disclose that information to a constable.

(2)   Where any person is a secondary recipient of information obtained by a supervisory authority, and that person forms such an opinion as is mentioned in paragraph (l)(b) above, that person may disclose the information to a constable.

(3)   Where any person within paragraph (6) below –

(a)   obtains any information whilst acting in the course of any investigation, or discharging any functions, to which his appointment or authorisation relates; and

(b)   is of the opinion that the information indicates that any person has or may have been engaged in money laundering,

that person shall, as soon as is reasonably practicable, either disclose that information to a constable or disclose that information to the supervisory authority by whom he was appointed or authorised.

(4)   Any disclosure made by virtue of the preceding provisions of this regulation shall not be treated as a breach of any restriction imposed by statute or otherwise.

(5)   Any information –

(a)   which has been disclosed to a constable by virtue of the preceding provisions of this regulation; and

(b)   which would, apart from the provisions of paragraph (4) above, be subject to such a restriction as is mentioned in that paragraph;

may be disclosed by the constable, or any person obtaining the information directly or indirectly from him, in connection with the investigation of any criminal offence or for the purposes of any criminal proceedings, but not otherwise.

(6)   Persons falling within this paragraph are –

(a)   a person or inspector appointed under section 17 of the Industrial Assurance Act 1923 [1923 c.8 (13 & 14 Geo.5); section 17 was amended by the Statute Law Revision Act 1950 (c.6), by sections 5(5) and 14(2) of, and Schedule 3 to, the Friendly Societies Act 1971 (c.66) and by section 100 of, and paragraphs 1, 5(2) and 6 of Schedule 19 to, the Friendly Societies Act 1992 (c.40)] or section 65 or 66 of the Friendly Societies Act 1992 [1992 c.40];

(b)   an inspector appointed under section 49 of the Industrial and Provident Societies Act 1965 [1965 c.12] or section 18 of the Credit Unions Act 1979 [1979 c.34];

(c)   an inspector appointed under section 431, 432, 442 or 446 of the Companies Act 1985 [1985 c.6; section 432 was amended by section 55 of the Companies Act 1989 (c.40); section 442 was amended by section 62 of the 1989 Act; there are amendments to section 446 in sections 182 and 212 of, and in paragraph 8 of Schedule 13, paragraph 21 of Schedule 16, Part I of Schedule 17 to the Financial Services Act 1986 (c.60), in section 212 of, and Schedule 24 to, the Companies Act 1989 (c.40) and in regulation 82 of, and in paragraph 16 of Schedule 10 to, the Banking Coordination (Second Council Directive) Regulations 1992 (S.I. 1992/3218)] or under Article 424, 425, 435 or 439 of the Companies (Northern Ireland) Order 1986 [S.I. 1986/1032 (N.I.6); Article 425 was amended by article 3 of the Companies (No.2) (Northern Ireland) Order 1990 (S.I. 1990/1504 (N.I.10)); Article 435 was amended by Article 10 of that Order; Article 439 was amended by Article 113 of, and Schedule 6 to, that Order];

(d)   a person or inspector appointed under section 55 or 56 of the Building Societies Act 1986 [1986 c.53];

(e)   an inspector appointed under section 94 or 177 of the Financial Services Act 1986 [1986 c.60; section 94 was amended by sections 72 and 212 of, and Schedule 24 to, the Companies Act 1989 (c.40); section 177 was amended by section 74 of that Act];

(f)   a person appointed under section 41 of the Banking Act 1987 [1987 c.22; section 41 was amended by regulation 37 of the Banking Coordination (Second Council Directive) Regulations 1992 (S.I. 1992/3218)]; and

(g)   a person authorised to require the production of documents under section 44 of the Insurance Companies Act 1982 [1982 c.50; section 44 was amended by section 77(1) and (2) of the Companies Act 1989 (c.40)], section 447 of the Companies Act 1985 [1985 c.6; section 447 was amended by sections 63(1)–(7) and 212 of, and Schedule 24 to, the Companies Act 1989 (c.40)], section 106 of the Financial Services Act 1986 [1986 c.60; section 106 was amended by section 73 of the Companies Act 1989 (c.40) and by regulation 55 of, and paragraph 29 of Schedule 9 to, the Banking Coordination (Second Council Directive) Regulations 1992], Article 440 of the Companies (Northern Ireland) Order 1986 [S.I. 1986/1032 (N.I.6); Article 440 was amended by Articles 11 and 113 of, and Schedule 6 to, the Companies (No.2) (Northern Ireland) Order 1990 (S.I. 1990/1504 (N.I.10))] or section 84 of the Companies Act 1989 [1989 c.40].

(7)   In this regulation "secondary recipient", in relation to information obtained by a supervisory authority, means any person to whom that information has been passed by the authority.

TRANSITIONAL PROVISIONS

Transitional provisions

17.(1)   Nothing in these Regulations shall require a person who is bound by regulation 5(1) above to maintain procedures in accordance with regulations 7 and 9 which require evidence to be obtained, in respect of any business relationship formed by him before the date on which these Regulations come into force, as to the identity of the person with whom that relationship has been formed.

(2)   For the purposes of regulation 2(6) above, any business relationship referred to in paragraph (1) above shall be treated as if it were an established business relationship.

(3)   In regulation 10(1)(g), the reference to the total payable in respect of any calendar year not exceeding ecu 1,000 shall, for the period commencing with the coming into force of these Regulations and ending with 30th December 1994, be construed as a reference to the total payable in respect of that period not exceeding ecu 750.

SCHEDULE

REGULATION 4(1)

"ANNEX

LIST OF ACTIVITIES SUBJECT TO MUTUAL RECOGNITION

1.   Acceptance of deposits and other repayable funds from the public.

2.   Lending [including *inter alia*:

– consumer credit

– mortgage credit

– factoring with or without recourse

– financing of commercial transactions (including forfaiting)].

3.   Financial leasing.

4.   Money transmission services.

5.   Issuing and administering means of payment (e.g. credit cards, travellers' cheques and bankers' drafts).

6.   Guarantees and commitments.

7.   Trading for own account or for account of customers in:

(a) money market instruments (cheques, bills, CDs, etc.);

(b) foreign exchange;

(c) financial futures and options;

(d) exchange and interest rate instruments;

(e) transferable securities.

8.   Participation in securities issues and the provision of services related to such issues [This paragraph represents the text as amended in accordance with a corrigendum published in the Official Journal of the European Communities No. L83 of 30 March 1990.].

9.   Advice to undertakings on capital structure, industrial strategy and related questions and advice and services relating to mergers and the purchase of undertakings.

10. Money broking.

11. Portfolio management and advice.

12. Safekeeping and administration of securities.

13. Credit reference services.

14. Safe custody services."

Annex 3C

Practice rule 13 (supervision and management of a practice) and Council statement on waivers

(see **3.08**, p.73)

[NOTE: On 23rd December 1999, rule 13 of the Solicitors' Practice Rules 1990 (supervision and management of an office) is replaced with the following rule. Guidance on the rule is available from Professional Ethics (see p.xv for contact details).]

In this rule, words in italics are defined in the notes.

(1) The *principals* in a practice must ensure that their practice is supervised and managed so as to provide for:

    (a) compliance with principal solicitors' duties at law and in conduct to exercise proper *supervision* over their admitted and unadmitted staff;

    (b) adequate *supervision* and direction of clients' matters;

    (c) compliance with the requirements of sections 22(2A) and 23(3) of the Solicitors Act 1974 as to the direction and *supervision* of unqualified persons;

    (d) effective *management* of the practice generally.

(2) Every practice must have at least one *principal* who is a solicitor *qualified to supervise.*

(3) (a) Except as provided in (b) below, every office of the practice must have at least one solicitor *qualified to supervise*, for whom that office is his or her normal place of work.

    (b) Without prejudice to the requirements of paragraph (1) of this rule, an office which undertakes only property selling and ancillary mortgage related services as defined in rule 6 of these rules, survey and valuation services, must be managed and supervised to the following minimum standards:

        (i) the day-to-day control and administration must be undertaken by a suitably qualified and experienced office manager who is a fit and proper person to undertake such work; and for whom that office is his or her normal place of work; and

        (ii) the office must be supervised and managed by a solicitor *qualified to supervise*, who must visit the office with sufficient frequency and spend sufficient time there to allow for adequate control of and consultation with staff, and if necessary consultation with clients.

(4) This rule is to be interpreted in the light of the notes, and is subject to the transitional provisions set out in note (k).

(5) (a) This rule applies to private practice, and to solicitors employed by a law centre.

(b) The rule also applies to other employed solicitors, but only:

(i) if they advise or act for members of the public under the legal aid scheme; or

(ii) if, in acting for members of the public, they exercise any *right of audience* or *right to conduct litigation,* or supervise anyone exercising those rights.

Notes

(a) *Principals' responsibility for the practice*

Principals are responsible at law and in conduct for their practices, and compliance with the rule does not derogate from this responsibility. Under rule 6 of these rules, property selling or mortgage related services to one party to a conveyance, and conveyancing services for the other party, may not be supervised by the same solicitor.

(b) *"Supervision" and "management"*

(i) *"Supervision" refers to the professional overseeing of staff and the professional overseeing of clients' matters.*

(ii) *"Management" is a wider concept, which encompasses the overall direction and development of the practice and its day-to-day control and administration. Management functions include business efficiency as well as professional competence.*

(iii) *Operationally, supervision and management may be delegated within an established framework for reporting and accountability. However, the responsibility under paragraph (1)(a) of the rule, and the responsibility referred to in note (a) above, remain with the principals.*

(iv) *"With sufficient frequency" in paragraph (3)(b)(ii) would normally mean daily; but if the office is open at weekends it may be possible to defer consultations with clients until a weekday and be available only at need to staff.*

(c) *Evidence of effective supervision and management*

Where a question arises as to compliance with paragraph (1) of the rule, principals will be expected to be able to produce evidence of a systematic and effective approach to the supervision and management of the practice. Such evidence may include the implementation by the practice of one or more of the following:

(i) *guidance on the supervision and execution of particular types of work issued from time to time by the Law Society including:*

(A) *guidance on solicitors' responsibilities for the supervision of clerks exercising rights of audience under section 27(2)(e) of the Courts and Legal Services Act 1990; and*

(B) *good practice guidelines on the recruitment and supervision of employees undertaking investment business;*

(ii) *the practice's own properly documented management standards and procedures;*

(iii) *practice management standards promoted from time to time by the Law Society;*

(iv) *accounting standards and procedures promoted from time to time by the Law Society;*

    (v)   *external quality standards such as BS EN ISO 9000 or Investors in People; and*

    (vi)   *in the case of solicitors employed by a law centre, any management standards or procedures laid down by its management committee.*

(d)   **"Qualified to supervise"**

A solicitor is qualified to supervise if he or she:

    (i)   *has held practising certificates for at least 36 months within the last ten years; and*

    (ii)   *has completed the training specified from time to time by the Law Society for the purpose of the rule.*

(e)   **"Normal place of work"**

    (i)   *A solicitor's "normal place of work" is the office from which he or she normally works, even though the day-to-day demands of practice may often take the solicitor out of the office.*

    (ii)   *If a solicitor normally works from a particular office for a part of the working week, that office is his or her "normal place of work" for that part of the week. The solicitor may have a different "normal place of work" for another part of the week.*

    (iii) *A solicitor who has a different "normal place of work" for different parts of the week could be the sole solicitor qualified to supervise at different offices at different times in the week. However, no solicitor can be the sole solicitor qualified to supervise at two different offices for the same part of the week.*

    (iv) *For compliance with paragraph (3) of the rule, an office must, for every part of the working week, have a solicitor qualified to supervise for whom that office is his or her "normal place of work" for that part of the week. This could be a different solicitor for different parts of the week.*

    (v)   *The working week of an office includes early mornings, late evenings and weekends if work is carried on, and if so the office must have a solicitor qualified to supervise for those times. However, it is not required that the solicitor qualified to supervise normally works at those times, provided that he or she:*

       (A)   *is available for emergency consultation; and*

       (B)   *pays occasional visits to the office during such times.*

(f)   **Working away from the office**

It is particularly important that systems of supervision and management encompass the work of:

    (i)   *those persons from time to time working away from the office – e.g. at home, visiting clients, at court, at a police station, at a consulting room open only for a few hours per week, or staffing a stand at an exhibition;*

    (ii)   *any person who normally works away from the office, such as a teleworker or homeworker.*

(g)   **Absence of solicitor qualified to supervise, or office manager**

    (i)   *When the solicitor qualified to supervise at an office is away on holiday, on sick leave, etc., suitable arrangements must be in place to ensure that any duties to clients and others are fully met. A similar standard applies to the absence of an office manager with responsibility for the day-to-day control and administration of a property selling office.*

    (ii)   *If the solicitor qualified to supervise will be away for a month or more, the arrangements will normally need to include the provision of another solicitor qualified to supervise at that office. A similar standard applies to the absence of an office manager with responsibility for the day-to-day control and administration of a property selling office.*

(h) **"Right of audience" and "right to conduct litigation"**

"Right of audience" and "right to conduct litigation" are to be interpreted in accordance with Part II and section 119 of the Courts and Legal Services Act 1990.

(i) **Recognised bodies**

"Principal", in relation to a recognised body, means a director of that body.

(j) **Registered foreign lawyers**

    (i) *A registered foreign lawyer who is a principal in the practice may fulfil the role of a "solicitor qualified to supervise" for the purpose of paragraph (2) of the rule, provided that:*

        (A) *the practice has at least one principal who is a solicitor; and*

        (B) *the practice does not exercise or assume responsibility for any right of audience or any right to conduct litigation; and*

        (C) *the registered foreign lawyer has practised as a lawyer for at least 36 months within the last ten years; and*

        (D) *he or she has completed the training specified under note (d)(ii) above.*

    (ii) *A registered foreign lawyer who is a principal in the practice may fulfil the role of a "solicitor qualified to supervise" for the purpose of paragraph (3) of the rule or note (k)(ii)(C) below, provided that:*

        (A) *no right of audience or right to conduct litigation is exercised or supervised from that office; and*

        (B) *the registered foreign lawyer has practised as a lawyer for at least 36 months within the last ten years; and*

        (C) *he or she has completed the training specified under note (d)(ii) above.*

(k) **Transitional provisions**

For a period of 10 years from 23rd December 1999:

    (i) *a solicitor or registered foreign lawyer who would not satisfy the requirements for a solicitor qualified to supervise can nevertheless fulfil that role for the purpose of paragraph (2) of the rule or note (k)(ii)(C) below, provided that:*

        (A) *immediately before 12th December 1996 he or she was qualified to supervise an office under practice rule 13(1)(a) as it then stood, or any waiver of that rule; and*

        (B) *any requirements of that rule or of any waiver continue to be met; and*

    (ii) *a person who would not satisfy the requirements for a solicitor qualified to supervise can nevertheless fulfil that role for the purpose of paragraph (3) of the rule, provided that:*

        (A) *immediately before 12th December 1996 he or she was managing or employed to manage an office in compliance with practice rule 13(1)(b) as it then stood, or any waiver of that rule; and*

        (B) *any requirements of that rule or of any waiver continue to be met; and*

        (C) *the office is attended on a daily basis by a solicitor qualified to supervise.*

Council statement on waivers of practice rule 13

On 23rd December 1999 a new version of practice rule 13 (supervision and management of a practice) will replace the "old" rule 13 (supervision and management of an office).

Existing waivers of the "old" rule granted in the period 1st September 1990 to 4th March 1999 are hereby extended, as waivers of the new rule 13, until the earlier of:

► any expiry date in the existing waiver; or

► 31st December 2001.

There are also important transitional provisions in the new rule itself, and the extension of a waiver is without prejudice to any transitional provision which may be applicable.

March 1999

Annex 3D

Solicitors' Incorporated Practice Rules 1988

(with consolidated amendments to 20th May 1998)

Rules dated 17th June 1988 made by the Council of the Law Society with the concurrence of the Master of the Rolls under section 9 of the Administration of Justice Act 1985, Part II of the Solicitors Act 1974 and Schedule 15 paragraph 6 of the Financial Services Act 1986, regulating the incorporated practices of solicitors and registered foreign lawyers in England and Wales and overseas.

1. Interpretation

In these Rules, except where the context otherwise requires:

(1) (a) "the Act" means the Administration of Justice Act 1985;

    (b) "authorised insurers", "the Council", "practising certificate", "the roll" and "the Society" shall have the meanings assigned to them in the Solicitors Act 1974;

    (c) "firm" means an unincorporated partnership consisting of solicitors or recognised bodies or both, or a multi-national partnership and includes also a solicitor who is a sole practitioner;

    (ca) "foreign lawyer" and "registered foreign lawyer" shall have the meanings assigned to them by section 89 of the Courts and Legal Services Act 1990;

    (d) "indemnity rules" means rules made under section 37 of the Solicitors Act 1974 and section 9 of the Act;

    (e) "member" means a person who agrees to become a member of a body corporate and whose name is entered in its register of members;

    (ea) "multi-national partnership" means an unincorporated partnership consisting of one or more registered foreign lawyers and one or more solicitors;

    (f) "person" includes a body corporate;

    (g) "recognised body" means a body corporate for the time being recognised by the Council under these Rules as being a suitable body to undertake the provision of professional services such as are provided by individuals practising as solicitors or by multi-national partnerships;

(h) "solicitor" means a person qualified to act as a solicitor under section 1 of the Solicitors Act 1974;

(i) "Solicitors Indemnity Fund" means the Fund established under the Solicitors' Indemnity Rules 1987.

(2) A reference to a Rule is a reference to one of the Solicitors' Incorporated Practice Rules 1988.

(3) A reference to any provision of an Act of Parliament includes a reference to any statutory modification or re-enactment of that provision for the time being in force.

(4) Words importing the masculine gender include the feminine and the neuter, words in the singular include the plural and words in the plural include the singular.

2. Requirement as to recognition by the Council

(1) Subject to the provisions of these Rules, a body corporate may carry on business consisting of the provision of professional services such as are provided by individuals practising as solicitors or by multi-national partnerships provided that before commencing any such business such body corporate shall have been recognised by the Council as being a suitable body to undertake the provision of such services and providing that at all times while carrying on such business it remains so recognised.

(2) A recognised body may carry on only such business as is referred to in paragraph (1) of this Rule.

3. Management and control

A recognised body shall at all times be managed and controlled by solicitors or recognised bodies, or by such persons together with one or more registered foreign lawyers provided that there shall be no breach of this Rule where the secretary of a recognised body is not a solicitor, a registered foreign lawyer or a recognised body.

4. Directors

A recognised body shall not have as a director any person who is not a solicitor or a registered foreign lawyer; provided that at all times at least one of the directors shall be a solicitor.

5. Shares

(1) A recognised body shall not have as a member any person who is not a solicitor, a registered foreign lawyer or a recognised body.

(2) (a) (i) Subject to paragraphs (4) and (5) of this Rule a member of a recognised body shall not hold any share in the body for another person save as nominee for a solicitor, a registered foreign lawyer or a recognised body or for a receiver appointed under section 99 of the Mental Health Act 1983 in respect of any such solicitor or registered foreign lawyer; and

(ii) at all times at least one share in the body must be held either by a member who or which is a solicitor or a recognised body and who or which beneficially owns that share; or by a member who or which holds that share as nominee for a solicitor or for a recognised body or for a receiver appointed under section 99 of the Mental Health Act 1983 in respect of a solicitor.

(b) A member of a recognised body shall disclose to the body the nature and extent of any interests in shares registered in his name and the persons by whom such interests are held. The recognised body shall maintain a record of the identity of all persons, other than the member in whose name a share is registered, holding such interests. The record shall be kept in respect of each person on it for at least three years from the date on which that person ceased to hold any interest in any share in the body.

(c) A member of a recognised body shall not create any charge or other third party interest (save as permitted by sub-paragraph (a) of this paragraph) over any share in the recognised body.

(3) In paragraphs (4) and (5) of this Rule references to the beneficial owner of a share do not include a person in whose name that share is registered and who beneficially owns that share.

(4) (a) Where a member of a recognised body dies the recognised body shall ensure that any shares registered in his name at the time of his death are within twelve months of his death registered in the name of a solicitor or a recognised body or (where permitted by paragraph (2)(a)(i) of this Rule) a registered foreign lawyer or (where the recognised body is a company limited by shares) are acquired by the recognised body itself.

(b) A solicitor, a registered foreign lawyer or a recognised body who or which is the personal representative of a deceased member of or beneficial owner of a share in a recognised body may elect to be entered in the register of members of the recognised body but no member shall hold any share as personal representative for longer than twelve months from the date of the death of the deceased.

(c) Where a beneficial owner of a share in a recognised body dies, a member may notwithstanding sub-paragraph (2)(a) of this Rule, continue to hold such share for the personal representative of the deceased for a period of not longer than twelve months from the date of the death; provided that voting rights shall only be exercised in respect of any share held in reliance on this sub-paragraph where the only personal representative in respect of the deceased beneficial owner's interest in the share is a solicitor, a registered foreign lawyer or a recognised body.

(5) (a) Where one of the following specified events happens, to a member of or a beneficial owner of a share in a recognised body, that is to say: (where such member or beneficial owner is a solicitor) his name is struck off or removed from the roll or his practising certificate is suspended (including automatic suspension on bankruptcy) or withdrawn; or (where such a member or beneficial owner is a registered foreign lawyer) his name is struck off the register or his registration is suspended (including automatic suspension on bankruptcy, or on striking off or suspension in his own jurisdiction) or

cancelled; or (where such a member or beneficial owner is a recognised body) its recognition is revoked or expires (including automatic expiry on liquidation, making of an administration order or appointment of an administrative receiver);

then –

(i) where the specified event happens in respect of a member, any share registered in his name may, notwithstanding paragraph (1) of this Rule, remain so registered for a period of not longer than six months from the date of the specified event; provided that no voting rights shall be exercised in respect of any such share while it remains so registered; and

(ii) where the specified event happens in respect of a beneficial owner of a share, a member may, notwithstanding sub-paragraph (2)(a) of this Rule, continue to hold such share for the beneficial owner or, as the case may be, his trustee in bankruptcy or liquidator for a period of not longer than six months from the date of the specified event; provided that no voting rights shall be exercised in respect of any share held in reliance on this sub-paragraph.

(b) A solicitor or registered foreign lawyer who is the trustee in bankruptcy or liquidator of a member of or a beneficial owner of a share in a recognised body may elect to be entered in the register of members of the recognised body but no member shall hold any share as trustee in bankruptcy or liquidator for longer than six months from the date of the bankruptcy order or winding-up order as the case may be.

(6) A member of a recognised body shall not exercise any voting rights in respect of any share held in breach of any part of this Rule and the chairman of a meeting shall not accept any vote tendered in breach of this paragraph or paragraph (7) of this Rule.

(7) For the purpose of attending and voting at meetings a member of a recognised body shall not appoint as a proxy or corporate representative any person other than a solicitor who is a member or officer of or who is working in the practice of, or a registered foreign lawyer who is a member or director of, (a) the recognised body or (b) a recognised body which is itself a member of the recognised body.

(8) A recognised body shall so far as possible ensure that its members comply with this Rule and Rule 6.

6.   Mental health

A recognised body shall not have as a director a solicitor or registered foreign lawyer while he is a patient as defined by section 94 of the Mental Health Act 1983 or while he is a person as to whom powers have been exercised under section 98 (emergency powers) of that Act and no voting rights shall be exercised in respect of any shares registered in the name of or beneficially owned by such a solicitor or registered foreign lawyer.

7.   Proper service to clients

A recognised body shall at all times remain able to provide a proper service to its clients.

8.   Registered office

The registered office of a recognised body shall be in England and Wales and at the place of business or one of the places of business of the body.

9.   Conditions which must at all times be satisfied

(1)   The following conditions shall at all times be satisfied by a recognised body and where any condition fails to be satisfied by a recognised body the recognition of the body by the Council shall expire:

(a)   a recognised body shall be registered in England and Wales under the Companies Act 1985 as an unlimited company having a share capital or as a company limited by shares;

(b)   a recognised body which is an unlimited company shall retain its status as an unlimited company, save where the Council consents to the body being re-registered as limited by shares under the Companies Act 1985;

(c)   a recognised body shall, notwithstanding sub-paragraphs (4)(c) and (5)(a) of Rule 5, at all times have at least one member holding a share or shares in the circumstances set out in Rule 5(2)(a)(ii) of these rules and able to exercise voting rights in respect of at least one share in the body, except that the recognition of a body shall not expire solely because:

(i)   the practising certificate of any member is withdrawn due to non-renewal under section 14(5) of the Solicitors Act 1974 provided that a new practising certificate is issued within two months of such expiry; or

(ii)   the death of a member has left a recognised body with no member able to exercise voting rights in respect of at least one share in the body provided (a) that within three months of the death the recognised body has at least one member able to exercise such voting rights, and (b) that until proviso (a) has been fulfilled either at least one share in the body is beneficially owned by a solicitor or a recognised body or the only personal representative in respect of at least one share in the body is a solicitor or a recognised body.

(2)   The recognition of a recognised body shall expire where a winding-up order or an administration order under Part II of the Insolvency Act 1986 is made with respect to the body or where a resolution for voluntary winding-up is passed with respect to the body or where a person is appointed administrative receiver of the body.

10. Revocation of recognition

The Council may revoke the recognition of a recognised body if that recognition was granted as a result of any error or fraud.

11. [repealed]

12. Application of principles and requirements of conduct to recognised bodies

All the principles and requirements of conduct affecting solicitors shall apply in all respects *mutatis mutandis* to recognised bodies.

13. Top-up insurance

(1)   A recognised body which is a company limited by shares shall insure with authorised insurers against the losses referred to in paragraph (3) of this Rule over and

above the maximum indemnity provided from time to time by the Solicitors Indemnity Fund.

(2)   The insurance required by paragraph (1) of this Rule shall provide, over and above that maximum indemnity, a minimum cover of either £500,000 on an each and every claim basis or £2,000,000 per annum on an aggregate basis.

(3)   The losses against which a recognised body is required to insure under this Rule are all losses arising from claims in respect of civil liability incurred in the practice of the recognised body by the recognised body or by any of its officers or employees or former officers or employees or by any solicitor or registered foreign lawyer who is or was a consultant to or associate in the body's practice or is or was working in the practice as an agent or a *locum tenens*; save that a recognised body shall not be required to insure against losses arising from claims of a type excluded, by the indemnity rules applicable from time to time to recognised bodies, from being afforded indemnity by the Solicitors Indemnity Fund.

(4)   The insurance required by paragraph (1) of this Rule shall cover the insured in respect of:

(a)   any claim first made or intimated during the period of insurance, and

(b)   any claim arising out of circumstances notified to the insurer during the period of insurance as circumstances which might give rise to a claim.

(5)   Provided that at all times

(i)   the "principals" of the recognised body, for the purposes of the Solicitors' Indemnity Rules, are the same in number and identity as the "principals" of an unincorporated practice, and

(ii)   the recognised body can act only as agent for the principals in that unincorporated practice, in their capacity as such,

the recognised body shall be exempt from compliance with paragraphs (1)–(4) of this Rule.

(6)   A recognised body which is a company limited by shares shall each twelve months after recognition is granted to it under these Rules, or at any other time when so required by the Council, submit to the Council evidence of compliance with, or exemption from, paragraphs (1)–(4) of this Rule.

14. Compensation Fund covenant

(1)   Each member of and each beneficial owner of a share in a recognised body shall submit to the Council, in such form as the Council may from time to time prescribe, a covenant under seal (referred to in these Rules as a "Compensation Fund covenant") that he or it will jointly and severally with the other members of and beneficial owners of any shares in the body reimburse the Society, when required to do so by the Council, in respect of any grant made out of the Compensation Fund under paragraph 6 of Schedule 2 to the Act where:

(a)   such grant is made in consequence of some act or default of the recognised body or any of its officers or employees; and

(b)   at the time of such act or default the covenantor is or was a member of or a beneficial owner of a share in the recognised body;

provided that a member or a beneficial owner of a share shall only be required to reimburse the Society to the extent that the Society has been unable to recover the amount of the grant from the recognised body or the officer or employee committing the act or default or the personal representative, trustee in bankruptcy or liquidator of any such person.

(2)   The Compensation Fund covenant shall include a covenant by the covenantor that before transferring any share or transferring a beneficial interest in any share or holding any share as nominee he or it will ensure that the intended transferee or beneficial owner submits a Compensation Fund covenant to the Council.

(3)   A recognised body shall not enter in its register of members any person until that person has submitted a Compensation Fund covenant to the Council and shall so far as possible ensure that all beneficial owners of any shares submit such a covenant to the Council.

15. Applications for recognition

A body corporate seeking recognition under these Rules shall submit to the Council:

(a)   a completed application signed by all the members and directors of the body (in the case of a member which is a recognised body two directors of that body shall sign on its behalf save that where a body has only one director that director shall sign on its behalf) in such form as the Council may from time to time prescribe, which application shall include:

   (i)   the names and addresses of all solicitors who are members of the body, and (separately designated) the names and addresses of all registered foreign lawyers who are members of the body;

   (ii)   the names and registered offices of all recognised bodies who are members of the body;

   (iii) the nature and extent of the interest held in any share by any person other than the member in whose name the share is registered and the identity of the person by whom such interest is held (including, separately designated, the identity of any such person who is a registered foreign lawyer);

   (iv)   the names and addresses of all directors of the body (including, separately designated, all directors who are registered foreign lawyers);

   (v)   the name, the registered office and any other proposed place or places of business of the body;

   (vi)   a statement as to whether the body is a company limited by shares or an unlimited company;

   (vii) reasonably sufficient information in respect of any of the matters referred to in Rule 16(2) except such information as has been provided by the body in a previous application under this Rule;

   (viii) a declaration:

      (a)   that the body complies with Rules 3–6, 8, 9 and 22 and that its members comply with Rules 5 and 6; and

      (b)   that the memorandum and articles of association of the body are such as to enable the body (i) to continue to comply with Rules 3–6 and (ii) so far as possible to ensure continued compliance by its members with Rules 5 and 6;

(b)   information or documentation, if required by the Society, to satisfy the Society that the recognised body or proposed recognised body complies, or will comply, with the indemnity rules applicable from time to time to recognised bodies;

(c)   in the case of a body which is a company limited by shares, evidence of compliance with, or exemption from, paragraphs (1)–(4) of Rule 13 (top-up insurance);

(d)   Compensation Fund covenants by all the members of the body and by all the beneficial owners of any shares in the body;

(e)   a copy of the certificate of incorporation of the body;

(f)   any other documentation or information which the Council may require;

(g)   such fee as the Council may from time to time prescribe in connection with such applications.

16. Grants and refusals of recognition

(1)   Where a body corporate has applied for recognition in accordance with Rule 15 the Council may recognise the body as a suitable body to undertake the provision of professional services such as are provided by individuals practising as solicitors or by multi-national partnerships where the Council is satisfied:

(a)   that the body complies with Rules 3–6, 8, 9 and 22 and that its members comply with Rules 5 and 6;

(b)   that the body complies with the indemnity rules applicable from time to time to recognised bodies; and

(c)   that, in the case of a body which is a company limited by shares, it complies with Rule 13 (top-up insurance).

(2)   Without prejudice to the generality of the Council's discretion under paragraph (1) of this Rule the Council may refuse to recognise a body where:

(a)   a director or member of the body is or has been a director or member of a recognised body which has been the subject of an order or direction under paragraphs 18 or 21 of Schedule 2 to the Act or the recognition of which has been revoked under Rule 10 of these Rules or has expired under Rule 9 of these Rules; or

(b)   a director or member has been the subject of an order under section 47(2)(a)–(c) of the Solicitors Act 1974 or Schedule 14 paragraph 15(4)(a)–(c) of the Courts and Legal Services Act 1990; or

(c)   the powers conferred by Part II of Schedule 1 to the Solicitors Act 1974 have been exercised in respect of the body or in respect of a firm or recognised body of which a director or member of the body applying for recognition is or has been a principal or a director or member as the case may be; or

(d)   a director or member:

(i)   has been convicted of a criminal offence involving fraud, dishonesty or violence; or

(ii) has had a bankruptcy order made against him or has made a composition or arrangement with his creditors or has made a proposal for a voluntary arrangement under Part VIII of the Insolvency Act 1986 or is or has been a director of a company in respect of which an administration order under Part II of the Insolvency Act 1986 or a winding-up order has been made or in respect of which a resolution for voluntary winding up has been passed or which has made a proposal for a voluntary arrangement under Part I of the Insolvency Act 1986 or in respect of which a person has been appointed receiver or administrative receiver; or

(iii) has had an order made against him which is not a bankruptcy order but which has the same or a similar effect under the law in force in any territory outside England and Wales; or

(iv) has been struck off or suspended from practice as a lawyer of a jurisdiction other than England and Wales; or

(e) for any other reason the Council thinks it proper in the public interest not to recognise the body.

17. Requirements on refusal; right of appeal if recognition neither granted nor refused within specified period

(1) Where the Council refuses an application for recognition it shall notify the applicant of the refusal and of the grounds on which it has been refused.

(2) Where the Council has within three months beginning with the date when an application for recognition was received by the Council neither granted nor refused recognition, an appeal to the Master of the Rolls may be brought under paragraph 2 of Schedule 2 to the Act as if the application had been refused by the Council. For the purpose of calculating the period of three months referred to in this paragraph time shall not run in August.

18. Duration of recognition

(1) Every recognition granted under these Rules shall, subject to paragraph (2) of this Rule, remain in force until the end of the third 31st May next after that recognition is granted except where prior to that time the recognition expires under Rule 9 or is revoked.

(2) Where an application is made in accordance with Rule 15 by a body which at the date of the application is already recognised under these Rules and the Council has neither granted nor refused a new recognition by the time when the body's existing recognition would, apart from this paragraph, expire in accordance with paragraph (1) of this Rule, the existing recognition shall not expire at that time but shall continue in force until a new recognition is granted or refused.

19. Duty to notify the Society of certain matters and to provide items required by the Council

(1) A recognised body shall notify the Society in writing:

(a) not less than 28 days before the change is implemented, of any change in the body's name, registered office or principal office if different from its registered office;

(b)   forthwith of any change:

  (i)   in the body's members, directors, or place or places of business other than those referred to in sub-paragraph (a) of this paragraph;

  (ii)   with respect to the interests held in any share in the body by a person other than the member in whose name the share is registered and in the identity of the person by whom any such interest is held;

(c)   forthwith of any of the occurrences referred to in Rule 9(2) or where a condition referred to in Rule 9(1) ceases to be satisfied.

(2)   The Council may (in order to ascertain whether or not any of these Rules or other rules, principles or requirements of conduct applicable to recognised bodies by virtue of these Rules or section 9 of the Act are being complied with) at any time by written notice require a recognised body or an officer or member of the body to submit to the Council any report, certificate, audit or other documentation or information which the Council may require and the recognised body or the officer or member as the case may be shall submit such item to the Council within such period as may be reasonably determined by the Council.

20. Certificate of recognition

Where the Council recognises a body under these Rules it shall issue to the body a certificate of recognition which shall state:

(a)   the name and registered office of the recognised body;

(b)   the dates of granting and expiry of recognition; and

(c)   whether the body is a company limited by shares or an unlimited company.

21. List of recognised bodies

The Society shall maintain a list containing the name, registered office and other place or places of business of every body for the time being recognised by the Council under these Rules, which list shall be available for inspection by the public.

22. Company name

The company name of a recognised body shall be governed by Rule 11 of the Solicitors' Practice Rules (names used by a firm).

23. Requirement to state certain matters on stationery, etc.

(1)   The names of all the directors of a recognised body shall be stated either on the body's stationery or in a list of the names of all the directors maintained at the body's registered office provided that in the latter case the body's stationery must state that such a list of all the directors' names is open to inspection at the body's registered office and must state the address of that office.

(1A)   In the case of a recognised body which has at least one registered foreign lawyer as a director, member or beneficial owner of a share, there must, in addition to paragraph (1) of this Rule, also be compliance with paragraph 7(b) of the Solicitors' Publicity Code.

(2)   A recognised body which is a company limited by shares shall comply with Chapter I (appearance of company name and other particulars on stationery, etc.) of Part XI of the Companies Act 1985.

(3)   On the stationery of a recognised body which is an unlimited company it shall be stated, either as part of the body's name or otherwise, that the body is a body corporate.

(4)   Where a recognised body which is an unlimited company is a partner in partnership with a solicitor or another recognised body it shall be stated on the stationery of the partnership, either as part of the body's name or otherwise, that the recognised body is a body corporate except where this is so stated on a list of the names of all the partners maintained by the partnership at its principal place of business in pursuance of section 4(3) of the Business Names Act 1985.

24. Duty of officers; application of Rules, etc., to officers, members, employees, etc.

(1)   It is the duty of a solicitor who or a recognised body which is an officer of a recognised body, or a registered foreign lawyer who is a director of a recognised body to take all reasonable steps to ensure compliance by any recognised body of which he or it is an officer with these Rules and any rules, principles or requirements of conduct applicable to recognised bodies by virtue of these Rules or section 9 of the Act.

(2)   A solicitor who is an officer, member or employee of or who is otherwise working in the practice of a recognised body, or a recognised body which is an officer or member of a recognised body, or a registered foreign lawyer who is a director or member of a recognised body, shall not by any act or omission by himself (or itself) or with any other person cause, instigate or connive at any breach of these Rules or any rules, principles or requirements of conduct applicable to recognised bodies by virtue of these Rules or section 9 of the Act and, for the avoidance of doubt, it is confirmed that a solicitor who is an officer, member or employee of or who is otherwise working in the practice of a recognised body remains personally subject to all the rules, principles and requirements of conduct affecting solicitors.

25. Waivers

In any particular case or cases the Council shall have power to waive in writing any of the provisions of these Rules for a particular purpose or purposes expressed in such waiver and to revoke such waiver.

26. Commencement

These Rules shall come into force on the coming into force of section 9 of the Administration of Justice Act 1985.

Annex 3E

Solicitors' Separate Business Code 1994

(with consolidated amendments to 20th May 1998)

Rules dated 4th February 1994 made by the Council of the Law Society with the concurrence of the Master of the Rolls under section 31 of the Solicitors Act 1974 and section 9 of the Administration of Justice Act 1985, regulating the circumstances in which practising solicitors, registered foreign lawyers and recognised bodies may provide certain services other than through their practices.

Section 1: Explanatory provisions

(1)   This code aims to ensure that members of the public know whether a service is provided by a solicitor practising as such (and thus regulated by the Law Society and affording clients certain statutory protections) or outside the scope of a solicitor's practice (and thus outside the regulation of the Law Society, and not affording any of the statutory protections extended to the clients of a solicitor).

(2)   This code prohibits a practising solicitor from providing certain legal services other than as a solicitor and requires that certain safeguards be observed where there is a connection between a solicitor's practice and his or her separate business. However, neither the Practice Rules nor this code regulate solicitors' separate businesses, and such separate businesses are not entitled to indemnity from the Solicitors' Indemnity Fund or underwritten by the Solicitors' Compensation Fund.

(3)   Practice Rule 5 and this code apply to solicitors practising as such in England and Wales, whether in private practice or employed practice.

(4)   A solicitor who is a partner in a firm of solicitors, or in a multi-national partnership, with an office in England and Wales is practising in England and Wales and is therefore subject to Practice Rule 5 and this code, even if he or she is based at an office outside the jurisdiction.

(5)   Rule 5 and this code do not apply to a solicitor solely by virtue of the fact that:

(a)   the solicitor is a non-executive director of a company; or

(b)   the solicitor, as the employee of a non-solicitor, does work permitted by virtue of Rule 4 of the Solicitors' Practice Rules 1990; or

(c)   the solicitor operates a separate practice as a notary public in conjunction with his or her practice as a solicitor.

(6)   This code applies whether a separate business is in England and Wales, or outside the jurisdiction, but nothing in Practice Rule 5 or this code applies to an overseas practice set up in accordance with the Solicitors' Overseas Practice Rules.

Section 2: Interpretation

In this code:

(a)   "separate business" means any business, other than a solicitor's practice or a multi-national partnership, which provides any service or services which may properly be provided by a solicitor's practice;

(b)   references to a solicitor who has a separate business are references to a solicitor who (alone, or by or with others) controls, actively participates in or operates a separate business;

(c)   Practice Rule 18 governs the application and interpretation of this code;

(d)   "investment business" means investment business as defined in the Financial Services Act 1986;

(e)   any reference to selling or buying property includes granting or taking a lease for value; and

(f)   "overseas" means in or of a jurisdiction other than England and Wales.

Section 3: Services which may only be provided through a solicitors' practice

Subject to the exceptions in Sections 4 and 5, a solicitor must not have a separate business which provides any of the following services:

(a)   the conduct of any matter which could proceed before any court, tribunal or inquiry, whether or not proceedings are commenced;

(b)   advocacy before any court, tribunal or inquiry;

(c)   instructing counsel;

(d)   acting as executor, trustee or nominee in England and Wales;

(e)   drafting any will or trust deed;

(f)   giving legal advice;

(g)   any activity reserved to solicitors (whether solely or together with other persons) by the Solicitors Act 1974 or any other statute; and

(h)   drafting any legal documents not already covered by (a) to (g) above.

Section 4: Safeguards and exceptions – separate businesses generally

Requirements:

(1)   A solicitor who has a separate business must do nothing in the course of practice, or in the course of making and accepting referrals, connected with that separate business, which is likely to compromise or impair any of the principles set out in Practice Rule 1. The requirements of the Solicitors' Introduction and Referral Code apply to referrals generally, including referral of a client by a solicitor to his or her own separate business.

(2)   A solicitor who has a separate business must ensure:

(a)   that the name of any practice of the solicitor has no substantial element in common with the name of that separate business;

(b)   that the words "solicitor(s)", "attorney(s)" or "lawyer(s)" are not used in connection with the solicitor's involvement with that separate business;

(c)   that paperwork and records relating to customers of the separate business are kept separately from paperwork and records relating to clients of the solicitor (whether or not those customers are also clients of the solicitor);

(d)   that all clients referred by any English or Welsh practice of the solicitor to the separate business are informed in writing of the solicitor's interest in the business and that, as customers of the separate business, they do not enjoy the statutory protections attaching to clients of a solicitor (or recognised body or multi-national partnership, as the case may be);

(e)   that where the separate business shares premises, office accommodation or reception staff with any English or Welsh practice of the solicitor, all customers of the separate business are informed in writing that, as customers of the separate business, they do not enjoy the statutory protections attaching to the clients of a solicitor (or a recognised body or multi-national partnership, as the case may be); and

(f)   that the solicitor does not hold on the client account of the solicitor's practice money held for customers of the separate business as such; or money held for the separate business.

Exceptions:

(3)   The prohibitions in Section 3(f) and (h) (giving legal advice and drafting certain legal documents) shall not apply to prevent a solicitor from having a separate business which provides such advice and drafts such documents if:

(a)   this is undertaken only as a necessary but subsidiary part of a main service or services provided by the separate business; and

(b)   the main service or services provided by the separate business do not include one or more of the services set out in Section 3(a)–(h).

Application to businesses covered by Section 5:

(4)   The requirements of Section 4(2) do not apply in relation to separate businesses covered by Section 5 except to the extent specifically stated in Section 5. Section 4(1) and (3) apply to all separate businesses including those covered by Section 5; except that those separate businesses covered by Section 5(3) are not subject to the restrictions in Sections 4(3)(a) and (b).

Section 5: Safeguards and exceptions – particular businesses

(1)   **Investment business**

Requirements:

A solicitor who has a separate business providing investment business services must ensure:

(a)   that the requirements of Section 4(2)(a), (b), (c) and (f) are observed; and

(b)   that the separate business is conducted from accommodation physically divided and clearly differentiated from that of any practice of the solicitor in England and Wales; and

(c)   that there is compliance with Practice Rule 12(1)(b) and (2); and

(d)   that all clients referred by any English or Welsh practice of the solicitor to the separate business are informed of the solicitor's interest in the business and that, as customers of the separate business, they do not enjoy the statutory protections attaching to clients of a solicitor (or recognised body or multi-national partnership, as the case may be) by the following steps:

   (i)   in a personal interview or telephone call and

   (ii)   in writing confirming the contents of that interview or call; and

(e)   that (without prejudice to (b) above) where the separate business shares premises or reception staff with any English or Welsh practice of the solicitor, all customers of the separate business are informed that, as customers of the separate business, they do not enjoy the statutory protections attaching to clients of a solicitor (or recognised body or multi-national partnership, as the case may be) by the following steps:

   (i)   in a personal interview or telephone call and

   (ii)   in writing confirming the contents of that interview or call.

Exceptions:

The prohibition in Section 3(d) will not apply to prevent such a separate business providing nominee services through its nominee company in England and Wales if this is ancillary to the main purpose of the business.

(2) **Estate agency**

Requirements:

A solicitor who has a separate business providing estate agency:

(a)   must comply with Section 4(2)(a), (b), (c) and (f); and

(b)   must ensure that the separate business is conducted from accommodation physically divided and clearly differentiated from that of any practice of the solicitor in England and Wales; and

(c)   must ensure that all clients referred by any English or Welsh practice of the solicitor to the separate business are informed of the solicitor's interest in the business and that, as customers of the separate business, they do not enjoy the statutory protections attaching to clients of a solicitor (or recognised body or multi-national partnership, as the case may be) by the following steps:

   (i)   in a personal interview or telephone call and

   (ii)   in writing confirming the contents of that interview or call; and

(d)   must ensure that (without prejudice to (b) above) where the separate business shares premises or reception staff with any English or Welsh practice of the solicitor, all customers of the separate business are informed that, as customers of the separate business, they do not enjoy the statutory protections attaching to clients of a solicitor (or a recognised body or multi-national partnership, as the case may be) by the following steps:

>   (i)   in a personal interview or telephone call and

>   (ii)   in writing confirming the contents of that interview or call; and

(e)   without prejudice to Practice Rule 6, must not act in the conveyance for the buyer of any property sold through the separate business, unless:

>   (i)   the solicitor's practice shares ownership of the separate business with at least one other firm, or other business, in which the solicitor or the solicitor's practice have no financial interest; and

>   (ii)   neither the solicitor nor any member or employee of his or her practice is dealing with or has dealt with the sale of the seller's property for the separate business; and

>   (iii) the buyer has given written consent to the solicitor acting, after the solicitor has explained his or her financial interest in the sale going through.

(3)   **Parliamentary agents, trade mark agents, patent agents, European patent attorneys and lawyers of jurisdictions other than England and Wales**

Requirements:

(a)   A solicitor who has a separate business as a parliamentary agent, trade mark agent, patent agent, European patent attorney or lawyer of an overseas jurisdiction must ensure that the requirements of Section 4(2)(d), (e) and (f) are observed.

Exceptions:

(b)   The prohibitions in Section 3 shall not apply to prevent a solicitor who is appropriately qualified from having such a separate business.

(4)   **Overseas executor, trustee and nominee companies**

Requirements:

A solicitor who has a separate business which is an overseas executor, trustee or nominee company (or other separate business set up overseas to act as executor, trustee or nominee) must ensure:

(a)   that the requirements of Section 4(2)(a), (b), (c) and (f) are observed; and

(b)   that all clients referred by any English or Welsh practice of the solicitor to the separate business are informed in writing of the solicitor's interest in the business and that, as customers of the separate business, they do not enjoy the statutory protections attaching to clients of a solicitor (or recognised body or multi-national partnership, as the case may be) by the following steps:

>   (i)   in a personal interview or telephone call and

>   (ii)   in writing confirming the contents of that interview or call; and

(c)   that where the separate business shares premises or reception staff with any English or Welsh practice of the solicitor, all customers of the separate business are informed that, as customers of the separate business, they do not enjoy the statutory protections attaching to clients of a solicitor (or a recognised body or multi-national partnership, as the case may be) by the following steps:

     (i)   in a personal interview or telephone call and

     (ii) in writing confirming the contents of that interview or call.

(5) **Separate businesses overseas (other than executor, trustee or nominee companies)**

Requirements:

(a)   A solicitor having any separate business overseas (other than one referred to in paragraph (4) above) must ensure that the requirements of Section 4(2)(a), (b), (c), (d), (e) and (f) are observed.

Exceptions:

(b)   The prohibitions in Section 3(a), (b), (c), (e), (f) and (h) shall not apply to prevent a solicitor having a separate business overseas if it does not provide services reserved to English solicitors, or offer services in England and Wales and there is no direct or indirect referral of clients to the separate business from any practice of the solicitor in England and Wales.

Section 6: Application to registered foreign lawyers

(1) A registered foreign lawyer who is a partner in a multi-national partnership or a director of a recognised body is subject to this code by virtue of Practice Rule 18(1A)(b) and (c); except that

(a)   where a registered foreign lawyer who is a partner in a multi-national partnership has a separate legal practice as a foreign lawyer:

     (i)   neither the prohibitions in Section 3 nor the requirements of Section 4(2)(a), (b), (c) and (f) shall apply in relation to the separate legal practice; and

     (ii) the registered foreign lawyer must ensure that the multi-national partnership does not hold on its client account money held for customers of the separate business as such; or money held for the separate business;

(b)   where a registered foreign lawyer who is a partner in a multi-national partnership has a separate business outside England and Wales, neither the prohibitions in Section 3 nor the requirements of Sections 4 or 5 shall apply provided:

     (i)   the registered foreign lawyer's involvement is not in breach of his or her own professional rules; and

     (ii) his or her solicitor partners do not (alone, or by or with others) operate, actively participate in or control the separate business; and

     (iii) the separate business does not offer, in England and Wales, any of the services set out in Section 3.

Section 7: Transitional provisions and commencement

(1) [Transitional provisions now expired]

(2) This code will come into force on 1st June 1994.

Annex 3F

Guidance – specimen letter where a firm ceases to practise as such and clients are required to be given a choice of solicitor

(see **3.11** note 5, p.77)

J & Co
64 High Street
Craxenford

Dear

I write to inform you that Mr J and I have agreed to dissolve our partnership and will each be setting up our own practice on 1st June.

Mr J will continue to practise from this address as J & Co.

I will be practising at 25 Market Street, Craxenford as A & Co.

Please let us know as soon as possible which of us you wish to act for you. You are, of course, free to instruct any solicitor of your choice.

It would be helpful if you could complete and sign the attached form and return it to this address preferably before 1st June. We will then be able to deal with your papers in accordance with your instructions.

For your information, we currently hold [your will], as well as [£15,000 (balance of sale proceeds of your former home)], in our client account.

Your will and other papers will remain in safekeeping at this address, and your money will remain on our client account until we receive your instructions, or until 1st June. If we have not heard from you by then, J & Co will assume responsibility for your papers, and hold your money on their client account, until they hear from you.

Yours sincerely

[Signed]

I wish *Mr J/Mr A/ (**other firm – please specify) to act for me, and instruct you to deal with my matters, papers and money accordingly.

Signed   ....

* Please delete as appropriate.

** If you wish to instruct another firm, we will ask you to settle any outstanding account first.

Annex 3G

Guidance – retiring solicitors, including solicitors who are professional trustees

There are several options open to a retiring solicitor – to continue to hold a practising certificate and perhaps to act as a consultant for a firm or to do occasional or part-time work; to cease holding a practising certificate but remain on the roll; or to have his or her name removed from the roll altogether.

Is a practising certificate necessary?

Section 1 of the Solicitors Act 1974 (the Act) defines a 'qualified person' as a person who is admitted, on the roll and has in force a current practising certificate (see **2.03**, p.33 in the Guide). The Act restricts certain activities to 'qualified persons', see sections 20–22 and 23–25 of the Act in Annex 2A at p.45. Therefore, without a practising certificate, a solicitor cannot carry out the following activities for fee, gain or reward:

(i)   conveyancing;

(ii) litigation, including drafting documents connected with litigation; and

(iii) applying for probate.

In addition, an uncertificated solicitor cannot use the title 'solicitor' without qualifying that statement with words such as 'non-practising' or 'uncertificated'.

To continue practising as a consultant in private practice, a practising certificate is essential. Section 1A of the Solicitors Act (see Annex 2A at p.42 in the Guide), provides that a solicitor who is admitted, on the roll and employed in connection with the provision of legal services must have a practising certificate.

For further information about when a certificate is necessary, see **2.03**, p.33 in the Guide.

If a solicitor remains on the roll, but does not have a practising certificate, can he or she use the title 'solicitor'?

Solicitors who remain on the roll, but do not hold a practising certificate, may, nevertheless, describe themselves as a solicitor provided it is not misleading. For example, if a solicitor has written a book there would be no objection to the solicitor being described on the title page as a solicitor even though he or she does not hold a practising certificate.

What steps does a solicitor need to take if he or she practises on his or her own account, or on a part-time or *ad hoc* basis?

A solicitor who wishes to practise must comply with:

▶ the relevant provisions of the Solicitors Act;

▶ the Solicitors' Practice Rules;

▶ the accounts rules;

▶ the indemnity rules; and

▶ the requirements of professional conduct generally.

Working without remuneration

If a solicitor works without remuneration for:

▶ relatives;

▶ personal friends;

▶ companies wholly owned by his or her family; or

▶ registered charities;

he or she will need a practising certificate but will not need to make contributions to the Solicitors' Indemnity Fund (SIF) if the client is told in writing that he or she will not be covered by that Fund (see rule 32 of the indemnity rules in Annex 29A at p.819).

Where a solicitor works without remuneration for any other client, indemnity cover must be effected through SIF.

Investment business authorisation

An investment business certificate may be necessary (see Chapter 27 in the Guide, p.522). Guidance on the question of authorisation may be obtained from Professional Ethics (see p.xv for contact details) and application forms for certificates may be obtained from Regulation and Information Services (see p.xv for contact details).

What are the requirements if a solicitor is a consultant with a firm?

▶ A practising certificate is essential (see above).

▶ A consultant to a firm will be covered:

  ▶ by a firm's indemnity cover for work carried out on behalf of the firm; and

  ▶ by a firm's investment business certificate for investment business undertaken on behalf of the firm.

What work can a solicitor do without a practising certificate?

Restrictions

(i) An uncertificated solicitor may not undertake any of the reserved activities under sections 20–22 and 23–24 of the Act or instruct counsel.

(ii) An uncertificated solicitor cannot be authorised by the Society to conduct investment business. Carrying on investment business without authorisation is a criminal offence under the Financial Services Act 1986.

(iii) A solicitor who gives legal advice (e.g. to friends or relatives) must make it clear to the person concerned that he or she is not a practising solicitor and cannot give advice or do any work on their behalf as such. In addition, the solicitor must make it clear that he or she is not insured against professional indemnity risks.

Closing down a practice

If a solicitor has closed down his or her practice and is trying to tie up loose ends by submitting bills of costs and continues to hold clients' money, the solicitor will not require a practising certificate, but will still be subject to the accounts rules (see below). However, the solicitor will have to be careful that he or she does not hold himself or herself out as a practising solicitor whilst sorting out these matters.

Accounts rules

▶ A solicitor who continues to hold clients' money remains subject to the Solicitors' Accounts Rules 1998 (Annex 28B, p.684 in the Guide).

▶ A solicitor requires a practising certificate to make a withdrawal from client account. Therefore, if a solicitor no longer holds a practising certificate, he or she:

    (i) will need to come to an arrangement with his or her bank, and with another solicitor who holds a practising certificate, to enable withdrawals to be made from client account; and

    (ii) must decide whether the certificated solicitor should be a sole signatory or whether the uncertificated solicitor wishes to remain as a counter signatory.

▶ The obligation to deliver an accountant's report under rules 35–39 of the Solicitors' Accounts Rules 1998 continues to apply to a solicitor until he or she stops holding clients' money and delivers a final accountant's report.

Can a solicitor without a practising certificate administer oaths?

No. A solicitor must hold a practising certificate to exercise the powers of a commissioner for oaths granted under section 81 of the Act. In addition, in order to use the title 'Commissioner for Oaths' granted under section 113(10) of the Courts and Legal Services Act 1990, a solicitor must have a practising certificate.

Who should a solicitor notify about his or her retirement?

▶ Clients (see **3.11**, p.77 in the Guide).

▶ Regulation and Information Services (see p.xv for contact details).

▶ Solicitors' Indemnity Fund (see p.xv for contact details) giving:

    (a) the date of retirement; and

    (b) the name of any successor practice.

Solicitors' Indemnity Fund – general points

A solicitor who retires from practice will receive free run-off cover, subject only to the standard deductible provisions in force at the date of the solicitor's retirement. There is an option to buy out the deductible for the run-off cover period and quotes can be obtained direct from SIF Ltd.

On retirement a sole principal's indemnity contribution is apportioned from the start of the indemnity year in which he or she retires (i.e. the previous 1st September) to the date of the solicitor's retirement. Any amount remaining outstanding immediately after the cessation is payable within 28 days, and similarly any amount overpaid will be refunded within 28 days. Once a solicitor has ceased to practise he or she will not be required to make contributions to the Indemnity Fund in respect of subsequent indemnity years.

Claims which occur following the retirement of a solicitor who was a principal will either be dealt with under the cover of the continuing partnership or in the case of a sole principal under the run-off cover.

What is the effect if a solicitor's name is removed from the roll?

A solicitor who does not remain on the roll cannot describe himself or herself as a solicitor, although the designation 'former solicitor' is acceptable. 'Retired solicitor' can be used provided it is not misleading in the circumstances.

How does a solicitor get his or her name removed from the roll?

If a solicitor does not renew his or her practising certificate, the solicitor will be asked to decide whether he or she wishes to retain his or her name on the roll. Under the Solicitors (Keeping of the Roll) Regulations 1999 (see Annex 2C, p.52 in the Guide), an enquiry form will normally be despatched annually at the beginning of March to the last address held on the Society's records.

If a solicitor wants to remain on the roll, he or she should complete the enquiry form and forward it to the Society with the appropriate annual enrolment fee. Regulation and Information Services should be kept informed of a solicitor's current address so that the solicitor can be sent renewal forms.

A solicitor can request the removal of his or her name from the roll on the same enquiry form. Application for restoration to the roll, subsequent to removal in accordance with the Solicitors (Keeping of the Roll) Regulations, is usually straightforward. Further information can be obtained from Regulation and Information Services (see p.xv for contact details).

If a solicitor does not continue to practise but remains on the roll, what are the effects?

A solicitor who remains on the roll has a continuing obligation not to behave in a manner unbefitting a solicitor, in his or her business and private life. The solicitor remains subject to the jurisdiction of the Compliance and Supervision Committee and the Solicitors Disciplinary Tribunal.

Membership

All solicitors on the roll are entitled to free Law Society membership. Those who are not currently members of the Society will need to complete a membership proposal form, and will need to find an existing member to support the application. Forms may be obtained from Regulation and Information Services. The *Gazette* is not provided free of charge unless the solicitor has a practising certificate. Non-practising solicitors may take out an annual subscription to the *Gazette*.

What are the requirements if a solicitor wants to continue to act as a professional trustee?

A retired solicitor who continues to hold monies as a professional trustee will hold clients' money or controlled trust money, therefore the solicitor must:

(i)   have a practising certificate;

(ii) comply with the accounts rules; and

(iii) have indemnity cover, unless rule 32 of the Solicitors' Indemnity Rules 1998 applies and/or a waiver of the rules has been obtained. Such a waiver and the exemption contained in rule 32 will not be available to a solicitor who is charging for his or her services. For further information, contact the Professional Indemnity Section (see p.xv for contact details).

The obligation to deliver an accountant's report

The obligation to deliver an accountant's report extends to a solicitor who holds controlled trust money, even if the solicitor does not hold clients' money.

Dispensation from the requirement to deliver an accountant's report

In limited circumstances a dispensation from this requirement may be granted. Dispensations can be applied for when the solicitor only holds clients' or controlled trust money on a few occasions during the accounting year. Regulation and Information Services should be contacted for information about obtaining a dispensation. If a dispensation is granted, this only relates to the requirement to deliver a report; a solicitor must still comply with the Solicitors' Accounts Rules in all other respects. Therefore, client records must be kept and reconciliations prepared in accordance with the rules.

Uncertificated solicitors

A solicitor who wishes to retire and not hold a practising certificate must cease to act, or charge for his or her work, as a professional trustee.

Revised February 1999

Annex 3H

Guidance – bankruptcy and voluntary arrangements: implications for practising certificates

Bankruptcy

Section 15(1) of the Solicitors Act 1974 automatically suspends any practising certificate when the holder is declared bankrupt. However, it is possible to apply for a termination of the suspension and this may be done even before a formal declaration of bankruptcy. Applications should be made to the Solicitors Practice Unit at the Office for the Supervision of Solicitors (OSS) (see p.xv for contact details).

If the suspension is terminated, the OSS has power to impose conditions on the certificate. It is almost inevitable that a condition will be imposed limiting the solicitor to partnership or employment approved by the OSS. The solicitor's next application is subject to section 12 of the Solicitors Act.

Bankruptcy is also a ground for an intervention under Schedule 1 to the Solicitors Act (see Annex 30A, p.850 in the Guide). An intervention will inevitably follow if all the principals are bankrupt unless either:

(a) the practice is disposed of before the bankruptcy is formally declared; **or**

(b) the suspension of the practising certificate of one or more principals is terminated as above; **and**

(c) the conditions imposed allow continued practice in an approved partnership; **and**

(d) some other person approved by the OSS can be persuaded to enter into partnership with those principals.

It should be noted that bankruptcy will terminate a partnership in any event.

Principals facing possible bankruptcy should consider what arrangements can be made either for the practice to be amalgamated with another, or for the clients to be referred to other firms. The costs of intervention are payable by the principal(s) and may be avoided or reduced if suitable arrangements to prevent an intervention are made in time.

Individual voluntary arrangement (IVA)

Unlike bankruptcy, an IVA does not suspend a solicitor's practising certificate. However, the OSS must be told that it has been entered into and may impose conditions on the practising certificate. Conditions are often imposed limiting the solicitor to practising only in approved employment or partnership, and requiring more frequent accountants' reports. Entering into an IVA is also a ground for intervention under Schedule 1 to the Solicitors Act, though that is not likely where there is no evidence of any risk to clients' money or the interests of the public or the profession.

Solicitors who are considering entering into an IVA would be wise to consult the OSS in advance to ensure that conditions are not likely to be imposed which would prevent the IVA from being effective.

Partnership voluntary arrangement (PVA)

The OSS takes the view that a PVA has the same effect on a practising certificate as an IVA. Similar advice therefore applies to all the principals involved.

Imposition of conditions: the process

The initial decision to impose conditions is taken by senior staff at the OSS. In considering this, the OSS follows guidance from the Court of Appeal in *Bolton* v. *Law Society* [1994] 2 All E.R. 486 and from the Master of the Rolls. It therefore has primary regard to the interests of the public and of the profession. Subject to that, the concern is to allow the solicitor an appropriate form of practice. (For further information see **31.09**, notes 2–4, p.859 in the Guide.)

Appeals

If an application for restoration of a practising certificate is refused, or is granted subject to conditions, an appeal lies to the Master of the Rolls within one month of the notification of the decision (see the Master of the Rolls (Appeals and Applications) Regulations 1991, Annex 2D, p.55 in the Guide).

Decision to stop practising

A principal who decides that he or she must stop practising should:

(a) give clients as much notice as possible;

(b) tell clients if another local firm has agreed to take matters over and of their right to go elsewhere if they wish;

(c) seek instructions from clients for the disposal of papers, wills, deeds and other documents held for them;

(d) obtain a receipt for all papers handed over;

(e) try to obtain an undertaking for payment of costs from solicitors to whom papers on outstanding cases are handed over;

(f) consider whether old and unclaimed papers can be destroyed (see Annex 12A, p.253 in the Guide);

(g) make arrangements for the storage of unclaimed papers in circumstances where confidentiality can be maintained;

(h) deliver an accountant's report within six months of the date when the solicitor ceases to hold clients' money; and

(i) tell both SIF and Regulation and Information Services of both the decision to stop practising and the date when that happens (see p.xv for contact details).

Financial assistance

Solicitors who, or whose families, are in severe financial difficulties may be able to get some help from the Solicitors Benevolent Association at 1 Jaggard Way, Wandsworth Common, London SW12 8SG.

Other help/SAS/SolCare

Solicitors who need to talk over their problems on a confidential basis with another practising solicitor may find it helpful to ask Professional Ethics for a contact with the Solicitors' Assistance Scheme (see p.xv for contact details). Where problems concerning stress or mind affecting disorders (such as alcoholism or drug related problems) are concerned, confidential help is available from SolCare, a registered charity independent of the Law Society. It may be contacted at P.O. Box 6, Porthmadog, Gwynedd LL49 9ZE or by telephone on 01766 512222.

Annex 3I

Whom to notify on change in composition of a firm – practice information

Where there has been a change in the composition of a firm, a solicitor may need to contact some or all of the organisations listed below. This list is meant as a guide only, and is not exhaustive.

Accountants

Bank/building society

Clients as specified in **3.11**, p.77 in the Guide

Companies using the office as a registered address

Counsel's chambers

Court offices/court records

Crown Prosecution Service/police

Data Protection Registrar

Directories – professional/telephone

Land Charges Registry (key number)

Landlord

Land Registry (re current matters)

Legal Aid area office and accounts department

Local authority (uniform business rate)

London Gazette and one other newspaper (not necessary for mergers)

Mortgage lenders

Owners of documents held by the firm

Regulation and Information Services, the Law Society* – where appropriate please provide address of storage of files

Solicitors Indemnity Fund Limited* and top-up insurers

Tax authorities

*(See p.xv for contact details)

December 1995, updated February 1999

Chapter 4

Employed solicitors

4.01   General principles

A solicitor employed by a non-solicitor is subject to the same principles of professional conduct as a solicitor in private practice.

1. For the purpose of this chapter, an 'employed solicitor' is a solicitor practising as a solicitor in the employment of a non-solicitor. If a solicitor is *not* practising as a solicitor he or she will not be subject to rules of conduct governing practising solicitors, but may still be disciplined for conduct unbefitting a member of the solicitors' profession. This chapter does not cover *all* the conduct requirements governing employed solicitors but highlights certain important requirements, some of which *only* apply to employed solicitors.

2. The relationship between an employed solicitor and his or her employer is that of solicitor and client. The practice rules and the general principles of professional conduct apply. For the Employed Solicitors Code ('the Code') see Annex 4A, p.152.

3. A solicitor who is employed by a non-solicitor would be practising as a solicitor, and would therefore need a practising certificate, in the following circumstances:

▶ where the solicitor is held out (on stationery or otherwise) as a solicitor for the employer;

▶ in administering oaths;

▶ where the solicitor appears before a court or a tribunal and in so appearing places reliance on his or her right of audience as a solicitor; and

unless that solicitor is supervised by and acting in the name of a certificated solicitor:

▶ in doing any of the acts prohibited to unqualified persons by the Solicitors Act 1974, save where there are statutory exceptions such as for certain work carried out by non-certificated solicitors employed by a local authority (see section 223 of the Local Government Act 1972) and see also section 22(2)(b) of the Solicitors Act 1974 (Annex 2A at p.46);

▶ in instructing counsel.

4. A solicitor acting only as a justice's clerk is not practising as a solicitor and can instruct counsel without a practising certificate.

5. An employed solicitor is personally bound by undertakings given in the course of his or her professional duties. In particular, **18.12** on undertakings (see p.356) should be noted.

6. An employed solicitor should not, when acting in the capacity of a solicitor (rather than, for example, as secretary to a company or local authority), communicate with third parties who are represented by a solicitor, except with that solicitor's consent; any communication should be made through the solicitor acting for the third party (see **19.02**, p.360).

7. An employed solicitor may use the stationery of, or stationery including the name of, his or her employer for professional work, provided:

   (a) either the letterhead or the signature makes it clear that the stationery is being used by a solicitor on legal professional business and that the solicitor is responsible for the contents of the letter; and

   (b) the stationery is being used for the business of the non-solicitor employer or for third parties in circumstances permitted by practice rule 4 (see paragraph 12(c) of the Solicitors' Publicity Code, Annex 11A at p.235).

8. An employed solicitor may as a solicitor use a style of stationery or description which appears to hold that solicitor out as a principal or solicitor in private practice. Note: if any employed solicitor held out as a principal on notepaper holds or receives clients' money, all those held out as principals on that notepaper will be required to pay the full contribution to the Compensation Fund. The Solicitors' Indemnity Fund does not cover work done by an employed solicitor acting in that capacity, and the Solicitors' Indemnity Rules do not apply. See, however, **4.05** note 3, p.149.

9. The address of a company's legal department is the place (or one of the places) where an employed solicitor practises and must therefore be notified to Regulation and Information Services as a practising address of the solicitor (see p.xv for contact details).

10. Employed solicitors who do not have offices open to the public are not required to comply with rule 13 of the Solicitors' Practice Rules 1990. However, an employed solicitor will be answerable in conduct for the acts of staff assisting in his or her practice as a solicitor.

11. A solicitor employed by a commercial organisation providing a telephone legal advice service may advise enquirers in accordance with paragraph 8 of the Code (see Annex 4A at p.157); where the service is open to telephone calls from the public practice rule 13 will apply (see **3.08**, p.73).

12. For an employed solicitor's obligation to pay counsel's fees see **20.06** note 6, p.368.

4.02   Accounts rules and accountants' reports

Employed solicitors who receive or hold clients' money must comply with the Solicitors' Accounts Rules 1998.

1. A solicitor who pays in or endorses over a cheque made out in his or her favour receives clients' money and must deal with it in accordance with the accounts rules (see Annex 28B, p.684). For the name of a client account, see rule 14(3), p.697. Even if a cheque is simply endorsed over to the employer, the solicitor will need to keep a record (see rule 32 of the accounts rules at p.715), submit an accountant's report, and pay the full contribution to the Solicitors' Compensation Fund. A solicitor who receives only his or her employer's money may seek to ensure that all cheques are made payable to the employer.

2. An in-house accountant may not prepare an accountant's report for an employed solicitor (see rule 37(2)(a) of the accounts rules – Annex 28B at p.723).

3. When only a small number of transactions are undertaken or a small volume of client money is handled in a year, a dispensation from the obligation to deliver an accountant's report may be sought from Regulation and Information Services, but will not be given as a matter of course (see p.xv for contact details).

4. (a) A solicitor when practising as an employee of:

    (i)   a local authority;

    (ii) an officer of statutory undertakers;

    (iii) a body whose accounts are audited by the Comptroller and Auditor General;

(iv) the Duchy of Lancaster;

(v)   the Duchy of Cornwall;

(vi) the Church Commissioners; or

(b) a solicitor who practises as the Solicitor of the City of London; or

(c) a solicitor when carrying out the functions of:

(i)   a coroner or other judicial office; or

(ii)   a sheriff or under sheriff,

need not comply with the accounts rules (see rule 5 at p.690) or submit an accountant's report, but will be required to pay the appropriate Compensation Fund contribution. However, if such a solicitor holds or receives clients' money, he or she must pay any additional contributions required to the Compensation Fund.

4.03   Practice rule 4 (employed solicitors)

'**(1) Solicitors who are employees of non-solicitors shall not:**

(a) choose an advocate; nor

(b) exercise any extended right of audience under one of the Law Society's higher courts qualifications; nor

(c) as part of their employment do for any person other than their employer work which is or could be done by a solicitor acting as such;

in any way which breaches the Employed Solicitors Code promulgated from time to time by the Council of the Law Society with the concurrence of the Master of the Rolls.

(2) Solicitors who are employees of multi-national partnerships shall not be regarded as "employees of non-solicitors" for the purpose of this rule.'

Solicitors' Practice Rules 1990, rule 4

4.04   Employed solicitors – additional guidance

Advocacy

1. The Employed Solicitors Code 1990 is set out in Annex 4A, p.152.

2. Employed solicitors may exercise higher rights of audience in certain circumstances – see paragraphs 1(g) and (h), p.153, and Annex 4B, p.159.

Acting for third parties

3. The Code governs the conduct of solicitors in the course of their practice as employees of non-solicitor employers. Paragraph 1 sets out general principles. Paragraphs 2–9 deal with specific circumstances where an employed solicitor, in the course of his or her employment, may act for persons or bodies other than the employer. Save as permitted by the Code, employed solicitors may not, in the course of their employment, act for third parties.

4

4.05   Separate private practice

An employed solicitor may act for private clients, including fellow employees, *outside* the course of the solicitor's employment.

1. For details regarding arrangements for the introduction of clients, see the Introduction and Referral Code at Annex 11B, p.238 and **11.05**, p.224.

2. An employed solicitor must not act for private clients where there is any conflict between the interests of the private client and the interests of the solicitor's employer.

3. An employed solicitor who also practises privately as a solicitor is a principal in private practice. In such circumstances contribution must be made to the Solicitors' Indemnity Fund. (For details of the Solicitors' Indemnity Rules see Chapter 29, p.782 and Annex 29A, p.793.)

4. An employed solicitor who carries on a private practice from home must take care not to breach the provisions of rule 13 of the Solicitors' Practice Rules 1990; see **3.08**, p.73.

5. An employed solicitor who holds or receives clients' money in the course of a private practice outside his or her employment must comply with the accounts rules. See Annex 28B, p.684.

6. An employed solicitor who also carries on private practice on his or her own account may agree to reimburse his or her employer for that proportion of the solicitor's salary and of the employer's other overhead expenses which is attributable to any private practice work carried out in the employer's time, on the employer's premises and/or with the assistance of staff and materials provided by the employer. It will be the responsibility of the solicitor in such cases to ensure that this allowance for overheads is properly computed; otherwise there could be a breach of practice rule 7 (fee-sharing) – see **3.03**, p.68.

4.06 Industrial action

It is not improper for an employed solicitor to strike or take other industrial action, but the solicitor must have regard to his or her duties to the court and third parties.

Before deciding to take industrial action a solicitor must:

(a) ensure that no client for whom the solicitor is acting in the course of his or her employment is prejudiced by the action in any crucial way, e.g. by missing a time limit;

(b) ensure that steps are taken to cover all court engagements;

(c) ensure compliance with his or her professional undertakings;

(d) promptly arrange to notify persons who may be affected by the proposed action.

4.07 Costs recovered from third parties

An employed solicitor, in putting forward a claim for costs against a third party, must have regard to the proper indemnity basis for costs.

1. Where an employed solicitor acts for his or her employer, there is no presumption that it is any cheaper to employ an in-house solicitor than to retain a solicitor in private practice. The court will therefore normally regard it as proper for an employed solicitor's bill to be drawn on the usual principles applicable to a solicitor in private practice. There may, however, be special cases where it is quite clear that a bill drawn on this basis would improperly remunerate the employer and should therefore be disallowed (see *Henderson* v. *Merthyr Tydfil U.D.C.* [1900] 1 Q.B. 434 and *Re Eastwood (deceased)* [1975] Ch. 112). There seems no reason in principle why such an approach should not also be applicable to non-contentious business, or to matters where the employed solicitor is acting for someone other than the employer.

2. Under certain circumstances the Code permits an employed solicitor to act for someone other than the employer, as part of the solicitor's employment. In such cases there will be no breach of practice rule 7 when the solicitor accounts to the employer for costs paid either by the client, the client's opponent or another third party (see rule 7(3) at **3.03**, p.68).

4.08   Direct access to client

A solicitor employed as the senior legal adviser of a company or a local authority must have direct access to the board or to the council and its committees.

1. A solicitor employed in this position should seek to ensure that his or her terms of employment provide for such access.

2. 'Direct access' does not mean that all instructions and advice must pass directly to and from the council, committee or board, but the solicitor must have direct access where necessary.

4.09   Advice services

A solicitor employed by a law centre, Citizens Advice Bureau or similar non-commercial organisation may, in accordance with paragraph 7 of the Employed Solicitors Code 1990, advise and act for members of the public; the solicitor must comply in all respects with the practice rules, the Code, and other principles of conduct.

1. At a law centre or other non-commercial advice service, advice may be given, and also casework handled, including legal proceedings. Solicitors employed in connection with the provision of such services are practising from offices which must be regarded as open to the public and must comply with rule 13 of the Solicitors' Practice Rules 1990 (see **3.08**, p.73). Difficulties for law centres in complying with rule 13 have resulted in frequent applications for waivers.

2. A solicitor employed by a non-commercial advice service is not employed in private practice. He or she is, therefore, outside the scope of the Solicitors' Indemnity Fund in respect of legal services provided through the advice centre. An advice service within the meaning of paragraph 7 of the Code (see Annex 4A at p.157) must have indemnity cover in accordance with paragraph 7(a)(v).

3. A solicitor who works as a volunteer for a non-commercial advice service may pay to the organisation any fees or costs he or she receives under the Legal Advice and Assistance ('green form') Scheme (see rule 7(4) of the Solicitors' Practice Rules 1990, at **3.03**, p.68). He or she must also have the benefit of indemnity cover through Solicitors Indemnity Fund Limited unless exempted by a waiver.

4. A service may also be offered through an honorary legal adviser scheme or rota scheme.

5. For restrictions on the charging of fees, see paragraph 7(a)(ii) of the Code (Annex 4A at p.157).

Annex 4A

Employed Solicitors Code 1990

(with consolidated amendments to 26th February 1997)

Code dated 18th July 1990 promulgated by the Council of the Law Society with the concurrence of the Master of the Rolls under rule 4 of the Solicitors' Practice Rules 1990, regulating the practices of employed solicitors.

1. General

(a) This code applies to solicitors employed by non-solicitor employers in the course of the solicitor's employment with such a non-solicitor employer. This code does not apply to any private practice of such solicitors. The code sets out the principles to be followed and the conditions which apply when an employed solicitor:

   (i) chooses an advocate; or

   (ii) exercises any extended right of audience under one of the Law Society's higher courts qualifications; or

   (iii) as part of his or her employment, acts for a person other than the employer in accordance with the provisions of the code.

Multi-national partnership

(aa) Nothing in this code applies to a solicitor employed by a multi-national partnership.

Conflict of interest

(b) Despite anything in this code employed solicitors must not act in any situation where they would be precluded from acting by an actual or potential conflict of interest.

Practice rules

(c) Nothing is this code should be taken as sanctioning conduct inconsistent with the principle of the solicitor's independence as embodied in rule 1 of the Solicitors' Practice Rules 1990 or with any other provisions of those rules.

THE GUIDE TO THE PROFESSIONAL CONDUCT OF SOLICITORS 1999

Best interests of client

(d)   The solicitor should, before accepting instructions to act for persons other than the employer in accordance with this code, consider whether the employer is able by way of insurance or otherwise to indemnify the client adequately in the event of a claim against the solicitor for which the employer would be vicariously liable.

Confidentiality

(e)   Where an employed solicitor is acting for a person other than the employer in accordance with this code any information disclosed to the solicitor by the client is confidential and cannot be disclosed to the employer without the express consent of the client.

Indemnity

(f)   The solicitor must ensure at the outset of the matter that the client has been made aware of the insurance position in that the solicitor is not covered by the Solicitors' Indemnity Fund in relation to professional negligence, and that the client receives or has received notice in writing of the position.

Choice of advocate

(g)   Practice rule 16B (choice of advocate) applies to employed solicitors. Where the employer delegates the choice of advocate to the solicitor, the criteria on which the choice is to be made should be set out in writing, and appropriate records should be kept as to how the choice is exercised. In relation to solicitors employed in the Government Legal Service or the Crown Prosecution Service, compliance with this rule is secured if the Head of the Government Legal Service or the Crown Prosecution Service or Director of Public Prosecutions publishes criteria and at least once in each year publishes records of how the choice has been exercised.

Advocacy in the higher courts

(h)   An employed solicitor may exercise additional rights of audience under one of the Law Society's higher court qualifications, but only where the following conditions are met:

 (i)   the solicitor holds a current practising certificate; and

 (ii)   the solicitor is appearing either on behalf of his or her employer, or under the terms of paragraph 7 below (law centres, charities and other non-commercial advice services); and

 (iii) the solicitor is wholly employed in a separate legal department which, however it may be described (but for present purposes referred to as a department) is concerned exclusively with providing services which may properly be provided as part of a solicitor's practice and meets the following conditions:

   (a)   that the most senior individual in the department with direct line management or professional responsibility for its day to day operations (the head of the department) is a lawyer (that is a solicitor who holds a current practising certificate, or an employed barrister);

(b) that the head of the department has practised as a lawyer for at least three years;

(c) that the head of the department has access to the highest level of decision-making authority;

(d) that the department has a normal establishment of at least three lawyers and is composed exclusively of lawyers, those qualified in professions ancillary to law (e.g. patent agents, trade mark agents, legal executives), and appropriate support staff who are answerable in terms of line management or professional responsibility to the head of the department;

(e) that the relationship between the department and those to whom advocacy and litigation services are provided is that of solicitor and client;

(iv) in relation to actions which are the subject matter of the litigation the solicitor has no responsibility for making executive decisions; and

(v) the employer has either made a public declaration in the form of a resolution of the board of directors (in the case of a company) or of the governing body or council (in the case of a public body, local authority, other corporation or law centre or advice centre), or by a Minister (in the case of a Government department), or has included in the solicitor's contract of employment or terms of appointment, a statement to the following or like effect:

"Solicitors employed by ...... to provide legal services are independent professionals with responsibilities as officers of the Court, and ethical standards set by their professional body, the Law Society. The management structure, lines of accountability and organisation of work will be such as to respect this status and to allow for the proper exercise of independent professional judgement. Where solicitors have any reason to doubt the propriety of any action or proposed course of action, they will have access to the highest levels of authority and the arrangements for securing this are [here set out the arrangements]. The solicitor will be entitled to ask the Law Society or a court of competent jurisdiction for a decision and the employer will accept the decision of the Law Society or a court of competent jurisdiction on a matter of conduct as binding on the employer as well as the solicitor. Where a solicitor is employed to conduct higher court advocacy it will be necessary to ensure that the solicitor has had no responsibility for making executive decisions in relation to actions which are the subject matter of litigation"; and

(vi) where the solicitor:

(a) has taken a post in the employed sector for the first time; or

(b) has taken a post with an employer who has not previously employed a higher court advocate; and

(c) the nature or structure or whose employment has altered significantly,

the solicitor has notified the Law Society of the event and has certified to the Society that he or she can comply with the provisions of this code;

(vii) where the claim being pursued or defended by the employer does not arise from or include reliance on rights assigned to it by another;

(viii) in cases requiring advocacy on behalf of the prosecution at the trial before a jury, or any subsequent appeal, of any defendant charged with:

    (a) an offence triable only on indictment, or

    (b) any other offence which magistrates have determined, under section 19 of the Magistrates' Courts Act 1980, is suitable for trial at the Crown Court,

the solicitor does not appear as the sole or senior advocate;

(ix) in cases requiring advocacy on behalf of a respondent in a substantive hearing of an application for judicial review or any subsequent appeal, the solicitor does not appear as the sole or senior advocate.

2. Fellow employees

Where it is not prohibited by the principles set out in paragraph 1 above, and subject to provisos (i)–(iv) below, an employed solicitor may act for:

(a) a fellow employee;

(b) a director, company secretary or board member of the solicitor's employer;

(c) an employee, director, company secretary, board member or trustee of a related body of the employer within the meaning of paragraphs 5(a) or 6(b) below;

(d) a contributor to a programme or periodical publication, broadcast or published by the solicitor's employer (or by a related body within the meaning of paragraphs 5(a) or 6(b) below), but only where the contributor is a defendant or potential defendant in a defamation case; and

(e) in conveyancing transactions, where acting in accordance with this code for any person in sub-paragraph (a) to (c) above, the employed solicitor may also act for a joint owner/buyer and for a mortgagee;

provided in every case that:

(i) the matter relates to or arises out of the work of the employee, director, company secretary, board member, trustee or contributor in that capacity; and

(ii) the matter does not relate to a claim arising as a result of a personal injury to the employee, director, company secretary, board member or trustee; and

(iii) the solicitor is satisfied that the employee, director, company secretary, board member, trustee or contributor does not wish to instruct some other solicitor or other qualified conveyancer; and

(iv) there is no charge to the employee, director, company secretary, board member, trustee or contributor in relation to the solicitor's costs insofar as they are not recoverable from any other source.

3. Associations

A solicitor who is the employee of an association may act for a member provided:

(a) the membership of the association is limited to persons engaged or concerned in a particular trade, occupation or activity or otherwise having a community of interest; and

(b)   the association is one formed *bona fide* for the benefit of its members and not formed directly or indirectly for the benefit of the solicitor or primarily for securing assistance in legal proceedings; and

(c)   there shall be no charge to the member in non-contentious matters; and in contentious matters the association shall indemnify the member in relation to the solicitor's costs and disbursements insofar as they are not recoverable from any other source.

4.   Insurance

(a)   A solicitor who is the employee of an insurer subrogated to the rights of an insured in respect of any matter may act on behalf of the insurer in relation to that matter in the name of the insured, and if he does so may:

   (i)   act on behalf of the insured in relation also to uninsured losses in respect of the matter;

   (ii)   act in proceedings both for the insured and for a defendant covered by another insurer where the insurers have agreed an apportionment of liability; and/or

   (iii) act in the matter on behalf of the employer and another insurer in the joint prosecution of a claim.

(b)   A solicitor who is the employee of a legal expenses insurer may handle on behalf of an insured a claim (other than a personal injury claim) the value of which does not exceed the "no costs" limit from time to time in operation in the county court, provided the insured gives specific consent.

5.   Related bodies

(a)   An employed solicitor may act for:

   (i)   the employer's holding, associated or subsidiary company;

   (ii)   a partnership, syndicate or company by way of joint venture in which the employer and others have an interest;

   (iii) a trade association of which the employer is a member;

   (iv)   a club, association, pension fund or other scheme operated for the benefit of employees of the employer.

(b)   Sub-paragraphs (a)(i) and (ii) above do not apply to local government.

6.   Local government

A solicitor employed in local government may act:

(a)   for another public body or statutory officer to which the employer is statutorily empowered to provide legal services; or

(b)   for a company limited by shares or guarantee of which the employer or nominee of the employer is a shareholder or guarantor in pursuance of its statutory powers and of which the solicitor or an officer of the employer is a director or secretary; together with any wholly owned subsidiary or associated companies of such a company; provided that in the case of a company limited by shares the majority of the shares are owned either by the employer or by the employer together with other public bodies; or

(c)   for lenders in connection with new mortgages arising from the redemption of mortgages to the local authority, provided:

    (i)   no employed solicitor or other employee acts on behalf of the borrowers; and

    (ii)   the borrowers are given the opportunity to be independently advised by a solicitor or other qualified conveyancer of their choice; or

(d)   in non-contentious matters for a charity or voluntary organisation whose objects relate wholly or mainly to the employer's area, provided there is no charge to the charity or organisation.

7.   Law centres, charities and other non-commercial advice services

(a)   A solicitor who is the employee of a law centre or advice service operated by a charitable or similar non-commercial organisation may give advice to and otherwise act for members of the public, provided:

    (i)   no funding agent has majority representation on the body responsible for the management of the service, which body must remain independent of central and local government; and

    (ii)   no fees are charged save:

        (A)   under the legal aid scheme; or

        (B)   where the organisation indemnifies the client in relation to the solicitor's costs insofar as they are not recoverable from any other source; and

    (iii)   all fees earned and costs recovered by the solicitor are paid to the organisation for furthering the provision of the organisation's services; and

    (iv)   the organisation is not described as a law centre unless it is a member of the Law Centres Federation; and

    (v)   the organisation effects indemnity cover reasonably equivalent to that available to solicitors from the Solicitors' Indemnity Fund.

(b)   Sub-paragraph (a) above does not extend to an association formed for the benefit of its members.

8.   Commercial legal advice services

A solicitor who is the employee of a commercial organisation providing a telephone legal advice service may advise enquirers, provided:

(a)   subject to paragraph 4(b) above, the advice comprises telephone advice only, together with a follow up letter to the enquirer when necessary; and

(b)   the solicitor is satisfied that there is indemnity cover reasonably equivalent to that available to solicitors from the Solicitors' Indemnity Fund.

9.   Government departments and regulatory bodies

A solicitor who is the employee of a government department or a regulatory body may in carrying out the functions of the employer give legal advice to other persons and in the case of statutory functions may act generally for such persons.

10. Interpretation

In this code:

(a) all words have the meanings assigned to them in rule 18 of the Solicitors' Practice Rules 1990;

(b) "act" includes the giving of legal advice;

(c) "holding company" and "subsidiary company" have the meanings assigned to them by the Companies Act 1985 (as amended by the Companies Act 1989) and two companies are "associated" where they are subsidiary companies of the same holding company;

(d) (i) save in paragraph 1, references to a solicitor's employer include the employer's holding, associated or subsidiary company; and references to an employee include references to an employee of such holding, associated or subsidiary company; and

    (ii) "employee" and "employment" shall include reference to service in an appointment under the Crown or as a Crown Prosecutor, and "employer" shall include reference as appropriate to the Director of Public Prosecutions and to the Head of the Government Legal Service; and

(e) all words or phrases have the meanings assigned to them in the Courts and Legal Services Act 1990.

Annex 4B

Guidance – additional restrictions on exercise of extended higher rights of audience for employed solicitors

By virtue of the decision of the Lord Chancellor and the four designated judges on 26th February 1997, extended higher rights of audience are not exercisable by employed solicitors in the following circumstances. All four restrictions apply to extended rights of audience only, not to pre-existing rights of audience.

Criminal proceedings

An employed solicitor may not appear as sole or senior advocate in any criminal proceedings which have been committed to trial at the Crown Court, or any subsequent appeal. Plea directions hearings and other preliminary proceedings are not included in this restriction.

Civil proceedings

An employed solicitor may not appear in open court as the sole or senior advocate in civil proceedings in the higher courts in any hearing where it is intended to dispose in whole or in part of the merits of the case.

Local authority solicitors – care proceedings

An employed solicitor may not appear as the sole or senior advocate on behalf of a local authority in a hearing of an application in care proceedings or any subsequent appeal.

Government solicitors

Solicitors who are employed by Government departments and who exercise a right of audience in a higher court (whether in a civil or criminal matter) must be persons who have a right of access to the Attorney General. It is recognised that the Crown Prosecution Service, the Serious Fraud Office and certain prosecutions by H.M. Customs and Excise are under the superintendence of the Attorney General.

Chapter 5

Legal aid

5.01 The duty to advise

A solicitor is under a duty to consider and advise the client on the availability of legal aid where the client might be entitled to assistance under the Legal Aid Act 1988.

1. This chapter deals with the conduct issues arising out of legal aid work. Solicitors should refer to the current *Legal Aid Handbook* for practical guidance on the application of all the legal aid regulations.

2. Failure to advise clients of their rights under the Legal Aid Act can amount to unbefitting conduct and may also lead to a claim in negligence against a solicitor for breach of duty owed to the client.

3. If the client is eligible for legal aid but no application is made for legal aid, it is prudent to keep a record on the client's file of the reasons for not making an application.

4. The duty to advise applies not only at the outset of the retainer but also as the matter proceeds. It is the duty of a solicitor to ensure that any material change in the client's means of which the solicitor becomes aware is at once taken into consideration in the context of eligibility for legal aid.

5. Where a solicitor considers that legal aid is likely to be available to the client, the availability of an emergency certificate should also be borne in mind. A solicitor who commences work without legal aid cover runs the risk of being unable to recover his or her pre-certificate costs.

6. In immigration cases, the client should be advised of the scope of legal aid in respect of representation at any appeal hearing before the immigration appellate authorities. The client should also be warned of the consequences in the event of the case having to go to appeal. The client should be advised of the existence and range of services for free representation. For guidelines for immigration practitioners, see Annex 12C, p.262.

7. Legally aided clients must be treated in the same way as privately funded clients and the same standards of care apply.

5.02 Information for clients on costs – civil legal aid

1. For information to be provided to clients on costs see practice rule 15 and the Solicitors' Costs Information and Client Care Code, Chapter 13, p.265.

2. In respect of tribunal cases it is particularly important to clarify which stages of the matter are covered by legal aid. It is good practice to put information about costs in writing (see the Solicitors' Costs Information and Client Care Code, **13.02**, p.266). If this is inappropriate, a contemporaneous file note may be helpful to record what information about costs has been given.

5.03 Confidentiality – civil

In certain circumstances in legally aided cases, a solicitor may be under a duty to report to the Legal Aid Board information concerning the client which is confidential or privileged.

1. The Area Director of the Legal Aid Board (under regulation 19 of the Legal Advice and Assistance Regulations 1989 (S.I. 1989 no. 340)) can require a solicitor to give information to the Area Director, and the solicitor shall not be precluded by reason of any privilege from disclosing the information to the Area Director.

2. Where a solicitor believes that the assisted person:

   (a) has required his or her case to be conducted unreasonably so as to incur unjustifiable expense;

   (b) has intentionally failed to comply with any provision made under the Legal Aid Act 1988 concerning information to be furnished by the client;

   (c) in furnishing information has knowingly made a false statement or representation;

   then the solicitor must report this to the Area Director (see regulation 67 of the Civil Legal Aid (General) Regulations 1989 (S.I. 1989 no. 339)).

Where the solicitor is uncertain as to whether it would be reasonable to continue acting for the assisted person, the solicitor must report the circumstances to the Area Director.

3. If solicitors wish to refuse to act for a legally aided client or to give up the case after being selected for it, there is a duty to report the reasons to the Area Director (see regulation 69 of the Civil Legal Aid (General) Regulations 1989).

4. Solicitors must report to the Area Director where assisted persons decline a reasonable settlement offer or a payment into court (see regulation 70 of the Civil Legal Aid (General) Regulations 1989).

5. Privilege and confidentiality are specifically overridden by regulation 73 of the Civil Legal Aid (General) Regulations 1989, which provides that solicitors shall not be precluded by reason of any privilege from providing any information or giving any opinion which the Area Director or the Area Committee require under the Legal Aid Act or the legal aid regulations.

6. For confidentiality in criminal proceedings, see **5.04** notes 1–2 below.

5.04   Confidentiality – criminal

Where the client is legally aided in a criminal matter the duty to disclose all relevant information remains with the client. However, if the solicitor becomes aware of information which indicates that the client's circumstances have changed, or that the client did not disclose relevant information at the outset, the solicitor must advise the client that unless the client informs or permits the solicitor to inform the clerk to the justices, or the appropriate officer in the Crown court, the solicitor will have to cease acting and may have to report the matter.

1. Regulation 56 of the Legal Aid in Criminal and Care Proceedings (General) Regulations 1989 (S.I. 1989 no. 343) provides that a solicitor with actual knowledge that an applicant or assisted person has intentionally failed to comply with any provision of the regulations, or has knowingly made a false statement, has a duty to report the fact that the client has abused legal aid to the clerk to the justices or the appropriate officer in the Crown court.

2. The regulation does not require a solicitor to provide details of the abuse to the Legal Aid Board but, if he or she chooses to do so, the Legal Aid (Disclosure of Information) Regulations 1991 (S.I. 1991 no. 1753) override the duty of confidentiality and privilege. However, this protection is available only if the information is disclosed to the Legal Aid Board and it does not protect the solicitor if he or she volunteers information to the Court.

5.05   Lien and termination of retainer

On termination of the retainer a solicitor should, subject to his or her lien, deliver to the client any papers and property to which the client is entitled or hold them to his or her order, and account for all of the client's funds which are not subject to the Legal Aid Board's statutory charge.

1.   Where there is a change of solicitor under a legal aid certificate, the original solicitor should not forward the file to the successor solicitor until the certificate has been transferred into that solicitor's name. However, subject to note 2 below, the papers should be made available for inspection in the meantime or copies provided.

2.   A lien will arise over a client's papers and documents delivered to a solicitor in his or her professional capacity for work done prior to the issue of a legal aid certificate where the client has not paid the pre-certificate costs. Consequently, a solicitor will be able to retain all papers, including those relating to work done under a legal aid certificate. However, the Society recommends that where proceedings are continuing the solicitor's papers should be released to the successor solicitor subject to the receipt of a satisfactory undertaking as to the costs already incurred. For guidance on ownership of documents see Annex 12A, p.253.

3.   Where the client is legally aided, the solicitor's costs are secured by a legal aid order or certificate and therefore it would be inappropriate to call for a professional undertaking from the successor solicitor to pay the costs except in respect of any outstanding pre-certificate costs.

4.   A solicitor who has acted in a legally aided matter may call for an undertaking from the successor solicitor either:

   (a)   to return the papers promptly at the end of the matter to enable a bill of costs to be drawn up; or

   (b)   that the successor solicitor will include the former solicitor's costs in a bill to be taxed, collect those costs and pay them over to the former solicitor.

5.   There is also provision under regulation 103(2), (3) and (4) of the Civil Legal Aid (General) Regulations 1989 for the Legal Aid Board to pay to the former solicitor who gives notice to the Board, the costs to which the former solicitor would have been entitled after a solicitor and own client taxation. This may assist to resolve a situation of deadlock where a solicitor is exercising a lien over legal aid papers for pre-certificate costs.

6.   If a legally aided client either terminates the retainer, or the Legal Aid Board revokes the client's certificate and the client decides to act for himself or herself, a problem can arise in respect of the release of the client's file. It is not misconduct for a solicitor to retain the file to get a bill drawn and taxed, but the client should be allowed access to the file and to take copies of papers at the client's expense.

5.06   Court and 24-hour duty solicitor schemes

A solicitor who provides police station advice as a duty solicitor or representation at a magistrates' court is bound by Parts VII and VIII of the Legal Aid Board Duty Solicitor Arrangements 1992 as to the scope of service to be provided, including paragraphs 51 (defendant's right to instruct other solicitor) and 60 (continued instructions).

1.   The Duty Solicitor Arrangements are contained in the *Legal Aid Handbook.*

2.   Solicitors attending at court or police stations as duty solicitors may have clients referred to them by court officers and others, may directly approach defendants at court and may subsequently act for the client at their office in the usual way.

3.   Where a solicitor is representing a client in a bail case under the duty solicitor scheme where legal aid has been refused, the duty solicitor should limit representation to re-applying for legal aid. This applies even where the duty solicitor feels the client has a good case for obtaining bail because, by refusing legal aid, the court has already decided the defendant does not require legal representation.

4.   For the position on gifts and inducements to clients, see **11.01** note 3, p.223.

Chapter 6

Legal expenses insurance

6.01 Acceptance of referrals
6.02 Confidentiality
6.03 Termination of retainer by legal expenses insurer or solicitor
6.04 Solicitors employed by legal expenses insurers

6

6.01 Acceptance of referrals

Solicitors may accept referrals from a legal expenses insurer to act for an insured provided they comply with provisions of the Solicitors' Introduction and Referral Code 1990.

1. The solicitor's principal duty is to the insured, not the legal expenses insurer but the insured has a duty to mitigate loss and keep the insurer informed of progress. The solicitor should remind the client of these obligations when necessary. The referred client must be dealt with in the same manner as any private client.

2. Solicitors must not enter into any arrangement in which the insurer insists that a particular solicitor must act. By virtue of rule 1 of the Solicitors' Practice Rules 1990 (see **1.01**, p.1) and the Solicitors' Introduction and Referral Code 1990 (see Annex 11B, p.238) the client has the right to instruct a solicitor of his or her choice. However, the client's right to instruct a solicitor of his or her choice may have been modified by the terms of the insurance policy and the Insurance Companies (Legal Expenses Insurance) Regulations 1990 (S.I. 1990 no. 1159).

3. The Insurance Companies (Legal Expenses Insurance) Regulations 1990 provide that the client's freedom of choice may be restricted except in two instances:

   (a) where there is a conflict of interest between the insurer and the insured, the insured has a free choice of solicitor;

   (b) where, under legal expenses insurance, the insured has recourse to a lawyer to defend, represent or serve his or her interest in any enquiry or proceedings.

4. It is a breach of the Solicitors' Introduction and Referral Code for solicitors to reward introducers by the payment of commission or otherwise.

5. Solicitors should make clear to the insured that the responsibility for the payment of the solicitor's costs remains with the insured and if for any reason the insurer refuses to make a payment for costs, the solicitor will look to the insured for payment.

6. For details of information that should be given at the outset of the retainer, see Chapter 13, p.265.

6.02   Confidentiality

A solicitor has a duty of confidentiality to the insured client.

1. The solicitor's duty of confidentiality is the same as in any privately funded matter but the insured client will normally be under an obligation to disclose relevant matters to the insurer.

2. A solicitor must obtain specific consent from the insured client before allowing the legal expenses insurer to inspect the file. The client should be reminded of his or her duties to the insurer when consent is sought.

6.03   Termination of retainer by legal expenses insurer or solicitor

The retainer with the insured client is not terminated when an insurer refuses to fund a matter further. Only the insured client or the solicitor can terminate the retainer. If funding is withdrawn, a solicitor has an obligation to advise as to the availability of legal aid, or otherwise advise as to costs if the insured wishes to continue as a private client.

As a matter of law, and subject to any provisions within the policy, where the insurer decides not to continue funding the proceedings, the normal position as to ownership of papers in the solicitor's possession will apply (for guidance on ownership of documents see Annex 12A, p.253).

6.04   Solicitors employed by legal expenses insurers

'Solicitors employed by a legal expenses insurer may with the insured's specific consent handle a claim (other than a personal injury claim) on the client's behalf provided that the value of the claim does not exceed the current county court "no costs" limit.'

Employed Solicitors Code 1990, paragraph 4

Further guidance on the position of employed solicitors can be found in Chapter 4 (p.145) and in the Employed Solicitors Code (Annex 4A, p.152).

Chapter 7
Avoiding discrimination

> **7.01** Solicitors' Anti-Discrimination Rule
> **7.02** Solicitors' Anti-Discrimination Code
> **7A** Law Society's model anti-discrimination policy

7.01 Solicitors' Anti-Discrimination Rule

'(1) Solicitors must not discriminate on grounds of race, sex or sexual orientation, and must not discriminate unfairly or unreasonably on grounds of disability, in their professional dealings with clients, staff, other solicitors, barristers or other persons.

(2) Principal solicitors in private practice must operate a policy dealing with the avoidance of such discrimination, and solicitors with management responsibilities in employed practice must use reasonable endeavours to secure the operation of such a policy.

(3) Principal solicitors in private practice who have not developed and adopted their own policy dealing with the avoidance of such discrimination will be deemed to have adopted the model anti-discrimination policy for the time being promoted for such purposes by the Law Society.

(4) Paragraph (1) applies to a recognised body as it applies to a solicitor, and paragraphs (2) and (3) apply to a recognised body as they apply to a principal solicitor in private practice.

(5) This rule comes into force on 18th July 1995.'

Solicitors' Anti-Discrimination Rule 1995

7.02 Solicitors' Anti-Discrimination Code

Solicitors must comply with the Solicitors' Anti-Discrimination Rule 1995.

1.   Solicitors and their staff must deal with all persons with the same attention, courtesy and consideration regardless of race, colour, ethnic or national origins, sex, creed, disability or sexual orientation.

2. (a) Solicitors must not discriminate on grounds of race, colour, ethnic or national origins, sex or sexual orientation, and must not discriminate unfairly or unreasonably on grounds of disability, in the selection, treatment or promotion of staff.

    (b) In relation to a position as partner in a firm, solicitors are reminded of the provisions of section 10 of the Race Relations Act 1976 and section 11 of the Sex Discrimination Act 1975 as amended by section 1(3) of the Sex Discrimination Act 1986 (provisions regarding discrimination in relation to a position as partner).

3. A solicitor is generally free to decide whether to accept instructions from any particular client, but any refusal to act must not be based upon the race, colour, ethnic or national origins, sex, creed, disability or sexual orientation of the prospective client.

4. (a) Barristers should be instructed on the basis of their skills, experience and ability. Solicitors must not, on the grounds of race, colour, ethnic or national origins, sex, or sexual orientation, or unfairly or unreasonably on the grounds of disability, avoid briefing a barrister and must not request barristers' clerks to do so.

    (b) Clients' requests for a named barrister should be complied with, subject to the solicitor's duty to discuss with the client the suitability of the barrister and to advise appropriately.

    (c) A solicitor has a duty to discuss with the client any request by the client that only a barrister of a particular racial group or sex be instructed. The solicitor must endeavour to persuade the client to modify instructions which appear to be given on discriminatory grounds. Should the client refuse to modify such instructions, the solicitor should cease to act.

    (d) In relation to the instruction of counsel, solicitors are reminded of the provisions of section 26A(3) of the Race Relations Act 1976 and section 35A(3) of the Sex Discrimination Act 1975 (provisions regarding discrimination in relation to the giving, withholding or acceptance of instructions to a barrister).

5. See also paragraph 2.4.1–2.4.2 of the Law Society's Code for Advocacy (Annex 21A at p.386) for additional requirements under the Advocacy Code (discrimination against clients).

6. See **30.03** note 5 (p.844) for victimisation of, or improper pressure on, complainants.

7. The Law Society's model anti-discrimination policy is at Annex 7A, p.169.

Annex 7A

Law Society's model anti-discrimination policy

(policy issued under paragraph (3) of the Solicitors' Anti-Discrimination Rule 1995)

A. Employees and partners

(1) General statements

The firm is committed to providing equal opportunities in employment. This means that all job applicants, employees and partners will receive equal treatment regardless of race, colour, ethnic or national origins, sex, marital status, sexual orientation or disability.

It is good business sense for the firm to ensure that its most important resource, its staff, is used in a fair and effective way.

(2) Legislation

It is unlawful to discriminate against individuals either directly or indirectly in respect of their race, sex or marital status; or to treat a person who has, or has had, a disability 'less favourably' without reasonable justification. The Race Relations Act 1976, the Sex Discrimination Act 1975 (both of which have been amended by subsequent legislation) and the Disability Discrimination Act 1995 are the relevant Acts. Regard must also be had for the Equal Pay Act 1970.

Codes of practice relating to race and sex discrimination have been produced by the Commission for Racial Equality, the Equal Opportunities Commission and the Law Society and have been used as the basis for this policy. There is also a code of practice for the elimination of discrimination in the field of employment against disabled persons or persons who have had a disability, published by the Department for Education and Employment. The firm is committed to implementing these codes.

(3) Forms of discrimination

The following are the kinds of discrimination which are against the firm's policy:

(a) **Direct discrimination**, where a person is less favourably treated because of race, colour, ethnic or national origins, sex, pregnancy, marital status, disability or sexual orientation.

(b) **Indirect discrimination**, where a requirement or condition which cannot be justified is applied equally to all groups but has a disproportionately adverse effect on one particular group.

(c)   **Victimisation**, where someone is treated less favourably than others because he or she has taken action against the firm under one of the relevant Acts, whether or not such victimisation is unlawful.

(4) Positive action

Although it is unlawful positively to discriminate in favour of certain groups on the grounds of race or sex, positive action to enable greater representation of under-represented groups is permitted by law and encouraged by the firm.

(5) Recruitment

The firm will take steps to ensure that applications are attracted from both sexes and all races and from people with disabilities, and regardless of sexual orientation, and will ensure that there are equal opportunities in all stages of the recruitment process.

(6) Targets

The firm is committed to compliance with Law Society policy on targets for the employment of ethnic minorities, as outlined in the Schedule to this policy.

(7) Promotion

Promotion within the firm (including to partnership) is made without regard to race, colour, ethnic or national origins, sex, marital status, sexual orientation or disability and is based solely on merit.

(8) Monitoring and review

This policy will be monitored periodically by the firm to judge its effectiveness. The firm will also appoint a senior person within it to be responsible for the operation of the policy. In particular, the firm will monitor the ethnic and sexual composition of existing staff and of applicants for jobs (including promotion), and the number of people with disabilities within these groups, and will review its equal opportunities policy in accordance with the results shown by the monitoring. If changes are required, the firm will implement them.

(9) Disciplinary and grievance procedures

Acts of discrimination or harassment on grounds of race, colour, ethnic or national origins, sex, marital status, sexual orientation or disability by employees or partners of the firm will result in disciplinary action. Failure to comply with this policy will be treated in a similar fashion. The policy applies to all who are employed in the firm and to partners.

The firm will treat seriously and take action when any employee or partner has a grievance as a result of discrimination or harassment on grounds of race, colour, ethnic or national origins, sex, marital status, sexual orientation or disability.

(10) Maternity policy

The maternity rights available to partners shall be no less favourable than those required by the Employment Protection (Consolidation) Act 1978 (as amended) for employees. In relation to its dealings with job applicants, employees or partners, the firm will be mindful of the provisions of the Sex Discrimination Act 1975, the Equal Pay Act 1970 and subsequent relevant legislation.

B. Clients

The firm is generally free to decide whether to accept instructions from any particular client, but any refusal to act will not be based upon the race, colour, ethnic or national origins, sex, creed, disability or sexual orientation of the prospective client.

C. Barristers

(1) Barristers should be instructed on the basis of their skills, experience and ability. The firm will not, on the grounds of race, colour, ethnic or national origins, sex, or sexual orientation, or unfairly or unreasonably on the grounds of disability, avoid briefing a barrister and will not request barristers' clerks to do so.

(2) Clients' requests for a named barrister should be complied with, subject to the firm's duty to discuss with the client the suitability of the barrister and to advise appropriately.

(3) The firm has a duty to discuss with the client any request by the client that only a barrister of a particular racial group or sex be instructed. The firm will endeavour to persuade the client to modify instructions which appear to be given on discriminatory grounds. Should the client refuse to modify such instructions, the firm will cease to act.

(4) In relation to the instruction of counsel, the firm will be mindful of the provisions of section 26A(3) of the Race Relations Act 1976 as inserted by section 64(2) of the Courts and Legal Services Act 1990 and section 35A(3) of the Sex Discrimination Act 1975 as inserted by section 64(1) of the Courts and Legal Services Act 1990 (provisions regarding discrimination in relation to the giving, withholding or acceptance of instructions to a barrister).

D. All dealings

The firm will deal with all persons with the same attention, courtesy and consideration regardless of race, colour, ethnic or national origins, sex, creed, disability or sexual orientation.

SCHEDULE

Targets for the employment of ethnic minority fee-earners by solicitors' firms

1. Introduction

As a result of continuing evidence of discrimination faced by job applicants of ethnic minority origin (particularly for training contracts), the Law Society has introduced a policy of setting targets for the number from ethnic minorities to be employed by solicitors' firms. The figures aim to give ethnic minority trainee and qualified solicitors as fair a chance of employment as their white counterparts, and are based on the available statistics relating to size of firm and to the proportion of ethnic minorities within the student and admitted sectors of the profession. These are not enforceable quotas which would be contrary to law, but targets to reach as good practice. The Law Society expects firms to participate wholeheartedly in this policy. Firms which take trainee solicitors will be monitored on their equal opportunities policies (including their adoption and implementation of targets) as part of the monitoring of authorised firms. This policy does not affect and should not be interpreted as affecting standards in recruitment in any way. Firms should clearly select staff on merit.

2. Small firms

Small firms – that is, where the total number of fee-earners is between six and ten – should have at least one fee-earner of ethnic minority origin. Where there are five or fewer fee-earners, firms should all the same have regard to this policy.

3. Large firms

Large firms – that is, where the number of fee-earners is eleven or more – should have at least 10% of their trainees and 5% of other fee-earners of ethnic minority origin.

4. Ethnic minority origin

For the purpose of these targets, ethnic minority origin means of Asian, African-Caribbean, African or Chinese origin.

18th July 1996, updated February 1999

PART II – INTERNATIONAL ASPECTS OF PRACTICE

Chapter 8

Multi-national legal practices

8.01 Formation of MNPs
8.02 Regulation of RFLs and MNPs

8.01 Formation of MNPs

Solicitors may practise in England and Wales in partnership and in incorporated practices with registered foreign lawyers.

1. Partnerships between solicitors and registered foreign lawyers (RFLs) are permitted (see practice rule 7(6) – **3.03**, p.68). This type of partnership is known as a multi-national partnership (MNP). The Solicitors' Incorporated Practice Rules 1988 permit RFLs to be shareowners and directors of recognised bodies (see **3.17**, p.85).

2. RFLs are foreign lawyers who are registered by the Society under section 89 of and Schedule 14 to the Courts and Legal Services Act 1990. A 'foreign lawyer' is a person who is not an English or Welsh solicitor or barrister but who is a member, and entitled to practise as such, of a legal profession regulated within a jurisdiction outside England and Wales.

3. Before a foreign lawyer may be registered, the Society must be satisfied that he or she is a member of a legal profession which is so regulated as to make it appropriate for solicitors to enter into MNPs with its members, and for its members to be officers of recognised bodies. The professional rules governing the applicant must not prohibit practice in partnership with English solicitors in England and Wales. The applicant must be of good standing with his or her professional body or bodies; and there must be no other circumstances which would make it undesirable to register the applicant.

4. RFL status does not confer any right of audience or right to conduct litigation in the courts of England and Wales, nor any right to undertake activities reserved to solicitors by the Solicitors Act 1974.

5. Solicitors practising wholly outside England and Wales may do so in partnership with lawyers of other jurisdictions, whether they are RFLs or not, and with English barristers practising under the Bar's overseas practice rules. Unless all the partners are solicitors or RFLs, the partnership may not practise in England and Wales. A solicitor overseas may practise in corporate form with lawyers of other jurisdictions, whether RFLs or not, unless the corporate practice also wishes to practise in England and Wales, in which case it would need to be a recognised body and have its registered office in England and Wales (see **3.17**, p.85).

6. An information pack on multi-national legal practices is available from Professional Ethics (see p.xv for contact details). This includes a list of foreign legal professions approved by the Society as appropriate for the formation of multi-national legal practices; and a list of foreign regulatory bodies whose rules do not prohibit the formation of multi-national legal practices in England and Wales. Forms of application to become an RFL, and for renewal of registration, are available from Regulation and Information Services (see p.xv for contact details).

8.02   Regulation of RFLs and MNPs

Registered foreign lawyers practising in partnership or in recognised bodies with solicitors are subject to the same rules and principles as solicitors, and multi-national legal practices are broadly subject to the same regulation as solicitors' practices.

1. Certain rules contain special provisions in respect of MNPs, in particular the Solicitors' Separate Business Code (Annex 3E, p.129), practice rule 11 on names used by a firm (**3.04**, p.69) and the Solicitors' Publicity Code (Annex 11A, p.229). The Solicitors' Overseas Practice Rules (Annex 9A, p.180) prohibit a solicitor practising overseas from sharing fees or entering into partnership with a foreign lawyer whose name has been struck off or suspended from the register. For special provisions relating to indemnity for MNPs with overseas offices, see **9.01** note 4, p.176, and **29.01**, p.782.

2. RFLs are subject to the jurisdiction of the Solicitors Disciplinary Tribunal. An RFL's registration is automatically suspended on the RFL being made bankrupt, or being struck off or suspended from practice in his or her own jurisdiction. It will be cancelled if the RFL is admitted as a solicitor or called to the Bar of England and Wales.

3. The regulatory powers of the Society, such as inspection of accounts and intervention, are exercisable in respect of MNPs.

4. RFLs must pay contributions to the Solicitors' Compensation Fund. The information pack (available from Professional Ethics – see p.xv for contact details) contains a list of the appropriate contributions and sets out the Solicitors' Compensation Fund (Foreign Lawyers' Contributions) Rules 1991.

5. The Lord Chancellor's Department has issued guidance to courts (circular B2272) which enables solicitors to go on the record in the name of an MNP. The relevant extract reads:

    'Registered foreign lawyers are not themselves permitted to conduct litigation in courts in England and Wales although litigation services may be provided through a multi-national partnership. The established practice is for solicitors to appear on the court record in the name of the partnership. The senior judiciary have been consulted and are content that this practice should also apply in the case of multi-national partnerships.'

6. Section 85 of the Solicitors Act 1974 gives protection to solicitors' client accounts against claims by banks, as well as protecting banks against certain claims in respect of client accounts. These protections are extended to client accounts of MNPs by the Registered Foreign Lawyers Order 1991 (S.I. 1991 no. 2831).

7. The consumer credit licence issued to the Society covers MNPs as well as solicitors and recognised bodies.

8. The Partnerships (Unrestricted Size) No. 8 Regulations 1991 (S.I. 1991 no. 2729) permit MNPs to have more than 20 partners.

Chapter 9

Practice outside England and Wales

9.01 Rules applicable outside England and Wales
9.02 General principles of conduct
9.03 Local law and rules of conduct
9.04 Partnerships with members of other legal professions
9.05 Providing services other than as a solicitor
9A Solicitors' Overseas Practice Rules 1990
9B International Code of Ethics of the IBA

9.01 Rules applicable outside England and Wales

The Solicitors' Overseas Practice Rules 1990 apply to solicitors practising as such outside England and Wales.

1. Throughout this chapter 'solicitor' means a solicitor of the Supreme Court of England and Wales. 'Overseas' means outside England and Wales.

2. The Solicitors' Overseas Practice Rules 1990 (SOPR) (see Annex 9A, p.180) are not the only conduct provisions applying to solicitors practising overseas. Some are highlighted in this chapter.

3. A solicitor who is practising overseas as a solicitor must have a practising certificate. The question whether a solicitor is practising as a solicitor is addressed in the explanatory note to rule 2 of the SOPR at p.181.

4. Some of the SOPR correspond to provisions in the Solicitors' Practice Rules 1990 and associated codes, and some have no equivalents. Where they correspond, the SOPR are often less specific, because the rules must apply in a variety of local conditions. Certain restrictions applying to solicitors in England and Wales do not apply overseas, so that:

   ▶ solicitors overseas may provide services, as solicitors, to a lawyer employer's clients (see rule 7 of the SOPR at p.183);

   ▶ solicitors overseas may share fees with barristers and practise in partnership with barristers and foreign lawyers (see rule 8 of the SOPR at p.183 and **9.04**, p.178);

- ▶ solicitors overseas may practise through a corporate body if it is wholly owned and directed by lawyers (see rule 9 of the SOPR at p.183);

- ▶ solicitors overseas practising through a corporate body in which non-solicitors own a controlling majority of shares are not subject to the accounts provisions in the SOPR (see rule 9 of the SOPR at p.183);

- ▶ a firm of solicitors practising wholly overseas is not subject to the Solicitors' Indemnity Rules, although the solicitors in the firm must comply with rule 17 of the SOPR (at p.189);

- ▶ the overseas office of an MNP with fewer than 75% solicitor principals is not subject to the Solicitors' Indemnity Rules, although the solicitors in that overseas office must comply with rule 17 of the SOPR (see also **29.01**, p.782).

5. The accounts provisions applying to solicitors overseas are in rules 12–16 of the SOPR, at p.185. A specimen form of accountant's report for overseas practices is available from Regulation and Information Services (see p.xv for contact details). See also **28.05–28.07**, p.678 *et seq.*

6. The Council may waive the provisions of any of the SOPR in particular cases. If a provision of the SOPR causes difficulty in particular local conditions a solicitor may write to Professional Ethics for guidance and in appropriate cases apply for a waiver (see p.xv for contact details).

9.02 General principles of conduct

A solicitor remains an officer of the Court when practising as a solicitor overseas, and the general principles of professional conduct apply to him or her.

1. The principles, notes and other guidance in the Guide may apply to overseas practice with modifications according to local conditions.

2. Rule 6 of the Solicitors' Practice Rules (avoiding conflicts of interest in conveyancing, etc.) does not apply overseas, but a solicitor practising overseas must not act in any situation where there is a conflict of interest.

3. Rules 8 and 9 of the Solicitors' Practice Rules (contingency fees and claims assessors) do not apply to an overseas practice; but see **9.03**, p.178.

4. Rule 10 of the Solicitors' Practice Rules (receipt of commissions from third parties) does not in terms apply to an overseas practice, but the general principle that a solicitor must account to his or her client for any commission or secret profit does apply.

5. The Council have adopted as the basic code for solicitors practising outside England and Wales the International Bar Association's International Code of Ethics (set out in Annex 9B, p.192). Not all foreign legal professions have done so and solicitors should not assume that all foreign lawyers are obliged to comply with it.

9.03   Local law and rules of conduct

A solicitor practising overseas must comply with the requirements of the local law, and must comply, where appropriate, with local requirements as to professional conduct.

1.   A solicitor is always bound by the local law of the jurisdiction in which he or she practises, but may not always be bound by the rules of conduct of the local legal professions.

2.   In certain cases, solicitors may have an express obligation to comply with the rules of a local legal profession:

(a)   if local law imposes an obligation on solicitors to observe those rules;

(b)   if a solicitor becomes a full member of a local legal profession, whether or not he or she also continues to practise as a solicitor;

(c)   if solicitors' rules require solicitors to observe particular local rules, for example:

▶   the obligation to observe local restrictions on publicity – paragraph 14(a)(ii) of the Solicitors' Publicity Code 1990 (see Annex 11A at p.236), rule 5(2)(b) of the SOPR (see Annex 9A at p.182), rule 8 of the IBA Code (see Annex 9B at p.193) and article 2.6.1 of the CCBE Code (see Annex 10B at p.211);

▶   the requirement that an EU lawyer who appears before a court or tribunal in another EU member state must comply with the rules of conduct applied before that court or tribunal (article 4.1 of the CCBE Code – see Annex 10B at p.217).

3.   Where there is no express obligation to comply with local rules, and it is inappropriate or impossible for a solicitor who is not a member of the local legal profession to do so, or it is doubtful which rules of conduct should be applied, a solicitor should observe the standards of conduct applicable to local lawyers so far as possible without breaching solicitors' conduct rules or hindering the proper exercise of his or her profession.

4.   Once the Establishment of Lawyers Directive 98/5/EC comes into effect, the conduct requirements for solicitors practising in other EU states will change.

9.04   Partnerships with members of other legal professions

A solicitor may practise overseas in partnership with a lawyer of another jurisdiction, or with an English barrister, subject to the local law and professional rules of conduct.

1.   See rule 8(2) of the SOPR (Annex 9A at p.183).

2. A solicitor may not practise in England and Wales in partnership with a lawyer of another jurisdiction unless that lawyer is a registered foreign lawyer (RFL) – see Chapter 8, p.173 – so any overseas partnership between a solicitor and a lawyer who is not an RFL must be kept distinct from any practice of that solicitor in England and Wales.

3. Subject to local law and any applicable local rules, a solicitor may practise overseas in partnership with an English barrister to the extent permitted by the overseas practice rules of the English Bar.

9.05   Providing services other than as a solicitor

If a solicitor practises wholly overseas and has an interest in a business which is not a legal or notarial practice but which provides 'solicitor-like' services, he or she must comply with rule 18A of the Solicitors' Overseas Practice Rules 1990.

1. Rule 18A (see Annex 9A at p.189) effectively applies only to solicitors practising wholly overseas, because solicitors who also practise in England and Wales have to comply with the Solicitors' Separate Business Code 1994 in relation to separate businesses (see **3.20–3.21**, p.89, and Annex 3E, p.129).

2. Accountants reporting on overseas practices must, *inter alia*, make test checks on controlled trust accounts (see rule 16 of the SOPR at p.187, and **28.06**, p.679). The checks apply to overseas executor, trustee or nominee companies if they are run as incorporated solicitors' practices in accordance with rule 9 of the SOPR (at p.183). They do not apply to overseas executor, trustee or nominee companies which are run outside a solicitor's practice, but a solicitor with an interest in such a company will be subject to rule 18A, or to the Solicitors' Separate Business Code.

9

Annex 9A

Solicitors' Overseas Practice Rules 1990

(with consolidated amendments to 3rd March 1999)

Rules dated 18th July 1990 made by the Council of the Law Society with the concurrence, where requisite, of the Master of the Rolls under Part II of the Solicitors Act 1974 and section 9 of the Administration of Justice Act 1985, regulating the overseas practices of solicitors and recognised bodies, together with explanatory notes not forming part of the rules.

Rule 1 – Ambit of the rules

(1)   These rules shall have effect in relation to the practice of solicitors, whether or not together with other lawyers, and whether as a principal in private practice, or in the employment of a solicitor, other lawyer, recognised body or other corporate practice, or of a non-lawyer employer, or in any other form of practice, and whether on a regular or an occasional basis.

(2)   Subject always to any requirements of the relevant law or of such local rules as may be applicable to him or her, a solicitor practising as such from an office outside England and Wales shall, in respect of that practice, comply with these rules and not be subject to any other rules made by the Council under sections 31, 32, 34 or 37 of the Act except where it is expressly provided to the contrary in any such rules or in these rules.

Explanatory notes

(i)   *These rules are not an exhaustive statement of the professional obligations of solicitors practising outside England and Wales. The Council considers that the principles of professional conduct which apply in England and Wales apply to all solicitors, even where no specific reference to a particular principle appears in these rules. For example, although these rules do not include any equivalent of Rule 10 of the Solicitors' Practice Rules (receipt of commissions from third parties), the general principle that a solicitor must account to his or her client for any commission or secret profit still applies. Similarly, a solicitor must not act in any situation where he or she would be involved in a conflict of interest.*

(ii)   *The Solicitors' Compensation Fund Rules, made under section 36 of the Act, apply to practices outside England and Wales.*

(iii) *The Solicitors' Investment Business Rules and Rule 12 of the Solicitors' Practice Rules (investment business) apply to the conduct of investment business within or into any part of the United Kingdom.*

Rule 2 – Obligation to hold a practising certificate

A solicitor shall not practise as such unless he or she has in force a practising certificate issued by the Law Society.

Explanatory note

The rules are directed at practice carried on by an English solicitor as such from an office outside England and Wales. Whether a person outside the jurisdiction is practising as an English solicitor depends on the circumstances. If a person is practising as a lawyer but with no other legal qualification than as an English solicitor, the presumption is that he or she is practising as such a solicitor. If a person describes him or herself as an English solicitor in the context of such practice, he or she must be treated as practising as such. If that person is also qualified as a member of another legal profession it is a question of fact and degree in each case whether he or she is practising as an English solicitor or as a member of the other legal profession. A person may be practising as both simultaneously, but will not be practising as an English solicitor when carrying on activities reserved to the local legal profession.

Rule 3 – Basic principles

A solicitor shall not do anything in the course of practising as a solicitor, or permit another person to do anything on his or her behalf, which compromises or impairs or is likely to compromise or impair any of the following:

(a)   the solicitor's independence or integrity;

(b)   a person's freedom to instruct a solicitor of his or her choice;

(c)   the solicitor's duty to act in the best interests of the client;

(d)   the good repute of the solicitor or of the solicitors' profession;

(e)   the solicitor's proper standard of work;

(f)   the solicitor's duty to the Court.

Rule 4 – Cross-border activities within the European Community

(1)   In relation to cross-border activities within the European Community solicitors shall, without prejudice to their other obligations under these rules or any other rules, principles or requirements of conduct, observe the rules codified in articles 2 to 5 of the CCBE Code of Conduct for Lawyers in the European Community adopted on 28th October 1988, as interpreted by article 1 (the preamble) thereof and the Explanatory Memorandum and Commentary thereon prepared by the CCBE's Deontology Working Party and dated May 1989.

(2)   In this Rule:

(a)   "cross-border activities" means:

(i)   all professional contacts with lawyers of member states of the European Community other than the United Kingdom; and

(ii)   the professional activities of the solicitor in a member state other than the United Kingdom, whether or not the solicitor is physically present in that member state; and

(b)   "lawyers" means lawyers as defined in Directive 77/249 of the Council of the European Communities dated 22nd March 1977 as amended from time to time.

Explanatory note

The Council's view is that a solicitor will fulfil his or her obligations under articles 2 to 5 of the code by observing the corresponding rules, principles and requirements of conduct otherwise applicable to solicitors (including these rules), and in addition articles 2.5 (incompatible occupations), 5.2 (co-operation among lawyers of different member states), 5.3 (correspondence between lawyers), 5.6 (change of lawyer) and 5.9 (disputes among lawyers in different member states), being articles having no such corresponding provision. This view is subject to any authoritative ruling to the contrary at Community level.

Rule 5 – Publicity

(1)   Solicitors may at their discretion publicise their practices or permit other persons to do so, or publicise the business or activities of other persons, provided there is no breach of paragraph (2) of this rule or any other provision of these rules, and provided there is compliance with the Solicitors' Publicity Code from time to time in force.

(2)   No publicity for a solicitor's practice may be conducted in another jurisdiction in any manner that would contravene either:

     (a)   the provisions of the Solicitors' Publicity Code; or

     (b)   any restrictions in force in that other jurisdiction concerning lawyers' publicity.

For the purposes of this paragraph, publicity shall be deemed to be conducted in the jurisdiction in which it is received. However, publicity shall not be regarded as being conducted in a jurisdiction in which such publicity would be improper if it is conducted for the purpose of reaching persons in a jurisdiction or jurisdictions where such publicity is permitted and its reception in the former jurisdiction is incidental.

Explanatory note

One of the provisions of the Solicitors' Publicity Code is the prohibition on unsolicited visits and telephone calls (paragraph 3). Attention is drawn not only to the corresponding provisions of the CCBE Code of Conduct for Lawyers in the European Community (article 2.6), but also to the International Code of Ethics of the International Bar Association, which the Council has adopted as the basic code of solicitors practising outside the jurisdiction. Rule 8 of the International Code provides: "A lawyer should not advertise or solicit business except to the extent and in the manner permitted by the rules of the jurisdiction to which that lawyer is subject. A lawyer should not advertise or solicit business in any country in which such advertising or soliciting is prohibited."

Rule 6 – Introductions and referrals

Solicitors may accept introductions and referrals of business from other persons and may make introductions and refer business to other persons, provided there is no breach of Rule 3 or any other provision of these rules.

Explanatory note

Assistance on complying with the provisions of Rule 3 can be obtained from the Solicitors' Introduction and Referral Code.

Rule 7 – Solicitors employed by non-lawyer employers

(1)   Solicitors who are employees of non-lawyer employers shall not as part of their employment do for any person other than their employer work which is or could be done by a solicitor acting as such.

(2)   Paragraph (1) of this rule shall not prevent a solicitor from acting for a company or organisation controlled by the employer or in which the employer has a substantial measure of control, or a company in the same group as the employer or which controls the employer.

Explanatory note

A body corporate wholly owned and controlled by lawyers for the purpose of practising law would not be a "non-lawyer employer".

Rule 8 – Fee sharing

(1)   A solicitor shall not share or agree to share his or her professional fees with any person except:

  (a)   a practising solicitor (which term includes a recognised body);

  (b)   a practising lawyer of another jurisdiction (other than a lawyer whose registration under section 89 of the Courts and Legal Services Act 1990 is suspended or whose name has been struck off the register);

  (c)   a member of the Bar of England and Wales acting in accordance with the overseas practice rules of the Bar;

  (d)   any body corporate (other than a recognised body) wholly owned and controlled by lawyers for the purpose of practising law;

  (e)   the solicitor's *bona fide* employee; or

  (f)   a retired partner or predecessor of the solicitor, or the dependants or personal representatives of a deceased partner or predecessor.

(2)   A solicitor shall not enter into partnership with any person other than those within sub-paragraphs (1)(a) to (c) of this rule.

(3)   In sub-paragraph (1)(f) of this rule, the references to a retired or deceased partner shall be construed, in relation to a recognised body, as including a retired or deceased director or member of that body or to a retired or deceased beneficial owner of any share in that body held by a member as nominee.

Explanatory note

Paragraph (2) of this rule allows a solicitor to be in partnership outside England and Wales with a lawyer of another jurisdiction. However, such a partnership may only practise in England and Wales, or hold itself out as so practising, if all the non-solicitor partners are on the register of foreign lawyers maintained by the Law Society under section 89 of the Courts and Legal Services Act 1990.

Rule 9 – Corporate practice

(1)   A solicitor shall not practise through a body corporate save one in which all the directors and the owners of all the shares are persons within Rule 8(1)(a) to (c) of these rules, or save as permitted under Rule 7 of these rules.

(2)   Notwithstanding Rule 1(2) of these rules, all the provisions of the Solicitors' Incorporated Practice Rules from time to time in force shall have effect where a recognised body practises outside England and Wales.

(3)   Where solicitors own a controlling majority of the shares in a corporate practice other than a recognised body, the provisions of Rules 12 to 16 of these rules shall apply to all solicitors who own shares in and all solicitors who are directors of that corporate practice as if all such solicitors and any other owners of shares and directors were practising in partnership as the principals of that practice.

(4)   The solicitor shareowners and directors in a corporate practice in which solicitors own a controlling majority of the shares (other than a recognised body) shall, where the corporate practice holds money as sole trustee or co-trustee with one or more of its officers or employees, be treated for the purposes of Rules 12, 13, 15 and 16 of these rules as holding money subject to a controlled trust.

Explanatory notes

(i)   A corporate practice operating both in England and Wales and in another jurisdiction needs to comply, in respect of its overseas practice, both with the Solicitors' Overseas Practice Rules and the Solicitors' Incorporated Practice Rules. A corporate practice operating solely outside England and Wales needs to comply with the Solicitors' Overseas Practice Rules but is not eligible for recognition under the Solicitors' Incorporated Practice Rules.

(ii)   The effect of paragraph (4) is that the solicitor shareowners and directors must ensure that the corporate practice complies with Rules 12 and/or 13 in relation to that money, which will be subject to the reporting accountant's check under Rule 16.

Rule 10 – Names used by a firm of solicitors

(1)   A firm of solicitors (which shall include the practice of a sole practitioner or a corporate practice of solicitors) must not use a name which:

(a)   is misleading; or

(b)   brings the profession into disrepute.

(2)   A name used by a firm of solicitors on any letterhead (or fax heading, or heading used for bills), if the name does not itself include the word "solicitor(s)" or "lawyer(s)", must be accompanied by either:

(a)   the words "solicitor(s)" or "English [or Welsh] lawyer(s)"; or

(b)   if appropriate the words "regulated by the Law Society of England and Wales".

(3)   Without prejudice to paragraph (1)(a) of this rule, a name used by a firm of solicitors shall not:

(a)   imply a connection with a business other than a legal practice; or

(b)   include the name of, or refer to, any actual person except:

(i)   a lawyer who is or was a principal in the firm or a predecessor firm; or

(ii)   an historical character unconnected with the practice.

(4)   Paragraphs (1) to (3) of this rule shall also apply to any other legal practice in which solicitors form a majority of the partners or own a controlling majority of the shares.

(5) Notwithstanding paragraphs (1) to (4) of this rule, the company name of a recognised body shall not be governed by this rule.

Explanatory notes

(i) For guidance on what is or is not misleading, see the notes to Rule 11 of the Solicitors' Practice Rules.

(ii) The words "regulated by the Law Society of England and Wales" would not be appropriate for:

(a) an incorporated practice which is not a recognised body; or

(b) a partnership of solicitors and other lawyers, unless it is a multi-national partnership with its head office in England and Wales and having at least 75% solicitor principals.

(iii) The company name of a recognised body is governed by Rule 11 of the Solicitors' Practice Rules – see Rule 9(2) of these rules and Rule 22 of the Solicitors' Incorporated Practice Rules.

Rule 11 – Supervision of offices

Solicitors shall ensure that every office from which their practice is carried on is supervised sufficiently to ensure that at all times the practice is properly conducted and the affairs of the clients receive proper attention.

Rule 12 – Solicitors' accounts

(1) (a) A solicitor shall keep any money held by him or her on behalf of clients separate from any other funds (save as provided in sub-paragraph (1)(d) of this rule) and in an account at a bank or similar institution subject to supervision by a public authority.

(b) All money received by a solicitor for or on behalf of a client shall be paid into such an account forthwith unless the client expressly or by implication agrees that the money shall be dealt with otherwise.

(c) Any such account in which clients' money is held in the name of the solicitor shall indicate in the title or designation that the funds belong to the client or clients of the solicitor.

(d) In such account may be kept money held subject to a controlled trust and paid into such account in accordance with Rule 13(1)(a) of these rules.

(2) A solicitor shall at all times keep, whether by written, electronic, mechanical or other means, such accounts as are necessary:

(a) to record all the solicitor's dealings with money dealt with through any such account for clients' money as is specified in sub-paragraph (1)(a) of this rule;

(b) to show separately in respect of each client all money received, held or paid by the solicitor for or on account of that client and to distinguish the same from any other money received, held or paid by the solicitor; and

(c) to ensure that the solicitor is at all times able without delay to account to clients for all money received, held or paid by the solicitor on their behalf.

(3) A solicitor shall not make any payment or withdrawal from money held on behalf of any client except where the money paid or withdrawn is:

9

    (a)   properly required for a payment to or on behalf of the client;

    (b)   properly required for or towards payment of a debt due to the solicitor from the client or in reimbursement of money expended by the solicitor on behalf of the client;

    (c)   paid or withdrawn on the client's authority; or

    (d)   properly required for or towards payment of the solicitor's costs where there has been delivered to the client a bill of costs or other written intimation of the amount of the costs incurred and it has thereby or otherwise in writing been made clear to the client that the money so paid or withdrawn is being or will be so applied.

(4)   A solicitor shall not make any payment or withdrawal from money held subject to a controlled trust and kept in an account in accordance with sub-paragraph (1)(d) of this rule except in proper execution of that trust.

(5)   Every solicitor shall preserve for at least six years from the date of the last entry therein all accounts, books, ledgers and records kept under this rule.

Explanatory note

Assistance in the keeping of solicitors' accounts may be derived from the Solicitors' Accounts Rules.

Rule 13 – Solicitors' trust accounts

(1)   A solicitor who holds or receives money subject to a controlled trust of which he or she is a trustee shall without delay pay such money either:

    (a)   into an account for clients' money such as is specified in Rule 12(1)(a) of these Rules; or

    (b)   into an account in the name of the trustee or trustees at a bank or similar institution subject to supervision by a public authority, which account shall be clearly designated as a trust account by use of the words "executor" or "trustee" or otherwise, and shall be kept solely for money subject to that particular trust;

provided that a solicitor shall not be obliged to comply with sub-paragraphs (1)(a) or (b) of this rule where money received is without delay paid straight over to a third party in the execution of the trust.

(2)   A solicitor shall at all times keep, whether by written, electronic, mechanical or other means, such accounts as are necessary:

    (a)   to show separately in respect of each controlled trust all the solicitor's dealings with money received, held or paid by the solicitor on account of that trust; and

    (b)   to distinguish the same from money received or paid by the solicitor on any other account.

(3)   A solicitor shall not make any payment or withdrawal from money held subject to a controlled trust except in proper execution of that trust.

(4)   Every solicitor shall preserve for at least six years from the date of the last entry therein all accounts, books, ledgers and records kept under this rule.

(5)   Every solicitor shall either:

    (i)   keep together, centrally, the accounts required to be kept under this rule; or

    (ii)   maintain a central register of controlled trusts.

Explanatory note

Assistance in keeping of trust accounts may be derived from the Solicitors' Accounts Rules.

Rule 14 – Deposit interest

Where a solicitor holds or receives for or on behalf of a client money on which, having regard to all the circumstances (including the amount and the length of the time for which the money is likely to be held and the law and prevailing custom of lawyers practising in the jurisdiction in which the solicitor practises) interest ought, in fairness, to be earned for the client, then, subject to any agreement to the contrary made in writing between solicitor and client, the solicitor shall either:

    (a)   deal with that money in such a way that proper interest is earned thereon; or

    (b)   pay to the client out of the solicitor's own money a sum equivalent to the interest which would have been earned for the benefit of the client had the money been dealt with in accordance with paragraph (a) of this rule.

Rule 15 – Investigation of accounts

(1)   In order to ascertain whether or not Rules 12 to 14 of these rules have been complied with, the Council may at any time in writing (including by telex or facsimile transmission) require any solicitor to produce at a time and place to be fixed by the Council all necessary documents for the inspection of any person appointed by the Council and to supply to such person any necessary information and explanations, and such person shall be directed to prepare a report on the result of such inspection.

(2)   Any requirement made by the Council of a solicitor under paragraph (1) of this rule shall be deemed to have been received by the solicitor upon proof of its having been delivered at or transmitted to the solicitor's practising address or last known practising address (or, in the case of a recognised body, its registered office).

(3)   Upon being required to do so a solicitor shall produce all necessary documents at the time and place fixed, and shall supply any necessary information and explanations.

(4)   Where a requirement is made by the Council of a recognised body under paragraph (1) of this rule such requirement shall, if so stated in the requirement, be deemed also to be made of any solicitor who is an officer or employee of that recognised body where such solicitor holds or has held client's money or money subject to a controlled trust of which he or she is or was a trustee.

Rule 16 – Accountants' reports

(1)   The accountant's report which a solicitor is required to deliver annually to the Council under section 34 of the Act shall be signed either by a qualified accountant (who may be an accountant qualified in the jurisdiction where the solicitor practises) or by such other person as the Council may think fit.

(2)   Such report shall be based on a sufficient examination of the relevant documents to give the person signing the report a reasonable indication whether or not the solicitor has complied with Rules 12(1) to (4) and 13 of these rules during the period covered by the report.

(3) Such report shall include:

(a) the name, practising addresses and practising style of the solicitor and any partners of the solicitor;

(b) the name, address and qualification of the person signing the report;

(c) an indication of the nature and extent of the examination made of the relevant documents by the said person;

(d) a statement to the effect that so far as may be ascertained from the examination the said person is satisfied (if this is indeed the case) that (save for trivial breaches) the solicitor has complied with Rules 12(1) to (4) and 13 of these rules during the period covered by the report;

(e) a statement of the total amount of money held at banks or similar institutions on behalf of clients on a date during the period under review, which date shall be selected by the accountant and which may be the last day of the period to which the report relates, and of the total liabilities to clients on such date, and an explanation of any difference; and

(f) details of any matters in respect of which the said person has been unable so to satisfy him or herself and any matters (other than trivial breaches) in respect of which it appears to the said person that the solicitor has not complied with Rules 12(1) to (4) and 13 of these rules.

(4) The delivery of an accountant's report shall be unnecessary in respect of any period during which the solicitor did not hold or receive money for or on behalf of clients or money subject to a controlled trust; provided that, except where the solicitor has no practising address outside England and Wales, the solicitor or a solicitor-partner of the solicitor (or, in the case of a recognised body, a director of that body) signs and delivers to the Council a declaration that no such money was held or received during that period.

(5) It shall be unnecessary to deliver an accountant's report until after the end of any period of twelve months ending 31st October during which the solicitor first held or received money for or on behalf of clients or money subject to a controlled trust, having not held or received any such money in the period of twelve months immediately preceding that period; provided that an accountant's report then delivered includes the period when such money was first held or received.

Explanatory notes

(i) *Assistance in the preparation of accountants' reports may be derived from the Accountant's Report Rules. Reference should also be made to section 34 of the Act.*

(ii) *Where a firm practises both in England and Wales and overseas, it would, if desired, be proper for a single report to be submitted covering both the "domestic" and overseas parts of the practice (provided that, in appropriate cases, there is also a declaration under paragraph (4) of this rule).*

(iii) *In checking controlled trust accounts, the reporting accountant may find it helpful to adopt the series of checks contained in Rule 4(1)(b) of the Accountant's Report Rules. Reference should also be made to the Law Society's Guidance on test checks on overseas controlled trust accounts.*

[Note: the Accountant's Report Rules 1991 can be found at Annex 28D of the seventh edition of the Guide. However, Part F of the Solicitors' Accounts Rules 1998, which contains equivalent provisions, will eventually supersede the 1991 rules – see Annex 28B (p.684) in this edition of the Guide.]

Rule 17 – Professional indemnity

(1)   A solicitor shall take out and maintain insurance or other indemnity against professional liabilities, or shall be covered by such insurance or other indemnity. The extent and amount of such insurance or other indemnity shall be reasonable having regard to the nature and extent of the risks the solicitor incurs in his or her practice, to the local conditions in the jurisdiction in which the solicitor practises and to the availability of insurance or other indemnity on reasonable terms, but need not exceed the current requirements of any other rules made by the Council under section 37 of the Act.

(2)   Paragraph (1) of this rule shall not apply to a solicitor who is the employee of a non-lawyer employer, provided the solicitor fully complies with Rule 7 of these rules in respect of that employment and conducts no professional business as a solicitor outside that employment.

(3)   Notwithstanding paragraphs (1) and (2) of this rule, a practice carried on both in England and Wales and in another jurisdiction shall be subject to all other rules made by the Council under section 37 of the Act; save that solicitors who are partners in a multi-national partnership of which fewer than 75% of the principals are solicitors shall be subject to paragraphs (1) and (2) of this rule in respect of any offices outside England and Wales and not any other rules made by the Council under section 37 of the Act.

(4)   A recognised body shall be governed in respect of professional indemnity not by this rule but by the indemnity rules applicable from time to time to recognised bodies and by the Solicitors' Incorporated Practice Rules from time to time in force, subject always to any requirements of the relevant law or of such local rules as may be applicable to the recognised body.

(5)   Notwithstanding paragraph (4) of this rule, a recognised body whose overseas offices are deemed by the Solicitors' Indemnity Rules to form a separate practice shall be subject to paragraph (1) of this rule in respect of its offices outside England and Wales.

Explanatory notes

(i)   *The statement in paragraph (1) that the extent and amount of insurance or other indemnity need not exceed the current requirements of any other rules made under section 37 of the Act ensures that the requirements of this rule are not more onerous than those of the Solicitors' Indemnity Rules, but the rule is subject to any more onerous requirements of the relevant law or of such local rules as may be applicable to the solicitor (see Rule 1(2) of these rules).*

(ii)   *Paragraph (3) provides that the Solicitors' Indemnity Rules shall continue to apply to* (inter alia) *a firm of solicitors (or a multi-national partnership of which at least 75% of the principals are solicitors) which has a head office in England and Wales and a branch office overseas.*

Rule 18 – Dual qualification

Where a solicitor is qualified as a member of a legal profession of another jurisdiction, nothing in these rules shall affect such duty as may be upon the solicitor to observe the rules of that profession.

Rule 18A – Providing services other than as a lawyer

(1)   A solicitor who, alone or with any other person, sets up, operates, actively participates in or controls a business which is not a legal (or notarial) practice but which

provides any service or services which may properly be provided by a solicitor practising as such, must ensure that:

(a)   the name of any practice of the solicitor has no substantial element in common with the name of the business;

(b)   the words "solicitor(s)", "attorney(s)", or "lawyer(s)" are not used in connection with the solicitor's involvement with the business;

(c)   paperwork and records relating to customers of the business are not kept with paperwork and records relating to clients of the solicitor;

(d)   all clients referred to the business by any practice of the solicitor outside England and Wales are informed in writing of the solicitor's interest in the business and that, as customers of the business, they do not enjoy the protections attaching to clients of a solicitor; and

(e)   the solicitor does not hold on the client account of the solicitor's practice money held for customers of the business as such, or money held for the business.

(2)   A solicitor who has a separate business as a European patent attorney is subject to paragraph (1)(d) and (e) only.

Rule 19 – Waivers

In any particular case or cases the Council shall have power to waive in writing any of the provisions of these rules for a particular purpose or purposes expressed in such waiver, and to revoke such waiver.

Rule 20 – Interpretation

In these Rules, except where the context otherwise requires:

(a)   the expressions "accounts", "books", "ledgers" and "records" include loose-leaf books and such cards or other permanent documents or records as are necessary for the operation of any system of book-keeping whether written, electronic, mechanical or otherwise;

(b)   "the Act" means the Solicitors Act 1974;

(c)   "another jurisdiction" means a jurisdiction other than England and Wales;

(d)   "controlled trust", in relation to a solicitor, means a trust of which he or she is a sole trustee or co-trustee only with one or more of his or her partners or employees;

(e)   "controlled trust", in relation to a recognised body, means a trust of which it is a sole trustee or co-trustee only with one or more of its officers, partners or employees;

(f)   "controlled trust", in relation to a solicitor or a recognised body, also includes, where that solicitor or recognised body is an officer or employee of a recognised body, a trust of which he, she or it is co-trustee only with one or more other officers or employees of that recognised body or the body itself;

(g)   "controlled trust", in relation to a solicitor who is an officer or employee of a corporate practice (other than a recognised body) of which solicitors own a controlling majority of the shares, also includes a trust of which he or she is a sole trustee or co-trustee only with one or more other officers or employees of that corporate practice or the corporate practice itself;

(h) "the Council" means the Council of the Law Society;

(i) "lawyer", except in Rule 4 of these rules, means a member of a regulated legal profession who is entitled to practise as such in the relevant jurisdiction (whether he or she is a member of the legal profession of that jurisdiction or of a different jurisdiction);

(j) "person" includes a body corporate or unincorporated association or group of persons;

(k) "recognised body" means a body corporate for the time being recognised by the Council under the Solicitors' Incorporated Practice Rules from time to time in force as being a suitable body to undertake the provision of professional services such as are provided by individuals practising as solicitors;

(l) "solicitor" means a solicitor of the Supreme Court of England and Wales and shall also be construed as including a firm of solicitors or a recognised body; and

(m) words in the singular include the plural, words in the plural include the singular, and words importing the masculine or feminine gender include the neuter.

Explanatory note

In connection with the definition of "lawyer", in some jurisdictions there may be uncertainty as to whether a particular profession can be regarded as a "regulated legal profession" in view of the differences in legal and professional structures. In case of doubt solicitors are invited to seek guidance from the Law Society.

9

Rule 21 – Repeal and commencement

(1) The Solicitors' Overseas Practice Rules 1987 are hereby repealed.

(2) These rules shall come into force on 1st September 1990.

Annex 9B

International Code of Ethics of the International Bar Association

adopted by the Council of the Law Society as the basic code for solicitors practising outside the jurisdiction – 1988 edition

Preamble

The International Bar Association is a federation of National Bar Associations and Law Societies with full or sustaining organisational members and individual members. Most of the full or sustaining organisational members have established Codes of Legal Ethics as models for or governing the practice of law by their members. In some jurisdictions these Codes are imposed on all practitioners by their respective Bar Associations or Law Societies or by the courts or administrative agencies having jurisdiction over the admission of individuals to the practice of law.

Except where the context otherwise requires, this Code applies to any lawyer of one jurisdiction in relation to his contacts with a lawyer of another jurisdiction or to his activities in another jurisdiction.

Nothing in this Code absolves a lawyer from the obligation to comply with such requirements of the law or of rules of professional conduct as may apply to him in any relevant jurisdiction. It is a re-statement of much that is in these requirements and a guide as to what the International Bar Association considers to be a desirable course of conduct by all lawyers engaged in the international practice of law.

The International Bar Association may bring incidents of alleged violations to the attention of relevant organisations.

Rules

1.   A lawyer who undertakes professional work in a jurisdiction where he is not a full member of the local profession shall adhere to the standards of professional ethics in the jurisdiction in which he has been admitted. He shall also observe all ethical standards which apply to lawyers of the country where he is working.

2.   Lawyers shall at all times maintain the honour and dignity of their profession. They shall in practice as well as in private life, abstain from any behaviour which may tend to discredit the profession of which they are members.

3.   Lawyers shall preserve independence in the discharge of their professional duty. Lawyers practising on their own account or in partnership where permissible, shall not

engage in any other business or occupation if by doing so they may cease to be independent.

4.   Lawyers shall treat their professional colleagues with the utmost courtesy and fairness.

Lawyers who undertake to render assistance to a foreign colleague shall always keep in mind that the foreign colleague has to depend on them to a much larger extent than in the case of another lawyer of the same country. Therefore their responsibility is much greater, both when giving advice and when handling a case.

For this reason it is improper for lawyers to accept a case unless they can handle it promptly and with due competence, without undue interference by the pressure of other work. To the fees in these cases Rule 19 applies.

5.   Except where the law or custom of the country concerned otherwise requires, any oral or written communication between lawyers shall in principle be accorded a confidential character as far as the court is concerned, unless certain promises or acknowledgements are made therein on behalf of a client.

6.   Lawyers shall always maintain due respect towards the court. Lawyers shall without fear defend the interests of their clients and without regard to any unpleasant consequences to themselves or to any other person.

Lawyers shall never knowingly give to the court incorrect information or advice which is to their knowledge contrary to the law.

7.   It shall be considered improper for lawyers to communicate about a particular case directly with any person whom they know to be represented in that case by another lawyer without the latter's consent.

8.   A lawyer should not advertise or solicit business except to the extent and in the manner permitted by the rules of the jurisdiction to which that lawyer is subject. A lawyer should not advertise or solicit business in any country in which such advertising or soliciting is prohibited.

9.   A lawyer should never consent to handle a case unless:

    (a)   the client gives direct instructions, or

    (b)   the case is assigned by a competent body or forwarded by another lawyer, or

    (c)   instructions are given in any other manner permissible under the relevant local rules or regulations.

10.   Lawyers shall at all times give clients a candid opinion on any case. They shall render assistance with scrupulous care and diligence. This applies also if they are assigned as counsel for an indigent person.

Lawyers shall at any time be free to refuse to handle a case, unless it is assigned by a competent body.

Lawyers should only withdraw from a case during its course for good cause, and if possible in such a manner that the client's interests are not adversely affected.

The loyal defence of a client's case may never cause advocates to be other than perfectly candid, subject to any right or privilege to the contrary which clients choose them to exercise, or knowingly to go against the law.

11. Lawyers shall, when in the client's interest, endeavour to reach a solution by settlement out of court rather than start legal proceedings.

Lawyers should never stir up litigation.

12. Lawyers should not acquire a financial interest in the subject matter of a case which they are conducting. Neither should they, directly or indirectly, acquire property about which litigation is pending before the court in which they practise.

13. Lawyers should never represent conflicting interests in litigation. In non-litigation matters, lawyers should do so only after having disclosed all conflicts or possible conflicts of interest to all parties concerned and only with their consent. This Rule also applies to all lawyers in a firm.

14. Lawyers should never disclose, unless lawfully ordered to do so by the court or as required by statute, what has been communicated to them in their capacity as lawyers even after they have ceased to be the client's counsel. This duty extends to their partners, to junior lawyers assisting them and to their employees.

15. In pecuniary matters lawyers shall be most punctual and diligent. They should never mingle funds of others with their own and they should at all times be able to refund money they hold for others. They shall not retain money they receive for their clients for longer than is absolutely necessary.

16. Lawyers may require that a deposit is made to cover their expenses, but the deposit should be in accordance with the estimated amount of their charges and the probable expenses and labour required.

17. Lawyers shall never forget that they should put first not their right to compensation for their services, but the interests of their clients and the exigencies of the administration of justice.

The lawyers' right to ask for a deposit or to demand payment of out-of-pocket expenses and commitments, failing payment of which they may withdraw from the case or refuse to handle it, should never be exercised at a moment at which the client may be unable to find other assistance in time to prevent irreparable damage being done.

Lawyers' fees should, in the absence or non-applicability of official scales, be fixed on a consideration of the amount involved in the controversy and the interest of it to the client, the time and labour involved and all other personal and factual circumstances of the case.

18. A contract for a contingent fee, where sanctioned by the law or by professional rules and practice, should be reasonable under all circumstances of the case, including the risk and uncertainty of the compensation and subject to supervision of a court as to its reasonableness.

19. Lawyers who engage a foreign colleague to advise on a case or to co-operate in handling it, are responsible for the payment of the latter's charges except where there is express agreement to the contrary. When lawyers direct a client to a foreign colleague they are not responsible for the payment of the latter's charges, but neither are they entitled to a share of the fee of this foreign colleague.

20. Lawyers should not permit their professional services or their names to be used in any way which would make it possible for persons to practise law who are not legally authorised to do so.

Lawyers shall not delegate to a legally unqualified person not in their employ and control any functions which are by the law or custom of the country in which they practise only to be performed by a qualified lawyer.

21.   It is not unethical for lawyers to limit or exclude professional liability subject to the rules of their local bar association and to there being no statutory or constitutional prohibitions.

Reproduced with the kind permission of the International Bar Association

Chapter 10

Cross-border practice in the European Union

> **10.01** Practice rule 16 (cross-border activities within the EC)
> **10.02** Cross-border activities – additional guidance
> **10.03** Local and EU legal requirements
> **10A** European Communities (Services of Lawyers) Order 1978
> **10B** CCBE Code of Conduct

10.01 Practice rule 16 (cross-border activities within the European Community)

'**(1)** In relation to cross-border activities within the European Community, solicitors shall, without prejudice to their other obligations under these rules or any other rules, principles or requirements of conduct, observe the rules codified in articles 2 to 5 of the CCBE Code of Conduct for Lawyers in the European Community adopted on 28th October 1988, as interpreted by article 1 (the Preamble) thereof and the Explanatory Memorandum and Commentary thereon prepared by the CCBE's Deontology Working Party and dated May 1989.

(2) In this rule:

(a) "cross-border activities" means:

(i) all professional contacts with lawyers of member states of the European Community other than the United Kingdom; and

(ii) the professional activities of the solicitor in a member state other than the United Kingdom, whether or not the solicitor is physically present in that member state; and

(b) "lawyers" means lawyers as defined in Directive 77/249 of the Council of the European Communities dated 22nd March 1977 as amended from time to time.'

Solicitors' Practice Rules 1990, rule 16

10.02 Cross-border activities – additional guidance

1. Solicitors practising overseas are also subject to the above requirements (see rule 4 of the Solicitors' Overseas Practice Rules 1990, Annex 9A at p.181).

2. The Council issued a statement in July 1990 to the effect that a solicitor will fulfil his or her obligations under articles 2–5 of the Code by observing the corresponding rules, principles and requirements of conduct otherwise applicable to solicitors (including the Solicitors' Practice Rules 1990), and in addition articles 2.5 (incompatible occupations), 5.2 (co-operation among lawyers of different member states), 5.3 (correspondence between lawyers), 5.6 (change of lawyer) and 5.9 (disputes among lawyers in different member states), being articles having no such corresponding provision. This view is subject to any authoritative ruling to the contrary at EU level.

3. References to European Community member states in the CCBE Code and the Explanatory Memorandum and Commentary may be taken to mean states of the European Union, the European Economic Area and Switzerland. The CCBE (the Council of the Bars and Law Societies of the European Union) is the officially recognised representative body in the European Union and the European Economic Area for the bars and law societies of the member states. Its objects include the study of all questions affecting the legal professions in the European Union and the formulation of solutions designed to co-ordinate and harmonise professional practice. The Law Society is represented on the UK delegation to the CCBE.

4. The CCBE Code as adopted on 28th October 1988 appears at Annex 10B, p.205. Relevant extracts from the Explanatory Memorandum and Commentary have been interspersed in the text of the Code as 'commentaries' rather than reproduced separately. They are shown in italics to distinguish them from the Code itself. There are also some Law Society notes, introduced to update the Code and the Explanatory Memorandum and Commentary. The full text of the Explanatory Memorandum and Commentary is available from Professional Ethics (see p.xv for contact details).

5. On 28th November 1998 the CCBE adopted a new version of its Code of Conduct. However, since this revised version of the Code has not yet been adopted by the Law Society as rules binding on solicitors, it does not appear in this edition of the Guide.

10.03 Local and EU legal requirements

A solicitor who practises in another jurisdiction within the European Union, or who acts in conjunction with a lawyer of another EU jurisdiction, must have regard to EU law and local law, including local provisions implementing EU directives.

1. References to the EU include the 15 members of the EU and the three additional member states of the European Economic Area.

2. A general discussion of the provisions of the law applicable to the cross-border practice of lawyers in the EU may be found in *Free Movement of Lawyers* by Hamish Adamson (2nd edition published by Butterworths).

3. Chapters 2 and 3 of the Treaty of Rome provide for the removal of restrictions on the freedom of nationals of one member state to establish themselves permanently, or to provide services on an occasional basis, in another member state. The provisions apply to lawyers.

Lawyers' Services Directive

4. The Lawyers' Services Directive 77/249/EEC requires all member states to allow a practising lawyer established in another member state to provide services (except conveyancing and probate services in the UK and Ireland) in a host member state on an occasional basis, which are otherwise reserved to a lawyer in the host jurisdiction. All host states which have adopted implementing legislation require that a visiting lawyer representing a client in legal proceedings must do so in conjunction with a host state lawyer. A solicitor should check the relevant implementing legislation of any host state in which he or she wishes to exercise rights under the Directive. The Directive has been extended to cover the whole of the European Economic Area and Switzerland.

5. A 'competent authority' in a host state may request proof of qualification from a visiting lawyer seeking to exercise rights under the Directive. A host lawyer who intends to appear in court with a visiting lawyer must check that the visiting lawyer is entitled to practise, and is of good standing. The lawyers' professional identity card, published in 1978 by the CCBE and issued by the bars and law societies of the member states, is officially recognised by the European Court of Justice, the Court of First Instance and national authorities as *prima facie* proof of a lawyer's right to practise. Solicitors holding practising certificates may obtain the card on application to Regulation and Information Services (see p.xv for contact details).

6. The implementing legislation in England and Wales is the European Communities (Services of Lawyers) Order 1978 (see Annex 10A, p.200). A solicitor acting as a host lawyer and representing a client in conjunction with a visiting lawyer should, as a matter of courtesy and to prevent the court being taken unawares, inform the court in advance of his or her intention to appear with the visiting lawyer.

Diplomas Directive

7. The 'Diplomas Directive' on the recognition of higher education diplomas (89/48/EEC) facilitates access by lawyers from one member state into the legal profession of another member state. It has been implemented in the UK by the European Communities (Recognition of Professional Qualifications) Regulations 1991 (S.I. 1991 no. 824) for the professions

generally. For access to the solicitors' profession in England and Wales, it has been implemented by the Qualified Lawyers Transfer Regulations 1990. Enquiries about these regulations should be addressed to Regulation and Information Services (see p.xv for contact details). Enquiries about the implementation of the Directive in other jurisdictions should be addressed to the International Directorate (see p.xv for contact details).

Establishment Directive

8. The Establishment of Lawyers Directive 98/5/EC is intended to facilitate practice of the profession of lawyer on a permanent basis in other member states. It confirms the right of lawyers from one member state to be established under their home title in other member states, subject to registration with, and regulation by, the local Bar or Law Society. The Directive is expected to take effect in the United Kingdom on 14th March 2000.

Solicitors and barristers

9. Although the legal profession in England and Wales is divided into solicitors and barristers, both have the same rights under the Treaty and the Directives, and are equally recognised as lawyers for all purposes under EU instruments, including practice before the European Court of Justice and the Court of First Instance. The same applies to practice before the European Court of Human Rights.

10. Lawyers from other member states exercising the right to provide services or to establish themselves in England and Wales must choose whether to practise in the sector of the Bar or of the solicitors' branch of the profession.

10

Annex 10A

European Communities (Services of Lawyers) Order 1978

(S.I. 1978 no. 1910)

(with consolidated amendments to 1st February 1981)

[Law Society note:

This Order has not been updated since 1981 but should be taken as applying to lawyers from the European Union, the European Economic Area and Switzerland. Section 39 of the Solicitors Act 1974 is referred to in Part III of the Schedule but it has now been repealed.]

Whereas a draft of this Order has been laid before Parliament and has been approved by a resolution of each House of Parliament:

Now, therefore, Her Majesty, in exercise of the powers conferred on Her by section 2(2) of the European Communities Act 1972, is pleased, by and with the advice of Her Privy Council, to order, and it is hereby ordered, as follows:

Citation and commencement

1.   This Order may be cited as the European Communities (Services of Lawyers) Order 1978 and shall come into operation on 1st March 1979.

Interpretation

2.   In this Order, unless the context otherwise requires –

"advocate", "barrister" and "solicitor" mean, in relation to any part of the United Kingdom, a person practising in that part as an advocate, barrister or solicitor as the case may be;

"the Directive" means the European Communities Council Directive no. 77/249/EEC to facilitate the effective exercise by lawyers of freedom to provide services;

"EEC lawyer" means a person entitled to pursue his professional activities under the designation, in Belgium of an avocat-advocaat, in Denmark of an advokat, in Germany of a Rechtsanwalt, in France of an avocat, in the Hellenic Republic of a dikigoros, in the Republic of Ireland of a barrister or solicitor, in Italy of an avvocato, in Luxembourg of an avocat-avoué, or in the Netherlands of an advocaat;

"member State of origin", in relation to an EEC lawyer, means the member State or States in which he is established; and

"own professional authority", in relation to an EEC lawyer, means an authority entitled to exercise disciplinary authority over him in his member State of origin.

3.   (1)   The Interpretation Act 1978 shall apply to this Order as it applies to subordinate legislation made after the commencement of that Act.

(2)   Unless the context otherwise requires, any reference in this Order to a numbered article or to the Schedule is a reference to an article of, or the Schedule to, this Order.

Purpose of Order

4.   The provisions of this Order shall have effect for the purpose of enabling an EEC lawyer to pursue his professional activities in any part of the United Kingdom by providing, under the conditions specified in or permitted by the Directive, services otherwise reserved to advocates, barristers and solicitors; and services which may be so provided are hereafter in this Order referred to as services.

Representation in legal proceedings

5.   No enactment or rule of law or practice shall prevent an EEC lawyer from providing any service in relation to any proceedings, whether civil or criminal, before any court, tribunal or public authority (including appearing before and addressing the court, tribunal or public authority) by reason only that he is not an advocate, barrister or solicitor; provided that throughout he is instructed with, and acts in conjunction with, an advocate, barrister or solicitor who is entitled to practise before the court, tribunal or public authority concerned and who could properly provide the service in question.

6.   Nothing in this Order shall enable an EEC lawyer –

(a)   if he is established in practice as a barrister in the Republic of Ireland, to provide in the course of any proceedings any service which could not properly be provided by an advocate or barrister;

(b)   if he is instructed with and acts in conjunction with an advocate or barrister in any proceedings, to provide in the course of those proceedings, or of any related proceedings, any service which an advocate or barrister could not properly provide;

(c)   if he is instructed with and acts in conjunction with a solicitor in any proceedings, to provide in the course of those proceedings, or of any related proceedings, any service which a solicitor could not properly provide.

7.   An EEC lawyer in salaried employment who is instructed with and acts in conjunction with an advocate or barrister in any proceedings may provide a service on behalf of his employer in those proceedings only in so far as an advocate or barrister in such employment could properly do so.

10

Drawing of documents, etc., not related to legal proceedings

8.   No enactment or rule of law or practice shall prevent an EEC lawyer from drawing or preparing for remuneration:

    (i)   in England, Wales or Northern Ireland, an instrument relating to personal estate, or

    (ii)   in Scotland, a writ relating to moveable property,

    by reason only that he is not an advocate, barrister or solicitor.

9.   Nothing in this Order shall entitle an EEC lawyer to draw or prepare for remuneration any instrument, or in Scotland any writ:

    (i)   creating or transferring an interest in land; or

    (ii)   for obtaining title to administer the estate of a deceased person.

Legal aid

10.   Services may be provided by an EEC lawyer by way of legal advice and assistance or legal aid under the enactments specified in Part 1 of the Schedule; and references to counsel and solicitors in those and any other enactments relating to legal advice and assistance or legal aid shall be construed accordingly.

Title and description to be used by EEC lawyers

11.   In providing any services, an EEC lawyer shall use the professional title and description applicable to him in his member State of origin, expressed in the language or one of the languages of that State, together with the name of the professional organisation by which he is authorised to practise or the court of law before which he is entitled to practise in that State.

Power to require an EEC lawyer to verify his status

12.   A competent authority may at any time request a person seeking to provide any services to verify his status as an EEC lawyer.

13.   Where a request has been made under article 12, the person to whom it is made shall not, except to the extent (if any) allowed by the competent authority making the request, be entitled to provide services in the United Kingdom until he has verified his status as an EEC lawyer to the satisfaction of that authority.

14.   For the purposes of articles 12 and 13, a competent authority is –

    (a)   where the services which the person concerned seeks to provide are reserved to advocates or barristers, or in any case where the person concerned claims to be a barrister established in practice in the Republic of Ireland, the Senate of the Inns of Court and the Bar, the Faculty of Advocates, or the Benchers of the Inn of Court of Northern Ireland, according to the part of the United Kingdom concerned; or

(b) where subparagraph (a) does not apply, the Law Society, the Law Society of Scotland, or the Incorporated Law Society of Northern Ireland, according to the part of the United Kingdom concerned; or

(c) in any case, any court, tribunal or public authority before which the person concerned seeks to provide services.

Professional misconduct

15. (1) A complaint may be made to a disciplinary authority that an EEC lawyer providing any services has failed to observe a condition or rule of professional conduct referred to in article 4 of the Directive and applicable to him.

(2) Where a complaint is made under paragraph (1), the disciplinary authority concerned shall consider and adjudicate upon it in accordance with the same procedure, and subject to the same rights of appeal, as apply in relation to an advocate, barrister or solicitor (as the case may be) over whom that authority has jurisdiction.

(3) For the purposes of this article and article 16, a disciplinary authority is –

(a) where the services in question are reserved to advocates or barristers, or in any case where the person whose conduct is in question is established in practice as a barrister in the Republic of Ireland, an authority having disciplinary jurisdiction over advocates or barristers (as the case may be) in the part of the United Kingdom concerned;

(b) where subparagraph (a) does not apply, an authority having disciplinary jurisdiction over solicitors in the part of the United Kingdom concerned.

16. (1) Where a disciplinary authority finds that an EEC lawyer against whom a complaint has been made under article 15(1) has committed a breach of a condition or a rule of professional conduct mentioned in that article, that authority –

(a) shall report that finding to the EEC lawyer's own professional authority; and

(b) may, if it thinks fit, direct him not to provide services in the United Kingdom, except to such extent and under such conditions (if any) as the disciplinary authority may specify in the direction.

(2) A disciplinary authority may at any time, if it thinks fit, vary, cancel or suspend the operation of a direction given by it under paragraph (1)(b).

17. An EEC lawyer in respect of whom a direction is made under article 16(1)(b) shall not be entitled to provide services in the United Kingdom except as allowed by the direction.

Modification of enactments

18. (1) Without prejudice to the generality of articles 5 and 8, the enactments specified in Part 2 of the Schedule (being enactments which reserve the provision of certain services to advocates, barristers, solicitors and other qualified persons) shall be construed subject to those articles.

(2) Notwithstanding anything in the Solicitors (Scotland) Act 1933, the Solicitors Act 1974 or the Solicitors (Northern Ireland) Order 1976, references to unqualified persons, however expressed, in the enactments specified in Part 3 of the Schedule (being enactments relating to unqualified persons acting as solicitors) shall not include an EEC lawyer providing services within the meaning of this Order.

(3) Nothing in section 42 of the Solicitors (Scotland) Act 1933 shall prevent an EEC lawyer from recovering any remuneration or expenses to which that section applies by reason only that he is not qualified as a solicitor.

Schedule

Article 10

PART I

Enactments Relating to the Provision of Legal Advice and Assistance and Legal Aid

Legal Aid and Advice Act (Northern Ireland) 1965 (c.8).
Legal Aid (Scotland) Act 1967 (c.43).
Legal Advice and Assistance Act 1972 (c.50).
Legal Aid Act 1974 (c.4).
Legal Aid, Advice and Assistance (Northern Ireland) Order 1977 (S.I. No. 1252 (N.I.19)).

Article 18(1)

PART II

Enactments Reserving the Provision of Services to Advocates, Barristers, Solicitors, etc.

Solicitors (Scotland) Act 1933 (c.21), section 39.
Magistrates' Courts Act 1952 (c.55), section 99.
Magistrates' Courts Act (Northern Ireland) 1964 (c.21(N.I.)), section 165(1).
County Courts Act 1959 (c.22), section 89.
County Courts Act (Northern Ireland) 1959 (c.25(N.I.)), section 139.
Solicitors Act 1974 (c.47), sections 20, 22.
Solicitors (Northern Ireland) Order 1976 (S.I. No. 582 (N.I.12)), articles 19, 23.

Article 18(2)

PART III

Enactments Relating to Unqualified Persons Acting as Solicitors

Solicitors (Scotland) Act 1933 (c.21), sections 37, 38.
Solicitors Act 1974 (c.47), sections 25(1), 39(1).
Solicitors (Northern Ireland) Order 1976 (S.I. No. 582 (N.I. 12)), articles 25(1), 27.

Annex 10B

CCBE Code of Conduct for Lawyers in the European Community

with extracts from the Explanatory Memorandum and Commentary

[Law Society note:

This is the version of the CCBE Code which was adopted on 28th October 1988. At the time of going to press, this is still the version of the Code which is binding on solicitors. In 1998 the CCBE adopted a revised version of the Code but this has not yet been adopted by the Council of the Law Society for the purposes of the practice rules or the overseas practice rules.

An Explanatory Memorandum and Commentary, dated May 1989, was prepared by the CCBE's deontology working party, who were responsible for the drafting of the Code itself. It seeks to explain the origin of the provisions of the Code, to illustrate the problems which they are designed to resolve, particularly in relation to cross-border activities, and to provide assistance to the competent authorities in the member states in the application of the Code.

Law Society notes and relevant extracts from the Explanatory Memorandum and Commentary have been integrated into the text of the Code as set out below, the relevant note or commentary appearing after each article. The notes and commentaries are not part of the Code, and in order to distinguish them they appear in italics.

The original languages of the Code are French and English.]

1. Preamble

1.1 The function of the lawyer in society

In a society founded on respect for the rule of law the lawyer fulfils a special role. His duties do not begin and end with the faithful performance of what he is instructed to do so far as the law permits. A lawyer must serve the interests of justice as well as those whose rights and liberties he is trusted to assert and defend and it is his duty not only to plead his client's cause but to be his adviser.

A lawyer's function therefore lays on him a variety of legal and moral obligations (sometimes appearing to be in conflict with each other) towards:

- the client;

- the courts and other authorities before whom the lawyer pleads his client's cause or acts on his behalf;

- the legal profession in general and each fellow member of it in particular; and

- the public for whom the existence of a free and independent profession, bound together by respect for rules made by the profession itself, is an essential means of safeguarding human rights in the face of the power of the state and other interests in society.

1.2   The nature of rules of professional conduct

1.2.1   Rules of professional conduct are designed through their willing acceptance by those to whom they apply to ensure the proper performance by the lawyer of a function which is recognised as essential in all civilised societies. The failure of the lawyer to observe these rules must in the last resort result in a disciplinary sanction.

1.2.2   The particular rules of each bar or law society arise from its own traditions. They are adapted to the organisation and sphere of activity of the profession in the member state concerned and to its judicial and administrative procedures and to its national legislation. It is neither possible nor desirable that they should be taken out of their context nor that an attempt should be made to give general application to rules which are inherently incapable of such application.

The particular rules of each bar and law society nevertheless are based on the same values and in most cases demonstrate a common foundation.

1.3   The purpose of the code

1.3.1   The continued integration of the European Community and the increasing frequency of the cross-border activities of lawyers within the Community have made necessary in the public interest the statement of common rules which apply to all lawyers from the Community whatever bar or law society they belong to in relation to their cross-border practice. A particular purpose of the statement of those rules is to mitigate the difficulties which result from the application of 'double deontology' as set out in Art 4 of EC Dir 77/249 of 22 March 1977.

1.3.2   The organisations representing the legal profession through the CCBE propose that the rules codified in the following articles:

- be recognised at the present time as the expression of the consensus of all the bars and law societies of the EC;

- be adopted as enforceable rules as soon as possible in accordance with national or Community procedures in relation to the cross-border activities of the lawyer in the EC; and

- be taken into account in all revisions of national rules of deontology or professional practice with a view to their progressive harmonisation.

They further express the wish that the national rules of deontology or professional practice be interpreted and applied whenever possible in a way consistent with the rules in this code.

After the rules in this code have been adopted as enforceable rules in relation to his cross-border activities the lawyer will remain bound to observe the rules of the bar or law society to which he belongs to the extent that they are consistent with the rules in this code.

1.4   Field of application *ratione personae*

The following rules shall apply to lawyers of the EC as they are defined by Dir 77/249.

[Law Society note:

The members of the EC (now the EU) are Austria, Belgium, Denmark, Finland, France, Germany, Greece, Ireland, Italy, Luxembourg, the Netherlands, Portugal, Spain, Sweden and the United Kingdom.

The Lawyer's Services Directive 77/249/EEC has been extended to Iceland, Liechtenstein and Norway (members of the European Economic Area) plus Switzerland.

All the above countries apart from Switzerland have full membership of the CCBE. The following legal professions are represented on the CCBE:

Austria – Rechtsanwalt;
Belgium – avocat/advocaat/Rechtsanwalt;
Denmark – advokat;
Finland – asianajaja/advokat;
France – avocat;
Germany – Rechtsanwalt;
Greece – dikigoros;
Iceland – logmadur;
Ireland – barrister, solicitor;
Italy – avvocato, procuratore;

Liechtenstein – Rechtsanwalt;
Luxembourg – avocat;
Netherlands – advocaat;
Norway – advokat;
Portugal – advogado;
Spain – abogado/advocat/ avogado/abokatu;
Sweden – advokat;
United Kingdom – advocate, barrister, solicitor.

The legal professions of the following countries have CCBE observer status and are required to comply with the Code: Cyprus, the Czech Republic, Hungary, Poland, the Slovak Republic, Slovenia, Switzerland and Turkey.]

1.5   Field of application *ratione materiae*

Without prejudice to the pursuit of a progressive harmonisation of rules of deontology or professional practice which apply only internally within a member state, the following rules shall apply to the cross-border activities of the lawyer within the EC. Cross-border activities shall mean:

–   all professional contacts with lawyers of member states other than his own; and

–   the professional activities of the lawyer in a member state other than his own, whether or not the lawyer is physically present in that member state.

Commentary

The rules are here given direct application only to 'cross-border activities', as defined of lawyers within the EC [...........]. The definition of cross-border activities would, for example, include contacts in state A even on a matter of law internal to state A between a lawyer of state A and a lawyer of state B; it would exclude contacts between lawyers of state A in state A on a matter arising in state B, provided that none of their professional activities takes place in state B; it would include any activities of lawyers of state A in state B, even if only in the form of communications sent from state A to state B.

1.6   Definitions

In these rules:

'home member state' means the member state of the bar or law society to which the lawyer belongs;

'host member state' means any other member state where the lawyer carries on cross-border activities; and

'competent authority' means the professional organisation(s) or authority(ies) of the member states concerned responsible for the laying down of rules of professional conduct and the administration of discipline of lawyers.

Commentary

The references to 'member state' include, where appropriate, separate jurisdictions within a single member state. The reference to 'the bar or law society to which the lawyer belongs' includes the bar or law society responsible for exercising authority over the lawyer. The reference to 'where the lawyer carries on cross-border activities' should be interpreted in the light of the definition of 'cross-border activities' in Art 1.5.

2.   General principles

2.1   Independence

2.1.1   The many duties to which a lawyer is subject require his absolute independence, free from all other influence, especially such as may arise from his personal interests or external pressure. Such independence is as necessary to trust in the process of justice as the impartiality of the judge. A lawyer must therefore avoid any impairment of his independence and be careful not to compromise his professional standards in order to please his client, the court or third parties.

2.1.2   This independence is necessary in non-contentious matters as well as in litigation. Advice given by a lawyer to his client has no value if it is given only to ingratiate himself, to serve his personal interests or in response to outside pressure.

2.2   Trust and personal integrity

Relationships of trust can only exist if a lawyer's personal honour, honesty and integrity are beyond doubt. For the lawyer these traditional virtues are professional obligations.

2.3   Confidentiality

2.3.1   It is of the essence of a lawyer's function that he should be told by his client things which the client would not tell to others, and that he should be the recipient of other information on a basis of confidence. Without the certainty of confidentiality there cannot be trust. Confidentiality is therefore a primary and fundamental right and duty of the lawyer.

2.3.2   A lawyer shall accordingly respect the confidentiality of all information given to him by his client, or received by him about his client or others in the course of rendering services to his client.

2.3.3   The obligation of confidentiality is not limited in time.

2.3.4   A lawyer shall require his associates and staff and anyone engaged by him in the course of providing professional services to observe the same obligation of confidentiality.

Commentary

This provision first restates, in Art 2.3.1, general principles laid down in the Declaration of Perugia and recognised by the ECJ in Australian Mining and Smelting Europe v. EC Commission *(155/79) 2 CMLR 264. It then, in Arts 2.3.2 to 4, develops them into a specific rule relating to the protection of confidentiality. Art 2.3.2 contains the basic rule requiring respect for confidentiality. Art 2.3.3 confirms that the obligation remains binding on the lawyer even if he ceases to act for the client in question. Art 2.3.4 confirms that the lawyer must not only respect the obligation of confidentiality himself but must require all members and employees of his firm to do likewise.*

2.4   Respect for the rules of other bars and law societies

Under Community law (in particular under Dir 77/249 of 22 March 1977) a lawyer from another member state may be bound to comply with the rules of the bar or law society of the host member state. Lawyers have a duty to inform themselves as to the rules which will affect them in the performance of any particular activity.

Commentary

Art 4 of the Lawyers' Services Directive of 1977 contains the provisions with regard to the rules to be observed by a lawyer from one member state providing services by virtue of Art 59 of the treaty in another member state as follows:

(a)   activities relating to the representation of a client in legal proceedings or before public authorities shall be pursued in each host member state under the conditions laid down for lawyers established in that state, with the exception of any conditions requiring residence, or registration with a professional organisation, in that state;

(b)   a lawyer pursuing these activities shall observe the rules of professional conduct of the host member state, without prejudice to his obligations in the member state from which he comes;

(c)   when these activities are pursued in the UK, 'rules of professional conduct of the host member state' means the rules of professional conduct applicable to solicitors, where such activities are not reserved for barristers and advocates. Otherwise the rules of professional conduct applicable to the latter shall apply. However, barristers from Ireland shall always be subject to the rules of professional conduct applicable in the UK to barristers and advocates. When these

10

activities are pursued in Ireland 'rules of professional conduct of the host member state' means, in so far as they govern the oral presentation of a case in court, the rules of professional conduct applicable to barristers. In all other cases the rules of professional conduct applicable to solicitors shall apply. However, barristers and advocates from the UK shall always be subject to the rules of professional conduct applicable in Ireland to barristers; and

(d) a lawyer pursuing activities other than those referred to in paragraph (a) shall remain subject to the conditions and rules of professional conduct of the member state from which he comes without prejudice to respect for the rules, whatever their source, which govern the profession in the host member state, especially those concerning the incompatibility of the exercise of the activities of a lawyer with the exercise of other activities in that state, professional secrecy, relations with other lawyers, the prohibition on the same lawyer acting for parties with mutually conflicting interests, and publicity. The latter rules are applicable only if they are capable of being observed by a lawyer who is not established in the host member state and to the extent to which their observance is objectively justified to ensure, in that state, the proper exercise of a lawyer's activities, the standing of the profession and respect for the rules concerning incompatibility.

In cases not covered by this Directive, the obligations of a lawyer under Community law to observe the rules of other bars and law societies are a matter of interpretation of the applicable provisions of the treaty or any other relevant Directive. A major purpose of the code is to minimise, and if possible eliminate altogether, the problems which may arise from 'double deontology', that is the application of more than one set of potentially conflicting national rules to a particular situation (see Art 1.3.1).

2.5   Incompatible occupations

2.5.1   In order to perform his functions with due independence and in a manner which is consistent with his duty to participate in the administration of justice a lawyer is excluded from some occupations.

2.5.2   A lawyer who acts in the representation or the defence of a client in legal proceedings or before any public authorities in a host member state shall there observe the rules regarding incompatible occupations as they are applied to lawyers of the host member state.

2.5.3   A lawyer established in a host member state in which he wishes to participate directly in commercial or other activities not connected with the practice of the law shall respect the rules regarding forbidden or incompatible occupations as they are applied to lawyers of that member state.

Commentary

There are differences both between and within member states on the extent to which lawyers are permitted to engage in other occupations, for example in commercial activities. The general purpose of rules excluding a lawyer from other occupations is to protect him from influences which might impair his independence or his role in the administration of justice. The variations in these rules reflect different local conditions, different perceptions of the proper function of lawyers and different techniques of rule-making. For instance in some cases there is a complete prohibition of engagement in certain named occupations, whereas in other cases engagement in other occupations is generally permitted, subject to observance of specific safeguards for the lawyer's independence.

Arts 2.5.2 and 3 make provision for different circumstances in which a lawyer of one member state is engaging in cross-border activities (as defined in Art 1.5) in a host member state when he is not a member of the host state legal profession.

Art 2.5.2 imposes full observation of host state rules regarding incompatible occupations on the lawyer acting in national legal proceedings or before national public authorities in the host state. This applies whether the lawyer is established in the host state or not.

Art 2.5.3, on the other hand, imposes 'respect' for the rules of the host state regarding forbidden or incompatible occupations in other cases, but only where the lawyer who is established in the host member state wishes to participate directly in commercial or other activities not connected with the practice of the law.

2.6 Personal publicity

2.6.1 A lawyer should not advertise or seek personal publicity where this is not permitted.

In other cases a lawyer should only advertise or seek personal publicity to the extent and in the manner permitted by the rules to which he is subject.

2.6.2 Advertising and personal publicity shall be regarded as taking place where it is permitted, if the lawyer concerned shows that it was placed for the purpose of reaching clients or potential clients located where such advertising or personal publicity is permitted and its communication elsewhere is incidental.

Commentary

The term 'personal publicity' covers publicity by firms of lawyers, as well as individual lawyers, as opposed to corporate publicity organised by bars and law societies for their members as a whole. The rules governing personal publicity by lawyers vary considerably in the member states. In some there is a complete prohibition of personal publicity by lawyers; in others this prohibition has been (or is in the process of being) relaxed substantially. Art 2.6 does not therefore attempt to lay down a general standard on personal publicity.

Art 2.6.1 requires a lawyer not to advertise or seek personal publicity in a territory where this is not permitted to local lawyers. Otherwise he is required to observe the rules on publicity laid down by his own bar or law society.

Art 2.6.2 contains provisions clarifying the question of the place in which advertising and personal publicity is deemed to take place. For example, a lawyer who is permitted to advertise in his home member state may place an advertisement in a newspaper published there which circulates primarily in that member state, even though some issues may circulate in other member states where lawyers are not permitted to advertise. He may not, however, place an advertisement in a newspaper whose circulation is directed wholly or mainly at a territory where lawyers are not permitted to advertise in that way.

10

2.7   The client's interests

Subject to due observance of all rules of law and professional conduct, a lawyer must always act in the best interests of his client and must put those interests before his own interests or those of fellow members of the legal profession.

3.   Relations with clients

3.1   Instructions

3.1.1   A lawyer shall not handle a case for a party except on his instructions. He may, however, act in a case in which he has been instructed by another lawyer who himself acts for the party or where the case has been assigned to him by a competent body.

3.1.2   A lawyer shall advise and represent his client promptly, conscientiously and diligently. He shall undertake personal responsibility for the discharge of the instructions given to him. He shall keep his client informed as to the progress of the matter entrusted to him.

3.1.3   A lawyer shall not handle a matter which he knows or ought to know he is not competent to handle, without co-operating with a lawyer who is competent to handle it.

A lawyer shall not accept instructions unless he can discharge those instructions promptly having regard to the pressure of other work.

3.1.4   A lawyer shall not be entitled to exercise his right to withdraw from a case in such a way or in such circumstances that the client may be unable to find other legal assistance in time to prevent prejudice being suffered by the client.

Commentary

The provisions of Art 3.1.1 are designed to ensure that a relationship is maintained between lawyer and client and that the lawyer in fact receives instructions from the client, even though these may be transmitted through a duly authorised intermediary. It is the responsibility of the lawyer to satisfy himself as to the authority of the intermediary and the wishes of the client.

Art 3.1.2 deals with the manner in which the lawyer should carry out his duties. The provision that he shall undertake personal responsibility for the discharge of the instructions given to him means that he cannot avoid responsibility by delegation to others. It does not prevent him from seeking to limit his legal liability to the extent that this is permitted by the relevant law or professional rules.

Art 3.1.3 states a principle which is of particular relevance in cross-border activities, for example when a lawyer is asked to handle a matter on behalf of a lawyer or client from another state who may be unfamiliar with the relevant law and practice, or when a lawyer is asked to handle a matter relating to the law of another state with which he is unfamiliar.

A lawyer generally has the right to refuse to accept instructions in the first place, but Art 3.1.4 states that, having once accepted them, he has an obligation not to withdraw without ensuring that the client's interests are safeguarded.

3.2 Conflict of interests

3.2.1　A lawyer may not advise, represent or act on behalf of two or more clients in the same matter if there is a conflict, or a significant risk of a conflict, between the interests of those clients.

3.2.2　A lawyer must cease to act for both clients when a conflict of interests arises between those clients and also whenever there is a risk of a breach of confidence or where his independence may be impaired.

3.2.3　A lawyer must also refrain from acting for a new client if there is a risk of a breach of confidences entrusted to the lawyer by a former client or if the knowledge which the lawyer possesses of the affairs of the former client would give an undue advantage to the new client.

3.2.4　Where lawyers are practising in association, paragraphs 3.2.1 to 3.2.3 above shall apply to the association and all its members.

Commentary

The provisions of Art 3.2.1 do not prevent a lawyer acting for two or more clients in the same matter provided that their interests are not in fact in conflict and that there is no significant risk of such a conflict arising. Where a lawyer is already acting for two or more clients in this way and subsequently there arises a conflict of interests between those clients or a risk of a breach of confidence or other circumstances where his independence may be impaired, then the lawyer must cease to act for both or all of them.

There may, however, be circumstances in which differences arise between two or more clients for whom the same lawyer is acting where it may be appropriate for him to attempt to act as a mediator. It is for the lawyer in such cases to use his own judgment on whether or not there is such a conflict of interest between them as to require him to cease to act. If not, he may consider whether it would be appropriate for him to explain the position to the clients, obtain their agreement and attempt to act as mediator to resolve the difference between them, and only if this attempt to mediate should fail, to cease to act for them.

Art 3.2.4 applies the foregoing provisions of Art 3 to lawyers practising in association. For example a firm of lawyers should cease to act when there is a conflict of interest between two clients of the firm, even if different lawyers in the firm are acting for each client. On the other hand, exceptionally, in the 'chambers' form of association used by English barristers, where each lawyer acts for clients individually, it is possible for different lawyers in the association to act for clients with opposing interests.

3.3 *Pactum de quota litis*

3.3.1　A lawyer shall not be entitled to make a *pactum de quota litis*.

3.3.2　By *pactum de quota litis* is meant an agreement between a lawyer and his client entered into prior to the final conclusion of a matter to which the client is a party, by virtue of which the client undertakes to pay the lawyer a share of the result regardless of whether this is represented by a sum of money or by any other benefit achieved by the client upon the conclusion of the matter.

3.3.3   The *pactum de quota litis* does not include an agreement that fees be charged in proportion to the value of a matter handled by the lawyer if this is in accordance with an officially approved fee-scale or under the control of the competent authority having jurisdiction over the lawyer.

Commentary

These provisions reflect the common position in all member states that an unregulated agreement for contingency fees (pactum de quota litis) *is contrary to the proper administration of justice because it encourages speculative litigation and is liable to be abused. The provisions are not, however, intended to prevent the maintenance or introduction of arrangements under which lawyers are paid according to results or only if the action or matter is successful, provided that these arrangements are under sufficient regulation and control for the protection of the client and the proper administration of justice.*

3.4   Regulation of fees

3.4.1   A fee charged by a lawyer shall be fully disclosed to his client and shall be fair and reasonable.

3.4.2   Subject to any proper agreement to the contrary between a lawyer and his client, fees charged by a lawyer shall be subject to regulation in accordance with the rules applied to members of the bar or law society to which he belongs. If he belongs to more than one bar or law society the rules applied shall be those with the closest connection to the contract between the lawyer and his client.

Commentary

Art 3.4.1 lays down a general standard of disclosure of a lawyer's fees to the client and a requirement that they should be fair and reasonable in amount. Art 3.4.2 deals with the question of the machinery for regulating the lawyers' fees. In many member states such machinery exists under national law or rules of conduct, whether by reference to a power of adjudication by the 'Batonnier' or otherwise. Art 3.4.1 applies the rules of the bar or law society to which the lawyer belongs (see Art 1.6) unless this has been varied by an agreement between lawyer and client which is in accordance with the relevant law or rules of conduct. It goes on to provide a 'choice of law' rule to deal with cases when the lawyer belongs to more than one bar or law society.

3.5   Payment on account

If a lawyer requires a payment on account of his fees and/or disbursements such payment should not exceed a reasonable estimate of the fees and probable disbursements involved.

Failing such payment, a lawyer may withdraw from the case or refuse to handle it, but subject always to para 3.1.4 above.

3.6   Fee-sharing with non-lawyers

3.6.1   Subject as after-mentioned a lawyer may not share his fees with a person who is not a lawyer.

3.6.2   This shall not preclude a lawyer from paying a fee, commission or other compensation to a deceased lawyer's heirs or to a retired lawyer in respect of taking over the deceased or retired lawyer's practice.

Commentary

In some member states lawyers are permitted to practise in association with members of certain other approved professions, whether legal professions or not. The provisions of Art 3.6.1 are not designed to prevent fee-sharing within such an approved form of association. Nor are the provisions designed to prevent fee-sharing by the lawyers to whom the code applies (see Art 1.4 above) with other 'lawyers', for example lawyers from non-member states or members of other legal professions in the member states such as notaries [...].

3.7   Legal aid

A lawyer shall inform his client of the availability of legal aid where applicable.

Commentary

There are widely differing provisions in the member states on the availability of legal aid. In cross-border activities a lawyer should have in mind the possibility that the legal aid provisions of a national law with which he is unfamiliar may be applicable.

3.8   Clients' funds

3.8.1   When lawyers at any time in the course of their practice come into possession of funds on behalf of their clients or third parties (hereinafter called 'clients' funds') it shall be obligatory:

3.8.1.1 that clients' funds shall always be held in an account in a bank or similar institution subject to supervision of public authority and that all clients' funds received by a lawyer should be paid into such an account unless the client explicitly or by implication agrees that the funds should be dealt with otherwise;

3.8.1.2 that any account in which the clients' funds are held in the name of the lawyer should indicate in the title or designation that the funds are held on behalf of the client or clients of the lawyer;

3.8.1.3 that any account or accounts in which clients' funds are held in the name of the lawyer should at all times contain a sum which is not less than the total of the clients' funds held by the lawyer;

3.8.1.4 that all clients' funds should be available for payment to clients on demand or upon such conditions as the clients may authorise;

3.8.1.5 that payments made from clients' funds on behalf of a client to any other person including payments made to or for one client from funds held for another client and payment of the lawyer's fees, are prohibited except to the extent that they are permitted by law or have the express or implied authority of the client for whom the payment is being made;

10

3.8.1.6 that the lawyer shall maintain full and accurate records, available to each client on request, showing all his dealings with his clients' funds and distinguishing clients' funds from other funds held by him; and

3.8.1.7 that the competent authorities in all member states should have powers to allow them to examine and investigate on a confidential basis the financial records of lawyers' clients' funds to ascertain whether or not the rules which they make are being complied with and to impose sanctions upon lawyers who fail to comply with those rules.

3.8.2 Subject as aforementioned, and without prejudice to the rules set out above, a lawyer who holds clients' funds in the course of carrying on practice in any member state must comply with the rules relating to holding and accounting for clients' funds which are applied by the competent authorities of the home member state.

3.8.3 A lawyer who carries on practice or provides services in a host member state may with the agreement of the competent authorities of the home and host member states concerned comply with the requirements of the host member state to the exclusion of the requirements of the home member state. In that event he shall take reasonable steps to inform his clients that he complies with the requirements in force in the host member state.

Commentary

The provisions of Art 3.8.1 reflect the recommendation adopted by the CCBE in Brussels in November 1985 on the need for minimum regulations to be made and enforced governing the proper control and disposal of clients' funds held by lawyers within the Community. [............................] Art 3.8.1 lays down minimum standards to be observed, while not interfering with the details of national systems which provide fuller or more stringent protection for clients' funds.

The provisions of Arts 3.8.2 and 3.8.3 deal with questions which arise where the rules on clients' funds of more than one member state may be applicable.

3.9   Professional indemnity insurance

3.9.1 Lawyers shall be insured at all times against claims based on professional negligence to an extent which is reasonable having regard to the nature and extent of the risks which lawyers incur in practice.

3.9.2.1 Subject as aftermentioned, a lawyer who provides services or carries on practice in a member state must comply with any rules relating to his obligation to insure against his professional liability as a lawyer which are in force in his home member state.

3.9.2.2 A lawyer who is obliged so to insure in his home member state and who provides services or carries on practice in any host member state shall use his best endeavours to obtain insurance cover on the basis required in his home member state extended to services which he provides or practice which he carries on in a host member state.

3.9.2.3 A lawyer who fails to obtain the extended insurance cover referred to in para 3.9.2.2 above or who is not obliged so to insure in his home member state and who provides services or carries on practice in a host member state shall in so far as possible obtain insurance cover against his professional liability as a lawyer whilst acting for clients in that host member state on at least an equivalent basis to that required of lawyers in the host member state.

3.9.2.4 To the extent that a lawyer is unable to obtain the insurance cover required by the foregoing rules, he shall take reasonable steps to draw that fact to the attention of such of his clients as might be affected in the event of a claim against him.

3.9.2.5 A lawyer who carries on practice or provides services in a host member state may with the agreement of the competent authorities of the home and host member states concerned comply with such insurance requirements as are in force in the host member state to the exclusion of the insurance requirements of the home member state. In this event he shall take reasonable steps to inform his clients that he is insured according to the requirements in force in the host member state.

Commentary

Art 3.9.1 reflects a recommendation, also adopted by the CCBE in Brussels in November 1985, on the need for all lawyers in the Community to be insured against the risks arising from professional negligence claims against them.

[...] Art 3.9.2 deals with questions which arise when the risks to be insured relate to more than one member state.

4.   Relations with the courts

4.1   Applicable rules of conduct in court

A lawyer who appears or takes part in a case before a court or tribunal in a member state must comply with the rules of conduct applied before that court or tribunal.

4.2   Fair conduct of proceedings

A lawyer must always have due regard for the fair conduct of proceedings. He must not, for example, make contact with the judge without first informing the lawyer acting for the opposing party or submit exhibits, notes or documents to the judge without communicating them in good time to the lawyer on the other side unless such steps are permitted under the relevant rules of procedure.

Commentary

This provision applies the general principle that in adversarial proceedings a lawyer must not attempt to take unfair advantage of his opponent, in particular by unilateral communications with the judge. An exception however is made for any steps permitted under the relevant rules of the court in question (see also 4.5).

4.3   Demeanour in court

A lawyer shall while maintaining due respect and courtesy towards the court defend the interests of his client honourably and in a way which he considers will be to the client's best advantage within the limits of the law.

4.4   False or misleading information

A lawyer shall never knowingly give false or misleading information to the court.

10

4.5   Extension to arbitrators, etc.

The rules governing a lawyer's relations with the courts apply also to his relations with arbitrators and any other persons exercising judicial or quasi-judicial functions, even on an occasional basis.

5.   Relations between lawyers

5.1   Corporate spirit of the profession

5.1.1   The corporate spirit of the profession requires a relationship of trust and co-operation between lawyers for the benefit of their clients and in order to avoid unnecessary litigation. It can never justify setting the interests of the profession against those of justice or of those who seek it.

5.1.2   A lawyer should recognise all other lawyers of member states as professional colleagues and act fairly and courteously towards them.

5.2   Co-operation among lawyers of different states

5.2.1   It is the duty of a lawyer who is approached by a colleague from another member state not to accept instructions in a matter which he is not competent to undertake. He should be prepared to help his colleague to obtain the information necessary to enable him to instruct a lawyer who is capable of providing the service asked for.

5.2.2   Where a lawyer of a member state co-operates with a lawyer from another member state, both have a general duty to take into account the differences which may exist between their respective legal systems and the professional organisations, competences and obligations of lawyers in the member states concerned.

5.3   Correspondence between lawyers

5.3.1   If a lawyer sending a communication to a lawyer in another member state wishes it to remain confidential or without prejudice he should clearly express this intention when communicating the document.

5.3.2   If the recipient of the communication is unable to ensure its status as confidential or without prejudice he should return it to the sender without revealing the contents to others.

Commentary

In certain member states communications between lawyers (written or by word of mouth) are normally regarded as confidential. This means that lawyers accept that those communications may not be disclosed to others and copies may not be sent to the lawyers' own client. This principle is recognised in Belgium, France, Greece, Italy, Luxembourg, Portugal and Spain. Such communications if in writing are often marked as 'confidentiel' *or* 'sous la foi du Palais'.

In the UK and Ireland the notion of 'confidentiality' is different in that it refers not to such communications between lawyers but to the lawyer's right and duty to keep his client's affairs confidential. However communications between lawyers made in order to attempt to settle a dispute are normally not regarded by a court as admissible evidence and the lawyer should not attempt to use them as evidence. If a lawyer wishes to indicate that he regards a document as such a communication he should indicate that it is sent 'without prejudice'. This means that the letter is sent without prejudice to and under reservation of the client's rights in the dispute.

In Denmark as a general rule, a lawyer has a right and duty to keep his client informed about all important correspondence from a lawyer acting for an opposing party, in practice normally by sending photocopies. This rule applies whether or not the letter is marked 'without prejudice' or 'confidential'. As an exception, lawyers may exchange views – normally by word of mouth only – on a case with a view to finding an amicable settlement, on the mutual understanding that such communications should be kept confidential and not disclosed to the clients. A lawyer is not legally bound by such a confidence, but to break it would prejudice his future participation in such confidential exchanges. Some lawyers do not wish to receive such communication in any form without having the right to inform their clients; in that event they should inform the other lawyer before he makes such a confidential communication to them. As a general rule also, all correspondence between lawyers may be freely produced in court. Normally, however, if such correspondence is marked 'without prejudice' or, even if not so marked, it is clearly of a 'without prejudice' nature, the court will disregard it and the lawyer producing it will be treated as being in contravention of the rules of professional conduct.

In the Netherlands legal recourse based on communications between lawyers may not be sought, unless the interest of the client requires it and only after prior consultation with the lawyer for the other party. If such consultation does not lead to a solution, the advice of the dean should be sought before recourse to law. The content of settlement negotiations between lawyers may not be communicated to the court without the permission of the lawyer for the other party, unless the right to do so was expressly reserved when the settlement proposal in question was made. There is however no general rule preventing a lawyer from sending copies of such communications to his client.

In Germany communications between lawyers are not confidential. The lawyer has an obligation to communicate them to his client and they may be admitted as evidence in court.

These differences often give rise to misunderstandings between lawyers of different member states who correspond with each other. For this reason lawyers should be particularly careful to clarify the basis upon which correspondence with lawyers in other member states is sent and received. In particular a lawyer who wishes to make a confidential or 'without prejudice' communication to a colleague in a member state where the rules may be different should ask in advance whether it can be accepted as such.

5.4 Referral fees

5.4.1 A lawyer may not demand or accept from another lawyer or any other person a fee, commission or any other compensation for referring or recommending a client.

5.4.2 A lawyer may not pay anyone a fee, commission or any other compensation as a consideration for referring a client to himself.

Commentary

This provision reflects the principle that a lawyer should not pay or receive payment purely for the reference of a client, which would risk impairing the client's free choice of lawyer or his interest in being referred to the best available service. It does not prevent fee-sharing arrangements between lawyers on a proper basis (see also Art 3.6 above).

In some member states lawyers are permitted to accept and retain commissions in certain cases provided the client's best interests are served, there is full disclosure to him and he has consented to the retention of the commission. In such cases the retention of the commission by the lawyer represents part of his remuneration for the service provided to the client and is not within the scope of the prohibition on referral fees which is designed to prevent lawyers making a secret profit.

5.5　Communication with opposing parties

A lawyer shall not communicate about a particular case or matter directly with any person whom he knows to be represented or advised in the case or matter by another lawyer, without the consent of that other lawyer (and shall keep the other lawyer informed of any such communications).

5.6　Change of lawyer

5.6.1　A lawyer who is instructed to represent a client in substitution for another lawyer in relation to a particular matter should inform that other lawyer and, subject to 5.6.2 below, should not begin to act until he has ascertained that arrangements have been made for the settlement of the other lawyer's fees and disbursements. This duty does not, however, make the new lawyer personally responsible for the former lawyer's fees and disbursements.

5.6.2　If urgent steps have to be taken in the interest of the client before the conditions in 5.6.1 above can be complied with, the lawyer may take such steps provided he informs the other lawyer immediately.

5.7　Responsibility for fees

In professional relations between members of bars of different member states, where a lawyer does not confine himself to recommending another lawyer or introducing him to the client but himself entrusts a correspondent with a particular matter or seeks his advice, he is personally bound, even if the client is insolvent, to pay the fees, costs and outlays which are due to the foreign correspondent. The lawyers concerned may, however, at the outset of the relationship between them make special arrangements on this matter. Further, the instructing lawyer may at any time limit his personal responsibility to the amount of the fees, costs and outlays incurred before intimation to the foreign lawyer of his disclaimer of responsibility for the future.

Commentary

Since misunderstandings about responsibility for unpaid fees are a common cause of difference between lawyers of different member states, it is important that a lawyer who wishes to exclude or limit his personal obligation to be responsible for the fees of his foreign colleague should reach a clear agreement on this at the outset of the transaction.

5.8   Training young lawyers

In order to improve trust and co-operation amongst lawyers of different member states for the clients' benefit there is a need to encourage a better knowledge of the laws and procedures in different member states. Therefore when considering the need for the profession to give good training to young lawyers, lawyers should take into account the need to give training to young lawyers from other member states.

5.9   Disputes among lawyers in different member states

5.9.1   If a lawyer considers that a colleague in another member state has acted in breach of a rule of professional conduct he shall draw the matter to the attention of his colleague.

5.9.2   If any personal dispute of a professional nature arises amongst lawyers in different member states they should if possible first try to settle it in a friendly way.

5.9.3   A lawyer shall not commence any form of proceedings against a colleague in another member state on matters referred to in 5.9.1 or 5.9.2 above without first informing the bars or law societies to which they both belong for the purpose of allowing both bars or law societies concerned an opportunity to assist in reaching a settlement.

Reproduced with the kind permission of the CCBE

10

PART III – RELATIONSHIP WITH THE CLIENT

Chapter 11

Obtaining instructions

11.01   Solicitor's independence and client's freedom of choice

It is fundamental to the relationship which exists between solicitor and client that a solicitor should be able to give impartial and frank advice to the client, free from any external or adverse pressures or interests which would destroy or weaken the solicitor's professional independence, the fiduciary relationship with the client or the client's freedom of choice.

1. A solicitor who suspects that a potential client has been improperly influenced in the choice of solicitor must satisfy himself or herself that the client's freedom of choice has not been restricted. Improper influence can come from the solicitor or from a third party.

2. A solicitor must not allow clients to override the solicitor's professional judgement, for example by insisting on the solicitor acting in a way which

is contrary to law or to a rule or principle of professional conduct (see **12.01**, p.244).

3. Gifts to potential clients, particularly those who are accused of criminal offences, or to people connected with them, in order to persuade them to become or remain the solicitor's clients, may amount to a breach of rule 1 of the Solicitors' Practice Rules 1990 (see **1.01**, p.1). Such gifts could compromise or impair the independence and integrity of the solicitor and the good repute of the solicitor and the solicitors' profession. The Criminal Law Committee strongly advise solicitors that neither they nor their representatives should directly or indirectly make a gift to a person who is accused of a criminal offence except by way of refreshments or cigarettes for the client's immediate consumption in the solicitor's presence.

11.02   Practice rule 2 (publicity)

'Solicitors may at their discretion publicise their practices or permit other persons to do so or publicise the businesses or activities of other persons, provided there is no breach of these rules and provided there is compliance with a Solicitors' Publicity Code promulgated from time to time by the Council of the Law Society with the concurrence of the Master of the Rolls.'

Solicitors' Practice Rules 1990, rule 2

11.03   Publicity – additional guidance

1. For the Solicitors' Publicity Code 1990 see Annex 11A, p.229. The code contains a number of restrictions.

2. Solicitors' publicity should comply with the Business Names Act 1985 and the Consumer Credit Act 1974 (see paragraph 1(d) of the code). Guidance on advertisements for mortgages is at **25.09** note 9, p.475. Solicitors will also need to take note of the British Codes of Advertising and Sales Promotion in relation to their publicity.

3. The Solicitors' Investment Business Rules 1995 apply to investment advertisements, both those approved by a solicitor and those issued by a solicitor. See rules 11 and 22 (Annex 27B at pp.574 and 580).

4. Solicitors may claim to be specialists or experts in a particular field, provided that they can justify such a claim (see paragraph 2(b) of the publicity code at p.230). The claim may be justified by the experience, competence and level of knowledge of the solicitor, membership of a Law Society panel or any additional qualifications held. The amount of time spent on a particular type of work will be relevant, but rarely the only consideration, as time does not necessarily indicate additional expertise. Where a firm as a whole claims a specialism, the number of individual specialists within the firm able to provide such a service will be relevant.

11

5.   Unsolicited mailshots may be sent and can be targeted. However, there are restrictions on unsolicited telephone calls and visits (see paragraph 3 of the publicity code at p.230).

6.   Publicity as to charges must be clearly expressed (see paragraph 5 of the publicity code at p.231). In particular, publicity including conveyancing charges may be misleading unless the charge is all inclusive (see paragraph 5(f) of the code). Care should be taken where an advertisement offers a discount as it could be open to criticism if there are no clear scales of charge included.

7.   A multi-national practice must comply with additional provisions in the code about the information that must be displayed on the firm's notepaper (see paragraph 7(b) of the code at p.233).

8.   Solicitors may name members of their staff on notepaper subject to the provisions of paragraph 7 of the publicity code at p.233. (See also **3.05**, p.70.)

9.   Oral and written representations about existing or former clients at a 'beauty parade' for prospective clients fall outside the definition of 'advertisement' for the purposes of paragraphs 4 (naming clients) and 16(ii) (interpretation) of the publicity code (at pp.231 and 237). What can be said is governed by the normal duty of confidentiality owed to existing or former clients, who must therefore consent to any disclosure which is not a matter of public knowledge. Both details of the clients' transactions and the fact that the firm acted for a client in a matter are subject to the duty of confidentiality (see also Chapter 16, p.323).

11.04   Practice rule 3 (introductions and referrals)

'Solicitors may accept introductions and referrals of business from other persons and may make introductions and refer business to other persons, provided there is no breach of these rules and provided there is compliance with a Solicitors' Introduction and Referral Code promulgated from time to time by the Council of the Law Society with the concurrence of the Master of the Rolls.'

Solicitors' Practice Rules 1990, rule 3

11.05   Introductions and referrals – additional guidance

1.   For the Solicitors' Introduction and Referral Code 1990 see Annex 11B, p.238. Sections 1–3A deal with the introduction of clients to solicitors. Sections 1 and 4 deal with the introduction of clients by solicitors to third parties.

2. The introduction and referral code applies to all arrangements for the referral of clients, other than introductions and referrals between solicitors, between solicitors and barristers or between solicitors and lawyers of other jurisdictions. Arrangements whereby the solicitor agrees to be paid by a third party to do work for the third party's customers are permitted, although these are subject to the additional requirements and restrictions set out in section 3A of the code in relation to conveyancing (see **25.10**, p.476) and section 3 in relation to other work.

3. Rule 12 of the Solicitors' Practice Rules 1990 (see **27.21**, p.533) makes provision in respect of introductions and referrals in connection with investment business and may restrict some forms of arrangement. In particular, the rule prevents a solicitor from acting as an appointed representative (as defined in the Financial Services Act 1986), other than by having a separate business which is the appointed representative of an independent financial adviser.

4. In accepting and making referrals in relation to mortgages or investment business, solicitors must also distinguish between appointed representatives (tied agents) and independent intermediaries (see **25.09**, p.474).

5. Section 2(3) of the introduction and referral code provides that a solicitor must not reward an introducer by the payment of commission or otherwise (see Annex 11B at p.239).

6. There is no objection to an employer recommending to employees the services of a particular solicitor in private practice. However, any arrangement must be in accordance with the introduction and referral code. It would not be proper for a solicitor to act for an employee in the knowledge that the employer has made it a condition of employment that the employee should instruct that solicitor.

7. Many insurance policies give the insurers the right to act in the name of the insured in the defence, prosecution or settlement of any claim falling within the policy cover, and also to nominate solicitors to provide legal services to the insured. Solicitors are permitted to act on the instructions of insurers who offer this form of policy. It must be recognised that in these circumstances a solicitor/client relationship is established between the solicitor and the insured. This note applies to indemnity insurance; it should not be taken as applying to legal expenses insurance, which is dealt with in **6.01**, p.165.

8. Where solicitors are asked to draft wills by will-writing companies, the introduction and referral code will apply, as the testator will be the client and the will-writing company the introducer. Principle **12.04**, p.246 applies in relation to the testator's instructions. Principle **11.07**, p.227 will also be relevant.

11

11.06　Acting for members of associations and in multi-party actions

A solicitor may act for members of an association or in a multi-party action subject to the provisions of the Solicitors' Introduction and Referral Code 1990.

Associations

1. Where the costs of an individual are to be paid by an association, the normal solicitor/client relationship will exist with the member client. Where the association for any reason decides not to continue to fund proceedings on its member's behalf, the position as to ownership of documents is governed, as always, by the law. The normal position is set out in Annex 12A, p.253. However, if statements were obtained by the association's officials before instructions were sent to the solicitor to act on behalf of the member client, the association may be able to claim ownership of those statements.

2. A solicitor may be instructed to act in a matter both for an association, club or trade union and for the association's members, or to act for a number of members of the association. The solicitor should be alert to the possibility of conflicting interests arising. In some circumstances, the solicitor should, at the outset, insist on one or more of the parties being separately represented. In other circumstances, the solicitor may be able to act for all the parties but may need to warn them at the outset that separate representation may at some stage be necessary.

Multi-party actions

3. Where there is a common interest between one or more individuals, but there is no formal association, it may be clear that to arrange for one solicitor to act for all those individuals whose rights are affected could save time and costs. Examples of such circumstances include common claims arising out of an air crash or certain neighbourhood disputes. Any solicitor accepting joint instructions should bear in mind the possibility of conflicting interests between the clients and may need to warn the prospective clients that at some later stage it may be necessary that each person is separately advised. The Law Society offers assistance in relation to multi-party actions. Advice is available from the Multi-Party Actions Co-ordinator (see p.xv for contact details).

11.07   Client denied choice of solicitor

A solicitor must not accept instructions knowing that a third party has stipulated that the solicitor must act.

1.   A breach of principle **11.07** would have the effect of denying the prospective client freedom of choice (see rule 1(b) of the Solicitors' Practice Rules 1990 at **1.01**, p.1 and **11.01**, p.222). Consequently, a solicitor must not act for a borrower where the solicitor knows or ought to know that the lender has stipulated that the solicitor must act for the borrower. In many cases, however, such conditions are imposed without the knowledge of the solicitor. A solicitor who has any doubts should satisfy himself or herself that the third party introductions are not tainted by such objectionable conditions, by making enquiries of the prospective client. For considerations where such a condition is imposed by a builder, see **25.02** note 2, p.467.

2.   Exceptions to this principle can be found in **6.01** (legal expenses insurance), p.165 and **11.05** note 7 (indemnity insurance), p.225.

11.08   Practice rule 9 (claims assessors)

'**(1) A solicitor shall not, in respect of any claim or claims arising as a result of death or personal injury, either enter into an arrangement for the introduction of clients with or act in association with any person (not being a solicitor) whose business or any part of whose business is to make, support or prosecute (whether by action or otherwise, and whether by a solicitor or agent or otherwise) claims arising as a result of death or personal injury and who in the course of such business solicits or receives contingency fees in respect of such claims.**

(2) The prohibition in paragraph (1) of this rule shall not apply to an arrangement or association with a person who solicits or receives contingency fees only in respect of proceedings in a country outside England and Wales, to the extent that a local lawyer would be permitted to receive a contingency fee in respect of such proceedings.'

Solicitors' Practice Rules 1990, rule 9

11

11.09   Claims assessors – additional guidance

1.   Rule 9 applies only where the claims assessor is charging a contingency fee. Contingency fees are defined in rule 18(2)(c) of the Solicitors' Practice Rules 1990 (see Annex 1A at p.29).

2. The prohibition only relates to claims arising as a result of death or personal injury. However, in other contentious matters, solicitors will need to consider whether the contingency fee arrangement between the claims assessor and the client will be enforceable as a matter of law and must be free to advise the client accordingly.

3. There is no prohibition under rule 9 where the proceedings take place outside England and Wales if a local lawyer would be able to receive a contingency fee.

Annex 11A

Solicitors' Publicity Code 1990

(with consolidated amendments to 3rd March 1999)

Code dated 18th July 1990 promulgated by the Council of the Law Society with the concurrence of the Master of the Rolls under Rule 2 of the Solicitors' Practice Rules 1990, regulating the publicity of solicitors and recognised bodies in England and Wales or overseas, and the publicity of registered foreign lawyers practising in England and Wales.

1. General principles

(a) Compliance with professional obligations

Nothing in this code shall be construed as authorising any breach of the Solicitors' Practice Rules, and in particular Rule 1 thereof, or any other professional obligation or requirement.

(b) Publicity in bad taste

Solicitors shall not publicise their practices in any manner which may reasonably be regarded as being in bad taste.

(c) Misleading or inaccurate publicity

Publicity must not be inaccurate or misleading in any way.

(d) Statutory requirements

As a matter of professional conduct the publicity of a solicitor must comply with the general law. Solicitors are reminded, *inter alia*, of the requirements of:

(i) any regulations made under the Consumer Credit Act 1974 concerning the content of advertisements;

(ia) sections 20 and 21 of the Consumer Protection Act 1987 concerning misleading price indications;

(ii) the Business Names Act 1985 concerning lists of partners and an address for service on stationery, etc.; and

(iii) Chapter 1 of Part XI of the Companies Act 1985 concerning the appearance of the company name and other particulars on stationery, etc.

(e) [repealed]

(f) *Solicitors' responsibility for publicity*

It is the responsibility of solicitors to ensure that all their publicity, and all publicity for their services which is conducted by other persons, complies with the provisions of this code. The responsibility cannot be delegated. Where solicitors become aware of any impropriety in any publicity appearing on their behalf, they must use their best endeavours to have the publicity rectified or withdrawn as appropriate.

2.   Contents of publicity – general

(a) *Solicitor to be identified*

Every advertisement by a solicitor must bear the solicitor's name or firm name (subject to paragraph 10 below on flag advertising).

(b) *Claims to specialisation or particular expertise*

It is not improper for a claim to be made that a solicitor (or a registered foreign lawyer) is a specialist, or an expert, in a particular field provided that such a claim can be justified.

(c) *Success rate*

No publicity may refer to a solicitor's success rate (or that of a registered foreign lawyer practising with the solicitor).

(d) *Comparisons and criticisms*

No publicity may make direct comparison or criticism in relation to the charges or quality of service of any other identifiable solicitor. However, a solicitor may participate in the preparation of a *bona fide* survey of legal services conducted by a third party which may make comparisons between the charges of or quality of service provided by different solicitors.

(e) *The Law Society's coat of arms*

The armorial bearings of the Law Society may not appear in a solicitor's publicity.

(f) *Legal aid logo*

Solicitors willing to undertake legal aid cases may use the legal aid logo in their publicity, but the logo must not be altered in any way. (Photographic copies of the logo can be obtained from the Legal Aid Board.)

3.   Unsolicited visits and telephone calls

Solicitors may not publicise their practices or properties for sale or to let by means of unsolicited visits or telephone calls except:

(i)   by means of a telephone call to a current or former client; or

(ii)   by means of a visit or telephone call to another solicitor or to an existing or potential professional connection; or

(iii) by means of a visit or telephone call made to publicise a specific commercial property or properties the solicitor has for sale or to let.

4.   Naming clients

Solicitors may name or identify their clients in advertisements for their practices or in the public media, or supply information about their clients to publishers of directories, provided that:

(i)   the client gives consent which, in the case of advertisements and directories, shall be in writing; and

(ii)   any such naming or identification of a client is not likely to prejudice the client's interests.

5.   Statements as to charges

(a) Clarity

Any publicity as to charges or a basis of charging must be clearly expressed. It must be stated what services will be provided for those charges or on that basis of charging. Any circumstances in which the charges may be increased or the basis altered must be stated. It must be clear whether disbursements and VAT are included.

(b) Fee from or upwards of a figure

It is prohibited to state a fee as being from or upwards of a certain figure.

(c) Service free of charge

Publicity may state that a particular service of a solicitor is free of charge, but this must not be conditional on the solicitor or any other person being given any other instructions, or receiving any commission or other benefit, in connection with that or any other matter.

(d) Composite fees

Solicitors may quote a composite fee for two or more separate services offered, but

(i)   the solicitor must if required quote separate fees for the individual services; and

(ii)   the solicitor must if required carry out any one only of those services on the basis of the separate fee quoted; and

(iii) except in relation to a composite fee for property selling and conveyancing services, the separate fees quoted may not total more than the composite fee.

11

(e) *Commissions from third parties*

In publicity for conveyancing or other services of a solicitor, fees must not be quoted which are intended to be net fees, i.e. fees which are reduced by the availability of any commission (such as that on an endowment policy). Any fee quoted in such circumstances must be the gross fee, although there is no objection to mentioning that the availability for the benefit of the client of a commission may reduce the net cost of the transaction to the client; provided that, where such mention is made in connection with mortgages, there must be no implication that endowment mortgages are appropriate in all circumstances, and there must be included an indication of the solicitor's willingness to advise as to the appropriate type of mortgage for the client's circumstances.

(f) *Fees for conveyancing services*

In publicity which includes references to charges for conveyancing services, regard must be had to paragraph 1(c) above (misleading or inaccurate publicity) and paragraph 5(a) above (clarity in statements as to charges).

The following are examples of publicity which would breach these provisions:

(i)   publicity which includes an estimated fee pitched at an unrealistically low level, if the solicitor then charges higher or additional fees;

(ii)   publicity which refers to an estimated or fixed fee plus disbursements, if the solicitor then charges as disbursements expenses which are in the nature of overheads such as normal postage and telephone calls, *unless* the publicity explicitly states that such charges will be made;

(iii) publicity which includes an estimated or fixed fee for conveyancing services, if the solicitor then makes an additional charge for work on a related mortgage loan or repayment, including work done for a lender, *unless* the publicity makes it clear that any such additional charge may be payable (e.g. by use of a formula like "excluding VAT, disbursements, mortgage related charges and fees for work done for a lender").

6. Description of a multi-national practice

In the case of a practice which has at least one registered foreign lawyer as a partner (or director, registered member or beneficial shareowner), a description of the firm appearing on any letterhead (or fax heading, or heading used for bills) of an English or Welsh office of the practice must, if the description includes the word "solicitor(s)", also include:

(i)   words denoting the countries or jurisdictions of qualification of the foreign lawyer partners (or directors, registered members and beneficial owners) and their professional qualifications; or

(ii)   the words "registered foreign lawyer(s)";

and the categories of lawyer must appear in order, with the largest group of partners (or directors, registered members and beneficial shareowners) placed first. There must be no breach of paragraph 14(b) below on the use of the word "lawyer(s)".

7. Naming and describing partners and staff

(a) Provisions applying to all practices

(i) A member of staff (including a partner or director) other than a solicitor who holds a current practising certificate may only be named in a practitioner's publicity, including stationery, if the status of that person is unambiguously stated.

(ii) The term "legal executive" may only be used in a practitioner's publicity, including stationery, to refer to a Fellow of the Institute of Legal Executives; and "trainee solicitor" to refer to a person training as a solicitor under a training contract registered with the Law Society.

(iii) Practitioners are reminded of the danger of inadvertently holding out persons as partners in a firm by inclusion of both partners' and non-partners' names in a list. The status of non-partners must be indicated for avoidance of doubt whenever a situation of inadvertent holding out might otherwise arise.

(iv) The following terms, used alone or in combination, will be deemed to indicate that a person is a solicitor holding a current practising certificate, unless it is made clear that the person is not so qualified:

(A) associate;

(B) assistant;

(C) consultant.

(v) The following terms, used alone or in combination, will be deemed to indicate that a person is not a solicitor holding a current practising certificate, unless a contrary indication appears:

(A) executive;

(B) clerk;

(C) manager;

(D) secretary;

(E) paralegal.

(vi) The appearance against a person's name of an indication that he or she is qualified in a jurisdiction other than England and Wales, or the title licensed conveyancer, or registered foreign lawyer, or the title of any other profession, will be deemed to indicate that the person is not a solicitor holding a current practising certificate, unless a contrary indication appears. (See also paragraph 14(b) below on the use of the word "lawyer(s)".)

(b) Additional provisions applying to multi-national practices

(i) In the case of a practice which has at least one registered foreign lawyer as a partner, director, registered member or beneficial owner of a share, the notepaper of an English or Welsh office of the practice must contain either:

(A) a list of the partners or directors; or

11

(B) a statement that a list of the partners or directors and their professional qualifications is open to inspection at that office (see also paragraph 1(d)(ii) above, the Business Names Act 1985 and Rule 23 of the Solicitors' Incorporated Practice Rules).

(ii) Any such list, as well as a list of the partners or directors in any other publicity conducted in England and Wales, must indicate the countries or jurisdictions of qualification of the partners or directors and their professional qualifications.

(iii) Any letterhead (or fax heading, or heading used for bills) of an English or Welsh office of the practice must bear either:

(A) a description of the firm which includes the word "solicitor(s)" and complies with paragraph 6 above; or

(B) a firm name which includes the word "Solicitor(s)" and complies with note (iv) to Practice Rule 11 (names used by a firm); or

(C) a list of the partners (or directors) which indicates their countries or jurisdictions of qualification and their professional qualifications as required by sub-paragraph (b)(ii) above; or

(D) a statement that the partners (or directors) are solicitors and others, described in a way, and in an order, which would comply with paragraph 6 above.

(iv) For the purpose of sub-paragraphs (b)(ii) and (iii) above:

(A) there must be no breach of the principle set out in paragraph 14(b) below on the use of the word "lawyer(s)"; and

(B) the word "solicitor(s)" is sufficient in itself to indicate that a solicitor's jurisdiction of qualification is England and Wales.

8. Directory headings

A firm may have an entry or advertisement in a directory or listing under any appropriate heading provided that either:

(i) the word "solicitor(s)"; or

(ii) as an additional option in the case of a directory referring wholly or mainly to practice outside England and Wales, the word "lawyer(s)" (but see paragraph 14(b) below);

appears *either* in the heading of the directory or listing *or* in a name *or* description of the practice appearing in the entry or advertisement itself.

9. Subsidiary practising style

[Repealed]

10. Flag advertising

(a) For the purpose of this paragraph, "flag advertising" means advertising conducted by or on behalf of solicitors under the logo of or in the name of a grouping or association including one or more firms of solicitors (or recognised bodies or multi-national partnerships) but without naming the firm or firms whose services are being advertised.

(b)   Any flag advertising must include the word "solicitor(s)" (or, as an additional option in the case of publicity conducted outside England and Wales, the word "lawyer(s)") and an address at which the names of all the firms involved are available. For the use of the word "lawyer(s)" see paragraph 14(b) below.

(c)   Notwithstanding anything in this paragraph, notepaper used on legal professional business must include the name of the firm concerned and not merely the name of a grouping or association.

11. Addresses to the court

It is not proper for solicitors to distribute to the press, radio or television copies of a speech or address to any court, tribunal or inquiry, except at the time and place of the hearing to persons attending the hearing to report the proceedings.

12. Professional stationery

(a) Application of the code to stationery

The provisions of this code apply to a solicitor's letterhead and matter similarly forming part of a solicitor's professional stationery.

(b) Practising address on stationery

Any stationery used by solicitors for their professional work must include a practising address and not merely a box number. Where a facsimile transmission is being sent, the frontsheet should contain the solicitor's address if this is not contained in some other part of the transmission.

(c) Use of client's or employer's stationery and client's or employer's name on solicitor's stationery

Solicitors may use for their professional work the stationery of, or stationery including the name of, a client or non-solicitor employer, provided that:

(i)   either the letterhead or the signature makes it clear that the stationery is being used by a solicitor on legal professional business and that the solicitor is responsible for the contents of the letter; and

(ii) the stationery is being used for the business of that client or non-solicitor employer or for third parties in circumstances permitted by Practice Rule 4.

(d) Stationery of a recognised body

The professional stationery of a recognised body and of a partnership which includes a recognised body as a partner must comply with the Solicitors' Incorporated Practice Rules from time to time in force.

11

13.   Professional announcements, advertisements for staff, etc.

Any professional announcement, advertisement for staff, advertisement offering agency services, or any other like advertisement by a solicitor (including any advertisement in the Law Society's *Gazette*) must comply with the provisions of this code.

14.   International aspects of publicity

(a)   No publicity for a solicitor's practice may be conducted in a jurisdiction other than England and Wales in any manner that would contravene either (i) the provisions of this code or (ii) any restrictions in force in that other jurisdiction concerning lawyers' publicity. For the purposes of this paragraph publicity shall be deemed to be conducted in the jurisdiction in which it is received. However, publicity shall not be regarded as being conducted in a jurisdiction in which such publicity would be improper if it is conducted for the purpose of reaching persons in a jurisdiction or jurisdictions where such publicity is permitted and its receipt in the former jurisdiction is incidental.

(b)   Whether in England and Wales or in any other jurisdiction, a solicitor's advertising (including stationery – see paragraph 16(ii) below) must not, except in the expression "registered foreign lawyer(s)", use the word "lawyer(s)" to refer to a person's qualification in a member state of the European Community unless the qualification is that of a "lawyer" as defined in the 1977 Lawyers' Services Directive as from time to time amended.

15.   Institutional publicity

(a)   Institutional publicity by the Law Society

This code does not apply to publicity by the Law Society, or any body established under the control of the Law Society, concerning the services of solicitors in general or any class or group of solicitors.

(b)   Institutional publicity by local law societies

This code does not apply to publicity by a local law society concerning the services of solicitors in general.

(c)   Publicity naming solicitors

Where any publicity referred to in (a) and (b) above names individual solicitors or firms, such publicity must comply with this code as if the publication were by individual solicitors.

16.   Interpretation

In this code:

(i)   all references to individual practice rules are references to the Solicitors' Practice Rules 1990 and all words have the meanings assigned to them in Rule 18 of those rules; and

    (ii)   "advertisement" and "advertising", except where the context otherwise requires, refer to any form of advertisement and include *inter alia* brochures, directory entries, stationery, and press releases promoting a solicitor's practice; but exclude press releases prepared on behalf of a client.

17. Commencement

This code will come into force on 1st September 1990.

Note: Breaches of the Publicity Code

Where contravention of this code is not serious, the Council encourages local law societies to bring breaches to the attention of the solicitors concerned. Serious or persistent cases should be reported to the Office for the Supervision of Solicitors.

11

Annex 11B

Solicitors' Introduction and Referral Code 1990

(with consolidated amendments to 29th March 1999)

Code dated 18th July 1990 promulgated by the Council of the Law Society with the concurrence of the Master of the Rolls under Rule 3 of the Solicitors' Practice Rules 1990, regulating the introduction of clients to and by solicitors, registered foreign lawyers and recognised bodies practising in England and Wales.

Introduction

(1) This code states the principles to be observed in relation to the introduction of clients by third parties to solicitors or by solicitors to third parties.

(2) The code does not apply to introductions and referrals between solicitors, between solicitors and barristers or between solicitors and lawyers of other jurisdictions.

(3) Non-compliance, evasion or disregard of the code could represent not only a breach of Practice Rule 3 (introductions and referrals) but also a breach of Practice Rule 1 (basic principles) or one of the other practice rules, and conduct unbefitting a solicitor.

(4) Those wishing to advertise the services of solicitors to whom they refer work should be encouraged to publicise their adherence to the code by means of a notice on the following lines:

"We comply with the Solicitors' Introduction and Referral Code published by the Law Society, and any solicitor to whom we may refer you is an independent professional from whom you will receive impartial and confidential advice. You are free to choose another solicitor."

(5) In this code all references to individual practice rules are references to the Solicitors' Practice Rules 1990 and all words have the meanings assigned to them in Rule 18 of those rules.

(6) The code will come into force on 1st September 1990.

Section 1: The basic principles

(1) Solicitors must always retain their professional independence and their ability to advise their clients fearlessly and objectively. Solicitors should never permit the requirements of an introducer to undermine this independence.

THE GUIDE TO THE PROFESSIONAL CONDUCT OF SOLICITORS 1999

(2)   In making or accepting introductions or referrals, solicitors must do nothing which would be likely to compromise or impair any of the principles set out in Practice Rule 1:

(a)   the solicitor's independence or integrity;

(b)   a person's freedom to instruct a solicitor of his or her choice;

(c)   the solicitor's duty to act in the best interests of the client;

(d)   the good repute of the solicitor or the solicitors' profession;

(e)   the solicitor's proper standard of work;

(f)   the solicitor's duty to the Court.

(3)   Practice Rule 9 prevents a solicitor from entering into any arrangement with a claims assessor for the introduction of personal injury clients to the solicitor.

(4)   Practice Rule 12 makes provision in respect of introductions and referrals in the field of investment business. In particular the rule prevents a solicitor from acting as an appointed representative as defined in the Financial Services Act 1986 other than by having a separate business which is the appointed representative of an independent financial adviser.

Note

An independent financial adviser is a financial adviser authorised under the Financial Services Act 1986, or subsequent relevant legislation, who is not constrained to recommend to clients or effect for them transactions in some investments but not others, with some persons but not others; or to refrain from doing so.

Section 2:   Introduction or referral of business to solicitors

(1)   Solicitors may discuss and make known to potential introducers the basis on which they would be prepared to accept instructions and the fees they would charge to clients referred.

(2)   Solicitors should draw the attention of potential introducers to the provisions of this code and the relevant provisions of the Solicitors' Publicity Code.

(3)   Solicitors must not reward introducers by the payment of commission or otherwise. However, this does not prevent normal hospitality. A solicitor may refer clients to an introducer provided the solicitor complies with Section 4 below.

(4)   Solicitors should not allow themselves to become so reliant on a limited number of sources of referrals that the interests of an introducer affect the advice given by the solicitor to clients.

(5)   Solicitors should be particularly conscious of the need to advise impartially and independently clients referred by introducers. They should ensure that the wish to avoid offending the introducer does not colour the advice given to such clients.

(6)   Where a tied agent refers to a solicitor a client who is proposing to take out a company life policy, the solicitor should, where necessary, have regard to the suitability of that policy in each particular case.

(7)   Solicitors must ensure that they alone are responsible for any decisions taken in relation to the nature, style or extent of their practices.

11

(8) This code does not affect the need for the solicitor to communicate directly with the client to obtain or confirm instructions, in the process of providing advice and at all appropriate stages of the transaction.

(9) Each firm should keep a record of agreements for the introduction of work.

(10) Each firm should conduct a review at six-monthly intervals, which should check:

(a) that the provisions of this code have been complied with;

(b) that referred clients have received impartial advice which has not been tainted by the relationship between the firm and the introducer; and

(c) the income arising from each agreement for the introduction of business.

(11) Where, so far as can be reasonably ascertained, more than 20 per cent of a firm's income during the period under review arises from a single source of introduction of business, the firm should consider whether steps should be taken to reduce that proportion.

(12) Factors to be taken into account in considering whether to reduce the proportion include:

(a) the percentage of income deriving from that source;

(b) the number of clients introduced by that source;

(c) the nature of the clients and the nature of the work; and

(d) whether the introducer could be affected by the advice given by the solicitor to the client.

Section 3:   Solicitor agreeing to be paid by a third party to do work for the third party's customers other than conveyancing work

(1) In addition to the other provisions of this code the following requirements should be observed in relation to agreements for the introduction of clients/business to solicitors under which the solicitor agrees with the introducer to be paid by the introducer to do work other than conveyancing work for the introducer's customers.

(2) The terms of the agreement should be set out in writing and a copy available for inspection by the Law Society or the Solicitors Complaints Bureau *[now the Office for the Supervision of Solicitors]*.

(3) The solicitor may agree to be remunerated by the introducer either on a case by case basis or on a hourly, monthly or any other appropriate basis.

(4) The solicitor should ensure that any agreement between the introducer and customer for the provision of services under this section includes:

(a) express mention of the independence of the solicitor's professional advice;

(b) a provision that control of the professional work should remain in the hands of the solicitor subject to the instructions of the client; and

(c) a provision that information disclosed by the client to the solicitor should not be disclosed to the introducer unless the client consents.

Section 3A: Contractual referrals for conveyancing

(1)   In addition to the other provisions of this code the following requirements must be observed in relation to agreements for the introduction of clients/business to solicitors under which the solicitor agrees with the introducer to be paid by the introducer to provide conveyancing services for the introducer's customers.

Agreements for referrals

(2)   Solicitors may enter into agreements under this section for referrals for conveyancing services only with introducers who undertake in such agreements to comply with the terms of this code.

(3)   Referrals under this section must not be made where the introducer is a seller or seller's agent and the conveyancing services are to be provided to the buyer.

(4)   The agreement between the solicitor and the introducer must be set out in writing. A copy of the agreement and of records of the six-monthly reviews carried out under paragraph 10 of Section 2 of this code in relation to transactions under the agreement must be retained by the solicitor for production on request to the Law Society or the Solicitors Complaints Bureau *[now the Office for the Supervision of Solicitors]*.

(5)   If the solicitor has reason to believe that the introducer is breaching terms of the agreement required by this section the solicitor must take all reasonable steps to procure that the breach is remedied. If the introducer persists in breaches the solicitor must terminate the agreement in respect of future referrals.

(6)   The agreement between the introducer and the solicitor must not include any provisions which would:

   (a)   compromise, infringe or impair any of the principles set out in Rule 1 of the Solicitors' Practice Rules or any duties owed by the solicitor to the introducer's customer by virtue of the solicitor/client relationship and/or the requirements of professional conduct; or

   (b)   restrict the scope of the duties which the solicitor owes to the customer in relation to the services agreed to be provided by virtue of the professional relationship between solicitor and client; or

   (c)   interfere with or inhibit the solicitor's responsibility for the control of the professional work.

Publicity as to conveyancing services

(7)   Publicity material of the introducer which includes reference to any service that may be provided by the solicitor must comply with the following:

   (a)   Any reference to the charge for the conveyancing service must be clearly expressed separately from charges for other services. Any circumstances in which the charges may be increased must be stated. It must be made clear whether disbursements and VAT are or are not included.

   (b)   The publicity must not suggest that the service is free, nor that different charges for the conveyancing services would be made according to whether the customer takes other products or services offered by the introducer or not.

11

(c)   Charges must not be stated as being from or upwards of a certain figure.

(d)   The publicity must not suggest that the availability or price of other services offered by the introducer are conditional on the customer instructing the solicitor.

Notice to customer

(8)   Before making a referral the introducer must give the customer in writing:

(a)   details of the conveyancing service to be provided under the terms of the referral;

(b)   notification of:

(i)   the charge payable by the customer to the introducer for the conveyancing services;

(ii)   the liability for VAT and disbursements and how these are to be discharged; and

(iii)   what charge if any is to be made if the transaction does not proceed to completion or if the solicitor is unable to continue to act;

(c)   notification of the amount the introducer will be paying to the solicitor for the provision of conveyancing services relating to the customer's transaction;

(d)   a statement to the effect that the charge for conveyancing services will not be affected whether or not the customer takes other products or services offered by the introducer, and that the availability and price of other services will not be affected whether the customer chooses to instruct a solicitor under the referral or decides to instruct another solicitor or conveyancer; and

(e)   a statement to the effect that the advice and service of the solicitor to whom the customer is to be referred will remain independent and subject to the instructions of the customer.

Solicitor's terms of business

(9)   Where a solicitor accepts instructions on referral under this section the solicitor must provide the client with written terms of business which must include:

(a)   details of the conveyancing service to be provided under the referral and if appropriate any other services the solicitor is to provide and on what terms;

(b)   a statement that any advice given by the solicitor will be independent and that the client is free to raise questions on all aspects of the transaction;

(c)   confirmation that information disclosed by the client to the solicitor will not be disclosed to the introducer unless the client consents; but that where the solicitor is also acting for the introducer in the same matter and a conflict of interest arises, the solicitor might be obliged to cease acting.

Definition

(10) In this section references to a conveyancing service or services include services to be provided to the introducer if the solicitor is also to be instructed to act for the introducer.

Section 4: Referral of clients by solicitors

(1)   If a solicitor recommends that a client use a particular firm, agency or business, the solicitor must do so in good faith, judging what is in the client's best interest. A solicitor should not enter into any agreement or association which would restrict the solicitor's freedom to recommend any particular firm, agency or business.

(2)   The referral to a tied agent of a client requiring life insurance would not discharge the solicitor's duty to give his/her client independent advice. In such circumstances, any referral should be to an independent intermediary.

(3)   If the best interests of the client require it, a solicitor may refer a client requiring a mortgage to a tied agent, provided that the client is informed that the agent offers products from only one company.

(4)   In relation to commission received for the introduction of clients' business to third parties, Practice Rule 10 applies.

11

Chapter 12

Retainer

12.01 Freedom to accept instructions

A solicitor is generally free to decide whether or not to accept instructions from any particular client.

1. Any refusal to act must not be based upon the race, colour, ethnic or national origins, sex, creed, disability or sexual orientation of the prospective client (**7.02** note 3, p.168). See also paragraphs 2.4.1–2.4.2 of the Law Society's Code for Advocacy (Annex 21A at p.386) for additional requirements for advocates.

2. A solicitor should generally accept instructions to bring an action against another solicitor. However, particular care is necessary where the solicitors or their partners are on friendly terms. If the solicitor feels unable to act he or she should assist the client, if possible, to obtain proper representation. See also **12.03**, below.

3. For clients who do not have mental capacity see **24.04**, p.453.

4. A solicitor must refuse to take action which he or she believes is solely intended to gratify a client's malice or vindictiveness.

5. For the position where a solicitor is likely to be called as a witness on behalf of the client see **21.12**, p.379.

12.02 When instructions must be refused

A solicitor must not act, or where relevant, must stop acting, where the instructions would involve the solicitor in a breach of the law or a breach of the principles of professional conduct, unless the client is prepared to change his or her instructions.

1. When acting for a client, a solicitor is under a duty to observe the rules and principles of professional conduct, such as those on conflict of interests, and a client must accept the limitations imposed by such rules.

2. A solicitor may need to consider whether he or she would be professionally embarrassed by acting in the matter; if so the solicitor should refuse the instructions.

3. A solicitor should be aware of becoming involved in, or becoming a victim of, fraud. For further details, see the 'Yellow card' warning on banking instrument fraud (Annex 12B, p.258).

12.03 Competence to act

A solicitor must not act, or continue to act, where the client cannot be represented with competence or diligence.

1. This would apply where a solicitor has insufficient time, experience or skill to deal with the instructions.

2. Principle **12.03** will not prevent a solicitor from acting if he or she is able to do so competently by, for example, instructing counsel.

3. Normally, a solicitor should not agree to represent a client where adequate preparation of the case is not possible. However, in cases of urgency such as immigration cases, the solicitor may agree to continue to act to apply for an adjournment. If the adjournment is refused, the solicitor must consider whether he or she can properly continue to act for the client. For guidelines for immigration practitioners, see Annex 12C, p.262.

12

12.04   Duress or undue influence

A solicitor must not accept instructions which he or she suspects have been given by a client under duress or undue influence.

In such a case the client must be seen alone. Particular care may need to be taken where a client is elderly or otherwise vulnerable to pressure from others.

12.05   Third party instructions

Where instructions are received from a third party, a solicitor should obtain written instructions from the client that he or she wishes the solicitor to act. In any case of doubt the solicitor should see the client or take other appropriate steps to confirm instructions.

1.   This principle applies to a joint retainer, e.g. when acting for a husband and wife in a conveyancing transaction.

2.   The solicitor must advise the client without regard to the interests of the introducer. See also **11.05** (p.224), **11.07** (p.227) and the Solicitors' Introduction and Referral Code (Annex 11B, p.238).

3.   When acting for a client who has language or other communication difficulties, and instructions are given through an interpreter, the solicitor should take reasonable steps to ensure that the interpreter is appropriate for the client's needs. Guidelines for solicitors dealing with immigration cases are set out in Annex 12C, p.262.

4.   In the case of elderly clients, a solicitor is sometimes put under pressure by the client's family to accept instructions which are not in accordance with the client's own intentions. In this case the solicitor should see the client.

12.06   Who is my client?

When instructions are received from a third party, a solicitor should consider whether both the third party and the person introduced are clients, or whether only the person introduced is the client.

1.   In some cases it is difficult for a solicitor to determine who is the client: for example, when a solicitor acts for an insurer with rights of subrogation, the insurer is the client as well as the insured. In practice the rights of the insurer are likely to supersede the rights of the insured, but the detail will depend on the contract of insurance. Alternatively, the solicitor may be acting for the insured on an uninsured loss claim funded by a separate insurance policy. In this case only the insured is the client. If instructions are received from a legal expenses insurer to act on behalf of the insured, only the insured is the client – see Chapter 6 (p.165).

2. A litigation friend (formerly *guardian ad litem*) who instructs a solicitor on behalf of a minor is normally a client, as is the minor. For guidance on what should happen if a conflict arises, see **15.03**, p.316.

3. If an introducer, for example, an estate agent, introduces a client for conveyancing services, only the individual, not the estate agent, will be the client. In this case the normal rules relating to confidentiality will apply (see Chapter 16, p.323) and the solicitor cannot disclose any information to the estate agent without the client's authority.

4. For guidance on the position in the administration of estates see Chapter 24, p.448.

12.07 Other solicitor instructed

A solicitor must not accept instructions where another solicitor is acting for the client in respect of the same matter until the first retainer has been determined.

1. Where the first retainer has been determined, there is no duty on the second solicitor to inform the first solicitor that he or she has been instructed, except in litigation where the first solicitor is on the record.

2. Provided he or she has sufficient information, a solicitor may give a second opinion without the first solicitor's knowledge.

12.08 Care and skill

A solicitor must carry out a client's instructions diligently and promptly.

1. A solicitor must act within his or her client's express or implied authority. It is essential at the outset for a solicitor to agree clearly with the client the scope of the retainer and subsequently to refer any matter of doubt to the client. If a solicitor limits the scope of the retainer it is good practice for the limits of the retainer to be precisely defined in writing to the client.

2. A solicitor has implied authority to bind the client in certain circumstances. As a matter of good practice, however, it would not be appropriate for a solicitor to rely upon implied authority for non-routine matters other than in exceptional circumstances, e.g. where it was impossible to obtain express authority.

3. For limitation of liability by contract see **12.11**, p.249.

4. For details of a solicitor's obligations to notify claims to Solicitors Indemnity Fund Limited and to advise the client to seek independent advice, see **29.08–29.09**, p.791.

5. Where there is a complaint of undue delay the Society has power to take possession of all papers and money relating to the matter and to deliver

12

them to the client or to the client's new solicitor (see Schedule 1, paragraph 3 of the Solicitors Act 1974, Annex 30A at p.851).

6. Where a solicitor is guilty of avoidable delay in litigation, the court may make a wasted costs order against the solicitor. Where the solicitor is guilty of gross misconduct or gross negligence, he or she risks being penalised by the court under its inherent jurisdiction. If the action is struck out, the solicitor may be ordered to pay costs and may be liable in damages. The Civil Procedure Rules 1998 contain additional powers for the courts to impose sanctions on solicitors and their clients (see Annex 21I, p.409, for a summary).

7. Delay can lead to a referral to the Office for the Supervision of Solicitors; for further details see Chapter 30, p.842.

12.09   Not taking advantage of client

A solicitor must not abuse the solicitor/client fiduciary relationship by taking advantage of the client.

1. A solicitor must not abuse his or her position to exploit a client by taking advantage of a client's age, inexperience, ill health, want of education or business experience, or emotional or other vulnerability. For example:

   (a) A solicitor must not induce a client to pay a sum of money on account of costs to be incurred which is out of proportion to what could be justified by the work which the solicitor has been instructed to do.

   (b) Whilst it would not necessarily be so, it may be an abuse of the solicitor/client fiduciary relationship for a solicitor to enter into a sexual relationship with a client (see also **15.04** note 9, p.317).

2. See also **15.04**, p.316 for a solicitor's interests conflicting with those of a client.

12.10   Dealing with letters and other communications

A solicitor should deal promptly with communications relating to the matter of a client or former client.

1. A solicitor who fails to answer and deal with the issues raised in communications from a client or former client on that client's business may be subject to disciplinary action.

2. Where a solicitor receives letters from third parties, or from solicitors acting on their behalf, relating to the business of a client or former client, instructions should be sought from the client. Unless instructed to provide a substantive reply, failure to do so would not normally amount to professional misconduct. As a matter of courtesy, however, the solicitor

should normally acknowledge such letters and may add that he or she will not entertain any further correspondence. For details on when it is permissible to contact another solicitor's client, see **19.02** note 3, p.360.

3. For a solicitor's obligation to deal with other correspondence received from a third party, and from other solicitors, see **17.01** note 7, p.347 and **19.03** (p.361).

12.11   Limitation of liability by contract

Although it is not acceptable for solicitors to attempt to exclude by contract all liability to their clients, there is no objection as a matter of conduct to solicitors seeking to limit their liability provided that such limitation is not below the minimum level of cover required by the Solicitors' Indemnity Rules.

1. The cover currently required by the Solicitors' Indemnity Rules is £1,000,000.

2. Principle **12.11** is subject to the position in law. The following points should be noted:

   (a) Liability for fraud or reckless disregard of professional obligations cannot be limited.

   (b) Existing legal restraints on solicitors cannot be overridden. In particular the courts will not enforce in the solicitor's favour an unfair agreement with his or her client.

   (c) Under section 60(5) of the Solicitors Act 1974 (see Annex 14A at p.286) a provision in a contentious business agreement that the solicitor shall not be liable for negligence, or that he or she shall be relieved from any responsibility to which he or she would otherwise be subject as a solicitor, is void.

   (d) By section 2(2) of the Unfair Contract Terms Act 1977, a contract term which seeks to exclude liability is of no effect except in so far as it satisfies the requirement of reasonableness set out in section 11, namely that the contract term must be a fair and reasonable one having regard to the circumstances which were or ought reasonably to have been known to or in the contemplation of the parties when the contract was made.

   (e) Section 11(4) of the Unfair Contract Terms Act 1977 provides that where a contractual term seeks to restrict liability to a specified sum of money, the question of whether the requirement of reasonableness has been satisfied must take into account the resources which the person seeking to impose it could expect to be available to him or her for the purpose of meeting the liability should it arise, and how far it was open to him or her to cover himself or herself by insurance.

12

(f) The Unfair Contract Terms in Consumer Contracts Regulations 1994 (S.I. 1994 no. 3159) have a comparable effect to the Unfair Contract Terms Act as to exclusions of liability but, unlike the Act, apply to all kinds of contract terms.

(g) When the retainer may be affected by foreign law, such matters may need to be considered according to the law applicable.

3. Any limitation must be brought clearly to the attention of the client and be understood and accepted by him or her.

4. It is preferable that the client's acceptance of the limitation should be evidenced in or confirmed by writing.

5. Practitioners are reminded that:

(a) Top-up indemnity insurance cover is not necessarily available on an each and every claim basis. It may only be available on an aggregate basis, so that there would be no guarantee that the amount of top-up cover maintained by the solicitor would be sufficient to meet any particular claim affected by a prospective limitation of liability.

(b) The insurance cover available to meet any particular claim is usually ascertained by reference to the claims year, i.e. the year in which the claim itself, or notice of circumstances which may give rise to a claim, is brought to the attention of insurers. This may mean that the top-up cover available when the contract is made may not be the same as the top-up cover available when the claim is actually brought (or notice of circumstances given).

6. As to the solicitor's liability to persons who are not his or her clients, the Council take the view that it may be reasonable in some circumstances for a solicitor to seek to limit or exclude altogether the liability he or she might otherwise incur to such persons under the principle in *Hedley Byrne & Co. Ltd* v. *Heller & Partners Ltd* [1964] A.C. 465 (H.L.).

12.12   Termination of retainer

A solicitor must not terminate his or her retainer with the client except for good reason and upon reasonable notice.

1. It is open to a client to terminate a solicitor's retainer for whatever reason. A solicitor must complete the retainer unless he or she has a good reason for terminating it.

2. Examples of good reasons include where a solicitor cannot continue to act without being in breach of the rules or principles of conduct, or where a solicitor is unable to obtain clear instructions from a client or where there is a serious breakdown in confidence between them.

3. For termination where the client fails to make a payment on account, see **14.01** notes 1–2, p.277.

4.   The retainer may be determined by operation of law, e.g. by the client's or solicitor's bankruptcy or mental incapacity. See *Cordery on Solicitors*. (For client's mental incapacity see **24.04** note 2, p.453.)

5.   For the situation where a solicitor knows or suspects that a client is involved in money laundering, see **16.07** note 7, p.334.

12.13   Client's papers and property

On termination of a retainer a solicitor should, subject to any lien, account to the client for any money still held on behalf of the client and, if so requested, deliver to the client all papers and property to which the client is entitled, or otherwise hold them to the client's order.

1.   Principle **12.13** applies whether the retainer is terminated during or at the conclusion of the matter.

2.   It is good practice to inform the client how his or her papers will be dealt with, particularly where documents are being passed to a third party, for example where deeds are being sent to the lender.

3.   When a solicitor has acted for joint clients the file belongs to both of those clients. Each client is entitled to a copy of the file, on payment of copying charges. However, the original file can only be released to one client with the other client's consent.

4.   When a client requires the file, a solicitor should not charge for removing it from storage, but a reasonable charge may be made for delivery or for chargeable work usually done by a fee-earner, such as retrieving documents from a file at the request of the client. For ownership and storage of documents, see Annex 12A, p.253.

5.   A solicitor should respond promptly to a request by a former client for his or her papers, especially where the matter has not been completed.

12.14   Lien

It is not unprofessional for a solicitor to retain papers and property belonging to the client, pending payment of professional costs owed by that client, where the retention is a proper exercise of a solicitor's lien.

1.   The lien is passive in nature and does not entitle the solicitor to sell or dispose of the client's property. For the effect of the general law, see *Cordery on Solicitors*.

2.   The lien will be challengeable unless the solicitor either delivers a bill or gives the client sufficient particulars to enable the client to calculate the amount owing. See also **14.07**, p. 280.

12

3. Despite the lien referred to above, the Society has certain powers to gain possession of a solicitor's documents and assets under Schedule 1 to the Solicitors Act 1974 (see Annex 30A, p.850).

4. The court has power to order a solicitor to deliver up a client's papers notwithstanding the existence of the solicitor's lien (see section 68 of the Solicitors Act 1974, Annex 14A at p.288).

5. Where a solicitor is properly exercising a lien in respect of unpaid costs following his or her discharge by the client during the course of proceedings, the Society recommends that the solicitor's papers should be released to the successor solicitor subject to a satisfactory undertaking as to the outstanding costs being given in lieu of the lien. There is, however, no duty on the original solicitor to accept an undertaking. See **5.05**, p.163 for the position where the client is legally aided. See Chapter 18, p.351 on the subject of undertakings generally.

Guidance – ownership, storage and destruction of documents

---

1. Is the client entitled to the whole file once the retainer is terminated?

Not necessarily. Most files will contain some documents which belong to you, some which belong to the client and possibly others belonging to a third party. Documents in existence before the retainer, held by you as agent for and on behalf of the client or a third party, must be dealt with in accordance with the instructions of the client or third party (subject to your lien). Documents coming into existence during the retainer fall into four broad categories (see also *Cordery on Solicitors*):

(a) **Documents prepared by you for the benefit of the client and which have been paid for by the client, either directly or indirectly, belong to the client.**

Examples: instructions and briefs; most attendance notes; drafts; copies made for the client's benefit of letters received by you; copies of letters written by you to third parties if contained in the client's case file and used for the purpose of the client's business. There would appear to be a distinction between copies of letters written to the client (which may be retained by you) and copies of letters written to third parties.

(b) **Documents prepared by you for your own benefit or protection, the preparation of which is not regarded as an item chargeable against the client, belong to you.**

Examples: copies of letters written to the client; copies made for your own benefit of letters received by you; copies of letters written by you to third parties if contained only in a filing system of all letters written in your office; tape recordings of conversations; inter-office memoranda; entries in diaries; time sheets; computerised records; office journals; books of account.

(c) **Documents sent to you by the client during the retainer, the property in which was intended at the date of despatch to pass from the client to you, belong to you.**

Examples: letters, authorities and instructions written or given to you by the client.

(d) **Documents prepared by a third party during the course of the retainer and sent to you (other than at your expense) belong to the client.**

Examples: receipts and vouchers for disbursements made by you on behalf of the client; medical and witness reports; counsel's advice and opinion; letters received by you from third parties.

12

2. Who owns the file where there has been a joint retainer?

In the Society's opinion the documents which fall into category (a) above belong to both or all of the clients jointly. Such documents can only be disclosed to third parties with the consent of both or all of the clients and the original papers can only be given to one client with the authority of the other(s). Each client is entitled to a copy of the relevant documents at their own expense. (See also **16.01** note 5, p.324 in the Guide.)

3. Who owns the file where there is a single file but two separate retainers?

This is usually the case where you have acted for the buyer/borrower and for the lender on a contemporaneous purchase and mortgage, or for the borrower and for the new lender on a re-mortgage. You will need to sort through the file to determine the ownership of the various papers (see question 1, above). There may, however, be documents which belong to the borrower but which the lender is nevertheless entitled to see as they relate to that part of your work where the lender and borrower can be said to have a common interest, such as the deduction of title, the acquisition of a good title to the property and ancillary legal issues such as the use of the property. See also **16.02** note 9 (p.326) in the Guide, and Annex 16C (p.341) in the Guide on the ownership of conveyancing documents.

4. How long should I retain old files?

The Society cannot specify how long individual files should be retained. It may be advisable to retain all files for a minimum of six years from when the subject matter was wholly completed. At the end of the six-year period, you should review the files again according to the nature of the particular transactions, and the likelihood of any claims arising. In cases where a party was under a disability at the time of the action or where judgement for provisional damages has been obtained, files should be retained for a minimum period of six years from the date on which the client would have a cause of action, or final judgement has been obtained.

The relevant statutory provisions should also be taken into account and some examples are given:

(a) Under Schedule 11, paragraph 6(3) of the Value Added Tax Act 1994, records and papers relevant to VAT liability have to be kept for six years; this obligation could cover all the papers in a solicitor's file and, subject to Customs and Excise agreeing the contrary in any particular case, the whole file should therefore be kept for this period. This obligation may be discharged by keeping the papers on microfilm or microfiche, but Customs and Excise's detailed requirements should first be checked with the local VAT office.

(b) Section 14A of the Limitation Act 1980 provides a special time limit for negligence actions where facts relevant to the cause of action are not known at the date of accrual. It prevents the bringing of such actions after six years from the date on which the cause of action accrued or three years from the date on which the plaintiff knew or ought to have known the facts, whichever is later. Section 14B provides an overriding time limit of 15 years from the defendant's breach of duty.

5. Can I destroy documents once I have held them for the relevant period?

Before deciding to destroy a file it is essential to consider who owns which documents (see question 1, above). No documents should be destroyed without the prior consent of the owner (but see question 6 below in respect of microfilming). You may always invite clients to take possession of their own papers, balancing the potential saving of space and expense against a possible loss of goodwill.

6. Can I store documents photographically or electronically, and destroy the originals?

Original documents, such as deeds, guarantees or certificates, which are not your own property, should not be destroyed without the express written permission of the owner. Where the work has been completed and the bill paid, other documents, including your file, may be stored, for example, on a CD ROM, computer system or microfilm and then destroyed after a reasonable time. In cases of doubt the owner's written permission should always be sought. If it is not possible to obtain such permission you will have to form a view and evaluate the risk. When seeking owners' permission to microfilm or store data electronically and destroy documents, you may wish to reserve the right to make a reasonable charge for preparing copies if they are later requested. See question 4(a) above for the requirements of Customs and Excise.

7. What is the evidential value of a photographically or electronically stored document where the original has been destroyed?

There is a dearth of judicial authority on this topic and, until the law and practice on the subject of microfilmed or electronically stored documents are clarified, it is only possible to provide general guidelines. The Society has been advised that:

(a) A microfilm of any document in a solicitor's file will be admissible evidence to the same extent, no more and no less, as the document itself, *provided that* there is admissible evidence of the destruction of the document and identification of the copy.

(b) Written evidence of the destruction of the original and of identification of the copy will enable the microfilm to be adduced in subsequent civil proceedings (under the Civil Evidence Act 1968) and in criminal proceedings (under the Police and Criminal Evidence Act 1984).

8. What procedures would the Society recommend where an original document is stored electronically or photographically and then the original is destroyed?

(a) Written evidence of the destruction of the original and of identification of the copy must always be preserved in case oral evidence is no longer available when needed (see question 7(b) above).

(b) There should be a proper system for:

    (i) identifying each file or document destroyed;

    (ii) recording that the complete file or document, as the case may be, has been photographed;

12

(iii) recording identification by the camera operator of the negatives as copies of the documents photographed; and

(iv) preserving and indexing the negatives.

(c) If a microfilm, electronically or photographically stored data is required to be produced in evidence, a partner or senior member of staff should be able to certify that:

(i) the document has been destroyed;

(ii) the microfilm, electronically or photographically stored data is a true record of that document; and

(iii) the enlargement is an enlargement of the microfilm, electronically or photographically stored data.

(d) Microfilm copies of some documents (e.g. coloured plans) can be unsatisfactory, in which case the originals should be preserved.

9. Will I be covered by the Solicitors' Indemnity Fund if I lose a client's file or destroy it without the client's consent?

If you incur liability either to a client or to a third party by the loss or destruction of documents, cover will normally be provided by the Solicitors' Indemnity Fund.

10. What happens if I lose a file relating to a claim against my firm?

If the handling or settlement of a claim has been prejudiced by non-compliance with any provision of the indemnity rules, Solicitors Indemnity Fund Limited (SIF) is entitled to recover from the firm (or from you personally) the difference between the sum payable by the Fund in respect of the claim and the sum that would have been payable but for the non-compliance (Annex 29A at p.793 in the Guide). This could happen if documents were destroyed after a claim had been made or after the firm had knowledge of circumstances likely to give rise to a claim. In such a case, the firm would be in breach of its obligation to allow SIF to take over and to conduct the defence or settlement of the claim. Extra care should, therefore, be taken of any papers that relate to a claim or possible claim.

11. Would the client have grounds for making a complaint if I lost a file, or destroyed it without the client's consent?

The Standards and Guidance Committee's view was that the storing of deeds and other legal documents for clients is a professional service. The loss or destruction of such documents could, therefore, give rise to an investigation by the Office for the Supervision of Solicitors on the basis of inadequate professional services.

12. What if I am holding documents which may be of historical or archival value?

Contact the county archivist to arrange a confidential inspection of the documents. If it is necessary to preserve the confidentiality of archival material due, for example, to the true ownership being in doubt, arrangements should be made with the county archivist for it to be deposited on that basis, so that if the ownership is later established, it can be returned. For further details contact the British Records Association, Records Preservation Section, c/o London Metropolitan Archives, 40 Northampton Road, London EC1R 0HB (0171 833 0428 or 020 7833 0428).

13. How can I ensure client confidentiality when destroying old files?

The best way to ensure confidentiality is to arrange for the old files to be shredded in the office sufficiently finely to avoid any risk. If that is not possible, while this responsibility remains with the solicitor, it should be possible to contract either with the local council or a member firm of the British Recovered Paper Association for their confidential destruction in sealed bags. The Association's address is Paper Makers House, Rivenhall Road, Swindon SN5 7BD (01793 889624).

December 1986, revised February 1999

12

Annex 12B

'Yellow card' warning on banking instrument fraud – practice information

Fraudulent investment schemes are on the increase. 'Prime bank guarantees', 'prime bank letters of credit' and 'zero coupon letters of credit' are not issued by the legitimate banking community. The legitimacy of such investments must always be questioned.

Solicitors should exercise extreme caution if approached by individuals promoting such transactions.

Example of schemes

Investors are often persuaded that these types of investment 'can be bought and sold by investing, say, $8.8m to purchase a prime bank instrument with a face value of $10m, issued by a prime bank, which will mature in one year and one day or can be traded in a second tier bond market for an immediate 7% profit'. The fraudster will often claim that these instruments are so special that the banks are keeping them secret and therefore will not discuss them with the general public.

There is no trading of such instruments in the legitimate financial market.

Solicitors may have read that the Salvation Army was a victim of a scheme involving fraudulent trading and standby letters of credit and is only one of a growing number of victims worldwide.

Clients anxious, perhaps desperate, to obtain substantial loans, should be warned about the dangers of making advance payments to brokers or individuals offering these types of instrument.

Why involve you as a solicitor?

The fraudster wants to be associated with the legitimacy and respectability which you as a solicitor can provide.

(a) He or she wants you to endorse the scheme by confirming that you will participate, and will act as his or her banker, solicitor, etc.

(b) He or she may ask you to provide a communication to someone he or she will nominate.

(c) The fraudster may seek a letter from you, addressed to his or her company, or a third party.

(d) He or she would like you to open an account, awaiting receipt of funds.

(e) The fraudster will frequently include, within the voluminous documentation accompanying such schemes, reference to the solicitor being insured with the Solicitors' Indemnity Fund.

Exercise caution in communicating with potential fraudsters

(a) **Never** send them anything – fax, letter, memo.

(b) **Never** even give them your visiting card.

(c) **Never** meet them on your own.

(d) **Never** assume that a 'bank's telephone number' given to you is actually that of a bank – it's probably not.

Common characteristics of banking instrument fraud

(a) Large transactions (ranging from US$1 million to US$100 million or much more).

(b) Promises of further sizeable transactions (often huge sums, US$100 billion); there may be reference to secret markets.

(c) Small first transaction with several subsequent tranches to follow.

(d) Unusual currencies (e.g. billions of new Kuwaiti dinars).

(e) Prime bank guarantees (PBGs) being offered or being the 'product' to be financed.

(f) Proposals received by fax.

(g) Letterheads of companies which could have been easily produced by laser printer.

(h) The issuing bank may not be identified, be geographically remote or licensed within a jurisdiction with little or no regulation. Letters, possibly forged, from respectable banks being used to support the documentation.

(i) Strange, weird, confusing and complex transactions, hazy descriptions.

(j) Overwhelming amount of transaction description along with supporting papers, and even flowcharts of the transaction.

(k) Large commission, even large 'bonus' or large 'discount' or 'spread' being offered to the bank.

(l) Suggestions that the scheme is supported by, or operates under the auspices of, a major international body (e.g. IMF, UN, Federal Reserve or Bank of England).

(m) Outlandish projects, difficult to verify e.g. financing of island resort on far away (unknown) island, retirement home village in a far away country, or good causes such as United Nations development or third world reconstruction.

(n) Documents will invariably be signed by 'The President' or 'The Chairman of the Board' or 'The Chief Executive Officer'.

(o) A power of attorney document may be produced, duly authenticated by a bank and/or lawyer.

12

Look for typical phrases, some of them meaningless:

Ready, willing and able.

Prime bank guarantees (PBGs).

Prime bank notes (PBNs).

Guarantees by top 100 world prime bank.

Unconditional SWIFT wire transfer.

Freely negotiable, irrevocable, clear SWIFT wire transfers.

Callable conditional sight drafts.

Closing bank.

Issuing bank.

Fiduciary bank.

Bank menu.

International banking days.

ICC (International Chamber of Commerce) 400.

UCC (uniform commercial code) form references.

Banking coordinates.

Fresh cut paper.

Seasoned paper.

Collateral houses, collateral source, collateral supplier.

Collateral first transaction.

Grand master collateral commitment.

Validation of the MCC (master collateral commitment).

Collateral purchase orders.

Collateral provider.

Instruments delivered free of all clients and/or encumbrances.

Non-circumvention and non-disclosure agreements.

Irrevocable pay order.

Irrevocable, irretractable commitment of funds to purchase instruments.

Lending bank, funding bank.

Good clean cleared funds of non-criminal origin.

With full corporate and legal responsibility.

Interest at seven and one half per cent, payable annually in arrears.

5, 10, 20 years, etc. plus one week or one day.

Fully binding commercial letter contract.

Client company principals.

Transaction tranches.

Millions or billions of US dollars with rolls and extensions.

Emissions, remission, commissions and fallout.

Transaction parameters.

There is to be no communication with our bank other than through the normal bank channels, no phone call allowed.

Request for details of client account

Beware of any scheme which requires the depositing of any substantial sums of money to you for safe keeping at lucrative rates for doing very little. **It may sound too good to be true and probably is.**

Beware of any scheme which requires you to send details of your bank, client account or blank letterheads. Such information may be used to make unauthorised payments from your client account.

Do not give any form of undertaking to guarantee a financial obligation unless you have funds or equivalent security. The word of someone backed by 'an international bank' is not enough. If asked to provide money from client account on the security of another firm's undertaking, ask that firm for evidence of their ability to comply. **NEVER** send a client account cheque on the basis of a verbal confirmation that the money is on its way into your client account – check it's there.

If you require further information concerning investment scams, especially those involving prime bank instruments or standby letters of credit, please contact the Fraud Intelligence Office on 0171 320 5703 (or 020 7320 5703) or Professional Ethics on 0171 242 1222 (or 020 7242 1222).

REMEMBER – if it sounds too good to be true, it probably is!

September 1997

12

Annex 12C

Guidelines for immigration practitioners – practice information

---

The following guidelines, approved by the Society's Immigration Law Sub-Committee in December 1998, constitute an amplification of the standard of practice that the Society considers essential for compliance with the rules of professional conduct when undertaking immigration, nationality and asylum work. The guidelines may be taken into account by the Office for the Supervision of Solicitors in its investigation and determination of complaints (including those made by third parties) alleging professional misconduct arising from immigration, nationality or asylum work.

General duties

1. Solicitors are expected to maintain the highest traditions of professional service in the conduct of activities as advisers and representatives in the field of immigration, nationality and asylum law and practice related matters. In particular:

    (a) They should give sound advice having familiarised themselves with the relevant law, the immigration rules (including details of any published concessions outside the rules), and the principal published materials that relate to the issue in question (e.g. the best practice guides published from time to time by the Immigration Law Practitioners' Association/the Law Society/Refugee Legal Group, and the published determinations of the Immigration Appeal Tribunal, etc.).

    (b) They should at all times show sensitivity to the particularly vulnerable position of those seeking immigration advice. Practitioners should pay due regard to the related difficulties faced by such a client, and should ensure that the client fully understands the implications for his or her position of any decision or proposed course of action, making full use of an appropriate interpreter, as necessary.

    (c) They must not deceive the immigration authorities or the courts or knowingly allow themselves to be used in any such deception.

    (d) They should consider whether, by virtue of their knowledge, skills and experience, they are competent to act in the particular case, and must not take on cases outside their area of competence or beyond their caseload capacity.

    (e) They must maintain proper records of their professional dealings, including records of the matters set out below.

Costs information

2.   Where a charge is to be made to a client for the provision of legal services, a written estimate of the costs should be supplied to the client, at the outset of the matter to which the charge relates, with a description of the work to be done to a specified stage and the method of calculation of such fee (unless the fee is fixed). Where the fee is likely to exceed the estimate given or requires variation, a written revision of the estimate and mode of calculation should be given as soon as it becomes apparent that the original estimate is likely to be exceeded or requires revision, and in any event before it is in fact exceeded. Solicitors must observe practice rule 15 and the Solicitors' Costs Information and Client Care Code (see Chapter 13, p.265 in the Guide).

Legal aid

3.   At the outset, the question of whether the client is eligible for advice under the legal aid scheme should be explored and discussed with the client. In particular, the client should be advised of the scope of legal aid in respect of representation at any appeal hearing before the immigration appellate authorities, and should be warned of the consequences in the event of the case having to go to appeal. The client should also be advised of the existence and range of services for free representation (e.g. the Refugee Legal Centre, the Immigration Advisory Service, and appropriate voluntary organisations).

Appeals

4.   Where a solicitor agrees to act for a client in the preparation of an appeal under the legal aid scheme, and where legal aid is not available to cover representation at the appeal hearing, adequate arrangements must be made:

▶   to comply with any pre-hearing directions;

▶   for the payment of fees to cover representation at the appeal or other hearing,

and these arrangements should be confirmed in writing to the client.

Practitioners should ascertain whether the client can pay for representation at the hearing. If not, adequate arrangements must be made either for the provision of such representation on a *pro bono* basis (by the solicitor or by, for example, the Free Representation Unit), or for the timely transfer of the case to the Immigration Advisory Service or the Refugee Legal Centre, or another provider of free representation, as appropriate.

These arrangements should be confirmed in writing to the client. A solicitor must not terminate a retainer except for good reason and upon reasonable notice. Therefore, if a practitioner has not been put in funds, it is unacceptable for the solicitor to terminate the retainer so soon before the date of the hearing as to prevent the client finding alternative representation, or to hinder the court or the immigration appellate authorities in adequately disposing of matters pending.

Lien (privately funded)

5.   If the client terminates the retainer just before a hearing date and a successor solicitor is appointed, the Society recommends the papers be released to the successor solicitor, subject to a satisfactory undertaking as to costs being given in lieu of the lien.

12

Lien (legally aided)

6.   (a)   A solicitor who has acted in a legally aided matter may call for an undertaking
from the successor solicitor either:

   (i)   to return the papers promptly at the end of the matter to enable a bill of
costs to be drawn up; or

   (ii)   that the successor solicitor will include the former solicitor's costs in a
bill to be taxed, collect those costs and then pay them over to the former
solicitor.

   (b)   If the client does not appoint a successor solicitor, it is not misconduct for a
solicitor to retain the file to get a bill drawn and taxed, but the client must be
allowed access to the file and to take copies of the papers at the client's
expense.

Standard of work

7.   A solicitor should not normally agree to represent a client where adequate
preparation of a case is not possible, but in cases of urgency the solicitor may agree
to act or continue to act for the purpose of applying for an adjournment. Where an
adjournment is refused, the solicitor must consider whether continuing to act
compromises effective standards of representation. If so, the solicitor should then
not participate further in the hearing.

Supervision

8.   These guidelines apply to anyone, including non-solicitors, supervised by the
solicitor.

9.   Solicitors must exercise care in the recruitment of non-solicitor staff whom it is
intended will undertake immigration work. Such staff should be of good standing
and repute and have proper knowledge and experience of the work for which they
are being recruited. Solicitors must ensure that staff are properly trained and
supervised.

Application of the guidelines

10.   Solicitors are subject to all the rules of professional conduct and any contractual
terms.

December 1998 – updated February 1999

Chapter 13

Client care

Introductory note

This chapter contains the new practice rule 15 and the Solicitors' Costs Information and Client Care Code 1999. These replace rule 15 of the Solicitors' Practice Rules 1990 and the costs information requirements previously contained in the written professional standards. The new rule and code come into force on 3rd September 1999. Compliance with the new rule 15 and the code will ensure compliance with the former rule 15 and the requirements of the written professional standards (see Chapter 13 of the seventh edition of the Guide). There is no change to the status quo in terms of sanctions and remedies. Both the conduct and inadequate professional services sanctions and remedies can be applied to breaches of the code as they were in the past. Specimen terms of business letters are available from Practice Advice Service, see p.xv for contact details.

13.01 Practice rule 15 (costs information and client care)

'Solicitors shall:

    (a) **give information about costs and other matters, and**

    (b) **operate a complaints handling procedure,**

in accordance with a Solicitors' Costs Information and Client Care Code made from time to time by the Council of the Law Society with the concurrence of the Master of the Rolls, but subject to the notes.

13

Notes

(i)   *A serious breach of the code, or persistent breaches of a material nature, will be a breach of the rule, and may also be evidence of inadequate professional services under section 37A of the Solicitors Act 1974.*

(ii) *Material breaches of the code which are not serious or persistent will not be a breach of the rule, but may be evidence of inadequate professional services under section 37A.*

(iii) *The powers of the Office for the Supervision of Solicitors on a finding of inadequate professional services include:*

   (a)   *disallowing all or part of the solicitor's costs; and*

   (b)   *directing the solicitor to pay compensation to the client up to a limit of £1,000.*

(iv) *Non-material breaches of the code will not be a breach of the rule, and will not be evidence of inadequate professional services under section 37A.*

(v)   *Registered foreign lawyers, although subject to Rule 15 as a matter of professional conduct, are not subject to section 37A. However, solicitor partners in a multi-national partnership are subject to section 37A for professional services provided by the firm.'*

13.02   Solicitors' Costs Information and Client Care Code

1.   Introduction

(a)   This code replaces the written professional standards on costs information for clients (see paragraphs 3–6) and the detail previously contained in Practice Rule 15 (client care) (see paragraph 7).

(b)   The main object of the code is to make sure that clients are given the information they need to understand what is happening generally and in particular on:

   (i)   the cost of legal services both at the outset and as a matter progresses; and

   (ii) responsibility for clients' matters.

(c)   The code also requires firms to operate a complaints handling procedure.

(d)   It is good practice to record in writing:

   (i)   all information required to be given by the code including all decisions relating to costs and the arrangements for updating costs information; and

   (ii) the reasons why the information required by the code has not been given in a particular case.

(e)   References to costs, where appropriate, include fees, VAT and disbursements.

2. Application

(a) The code is of general application, and it applies to registered foreign lawyers as well as to solicitors. However, as set out in paragraph 2(b), parts of the code may not be appropriate in every case, and solicitors should consider the interests of each client in deciding which parts not to apply in the particular circumstances.

(b) The full information required by the code may be inappropriate, for example:

    (i) in every case, for a regular client for whom repetitive work is done, where the client has already been provided with the relevant information, although such a client should be informed of changes; and

    (ii) if compliance with the code may at the time be insensitive or impractical. In such a case relevant information should be given as soon as reasonably practicable.

(c) Employed solicitors should have regard to paragraphs 3–6 of the code where appropriate, e.g. when acting for clients other than their employer. Paragraph 7 does not apply to employed solicitors.

(d) Solicitors should comply with paragraphs 3–6 of the code even where a client is legally aided if the client may have a financial interest in the costs because contributions are payable or the statutory charge may apply or they may become liable for the costs of another party.

(e) The code also applies to contingency fee and conditional fee arrangements and to arrangements with a client for the solicitor to retain commissions received from third parties.

3. Informing the client about costs

(a) Costs information must not be inaccurate or misleading.

(b) Any costs information required to be given by the code must be given clearly, in a way and at a level which is appropriate to the particular client. Any terms with which the client may be unfamiliar, for example "disbursement", should be explained.

(c) The information required by paragraphs 4 and 5 of the code should be given to a client at the outset of, and at appropriate stages throughout, the matter. All information given orally should be confirmed in writing to the client as soon as possible.

4. Advance costs information – general

The overall costs

(a) The solicitor should give the client the best information possible about the likely overall costs, including a breakdown between fees, VAT and disbursements.

13

(b) The solicitor should explain clearly to the client the time likely to be spent in dealing with a matter, if time spent is a factor in the calculation of the fees.

(c) Giving "the best information possible" includes:

   (i)   agreeing a fixed fee; or

   (ii) giving a realistic estimate; or

   (iii) giving a forecast within a possible range of costs; or

   (iv) explaining to the client the reasons why it is not possible to fix, or give a realistic estimate or forecast of, the overall costs, and giving instead the best information possible about the cost of the next stage of the matter.

(d) The solicitor should, in an appropriate case, explain to a privately paying client that the client may set an upper limit on the firm's costs for which the client may be liable without further authority. Solicitors should not exceed an agreed limit without first obtaining the client's consent.

(e) The solicitor should make it clear at the outset if an estimate, quotation or other indication of cost is not intended to be fixed.

Basis of firm's charges

(f) The solicitor should also explain to the client how the firm's fees are calculated except where the overall costs are fixed or clear. If the basis of charging is an hourly charging rate, that must be made clear.

(g) The client should be told if charging rates may be increased.

Further information

(h) The solicitor should explain what reasonably foreseeable payments a client may have to make either to the solicitor or to a third party and when those payments are likely to be needed.

(i) The solicitor should explain to the client the arrangements for updating the costs information as set out in paragraph 6.

Client's ability to pay

(j) The solicitor should discuss with the client how **and when** any costs are to be met, and consider:

   (i) whether the client may be eligible and should apply for legal aid (including advice and assistance);

   (ii) whether the client's liability for their own costs may be covered by insurance;

(iii) whether the client's liability for another party's costs may be covered by pre-purchased insurance and, if not, whether it would be advisable for the client's liability for another party's costs to be covered by after the event insurance (including in every case where a conditional fee or contingency fee arrangement is proposed); and

(iv) whether the client's liability for costs (including the costs of another party) may be paid by another person e.g. an employer or trade union.

Cost-benefit and risk

(k) The solicitor should discuss with the client whether the likely outcome in a matter will justify the expense or risk involved including, if relevant, the risk of having to bear an opponent's costs.

5. Additional information for particular clients

Legally aided clients

(a) The solicitor should explain to a legally aided client the client's potential liability for the client's own costs and those of any other party, including:

(i) the effect of the statutory charge and its likely amount;

(ii) the client's obligation to pay any contribution assessed and the consequences of failing to do so;

(iii) the fact that the client may still be ordered by the court to contribute to the opponent's costs if the case is lost even though the client's own costs are covered by legal aid; and

(iv) the fact that even if the client wins, the opponent may not be ordered to pay or be capable of paying the full amount of the client's costs.

Privately paying clients in contentious matters (and potentially contentious matters)

(b) The solicitor should explain to the client the client's potential liability for the client's own costs and for those of any other party, including:

(i) the fact that the client will be responsible for paying the firm's bill in full regardless of any order for costs made against an opponent;

(ii) the probability that the client will have to pay the opponent's costs as well as the client's own costs if the case is lost;

13

(iii) the fact that even if the client wins, the opponent may not be ordered to pay or be capable of paying the full amount of the client's costs; and

(iv) the fact that if the opponent is legally aided the client may not recover costs, even if successful.

Liability for third party costs in non-contentious matters

(c) The solicitor should explain to the client any liability the client may have for the payment of the costs of a third party. When appropriate, solicitors are advised to obtain a firm figure for or agree a cap to a third party's costs.

6. Updating costs information

The solicitor should keep the client properly informed about costs as a matter progresses. In particular, the solicitor should:

(a) tell the client, unless otherwise agreed, how much the costs are at regular intervals (at least every six months) and in appropriate cases deliver interim bills at agreed intervals;

(b) explain to the client (and confirm in writing) any changed circumstances which will, or which are likely to, affect the amount of costs, the degree of risk involved, or the cost-benefit to the client of continuing with the matter;

(c) inform the client in writing as soon as it appears that a costs estimate or agreed upper limit may or will be exceeded; and

(d) consider the client's eligibility for legal aid if a material change in the client's means comes to the solicitor's attention.

7. Client care and complaints handling

Information for clients

(a) Every solicitor in private practice must ensure that the client:

(i) is given a clear explanation of the issues raised in a matter and is kept properly informed about its progress (including the likely timescale);

(ii) is given the name and status of the person dealing with the matter and the name of the principal responsible for its overall supervision;

(iii) is told whom to contact about any problem with the service provided; and

(iv) is given details of any changes in the information required to be given by this paragraph.

Complaints handling

(b) Every principal in private practice must:

  (i) ensure the client is told the name of the person in the firm to contact about any problem with the service provided;

  (ii) have a written complaints procedure and ensure that complaints are handled in accordance with it; and

  (iii) ensure that the client is given a copy of the complaints procedure on request.

Costs information and client care – additional guidance

The following notes are additional general comments related to the giving of advance information on costs. Some refer to legal matters, others cross refer to relevant conduct issues. They have been grouped to relate to the most relevant part of the code.

13.03   Advance costs information – general (paragraph 4 of the code)

Overall costs and basis of charges

1. It is an implied term in law that solicitors will be paid reasonable remuneration for their services (see section 15 of the Supply of Goods and Services Act 1982). Solicitors should not, however, rely solely upon this implied term but should explain to the client, so far as is possible, the work which is likely to be involved in carrying out the instructions and the time which may be taken, both of which will have direct relevance to the likely amount of fees.

2. Wherever possible, a solicitor should give an estimate of the likely cost of acting in a particular matter. When giving such an estimate or forecast, regard should be had to Part III of the Consumer Protection Act 1987 which deals with misleading price indications. To give an estimate which has been pitched at an unrealistically low level solely to attract the work and subsequently to charge a higher fee for that work is improper because it misleads the client as to the true or likely cost.

3. Oral estimates should be confirmed in writing and clients should be informed immediately it appears that the estimate will be or is likely to be exceeded. In most cases this should happen before undertaking work that exceeds the estimate. Solicitors should not wait until submitting the bill of costs. The Office for the Supervision of Solicitors deals with many complaints that have arisen simply because the solicitor does not have a system for tracking costs, and estimates are exceeded without the client's authority.

13

4. The Conditional Fee Agreement Regulations 1995 prescribe both information to be given to the client and matters to be contained in a written agreement in conditional fee cases (see **14.05**, p.279 and Annex 14B, p.292). In non-contentious matters, regard must be had to the Solicitors' (Non-Contentious Business) Remuneration Order 1994 (see Annex 14D, p.296).

5. If the agreement is for the solicitor to be remunerated by an agreed fee, the solicitor is bound to do the work covered by the agreement for that fee, even though circumstances arise which make the work unremunerative for the solicitor. Under rule 19(5) of the Solicitors' Accounts Rules 1998, money received for or on account of an agreed fee which is paid by the client to the solicitor must not be paid into client account (see Annex 28B at p.702).

6. Section 57(3) of the Solicitors Act 1974 (see Annex 14A at p.284) requires a non-contentious business agreement to be in writing and signed by the person to be bound by it. Under section 59(1) a contentious business agreement must also be in writing. (See Annex 14A at p.285.)

7. A solicitor providing property selling services must, when accepting instructions to act in the sale of a property, give the client a written statement setting out certain details of their agreement. See **26.09**, p.515, for further details.

8. Where clients want to set a limit on costs solicitors should warn of the consequences before accepting instructions. Any limit cannot be exceeded without the authority of the client. Further, where the limit imposed on the expenditure is insufficient the solicitor must, as soon as possible, obtain the client's instructions as to whether to continue with the matter.

9. Where a solicitor continues to act in such circumstances regardless of the limit and then presents a bill for a sum which exceeds that limit, he or she may be guilty of professional misconduct as well as having the excess disallowed on an application for a remuneration certificate and/or taxation.

10. In non-contentious matters, a solicitor may render an interim bill if the client has agreed or acquiesced. In contentious matters, the question of an interim bill in respect of costs incurred is dealt with by reference to section 65(2) of the Solicitors Act 1974.

Ability to pay

11. When discussing costs with the client, not only should the solicitor discuss the various ways of funding the case, but he or she should also explain when the costs are due. It should be clear whether payments on account will be necessary and how payment of disbursements will be dealt with.

12. Where a client may be eligible for legal aid, the availability of an emergency certificate or the 'green form' scheme should be considered. A

solicitor who commences or continues work without legal aid cover runs the risk of being unable to recover pre-certificate costs.

13. The duty to advise as to legal aid applies throughout the retainer. Solicitors should ensure that any material change in a client's means, of which they become aware, is at once taken into consideration in the context of eligibility for legal aid.

14. Other methods of funding the matter should be explored with the client. The client may have insurance that will cover the matter. In respect of covering another party's costs, the solicitor should find out if the client has pre-purchased insurance, or whether it is advisable for the client to purchase after-the-event insurance. These possibilities should be explored in all cases, as well as when a conditional fee or contingency arrangement is proposed.

15. For the position where a solicitor requires a client to make a payment on account of costs see **14.01**, p.277.

16. There is no objection to solicitors accepting payment for their fees by the use of a credit card facility. See **14.02** note 3, p.277.

13.04 Cost-benefit and risk (paragraph 4(k) of the code)

1. It is in the interests of both the solicitor and the client that advice on the risks should be in writing, and that the advice is repeated at appropriate times throughout the transaction.

2. Breach of this standard will amount *prima facie* to inadequate professional services, giving the Office for the Supervision of Solicitors (OSS) power, *inter alia*, to reduce the solicitor's bill.

13.05 Responsibility for client's matter (paragraph 7(a) of the code)

1. The code requires that the client be informed of both the name and status of the person responsible for conduct of the matter. Status refers to qualification as well as partnership status, e.g. whether the person is a solicitor or a legal executive. For restriction of the term 'legal executive' to Fellows of the Institute of Legal Executives see paragraph 7(a)(ii) of the publicity code, Annex 11A at p.233.

2. If the conduct or the overall supervision of the whole or part of the client's matter is transferred to another person in the firm the client should be informed and the reasons must be explained.

13

13.06   General information for clients (paragraph 7(a) of the code)

1.   One of the objects of the code is to help clients who are unfamiliar with the law to understand what is happening. This will reduce areas of potential conflict and complaint. Different levels of information may be agreed or may be appropriate for different clients.

2.   The client should normally be told in appropriate language at the outset of a matter, or as soon as possible thereafter, the issues in the case and how they will be dealt with. In particular, the immediate steps to be taken must be clearly explained. It may be helpful to give an explanatory leaflet to the client.

3.   Solicitors should keep clients informed of the progress of matters. This may often be assisted by sending to clients copies of letters. In particular, it is important to tell clients of the reason for any serious delay. Requests for information should be answered promptly.

4.   The solicitor should advise the client when it is appropriate to instruct counsel. Whenever clients are to attend hearings at which they are to be represented, they must be told the name of the advocate who it is intended will represent them.

5.   Solicitors should normally explain to clients the effect of important and relevant documents. Information to be given also includes recent changes in law where those changes affect the subject matter of the retainer. At the end of the matter solicitors should normally write to clients confirming that it has been completed and summarising any future action to be taken by the client or the solicitor.

6.   Solicitors should consider whether it is appropriate to confirm in writing the advice given and instructions received. Confirmation in writing of key points will both reduce the risk of misunderstanding by clients and assist colleagues who may have to deal with the matter.

13.07   Complaints handling (paragraph 7(b) of the code)

1.   Paragraph 7(b) applies to firms; paragraph 7(a) applies to all solicitors in private practice. The firm's complaints handling procedure should be in writing, and all staff should be aware of the procedure. If a complaint is made to the Office for the Supervision of Solicitors (OSS) a firm will have to explain its procedure and whether it had been followed. *Keeping Clients, a Client Care Guide for Solicitors*, published by the OSS, contains advice on compliance with the code. Information on avoiding complaints and on complaints procedures is available from the OSS (see p.xv for contact details).

2.   The following are the basic elements of a complaints handling procedure:

   (a)   Clients should be told that if they have any problem with the service provided, they should make it known.

   (b)   Clients should be told whom to inform in the event of such a problem. This may be the fee-earner handling the case. It may be the senior partner, sole practitioner, principal with overall responsibility for the matter or another person within the practice nominated for the purpose. It could be someone outside the firm altogether.

   (c)   The procedure should ensure that any complaint is investigated promptly and thoroughly, that an explanation of the investigation is given to the client and any appropriate action taken. It is advisable to keep a record of all stages.

   (d)   Clients should be given details in writing of the firm's response to the complaint. If the client is not satisfied (or if there is any doubt) the client should be given information about the OSS. (The OSS can supply leaflets for this purpose.)

3.   The client may be informed about the whole complaints procedure at the start of the matter, e.g. in any general information about the firm given to new clients. The code requires that the client must be told at the outset at least the name of the person with whom any problems should be raised and this should preferably be confirmed in writing. The code requires the client to be given a copy of the complaints procedure on request. If a problem does arise which cannot be resolved almost immediately, the full procedure should be explained, in writing.

4.   Paragraph 2 of the code (application) states that parts of the code may not be appropriate in every case. For example, it may not be necessary to tell established clients the complaints handling requirements (paragraph 7(b)) each time they confirm new instructions, provided that they know whom to contact. If a complaint is subsequently investigated by the OSS, the firm will have to show that the client has been informed or why it was inappropriate to give the information.

13

Chapter 14

Professional fees

14.01 Payments on account

In contentious matters, a solicitor may require the client to make payments on account of costs and disbursements. In non-contentious matters, a solicitor may require the client to make payments on account of disbursements; there is no right to require payment on account of costs, as distinct from disbursements, unless such a right has been agreed with the client.

1. In non-contentious matters, a solicitor must make any requirement for a payment on account of costs, as distinct from disbursements, a condition of accepting instructions. Without this condition (or the client's subsequent agreement), a solicitor cannot terminate the retainer if the client refuses to make such a payment. This is something to be considered at the outset of the retainer when terms of business are being agreed. With regard to termination generally see **12.12**, p.250.

2. In contentious matters, section 65(2) of the Solicitors Act 1974 provides that where a solicitor requests the client to make a payment of a reasonable sum on account of the costs incurred or to be incurred, and the client refuses or fails within a reasonable time to make that payment, then the solicitor may terminate the retainer upon giving reasonable notice.

3. Where a solicitor requests a payment on account of costs or disbursements it should be made clear to the client that the total costs may be greater than the sum paid in advance. Any sum requested must be reasonable (see **14.12**, p.282).

4. Money paid on account of costs must be paid into client account pending delivery of the bill or interim bill or written notification of costs, see rule 19(4) of the Solicitors' Accounts Rules 1998, Annex 28B at p.702. An agreed fee must be paid into office account (see rule 19(5) of the Solicitors' Accounts Rules 1998, Annex 28B at p.702).

14.02 Fee sharing – commissions and credit card payments

1. A solicitor can share fees only with another solicitor or other person described in practice rule 7 (see **3.03**, p.68).

2. The term 'professional fees' in practice rule 7 (fee sharing) does not include commissions received by a solicitor from any third party, but it does include negotiation fees. Note also rule 10 of the Solicitors' Practice Rules 1990 which deals with a solicitor's duty to account to clients for commissions and secret profits (see **14.13**, p.283).

3. Payment may be made by credit card. However, solicitors should ensure that any agreements with credit card companies address confidentiality and

14

the resolution of disputes. If solicitors wish to refuse payment of disbursements by credit card, this will need to be addressed in the agreements. Any publicity for the credit card facility must not imply that the service is available for all legal services, if that is not the case.

14.03   Practice rule 8 (contingency fees)

'(1) A solicitor who is retained or employed to prosecute or defend any action, suit or other contentious proceeding shall not enter into any arrangement to receive a contingency fee in respect of that proceeding, save one permitted under statute or by the common law.

(2) Paragraph (1) of this rule shall not apply to an arrangement in respect of an action, suit or other contentious proceeding in any country other than England and Wales to the extent that a local lawyer would be permitted to receive a contingency fee in respect of that proceeding.'

Solicitors' Practice Rules 1990, rule 8

14.04   Contingency fees – additional guidance

1.   A contingency fee is any sum (whether fixed, or calculated either as a percentage of the proceeds or otherwise howsoever) payable only in the event of success in the prosecution or defence of any action, suit or other contentious proceeding. The fact that an agreement further stipulates a minimum fee in any case, win or lose, will not prevent it from being an arrangement for a contingency fee. See rule 18(2)(a)–(c) of the Solicitors' Practice Rules 1990 (Annex 1A at p.29).

2.   Rule 8 came into force on 7th January 1999. It allows a contingency fee to the extent that it is permitted by the common law. It seems, at present, that the decision in *Thai Trading Co (a firm)* v. *Taylor* [1998] 2 W.L.R. 893 represents the common law. This case permits a solicitor to seek no more than ordinary profit costs in a winning case, and less (but not necessarily nothing) if the case is lost. Other cases currently before the courts or awaiting appeal may change the position.

3.   It is anticipated that the Access to Justice Bill will put those contingency fee arrangements that are now permitted by common law on a similar statutory basis to conditional fee agreements, but this is unlikely to become law before the end of 1999. Any solicitor proposing to enter into a contingency fee arrangement must, therefore, satisfy himself or herself as to the current position at law. Any solicitor who is in doubt as to the legal position may contact the Practice Advice Service for guidance (see p.xv for contact details).

4.   The reference in rule 8 to a contingency fee arrangement permitted by statute refers to a conditional fee agreement which complies with the Conditional Fee Agreements Order 1998 (see **14.05** below and Annex 14C, p.294).

5.   Prior to the conclusion of a matter (contentious or non-contentious) a solicitor should not agree with a client to acquire an interest in the publication rights with respect to that matter (see **15.04** note 2, p.317).

6.   A solicitor may enter into an agreement to be paid on a commission basis to recover debts due to a client, provided that the agreement is limited to debts which are recovered without the institution of legal proceedings or forms a legally binding contingency fee agreement.

7.   Section 59(2) of the Solicitors Act 1974 (contentious business agreements) provides *inter alia* that nothing in the Act shall give validity to a contingency fee agreement (see Annex 14A at p.285). For conditional fee agreements see **14.05** below.

14.05   Conditional fee agreements – additional guidance

1.   Under practice rule 8 solicitors may enter into conditional fee agreements in relation to all proceedings except criminal proceedings and specified family proceedings. See section 58 of the Courts and Legal Services Act 1990 and the Conditional Fee Agreements Order 1998 (S.I. 1998 no. 1860).

2.   Solicitors may not enter into conditional fee agreements where the client has legal aid. Where legal aid is granted in respect of proceedings to which a conditional fee agreement relates, that agreement cannot apply to costs incurred whilst the client is in receipt of legal aid.

3.   The maximum percentage by which fees may be increased in respect of the proceedings which are the subject of the conditional fee agreement is 100%.

4.   The Conditional Fee Agreements Regulations 1995 prescribe matters which solicitors must deal with before entering into a conditional fee agreement and set out certain minimum requirements of the agreement itself (see Annex 14B, p.292). The regulations also apply with modifications to an agreement between solicitors and barristers.

5.   See Annex 14F (p.303) for a statement of the application of the rules and principles of professional conduct to conditional fee agreements.

6.   Copies of the Society's model agreement for use in personal injury cases, leaflets for clients and *Conditional Fees – A Survival Guide* by Bawdon and Napier may be ordered from Marston Book Services (see p.xv for contact details).

14

14.06 When to bill

A solicitor should render a bill of costs to a client within a reasonable time of concluding the matter to which the bill relates.

1. In a contentious matter, where the court has made an order for costs or there is a legal aid taxation, the bill must be lodged for taxation or assessment within three months of the end of the proceedings, as provided by the Civil Procedure Rules and legal aid regulations.

2. Principle **14.06** is particularly important where a solicitor is holding sums of money on behalf of a client and awaits approval of the costs before accounting to the client, or where the client has asked for the papers and the solicitor claims a lien.

14.07 Content of bill

A solicitor's bill of costs should contain sufficient information to identify the matter and period to which it relates.

1. The bill or letter accompanying the bill should be signed by the principal or a partner of the firm – see section 69 of the Solicitors Act 1974 (Annex 14A at p.289).

2. In order to comply with the VAT regulations when a third party is paying the solicitor's costs, the bill must be made out to the client, but it should state that the bill is payable by a third party.

3. The bill should show disbursements separately from the solicitor's fees. Section 67 of the Solicitors Act 1974 (Annex 14A at p.288) provides that unpaid disbursements be described in the bill as not then paid and, if the bill is to be taxed, requires the disbursements to be paid before the taxation is completed.

4. A client in receipt of a gross sum bill in a contentious matter has the right, in certain circumstances, to demand a detailed bill (see section 64 of the Solicitors Act 1974, at Annex 14A at p.287). Once such a request has been made the original gross sum bill is of no effect. The solicitor must render a detailed bill within a reasonable time.

5. Sections 57 and 59–63 of the Solicitors Act 1974 make provision respectively for non-contentious and contentious business agreements, which may be based on an hourly rate. See Annex 14A, p.284.

14.08 Recovery of fees – non-contentious

In a non-contentious matter, a solicitor may not sue the client until the expiration of one month from the delivery of the bill, unless the solicitor has been given leave to do so on the grounds set out in section 69 of the Solicitors Act 1974. Further, a solicitor must not sue or threaten to sue

unless he or she has first informed the client in writing of the right to require a remuneration certificate and of the right to seek taxation (now assessment) of the bill.

1.   Any judgement obtained against a client is unenforceable unless **14.08** has been complied with. For section 69, see Annex 14A at p.289.

2.   A statutory demand is not a proceeding and can be served prior to service of the notice upon the client (*Re a debtor; Marshalls (a firm)* v. *A debtor* [1992] 4 All E.R. 301).

3.   The Solicitors' (Non-Contentious Business) Remuneration Order 1994 (Annex 14D, p.296) regulates a solicitor's remuneration for non-contentious business where the costs are not more than £50,000. Solicitors who fail to comply with the terms of the Remuneration Order may be guilty of unprofessional conduct and liable to disciplinary proceedings.

4.   A form of notice to the client and entitled third parties under article 6 of the Solicitors' (Non-Contentious Business) Remuneration Order 1994 is contained in Annex 14E, p.302.

5.   As an alternative, or in addition to seeking a remuneration certificate, a client who is dissatisfied with the amount of a solicitor's bill in respect of a non-contentious matter may apply to have the bill taxed by the High Court – see section 68(1) of the Solicitors Act 1974 (Annex 14A at p.288).

6.   A third party who has paid or is liable to pay a solicitor's bill may apply for taxation (e.g. a tenant paying a landlord's costs) – see section 71 of the Solicitors Act 1974 (see Annex 14A at p.291).

7.   Although a solicitor may apply for taxation, either of his or her own volition or at the request of the client or a third party liable to pay the bill, he or she is under no duty to do so.

14.09   Recovery of fees – contentious

In a contentious matter, a solicitor may not sue the client until the expiration of one month from the delivery of the bill, unless the solicitor has been given leave to do so on the grounds set out in section 69 of the Solicitors Act 1974. Section 61 of the Act provides that a solicitor may not bring an action on a contentious business agreement without leave of the court.

1.   For sections 69 and 61 of the Act, see Annex 14A at pp.289 and 286.

2.   It is the Society's view that there is no need for leave of the court under section 61 before suing on a bill calculated in accordance with agreed rates.

3.   A contentious business agreement does not include a conditional fee agreement – see **14.05**, p.279 and section 58(1)(d) of the Courts and Legal Services Act 1990.

14

4.   Where there is no contentious business agreement, a client may apply for a statutory taxation (now assessment) of the bill pursuant to section 70 of the Solicitors Act (see Annex 14A at p.289). Whilst there is no duty upon a solicitor to inform clients of their right to apply for taxation, when a solicitor sues on a contentious bill it may be prudent to inform the client in a letter before action of the right to apply for a taxation.

5.   A third party who has paid or is liable to pay a solicitor's bill may apply for taxation – section 71 of the Solicitors Act (see Annex 14A at p.291).

14.10   Interest – non-contentious

In a non-contentious matter, a solicitor may charge interest on the whole or outstanding part of an unpaid bill with effect from one month after delivery of the bill, provided that notice as mentioned in 14.08 has been given to the client.

1.   The right to charge interest and the rate chargeable are governed by article 14 of the Solicitors' (Non-Contentious Business) Remuneration Order 1994 (see Annex 14D at p.300). Terms of business may provide for a different rate of interest.

2.   If a bill is reduced, whether as a result of a remuneration certificate or of taxation, the rate of interest may only be applied to the reduced bill.

14.11   Interest – contentious

In a contentious matter, a solicitor may charge interest on an unpaid bill:

(a)   **if the right to charge interest has been expressly reserved in the original retainer agreement, or**

(b)   **if a client has later agreed to pay it for a contractual consideration, or**

(c)   **where the solicitor has sued the client and claimed interest under section 35A of the Supreme Court Act 1981.**

14.12   Overcharging

A solicitor must not take unfair advantage of the client by overcharging for work done or to be done.

1.   It is a question of fact in each case whether the charge is so excessive as to amount to culpable overcharging.

2.   If an agreement between solicitor and client is found to be wholly unreasonable as to the amount of the fees charged or to be charged,

disciplinary action could be taken against the solicitor on the grounds that the solicitor had taken unfair advantage of the client.

3. Under article 5(1) of the Solicitors' (Non-Contentious Business) Remuneration Order 1994 (see Annex 14D at p.298), if a taxing (now costs) officer allows less than one-half of the sum charged in a non-contentious bill, the officer is under a duty to bring the facts of the case to the attention of the Society.

4. Where a solicitor has a bill of costs prepared by a costs draftsman, the bill remains the responsibility of the solicitor.

14.13 Practice rule 10 (receipt of commissions from third parties)

'(1) Solicitors shall account to their clients for any commission received of more than £20 unless, having disclosed to the client in writing the amount or basis of calculation of the commission or (if the precise amount or basis cannot be ascertained) an approximation thereof, they have the client's agreement to retain it.

(2) Where the commission actually received is materially in excess of the amount or basis or approximation disclosed to the client the solicitor shall account to the client for the excess.

(3) This rule does not apply where a member of the public deposits money with a solicitor who is acting as agent for a building society or other financial institution and the solicitor has not advised that person as a client as to the disposition of the money.'

Solicitors' Practice Rules 1990, rule 10

14.14 Receipt of commissions from third parties – additional guidance

1. Detailed guidance on the application of rule 10 is contained in Annex 14G, p.308.

2. Rule 10 follows the position at law from which it is clear that a solicitor may not make a secret profit but must disclose to the client fully the receipt of any such profit. It may only be retained provided the client agrees. The rule also applies to the receipt by solicitors of, for example, commissions on insurances and from the Stock Exchange.

3. Appendix 7 of the Solicitors' Investment Business Rules 1995 will apply in connection with any transaction or contemplated transaction relating to a life policy (see Annex 27B at p.601).

14

Annex 14A

Solicitors Act 1974

sections 57, 59–61, 64 and 66–71 (remuneration of solicitors)

(with consolidated amendments to May 1995)

57. Non-contentious business agreements

(1) Whether or not any order is in force under section 56, a solicitor and his client may, before or after or in the course of the transaction of any non-contentious business by the solicitor, make an agreement as to his remuneration in respect of that business.

(2) The agreement may provide for the remuneration of the solicitor by a gross sum or by reference to an hourly rate, or by a commission or percentage, or by a salary, or otherwise, and it may be made on the terms that the amount of the remuneration stipulated for shall or shall not include all or any disbursements made by the solicitor in respect of searches, plans, travelling, stamps, fees, or other matters.

(3) The agreement shall be in writing and signed by the person to be bound by it or his agent in that behalf.

(4) Subject to subsections (5) and (7), the agreement may be sued and recovered on or set aside in the like manner and on the like grounds as an agreement not relating to the remuneration of a solicitor.

(5) If on any taxation of costs the agreement is relied on by the solicitor and objected to by the client as unfair or unreasonable, the taxing officer may enquire into the facts and certify them to the court, and if from that certificate it appears just to the court that the agreement should be set aside, or the amount payable under it reduced, the court may so order and may give such consequential directions as it thinks fit.

(6) Subsection (7) applies where the agreement provides for the remuneration of the solicitor to be by reference to an hourly rate.

(7) If, on the taxation of any costs, the agreement is relied on by the solicitor and the client objects to the amount of the costs (but is not alleging that the agreement is unfair or unreasonable), the taxing officer may enquire into –

(a) the number of hours worked by the solicitor; and

(b) whether the number of hours worked by him was excessive.

[NOTE

For the application of section 57 to a recognised body (i.e. an incorporated practice recognised under section 9 of the Administration of Justice Act 1985) see paragraph 22 of Schedule 2 to the Administration of Justice Act 1985.]

59. Contentious business agreements

(1) Subject to subsection (2), a solicitor may make an agreement in writing with his client as to his remuneration in respect of any contentious business done, or to be done, by him (in this Act referred to as a "contentious business agreement") providing that he shall be remunerated by a gross sum or by reference to an hourly rate, or by a salary, or otherwise, and whether at a higher or lower rate than that at which he would otherwise have been entitled to be remunerated.

(2) Nothing in this section or in sections 60 to 63 shall give validity to –

    (a) any purchase by a solicitor of the interest, or any part of the interest, of his client in any action, suit or other contentious proceeding; or

    (b) any agreement by which a solicitor retained or employed to prosecute any action, suit or other contentious proceeding, stipulates for payment only in the event of success in that action, suit or proceeding; or

    (c) any disposition, contract, settlement, conveyance, delivery, dealing or transfer which under the law relating to bankruptcy is invalid against a trustee or creditor in any bankruptcy or composition.

[NOTES

1. Section 59(2)(b) must be read in the light of section 58 of the Courts and Legal Services Act 1990. Section 58(1) provides a definition of 'a conditional fee agreement' and subsection (3)–(4) of section 58 provide:

'(3) Subject to subsection (6), a conditional fee agreement which relates to specified proceedings shall not be unenforceable by reason only of its being a conditional fee agreement.

(4) In this section "specified proceedings" means proceedings of a description specified by order made by the Lord Chancellor for the purposes of subsection (3).'

2. For the application of section 59 to a recognised body (i.e. an incorporated practice recognised under section 9 of the Administration of Justice Act 1985) see paragraph 22 of Schedule 2 to the Administration of Justice Act 1985.]

60. Effect of contentious business agreements

(1) Subject to the provisions of this section and to sections 61 to 63, the costs of a solicitor in any case where a contentious business agreement has been made shall not be subject to taxation or (except in the case of an agreement which provides for the solicitor to be remunerated by reference to an hourly rate) to the provisions of section 69.

(2) Subject to subsection (3), a contentious business agreement shall not affect the amount of, or any rights or remedies for the recovery of, any costs payable by the client to, or to the client by, any person other than the solicitor, and that person may, unless he has otherwise agreed, require any such costs to be taxed according to the rules for their taxation for the time being in force.

(3) A client shall not be entitled to recover from any other person under an order for the payment of any costs to which a contentious business agreement relates more than the amount payable by him to his solicitor in respect of those costs under the agreement.

(4) A contentious business agreement shall be deemed to exclude any claim by the solicitor in respect of the business to which it relates other than –

    (a) a claim for the agreed costs; or

    (b) a claim for such costs as are expressly excepted from the agreement.

14

(5)   A provision in a contentious business agreement that the solicitor shall not be liable for negligence, or that he shall be relieved from any responsibility to which he would otherwise be subject as a solicitor, shall be void.

[NOTE

For the application of section 60 to a recognised body (i.e. an incorporated practice recognised under section 9 of the Administration of Justice Act 1985) see paragraphs 22 and 24 of Schedule 2 to the Administration of Justice Act 1985.]

61. Enforcement of contentious business agreements

(1)   No action shall be brought on any contentious business agreement, but on the application of any person who –

(a)   is a party to the agreement or the representative of such a party; or

(b)   is or is alleged to be liable to pay, or is or claims to be entitled to be paid, the costs due or alleged to be due in respect of the business to which the agreement relates,

the court may enforce or set aside the agreement and determine every question as to its validity or effect.

(2)   On any application under subsection (1), the court –

(a)   if it is of the opinion that the agreement is in all respects fair and reasonable, may enforce it;

(b)   if it is of the opinion that the agreement is in any respect unfair or unreasonable, may set it aside, and order the costs covered by it to be taxed as if it had never been made;

(c)   in any case, may make such order as to the costs of the application as it thinks fit.

(3)   If the business covered by a contentious business agreement (not being an agreement to which section 62 applies) is business done, or to be done, in any action, a client who is a party to the agreement may make application to a taxing officer of the court for the agreement to be examined.

(4)   A taxing officer before whom an agreement is laid under subsection (3) shall examine it and may either allow it, or, if he is of the opinion that the agreement is unfair or unreasonable, require the opinion of the court to be taken on it, and the court may allow the agreement or reduce the amount payable under it, or set it aside and order the costs covered by it to be taxed as if it had never been made.

(4A) Subsection (4B) applies where a contentious business agreement provides for the remuneration of the solicitor to be by reference to an hourly rate.

(4B) If on the taxation of any costs the agreement is relied on by the solicitor and the client objects to the amount of the costs (but is not alleging that the agreement is unfair or unreasonable), the taxing officer may enquire into –

(a)   the number of hours worked by the solicitor; and

(b)   whether the number of hours worked by him was excessive.

(5)   Where the amount agreed under any contentious business agreement is paid by or on behalf of the client or by any person entitled to do so, the person making the payment may at any time within twelve months from the date of payment, or within such further

time as appears to the court to be reasonable, apply to the court, and, if it appears to the court that the special circumstances of the case require it to be re-opened, the court may, on such terms as may be just, re-open it and order the costs covered by the agreement to be taxed and the whole or any part of the amount received by the solicitor to be repaid by him.

(6)   In this section and sections 62 and 63 "the court" means –

    (a)   in relation to an agreement under which any business has been done in any court having jurisdiction to enforce and set aside agreements, any such court in which any of that business has been done;

    (b)   in relation to an agreement under which no business has been done in any such court and under which more than £50 is payable, the High Court;

    (c)   in relation to an agreement under which no business has been done in any such court, and under which not more than £50 is payable, any county court which would, but for the provisions of subsection (1) prohibiting the bringing of an action on the agreement, have had jurisdiction in any action on it;

and for the avoidance of doubt it is hereby declared that in paragraph (a) "court having jurisdiction to enforce and set aside agreements" includes a county court.

[NOTE

For the application of section 61 to a recognised body (i.e. an incorporated practice recognised under section 9 of the Administration of Justice Act 1985) see paragraph 22 of Schedule 2 to the Administration of Justice Act 1985.]

64. Form of bill of costs for contentious business

(1)   Where the remuneration of a solicitor in respect of contentious business done by him is not the subject of a contentious business agreement, then, subject to subsections (2) to (4), the solicitor's bill of costs may at the option of the solicitor be either a bill containing detailed items or a gross sum bill.

(2)   The party chargeable with a gross sum bill may at any time –

    (a)   before he is served with a writ or other originating process for the recovery of costs included in the bill, and

    (b)   before the expiration of three months from the date on which the bill was delivered to him,

require the solicitor to deliver, in lieu of that bill, a bill containing detailed items; and on such a requirement being made the gross sum bill shall be of no effect.

(3)   Where an action is commenced on a gross sum bill, the court shall, if so requested by the party chargeable with the bill before the expiration of one month from the service on that party of the writ or other originating process, order that the bill be taxed.

(4)   If a gross sum bill is taxed, whether under this section or otherwise, nothing in this section shall prejudice any rules of court with respect to taxation, and the solicitor shall furnish the taxing officer with such details of any of the costs covered by the bill as the taxing officer may require.

[NOTE

For the application of section 64 to a recognised body (i.e. an incorporated practice recognised under section 9 of the Administration of Justice Act 1985) see paragraph 22 of Schedule 2 to the Administration of Justice Act 1985.]

14

66. Taxation with respect to contentious business

Subject to the provisions of any rules of court, on every taxation of costs in respect of any contentious business, the taxing officer may –

(a) allow interest at such rate and from such time as he thinks just on money disbursed by the solicitor for the client, and on money of the client in the hands of, and improperly retained by, the solicitor; and

(b) in determining the remuneration of the solicitor, have regard to the skill, labour and responsibility involved in the business done by him.

[NOTE

For an analogous provision in the case of a recognised body (i.e. an incorporated practice recognised under section 9 of the Administration of Justice Act 1985) see paragraph 26 of Schedule 2 to the Administration of Justice Act 1985.]

67. Inclusion of disbursements in bill of costs

A solicitor's bill of costs may include costs payable in discharge of a liability properly incurred by him on behalf of the party to be charged with the bill (including counsel's fees) notwithstanding that those costs have not been paid before the delivery of the bill to that party; but those costs –

(a) shall be described in the bill as not then paid; and

(b) if the bill is taxed, shall not be allowed by the taxing officer unless they are paid before the taxation is completed.

[NOTE

For the application of section 67 to a recognised body (i.e. an incorporated practice recognised under section 9 of the Administration of Justice Act 1985) see paragraph 22 of Schedule 2 to the Administration of Justice Act 1985.]

68. Power of court to order solicitor to deliver bill, etc.

(1) The jurisdiction of the High Court to make orders for the delivery by a solicitor of a bill of costs, and for the delivery up of, or otherwise in relation to, any documents in his possession, custody or power, is hereby declared to extend to cases in which no business has been done by him in the High Court.

(2) A county court shall have the same jurisdiction as the High Court to make orders making such provision as is mentioned in subsection (1) in cases where the bill of costs or the documents relate wholly or partly to contentious business done by the solicitor in that county court.

(3) In this section and in sections 69 to 71 "solicitor" includes the executors, administrators and assignees of a solicitor.

[NOTE

For the application of section 68 to a recognised body (i.e. an incorporated practice recognised under section 9 of the Administration of Justice Act 1985) see paragraph 27 of Schedule 2 to the Administration of Justice Act 1985. Paragraph 28 of Schedule 2 provides that any jurisdiction of the High Court to make, in the case of a solicitor who is acting or has acted as such for a client, an order requiring the payment or delivery up of, or otherwise relating to, money or securities which the solicitor has in his possession or control on behalf of the client, shall be exercisable in like manner in the case of a recognised body which is acting or has acted as such for a client.]

69. Action to recover solicitor's costs

(1) Subject to the provisions of this Act, no action shall be brought to recover any costs due to a solicitor before the expiration of one month from the date on which a bill of those costs is delivered in accordance with the requirements mentioned in subsection (2); but if there is probable cause for believing that the party chargeable with the costs –

 (a) is about to quit England and Wales, to become bankrupt or to compound with his creditors, or

 (b) is about to do any other act which would tend to prevent or delay the solicitor obtaining payment,

the High Court may, notwithstanding that one month has not expired from the delivery of the bill, order that the solicitor be at liberty to commence an action to recover his costs and may order that those costs be taxed.

(2) The requirements referred to in subsection (1) are that the bill –

 (a) must be signed by the solicitor, or if the costs are due to a firm, by one of the partners of that firm, either in his own name or in the name of the firm, or be enclosed in, or accompanied by, a letter which is so signed and refers to the bill; and

 (b) must be delivered to the party to be charged with the bill, either personally or by being sent to him by post to, or left for him at, his place of business, dwelling-house, or last known place of abode;

and, where a bill is proved to have been delivered in compliance with those requirements, it shall not be necessary in the first instance for the solicitor to prove the contents of the bill and it shall be presumed, until the contrary is shown, to be a bill bona fide complying with this Act.

(3) Where a bill of costs relates wholly or partly to contentious business done in a county court and the amount of the bill does not exceed £5,000, the powers and duties of the High Court under this section and sections 70 and 71 in relation to that bill may be exercised and performed by any county court in which any part of the business was done.

[NOTE

For the application of section 69 to a recognised body (i.e. an incorporated practice recognised under section 9 of the Administration of Justice Act 1985) see paragraphs 22 and 29 of Schedule 2 to the Administration of Justice Act 1985.]

70. Taxation on application of party chargeable or solicitor

(1) Where before the expiration of one month from the delivery of a solicitor's bill an application is made by the party chargeable with the bill, the High Court shall, without requiring any sum to be paid into court, order that the bill be taxed and that no action be commenced on the bill until the taxation is completed.

(2) Where no such application is made before the expiration of the period mentioned in subsection (1), then on an application being made by the solicitor or, subject to subsections (3) and (4), by the party chargeable with the bill, the court may on such terms, if any, as it thinks fit (not being terms as to the costs of the taxation), order –

 (a) that the bill be taxed; and

 (b) that no action be commenced on the bill, and that any action already commenced be stayed, until the taxation is completed.

14

(3)   Where an application under subsection (2) is made by the party chargeable with the bill –

(a)   after the expiration of 12 months from the delivery of the bill, or

(b)   after a judgment has been obtained for the recovery of the costs covered by the bill, or

(c)   after the bill has been paid, but before the expiration of 12 months from the payment of the bill,

no order shall be made except in special circumstances and, if an order is made, it may contain such terms as regards the costs of the taxation as the court may think fit.

(4)   The power to order taxation conferred by subsection (2) shall not be exercisable on an application made by the party chargeable with the bill after the expiration of 12 months from the payment of the bill.

(5)   An order for the taxation of a bill made on an application under this section by the party chargeable with the bill shall, if he so requests, be an order for the taxation of the profit costs covered by the bill.

(6)   Subject to subsection (5), the court may under this section order the taxation of all the costs, or of the profit costs, or of the costs other than profit costs and, where part of the costs is not to be taxed, may allow an action to be commenced or to be continued for that part of the costs.

(7)   Every order for the taxation of a bill shall require the taxing officer to tax not only the bill but also the costs of the taxation and to certify what is due to or by the solicitor in respect of the bill and in respect of the costs of the taxation.

(8)   If after due notice of any taxation either party to it fails to attend, the officer may proceed with the taxation ex parte.

(9)   Unless –

(a)   the order for taxation was made on the application of the solicitor and the party chargeable does not attend the taxation, or

(b)   the order for taxation or an order under subsection (10) otherwise provides,

the costs of a taxation shall be paid according to the event of the taxation, that is to say, if one-fifth of the amount of the bill is taxed off, the solicitor shall pay the costs, but otherwise the party chargeable shall pay the costs.

(10)   The taxing officer may certify to the court any special circumstances relating to a bill or to the taxation of a bill, and the court may make such order as respects the costs of the taxation as it may think fit.

(11)   Subsection (9) shall have effect in any case where the application for an order for taxation was made before the passing of the Solicitors (Amendment) Act 1974 and –

(a)   the bill is a bill for contentious business, or

(b)   more than half of the amount of the bill before taxation consists of costs for which a scale charge is provided by an order for the time being in operation under section 56,

as if for the reference to one-fifth of the amount the bill there were substituted a reference to one-sixth of that amount.

(12) In this section "profit costs" means costs other than counsel's fees or costs paid or payable in the discharge of a liability incurred by the solicitor on behalf of the party chargeable, and the reference in subsection (9) to the fraction of the amount of the bill taxed off shall be taken, where the taxation concerns only part of the costs covered by the bill, as a reference to that fraction of the amount of those costs which is being taxed.

[NOTE

For the application of section 70 to a recognised body (i.e. an incorporated practice recognised under section 9 of the Administration of Justice Act 1985) see paragraph 22 of Schedule 2 to the Administration of Justice Act 1985.]

71. Taxation on application of third parties

(1)   Where a person other than the party chargeable with the bill for the purposes of section 70 has paid, or is or was liable to pay, a bill either to the solicitor or to the party chargeable with the bill, that person or his executors, administrators or assignees may apply to the High Court for an order for the taxation of the bill as if he were the party chargeable with it, and the court may make the same order (if any) as it might have made if the application had been made by the party chargeable with the bill.

(2)   Where the court has no power to make an order by virtue of subsection (1) except in special circumstances it may, in considering whether there are special circumstances sufficient to justify the making of an order, take into account circumstances which affect the applicant but do not affect the party chargeable with the bill.

(3)   Where a trustee, executor or administrator has become liable to pay a bill of a solicitor, then, on the application of any person interested in any property out of which the trustee, executor or administrator has paid, or is entitled to pay, the bill the court may order –

   (a)   that the bill be taxed on such terms, if any, as it thinks fit; and

   (b)   that such payments in respect of the amount found to be due to or by the solicitor and in respect of the costs of the taxation, be made to or by the applicant, to or by the solicitor, or to or by the executor, administrator or trustee, as it thinks fit.

(4)   In considering any application under subsection (3) the court shall have regard –

   (a)   to the provisions of section 70 as to applications by the party chargeable for the taxation of a solicitor's bill so far as they are capable of being applied to an application made under that subsection;

   (b)   to the extent and nature of the interest of the applicant.

(5)   If an applicant under subsection (3) pays any money to the solicitor, he shall have the same right to be paid that money by the trustee, executor or administrator chargeable with the bill as the solicitor had.

(6)   Except in special circumstances, no order shall be made on an application under this section for the taxation of a bill which has already been taxed.

(7)   If the court on an application under this section orders a bill to be taxed, it may order the solicitor to deliver to the applicant a copy of the bill on payment of the costs of that copy.

[NOTE

For the application of section 71 to a recognised body (i.e. an incorporated practice recognised under section 9 of the Administration of Justice Act 1985) see paragraph 22 of Schedule 2 to the Administration of Justice Act 1985.]

14

Annex 14B

Conditional Fee Agreements Regulations 1995

(S.I. 1995 no. 1675)

Whereas a draft of the above regulations has been laid before and approved by resolution of each House of Parliament;

Now, therefore, the Lord Chancellor, in exercise of the powers conferred on him by sections 58(1) and 119 of the Courts and Legal Services Act 1990 [1990 c.41; section 119 is an interpretation provision and is cited because of the meaning assigned to the word "prescribed"], hereby makes the following Regulations:–

Citation, commencement and interpretation

1.(1) These Regulations may be cited as the Conditional Fee Agreements Regulations 1995 and shall come into force on 5th July 1995.

(2)   In these Regulations –

"agreement", in relation to an agreement between a legal representative and an additional legal representative, includes a retainer;

"legal aid" means representation under Part IV of the Legal Aid Act 1988 [1988 c.34.];

"legal representative" means a person providing advocacy or litigation services.

Agreements to comply with prescribed requirements

2.   An agreement shall not be a conditional fee agreement unless it complies with the requirements of the following regulations.

Requirements of an agreement

3.   An agreement shall state –

(a)   the particular proceedings or parts of them to which it relates (including whether it relates to any counterclaim, appeal or proceedings to enforce a judgment or order);

(b)   the circumstances in which the legal representative's fees and expenses or part of them are payable;

(c)   what, if any, payment is due –

    (i)   upon partial failure of the specified circumstances to occur;

    (ii)   irrespective of the specified circumstances occurring; and

    (iii)   upon termination of the agreement for any reason;

(d)   the amount payable in accordance with sub-paragraphs (b) or (c) above or the method to be used to calculate the amount payable; and in particular whether or not the amount payable is limited by reference to the amount of any damages which may be recovered on behalf of the client.

Additional requirements

4.(1) The agreement shall also state that, immediately before it was entered into, the legal representative drew the client's attention to the matters specified in paragraph (2).

(2)   The matters are –

(a)   whether the client might be entitled to legal aid in respect of the proceedings to which the agreement relates, the conditions upon which legal aid is available and the application of those conditions to the client in respect of the proceedings;

(b)   the circumstances in which the client may be liable to pay the fees and expenses of the legal representative in accordance with the agreement;

(c)   the circumstances in which the client may be liable to pay the costs of any other party to the proceedings; and

(d)   the circumstances in which the client may seek taxation of the fees and expenses of the legal representative and the procedure for so doing.

Application of regulation 4

5.   Regulation 4 shall not apply to an agreement between a legal representative and an additional legal representative.

Form of agreement

6.   An agreement shall be in writing and, except in the case of an agreement between a legal representative and an additional legal representative, shall be signed by the client and the legal representative.

Amendment of agreement

7.   Where it is proposed to extend the agreement to cover further proceedings or parts of them regulations 3 to 6 shall apply to the agreement as extended.

14

Annex 14C

Conditional Fee Agreements Order 1998

(S.I. 1998 no. 1860)

The Lord Chancellor, in exercise of the powers conferred on him by sections 58(4) and (5) of the Courts and Legal Services Act 1990 [1990 c.41], having consulted in accordance with section 58(7) of that Act, makes the following Order, a draft of which has been laid before and approved by resolution of each House of Parliament:

Citation, commencement and interpretation

1.(1) This Order may be cited as the Conditional Fee Agreements Order 1998 and shall come into force on the day after the day on which it is made.

(2) In this Order "the Act" means the Courts and Legal Services Act 1990.

Revocation of 1995 Order

2. The Conditional Fee Agreements Order 1995 [S.I. 1995/1674] is revoked.

Specified proceedings

3.(1) All proceedings are proceedings specified for the purposes of section 58(3) of the Act (conditional fee agreements in respect of specified proceedings not to be unenforceable).

(2) Proceedings specified in paragraph (1) shall be specified proceedings notwithstanding that they are concluded without the commencement of court proceedings.

Maximum permitted percentage increase on fees

4. For the purposes of section 58(5) of the Act the maximum permitted percentage by which fees may be increased in respect of any proceedings designated by article 3 as proceedings specified for purposes of section 58(3) of the Act is 100%.

Explanatory note

(This note is not part of the Order)

Section 58 of the Courts and Legal Services Act 1990 provides that a conditional fee agreement which relates to specified proceedings shall not be unenforceable by reason only of its being a conditional fee agreement. Section 58(1)(a) excludes agreements in respect of criminal proceedings and specified family proceedings from the scope of section 58. This Order replaces the Conditional Fee Agreements Order 1995, which specified a limited number of categories of proceedings, and specifies instead all proceedings (within the scope of section 587) without any exceptions.

The Order also specifies (as did the 1995 Order) that the maximum percentage by which fees may be increased in respect of the specified proceedings is 100%.

August 1998

14

Annex 14D

Solicitors' (Non-Contentious Business) Remuneration Order 1994

(S.I. 1994 no. 2616)

The Lord Chancellor, the Lord Chief Justice, the Master of the Rolls, the President of the Law Society, the president of Holborn law society and the Chief Land Registrar (in respect of business done under the Land Registration Act 1925 [1925 c.21.]), together constituting the committee authorised to make orders under section 56 of the Solicitors Act 1974 [1974 c.47, as modified by the Administration of Justice Act 1985 (c.61), Schedule 2, paragraphs 22 and 23.], in exercise of the powers conferred on them by that section and having complied with the requirements of section 56(3), hereby make the following Order:–

Citation, commencement and revocation

1.   (1)   This Order may be cited as the Solicitors' (Non-Contentious Business) Remuneration Order 1994.

(2)   This Order shall come into force on 1st November 1994 and shall apply to all non-contentious business for which bills are delivered on or after that date.

(3)   The Solicitors' Remuneration Order 1972 [S.I. 1972/1139] is hereby revoked except in its application to business for which bills are delivered before this Order comes into force.

Interpretation

2.   In this Order:–

'client' means the client of a solicitor;

'costs' means the amount charged in a solicitor's bill, exclusive of disbursements and value added tax, in respect of non-contentious business or common form probate business;

'entitled person' means a client or an entitled third party;

'entitled third party' means a residuary beneficiary absolutely and immediately (and not contingently) entitled to an inheritance, where a solicitor has charged the estate for his professional costs for acting in the administration of the estate, and either

(a)   the only personal representatives are solicitors (whether or not acting in a professional capacity); or

(b) the only personal representatives are solicitors acting jointly with partners or employees in a professional capacity;

'paid disbursements' means disbursements already paid by the solicitor;

'recognised body' means a body corporate recognised by the Council under section 9 of the Administration of Justice Act 1985 [1985 c.61];

'remuneration certificate' means a certificate issued by the Council pursuant to this Order;

'residuary beneficiary' includes a person entitled to all or part of the residue of an intestate estate;

'solicitor' includes a recognised body;

'the Council' means the Council of the Law Society.

Solicitors' costs

3.   A solicitor's costs shall be such sum as may be fair and reasonable to both solicitor and entitled person, having regard to all the circumstances of the case and in particular to:–

(a) the complexity of the matter or the difficulty or novelty of the questions raised;

(b) the skill, labour, specialised knowledge and responsibility involved;

(c) the time spent on the business;

(d) the number and importance of the documents prepared or perused, without regard to length;

(e) the place where and the circumstances in which the business or any part thereof is transacted;

(f) the amount or value of any money or property involved;

(g) whether any land involved is registered land;

(h) the importance of the matter to the client; and

(i) the approval (express or implied) of the entitled person or the express approval of the testator to:–

    (i) the solicitor undertaking all or any part of the work giving rise to the costs or

    (ii) the amount of the costs.

Right to certification

4.   (1)   Without prejudice to the provisions of sections 70, 71, and 72 of the Solicitors Act 1974 (which relate to taxation of costs), an entitled person may, subject to the provisions of this Order, require a solicitor to obtain a remuneration certificate from the Council in respect of a bill which has been delivered where the costs are not more than £50,000.

(2)   The remuneration certificate must state what sum, in the opinion of the Council, would be a fair and reasonable charge for the business covered by the bill

14

(whether it be the sum charged or a lesser sum). In the absence of taxation the sum payable in respect of such costs is the sum stated in the remuneration certificate.

Disciplinary and other measures

5.   (1)   If on a taxation the taxing officer allows less than one half of the costs, he must bring the facts of the case to the attention of the Council.

    (2)   The provisions of this Order are without prejudice to the general powers of the Council under the Solicitors Act 1974.

Commencement of proceedings against a client

6.   Before a solicitor brings proceedings to recover costs against a client on a bill for non-contentious business he must inform the client in writing of the matters specified in article 8, except where the bill has been taxed.

Costs paid by deduction

7.   (1)   If a solicitor deducts his costs from monies held for or on behalf of a client or of an estate in satisfaction of a bill and an entitled person objects in writing to the amount of the bill within the prescribed time, the solicitor must immediately inform the entitled person in writing of the matters specified in article 8, unless he has already done so.

    (2)   In this article and in article 10, 'the prescribed time' means:–

        (a)   in respect of a client, three months after delivery of the relevant bill, or a lesser time (which may not be less than one month) specified in writing to the client at the time of delivery of the bill, or

        (b)   in respect of an entitled third party, three months after delivery of notification to the entitled third party of the amount of the costs, or a lesser time (which may not be less than one month) specified in writing to the entitled third party at the time of such notification.

Information to be given in writing to entitled person

8.   When required by articles 6 or 7, a solicitor shall inform an entitled person in writing of the following matters:–

        (a)   where article 4(1) applies:–

            (i)   that the entitled person may, within one month of receiving from the solicitor the information specified in this article or (if later) of delivery of the bill or notification of the amount of the costs, require the solicitor to obtain a remuneration certificate; and

            (ii)   that (unless the solicitor has agreed to do so) the Council may waive the requirements of article 11(1), if satisfied from the client's written application that exceptional circumstances exist to justify granting a waiver;

        (b)   that sections 70, 71 and 72 of the Solicitors Act 1974 set out the entitled person's rights in relation to taxation;

        (c)   that (where the whole of the bill has not been paid, by deduction or otherwise) the solicitor may charge interest on the outstanding amount of the bill in accordance with article 14.

Loss by client of right to certification

9.   A client may not require a solicitor to obtain a remuneration certificate:–

(a)   after a bill has been delivered and paid by the client, other than by deduction;

(b)   where a bill has been delivered, after the expiry of one month from the date on which the client was informed in writing of the matters specified in article 8 or from delivery of the bill if later;

(c)   after the solicitor and client have entered into a non-contentious business agreement in accordance with the provisions of section 57 of the Solicitors Act 1974;

(d)   after a court has ordered the bill to be taxed;

(e)   if article 11(2) applies.

Loss by entitled third party of right to certification

10.   An entitled third party may not require a solicitor to obtain a remuneration certificate:–

(a)   after the prescribed time (within the meaning of article 7(2)(b)) has elapsed without any objection being received to the amount of the costs;

(b)   after the expiry of one month from the date on which the entitled third party was (in compliance with article 7) informed in writing of the matters specified in article 8 or from notification of the costs if later;

(c)   after a court has ordered the bill to be taxed.

Requirement to pay a sum towards the costs

11.   (1)   On requiring a solicitor to obtain a remuneration certificate a client must pay to the solicitor the paid disbursements and value added tax comprised in the bill together with 50% of the costs unless: –

(a)   the client has already paid the amount required under this article, by deduction from monies held or otherwise; or

(b)   the solicitor or (if the solicitor refuses) the Council has agreed in writing to waive all or part of this requirement.

(2)   The Council shall be under no obligation to provide a remuneration certificate, and the solicitor may take steps to obtain payment of his bill if the client, having been informed of his right to seek a waiver of the requirements of paragraph (1), has not:–

(a)   within one month of receipt of the information specified in article 8, either paid in accordance with paragraph (1) or applied to the Council in writing for a waiver of the requirements of paragraph (1); or

(b)   made payment in accordance with the requirements of paragraph (1) within one month of written notification that he has been refused a waiver of those requirements by the Council.

14

Miscellaneous provisions

12. (1) After an application has been made by a solicitor for a remuneration certificate the client may pay the bill in full without invalidating the application.

(2) A solicitor and entitled person may agree in writing to waive the provisions of sub-paragraphs (a) or (b) of articles 9 or 10.

(3) A solicitor may take from his client security for the payment of any costs, including the amount of any interest to which the solicitor may become entitled under article 14.

Refunds by solicitor

13. (1) If a solicitor has received payment of all or part of his costs and a remuneration certificate is issued for less than the sum already paid, the solicitor must immediately pay to the entitled person any refund which may be due (after taking into account any other sums which may properly be payable to the solicitor whether for costs, paid disbursements, value added tax or otherwise) unless the solicitor has applied for an order for taxation within one month of receipt by him of the remuneration certificate.

(2) Where a solicitor applies for taxation, his liability to pay any refund under paragraph (1) shall be suspended for so long as the taxation is still pending.

(3) The obligation of the solicitor to repay costs under paragraph (1) is without prejudice to any liability of the solicitor to pay interest on the repayment by virtue of any enactment, rule of law or professional rule.

Interest

14. (1) After the information specified in article 8 has been given to an entitled person in compliance with articles 6 or 7, a solicitor may charge interest on the unpaid amount of his costs plus any paid disbursements and value added tax, subject to paragraphs (2) and (3) below.

(2) Where an entitlement to interest arises under paragraph (1), and subject to any agreement made between a solicitor and client, the period for which interest may be charged may run from one month after the date of delivery of a bill, unless the solicitor fails to lodge an application within one month of receipt of a request for a remuneration certificate under article 4, in which case no interest is payable in respect of the period between one month after receiving the request and the actual date on which the application is lodged.

(3) Subject to any agreement made between a solicitor and client, the rate of interest must not exceed the rate for the time being payable on judgment debts.

(4) Interest charged under this article must be calculated, where applicable, by reference to the following: –

    (a) if a solicitor is required to obtain a remuneration certificate, the total amount of the costs certified by the Council to be fair and reasonable plus paid disbursements and value added tax;

    (b) if an application is made for the bill to be taxed, the amount ascertained on taxation;

(c) if an application is made for the bill to be taxed or a solicitor is required to obtain a remuneration certificate and for any reason the taxation or application for a remuneration certificate does not proceed, the unpaid amount of the costs shown in the bill or such lesser sum as may be agreed between the solicitor and the client, plus paid disbursements and value added tax.

Application by solicitor

15.　A solicitor, when making an application for a remuneration certificate in accordance with the provisions of this Order, must deliver to the Council the complete relevant file and working papers, and any other information or documentation which the Council may require for the purpose of providing a remuneration certificate.

Annex 14E

Guidance – specimen information for entitled persons under the Solicitors' (Non-Contentious Business) Remuneration Order 1994

The specimen information for the entitled person is not part of the Order and solicitors may use any form of words which complies with the requirements of the Order.

Remuneration certificates

(1)   If you are not satisfied with the amount of our fee you have the right to ask us to obtain a remuneration certificate from the Law Society.

(2)   The certificate will either say that our fee is fair and reasonable, or it will substitute a lower fee.

(3)   If you wish us to obtain a certificate you must ask us to do so *within a month* of receiving this notice.

(4)   We may charge interest on unpaid bills and we will do so at [the rate payable on judgment debts, from one month after delivery of our bill].

(5)   (i)   If you ask us to obtain a remuneration certificate, then unless we already hold the money to cover these, you must first pay:

▶   half our fee shown in the bill;

▶   all the VAT shown in the bill;

▶   all the expenses we have incurred shown in the bill – sometimes called 'paid disbursements'.

(ii)   However, you may ask the Office for the Supervision of Solicitors at 8 Dormer Place, Leamington Spa, Warwickshire CV32 5AE to waive this requirement so that you do not have to pay anything for the time being. You would have to show that exceptional circumstances apply in your case.

(6)   Your rights are set out more fully in the Solicitors' (Non-Contentious Business) Remuneration Order 1994.

Taxation

You may be entitled to have our charges reviewed by the court. (This is called 'taxation' or 'assessment'.) The procedure is different from the remuneration certificate procedure and it is set out in sections 70, 71 and 72 of the Solicitors Act 1974.

Annex 14F

Guidance – conditional fee agreements

Introduction

1.   The Conditional Fee Agreements Regulations (see Annex 14B, p.292 in the Guide) came into force on 5th July 1995, as did the Conditional Fee Agreements Order. The order has now been replaced by the Conditional Fee Agreements Order 1998 (see Annex 14C, p.294 in the Guide). The effect of the new order and regulations together with the recent amendment made to rule 8 of the Solicitors' Practice Rules 1990 (**14.03**, p.278 in the Guide) is to permit solicitors to enter into conditional fee agreements ('no win, no fee') in respect of all proceedings, except family and criminal matters and all non-contentious matters.

2.   The Council has considered whether any new practice rule or formal guidance is required in respect of conditional fee agreements. The Council is of the view that this is not necessary at this stage as, together with the regulations, existing rules and guidance deal adequately with the issues likely to arise. This note draws attention to the relevant provisions. The Council will keep the matter under review and, if experience of the operation of conditional fee agreements indicates that new issues are arising that should be addressed through rules or guidance, appropriate measures will be brought forward.

Specimen agreement

3.   The Society has produced an example of a conditional fee agreement which solicitors may choose to adapt as appropriate. It is emphasised that the form of agreement is not mandatory but it is intended to be of help to solicitors in producing a form of agreement which is appropriate to particular circumstances, including the requirements of an individual case.

Making an effective agreement

4.   The regulations prescribe matters which solicitors must deal with before entering a conditional fee agreement, as well as certain minimum requirements of the agreement itself:

(A) *Requirements preliminary to an agreement*

Before any agreement is entered into, the solicitor shall draw to the client's attention each of the following matters:

(a) whether the client might be entitled to legal aid in respect of the proceedings to which the agreement relates, the conditions upon which legal aid is available and the application of those conditions to the client in respect of the proceedings;

(b) the circumstances in which the client may be liable to pay the fees and expenses of the solicitor in accordance with the agreement;

(c) the circumstances in which the client may be liable to pay the costs of any other party to the proceedings; and

(d) the circumstances in which the client may seek taxation of the fees and expenses of the legal representative and the procedure for so doing.

(B) *Requirements of an agreement*

Any agreement shall state:

(a) the particular proceedings or parts of them to which it relates (including whether it relates to any counterclaim, appeal or proceedings to enforce a judgment or order);

(b) the circumstances in which the legal representative's fees and expenses or part of them are payable;

(c) what, if any, payment is due:

(i) upon partial failure of the specified circumstances to occur;

(ii) irrespective of the specified circumstances occurring; and

(iii) upon termination of the agreement for any reason;

(d) the amount payable in accordance with sub-paragraphs (b) or (c) above or the method to be used to calculate the amount payable; and in particular whether or not the amount payable is limited by reference to the amount of any damages which may be recovered on behalf of the client.

(C) *Form of agreement*

Any agreement shall be in writing and shall be signed by the client and the solicitor.

5.   Solicitors are reminded that practice rule 8 disapplies the prohibition on conditional fees only when the agreement allows for a contingency fee that is permitted under statute or by the common law. An attempt to make a conditional fee agreement, which fails because the regulations or law have not been complied with, would put the solicitor in breach of rule 8, and might be rendered unenforceable by reason of public policy. A solicitor will not be able to recover costs under an unenforceable agreement; thus particular care should be taken to ensure that any agreement conforms strictly to the regulations.

Conduct issues

6.   In addition to rule 8 itself, a number of the provisions contained in the Guide may be applied in relation to issues of professional conduct which arise in respect of conditional fee agreements. The essential starting point is rule 1 of the Solicitors' Practice Rules (see **1.01**, p.1 in the Guide).

7.   The general principles enshrined in practice rule 1 are reinforced by and elaborated upon in a number of principles contained in the Guide which are relevant to conditional fee agreements. Practice rule 15 (see **13.01**, p.265 in the Guide) and the Solicitors' Costs Information and Client Care Code are also of particular importance.

The Solicitors' Costs Information and Client Care Code

8. The Solicitors' Costs Information and Client Care Code (see **13.02**, p.266 in the Guide) requires solicitors to give clients detailed advance information on costs, so that clients receive all the information needed to understand and make informed decisions as to agreements on costs. The code applies to conditional fees as it applies to any other basis of charging.

9. Solicitors are reminded that a breach of the code could lead to a finding that the solicitor has provided inadequate professional services (IPS) or, in a serious or persistent case, a finding of professional misconduct. See also **5.01**, p.160 in the Guide, regarding the availability of legal aid. Unreasonable failure to advise a client properly on some matters, particularly as to costs in litigation or the availability of legal aid, may well also give rise to a claim in negligence.

10. The Office for the Supervision of Solicitors treat a material breach of the code as *prima facie* evidence of IPS. Therefore, in the event of a complaint, the burden will be upon the solicitor to establish that the client was given full information about the risks and costs issues.

Taking unfair advantage

11. In accordance with **11.01**, p.222 in the Guide: 'It is fundamental to the relationship which exists between solicitor and client that a solicitor should be able to give impartial and frank advice to the client, free from any external or adverse pressures or interests which would destroy or weaken the solicitor's professional independence, the fiduciary relationship with the client or the client's freedom of choice.'

12. Because of the fiduciary relationship which exists between solicitor and client, the solicitor must not take advantage of the client (see also **12.09**, p.248 and **15.04**, p.316 in the Guide). In considering, therefore, whether a conditional fee arrangement would be appropriate in the circumstances of any particular case, a solicitor should take care to ensure that his or her own financial interests are not placed above the general interests of the client.

13. Whilst a solicitor is generally free to decide whether to accept instructions from any particular client and the terms upon which instructions will be accepted (**12.01**, p.244 in the Guide), it is important that all the options available to the client for financing the proceedings should be explained and discussed, including the availability of legal aid. As with all litigation, the client's potential exposure to pay another party's costs should also be explained and discussed. The code in paragraph 3 (c) provides that the information in paragraph 4 (advance costs) and 5 (additional information for particular clients) should be given at the outset and at appropriate stages throughout the matter, as do the regulations themselves. In particular, paragraph 4(j)(ii) requires that the solicitor should consider whether the client's liability for the costs may be covered by insurance; in this context such insurance may include 'after the event' insurance. Paragraph 4(j) requires the solicitor to discuss with clients how legal charges and disbursements are to be met; in this context an explanation may be appropriate of how a conditional fee agreement differs from the more usual basis of charging, where the client bears the risks of failure.

Fair and reasonable terms

14. Should the client opt to proceed on a conditional fee basis, the contents of the agreement should be clearly explained and care must be taken to ensure that the terms are

14

fair and reasonable in the circumstances. Any attempt to take unfair advantage of the client by overcharging for work done or to be done (contrary to **14.12**, p.282 in the Guide) raises an issue of conduct for the solicitor, quite apart from the remedies available to the client in relation to taxation. The taxation (now assessment) rules are in Part 47 of the Civil Procedure Rules.

Client's risk

15. Paragraph 6(b) of the code provides that in all matters a solicitor should consider with clients whether the likely outcome will justify the expense or risk involved in relation to the matter. Specifically, the client must fully understand the nature and extent of his or her risk in relation to costs, including the costs of his or her opponent, in accordance with paragraphs 5(b) and (c) of the code.

16. Solicitors may wish the agreement to provide for a cap on the success fee for the benefit of the client to limit the possibility of the client suffering a net financial loss, even where successful in the proceedings, and the model agreement contains a suggested provision. The regulations require that the agreement must state whether or not such a provision applies.

Solicitor's risk

17. An important issue which arises is that of the percentage 'uplift' applicable. Solicitors may well not wish to apply the same uplift to all cases, or to all elements within an individual case. The principles applicable on taxation in relation to the uplift relate the risk to the individual case. In considering what uplift to stipulate in any particular case, solicitors will wish to take into account the degree of risk of the case being lost and the cost of funding the litigation over a period of time. Paragraph 4(k) of the code, and **14.12** (see 14 above) are also relevant. The financial risk assumed by the solicitor may be a factor in deciding on the appropriate uplift, but in determining this the solicitor 'must not take unfair advantage of the client by overcharging for work to be done' (**14.12**, p.282), 'should discuss with the client whether the likely outcome in a matter will justify the expense involved' (see paragraph 4(k) of the code), and 'must not abuse his or her position to exploit a client by taking advantage of a client's inexperience . . . want of . . . business experience' (see **12.09** note 1, p.248).

Advising on settlement

18. In advising clients on matters of settlement, solicitors are reminded of the principles referred to in 11–12 above. Solicitors should always consider their overriding duty to act in the best interests of the client in achieving a suitable settlement *for the client* irrespective of the solicitor's own interest in receiving early payment of costs in accordance with the agreement.

Publicity

19. Although conditional fee agreements have commonly been referred to in the media as 'no win, no fee' agreements, solicitors are reminded of the provisions of the Solicitors' Publicity Code (Annex 11A, p.229 in the Guide). Paragraph 5(a) of the code specifically requires any publicity as to charges or a basis of charging to be clearly expressed, and under paragraph 10(c) of the code publicity must not be inaccurate or misleading in any

way. Further, paragraph 5(c) of the code restricts advertising that a service is 'free' of charge where the conditions which are attached to that service effectively mean that the client will be required to make some payment in respect of the service.

20. Advertisements which purport to offer a solicitor's services on the basis that the client is, for example, able to litigate 'at no financial risk' would be misleading.

January 1996, updated February 1999

Annex 14G

Guidance – commissions

1. Why did the Society make a rule to prevent solicitors keeping commissions unless their clients consent?

Practice rule 10 (see **14.13**, p.283 in the Guide) simply put into practice rule form what had long been required of solicitors both as a matter of law and of professional conduct. The position at law results from the fiduciary and agency relationships which exist between the solicitor and the client. One of the consequences of these relationships is that a solicitor cannot, unless otherwise authorised by law, contract or a trust deed, keep a secret remuneration or financial benefit arising from the use of client's property.

2. To what sort of commissions does the rule apply?

Any financial benefit which you obtain by reason of and in the course of the relationship of solicitor and client is caught by the rule. Examples include commission on life policies, stocks and shares, pensions and general insurances such as household contents and fire policies (including renewals). Also caught is a payment made to you for introducing a client to a third party (unless the introduction was unconnected with any particular matter which you were currently or had been handling for the client) or for opening a building society account.

3. What exactly is meant by 'account to' the client?

'Account to' does not mean simply telling the client that you will receive commission. It means that unless the client agrees to you keeping the commission it belongs to and must be paid to the client. In this respect, the general law relating to solicitors requires a higher duty from solicitors than from, for example, others in the financial service industry.

4. Why must disclosure be in writing?

To protect the interests of both the solicitor and the client. The rule does not require the client's *consent* to be in writing, but this would be advisable (see next question).

5. Can I write to clients setting out details of the commission I will receive and saying that if I do not hear from them within seven days I will assume that they agree to me keeping the commission?

Firstly, it is unlikely that this would constitute the agreement of the client for the purpose of practice rule 10. Secondly, it would be unwise to rely on this as it would be an attempt to impose an agreement on the client unilaterally. The case of *Jordy* v. *Vanderpump* (1920) S.J. 324 made clear that the onus is on the solicitor to show the client's consent. Therefore it is advisable to obtain the client's written consent to keep commission.

6. Exactly what has to be disclosed to the client?

The rule requires that the client be told the amount or basis of calculation of the commission or (if the precise amount or basis cannot be ascertained) an approximation thereof. Although the rule gives you a choice of disclosing the actual amount or the basis of calculation, if the actual amount is known then it should be disclosed to the client when you are seeking consent, bearing in mind your duty to act in the best interests of the client. This is particularly so where the basis of calculation of the commission is very complicated. If the exact amount is not known then the calculation should be explained to the client, and in some cases it may be that an approximation would be more helpful than the basis of the calculation, or should be given as well as the basis of calculation. This may depend on the level of understanding of the client. It is also acceptable for a range to be given into which the amount of the commission is likely to fall, provided that the range is not unreasonably wide.

7. What if the estimate I give turns out to have been too low?

If the commission actually received by you is *materially* in excess of the estimate given by you, or indeed the amount or basis originally disclosed to the client, the rule provides that you must account to the client for the excess. Whether the commission is 'materially in excess' of the original figure will depend on the circumstances of each case, and consideration should be given to the amount of any excess, both on its own and as a proportion of the amount which the client has agreed to you keeping, and the client's financial circumstances. The main reason for the use of the word 'material' in the rule is to avoid situations where the cost to the solicitor of accounting to the client for the excess would be greater than the actual amount of the excess. You may prefer simply to have a policy of accounting for all excesses rather than having to worry about whether the sums involved are materially in excess of the original figure, or it may be possible to use the £20 *de minimis* figure as a guideline (see next question).

8. What is the significance of the £20 figure in the rule?

The £20 figure set out in the rule attempts to define for practical purposes what would be acceptable in law as being *de minimis*.

9. What if I receive a number of commissions of less than £20 in the course of acting for one client?

Whether such commissions can be treated separately for the purposes of the rule will depend on the facts of the particular case. Where the commissions are received in respect of separate transactions they can generally be treated separately. It would be wrong, however, to attempt to split up a transaction for the purpose of creating several commissions of £20 or less as this would not be acting in the best interests of the client. Also the commission would probably not, as a matter of law, be retainable on the basis of the *de minimis* principle. Similarly, you may carry out for

14

a client a number of small transactions as part of a single retainer, each of which results in you receiving a commission of less than £20. It may be difficult to argue that the total of the commission is retainable by you on the *de minimis* principle. Such difficulties could be avoided by obtaining the client's consent to retain the commission at the outset of the retainer.

10. When should the client's consent be obtained?

Although the rule does not contain any specific requirements on timing, as a matter of law the best time to obtain the client's consent is before you do the work which results in the commission being payable. Under the law of contract it is likely to be your agreement to do the work which amounts to the consideration for the client's agreement. Therefore, if the client has not consented when you receive the commission, arguably it belongs to the client. Further, it cannot be in keeping with a duty to act in the best interests of the client for a solicitor, having received a commission, to then seek the client's consent to keep it, when the client is entitled in law to receive it.

11. When commissions are received should they be placed on office or client account?

If the client has consented to you retaining the commission then the money belongs to you and can be placed on office account. When no such agreement has been obtained the money is the property of the client and must be placed on client account. However, if you have any outstanding costs against the client in respect of this or any other matter, you may, provided a bill or some other written notification of costs has been submitted to the client, withdraw from client account the sum of money owed in accordance with rule 19 of the Solicitors' Accounts Rules 1998 (see Annex 28B at p.701 in the Guide).

12. If the client does not consent to me keeping the commission can I still charge him or her for the work which leads to the commission being payable?

Yes. If a bill is submitted for an amount equal to the amount of commission received and this cannot be justified by the factors set out in the Solicitors (Non-Contentious Business) Remuneration Order 1994 (see Annex 14D, p.296 in the Guide), the bill may be reduced under the remuneration certifying procedure or on taxation (now assessment). The Order would not apply if there was a non-contentious business agreement under section 57 of the Solicitors Act 1974 (see Annex 14A, p.284 in the Guide) – although the agreement could be set aside if the court considered it to be unfair or unreasonable.

13. If I am charging the client on a fee basis can I take my fee out of the commission?

Yes, providing that you have not agreed with the client to utilise any commission received for some other specific purpose and providing the client has been sent a bill or some other written notification of costs. In this situation there is no requirement for prior disclosure of the amount of commission or for the client's agreement, as you are, in effect, accounting to the client for the commission and the offsetting is merely a convenient accounting arrangement.

14. Can I advertise 'free conveyancing' where I propose to offset commission against my fees?

No. See paragraph 5 of the Solicitors' Publicity Code 1990 (Annex 11A at p.231 in the Guide).

15. What is the position regarding VAT if I offset commission against costs?

Where you receive commission from a third party (e.g. an insurance broker) in connection with making a supply to a client, and the commission is to be set against the fee to be charged to the client, VAT is calculated on the *net* amount of the fee, following the setting off of the commission against the fee.

16. If the client signs a section 57 agreement will this also meet the requirements of rule 10?

Provided the agreement contains disclosure of the amount or basis of calculation of commission and a clause that the client consents to you retaining the commission, there will normally have been compliance with rule 10.

17. Could I choose to offer financial services on a commission only basis?

Yes. At the outset of a transaction you may state that you are only prepared to act on the basis that you retain any or part of any commission received, provided this does not conflict with your duty to act in the best interests of the client. Simply obtaining the client's agreement to you acting on a commission only basis will not satisfy the requirements of rule 10 where the amount or basis of calculation of the commission is not known or an approximation cannot be given. The client's informed consent is still required. A drawback of working on a commission only basis is that you could find that either the most suitable product does not generate a commission, or that the client does not proceed. In such a situation you could only charge a fee for the work done if you had made clear at the outset your intention to do so.

18. What if the client defaults on a life policy and I become liable to repay some of the commission?

This can cause difficulties where you have accounted to the client for the commission. One option is to agree with the client that the client will be liable for the amount which you have to repay. The prospects of recovering from the client may not be very good. Other options would be to come to an agreement with the client for the late payment of the commission to the client (in which case the money should be kept on client account) or for you to elect to receive the commission from the insurer on a non-indemnity basis, in which case the commission is paid to you in instalments and if the client defaults no refund is necessary.

19. What if the insurance company prohibits me from passing the commission on to the client?

Some insurance companies have been known to state in their agreements with solicitors that the solicitors must not pass any commission on to their clients. In this

14

case, if you cannot obtain the client's agreement to retain the commission you will normally have to decline to accept the commission, and to charge the client a fee instead. It may be possible for you to offset the commission against your fee, but this will depend on the exact nature of the agreement with the insurance company.

20. Surely if I am acting in the renewal of an insurance policy I am not acting as the client's solicitor but as the agent of the insurance company and therefore I am entitled to the commission?

Wrong. See *Copp* v. *Lynch and Law Life Assurance Co.* (1882) 26 S.J. 348 where it was held that the plaintiff was acting as the defendant's solicitor upon renewal of a life policy, and not as agent for the insurance company. Where solicitors are instructed by insurance companies to send out renewal notices and collect premiums, whilst solicitors might be effectively acting as agent for the insurance company, they are still the policy holder's solicitor and therefore rule 10 applies.

21. What if the insurance company sends me one cheque in respect of various clients and I cannot attribute the commission to individual clients?

In *Brown* v. *I.R.C.* [1965] A.C. 244 Lord Reid said, 'I do not see how the difficulty in discovering who is the owner can make the money the property of the solicitor.' Either make a reasonable estimate as to how much is attributable to each individual client or decline to accept the commission.

22. If I am the sole executor of a will can I consent to myself retaining any commission earned in dealing with the estate?

No. A trustee cannot profit from the trust and rule 10 does not permit a solicitor to retain a commission where this would not be permitted at law. Therefore any commission earned in dealing with the estate should be accounted for to the estate. The same principle would apply to a solicitor who was the donee of a power of attorney.

March 1992, updated February 1999

Chapter 15

Conflict of interests

Introductory note

Two forms of conflict of interests are described in this chapter:

▶ *a solicitor must not act where the solicitor's own interests conflict with the client's; and*

▶ *a solicitor must not act where a conflict of interests (or a significant risk of conflict) arises between two or more clients.*

The prohibition against a solicitor acting where his or her personal interests actually conflict with those of a client is absolute. Too often a solicitor believes that merely informing a client that independent advice should be sought is sufficient to discharge his or her duties to the client. This is not normally the case and, in most instances, if the client will not get independent advice, the solicitor must not proceed with the transaction.

The number of enquiries to Professional Ethics suggests that many solicitors have difficulty in identifying when a conflict of interests between clients has arisen or may arise. Two important points to bear in mind are:

▶ *Where a solicitor is acting for two or more clients, whether they be a husband and wife, partners or a corporation embarking on a joint venture, the solicitor always owes a duty to each individual body or person and he or she must advise each individual what is in that individual's interests.*

15

▶ *A possible initial test to apply to the above circumstances to assist in
   identifying if a conflict exists, is: what would occur if the solicitor
   were acting for only one of the parties?*

   ▶ *Would the advice be different?*

   ▶ *Do the parties have different interests?*

   ▶ *Has one of the parties given the solicitor a piece of information
      on a 'confidential' basis that would affect the advice given to
      other clients, if the solicitor could disclose it?*

If these factors apply, a conflict of interests has arisen.

15.01   When instructions must be refused

**A solicitor or firm of solicitors should not accept instructions to act for two
or more clients where there is a conflict or a significant risk of a conflict
between the interests of those clients.**

1. Where a solicitor already acts for one client and is asked to act for another
    client whose interests conflict or are likely to conflict with those of the first
    client, the solicitor must refuse to act for the second client.

2. Even if an actual conflict of interests exists and is disclosed to the client
    and the client consents to the solicitor acting, the solicitor must not accept
    the instructions.

3. There is no objection to a solicitor acting as a conciliator or mediator
    between parties in a domestic dispute. See Chapter 22, p.417 for further
    guidance.

4. For the position of a solicitor acting for seller and buyer, or lender and
    borrower, see practice rule 6 (**25.01**, p.455). For ownership of documents in
    conveyancing, see **16.02** note 9, p.326 and Annex 16C, p.341.

15.02   Relevant confidential information

**If a solicitor or firm of solicitors has acquired relevant confidential
information about an existing or former client during the course of acting
for that client, the solicitor or the firm must not accept instructions to act
against the client.**

1. Any information acquired by a solicitor whilst acting for a client is
    confidential and cannot be disclosed without that client's consent (see
    16.01, p.324). However, a solicitor is under a duty to a client to inform the
    client of all matters which are material to the retainer (see **16.06**, p.331).
    Consequently, a solicitor in possession of confidential information
    concerning a client which is or might be relevant to another client, is put in
    an impossible position and cannot act against that client.

2.   A solicitor who has acted jointly for both husband and wife in matters of common interest, must not act for one of them in matrimonial or other proceedings where the solicitor is in possession of relevant confidential information concerning the other. Usually, where a solicitor has acted jointly for the parties, the solicitor will not have obtained any confidential information, as between the two parties. If the parties consult the solicitor separately on the joint matter, a conflict may arise at this point.

3.   Care must be taken where a solicitor has acted for members of a family and is then asked to act against one or more of them. If the solicitor is obliged by principle **15.02** to refuse to act for a particular member of the family who is under a legal disability, then the solicitor should make reasonable efforts to ensure that that person is separately advised; it is not sufficient for the solicitor merely to cease to act.

4.   Where a solicitor has acted for both lender and borrower in the making of a loan, the solicitor should not subsequently act for the lender against the borrower to enforce repayment if the solicitor has obtained relevant confidential information, e.g. of the borrower's financial position, when acting for the borrower in connection with the original loan. See also practice rule 6 (**25.01**, p.455).

5.   If a solicitor has acted either for a partnership or in its formation, the solicitor may only accept instructions to act against an individual partner or former partner provided no relevant confidential information has been obtained about that individual whilst acting for the partnership, or in its formation.

6.   A solicitor who has acted for a company in a particular matter and has also separately acted for directors or shareholders in their personal capacity in the same matter is unlikely to be able to act for either the company or the other parties if litigation ensues between them in respect of that matter.

7.   When tendering for local authority work, a solicitor will need to consider how frequently the range of work involved is likely to give rise to conflicts between existing clients and the local authority, for example, in housing and custody matters where the solicitor acts against the local authority.

8.   Where a partner changes firm, the test to be applied before that firm may act against a client of the former firm is whether he or she personally has relevant confidential information. If challenged, the burden of proof is on the solicitor to show that he or she has no such information (see *Re: a firm of solicitors* [1995] 3 All E.R. 482).

9.   Where an assistant solicitor changes firms and the firm he or she moves to is acting against a client of the solicitor's former employer, that solicitor cannot act for the new firm's client on that matter. The solicitor owes a duty of confidentiality to his or her former employer and former clients. The solicitor cannot use any information obtained about a former client to assist his or her new employer's client. The new employer can continue acting for the client only if the solicitor can be adequately isolated from the matter.

15

15.03 Conflict arising between two or more current clients

A solicitor or firm of solicitors must not continue to act for two or more clients where a conflict of interests arises between those clients.

1. If a solicitor has already accepted instructions from two clients in a matter or related matters and a conflict subsequently arises between the interests of those clients, the firm must usually cease to act for both clients. A solicitor may only continue to represent one client if not in possession of relevant confidential information concerning the other obtained whilst acting for the other. For guidance on professional embarrassment, see **12.02** note 2 at p.245.

2. Where a solicitor acts for two or more co-defendants in criminal proceedings and one or more of them changes his or her plea, the solicitor must consider carefully whether it is proper to continue to represent any of them. In reaching a decision, the solicitor must bear in mind that if his or her duty of disclosure to the retained client or clients conflicts with his or her duty of confidentiality to the other client or clients, the solicitor must cease to act for all of them. Before agreeing to continue to represent one client the solicitor must, therefore, examine carefully whether there is any information in his or her possession relating to the other clients which may be relevant to the retained client (see *R*. v. *Ataou* [1988] Q.B. 798).

3. Following the amalgamation of two or more firms, the clients of the individual firms will, as a result of an express or implied change of retainer, become clients of the new firm; care must be taken to ensure that the interests of the clients of the new firm do not conflict. If they do, the firm must cease to act for both clients unless they are able, within the terms of note 1 above, to continue to act for one. In certain exceptional circumstances the amalgamated firm may continue to act for one or both clients after erecting a 'Chinese wall'. Further guidance can be found in Annex 15A, p.322.

4. It is doubtful whether, in circumstances other than where there has been an amalgamation of two or more firms, a 'Chinese wall' can be erected so that a firm can continue to represent the interests of two clients whose interests conflict. The courts have expressed doubts on whether an impregnable wall can ever be created because of the practical difficulties of ensuring the absolute confidentiality of each client's affairs (see *Re: a firm of solicitors* [1992] 1 All E.R. 353).

15.04 Solicitor's interests conflicting with client's

A solicitor must not act where his or her own interests conflict with the interests of a client or a potential client.

1. Because of the fiduciary relationship which exists between solicitor and client, a solicitor must not take advantage of the client nor act where there is a conflict of interest or potential conflict of interest between the client and the solicitor. In conduct there is a conflict of interest where a solicitor in his or her personal capacity sells to, or purchases from or lends to or borrows from his or her own client. The solicitor should in these cases ensure that the client takes independent legal advice. If the client refuses to do so, the solicitor must not proceed with the transaction. The fact that the client accepts the conflict does not permit a solicitor to continue to act. It is generally proper for a solicitor to provide short term bridging finance for a client in a conveyancing transaction (see **25.03**, p.469).

2. A solicitor should not enter into any arrangement or understanding with a client or prospective client prior to the conclusion of the matter giving rise to the retainer by which the solicitor acquires an interest in the publication rights with respect to that matter. This applies equally to non-contentious business.

3. A solicitor is entitled to take security for costs but should be aware of the risk of the court finding undue influence. Where taking a charge it is advisable, therefore, to suggest that the client consider seeking independent legal advice. Such advice would not normally be essential unless the terms of the charge are to be particularly onerous or to give the solicitor some benefit or profit. It is important always to ensure that the client understands that a charge is being taken and the effect of such a charge.

4. A solicitor must at all times disclose with complete frankness whenever the solicitor has or might obtain any personal interest or benefit in a transaction in which he or she is acting for the client. In such circumstances, it is incumbent upon a solicitor to insist that the client receives independent advice. Failure to do so may lead to civil action by the client for account.

5. Independent advice means not only legal advice but, where appropriate, competent advice from a member of another profession, e.g. a chartered surveyor.

6. The interests of the solicitor referred to in principle **15.04** may be direct (for example, where a solicitor seeks to sell or buy property from the client or lends to, or borrows from, the client), or indirect (for example, where the solicitor's business interests lead the solicitor to recommend the client to invest in a concern in which the solicitor is interested).

7. Principle **15.04** applies not only where a solicitor is personally interested in a transaction, but equally where a partner or a member of the solicitor's staff is so interested.

8. A solicitor must also consider whether any personal relationship, office or appointment inhibits his or her ability to advise the client properly and impartially (see **15.06**, p.319).

9. The interests envisaged by principle **15.04** are not restricted to those of a primarily economic nature only. For example, a solicitor who becomes

15

involved in a sexual relationship with a client must consider whether this may place his or her interests in conflict with those of the client or otherwise impair the solicitor's ability to act in the best interests of the client. (See also **12.09** note 1(b), p.248.)

10. A solicitor who is a director or shareholder of a company for which the solicitor also acts must consider whether he or she is in a position of conflict when asked to advise the company upon steps it has taken or should take. It may be necessary for the solicitor to resign from the board or for another solicitor to advise the company in that particular matter. A solicitor acting for a company in which he or she has a personal interest should always ensure that his or her ability to give independent and impartial advice is not thereby impaired.

11. A solicitor who holds a power of attorney from a client must not use that power to gain a benefit which, if acting as a professional adviser to that client, he or she would not be prepared to allow to an independent third party. This applies regardless of the legal position, e.g. as to whether a solicitor acting under a power of attorney may lend the donor's money to himself or herself.

12. A solicitor who is in breach of principle **15.04** may be subject to disciplinary action. In some circumstances, failure to comply with the principle may also lead to legal difficulties. For the legal position in respect of sales to, and purchases from, clients and loans by the solicitor to, and borrowing from, the client see, e.g., *Cordery on Solicitors*.

13. Chapter 23 (p.439) deals with the conflict issues arising where a solicitor is acting as an insolvency practitioner.

14. Practice rule 10 (receipt of commissions from third parties – see **14.13**, p.283) follows the position at law from which it is clear that a solicitor must not make a secret profit and must disclose to the client fully the receipt of any such profit. It may only be retained provided the client agrees. See *Brown* v. *I.R.C.* [1965] A.C. 244, *Copp* v. *Lynch and Law Life Assurance Co.* (1882) 26 S.J. 348 and *Jordy* v. *Vanderpump* (1920) 64 S.J. 324. The rule applies to the receipt by solicitors of, for example, commissions on insurances and from the Stock Exchange. Further guidance on commissions is in Annex 14G, p.308.

15.05 Gifts to solicitor

Where a client intends to make a gift *inter vivos* or by will to his or her solicitor, or to the solicitor's partner, or a member of staff or to the families of any of them and the gift is of a significant amount, either in itself or having regard to the size of the client's estate and the reasonable expectations of prospective beneficiaries, the solicitor must advise the client to be independently advised as to that gift and if the client declines, must refuse to act.

1. A solicitor must also ensure that members of staff do not embody in any will or document a gift to themselves without the approval of the solicitor. If the member of staff seeks the solicitor's approval, the same rule as to independent advice applies.

2. Where a client wishes to leave a legacy to the solicitor which is not of a significant amount, there is no need for independent advice. However, the solicitor should be satisfied that the client does not feel obliged to make such a gift.

3. Occasionally, a testator may wish to leave all or a substantial part of his or her estate to a solicitor to be dealt with in accordance with the testator's wishes as communicated to the solicitor either orally or in a document, or as a secret trust. The Council of the Law Society consider that where a solicitor in such circumstances will not benefit personally and financially, there is no need to ensure the testator receives independent advice. However, solicitors should preserve the instructions from which the will was drawn and should also see that the terms of such secret trusts are embodied in a written document signed or initialled by the testator.

4. Where the donor or testator is a relative of the solicitor and wishes to make a gift or leave a legacy to the solicitor, the solicitor must consider whether in these circumstances independent advice is desirable. The same principle will apply if the intended recipient is a partner of the solicitor, or a member of staff and the donor or testator is a relative of the intended recipient.

15.06 Appointment leading to conflict

A solicitor must decline to act where either the solicitor or a partner, employer, employee or relative of the solicitor holds some office or appointment as a result of which:

(a) a conflict of interests or a significant risk of a conflict arises, or

(b) the public might reasonably conclude that the firm had been able to make use of the office or appointment for the advantage of the client, or

(c) the solicitor's ability to advise the client properly and impartially is inhibited.

1. The expression 'relative' includes spouse, parent, child, brother, sister, or spouse of any of them.

2. Examples of offices and appointments to which principle **15.06** relates are:

Local authority councillors

(a) A solicitor must consider carefully whether the firm can properly act either for the local council or for other clients in relation to matters involving that local council.

15

Acting for the local council

(i)   There is generally no objection to the firm acting for, or tendering to provide legal services to, the council. However, the firm must consider whether it will be able to advise the council impartially and independently of any personal interest of the councillor. Much will depend upon the nature of the work being undertaken, e.g. whether the firm will be required to have any input on policy/political matters in which the councillor may have a political or other interest.

Acting against the local council

(ii) The conflict referred to in principle **15.06** will include any conflict between the individual's duties to the council as councillor (as detailed in the National Code of Local Government Conduct) and the duty of the firm to act in the best interests of the client.

(iii) In practice the firm will be precluded from acting in any matter involving the council which comes within the councillor's sphere of activity as councillor.

Local authority prosecutions

(iv) A solicitor councillor should not appear as an advocate for the prosecution or for the defence in prosecutions brought by the local authority.

Judicial appointments

(b)   Where a solicitor holds a part-time judicial appointment (including chairman of an industrial tribunal) the terms and conditions of the appointment will contain restrictions as to the circumstances in which the solicitor can properly sit in a particular court, or appear as an advocate in that court or adjudicate on a particular case. The Lord Chancellor's Department (see p.xv for contact details) can advise on this.

Justices and clerks to justices

(c)   Section 38 of the Solicitors Act 1974 restricts a solicitor who is a Justice of the Peace from acting in certain proceedings. In addition, the Council of the Law Society take the view that the section should be deemed to apply to a solicitor who is a clerk or deputy clerk to the justices and to any partner, assistant solicitor or other employee in the firm.

Gaming Board

(d) A solicitor who is a member of the Gaming Board, or any partner or employee, should not act in connection with any application made to the Board, or in any subsequent or consequential licensing applications in which the Board has an interest.

Coroners

(e) A solicitor who is a coroner or deputy or assistant deputy coroner should not appear on behalf of a client before a coroner's court for the area or district for which he or she is appointed. Nor should such a solicitor (or any partner or employee of the solicitor) act professionally in any civil or criminal proceedings resulting from a death where the solicitor has held an inquest into the circumstances of such death. Further, since the coroner acts in a judicial capacity, such a solicitor must make arrangements for another person to carry out an inquest into the death of a person where it might be thought that some bias could arise out of his or her personal or professional connection with the deceased, or with a near relative of the deceased.

Police authority

(f) A solicitor who is a member of a police authority should not appear as an advocate for the prosecution or for the defence in prosecutions brought by the Crown Prosecution Service in that authority's area.

Legal Aid Committees

(g) A solicitor member of an Area Legal Aid Committee may act (or continue to act) for the applicant in a case coming before that Committee, provided he or she declares an interest in the case and withdraws from the adjudication. Where a solicitor has adjudicated on an application submitted to a Legal Aid Committee, he or she must not act or continue to act for the opponent of the applicant. Even if the solicitor does not remember details of the case, it would be undesirable for the solicitor to act. Adjudication by a member of a Legal Aid Committee should not inhibit the solicitor's partners or other members of the firm dealing with the matter.

Criminal Injuries Compensation Board

(h) Firms in which a member of the Criminal Injuries Compensation Board is a partner or employee should not accept instructions to act before the Board.

15

Annex 15A

Guidance – conflict arising on the amalgamation of firms of solicitors

---

1. Amalgamating firms must be alert to the high risk of conflicts of interest arising on amalgamation. Usually, the new firm must cease acting for both clients where there is a conflict of interests between them. However, there may be exceptional circumstances (except in litigation) where the best interests of the client(s) permit the new firm to continue acting for one or, occasionally, both clients.

2. In order to continue to act the firm has to be able to erect a 'Chinese wall'. This does not eliminate the conflict but provides a method of dealing with it.

3. Before continuing to act the following conditions must be satisfied:

    3.1 both clients must have consented (if one does not, that is an absolute bar to the firm acting for either);

    3.2 it must be in the client's best interests that the new firm continue acting despite the conflict of interest;

    3.3 there must be no embarrassment to the solicitors, who must not favour one client to the detriment of the other;

    3.4 the clients must have the risks fully explained.

4. The purpose of the wall is to preserve confidentiality in relation to the affairs of each client. There will be a heavy onus on the firm to show the wall is effective, which will require the following minimum safeguards:

    4.1 If acting for one or both clients, the relevant personnel must adopt appropriate guidelines.

    4.2 If acting for both clients, complete physical separation into different rooms (which should be as far apart as can reasonably be achieved) of:

        4.2.1 all papers relating to each client; and

        4.2.2 all property of or relating to each client; and

        4.2.3 all personnel dealing with each client.

5. If, once set up, the wall cannot be maintained effectively, the client(s) must be told to instruct other solicitors and the firm must stop acting.

6. The Court, under its inherent jurisdiction to supervise the conduct of its officers, can order a solicitor to cease acting. The Court can order a solicitor to pay to his or her client or another party any costs unreasonably incurred as a result of the solicitor acting improperly.

May 1987, revised February 1999

THE GUIDE TO THE PROFESSIONAL CONDUCT OF SOLICITORS 1999

Chapter 16

Confidentiality

Introductory note

The duty of confidentiality is fundamental to the relationship of solicitor and client. It exists as an obligation both in law, having regard to the nature of the contract of retainer, and as a matter of conduct. All the information a solicitor discovers about a client in the course of a retainer is confidential; whether the information is also privileged is a separate legal issue.

In considering this chapter, solicitors should have in mind the fundamental nature of the duty and remember that the circumstances in which confidentiality can be overridden are rare. A solicitor who volunteers confidential information must be prepared to show powerful justification for breaching the client's confidentiality.

16.01   General duty of confidentiality

A solicitor is under a duty to keep confidential to his or her firm the affairs of clients and to ensure that the staff do the same.

1. It is important to bear in mind the distinction between the duty to keep client affairs confidential and the concept of law known as legal professional privilege. The duty in conduct extends to all matters communicated to a solicitor by the client or on behalf of the client, except as detailed in **16.02** (p.325), **16.03** (p.327) and **16.07** (p.333). Legal professional privilege protects communications between a client and solicitor from being disclosed, even in a court of law. Certain communications, however, are not protected by legal professional privilege and reference should be made to an appropriate authority on the law of evidence. Non-privileged communications remain subject to the solicitor's duty to keep the client's affairs confidential.

2. Disclosure of a client's confidences which is unauthorised by the client or by the law could lead to disciplinary proceedings against a solicitor and could also render a solicitor liable, in certain circumstances, to a civil action by the client arising out of the misuse of confidential information.

3. The duty of confidentiality applies to information about a client's affairs irrespective of the source of the information. It continues despite the end of the retainer or the death of the client when the right to confidentiality passes to the client's personal representatives. As to when the right passes to the personal representatives, and for disclosures to attorneys, or where a will is in dispute, see Chapter 24, p.448.

4. A solicitor who acquires information on behalf of a prospective client may be bound by the duty of confidentiality even if there is no subsequent retainer at law.

5. Information given to the solicitor in the context of a joint retainer must be available between the clients; they must, however, all consent to a waiver of the duty of confidentiality before that information may be disclosed to a third party. However, information communicated to the solicitor in the capacity of solicitor for only one of the clients in relation to a separate matter must not be disclosed to the other clients without the consent of that client.

6. Where firms amalgamate, information which each firm has obtained when acting for its clients will pass to the new firm as a result of any express or implied retainer of the new firm, and conflicts of interest could arise from the competing duties of confidentiality and disclosure. For conflicts of interests see Chapter 15, p.313; for 'Chinese walls' see Annex 15A, p.322.

7. Problems with confidentiality can arise where more than one practice share office services, computers or other equipment or use a common typing agency. Solicitors should only make use of these where strict confidentiality of client matters can be ensured.

8. A solicitor should not sell book debts to a factoring company because of the special confidential nature of a solicitor's bill and the danger of breaches of confidence which might occur. Such factoring might also lead to a breach of rule 7 of the Solicitors' Practice Rules 1990 (see **3.03**, p.68).

9. Where a solicitor sends postcards to acknowledge receipt of communications, care must be taken to ensure that no confidential information of any kind appears on them.

16.02 Circumstances which override confidentiality

The duty to keep a client's confidences can be overridden in certain exceptional circumstances.

1. The duty of confidentiality does not apply to information acquired by a solicitor where he or she is being used by the client to facilitate the commission of a crime or fraud, because that is not within the scope of a professional retainer. If the solicitor becomes suspicious about a client's activities the solicitor should normally assess the situation in the light of the client's explanations and the solicitor's professional judgement.

2. Express consent by a client to disclosure of information relating to his or her affairs overrides any duty of confidentiality, as does consent by the personal representatives of a deceased client.

3. A solicitor may reveal confidential information to the extent that he or she believes necessary to prevent the client or a third party committing a criminal act that the solicitor believes on reasonable grounds is likely to result in serious bodily harm.

4. There may be exceptional circumstances involving children where a solicitor should consider revealing confidential information to an appropriate authority. This may be where the child is the client and the child reveals information which indicates continuing sexual or other physical abuse but refuses to allow disclosure of such information. Similarly, there may be situations where an adult discloses abuse either by himself or herself or by another adult against a child but refuses to allow any disclosure. The solicitor must consider whether the threat to the child's life or health, both mental and physical, is sufficiently serious to justify a breach of the duty of confidentiality.

5. In proceedings under the Children Act 1989 solicitors are under a duty to reveal experts' reports commissioned for the purposes of proceedings, as these reports are not privileged. The position in relation to voluntary disclosure of other documents or solicitor/client communications is uncertain. Clearly advocates are under a duty not to mislead the court (see **21.01**, p.374). Therefore, if an advocate has certain knowledge which he or she realises is adverse to the client's case, the solicitor may be extremely limited in what can be stated in the client's favour. In this situation, the

solicitor should seek the client's agreement for full voluntary disclosure for three reasons:

(i)   the matters the client wants to hide will probably emerge anyway;

(ii) the solicitor will be able to do a better job for the client if all the relevant information is presented to the court;

(iii) if the information is not voluntarily disclosed, the solicitor may be severely criticised by the court.

If the client refuses to give the solicitor authority to disclose the relevant information, the solicitor is entitled to refuse to continue to act for the client if to do so will place the solicitor in breach of his or her obligations to the court.

6.   A solicitor should reveal matters which are otherwise subject to the duty to preserve confidentiality where a court orders that such matters are to be disclosed or where a warrant permits a police officer or other authority to seize confidential documents. If a solicitor is of the opinion that the documents are subject to legal privilege or that for some other reason the order or warrant ought not to have been made or issued, he or she without unlawfully obstructing its execution should normally discuss with the client the possibility of making an application to have the order or warrant set aside. Advice may be obtained from the Professional Adviser (see p.xv for contact details).

7.   The civil justice reforms have an impact on the treatment of material which is subject to legal professional privilege. See Annex 21I (p.409) for further details.

8.   Occasionally a solicitor is asked by the police or a third party to give information or to show them documents which the solicitor has obtained when acting for a client. Unless the client is prepared to waive confidentiality, or where the solicitor has strong *prima facie* evidence that he or she has been used by the client to perpetrate a fraud or other crime and the duty of confidence does not arise, the solicitor should insist upon receiving a witness summons or subpoena so that, where appropriate, privilege may be claimed and the court asked to decide the issue. If the request is made by the police under the Police and Criminal Evidence Act 1984 the solicitor should, where appropriate, leave the question of privilege to the court to decide on the particular circumstances. See also Annex 16A, p.335. Advice may be obtained from the Professional Adviser (see p.xv for contact details).

9.   When a lender asks for a conveyancing file and the solicitor has kept a joint file for both borrower and lender clients, the solicitor must not, without the consent of the borrower, send the whole file to the lender. If the lender can show evidence of a *prima facie* case of fraud, the solicitor can follow the guidance in note 1 above. For guidance on ownership of conveyancing documents, see Annex 16C, p.341.

10. Certain communications from a client are not confidential if they are a matter of public record. For example, the fact that a solicitor has been instructed by a named client in connection with contentious business for which that client's name is on the public record is not confidential, but the type of business involved will usually be confidential.

11. In the case of a legally aided client, a solicitor may be under a duty to report to the Legal Aid Board information concerning the client which is confidential and privileged. See regulations 67 and 70 of the Civil Legal Aid (General) Regulations 1989, regulation 56 of the Legal Aid in Criminal and Care Proceedings (General) Regulations 1989 and **5.03–5.04**, p.161.

12. A solicitor may reveal confidential information concerning a client to the extent that it is reasonably necessary to establish a defence to a criminal charge or civil claim by the client against the solicitor, or where the solicitor's conduct is under investigation by the Office for the Supervision of Solicitors, or under consideration by the Solicitors Disciplinary Tribunal.

13. Under section 18 of the Prevention of Terrorism (Temporary Provisions) Act 1989 it is an offence for a person who has certain information about acts of terrorism to fail without reasonable excuse to disclose that information. The Society takes the view that, in the light of the reasonable excuse defence, a solicitor is not obliged to disclose confidential or privileged information under this provision other than in wholly exceptional circumstances.

14. A number of statutes empower government and other bodies, for example the Inland Revenue, to require any person to disclose documents and/or information. This could include a client's solicitor but such information would normally be subject at least to a duty of confidentiality and possibly privileged. Should a solicitor be approached he or she should ask under which statutory power the information is being sought, consider the relevant provisions and consider whether privileged information is protected from disclosure in the absence of the client's specific consent. Further advice may be obtained from the Professional Adviser (see p.xv for contact details).

15. For guidance on the application of principle **16.02** in relation to money laundering, see **16.07**, p.333.

16.03 Insolvency of client

If a client becomes insolvent, the solicitor should consider to whom the duty of confidentiality is owed.

Company insolvency

1. Where insolvency proceedings are begun in relation to a company client, or former client, and an 'office holder' is appointed, the Insolvency Act 1986

gives the 'office holder' extensive powers and duties to gather in the company's property and to obtain, from anyone who may be in possession of it, information about its affairs. The most significant sections of the Act for this purpose are sections 234, 235, 236 and 237. An office holder is: a liquidator, a provisional liquidator, an administrator or an administrative receiver. For a number of purposes, an official receiver has similar powers (though an official receiver may be appointed as liquidator, in which case the sections apply directly).

2.   Under section 234, the office holder is entitled to 'such information concerning the company and its promotion, formation, business dealings, affairs, or property' as he or she 'may . . . reasonably require' from certain categories of people; and under section 236, with the authority of the court, to a still wider range of information, books, papers, etc., from a wider range of people. This effectively means that the office holder is entitled to any information whatsoever relating to the company which the company itself would have been entitled to, and from whomever holds it (including information in the possession of a solicitor which would otherwise have been protected by confidentiality or privilege).

3.   Section 246 of the Act makes any lien which a solicitor may have over 'books, papers or other records of the company' unenforceable against an office holder. There is an exception for documents of title to property which the solicitor holds 'as such' – as to the meaning of this term, see *Re SEIL Trade Finance Ltd* [1992] B.C.C. 538. However, the court has power under sections 236 and 237 to order disclosure of information in, and, if it thinks fit, production of, documents which would otherwise be protected by the exception in section 246 (though the court will do what it can to protect the lien if it makes an order of this kind).

4.   Where the solicitor's client, or former client, was not the company itself but a director or other officer personally (i.e. other than on behalf of the company), the powers given by the Insolvency Act to the court and office holder do not override privilege or confidentiality and communications are protected according to the normal rules. (There is an Australian case, *Re Compass Airlines Pty Ltd* [1992] 10 A.C.L.C. 1380, on this point.)

5.   However, a solicitor might have given certain advice on some occasion to a director both personally and as an officer of the company, or it may not be clear in what capacity the director was acting at the time. In either of these situations, the solicitor may not be entitled to refuse to disclose information about the advice to the office holder. There is, unfortunately, little judicial authority on borderline situations of this kind but a solicitor faced with the problem might find it worth looking at *Butts Gas and Oil Co.* v. *Hammer (No. 3)* [1981] Q.B. 223 and, on appeal, [1982] A.C. 888; and an Australian case, *Farrow Mortgage Services (Pty) Ltd* v. *Webb* [1995] 13 A.C.L.C. 1329. When a solicitor has acted for, or given advice to, both a company and a director or other officer as joint clients, the rule on privilege as between joint clients is likely to apply – i.e. one client cannot assert privilege against the other (*Re Konigsberg* [1989] 1 W.L.R. 1257 and

[1989] 3 All E.R. 289), in which case the office holder would be entitled to require disclosure.

Individual insolvency

6. The position is more difficult in relation to a client against whom a bankruptcy order has been made. Section 312(3) of the Insolvency Act 1986 places an obligation on any person, including a solicitor, 'who holds any property to the account of, or for, the bankrupt' to 'pay or deliver to the trustee all property in his possession or under his control which forms part of the bankrupt's estate'. Section 311 of the Act makes it clear that this includes 'all books, papers and other records which relate to the bankrupt's estate or affairs and which belong to him' and that this applies even to privileged communications. Broadly, the trustee is entitled to all those papers and other property which are legitimately needed in order to carry out effectively the trustee's function, which is to gather in and then distribute the bankrupt's estate. Thus, where a bankrupt client's (or former client's) financial affairs are concerned, the trustee in bankruptcy is in the same position in relation to the solicitor as the client would have been had he or she not been made bankrupt. A solicitor should therefore comply with a trustee's requests about matters relating to the client's financial affairs regardless of the client's wishes or instructions.

7. It is a contempt of court for the bankrupt or any other person without reasonable excuse to decline to hand over papers or other property to the trustee – section 312(4) – and a solicitor should also draw the client's attention to the series of sections starting with section 351, which create bankruptcy offences. For example, under section 353, a bankrupt is guilty of an offence if he or she does not, to the best of his or her knowledge and belief, disclose all the property comprised in his or her estate to the trustee. This includes property acquired by, or which has devolved on, the bankrupt since the bankruptcy (section 307). A solicitor should take care to avoid becoming a party to the commission of any of these offences by a client.

8. Sections 366 and 367 give trustees, through the courts, wide powers to obtain information about the bankrupt's affairs, and further means of getting possession of property 'comprised in' the bankrupt's estate.

9. Since a trustee's powers to obtain property apply to property belonging to the bankrupt, a solicitor is obliged to give the trustee only those papers on the solicitor's file which belong to the bankrupt. However, there are differences of views about which papers belong to the client and which to the solicitor and it might be unwise to place too much reliance on a claim to ownership as a ground for refusing to hand documents over to a trustee. In any case, the solicitor could be compelled, under section 366, to produce the documents. A solicitor's right of lien over documents belonging to a bankrupt is very much restricted by section 349 and applies only to documents of title which the solicitor holds 'as such'. For the meaning of this phrase, see the decision in *Re SEIL Trade Finance Ltd* [1992] B.C.C. 538.

10. The Insolvency Act gives official receivers similar, but not identical, powers to those of trustees.

11. Trustees may ask for information about bankrupt clients which is not, or not obviously, related to those clients' financial affairs. There is little statutory guidance as to how far the removal of privilege by the Insolvency Act is intended to extend, and judicial guidance is scarce and inconclusive. The Society suggests, however, that:

    (a) Where the information sought relates to a bankrupt's financial affairs, the solicitor should comply with the trustee's request regardless of the client's wishes.

    (b) As it is unclear how the rules on privilege and confidentiality apply where the information sought falls within any of the following cases:

        ▶ it concerns personal affairs of the bankrupt, which have no ostensible relevance to the trustee's functions;

        ▶ its disclosure could be incriminatory of the bankrupt and expose him or her to the risk of criminal prosecution;

        ▶ it relates to legal advice taken by the bankrupt for the purpose of resisting the bankruptcy petition or appealing against the order;

        ▶ it relates to legal advice taken by the bankrupt after the commencement of the bankruptcy;

        the solicitor should in such cases explain to the trustee that the solicitor regards himself or herself as unable to comply with the trustee's request without either the client's authority or an order of the court under section 366, giving the reasons why the solicitor takes this view.

12. If the trustee decides to make a section 366 application against the solicitor, the question of costs may arise; the solicitor may expose himself or herself to the risk of an adverse costs order by resisting a trustee's application. The Society suggests that the solicitor should inform the client of the application or possible application, explaining the powers given to the court by section 366 (in particular, the power to require disclosure) and that, unless the client instructs the solicitor to the contrary and puts the solicitor in funds, the solicitor will not resist the application. It is not the solicitor's duty to bear the cost of opposing the trustee, or the risk of a costs order, without the client's instructions and funding. This should be explained to the client, which gives the client the opportunity to take action, either through the solicitor or in person.

13. The Society's view is that a solicitor who has acted in this way should not be at risk of an adverse costs order, provided the reasons for so acting are explained to the court, and that the solicitor would be safe from any complaint which the client might make for breach of confidence or privilege.

16.04 Client's address

A solicitor must not disclose a client's address without the client's consent.

> The solicitor may, as a matter of courtesy, offer to send on to the client a letter from the enquirer addressed to the client c/o the solicitor.

16.05 Duty not to profit

A solicitor must not make any profit by the use of confidential information for his or her own purposes.

1. In such circumstances a solicitor may be liable to civil action by the client in an action for account and could also be liable to disciplinary proceedings or, in some cases, criminal proceedings. See also **14.14** note 2, p.283.

2. For a solicitor acquiring publication rights, see **15.04** note 2, p.317.

16.06 Duty to disclose all relevant information to client

A solicitor is usually under a duty to pass on to the client and use all information which is material to the client's business regardless of the source of that information. There are, however, exceptional circumstances where this duty does not apply.

1. A breach of this duty may be actionable in law and might involve the solicitor in disciplinary action.

2. Some provisions in the money laundering legislation effectively prohibit solicitors from passing on information to clients in certain circumstances. See **16.07**, p.333.

3. In general terms, since the solicitor is the agent of the client, all information coming into his or her possession relating to the client's affairs must be disclosed to the client. Consequently, it is undesirable that a solicitor should seek to pass on to the solicitor on the other side information which is not to be disclosed to the other side's client. Equally, the recipient should decline to accept or receive confidential information on the basis that it will not be disclosed. If a confidential letter is written to the solicitor on the other side, the writer cannot insist on the letter not being shown to the client. When offered information from another solicitor, or any other source, which the solicitor is asked to treat as confidential and not to disclose to the client, the solicitor should consider carefully before accepting such confidential information. For correspondence with lawyers of other EU jurisdictions, see article 5.3 of the CCBE Code and commentary (Annex 10B at p.218).

16

4. There might, however, be certain circumstances where the imparting to the client of information received by the solicitor could be harmful to the client because it will affect the client's mental or physical condition. Consequently, it will be necessary for a solicitor to decide whether to disclose such information to the client, e.g. a medical report disclosing a terminal illness.

5. Generally, a solicitor should not seek, or encourage a client to obtain access to, information from private confidential correspondence or documents belonging to, or intended for, the other side. This includes not opening or reading letters addressed to someone other than himself or herself or the firm. If, however, the contents of such documents otherwise come to the solicitor's knowledge (and other than in circumstances described in notes 6 and 7 below), the solicitor is entitled, and may have a duty, to use the information for the benefit of the client. The intention to do so should, however, be disclosed to the other side. Where it is **not obvious** either that a document has been mistakenly disclosed, or that it is subject to legal professional privilege, rule 31.20 of the Civil Procedure Rules confirms that the party who has inspected the document may use it or its contents only with the court's permission.

6. Where it **is obvious** that privileged documents have been mistakenly disclosed to a solicitor, the solicitor should immediately cease to read the document, inform the other side and return the documents. The solicitor may tell the client what has happened. As to the use of privileged documentation and possible repercussions as to costs should injunctions be necessary, see any text on the law of evidence. See also *English and American Insurance Company Limited* v. *Herbert Smith* [1988] F.S.R. 232 and *Ablitt* v. *Mills and Reeve,* The Times, 25th October 1995 for cases where counsel's papers have accidentally been sent to the wrong side. Advice may be obtained from the Professional Adviser (see p.xv for contact details).

7. Where a solicitor comes into possession of information relating to state security or intelligence matters to which the Official Secrets Act 1989 applies, and which is pertinent to a client's affairs, the solicitor should not disclose such information to the client without lawful authority unless satisfied that the information was itself disclosed by someone with lawful authority to do so. Section 5 of the Act makes such disclosure a criminal offence where the disclosure will be 'damaging' within the terms of the Act. It is unclear what is meant by lawful authority, although that term obviously includes the authority of the appropriate government department. Advice may be obtained from the Professional Adviser (see p.xv for contact details).

8. Where a solicitor acts for two or more clients on related matters, a conflict may arise between the duty of disclosure owed to a client under one retainer and the duty of confidentiality owed to a client under another retainer. For example, a solicitor acting for borrower and lender in the same

transaction has two separate retainers and if the borrower does not consent to relevant but confidential facts being brought to the attention of the lender, the solicitor must honour the duty of confidentiality to the borrower. See also practice rule 6 (**25.01**, p.455). Should that situation arise, however, the solicitor will be faced with a conflict of interests and must cease to act for the lender and probably also the borrower (see **15.03**, p.316). For cases where there is, or may be, property fraud see **16.02** note 1, p.325. Annex 25G, p.501, contains the Society's 'green card' warning on property fraud; Annex 25F, p.500, contains guidance on a solicitor's duty in conduct when acting for a lender and borrower when there is some variation in the purchase price.

16.07 Money laundering

A solicitor's duty of confidentiality and duty of disclosure are varied by statutory provisions relating to money laundering.

1. The Criminal Justice Act 1993 amended existing legislation and introduced new criminal offences designed to prevent those who seek to launder the proceeds of crime, drug trafficking and terrorism from being able to use legitimate professional services for this purpose. The legislation contains important exceptions to the solicitor's normal duty of confidentiality to clients and to the duty to disclose relevant information to a client. A summary of the substantive law on money laundering is contained in Annex 16B, p.337.

2. The substantive law applies to all practising solicitors and not simply to solicitors who conduct investment business under the Financial Services Act 1986. The money laundering legislation does not require solicitors to be suspicious of clients without cause, or to detect money laundering, but solicitors should be aware of the legislation, be alert to any unusual circumstances, and make further enquiries of their clients where appropriate. The 'blue card' warning on money laundering, first issued by the Society in April 1994, is at Annex 16D, p.343.

3. The Money Laundering Regulations 1993 (see Annex 3B, p.95) apply in relation to certain services provided by solicitors (see **3.16**, p.84). They contain requirements relating to:

    ▶ the training of staff in the recognition and handling of suspicious transactions;

    ▶ the appointment of a reporting officer and the establishment of internal reporting procedures;

    ▶ the establishment of procedures for obtaining and keeping evidence of client's identity where necessary; and

    ▶ the keeping of records of transactions undertaken for a minimum period.

16

4. The legislation makes it a criminal offence for a person to assist anyone
    known or suspected of being engaged in money laundering – see section
    93A of the Criminal Justice Act 1988, section 50 of the Drug Trafficking
    Act 1994 and section 11 of the Prevention of Terrorism (Temporary
    Provisions) Act 1989 – or to acquire property known to be the proceeds of
    crime or drug trafficking. It is a statutory defence that disclosure of any
    knowledge or suspicion was made to 'a constable' (see note 5 below), and
    the statutes provide immunity for a breach of the solicitor's professional
    and contractual duty of confidence. Further, under section 26B of the Drug
    Trafficking Offences Act 1986 and section 18A of the Prevention of
    Terrorism (Temporary Provisions) Act 1989 it is a criminal offence, in
    certain circumstances, *not* to disclose to a constable information gained in
    the course of any profession relating to the laundering of funds from drug
    trafficking or terrorism. See also Annex 16B, p.337.

5. If a solicitor decides to make disclosure to 'a constable', such disclosure
    may be made to the Financial Unit, National Criminal Intelligence Service,
    Spring Gardens, Vauxhall, London SE11 5EN; telephone 0171 238 8271 or
    020 7238 8271 (outside office hours 0171 238 8607 or 020 7238 8607), fax
    0171 238 8286 or 020 7238 8286.

6. The legislation also affects the solicitor's duty to disclose all relevant
    information to the client (see **16.06**, p.331). The 'tipping-off' provisions
    would effectively prohibit a solicitor from passing on information to the
    client should the solicitor know or suspect that a report has been made or
    that there is or is about to be an investigation into money laundering, if that
    tipping-off is likely to prejudice the investigation. See section 53 of the
    Drug Trafficking Act 1994, section 17 of the Prevention of Terrorism
    (Temporary Provisions) Act 1989, section 93D of the Criminal Justice Act
    1988 and Annex 16B, p.337. Until there is clear authority on the point, it
    would be prudent for a solicitor not to disclose to the client that an
    investigation is under way unless the solicitor has ascertained that the
    investigating authorities have no objection. Advice may be obtained from
    the Professional Adviser (see p.xv for contact details).

7. Where a solicitor knows or suspects that a client is involved in money
    laundering and a report is made, the solicitor should consider whether the
    'tipping-off' provisions so affect the trust and confidentiality necessary
    between solicitor and client that the retainer should be terminated. The
    Society takes the view that there is no necessary objection to a solicitor
    continuing to act. Whether or not the solicitor feels able to do so will
    depend upon all the circumstances. Advice may be sought from
    Professional Ethics (see p.xv for contact details).

8. Advice may be obtained from the Professional Adviser and an information
    pack containing detailed guidance on the money laundering legislation may
    be obtained from Professional Ethics.

Annex 16A

Guidance – Police and Criminal Evidence Act 1984 – production orders and client confidentiality

It is usually solicitors concerned in non-contentious matters who find themselves a party to an application by the police under section 9 of and Schedule 1 to the Police and Criminal Evidence Act 1984 (PACE) for a production order. Such solicitors are not at ease with criminal matters and will frequently telephone the Society for advice. Most criminal law practitioners have already got to grips with this part of the Act, but just in case there are any of you out there who have been fortunate enough not to be involved in such an application, here is some advice on the professional conduct issues to be considered when an application is received.

The Guide, at Chapter 16, p.323, deals with the solicitor's duty to keep confidential the affairs of clients. But what exactly should a solicitor do when served with a notice of application for a production order?

The solicitor should remember that he or she is the party to the application; the client is not a party and has no locus in the matter. However, the solicitor must inform the client of the existence of the notice of application; a solicitor is under a professional duty to keep the client properly informed of matters affecting the client's affairs (**13.06**, p.274 in the Guide). The solicitor should seek instructions from the client as to whether or not the client would like the application to be opposed. However, as the client is not a party to the proceedings, the solicitor is not under any obligation to oppose the application unless and until he or she is put in funds by the client to do so.

Once the production order is made and served upon a solicitor, the solicitor must comply with the order, unless there is a clear error on the face of the order or the solicitor has instructions and funds to appeal against the terms of the order. In *Barclays Bank plc* v. *Taylor; Trustee Savings Bank of Wales and Border Counties* v. *Taylor* [1989] 1 W.L.R. 1066, the Court of Appeal reminded banks that they must comply with the terms of a production order because a court order which is valid on its face is fully effective and demands compliance, unless or until it is set aside by due process of law.

However, the solicitor should scrutinise the terms of the order very carefully. If the order contains words which exclude from production items subject to legal professional privilege, the solicitor must consider what items he or she has on the file which would come within that definition. There is a difference between items which are subject to legal professional privilege on a contentious file and those which are subject to legal professional privilege on a non-contentious file. If, however, the order is silent as to the exclusion of items subject to legal privilege, the whole of the file and other documents listed in the production order must be disclosed. This is because the judge hearing the application is under a duty to consider whether all of the access conditions in Schedule 1 to PACE have been fulfilled. Amongst other matters, the judge must consider whether or not there are items or materials subject to legal professional privilege. To assist in those deliberations, the judge will have considered section 10 of PACE where at subsection (2) it is clear that items held with the intention of furthering a criminal purpose are not items subject to legal privilege. (See also *R.* v. *Central Criminal Court ex p. Francis & Francis* [1988] 3 All E.R. 775.)

Section 55 of the Drug Trafficking Act 1994 also provides a mechanism for production orders. Should such an order or approach be made, the solicitor must consider his or her position carefully before contacting the client. The solicitor may run the risk of committing a 'tipping-off' offence under section 53 or an offence under section 58 of the Drug Trafficking Act 1994 if this would prejudice the investigation.

Advice may be obtained from the Professional Adviser (see p.xv for contact details).

May 1991, revised February 1999

Annex 16B

Guidance – money laundering – summary of the substantive law

Drug Trafficking Act 1994

Section 49 makes it an offence to conceal, disguise, convert or transfer the proceeds of drug trafficking for the purpose of avoiding prosecution for a drug trafficking offence, or the making or enforcing of a confiscation order. It is also an offence to conceal, etc., another's proceeds of drug trafficking, knowing or having reasonable grounds to suspect that they are such proceeds. Conviction on indictment for the offence is punishable by up to 14 years' imprisonment, or a fine, or both.

Section 51 makes it an offence to acquire, possess or use another person's proceeds of drug trafficking, knowing that they are such proceeds. A defence to a charge for this offence exists if the person charged acquired, used or had possession of the property for adequate consideration. Consideration is not adequate if its value is significantly less than the value of the property acquired, or the value of its possession or use; the provision of services or goods in return for the property is not treated as consideration if it is of assistance to the other person in drug trafficking. The offence is not committed if the person acquiring, possessing or using the property reports his or her suspicions about the origin of the property to a constable or to a supervisor in accordance with his or her employer's established system, and is given permission to acquire, possess or use the property; or he or she makes the report as soon as possible after the acquisition, etc. and on his or her own initiative; or he or she can show that he or she intended to make the report, but had a reasonable excuse for failing to do so. Such a report is not a breach of any restriction on the disclosure of confidential information. Conviction on indictment for the offence is punishable by up to 14 years' imprisonment, or a fine, or both.

Section 50 makes it an offence to enter into an arrangement which facilitates the retention or control by or on behalf of another of his or her proceeds of drug trafficking, or which allows the other's proceeds of drug trafficking to be used to secure funds for him or her, or to be used for his or her benefit to acquire property by way of investment, knowing or suspecting that the person concerned carries on or has carried on drug trafficking, or that he or she had benefited from drug trafficking. The offence is not committed if the person assisting the drug trafficker reports his or her suspicions or belief about the origin of the funds to a constable, or to a supervisor in accordance with his or her employer's established system, and is given permission to carry out the activity concerned; or he or she makes the report as soon as possible after the activity and on his or her own initiative; or he or she can show that he or she intended to make the report, but had a reasonable excuse for failing to do so. Such a report is not a breach of any restriction on the disclosure of confidential information. It is also a defence to prove that the person assisting the drug trafficker did not know or suspect that his or her actions related to the proceeds of drug trafficking, or that he or she did not know or suspect that he or she was assisting the trafficker. Conviction on indictment for the offence is punishable by up to 14 years' imprisonment, or a fine, or both.

Section 52 makes it an offence to fail to report knowledge or suspicions of drug money laundering gained in the course of trade, profession, business or employment to a constable, or to a supervisor in accordance with an employer's established system. The offence does not apply to a professional legal adviser who fails to disclose information which has come to him or her in privileged circumstances. It is a defence to prove that there was a reasonable excuse for failing to make the necessary report. Such a report does not breach any restriction on the disclosure of confidential information. Conviction on indictment for the offence is punishable by up to five years' imprisonment, or a fine, or both.

Section 53 makes it an offence to prejudice an investigation, or possible investigation, by disclosing to another person information or any other matter likely to be prejudicial, knowing or suspecting that a constable is acting or is proposing to act in connection with an investigation into drug trafficking; or knowing or suspecting that a report under sections 50, 51 or 52 has been made to a constable or to a supervisor. The offence does not apply to a professional legal adviser who discloses information to his or her client in connection with giving legal advice, or who discloses information to anybody in contemplation of or in connection with, and for the purpose of, legal proceedings. It is a defence to prove that the person making the disclosure did not know or suspect that it would be prejudicial. Conviction on indictment for the offence is punishable by up to five years' imprisonment.

Section 55 provides for an order to be made by a circuit judge for the production of material which may be relevant to an investigation into drug trafficking, on the application of a constable or officer of the Customs and Excise. The material must be specified, or must be material of a particular kind. The circuit judge must be satisfied of the matters set out in section 55(4). The order may be made against any person holding the material to which the order relates, not necessarily the person who is suspected of having carried on or benefited from drug trafficking, but the name of that person must be specified in the order. An application may be made at any time in relation to the criminal proceedings against the person suspected of drug trafficking before or during the criminal proceedings, or after conviction. Normally, the application will be made *ex parte* to the court. Normally, the order will give the person to whom it is addressed seven days in which to produce the material for the constable to take away or, if the order states, to give a constable access to it. An order may not be made in relation to material which is subject to legal privilege or is 'excluded material' as defined in sections 10 and 11 of the Police and Criminal Evidence Act 1984. Apart from this, an order will override any obligation as to secrecy or confidentiality imposed on the holder of the material.

Section 58 makes it an offence to make any disclosure which is likely to prejudice an investigation into drug trafficking, where an order under section 55 has been made or applied for. A person who, knowing or suspecting the investigation is taking place, makes such a disclosure, will be guilty of an offence punishable by up to five years' imprisonment on conviction on indictment.

Criminal Justice Act 1988

Section 93A reads across to the proceeds of criminal conduct the offence at section 50 of the Drug Trafficking Act 1994 (see above) of assisting another to retain the benefit of drug trafficking.

Section 93B reads across to the proceeds of criminal conduct the offence at section 51 of the Drug Trafficking Act 1994 (see above) of acquiring, possessing or using the proceeds of drug trafficking.

Section 93C reads across to the proceeds of criminal conduct the offence at section 49 of the Drug Trafficking Act 1994 (see above) of concealing or transferring proceeds of drug trafficking.

Section 93D reads across as to the offences of money laundering the proceeds of criminal conduct the offence at section 53 of the Drug Trafficking Act 1994 (see above) of 'tipping-off' any person.

Prevention of Terrorism (Temporary Provisions) Act 1989

Section 11 makes it an offence to enter into or be otherwise concerned in an arrangement whereby the retention or control by or on behalf of another person of terrorist funds is facilitated. It is a defence to prove that the person did not know and had no reasonable cause to suspect that the arrangement related to terrorist funds.

Section 12 provides that the offence in section 11 is not committed if the person who enters into or is otherwise concerned in the arrangement reports his or her suspicion or belief that any money or other property is or is derived from terrorist funds to a constable, or to a supervisor in accordance with his or her employer's established system, and is given permission to carry out the act concerned; or he or she makes the report as soon as is reasonable after the act and on his or her own initiative; or he or she can show that he or she intended to make the report, but had a reasonable excuse for failing to do so. Such a report is not a breach of any restriction on the disclosure of information.

Section 13 provides that conviction on indictment of an offence under section 11 is punishable by up to 14 years' imprisonment, or a fine, or both.

Section 17 makes it an offence to disclose to another person information or any other matter which is likely to prejudice a terrorist investigation or proposed investigation, or to falsify, conceal, or destroy or otherwise dispose of material which is or is likely to be relevant to such an investigation, knowing or having reasonable cause to suspect that a constable is acting or is proposing to act in connection with a terrorist investigation or knowing or having reasonable cause to suspect that a report has been made to a constable or supervisor.

The offence does not apply to professional legal advisers who disclose information to their clients in connection with giving them legal advice, or who disclose information to anybody in contemplation of or in connection with, and for the purpose of, legal proceedings. It is a defence to prove that the person did not know and had no reasonable cause to suspect that his or her disclosure was likely to prejudice the investigation, or that he or she had lawful authority or reasonable excuse for making his or her disclosure, or to prove that the person had no intention of concealing any information contained in the material from any person who might carry out the investigation. Conviction on indictment for the offence is punishable by up to five years' imprisonment, or a fine, or both.

Section 18A makes it an offence to fail to report knowledge or suspicion of an offence under section 11 gained in the course of trade, profession, business or employment to a constable, or to a supervisor in accordance with an employer's established system. The offence does not apply to professional legal advisers who fail to disclose any information which has come to them in privileged circumstances. It is a defence to prove that there was a reasonable excuse for failing to make the necessary report. Such reports do not breach any restriction on the disclosure of information. Conviction on indictment for the offence is punishable by up to five years' imprisonment, or a fine, or both.

Criminal Justice Act 1993

This Act amends and adds to most of the Acts mentioned above. The summaries above concern the provisions as amended by the 1993 Act.

[Note: The Money Laundering Regulations 1993 are at Annex 3B, p.95 in the Guide.]

April 1994, revised February 1999

Annex 16C

Guidance – disclosure of conveyancing files to lenders

The Society continues to receive queries from solicitors who have been asked to produce conveyancing files to lenders. It appears that in some cases lenders, and their solicitors, are suggesting that they are entitled to see the whole file and that the borrower's consent is not required. Some lenders justify this by claiming that there is a joint retainer between borrower and lender. The Society's view, confirmed by the Land Law and Succession Committee, is that there are two separate retainers. Some time ago the Land Law and Succession Committee approved guidance on which documents the lender is entitled to see, either because they belong to the lender or because they are relevant to the lender's retainer. That advice is set out below.

The following guidance relates to the position where the same firm of solicitors acted for the buyer/borrower and for the lender on a contemporaneous purchase and mortgage, and the lender asks to see documents on the 'conveyancing file'. There are, in these circumstances, two separate retainers and so, in theory, two files.

Where all the documentation is kept on one file, the solicitors will have to sort through the file to determine ownership of the various papers. Annex 12A in the Guide, p.253, contains guidance on the legal subject of ownership of documents on a solicitor's file.

It is considered that the documents which the **lender** will be entitled to see fall into two categories:

  (1) documents prepared or received by the solicitor as solicitor for the lender;

  (2) documents prepared or received by the solicitor as solicitor for the borrower which, it is considered, the lender is nonetheless entitled to see because they relate to that part of the solicitor's work where the lender and borrower can be said to have a common interest, i.e. the deduction of title, the acquisition of a good title to the property and ancillary legal issues such as the use of the property.

Examples of the most common items in these two categories are set out below.

  (1) **Documents prepared or received by the solicitor as solicitor for the lender:**

  (a) the lender's instructions to the solicitor;

  (b) copy mortgage deed;

  (c) copy report on title;

  (d) any correspondence between the solicitor and the lender or between the solicitor and a third party written or received on the lender's behalf.

(2) **Documents prepared or received by the solicitor as solicitor for the borrower which the lender is entitled to see:**

   (a)   contract for sale;

   (b)   property information form/enquiries before contract;

   (c)   abstract or epitome of title/office copy entries and plan;

   (d)   requisitions on title;

   (e)   draft purchase deed;

   (f)   draft licence to assign (where appropriate);

   (g)   Land Registry application forms;

   (h)   correspondence with local authority – re: matters raised in local search;

   (i)   correspondence with Land Registry – re: registration of title.

The only circumstances where a duty of confidentiality to the borrower would not arise is where the solicitor holding the information is satisfied that there is strong *prima facie* evidence that the borrower has used the solicitor's services in relation to a criminal fraudulent activity. In all other cases the borrower's consent or a court order will be required before the solicitor is able to pass documents to the lender which would otherwise be confidential to the borrower.

January 1997

Annex 16D

'Blue card' warning on money laundering – practice information

---

Could you be involved?

Could you or your firm be unwittingly assisting in the laundering of proceeds of crime? The Criminal Justice Act 1993 (see Annex 16B, p.337 in the Guide) and the Money Laundering Regulations 1993 (Annex 3B, p.95 in the Guide) mark an important step in the fight against serious crime, in particular against the drugs trade. All solicitors should be aware of the money laundering provisions in the Criminal Justice Act 1993. *Additionally,* solicitors who engage in investment business within the meaning of the Financial Services Act 1986 are subject to the Money Laundering Regulations 1993, and must take the steps required by the Regulations to ensure that they and their firms cannot be used by money launderers.

Might YOU commit a criminal offence?

If solicitors do not take steps to learn about the provisions of the Criminal Justice Act 1993, they may commit criminal offences, by assisting someone known or suspected to be laundering money generated by any serious crime, by telling clients or anyone else that they are under investigation for an offence of money laundering, or by failing to report a suspicion of money laundering in the case of drug trafficking or terrorism, unless certain exceptions apply. *Additionally,* solicitors who engage in investment business within the meaning of the Financial Services Act 1986 will commit criminal offences unless they take the steps required by the Money Laundering Regulations 1993. The Regulations may also apply in certain other circumstances – see **3.16**, p.84 in the Guide.

As well as the Money Laundering Regulations 1993, the law relating to money laundering in England and Wales is contained in several different Acts:

▶ the Drug Trafficking Offences Act 1986

▶ the Criminal Justice Act 1988

▶ the Prevention of Terrorism (Temporary Provisions) Act 1989

▶ the Drug Trafficking Act 1994

The Criminal Justice Act 1993 amended parts of these Acts.

Guidance on these Acts and their effect on solicitors can be found in **16.07**, p.333 and Annex 16B, p.337 in the Guide. *Remember* – the Criminal Justice Act 1993 in some cases affected the client's right to confidentiality.

Could you spot a money laundering transaction?

The signs to watch for:

1. **UNUSUAL SETTLEMENT REQUESTS** – Settlement by cash of any large transaction involving the purchase of property or other investment should give rise to caution. Payment by way of third party cheque or money transfer where there is a variation between the account holder, the signatory and a prospective investor should give rise to additional enquiries.

2. **UNUSUAL INSTRUCTIONS** – Care should always be taken when dealing with a client who has no discernible reason for using the firm's services, e.g., clients with distant addresses who could find the same service nearer their home base; or clients whose requirements do not fit into the normal pattern of the firm's business and could be more easily serviced elsewhere.

3. **LARGE SUMS OF CASH** – Always be cautious when requested to hold large sums of cash in your client account, either pending further instructions from the client or for no other purpose than for onward transmission to a third party.

4. **THE SECRETIVE CLIENT** – A personal client who is reluctant to provide details of his or her identity. Be particularly cautious about the client you do not meet in person.

5. **SUSPECT TERRITORY** – Caution should be exercised whenever a client is introduced by an overseas bank, other investor or third party based in countries where production of drugs or drug trafficking may be prevalent.

Investment business – what the law says you must do

Solicitors who engage in investment business within the meaning of the Financial Services Act 1986 must comply with the provisions of the Money Laundering Regulations 1993 (Annex 3B, p.95 in the Guide). Every firm should keep a copy of the Regulations. In particular, every firm affected by the Regulations must:

1. Ensure that all staff who handle investment business are given training in the recognition and handling of suspicious transactions. Every firm must ensure that employees are aware of the firm's policies and procedures for preventing money laundering.

2. Appoint an individual to whom staff can report suspicions of money laundering, and who will be responsible for making a decision on reporting the suspicions to the appropriate authorities.

3. Ensure that they have in place a recognised procedure for obtaining satisfactory evidence of the identity of those with whom they do business, and that records of that evidence of identity are established and kept in respect of each transaction for five years. There are exceptions set out in regulation 10.

4. Establish and maintain for at least five years from the date of the completion of the transaction, a record of each transaction undertaken.

5. Report knowledge or suspicions to the Financial Unit, National Criminal Intelligence Service (see below).

Useful addresses

Disclosure to a constable under the money laundering legislation may be made to the Duty Officer, Economic Crime Unit, National Criminal Intelligence Service, PO Box 800, London SE11 5EN. Telephone 0171 238 8271 or 020 7238 8271 (outside office hours 0171 238 8607 or 020 7238 8607), fax 0171 238 8286 or 020 7238 8286.

Further advice and guidance can be obtained from:

The Professional Adviser, Policy Directorate, The Law Society, 113 Chancery Lane, London WC2A 1PL. Telephone 0171 320 5712 or 020 7320 5712; fax 0171 320 5918 or 020 7320 5918.

The Joint Money Laundering Steering Group, Pinners Hall, 105–108 Old Broad Street, London EC2N 1EX. Telephone 0171 216 8863 or 020 7216 8863; fax 0171 216 8907 or 020 7216 8907.

April 1994, revised February 1999

PART IV – OBLIGATIONS TO OTHERS

Chapter 17

Relations with third parties

17.01   Fairness

Solicitors must not act, whether in their professional capacity or otherwise, towards anyone in a way which is fraudulent, deceitful or otherwise contrary to their position as solicitors. Nor must solicitors use their position as solicitors to take unfair advantage either for themselves or another person.

1. A solicitor must not deceive anyone; however, any information disclosed must be consistent with the solicitor's duty of confidentiality.

2. When dealing with an unrepresented third party a solicitor must take care to ensure that no retainer arises by implication between the solicitor and the third party.

3. A solicitor may be aware of the name and address of the other party, but not of the other party's solicitor. The normal practice is for the solicitor to write to the other party asking to be put in touch with his or her solicitor. For making initial contact with another party's solicitor, see **19.02** note 2, p.360.

4. When dealing with an unrepresented third party, any draft document received should be amended if it contains errors which could be put right by a reasonable amount of correction, provided that it is in the client's interests to do so. If the document is so badly drawn as to be inappropriate,

there is no objection to returning it to the lay party and advising that a solicitor should be consulted on its preparation.

5. When giving a reference as to character and financial standing, a solicitor must take care to give one that is true. A solicitor may be guilty of unbefitting conduct and may incur a liability where a false or misleading reference is given. The same principle applies where a solicitor makes or corroborates a statement on an application by another person for a passport.

6. It is a breach of rule 1 of the Solicitors' Practice Rules (see p.1) for a solicitor to write offensive letters to third parties. The same principle applies to offensive behaviour. (With regard to offensive letters written to other solicitors see **19.01** note 3, p.359.)

7. Where a solicitor receives a letter from a person who is not a client and to whom no professional duty is owed, and which does not relate to the business of a client or former client, failure to reply does not normally amount to professional misconduct. As a matter of courtesy the solicitor should acknowledge such letters.

8. For dealing with letters relating to the matters of a client or former client, see **12.10** note 2, p.248.

17.02   Stopping client account cheques

To stop a client account cheque is not inevitably professional misconduct, but may be if notice of intention to stop the cheque is not given promptly and effectively to the recipient.

1. Notice will be 'prompt and effective' if it is received before the recipient has committed himself or herself to an action which was reasonably foreseeable by the giver as likely to follow the receipt of the cheque, e.g. effecting exchange of contracts.

2. Where the recipient of the cheque is another solicitor who has paid it into his or her client account, it is open to the giver to stop the cheque, even where the other solicitor has not awaited clearance before accounting to the client.

3. Principle **17.02** does not affect any right in law which the recipient may have if the cheque is stopped.

17.03   Agreeing costs with another party

When stipulating, as a term of any settlement or agreement between a client and another party, that costs should be paid by the other party, a solicitor should give the other party sufficient opportunity to agree those costs on an informed basis, or to apply for taxation (now assessment).

1. A solicitor should not use a client's bargaining position to prevent agreement on costs being reached on a reasonably informed basis, nor must unfair advantage be taken of another party for the solicitor's own benefit by overcharging. The solicitor should, if requested, offer the other party a sufficient breakdown of the calculation.

2. Principle **17.03** also applies in relation to non-contentious matters, e.g. where a landlord or lender demands an undertaking in respect of costs. Solicitors should consider carefully whether it is possible to comply with any undertaking given.

3. A solicitor requesting an undertaking should give sufficient indication as to the basis of charging or an estimate of the amount, together in any case with a cap on the amount to be covered by the undertaking. This cap will not affect any right to charge the client the full amount of costs. As it relates only to the amount to be covered by the undertaking, a further undertaking may be sought if it subsequently appears that the cap will be exceeded. It is advisable for the solicitor giving the undertaking to set a limit on the amount (see also Chapter 18 on undertakings, p.351).

17.04   Dealing with unqualified persons

If a solicitor discovers that another party is represented by an unqualified person who is carrying out reserved activities, the solicitor's proper course is to decline to communicate with the unqualified person.

1. The provision of advocacy, litigation, probate and conveyancing services is limited to certain categories of persons by the Solicitors Act 1974 (see Annex 2A, p.42), the Administration of Justice Act 1985 and the Courts and Legal Services Act 1990. For guidance on dealing with unqualified conveyancers see Annex 25A, p.482.

2. Solicitors are asked to report to the Professional Adviser any cases where it appears that an unqualified person has acted in breach of the law (see p.xv for contact details).

17.05   Letters before action

When writing a letter before action (now letter of claim), a solicitor must not demand anything other than that recoverable under the due process of law.

1. For example, where a solicitor is retained to collect a simple debt, he or she must not demand from the debtor the cost of the letter before action, since it cannot be said, at that stage, that such costs are legally recoverable.

2. Where a solicitor is instructed by a creditor to collect a debt, there is nothing improper in the solicitor communicating with the employer of the debtor in order to obtain information as to the debtor's status or means. A

solicitor should not, however, use the threat of contacting the employer or the media as a means of obtaining payment. (As to a solicitor instructing an enquiry agent to enquire into the means of a debtor, see **19.02** note 5, p.360.)

3.   Under the new civil litigation regime, litigation should be seen as a last resort. To further this aim, solicitors will be expected to comply with new pre-action protocols. Both the pre-action protocol for personal injury claims and the pre-action protocol for the resolution of clinical disputes provide templates for letters before action (now called 'letters of claim'). For further details, see Annex 21I (p.409).

4.   A solicitor must not seek to enforce a gaming debt, except in cases permitted by the Gaming Acts.

17.06   Administering oaths

When administering oaths and affirmations or taking declarations, a solicitor is under a duty to ascertain:

(a)   that the deponent is in the solicitor's presence, by enquiring whether the signature to the document before the solicitor is the name and in the handwriting of the deponent;

(b)   that the deponent is apparently competent to depose to the affidavit or declaration;

(c)   that the deponent knows he or she is about to be sworn or declared by the solicitor to the truth of the statement; and

(d)   that the exhibits, if any, are the documents referred to.

1.   Section 81(1) of the Solicitors Act 1974 enables any solicitor holding a practising certificate to exercise the powers of a commissioner for oaths. Under section 113(10) of the Courts and Legal Services Act 1990 any such solicitor may use the title 'Commissioner for Oaths'.

2.   The responsibility for the contents of the affidavit or declaration rests with the deponent and the solicitor who prepared it. The solicitor administering the oath has a duty to be satisfied that the oath is in a proper form and, upon the face of it, an oath which the solicitor is authorised to administer. If the affidavit or declaration is incomplete, e.g. containing blanks, the solicitor should refuse to administer it.

3.   Although a solicitor is under no duty to read through the oath or declaration, if a solicitor has good reason to believe that the oath or declaration is false (even if that was unknown to the deponent), the solicitor must refuse to administer it.

4.   It is improper for a solicitor to share any part of the fees received for administering the oath with the deponent or the deponent's solicitor.

17.07   Circumstances where an oath should not be administered

A solicitor should not administer oaths and affirmations nor take declarations in a proceeding in which the solicitor or the solicitor's firm is acting for any of the parties, or is otherwise interested.

1. Principle **17.07** derives from section 1(3) of the Commissioners for Oaths Act 1889 and section 81(2) of the Solicitors Act 1974, and applies to both contentious and non-contentious matters.

2. In relation to the administering of oaths and affirmations and the taking of declarations, principle **17.07** prevents, e.g.:

    (a) a solicitor from exercising these powers in relation to a local authority's business where the solicitor is a member or employee of that local authority;

    (b) a solicitor from exercising these powers regarding proofs in bankruptcy when acting for that proving creditor or regarding the winding-up of an estate when acting for the personal representatives;

    (c) a solicitor who is employed part-time by another solicitor from exercising these powers for a client of that employer;

    (d) a solicitor who is in the full or part-time employment of a company from exercising these powers in matters in which the company is concerned.

3. It is not necessarily improper for a solicitor to administer an oath to his or her spouse who is also a solicitor where the oath arises out of a matter connected with that spouse's practice. However, doubts could arise as to the impartiality of the solicitor administering the oath, and this could lead to a challenge to the admissibility of the affidavit.

4. On the other hand, section 81(2) of the Solicitors Act 1974 prevents a solicitor from administering an oath to his or her spouse (who may or may not be a solicitor) arising out of a matter personal to the spouse (for example, a claim for damages for personal injury suffered by the spouse) if, by reason of their personal relationship, it could be said that the solicitor administering the oath had an interest in the proceedings.

Chapter 18

Professional undertakings

18.01   Definition of undertaking

An undertaking is any unequivocal declaration of intention addressed to someone who reasonably places reliance on it and made by:

(a)   a solicitor or a member of a solicitor's staff in the course of practice; or

(b)   a solicitor as 'solicitor', but not in the course of practice.

1.   An undertaking is personally binding on the solicitor – see **18.02**, p.352.

2.   An undertaking may be given orally or in writing and need not necessarily include the word 'undertake'.

3.   Although an oral undertaking has the same effect as a written one, there may be evidential problems as to its existence unless there is available a contemporaneous note, transcript or written confirmation of its terms. If the recipient confirms the terms of an oral undertaking and the giver does not promptly repudiate those terms, the Office for the Supervision of Solicitors

(OSS) is likely to accept this as sufficient evidence of the terms of any undertaking.

4. The OSS will treat a promise to give an undertaking as an undertaking, provided the promise sufficiently identifies the terms of the undertaking and provided any conditions precedent have been satisfied. If the promise refers to the 'usual undertaking', the OSS will take into account current practice but discourages the giving of such vague undertakings.

5. The Society's formulae for exchanging contracts and its code for completion by post embody undertakings – see **25.11**, p.477 and Annexes 25D (p.492) and 25E (p.496). For forms of undertakings used in conveyancing, see Annexes 25B (p.487) and 25C (p.488).

6. A solicitor may be subject to professional obligations even though he or she has not given an undertaking. For example:

(a) If a person sends documents or money to a solicitor subject to an express condition, the recipient is subject to a professional obligation to return the documents or money if unwilling or unable to comply with the condition.

(b) If documents or money are sent to a solicitor on condition that they should be held to the sender's order, the recipient has a professional obligation to return the documents or money to the sender on demand. Any cheque or draft must not be presented for payment without the consent of the sender.

(c) Where a solicitor asks another solicitor to supply copies of documents, there is a professional obligation to pay a proper charge for them.

(d) For the stopping of client account cheques, see **17.02**, p.347.

18.02   Breach and misconduct

A solicitor who fails to honour an undertaking is *prima facie* guilty of professional misconduct. Consequently, the Office for the Supervision of Solicitors will expect its implementation as a matter of conduct.

1. Professional conduct obligations can be more onerous than legal obligations. For example, if an undertaking is given in the course of representing a party to a dispute, the resolution of the dispute will not necessarily discharge the undertaking.

2. Neither the OSS nor the Solicitors Disciplinary Tribunal have power to order payment of compensation or to procure the specific performance of an undertaking. The only step open to the OSS is to take disciplinary action for failure to honour the undertaking. See Chapter 30, p.842 and Chapter 31, p.856 for details of the disciplinary process. For enforcement by the Court see **18.16**, p.358.

3. The OSS expects solicitors to honour undertakings for so long as their names remain on the roll and regardless of whether or not they hold practising certificates. The Tribunal has power to consider allegations against a former solicitor relating to a time when he or she was a solicitor.

4. The giver cannot unilaterally withdraw from an undertaking once the recipient has placed reliance on it.

5. The OSS has no power to order the release of a solicitor from the terms of an undertaking. This is a matter for the Court, or the person entitled to the benefit of the undertaking.

6. In certain circumstances, the OSS can give notice, on receipt of a request from the giver of an undertaking, that, unless steps are taken within a specified time by the recipient, the OSS will not consider a complaint in respect of it, e.g. where the recipient is required to take some action, but has not done so. The request should be made in writing to the OSS (see p.xv for contact details).

7. Subject to note 6 above, a solicitor cannot claim to be released from an undertaking on the basis that the recipient has been slow in drawing attention to the breach, although this is a matter to which the OSS may have regard if a complaint is made.

8. The OSS will not become involved where:

   (a) the undertaking has been procured by fraud, deceit or, in certain circumstances, by innocent misrepresentation; or

   (b) the performance of the undertaking turns on a disputed point of law.

18.03   No obligation to give or accept

There is no obligation on a solicitor either to give or accept an undertaking.

Although there is a duty to act in a client's best interests, this does not imply a duty to assume or underwrite a client's financial or other obligations.

18.04   Performance outside solicitor's control

An undertaking is binding even if it is to do something outside the solicitor's control.

1. Solicitors should consider whether they will be able to implement an undertaking before giving it, and they should have regard to all eventualities which might affect their ability to perform the undertaking. For example, unless the undertaking is suitably qualified, it will be no defence to a complaint of professional misconduct that:

   ▶ a third party was required to take some action but has failed to do so; or

   ▶ the client has terminated the retainer.

2. Solicitors who give an undertaking involving the payment of money can be required in conduct to discharge this out of their own and their partners' resources. In particular, it should be noted that:

   (a) The client's bankruptcy will not discharge the undertaking.

   (b) Others may have a prior claim over the fund from which the solicitor agreed to remit monies, such as the client's trustee in bankruptcy or a garnishee.

18.05   Indemnity

A solicitor who incurs loss which arises directly from a claim based on an undertaking given by the solicitor (or by a partner or member of staff) in the course of private practice may be entitled to an indemnity out of the Solicitors' Indemnity Fund.

1. Although it is the solicitor giving the undertaking (or his or her firm) who is entitled to any indemnity under the Solicitors' Indemnity Rules, in practice Solicitors Indemnity Fund Limited would usually make payment to the person to whom money was due by the terms of the undertaking.

2. Even if cover is provided by the Indemnity Fund, this does not remove the possibility of disciplinary action for failure to honour the undertaking.

3. No cover is provided for a trading debt incurred by a practice or by any of its members, nor (in general) for an undertaking given in connection with the provision of finance, property, assistance or other advantage for the benefit of the solicitor or certain connected persons or organisations (see rule 14.1(e) of the Solicitors' Indemnity Rules 1998 in Annex 29A at p.803). For these reasons:

   (a) Where a solicitor borrows money on the basis of an undertaking to repay it, and then re-lends the money to a client who subsequently defaults, the solicitor would have no cover from the Indemnity Fund.

   (b) A solicitor will have no cover from the Indemnity Fund in respect of an undertaking which amounts to a bare guarantee or underwriting of the financial obligations of a client or third party.

18.06   Who is bound? – who may complain?

Normally only the giver of an undertaking will be expected to honour it and only the recipient of an undertaking may complain of a breach.

1. Where a solicitor has received an undertaking for the benefit of a client who instructs another solicitor in his or her place then, unless for good reason the former solicitor objects, the benefit of the undertaking will remain vested in the client and any complaint can be made at the client's request by the new solicitor.

2. A solicitor cannot assign the burden of an undertaking (and thus claim to be released from its terms) without the approval of the recipient.

3. Where a solicitor acquires a practice from another and consequently takes over the conduct of a matter in which there is an undertaking outstanding, the acquiring solicitor is not liable on the undertaking unless it is expressly or impliedly adopted. If the solicitor adopts the undertaking, the solicitor who gave the undertaking nevertheless remains liable under it unless the giver obtains a release from the recipient.

18.07 Ambiguous undertakings

An ambiguous undertaking is generally construed in favour of the recipient.

1. Principle **18.07** is particularly applicable if the undertaking is given to a lay person. Only in limited circumstances will the Office for the Supervision of Solicitors consider extraneous evidence to clarify an ambiguity (see also **18.15**, p.357).

2. Care should be taken when giving or accepting an undertaking which includes the words 'to use best endeavours'. What constitutes 'best endeavours' is arguable and each case must be construed on its own facts. It may well involve the giver of the undertaking in making a payment, for example to discharge a mortgage – see **25.11** note 1, p.477).

18.08 Consideration

An undertaking does not have to constitute a legal contract in order for disciplinary action to be taken in respect of a breach.

If an undertaking is expressed to be given for consideration but, through no fault of the giver, that consideration has failed, the undertaking will be discharged. Consequently, where there is consideration, it should be expressly stated in the undertaking itself.

18.09 Undertakings 'on behalf of' clients

A solicitor will be held personally liable to honour an undertaking given 'on behalf of' anyone unless such liability is clearly disclaimed in the undertaking itself.

1. Accordingly, where it is not the solicitor's intention to be personally bound, the undertaking should be worded so as to exclude personal liability on the part of the solicitor.

2. There is a distinction between an undertaking (including one given 'on behalf of' a client) and a mere statement of a client's intentions, or an agreement between solicitors as agents for their clients, which is manifestly without the assumption of any personal liability.

18.10 Liability of partners

Where a solicitor in partnership gives an undertaking in the course of his or her practice, all partners are responsible for its performance.

1. A partner will remain responsible for the firm's undertakings even after he or she leaves the firm or the partnership is dissolved.

2. As a matter of conduct no liability will normally attach to a solicitor who becomes a partner after an undertaking was given.

18.11 Liability for undertakings of staff

A solicitor employer is responsible for honouring an undertaking given by any member of staff, including unadmitted staff.

1. Where an assistant solicitor gives the undertaking, his or her own conduct may also be called into question by the Office for the Supervision of Solicitors.

2. In view of their own liability, principals should limit those members of staff who are permitted to give undertakings and should prescribe the manner in which any undertaking is given.

18.12 Employed solicitors

A solicitor in employment outside private practice will be held personally liable as a matter of conduct on a professional undertaking, whether or not given in the course of employment.

1. A solicitor employed outside private practice must consider the personal implications of giving an undertaking, particularly in commerce or industry, because of the possibility that the employer might become insolvent. The employer's insolvency will not affect the personal responsibility of the solicitor for an undertaking.

2. Where the head of a legal department in e.g. commerce, industry or local or central government is a solicitor, that person has the primary liability for an undertaking given by the department. This applies whether the undertaking is given over the signature of an admitted or unadmitted staff member.

3. Solicitors who are offered undertakings from such legal departments should take care where the head of the department is an unadmitted person. The Office for the Supervision of Solicitors can consider a complaint only where an undertaking is given by a solicitor or a member of a solicitor's staff.

18.13   Client's instructions

A solicitor cannot avoid liability on an undertaking by pleading that to honour it would be a breach of the duty owed to a client.

1. It is important that before giving an undertaking the solicitor has the client's express or implied authority.

2. Where a solicitor gives an undertaking without the client's authority and, as a result, the client suffers loss, the client's remedies may include a claim in negligence against the solicitor.

3. If a solicitor has received written instructions from a client which are expressed to be irrevocable, those instructions are nonetheless revocable unless the solicitor has acted on them in such a way as to change the solicitor's personal position; the instructions may be revoked before the solicitor has given the undertaking but not afterwards.

4. In conduct a solicitor cannot avoid the obligations on an undertaking by claiming set-off or lien.

18.14   Conditional undertakings

A solicitor who gives an undertaking which is dependent upon the happening of a future event must notify the recipient immediately if it becomes clear that the event will not occur.

18.15   Implied terms and extraneous evidence

In general, no terms will be implied into a professional undertaking and extraneous evidence will not be considered.

1. Terms will be implied as follows:

    (a) When a solicitor gives an undertaking to pay another solicitor's costs the undertaking will be discharged if the matter does not proceed unless, in the body of the undertaking, or in a separate agreement, there is an express provision that the costs are payable in any event.

    (b) An undertaking to pay another solicitor's costs is an undertaking to pay 'proper costs' unless otherwise stated; consequently, it is open to the giver of the undertaking to apply for taxation (now assessment) of the bill and, provided that the recipient is notified of this promptly, the undertaking will take effect on the bill as taxed. A remuneration certificate is not normally available unless the client of the solicitor who has received the undertaking consents to an application being made.

(c)   An undertaking to pay the costs of a professional agent other than a solicitor is similarly an undertaking to pay 'proper costs'. However, unless the agent's professional body can determine whether the costs are proper, the Office for the Supervision of Solicitors may be unwilling to take disciplinary action in respect of such an undertaking and a *bona fide* dispute as to quantum will have to be resolved through the court (see also **20.01**, p.363).

(d)   If an undertaking is given to pay money out of a fund at some specified time, there is an implied warranty that the fund will be sufficient for that purpose. Accordingly, if so desired, it is crucial that this warranty is negatived in the body of the undertaking itself.

(e)   Where an undertaking is given to pay a sum of money out of the proceeds of sale of an asset, there is no implied term that the sum is payable out of the net proceeds. Consequently, it is essential that any undertaking of this nature should stipulate what deductions have been agreed.

(f)   There is an implied term that an undertaking is to be performed within a reasonable time having regard to its nature. If there is any delay, the giver is under an obligation in conduct to keep the recipient informed.

(g)   A solicitor who has undertaken to accept service of court proceedings on behalf of a client should, as far as practicable, reach agreement with the serving party in advance of issue or service (particularly if service by fax or e-mail is intended); but, in any event, should accept or acknowledge service, if possible, on the day of receipt of the proceeding.

2.   An undertaking will not be affected by events which occur subsequently, unless these events are provided for in the undertaking itself.

3.   The terms of a written undertaking may be contained in more than one document (see *Goldman* v. *Abbot* [1989] 139 New L.J. 828).

4.   See **25.11**, p.477 for undertakings relating to conveyancing matters.

18.16   Enforcement by the Court

The Court, by virtue of its inherent jurisdiction over its own officers, has power to enforce undertakings.

1.   The Office for the Supervision of Solicitors (OSS) will not take disciplinary steps in relation to any breach where a solicitor gives an undertaking to the Court.

2.   The OSS takes the view that where a solicitor gives an undertaking to the Court, enforcement is a matter for the Court; for this reason the OSS will not normally take any action.

Chapter 19

Relations with other solicitors

19.01 Duty of good faith

A solicitor must act towards other solicitors with frankness and good faith consistent with his or her overriding duty to the client.

1. Any fraudulent or deceitful conduct by one solicitor towards another will render the offending solicitor liable to disciplinary action, in addition to the possibility of civil or criminal proceedings.

2. A solicitor must honour his or her word given either personally, or by partners or by any other member of the solicitor's firm, and whether or not in writing. For solicitors' undertakings see Chapter 18, p.351.

3. A solicitor must maintain his or her personal integrity and observe the requirements of good manners and courtesy towards other members of the profession or their staff, no matter how bitter the feelings between clients. A solicitor must not write offensive letters to other members of the profession.

4. A solicitor will normally warn the other party to a telephone conversation if it is going to be recorded. This warning may, however, be dispensed with in cases where the solicitor believes that considerations of courtesy are outweighed by other factors. Regard should be had to the legislation relating to telecommunications systems and any requirement to give notice prior to recording any conversation.

5. In the absence of an agreement, a solicitor is personally responsible for paying the proper costs of solicitor agents instructed on behalf of his or her client (see **20.01**, p.363).

19.02   Contacting other party to a matter

A solicitor should not communicate with any party who to the solicitor's knowledge has retained a solicitor to act in the matter except with that other solicitor's consent.

1. A solicitor who has been instructed by a client should not write on that matter directly to the client of another solicitor where the solicitor has reason to believe that the other solicitor's retainer still exists.

2. A solicitor may be aware of the name and address of the other party, but not of the other party's solicitor. The normal practice is for the solicitor to write to the other party asking to be put in touch with his or her solicitor.

3. A solicitor may be justified in writing direct to the client of another solicitor if that solicitor fails to reply to a letter, or where the solicitor has refused for no adequate reason to pass on any messages to his or her client. However, this step should only be taken after warning the other solicitor of the intention to write direct to his or her client. It is also courteous to copy such correspondence to the other solicitor.

4. Principle **19.02** does not prevent a solicitor suggesting to a client that the client should communicate directly with the solicitor's client on the other side.

5. Principle **19.02** does not prevent a solicitor from instructing an enquiry agent to ascertain, for example, the whereabouts or means of the other side, or to serve documents. However, where a third party is already represented, a solicitor should not instruct an enquiry agent to approach the other party to obtain a statement until notice of the intention to do so has been given to the other party's solicitor.

6. Principle **19.02** extends to employed solicitors. Thus, for example, a solicitor acting for a client in a matter concerning a local authority who has express or implied notice that the authority's solicitor has been instructed to act in the matter, must not discuss that matter directly with the appropriate committee chairman, any individual councillor or any political group on the authority. However, the principle does not prevent political lobbying of individual councillors or a political group on the authority by a solicitor on behalf of a client, even where the solicitor knows that the authority's solicitor has been instructed to deal with the legal issues.

7. In the context of **19.02**, only those employees or officers of a corporation who are responsible for the giving of instructions are to be regarded as the client of the corporation's solicitor. See also **21.10**, p.377.

8. Save as stated in note 7, it is not a breach of **19.02** to interview employees of an organisation on the other side in a matter. When contemplating interviewing such an employee, the solicitor should have regard to the employee's position *qua* employee and in appropriate circumstances should advise the employer or its solicitor of the intention to interview the employee. This would enable the employee to be advised as to his or her position. Before making the decision to interview an employee, the interviewing solicitor should have regard to:

    (a) the liability of the employee;

    (b) the fact that the information sought may be confidential to the employer and, if disclosed, may place the employee in breach of his or her contract or the common law; similarly, the position as to privileged information may be relevant.

9. Solicitors may write, on behalf of a client, direct to the Legal Aid Board complaining about the grant of legal aid to another party, as the Legal Aid Board is not a client of the solicitor, merely the funding agent of the other solicitor's client.

10. Where a solicitor is instructed in his or her capacity as an estate agent to act for a seller, it is not a breach of **19.02** if the solicitor contacts the buyer direct solely about estate agency matters. Similarly, where a solicitor is providing a relocation service to a corporate client who is buying a property from an employee, the solicitor may contact the employee, but only to discuss administrative matters arising out of the relocation.

19.03 Dealing with letters from solicitors

Purely as a matter of courtesy, a letter from another solicitor should normally be acknowledged. Failure to give a full reply to a letter from another solicitor is not misconduct if the client has instructed his or her solicitor not to reply.

For dealing with letters and communications generally, see **12.10**, p.248, and for dealing with letters from third parties, see **17.01** note 7, p.347.

19.04 Duty to report another solicitor

A solicitor is under a duty to report to the Office for the Supervision of Solicitors any serious misconduct. Where necessary the solicitor must obtain his or her client's consent to report the other solicitor.

1. Where a solicitor has reason to believe that another solicitor may be in financial difficulty or where the solicitor's integrity is in question, the solicitor should report those suspicions to the OSS (see p.xv for contact details).

2. A solicitor has a duty to inform the OSS of serious misconduct in the solicitor's own firm, e.g. theft by members of his or her staff whether solicitors or not. Unadmitted staff can have orders made against them under section 43 of the Solicitors Act 1974, see Annex 3A at p.93 restricting their employment in solicitors' offices.

3. The Society's Monitoring and Investigation Unit and Fraud Intelligence Officer will receive information on an anonymous basis from a solicitor, or member of a solicitor's firm, which suggests that a solicitor is in financial difficulties (see p.xv for contact details).

4. The OSS should be informed where a solicitor is charged with an offence involving dishonesty or deception or a serious arrestable offence, as defined by section 116 of the Police and Criminal Evidence Act 1984.

19.05   Signing certificates

Where a solicitor signs a certificate or otherwise gives information concerning another solicitor, he or she must give a full and frank assessment of that other solicitor and must not mislead.

Principle **19.05** applies particularly where a solicitor agrees to sign a certificate to the effect that an individual is a proper person:

(a) to be admitted as a solicitor;

(b) to hold a practising certificate;

(c) to be restored to the roll; or

(d) to be employed as a solicitor.

Chapter 20

Relations with the Bar, other lawyers and professional agents

20.01 Duty to pay agents' fees

A solicitor is personally responsible for paying the proper costs of any professional agent or other person whom he or she instructs on behalf of a client, whether or not the solicitor receives payment from the client, unless the solicitor and the person instructed make an express agreement to the contrary.

Costs

1. Principle **20.01** covers the proper costs of experts as well as professional and ordinary witnesses and enquiry agents.

2. Disputes as to the proper fee cannot usually be determined by the Society.

3. If the solicitor and the agent have agreed a fee in advance, this will be the sum which will be payable.

Legal aid

4. Where the solicitor wishes to restrict liability to an agent to whatever sums are allowed on taxation (now assessment), or to delay payment until put in funds by e.g. the Legal Aid Board, this should be made clear to the agent before instructions are given.

Witnesses

5. A solicitor is not personally responsible for payment of the fees of witnesses who have declined an invitation to give evidence and have had to be subpoenaed or summonsed (see also **21.11**, p.378).

Counsel's fees

6. For the position as to counsel's fees, see **20.06**, p.367.

20.02　Fees of foreign lawyers

A solicitor who instructs a lawyer of a jurisdiction other than England and Wales is liable personally to pay that lawyer's proper fees, unless there has been an express agreement to the contrary.

1. The Society accepts rule 19 of the International Code of Ethics of the International Bar Association (see Annex 9B at p.194). Corresponding provisions are in article 5.7 of the CCBE Code of Conduct for Lawyers in the European Community (see Annex 10B at p.220).

2. Difficulties may sometimes arise in ascertaining what are the proper fees of a foreign lawyer. Such fees may be regulated by a scale approved by the relevant bar association or law society. In case of doubt contact the International Directorate (see p.xv for contact details).

3. The CCBE Code of Conduct provides that where a lawyer considers that a colleague in another member state has acted in breach of a rule of professional conduct, or any personal dispute of a professional nature has arisen between them, he or she must not commence any form of proceedings against the colleague without first informing the bars or law societies to which they both belong, so as to afford an opportunity for those bodies to assist in reaching a settlement (see article 5.9 set out in Annex 10B at p.221).

20.03　Instructing counsel or other advocate

When instructing counsel or other advocate, it is the solicitor's responsibility to ensure, so far as practicable, that adequate instructions, supporting statements and documents are sent in good time.

For the rules of conduct affecting barristers, see the *Code of Conduct of the Bar of England and Wales 1998* published by the General Council of the Bar (see p.xv for contact details).

20.04   Attending advocates at court

Where counsel has been instructed, the instructing solicitor is under a duty to attend or arrange for the attendance of a responsible representative throughout the proceedings; save that attendance may be dispensed with in the magistrates' court or in certain categories of Crown court proceedings, where, in either case, the solicitor is satisfied that it is reasonable in the particular circumstances of the case that counsel be unattended. The solicitor will be so satisfied where it is clear that the interests of the client and the interests of justice will not be prejudiced by counsel appearing alone.

Where a solicitor advocate has been instructed in a Crown court case, the instructing solicitor should attend or arrange for the attendance of a responsible representative where this is necessary for the proper conduct of the case.

1.   Attendance on counsel may be dispensed with in the Crown court only in the following categories of hearing:

    (a)   trials;

    (b)   hearings of cases listed for pleas of guilty;

    (c)   sentencing hearings following committals for sentence;

    (d)   hearings of appeals against conviction or sentence.

2.   Attendance on counsel in the Crown court will not normally be dispensed with:

    (a)   where the client is charged with an offence included in Class 1 or 2 as determined pursuant to section 75(2) of the Supreme Court Act 1981;

    (b)   if the proceedings have been instituted or taken over by the Serious Fraud Office, or are before the Crown court by reason of a notice of transfer given under section 4 of the Criminal Justice Act 1987;

    (c)   where the client was a child or young person at the time the Crown court acquired jurisdiction;

    (d)   where the client is unable to understand the proceedings or give adequate instructions to counsel because of inadequate knowledge of English, mental illness or other mental or physical disability;

    (e)   on the last day of a trial if the client was likely if convicted to receive a custodial sentence and it is expected that sentence will then take place; and the day on which the client is in fact sentenced, whether or not it coincides with the last day of any trial;

    (f)   on days where a significant number of defence witnesses are to be marshalled;

    (g) in a trial where there are a substantial number of defence documents;

    (h) where counsel is representing more than one defendant;

    (i) where the client was likely to disrupt proceedings if counsel were to appear alone;

    (j) on days where counsel is likely to require notes of the proceedings to be taken for the proper conduct of the defence;

    (k) in cases outside the above criteria where there are exceptional circumstances such that it was desirable that counsel should be attended.

3.   Where it is necessary to take a proof of evidence from an unexpected witness during a trial or to hold a conference at court due to a late change of advocate, attendance on counsel for that part of the preparation of a case will not normally be dispensed with.

4.   Where a solicitor proposes that counsel should appear unattended he or she must:

    (a) so inform counsel and deliver a full and detailed brief sufficiently early before the hearing to enable counsel to consider the papers and to decide whether it would be appropriate for counsel to attend alone (guidelines issued by the Criminal Law Committee as to the contents and handling of such briefs and remuneration are to be found in Annex 20A, p.370); and

    (b) inform the client that counsel will be unattended and tell the client both the name of counsel and how instructions may be given; and

    (c) attend on counsel or send a representative where:

        (i) counsel originally instructed or subsequently substituted informs the solicitor, either before or during the proceedings, that he or she does not believe that it is appropriate for counsel to be unattended; and

        (ii) attendance is necessary in the proper and efficient administration of justice.

5.   The Council, when considering any complaint that **20.04** has not been observed, will take into account all the practical difficulties and any legal aid regulations affecting the position.

6.   The Council is currently reviewing the obligation to attend counsel in civil proceedings. For further information contact Professional Ethics (see p.xv for contact details).

20.05   Solicitors' responsibility to clients

Solicitors may not abrogate their responsibility to clients by instructing counsel or other advocate.

1. A solicitor should take care in the selection of suitable counsel or other advocate and must, when considering the advice of counsel or other advocate, ensure that it contains no obvious errors. If the advice conflicts with previous advice, it may be necessary to seek clarification.

2. Solicitors must use their best endeavours to ensure that the barrister or other advocate carries out instructions within a reasonable time and that the claim does not become statute barred or liable to be struck out. Where appropriate, a solicitor must ask for the return of the papers in order to instruct another barrister or other advocate.

3. The Bar's code requires that where a barrister has received instructions and it is or becomes apparent that the work cannot be done within a reasonable time, the barrister should inform the instructing solicitor forthwith. Where a brief has been delivered, immediately that there is an appreciable risk that the barrister may not be able to undertake the case, the brief should be returned in sufficient time to allow another barrister to be engaged and to master the brief.

20.06   Solicitors' liability for counsel's fees

Except in legal aid cases, solicitors are personally liable as a matter of professional conduct for the payment of counsel's proper fees, whether or not they have been placed in funds by the client.

1. A barrister is entitled to demand payment of a fee with a brief, except in legal aid cases.

2. In non-legal aid cases, and unless there is a special agreement, a solicitor must pay or challenge counsel's fees within three months of the delivery of the fee note at the conclusion of the case, whether or not the solicitor has been put in funds by the client or the costs have been taxed or assessed.

3. In legal aid cases, a delay on the part of a solicitor in submitting the bill and papers for taxation or assessment, which results in counsel not receiving fees within a reasonable time after submission of the fee note, can amount to unbefitting conduct.

4. If a solicitor wishes to challenge counsel's fees, this must be done promptly upon receipt of the fee note. It would usually be appropriate for a solicitor to ensure that the client has an opportunity to consider whether the fees should be challenged. For details of the procedure for resolving disputes see **20.07**, p.369.

5. The Law Society and the General Council of the Bar have published an agreed statement concerning the liability of solicitors for the payment of counsel's fees following a transfer of practice or the disappearance, death or bankruptcy of a solicitor. The statement, first published on 23rd March 1988, says:

    'The Bar Council has expressed concern to the Council of the Law Society about cases where an outstanding liability to pay counsel is overtaken by a transfer of practice or the disappearance, death or bankruptcy of a solicitor.

    The general principle to be recognised in all cases is as follows:

    A solicitor is personally liable for payment of counsel's proper fees whether or not the solicitor has received the money from the client with which to pay the fees. Where instructions have been given in the name of a firm, all partners at that date incur personal liability.

    The liability of a sole practitioner and of partners for the liabilities of their co-partners is a continuing one and is not cancelled or superseded by any transfer of the practice, without counsel's express consent. Equally, a partner or partners in a firm remain liable for the payment of counsel's fees incurred on behalf of the firm by a deceased, bankrupt or otherwise defaulting former partner of the firm.

    If a transfer of a practice is contemplated, consideration should be given to outstanding counsel's fees on files taken over.'

6. Principle **20.06** applies equally to solicitors employed by lay-employers. Such a solicitor should ensure that counsel and counsel's clerk are made aware at the outset of the matter that the solicitor is employed.

7. The Bar keep a list of solicitors whom they consider to be in default. The Bar may consider that a default has occurred in circumstances which would not necessarily constitute professional misconduct. The list may be operated against future partners or employers of a listed solicitor.

8. Solicitors are exonerated from liability for payment of counsel's fees where counsel is instructed to appear before a court or tribunal outside England and Wales if:

    (a) the solicitor is acting, whether as agent or not, for a client who is normally resident outside England and Wales; and

    (b) the solicitor informs counsel in writing a reasonable time before the date planned for counsel's departure abroad that the solicitor has not been put in funds.

20.07   Counsel's fees: challenge and dispute resolution

If a solicitor wishes to challenge counsel's fees this must be done promptly upon receipt of the fee note. If the dispute cannot be resolved, it may be referred to a Joint Tribunal consisting of a member of the Council and a Queen's Counsel nominated respectively by the President of the Law Society and the Chairman of the Bar.

20

1.   It would usually be appropriate for the solicitor to ensure that the client has an opportunity to consider whether the fees should be challenged.

2.   Solicitors wishing to invoke the procedure should inform counsel within three months of the delivery of the fee note and apply to the Office for the Supervision of Solicitors (OSS) (see p.xv for contact details).

3.   Where a dispute as to fees is referred to it, the Joint Tribunal's task is to look at all the circumstances in dispute. Where matters touching counsel's competence amounting to professional misconduct are in issue, such matters are first considered by the Professional Conduct Committee of the General Council of the Bar (see p.xv for contact details).

4.   The Joint Tribunal is an informal body, fixing its own procedure which may or may not involve a hearing of the parties. Both parties are asked to agree the documentation to be submitted to the Joint Tribunal and, where possible, the Tribunal will reach a decision on that documentation. The parties to an adjudication bear their own expenses, unless these are otherwise awarded. The parties are required to undertake to abide by the decision of the Tribunal. Failure on the part of a solicitor to comply with the award of a Tribunal is regarded by the OSS as unbefitting conduct and can lead to disciplinary proceedings.

20.08   Barrister employees

A non-practising barrister may be an employee in a solicitor's office.

Annex 20A

Preparation of cases where counsel is unattended – practice information

The Council have, in certain circumstances, relaxed the requirement that an instructing solicitor or a responsible representative attend on counsel in the Crown court. The circumstances in which attendance may be dispensed with are set out at **20.04** (p.365 in the Guide).

Content and handling of briefs

The Society's Criminal Law Committee have considered the content and handling of briefs where a solicitor proposes that counsel be unattended and believe that the following guidelines will be of assistance to the profession.

Note 4 to **20.04** provides that where a solicitor proposes that counsel be unattended the solicitor must so inform counsel and deliver a full and detailed brief sufficiently early before the hearing to enable counsel to consider the papers and to decide whether it would be appropriate for counsel to attend alone. The Committee take the view that whenever possible such briefs should be delivered not later than seven days in advance of the case. In order to alert counsel and their clerks, briefs should be clearly marked with a red star where solicitors propose that counsel should be unattended.

The brief will need to contain more than it would if the solicitor or a representative was in attendance, as counsel will have to undertake those duties normally carried out by the solicitor or the representative in attending court. Solicitors should insert clear instructions in the brief so that counsel is aware of precisely what duties will have to be fulfilled in the absence of the solicitor or a representative. Broadly, such instructions should cover actions required and details needed in respect of dealings with the client and witnesses, and recording and reporting what takes place in court. Thus the instructions should, where appropriate:

(a) deal with counsel's early arrival at court in order to see the client;

(b) include sufficient details about the defendant and any witnesses to enable counsel to contact them if they do not appear;

(c) require the judge's comments on sentence to be fully recorded;

(d) require notes to be provided of the headings of counsel's speech in mitigation;

(e) require a telephone report to the solicitor after the case ends;

(f) require counsel to deal with witnesses' expenses;

(g) require counsel to deal with the client and any relatives who may be present after the case has been concluded;

(h) require counsel to find out where the client has been taken, if in custody, and pass that information to the solicitor; and

(i) require counsel to endorse on the brief within two days what oral advice on appeal has been given to the client.

Remuneration

The Legal Aid in Criminal and Care Proceedings (General) (Amendment) Regulations 1999 (S.I. 1999 no. 346) and (Costs) Amendment Regulations 1999 (S.I. 1999 no. 345) came into force on 1st April 1999. These apply to all proceedings in the Crown court initiated by committal or otherwise on or after that date. The regulations apply to all proceedings in the Crown court initiated by committal on or after 1st April, and restrict the circumstances in which remuneration can be paid for attendance, but apply the same principles to solicitor advocates and counsel. They provide also for additional payments to the instructing solicitor and the advocate in non-attendance cases.

In 1997 the then Lord Chancellor, Lord Mackay, proceeded with proposals which he had put forward in 1994 (see [1997] *Gazette*, 5 March, 4). During that time the Law Society, while agreeing that wasteful expenditure should be eliminated, had argued that there must be adequate support where the interest of the defendant necessarily required attendance. Accordingly, as well as specifying the circumstances where attendance will always be remunerated, a role was secured for a judge to certify in advance that attendance was required.

It was agreed that the legal aid changes should not come into effect before changes to the professional obligations to attend on counsel contained in the principles of conduct. Those were eventually approved. Principle **20.04** matches the legal aid provisions. The main elements of the regulations are:

▶ Remuneration for attendance on an advocate, whether solicitor or counsel, will automatically be allowed at trials, guilty pleas following plea and direction hearings, committals for sentence and appeals, in the circumstances specified in note 2(a)–(e) of **20.04**.

▶ Remuneration will not be allowed in other cases unless a judge has certified that attendance on the advocate is required for the whole or part of any hearing. Application may be made orally or in writing. A non-exhaustive list of factors is set out in the regulations which match notes 2(f)–(j) of **20.04**.

The changes do not apply to preliminary hearings such as bail applications, plea and direction hearings, mentions and other interlocutory applications. Existing arrangements remain in place.

The regulations do not change existing provisions for attendance at a conference at court with the advocate where this is necessary. However, if it is then proposed that the representative should remain at court for the hearing, an application for a certificate must be made to the judge if the case does not come within one of the automatic circumstances.

In standard fee cases for preparation, an additional fee of £30 (£32 within Legal Aid Area 1) will be paid for guilty pleas, committals and appeals; £60 (£64 in Area 1) for trials or cases prepared for trial. In *ex post facto* determinations the additional amount allowed will depend on the work done bearing in mind the extra instructions which the brief will need to contain for the advocate.

For advocates appearing unattended, the additional fees are £19.25 for fixed fee cases, and £38.50 for graduated fees.

Amendments to the Directions for Determining Officers have been made. These are essential reading. They set out examples of the likely extra work which is to be taken into account on determinations of litigation and advocacy fees. These directions should be available on request from Crown courts. In cases of difficulty, copies can also be requested from Practice Advice Service (see p.xv for contact details).

January 1989, updated March 1999

PART V – PARTICULAR AREAS OF PRACTICE

Chapter 21

Litigation and advocacy

21

21.01   Duty not to mislead court

Solicitors who act in litigation, whilst under a duty to do their best for their client, must never deceive or mislead the court.

1. Principle **21.01** applies equally to proceedings before tribunals and inquiries as well as to proceedings before the courts.

2. See also paragraph 2.2 of the advocacy code (Annex 21A at p.386).

3. Although a solicitor is entitled to take every point, technical or otherwise, that is fairly arguable on behalf of the client, the court must be advised of relevant cases and statutory provisions by the advocates on both sides; if one of them omits a case or provision or makes an incorrect reference to a case or provision, it is the duty of the other to draw attention to it even if it assists the opponent's case. See also paragraph 7.1(c) of the advocacy code at p.392. For the effect of changes brought about by the Civil Procedure Rules 1998, see Annex 21I, p.409.

4. Except when acting or appearing for the prosecution (see **21.19**, p.381), a solicitor who knows of facts which, or of a witness who, would assist the adversary is not under any duty to inform the adversary or the court of this to the prejudice of his or her own client. But if the solicitor knows that a relevant affidavit or statement has been filed in the proceedings and is therefore notionally within the knowledge of the court, then there is a duty to inform the judge of its existence.

5. A solicitor would be guilty of unbefitting conduct if he or she called a witness whose evidence is untrue to the solicitor's knowledge, as opposed to his or her belief. For further guidance see Annex 21F, p.403.

6. See also Annex 21I, p.409, for guidance on certifying truthfulness of witness statements.

21.02   Practice rule 16A (solicitors acting as advocates)

'Any solicitor acting as advocate shall at all times comply with the Law Society's Code for Advocacy.'

Solicitors' Practice Rules 1990, rule 16A

21.03   Solicitors acting as advocates – additional guidance

1. The advocacy code applies to advocacy before any court and not merely to advocacy in the higher courts or advocacy under extended rights of audience.

2. The advocacy code appears at Annex 21A, p.385. Guidance on paragraphs 2.4–2.5 of the code (non-discrimination provisions) appears at Annex 21B, p.393. Guidance on paragraph 4.1(e) of the code (not accepting brief where solicitor responsible for course of action) appears at Annex 21C, p.395.

3. Paragraph 3.3 of the advocacy code refers to the Solicitors' Publicity Code 1990, see Annex 11A, p.229.

21.04   Practice rule 16B (choice of advocate)

'(1) A solicitor shall not make it a condition of providing litigation services that advocacy services shall also be provided by that solicitor or by the solicitor's firm or the solicitor's agent.

(2) A solicitor who provides both litigation and advocacy services shall as soon as practicable after receiving instructions and from time to time consider and advise the client whether having regard to the circumstances including:

(i) the gravity, complexity and likely cost of the case;

(ii) the nature of the solicitor's practice;

(iii) the solicitor's ability and experience;

(iv) the solicitor's relationship with the client;

the best interests of the client would be served by the solicitor, another advocate from the solicitor's firm, or some other advocate providing the advocacy services.'

Solicitors' Practice Rules 1990, rule 16B

21.05   Choice of advocate – additional guidance

1. Rule 16B applies to advocacy before any court and not merely to advocacy in the higher courts or advocacy under extended rights of audience.

2. Practice information on the choice of advocate appears at Annex 21H, p.408.

3. For the duty to attend court with counsel, see **20.04**, p.365.

21.06   Exercise of extended rights of audience

Solicitors who have been granted a qualification of a right of audience in the higher courts may exercise their extended rights of audience whether they are engaged in private practice or employed as in-house solicitors. However, additional restrictions apply to in-house advocates.

1. For the position relating to employed solicitors see practice rule 4 (**4.03**, p.148) and Annexes 4A and 4B, pp.152 and 159.

2. Solicitors wishing to apply for a higher courts qualification should contact Regulation and Information Services (see p.xv for contact details).

21.07 Supervision of clerks exercising rights of audience

Solicitors are responsible for supervising their clerks who exercise rights of audience under section 27 of the Courts and Legal Services Act 1990.

For guidance, see Annex 21G, p.407.

21.08 Improper allegations

A solicitor must not make or instruct an advocate to make an allegation which is intended only to insult, degrade or annoy the other side, the witness or any other person.

1. Principle **21.08** would also preclude a solicitor from making or instructing an advocate to make an allegation which is merely scandalous. See also paragraph 7.1(e) of the advocacy code (Annex 21A at p.392).

2. In any litigation a solicitor should, if possible, avoid naming in open court persons who are neither parties nor witnesses if their characters would thereby be impugned. The court should be invited to receive in writing the names, addresses and other details of such third parties. See also paragraph 7.1(f) of the advocacy code (at p.392).

3. A solicitor should not, in a plea in mitigation, make or instruct counsel to make an allegation which is likely to vilify or insult any person, without first being satisfied that there are reasonable grounds for making the statement. See also paragraph 7.1(h) of the advocacy code (at p.392).

21.09 Private communications with judge

Except when making an application to the court, a solicitor must not discuss the merits of the case with a judge, magistrate or other adjudicator before whom a case is pending or may be heard, unless invited to do so in the presence of the solicitor or counsel for the other side or party.

1. If a written communication is to be made to the judge, magistrate or other adjudicator at any time, the solicitor should at the same time deliver a copy of it to his or her professional adversary or to the opposing party if not legally represented. Where oral communication is proper, prior notice to the other party or that party's solicitor or counsel should be given.

2.   Where, after a hearing, judgement is reserved and a relevant point of law is subsequently discovered, a solicitor who intends to bring it to the judge's attention should inform the advocate on the other side, who should not oppose this course of action, even if that advocate knows that the point of law is against his or her client.

21.10   Interviewing witnesses

It is permissible for a solicitor acting for any party to interview and take statements from any witness or prospective witness at any stage in the proceedings, whether or not that witness has been interviewed or called as a witness by another party.

1.   Principle **21.10** stems from the fact that there is no property in a witness and applies both before and after the witness has given evidence at the hearing.

2.   A solicitor must not, of course, tamper with the evidence of a witness or attempt to suborn the witness into changing evidence. Once a witness has given evidence, the case must be very unusual in which a solicitor acting for the other side needs to interview that witness without seeking to persuade the witness to change evidence. See also paragraph 6.5 of the advocacy code (Annex 21A at p.391).

3.   A solicitor should be aware that, in seeking to exercise the right to interview a witness who has already been called by the other side or who to the solicitor's knowledge is likely to be called by them, the solicitor may well be exposed to the suggestion that he or she has improperly tampered with the evidence. This may be so particularly where the witness subsequently changes his or her evidence.

4.   In order to avoid allegations of tampering with evidence, it is wise for a solicitor to offer to interview the witness in the presence of a representative of the other side. If this is not possible a solicitor may record the interview, ask the witness to bring a representative and ask the witness to sign an additional statement to the effect that the witness has freely attended the interview, and has not been coerced into giving the statement or changing his or her evidence.

5.   In interviewing an expert witness or professional agent instructed by the other side, there should be no attempt to induce the witness to disclose privileged information. In these circumstances also it would be wise to offer to interview the witness in the presence of the other solicitor's representative.

6.   As a general rule, it is not improper for a solicitor to advise a witness from whom a statement is being sought that he or she need not make such a statement. The advice that the solicitor should give must depend upon the client's interests and the circumstances of the case.

7. A solicitor must not, without leave of the court, or without the consent of counsel or solicitor for the other party, discuss the case with a witness, whether or not the witness is the client, whilst the witness is in the course of giving evidence. This prohibition covers the whole of the relevant time including adjournments and weekends.

8. A solicitor, on the client's instructions, may insert advertisements for witnesses to come forward as to a particular occurrence. However, care must be taken to draft the advertisement so that, so far as practicable, it does not suggest the detailed testimony sought.

21.11 Payments to witnesses

A solicitor must not make or offer to make payments to a witness contingent upon the nature of the evidence given or upon the outcome of a case.

1. There is no objection to the payment of reasonable expenses to witnesses and reasonable compensation for loss of time attending court. In the case of an expert witness, there is an implied obligation to pay a reasonable fee.

2. For the solicitor's professional responsibility for payment of fees to witnesses, see **20.01**, p.363. The obligation includes witnesses who have been subpoenaed where they have been invited to give evidence and have agreed to do so. Therefore, a solicitor who does not wish to accept such responsibility should make this clear to the witness in advance. In criminal cases in the Crown court all witnesses other than expert witnesses can obtain payment of their fees and expenses, within the limits of the statutory scale, from the Court Office. It is good practice to inform such witnesses of this and to agree in advance whether the solicitor will accept responsibility for any sum in excess of such scale.

3. In legal aid cases, whether civil or criminal, a solicitor should draw the attention of the witness to the fact of legal aid and that the witness's fees and disbursements will have to be taxed or assessed, and that only such amounts can be paid to the witness. A solicitor should expressly disclaim personal responsibility for payment of fees beyond those allowed on taxation or assessment. It should be noted that:

   (a) prior authority is not mandatory;

   (b) Area Committees do not have the power to grant prior authority for the costs of tendering expert evidence in criminal cases;

   (c) witness expenses are not payable under a criminal legal aid order unless the court directs that they may not be paid from Central Funds (see Practice Direction on Costs in Criminal Proceedings, 3rd May 1991 [1991] 2 All E.R. 924).

4. The court has disapproved of arrangements whereby expert witnesses are instructed to provide a report on a contingency basis. It is possible (subject to prior agreement, see **20.01**, p.363) to delay paying an expert until the case has concluded, but the fee must not be calculated dependent upon the outcome.

21.12   Solicitor called as witness

A solicitor must not accept instructions to act as advocate for a client if it is clear that he or she or a member of the firm will be called as a witness on behalf of the client, unless the evidence is purely formal.

1. A solicitor must exercise judgement as to whether to cease acting where he or she:

    (a) has already accepted instructions as advocate and then becomes aware that he or she or a member of the firm will be called as a witness on behalf of the client; or

    (b) is instructed to act as litigator and knows that he or she must give evidence.

2. The circumstances in which a solicitor should continue to act as advocate, or as a litigator, must be extremely rare where it is likely that he or she will be called to give evidence other than that which is purely formal. Factors to be taken into consideration include whether giving the evidence will create a conflict of interest between the solicitor and the client, or whether the solicitor's duty to the court is likely to be impaired. See practice rule 1, p.1.

3. It may be possible for a solicitor to continue to act as an advocate if a member of the firm will be called to give evidence as to events witnessed whilst advising or assisting a client, for example at a police station or at an identification parade. In exercising judgement, the solicitor should consider the nature of evidence to be given, its importance to the case overall and the difficulties faced by the client if the solicitor were to cease to act. The decision should be taken in the interests of justice as a whole and not solely in the interests of the client. See also paragraph 4.1(d) of the advocacy code (Annex 21A at p.388).

21.13   Client's perjury

Where a client, prior to or in the course of any proceedings, admits to his or her solicitor that the client has committed perjury or misled the court in any material matter in continuing proceedings in relation to those proceedings, the solicitor must decline to act further in the proceedings, unless the client agrees fully to disclose his or her conduct to the court.

See also paragraph 5.1(e) of the advocacy code (Annex 21A at p.389).

21.14   Duty to obey court

A solicitor must comply with any order of the court which the court can properly make requiring the solicitor or the firm to take or refrain from taking some particular course of action; equally, a solicitor is bound to honour an undertaking given to any court or tribunal.

1.   A breach of principle **21.14** may amount to contempt of court (see also **18.16**, p.358).

2.   A solicitor must not aid and abet a client where the client refuses to obey a lawful court order.

3.   The Society has issued guidance as to the steps a solicitor should take to secure the attendance of a client at the Crown court for trial (see Annex 21E, p.400).

4.   The civil justice rules give judges wider powers to make directions and orders; for details of these and information about the sanctions available to the court, see Annex 21I, p.409.

21.15   Solicitor standing bail

It is undesirable for a solicitor to offer to stand bail for a person for whom the solicitor or any partner is acting as solicitor or agent.

It is unlawful for any person, including a solicitor, to be a party to a bargain to indemnify a surety for bail.

21.16   Tapes and videos of children's evidence

When solicitors act in the defence or prosecution of an accused and have in their possession a copy of an audio or video recording of a child witness, which has been identified as having been prepared to be admitted in evidence at a criminal trial in accordance with section 54 of the Criminal Justice Act 1991, they must comply with the Council statement on access to recordings of a child witness's evidence dated 25th November 1992.

The Council statement and recommended form of undertaking, together with practice notes, are set out in Annex 21D, p.398.

21.17   Court dress

A solicitor appearing in court as an advocate should appear duly robed where this is customary and must always wear suitable clothing.

1.   Whilst it is proper for a solicitor or firm of solicitors to act as solicitors in a matter where the solicitor or the firm have an interest, they must, when

engaged in such litigation, sue or appear as litigants in person. If they appear before the court in such a capacity they should not be robed, so that it is clear that they are not acting as professional advocates.

2.   Where a solicitor, an employee or the firm is one of a number of plaintiffs (now claimants) or defendants, the firm is permitted to go on the record as the solicitors, but a solicitor or employee who is a party to the litigation should not appear as a professional advocate on behalf of the parties either in chambers or in open court. If the solicitor does appear he or she must not be robed; the alternative being for the litigants to be represented by some other person who can act as a professional advocate.

21

21.18   Statements to the press

A solicitor who on the client's instructions gives a statement to the press must not become in contempt of court by publishing any statement which is calculated to interfere with the fair trial of a case which has not been concluded.

See also paragraph 6.3 of the advocacy code (Annex 21A at p.391).

21.19   Solicitor for prosecution

Whilst a solicitor prosecuting a criminal case must ensure that every material point is made which supports the prosecution, the evidence must be presented dispassionately and with scrupulous fairness.

1.   The prosecutor should state all relevant facts and should limit expressions of opinion to those fairly required to present the case. He or she should reveal any mitigating circumstances and should inform the court of its sentencing powers if invited to do so and whenever it appears to be under a misapprehension about those powers. See also paragraph 7.1(b)–(c) of the advocacy code (Annex 21A at p.392).

2.   If a prosecutor obtains evidence which he or she does not intend to use but which may assist the defence, the prosecutor must supply particulars of witnesses to the defence, but is not obliged to supply copies of the statements made by those witnesses. If, however, the prosecutor knows of a credible witness who can speak to material facts which tend to show the accused to be innocent, he or she must either call that witness or make the statement available to the defence. Further, if the prosecutor knows, not of a credible witness, but a witness whom he or she does not accept as credible, the prosecutor should tell the defence about the witness so that they can call that person if they wish. The prosecutor must reveal to the defence factual evidence of which he or she has knowledge and which is inconsistent with that which he or she, as prosecutor, has presented or proposes to present to the court. See also paragraph 2.2 of the advocacy code (at p.386).

3.   The prosecutor must reveal all relevant cases and statutory provisions known to him or her whether it be for or against the prosecution's case. This is so whether or not the prosecutor has been called upon to argue the point in question. See also **21.01** note 3, p.374, and paragraph 2.2 of the advocacy code (at p.386).

21.20   Solicitor for defence

A solicitor who appears in court for the defence in a criminal case is under a duty to say on behalf of the client what the client should properly say for himself or herself if the client possessed the requisite skill and knowledge. The solicitor has a concurrent duty to ensure that the prosecution discharges the onus placed upon it to prove the guilt of the accused.

1.   Unlike the advocate for the prosecution, a solicitor who appears for the defendant is under no duty of disclosure to the prosecution or the court, save that he or she is bound to reveal all relevant cases and statutory provisions. Moreover, save in exceptional and specific circumstances, the client's privilege precludes the solicitor from making a disclosure of privileged material without the client's consent. Consequently, the solicitor must not, without instructions, disclose facts known to him or her regarding the client's character or antecedents, nor must the solicitor correct any information which may be given to the court by the prosecution if the correction would be to the client's detriment. The solicitor must not, however, knowingly put forward or let the client put forward false information with intent to mislead the court. Similarly, the solicitor must not indicate agreement with information that the prosecution puts forward which the solicitor knows to be false. For further guidance see Annex 21F, p.403. See also the advocacy code (Annex 21A) paragraphs 2.2 (at p.386) and 7.1(c) (at p.392).

2.   It is an implied term of the retainer that the advocate is free to present the client's case at the trial or hearing in such a way as he or she considers appropriate. If the client's express instructions do not permit the solicitor to present the case in a manner which the solicitor considers to be the most appropriate, then unless the instructions are varied, the solicitor may withdraw from the case after seeking the approval of the court to that course, but without disclosing matters which are protected by the client's privilege. See also paragraph 5.1(e) of the advocacy code (at p.389).

3.   If the client instructs the solicitor that he or she is not guilty, the solicitor must put before the court the client's defence, even if the client decides not to give evidence and must, in any event, put the prosecution to proof. Whilst a solicitor may present a technical defence which is available to the client, he or she must never fabricate a defence on the facts. See also the advocacy code, paragraphs 6.6 (at p.391), 7.1(d) (at p.392) and 7.1(h) (at p.392).

4. In general, there is no duty upon a solicitor to enquire in every case as to whether the client is telling the truth. However, where instructions or other information are such as should put the solicitor upon enquiry, he or she must, where practicable, check the truth of what the client says to the extent that such statements will be relied upon before the court or in pleadings or affidavits.

5. Where, prior to the commencement or during the course of the proceedings, a client admits to the solicitor that he or she is guilty of the charge, the solicitor must decline to act in the proceedings if the client insists on giving evidence in the witness box in denial of guilt or requires the making of a statement asserting his or her innocence. The advocate who acts for a client who has admitted guilt but has pleaded not guilty (as the client is entitled), is under a duty to put the prosecution to proof of its case and may submit that there is insufficient evidence to justify a conviction. Further, the advocate may advance any defence open to the client other than protesting the client's innocence or suggesting, expressly or by implication, that someone other than the client committed the offence.

6. If, either before or during the course of proceedings, the client makes statements to the solicitor which are inconsistent, this is not of itself a ground for the solicitor to refuse to act further on behalf of the client. Only where it is clear that the client is attempting to put forward false evidence to the court should the solicitor cease to act. In other circumstances, it would be for the court, and not the solicitor, to assess the truth or otherwise of the client's statement.

7. If the client wishes to plead guilty, but at the same time asserts the truth of facts which, if true, would or could lead to an acquittal, the solicitor should use his or her best endeavours to persuade the client to plead not guilty. However, if the client insists on pleading guilty, despite being advised that such a plea may or will restrict the ambit of any plea in mitigation or appeal, then the solicitor is not prevented from continuing to act in accordance with the client's instructions, doing the best he or she can. The solicitor will not, in mitigation, be entitled to suggest that the facts are such . that the ingredients of the offence have not been established.

21.21 Solicitor in civil proceedings

A solicitor who appears in court or in chambers in civil proceedings is under a duty to say on behalf of the client what the client should properly say for himself or herself if the client possessed the requisite skill and knowledge.

1. A solicitor who appears as advocate for the plaintiff (now claimant), the defendant or any other party in civil proceedings is under no duty of disclosure to the other parties or the court, save that he or she is bound to reveal all relevant cases and statutory provisions. Moreover, save in

exceptional and specific circumstances, the client's privilege precludes the solicitor from making a disclosure of privileged material without the client's consent. However, the advocate should not act in such a way that, in the context of the language used, failure to disclose amounts to a positive deception of the court. See also paragraph 2.2 of the advocacy code (Annex 21A at p.386).

2.   It is an implied term of the advocate's retainer that he or she is free to present the client's case at the trial or hearing in such a way as the advocate considers appropriate. If the client's express instructions do not permit the solicitor to present the case in what the solicitor considers to be the most appropriate manner, then unless the instructions are varied, the solicitor may withdraw from the case after seeking the approval of the court to that course, but without disclosing matters which are protected by the client's privilege. See also paragraph 5.1(e) of the advocacy code (at p.389).

3.   Whilst a solicitor may present any technical argument which is available to the client, he or she must never fabricate an argument on the facts for the client. See also paragraphs 6.6 (at p.391) and 7.1(d) (at p.392) of the advocacy code.

4.   In general, there is no duty upon a solicitor to enquire in every case where he or she is instructed as to whether the client is telling the truth. However, where the solicitor's instructions or other information are such as should put him or her upon enquiry, a solicitor must, where practicable, check the truth of what the client says to the extent that such statements will be relied on before the court or in pleadings (now statements of case) or affidavits. See Annex 21I (p.409) for statements of truth in civil proceedings.

5.   If, either before or during the course of proceedings, the client makes statements to the solicitor which are inconsistent, this is not of itself a ground for the solicitor to refuse to act further on behalf of the client. Only where it is clear that the client is attempting to put forward false evidence to the court should the solicitor cease to act. In other circumstances, it would be for the court, and not the solicitor, to assess the truth or otherwise of the client's statement.

Annex 21A

Law Society's Code for Advocacy

Part I – Introduction

1.1 For the purpose of maintaining the proper and efficient administration of justice this Code sets out the principles and standards to be observed by all solicitor advocates when acting as such. These obligations are in addition to and do not replace those imposed by law or required by other Law Society rules.

1.2 In this Code except where otherwise indicated:

"the Act" means the Courts and Legal Services Act 1990 and where the context permits includes any orders or regulations made pursuant to powers conferred thereby;

"advocacy services" means advocacy services as defined in Section 119 of the Act;

"advocate" means an authorised advocate as defined in Section 119 of the Act;

"brief" means instructions to an advocate to appear in person at or before a court;

"client" means the lay client and also (in the case of an advocate with a professional intermediary) the professional client and where the context permits includes a prospective client;

"court" means:

(i) any court of record (the House of Lords, the Court of Appeal, the High Court, the Crown Court, county courts, magistrates' courts, coroners' courts);

(ii) any tribunal which the Council on Tribunals is under a duty to keep under review;

(iii) any court martial; and

(iv) a statutory inquiry within the meaning of Section 19(1) of the Tribunals and Enquiries Act 1971;

"litigator" means an authorised litigator as defined in Section 119 of the Act;

"member" in relation to any authorised body means a member as defined in Section 119 of the Act;

"rules of conduct" means rules of conduct as defined in Section 27(9) of the Act.

Part II – Fundamental principles

2.1   Advocates must not:

     (a)   engage in conduct whether in pursuit of their profession or otherwise which is:

         (i)   dishonest or otherwise discreditable to an advocate;

         (ii)   prejudicial to the administration of justice; or

         (iii)   likely to diminish public confidence in the legal profession or the administration of justice or otherwise bring the legal profession into disrepute;

     (b)   engage directly or indirectly in any occupation if their association with that occupation may adversely affect the reputation of advocates or prejudice their ability to attend properly to the interests of clients.

2.2   Advocates have an overriding duty to the court to ensure in the public interest that the proper and efficient administration of justice is achieved: they must assist the court in the administration of justice and must not deceive or knowingly or recklessly mislead the court.

2.3   Advocates:

     (a)   must promote and protect fearlessly and by all proper and lawful means the clients' best interests and do so without regard to their own interests or to any consequences to themselves or to any other person (including professional clients or fellow advocates or members of the legal profession);

     (b)   subject only to compliance with the specific provisions of Legal Aid Regulations owe their primary duty:

         (i)   as between their lay client and their professional client; and

         (ii)   as between the legal aid authorities and the lay client

     to the lay client and must not permit the legal aid authorities or professional clients to limit their discretion as to how the interests of the lay client can best be served;

     (c)   must act towards clients at all times in good faith.

2.4.1 Advocates must not in relation to any other person (including a client or another advocate) on grounds of race, ethnic origin, gender, religion, sexual orientation or political persuasion treat that person for any purpose less favourably than they would treat other such persons.

2.4.2 Advocates must not decline to accept instructions to act as such:

     (a)   on grounds relating to the race, colour, ethnic or national origins, creed, gender or sexual orientation of the client;

     (b)   on the grounds that the nature of the case is objectionable to the advocate or to any section of the public;

     (c)   on the grounds that the conduct, opinions or beliefs of the client are unacceptable to the advocate or to any section of the public;

     (d)   on any ground relating to the source of any financial support which may properly be given to the client for the proceedings in question (for example on the grounds that such support will be available under the Legal Aid Act 1988).

2.5 Nothing in this Code is to be taken as requiring an advocate to accept instructions if there are reasonable grounds for the advocate to consider that having regard to:

(i) the circumstances of the case;

(ii) the nature of the advocate's practice; or

(iii) the advocate's experience and standing;

the advocate is not being offered a proper fee.

2.6 Advocates must not:

(a) permit their absolute independence and freedom from external pressures to be compromised;

(b) do anything (for example accept a present) in such circumstances as may lead to any inference that their independence may be compromised;

(c) compromise their professional standards in order to please their clients, the court or a third party;

(d) except as permitted by the Act, accept a brief on terms that payment of fees shall depend upon or be related to or postponed on account of the outcome of the case or of any hearing.

2.7 Advocates are individually and personally responsible for their own conduct and for professional work: they must exercise their own personal judgement in all their professional activities and must not delegate such responsibility to another advocate.

Part III – Organisation of the advocate's practice

3.1 Advocates must have or have ready access to library facilities which are adequate having regard to the nature of their practice.

3.2 Advocates must take all steps which it is reasonable in the circumstances to take to ensure that:

(a) their practices are administered competently and efficiently and properly staffed having regard to the nature of the practice;

(b) proper records are kept;

(c) all employees and staff in the practice:

(i) carry out their duties in a correct and efficient manner; and

(ii) are made clearly aware of such provisions of this Code as may affect or be relevant to the performance of their duties.

3.3 Advocates may engage in any advertising or promotion in connection with their practice which conforms to the Solicitors' Publicity Code (and such advertising or promotion may include photographs or other illustrations of the advocate, statements of rates and methods of charging, statements about the nature and extent of the advocate's services and with that client's express written consent the name of any client) but advertising or promotion must not:

(a) be inaccurate or likely to mislead;

(b) be likely to diminish public confidence in the legal profession or the administration of justice or otherwise bring the legal profession into disrepute;

(c)   make comparison with or criticisms of other advocates;

(d)   include statements about the advocate's success rate;

(e)   indicate or imply any willingness to accept a brief, or any intention to restrict the persons from whom a brief may be accepted otherwise than in accordance with this Code;

(f)   be so frequent or obtrusive as to cause justifiable annoyance to those to whom it is directed.

Part IV – The decision to appear

4.1   Advocates must not accept any brief if to do so would cause them to be professionally embarrassed and for this purpose advocates will be professionally embarrassed:

(a)   if they lack sufficient experience or competence to handle the matter, or if their experience of advocacy in the relevant court or proceedings has been so infrequent or so remote in time as to prejudice their competence;

(b)   if having regard to their other professional commitments they will be unable to do or will not have adequate time and opportunity to prepare that which they are required to do;

(c)   if the brief seeks to limit the ordinary authority or discretion of an advocate in the conduct of proceedings in court or to impose on an advocate an obligation to act otherwise than in conformity with the provisions of this Code;

(d)   if the matter is one in which they have reason to believe that they are likely to be witnesses or in which, whether by reason of any connection of the advocate (or of any partner or other associate of the advocate) with the client or with the court or a member of it or otherwise, it will be difficult for them to maintain professional independence or the administration of justice might be or appear to be prejudiced;

(e)   if they have been responsible for deciding on a course of action and the legality of that action is in dispute in the proceedings; if they are company directors and the company is a party to the proceedings;

(f)   if there is or appears to be some conflict or a significant risk of some conflict either between the interests of the advocate (or of any partner or other associate of the advocate) and some other person or between the interests of any one or more of their clients;

(g)   if the matter is one in which there is a risk of a breach of confidences entrusted to them (or to any partner or other associate) by another client or where the knowledge which they possess of the affairs of another client would give an undue advantage to the new client.

4.2   Queen's Counsel are not obliged to accept a brief to act without a junior if they consider that the interests of the lay client require that a junior should also be instructed.

4.3.1 Advocates (whether or not they are also litigators and whether they are instructed on their own or with another advocate) must in the case of each brief consider whether consistently with the proper and efficient administration of justice and having regard to:

    (i)   the circumstances including the gravity, complexity and likely cost of the case;

    (ii)   the nature of their practice;

    (iii) their ability, experience and seniority;

    (iv) their relationship with the client;

the best interests of the client would be served by instructing or continuing to instruct them in that matter.

4.3.2 Where more than one advocate is instructed in any matter each advocate must in particular consider whether the best interests of the client would be served by:

    (a)   the advocate representing the client together with the other advocate or advocates; or

    (b)   the advocate representing the client without the other advocate or advocates; or

    (c)   the client instructing only the other advocate or advocates; or

    (d)   the client instructing some other advocate.

4.3.3 If they consider that the best interests of the client would not be served by their continuing to represent the client (together with any other advocate instructed with them) advocates must immediately advise the lay client accordingly.

Part V – Withdrawal from a case

5.1   Advocates must cease to act and return any brief:

    (a)   if continuing to act would cause them to be professionally embarrassed within the meaning of paragraph 4.1 provided that if they would be professionally embarrassed only because it appears to them that they are likely to be witnesses on a material question of fact they may retire or withdraw only if they can do so without jeopardising the clients' interests;

    (b)   if having accepted a brief on behalf of more than one client there is or appears to be:

        (i)   a conflict or a significant risk of a conflict between the interests of any one or more of such clients; or

        (ii) a risk of a breach of confidence;

and the clients do not all consent to them continuing to act;

    (c)   if in any legally aided case (whether civil or criminal) it has become apparent to them that legal aid has been wrongly obtained by false or inaccurate information and action to remedy the situation is not immediately taken by the client;

    (d)   if the circumstances set out in Regulation 67 of the Civil Legal Aid (General) Regulations 1989 arise at a time when it is impracticable for the Area Committee to meet in time to prevent an abuse of the Legal Aid Fund;

    (e)   if the client refuses to authorise them to make some disclosure to the court which their duty to the court requires them to make;

(f)   if having become aware during the course of a case of the existence of a document which should have been but has not been disclosed on discovery the client fails forthwith to disclose it;

(g)   if having come into possession of a document belonging to another party by some means other than the normal and proper channels and having read it before they realise that it ought to have been returned unread to the person entitled to possession of it they would thereby be embarrassed in the discharge of their duties by their knowledge of the contents of the document provided that they may retire or withdraw only if they can do so without jeopardising the client's interests.

5.2   Advocates may withdraw from a case where they are satisfied that:

(a)   the brief has been withdrawn or their retainer terminated;

(b)   their professional conduct is being impugned; or

(c)   there is some other substantial reason for so doing.

5.3   Advocates must not:

(a)   cease to act or return a brief without having first explained to their client their reasons for doing so;

(b)   return a brief to another advocate without the consent of the client;

(c)   return a brief which they have accepted and for which a fixed date has been obtained or (except with the consent of the client and where appropriate the court) break any other professional engagement so as to enable them to attend a social or non-professional engagement;

(d)   save as provided above return any brief or withdraw from a case in such a way or in such circumstances that their client may be unable to find other legal assistance in time to prevent prejudice being suffered by the client.

Part VI – Conduct of work: the client

6.1   Advocates:

(a)   must in all their professional activities be courteous and act promptly, conscientiously, diligently and with reasonable competence and take all reasonable and practicable steps to avoid unnecessary expense or waste of the court's time and to ensure that professional engagements are fulfilled;

(b)   must not undertake any task which:

     (i)   they know or ought to know they are not competent to handle;

     (ii)   they do not have adequate time and opportunity to prepare for or perform; or

     (iii)   they cannot discharge within a reasonable time having regard to the pressure of other work;

(c)   must read all briefs delivered to them expeditiously;

(d)   must have regard to any relevant written standards adopted by the Law Society for the conduct of professional work;

(e)   must inform the client forthwith:

    (i)   if it becomes apparent that they will not be able to do the work within a reasonable time after receipt of instructions;

    (ii)   if there is an appreciable risk that they may not be able to undertake a brief or fulfil any other professional engagement which they have accepted.

6.2   Whether or not the relation of advocate and client continues, advocates must preserve the confidentiality of their clients' affairs and must not without the prior consent of the client or as permitted by law lend or reveal the contents of the papers in any brief to or communicate to any third person (other than an associate or any of the staff in their practice who need to know it for the performance of their duties) information which has been entrusted to them in confidence or use such information to their clients' detriment or to their own or another client's advantage.

6.3   Advocates must not in relation to any current matter in which they are or have been briefed offer their personal views or opinions to or in any news or current affairs media upon the facts of or the issues arising in that matter.

6.4   Advocates who form the view that there is a conflict of interest between their lay client and their professional client must advise that it would be in the lay client's interest to instruct another professional adviser and such advice must be given either in writing or at a conference at which both the professional client and the lay client are present.

6.5   Advocates must not when interviewing a witness out of court:

(a)   place witnesses who are being interviewed under any pressure to provide other than a truthful account of their evidence;

(b)   rehearse, practise or coach witnesses in relation to their evidence or the way in which they should give it.

6.6   Advocates must not devise facts which will assist in advancing their client's case and must not draft any originating process, pleading, affidavit, witness statement or notice of appeal containing:

(a)   any statement of fact or contention (as the case may be) which is not supported by the client or by their brief or instructions;

(b)   any contention which they do not consider to be properly arguable;

(c)   any allegation of fraud unless they have clear instructions to make such allegation and have before them reasonably credible material which as it stands establishes a *prima facie* case of fraud;

(d)   in the case of an affidavit or witness statement any statement of fact other than the evidence which in substance according to their instructions the advocate reasonably believes the witness would give if the evidence contained in the affidavit or witness statement were being given *viva voce*;

provided that nothing in this paragraph shall prevent an advocate drafting a pleading, affidavit or witness statement containing specific facts, matters or contentions included by the advocate subject to the client's confirmation as to their accuracy.

Part VII – Conduct of work: the court

7.1 Advocates when conducting proceedings at court:

(a) are personally responsible for the conduct and presentation of their case and must exercise personal judgement upon the substance and purpose of statements made and questions asked;

(b) must not unless invited to do so by the court or when appearing before a tribunal where it is their duty to do so assert a personal opinion on the facts or the law;

(c) must ensure that the court is informed of all relevant decisions and legislative provisions of which they are aware whether the effect is favourable or unfavourable towards the contention for which they argue and must bring any procedural irregularity to the attention of the court during the hearing and not reserve such matter to be raised on appeal;

(d) must not adduce evidence obtained otherwise than from or through their client or devise facts which will assist in advancing their client's case;

(e) must not make statements or ask questions which are merely scandalous or intended or calculated only to vilify, insult or annoy either a witness or some other person;

(f) must if possible avoid the naming in open court of third parties whose character would thereby be impugned;

(g) must not by assertion in a speech impugn a witness whom they have had an opportunity to cross-examine unless in cross-examination they have given the witness an opportunity to answer the allegation;

(h) must not suggest that a witness or other person is guilty of crime, fraud or misconduct or attribute to another person the crime or conduct of which their client is accused unless such allegations go to a matter in issue (including the credibility of the witness) which is material to their client's case and which appear to them to be supported by reasonable grounds.

Part VIII – Communications with clients

8.1 Advocates must have proper lines of communications. When instructed by a litigator they are normally entitled to rely on the litigator to communicate with the client. When instructed direct by a representative of the client who is not a litigator, they should ensure that the representative is properly authorised.

8.2 Where there is any reason to doubt the propriety of any action or proposed course of action, advocates should satisfy themselves that the client has received and understood any warnings or advice which it may be appropriate to offer. Where the client is a public or corporate body, this duty may include ensuring that the council, the board of directors, the governing body or others in positions of like authority have received the warnings or advice and that consequent instructions have their approval.

8th December 1993 – made under Solicitors' Practice Rules 1990, rule 16A

Annex 21B

Guidance – advocacy code, paragraphs 2.4–2.5 (non-discrimination provisions)

The Courts and Legal Services Act 1990 section 17 requires that rules of professional bodies whose members provide advocacy services shall include a non-discrimination rule. The Law Society's Code for Advocacy, paragraphs 2.4–2.5 (see Annex 21A at p.386 in the Guide) follows closely the wording of the Act. Although all advocates are bound by the code for advocacy, it is likely that those who hold themselves out as willing to provide advocacy services alone, for example as solicitor agents, will be more directly affected by the impact of paragraphs 2.4–2.5. In addition to the code for advocacy, solicitor advocates are also bound by the Solicitors' Anti-Discrimination Rule 1995 and the Solicitors' Anti-Discrimination Code (**7.01–7.02**, p.167 in the Guide) – see paragraph 1.1 of the code for advocacy. The code for advocacy only applies to the provision of advocacy services and not to the provision of litigation services. In deciding whether or not to act for a client in litigation matters, a solicitor is bound by the Solicitors' Anti-Discrimination Rule 1995 and the Solicitors' Anti-Discrimination Code and the statutory provisions relating to race and sex discrimination, but is otherwise free to determine whether to accept instructions to act.

Paragraph 2.5 of the code for advocacy contains a proviso which entitles a solicitor to a proper fee, and this is similar to the rule contained in the Code of Conduct of the General Council of the Bar. Although the code for advocacy refers to a solicitor being 'offered' a proper fee, the context of the provision as a whole, particularly the reference to legal aid in paragraph 2.4.2(d), makes it clear that the provision applies to legal aid cases even though the remuneration is prescribed by regulations. During the debates in Parliament, however, the Government made it quite clear that the wording of section 17 had been specifically drafted so as not to impose on advocates any requirement to undertake legal aid work. The Attorney-General stated:

> 'It is not possible to refuse a case simply because it is legally aided, but it is open to a solicitor to decide whether the amount, from whatever source, is sufficient given the nature of the case and his standing, seniority and experience.' (Standing Committee D, 17th May 1990, Col. 129)

The Lord Chancellor stated:

> 'Under the approach which Parliament approved in the Legal Aid Act 1988, it must be for each individual advocate to decide whether the rates on offer under the Legal Aid Regulations for the time being in force are appropriate for him to undertake such cases.' (House of Lords, 24th October 1990, Col. 1385)

If therefore the fee likely to be received from legal aid is lower than the normal charging rate of the solicitor, the solicitor is entitled to decline to act.

Where no separate advocacy fee is payable, for example in standard fee magistrates' court cases, there are underlying hourly rates which are used to assess whether a case comes within a particular standard fee band, and these can be used. In some cases rates are prescribed subject to a discretion on the part of taxing or assessment authorities to exceed them. Where there can be no certainty that the prescribed rates will be exceeded it would be reasonable to rely only on the rates as prescribed. In some instances there are significant delays in receiving payment from the legal aid authorities, whereas a solicitor in a private case is entitled to ask for costs on account. If therefore the fee receivable from the legal aid authorities is likely to be diminished in value as a result of the late payment, it would be reasonable for solicitors to apply the diminished value of the fee when comparing it with their normal charging rate.

January 1994, updated January 1996

Annex 21C

Guidance – advocacy code, paragraph 4.1(e) (not accepting brief where solicitor responsible for course of action)

Paragraph 4.1(e) of the advocacy code (Annex 21A at p.388 in the Guide) is designed to prevent the situation arising where a solicitor, whether in-house or in private practice, is so identified with a policy or a course of action which is itself the subject of litigation that if the solicitor appeared as an advocate to defend the policy or action he or she would be, and would appear in the eyes of the court to be, in a professionally embarrassing situation.

The provision derives from the principle (see paragraph 4.1(d) of the code) which prohibits advocates appearing if they are likely to be witnesses. This is perhaps the most obvious example of a professional embarrassment. The purpose of paragraph 4.1(e) is to protect the judge from the difficulty of having to deal with an advocate who has an interest in the outcome of the case over and above the normal professional concern. An advocate before the court must be ready to deal with comments or questions from the bench which may touch on the evidence given by a witness. An advocate must also be prepared, in exchanges with the court, to see where concessions may in the client's interest need to be made in the light of the way the case has developed. A judge must be confident that an advocate will not be inhibited by any personal interests from debating the merits and weaknesses of his or her case.

The provision disqualifies solicitors from acting as advocates in two situations:

(1) *'if they are company directors and the company is a party to the proceedings'*

This applies to all solicitors, both in-house and in private practice; it applies to advocacy before all courts.

(2) *'if they have been responsible for deciding on a course of action and the legality of that action is in dispute in the proceedings'*

In the case of situation (2), it is only if both limbs of the test are applicable that the solicitor is prevented from accepting a brief. The fact that an advocate may have been responsible for a decision will not mean that it is wrong for him or her to appear unless the legality of the action is also in issue. Nor is there any objection to an advocate appearing to defend the legality of an action taken by his or her client if the advocate has not been responsible for deciding on the action.

Each limb of (2) will be considered in turn:

'if they have been responsible for deciding on a course of action'

This applies to all solicitors and to all advocacy. As far as solicitors in private practice are concerned, the provision will rarely affect them since there are very few actions which they take in their own name and under their own authority; most relevant decisions are taken by clients on advice from the solicitor (or more often will have been taken without the benefit of legal advice at all). In some cases, however, the private practice solicitor will be affected, for instance where the solicitor is a governor of a school or a trustee of a charity. Here the solicitor may have participated in the decision-making himself or herself, or even if not, cannot be dissociated from the decision since the body acts collectively. In such a case the solicitor may not appear if the legality of the action is an issue.

The other situation where a private practice solicitor could make decisions which may later be the subject of litigation would be where his or her firm is sued for negligence, is suing to recover fees, or is in dispute with a landlord, office supplier or other non-client. Principle **21.17** note 1 in the Guide (p.380) tells solicitors that:

> 'Whilst it is proper for a solicitor or firm of solicitors to act as solicitors in a matter where the solicitor or the firm have an interest, they must, when engaged in such litigation, sue or appear as litigants in person. If they appear before the court in such a capacity, they should not be robed, so that it is clear that they are not acting as professional advocates.'

As far as solicitors employed in legal departments in central or local government or in commerce or industry are concerned, most have functions which are solely or primarily legal. Their job descriptions and terms of service engage them only to offer legal advice and to provide legal services. In these situations their position will be the same as that of solicitors in private practice: they will rarely if ever be responsible for decisions which are subsequently in issue. The managers whom they are advising or for whom they are providing the legal service will be responsible for the policy decisions. In the Government Legal Service, and in local government and commerce, most solicitors are engaged in work which is exclusively legal.

Sometimes they may have a managerial role – indeed most will have a role in supervising more junior staff whether lawyers or other support staff. Where a solicitor has a managerial or executive responsibility for a non-legal function, e.g. insurance or estate management, paragraph 4.1(e) of the advocacy code means that where a solicitor has in that capacity taken a decision which is later the subject of litigation, he or she may not appear in court to defend the legality of the decision. The rule does not affect the common situation where the formal decision to institute or to defend proceedings, or to take relevant steps in those proceedings, is delegated to a local authority solicitor or company solicitor unless he or she has also exercised a managerial or executive role in relation to the subject in question.

'and the legality of that action is in dispute in the proceedings'

The legality, or lawfulness, of a decision would be regarded as being in dispute when any aspect of it is subject to challenge in litigation. A challenge to lawfulness does not simply arise where the action or decision of the organisation is claimed to be *ultra vires* or judicially reviewable. It arises at any time when it is claimed that the action was wrong in law, e.g. in breach of contract or of a civil obligation. Thus where a company's products are challenged as unsafe or where a system of work caused injury to an employee, the legality of the action of the company, and of the managers responsible for designing and marketing the products or approving the work system, would be regarded as being in dispute. Where a local authority decides that a child should be taken into care, to evict tenants or to refuse planning permission, those decisions if challenged during the ordinary course of proceedings before any court would be in dispute.

It would be otherwise, however, if the company had sold products and was seeking simply to recover the sale price from a debtor who sought additional time to pay; or where the company admitted that the system of work was unsafe but challenged the employee's assessment of the amount of damages claimed. By the same reasoning a local authority's decision would not be in dispute if the proposal for a care order was not challenged (for instance it was being made at the instance of the parents), or the amount of rent owing was the only matter in issue, or if the refusal of planning permission itself was not challenged or appealed against.

8th December 1993, revised January 1996

21

Annex 21D

Guidance – access to recordings of a child witness's evidence

Council statement

When solicitors act in the defence or prosecution of an accused and have in their possession a copy of an audio or video recording of a child witness which has been identified as having been prepared to be admitted in evidence at a criminal trial in accordance with section 54 of the Criminal Justice Act 1991, they must:

(a) not make or permit any person to make a copy of the recording;

(b) not release the recording to the accused;

(c) not make or permit any disclosure of the recording or its contents to any person except when in the opinion of the solicitor it is necessary in the course of preparing the prosecution, defence or appeal against conviction and/or sentence;

(d) ensure that the recording is always kept in a locked, secure container when not in use;

(e) return the recording when they are no longer instructed in the matter.

Undertaking

Form of undertaking recommended by the Law Society for use by solicitors when receiving recorded evidence of a child witness prepared to be admitted in evidence at criminal trials in accordance with section 54 of the Criminal Justice Act 1991:

I/We acknowledge receipt of the recording marked 'evidence of....'.

I/We undertake that whilst the recording is in my/our possession I/we shall:

(a) not make or permit any other person to make a copy of the recording;

(b) not release the recording to [name of the accused];

(c) not make or permit any disclosure of the recording or its contents to any person except when in my/our opinion it is necessary in the course of preparing the prosecution, defence, or appeal against conviction and/or sentence;

(d) ensure that the recording is always kept in a locked, secure container when not in use;

(e) return the recording to you when I am/we are no longer instructed in the matter.

Practice notes

1. Recordings should preferably be delivered to third parties by hand but where this is not possible (e.g. because a solicitor may practise a long distance away from the barrister or expert instructed) the recording should be sent by recorded delivery post (it should not be sent by document exchange). To avoid the risk of theft, the contents of the package should not be apparent from the outside. If a solicitor or staff member personally collects a recording, he or she should be able to produce a proper form of identification.

2. 'Locked, secure container' – no special type of container is defined. Because of the ease and prevalence of theft from and of cars, a locked car cannot be considered as being a 'locked, secure container' and a recording should not be left unattended in a car.

3. The Home Office has published a memorandum of good practice to help those making such recordings. The memorandum contains a form of undertaking which it recommends be required of anyone who receives a copy of a recording (e.g. a barrister or expert who receives a recording from a solicitor). The terms are broadly similar to those of the Law Society's recommended undertaking. It is possible that solicitors may be asked to provide an undertaking in the form of that recommended by the Home Office. As with the giving of any undertaking, solicitors should first ensure that they can comply with its terms.

25th November 1992, revised January 1996

21

Annex 21E

Guidance – client's failure to attend court – a solicitor's duties

---

The Law Society guidance issued by the Standards and Guidance Committee and the Criminal Law Committee

It is accepted that there is a duty to provide reasonable assistance in the smooth running of the court lists, but the duty of confidentiality and the right of privilege override the duty to the court and, therefore, the solicitor should provide only such assistance to the court as is consistent with the duty to the client.

The Society has received enquiries from solicitors as to the lengths to which they should go to ensure that clients receive notification of listing arrangements of matters to be tried in the Crown court. The Society's view is that, while a solicitor ought to take reasonable steps to ensure that the client is aware of the date for attendance at the Crown court and of the client's duty to attend, the solicitor is not under an obligation to take all possible steps to secure attendance.

Should a client fail to attend for trial, a solicitor should, as mentioned above, consider the limitations imposed upon him or her by the duty of confidentiality and the client's privilege when deciding what information might be revealed to the court. There would be no objection to a solicitor stating that he or she had written to the client about the hearing and that the letter had not been returned undelivered. Where a solicitor believes that a client is unlikely to attend court it is reasonable for the solicitor to advise the court accordingly, although he or she might not be able to state the grounds for this belief. If the client has failed to respond to requests to attend the solicitor's office, it might be reasonable, depending on the facts, for the solicitor to advise the court that he or she is without instructions and/or that it would be desirable to list the case.

With reference to the above guidance, the Criminal Law Committee take the view that different circumstances will make different steps reasonable. The following are some examples.

Notification by post will be reasonable if the client can read English or such other language as the solicitor might reasonably be expected to use; and only if there are sufficient days between the date of posting and date of hearing for the client to be warned in time (bearing in mind postal conditions at the time) and to advise the solicitor that he or she has received the notice.

A request to clients to telephone daily after a case appears in the warned list should be used with great caution. It will only be appropriate for clients with ready access to a private telephone and for offices where a responsible fee-earner will be readily available to take the calls.

If it is not reasonable to expect the client to telephone the solicitor's office daily to check the position of the case in the warned list, then some other method may be reasonable, such as delivery of a letter by taxi or courier. These should also be considered if there has been no acknowledgement of a written notice.

In cases where personal service is reasonable the solicitor may need to consider who should or can effect such service. It may need to be done by a person who knows the client; the time of day or type of area in which the client lives, or some other factor, may make it unreasonable to expect a junior or female employee or colleague, or perhaps any person alone, to undertake the task.

The Criminal Law Committee are continuing to press for an end to short-notice listing of cases for hearing in the Crown court. Although there have been some improvements in some places, the position remains far from satisfactory.

The Criminal Law Committee were concerned at the incidence of judicial criticism of defendants' solicitors in public, particularly where such criticism was unjustified, and asked the Lord Chancellor's Department (LCD) to remind members of the judiciary that these issues should be dealt with in chambers.

Practitioners are reminded that the Society's support is available to solicitors who are unjustly criticised or penalised by the court; or who, after taxation, wish to take further a claim against unjustified disallowance or reduction of costs. In appropriate cases, financial assistance from the Society will be given.

With reference to the LCD guidance (reproduced below), the Criminal Law Committee take the view that 'several days' normally means four to six days and 'very short notice' normally means three days or less; and that Sundays cannot count for this purpose.

In regard to criminal legal aid costs generally, practitioners are reminded of the need to record every telephone call to ensure that none is forgotten when drawing the bill. Dealing with a telephone call from the client or from witnesses, for example, is normally done by a fee-earner and, if reasonable, is normally paid for.

The Remuneration Team in the Policy Directorate wish to be kept informed of any disallowances thought to be unfair of items of costs claimed in Crown court cases; in particular, please inform the Remuneration Team (see p.xv for contact details) of any difficulties encountered concerning items of costs or disbursements claimed for informing or attempting to inform the client of the date for attendance at court.

October 1988, updated February 1999

Lord Chancellor's Department guidance to circuit taxing co-ordinators and determining officers

Notification of defendant for court hearings

The Law Society has written to the department expressing the concern of many practitioners about the seeming lack of consistency between Crown courts when considering claims by solicitors for notifying defendants of court hearings.

This subject was discussed at the recent circuit taxing co-ordinators meeting. Those present were surprised by the letter, being under the impression that in cases where it was reasonable to make payment for warning the defendant, determining officers were doing so.

I would ask you to bring this matter to the attention of all determining officers reminding them of the tests to be applied when considering such a claim.

Where a case is included in a fixed list which is published far enough in advance for the defendant to be warned by correspondence then a letter (allowed at unit cost) should usually suffice. But it might also be reasonable to allow an occasional telephone call in from the defendant to the solicitor to check that the position is unchanged.

Where a case is brought into a list at shorter notice and assuming the defendant is not on the telephone the determining officer should consider:

(a) was there reasonably sufficient time for the solicitor to warn the defendant by letter;

(b) if not, was the method of warning chosen reasonable.

As to (b), if the notice of listing is several days in advance it might be considered:

(a) that notification should have reasonably been covered by adequate arrangements made by the solicitor for the defendant to telephone or call in at the office;

(b) that a form of notice other than personal service would have been reasonable (e.g. a letter sent by taxi);

(c) that in the circumstances of the particular case personal service was reasonable.

If a case is brought into a list at very short notice then personal service would normally be reasonable and should be allowed. Personal service should generally be regarded as fee-earner work and in normal circumstances would be appropriate to a grade C fee-earner. It is, as always, for the solicitor to provide the determining officer with full details in support of his claim.

1988

Annex 21F

Guidance – citation of criminal convictions – misleading the court

Whilst it is true that a person can call himself or herself by whatever name he or she chooses, a solicitor (in the context of court proceedings) must be satisfied that the client is not adopting a name other than that with which he or she was born (or subsequently acquired by marriage, deed poll or statutory declaration, etc.) with the intention of deceiving the court so that the client could avoid previous convictions becoming known to the court and thereby obtain a lighter sentence than would otherwise be the case, or some other benefit (such as the grant of bail) that would not otherwise have been obtained. (See the disciplinary proceedings against solicitor *John Francis Bridgwood* [1988] reported in the *Gazette,* 9 November, 53). Similarly, an address given is not 'false' simply because it is not the person's main or only residence (provided that it is an address at which correspondence can reach the client or at which contact with the client can be made), but the solicitor must be satisfied that the client has not given it for the purpose of deceiving the court in the sense described above.

Principle **21.01** (p.374 in the Guide) provides that solicitors who act in litigation, whilst under a duty to do their best for their client, must never deceive or mislead the court. This is developed further in paragraph 2.2 of the Law Society's code for advocacy (p.386) which provides that solicitors acting as advocates must not deceive or knowingly mislead the court. This obligation must be considered in the context of other duties placed on solicitors:

(a) If the duty not to deceive or mislead the court conflicts with the duty of a solicitor to say on behalf of the client what the client should properly say for himself or herself (see **21.20**, p.382, in the Guide, and paragraphs 2.2 and 7.1(c) of the code for advocacy, pp.386 and 392 in the Guide), the solicitor must decline to act for the client.

(b) Whilst the defence solicitor has a duty to ensure that the prosecution discharges the onus placed upon it to prove the guilt of the accused (**21.20** in the Guide) and is entitled to take every point, technical or otherwise, that is fairly arguable on behalf of the client, the solicitor must ensure that the court is informed of all relevant decisions and legislative provisions of which he or she is aware whether favourable or unfavourable to the client (**21.01**, p.374 in the Guide and paragraph 7.1(c) of the code for advocacy, p.392 in the Guide).

(c) However, a defence solicitor is under no duty to inform the court of facts which would assist the prosecution and must, subject to the client's instructions, keep confidential information about a client and his or her affairs (**21.01** and **16.01**, pp.374 and 324 in the Guide).

A solicitor deceives, or knowingly or recklessly misleads, the court when he or she puts forward to the court, or lets the client put forward, information which the solicitor knows to be false, or is reckless as to its truth, with the intention of securing a result which would not otherwise be secured. The defence solicitor need not correct the information given to the court by the prosecution or any other party which the solicitor knows will have the effect of allowing the court to make incorrect assumptions about the client or the case, provided the solicitor does not indicate in any way his or her agreement with that information.

Law Society advice

The Criminal Law Committee has considered the specific problems raised by *Bridgwood* and advises practitioners as follows.

Where, to the knowledge of the solicitor, the client seeks to deceive or mislead the court by giving a false name, address and/or date of birth, the solicitor's first duty is to warn the client of the implications of doing so. These include the fact that the client may be committing an offence. The solicitor should also explain to the client that, unless he or she changes his or her mind, and is willing to give the correct details to the court, the solicitor will have to stop acting. The client should be further advised that if the solicitor withdraws from acting there could be problems with the client's legal aid order. If the client does not accept this advice and intends to continue with the deception, the solicitor should stop acting. Note that in certain circumstances the solicitor may be under a duty to report the fact that the client has given false information in a legal aid application (see below) and, if relevant, the solicitor should explain this to the client.

Since a solicitor must not deceive or knowingly mislead the court, the above advice also applies where a client intends to give some false information, such as his or her correct name, but a false address and/or false date of birth. Solicitors will be aware that the defendant's address is crucial in the proper administration of justice, is relevant to consideration of bail, and is the point of contact between the court, the solicitor and the police and the client. The date of birth is the key to establishing the correct record of convictions.

Special difficulties may arise where a solicitor is obliged to withdraw from a case where the client is legally aided. The solicitor must apply to the court to be released from the legal aid order, but the duty of confidentiality (which continues after a solicitor stops acting) prevents the solicitor from revealing the reasons for the application. In these circumstances, the solicitor should, if necessary, inform the court that in view of the duty of confidentiality, the solicitor cannot give reasons for the application and should ask the court to accept, without further explanation, that circumstances have arisen to make it impossible for him or her to continue to act. The Committee advises that solicitors must be firm in such circumstances. The solicitor should explain the situation to the client in advance so that the client is not taken unawares.

Solicitors' attention is drawn to regulation 56 of the Legal Aid in Criminal and Care Proceedings (General) Regulations 1989. The regulation places a duty on solicitors, notwithstanding the duty of confidentiality, to report forthwith to the 'proper officer' (the 'proper officer' in respect of proceedings in the magistrates' court is the justices' clerk) if the solicitor knows or suspects that a legally aided client has intentionally failed to comply with any provision of the regulations made under the Legal Aid Act 1988 concerning information to be supplied by him or her, or, in supplying such information, has knowingly made a false statement or false representation. Where such a report is required, it should not be made in open court, and should be dealt with separately from the application to withdraw. There is no obligation to report the detail of the abuse (see **5.04**, p.162 in the Guide).

Solicitors should try to obtain a list of their client's previous convictions in good time in order to take the client's instructions on them before going to court. If a list of previous convictions is inaccurate, a solicitor should consider the following:

▶ If the inaccuracy results from the client having given a false name, address and/or date of birth, the solicitor should act in accordance with the advice given above.

▶ If the inaccuracy does not appear to result from false information given by the client, the solicitor should consider the following:

  ▶ If the list contains convictions which are not those of the client the solicitor should, subject to instructions, make this known to the court.

  ▶ If the list omits convictions, the solicitor should consider whether he or she can represent the client appropriately without disclosing the omission to the court. In doing so, the solicitor must have regard to the duty not to mislead the court and the duty not to disclose confidential information relating to the client, e.g. a bail application may be made provided there is no explicit or implicit assertion by the solicitor that the client has not been convicted of additional offences omitted from the list of previous convictions.

  ▶ Similarly, a plea in mitigation may be made by the solicitor provided there is no explicit or implicit assertion by the solicitor that the client has not been convicted of additional offences omitted from the list of previous convictions. Where the solicitor has a professional difficulty in presenting full mitigation, without referring to the omitted convictions, or the solicitor considers that the omitted convictions are likely to be disclosed in any event (for example, if the client is currently subject to a probation or community service order, and/or if a pre-sentence report is likely to be required), he or she should advise the client of the professional difficulty and, if appropriate, obtain the client's instructions to disclose the omitted conviction(s) to the court.

  ▶ If the client does not consent to disclosure, the solicitor may take the view that he or she cannot continue to act.

Magistrates' clerks should no longer ask solicitors to confirm the accuracy of previous convictions, or to accept previous convictions on the client's behalf, or to confirm that the list submitted by the prosecution is a full list of previous convictions. The Justices' Clerks' Society advised their members (JCS News Sheet No. 98/11) that in relation to the citing of previous convictions, only one question should be put to the defence by the bench or the clerk: 'Have you seen this list?' All other questions are superfluous and inappropriate.

If other questions are asked, and solicitors habitually confirm the accuracy of the list (except when there is an omission), then when a solicitor refuses to comment, it will then be clear to the court and the prosecution that the list is likely to contain omissions. This, in effect, may amount to disclosing information concerning the client which is contrary to the duty of confidentiality. On the other hand, if the solicitor, by his or her reply to the court, implies that an inaccurate list is accurate, this will amount to deceiving the court. The appropriate response will depend, in part, on the form of the question, but solicitors should consider the following advice:

21

► Solicitors should normally decline to comment on the accuracy of the list. Solicitors may do so by referring to this guidance and/or by stating that they have no comment. Solicitors should be careful not to deceive the court inadvertently. Expressions such as 'It is not disputed' may falsely imply that the list is accurate.

► Where relevant, solicitors should advise their clients that they are under no duty to comment on the accuracy of lists of previous convictions.

► If, however, the list is inaccurate in that it contains convictions which are not those of the client, or there is some other good reason for indicating any inaccuracy then, subject to the client's instructions, the solicitor should indicate the inaccuracy in the list.

July 1989, updated February 1999

Annex 21G

Guidance – solicitors' clerks – rights of audience – solicitors' supervision responsibilities

Solicitors' clerks have a common law right of audience in chambers in the High Court and by long custom and usage they are heard in chambers in the county court. The Courts and Legal Services Act 1990 gives statutory recognition to the position. Section 27(2)(e) gives a person a right of audience in chambers in the High Court or a county court where:

'he is employed (whether wholly or in part), or is otherwise engaged, to assist in the conduct of litigation and is doing so under instructions given (either generally or in relation to the proceedings) by a qualified litigator'.

This provision makes it clear that a person instructed by a solicitor to appear in chambers may be either an employee of the solicitor or an independent contractor.

The Standards and Guidance Committee issued guidance that under **3.07** (p.72) of the Guide a solicitor is responsible for exercising supervision over both admitted and unadmitted staff. The duty to supervise extends to independent contractors as much as to employees. Note 1 to **3.07** makes it clear that solicitors remain responsible for work carried out by their firm and that this extends to the acts or omissions of their staff, which term would include an independent contractor as well as an employee.

Accordingly, as a matter of professional conduct, when instructing an unadmitted person (whether an employee or an independent contractor) to appear in chambers in the High Court or the county court, a solicitor should:

▶ be satisfied that the person is responsible and competent to carry out the instructions;

▶ give the person sufficiently full and clear instructions to enable him or her to carry out those instructions properly;

▶ afford appropriate supervision.

Solicitors' attention is drawn to section 27(4) which explicitly preserves the power of any court to refuse to hear a person who would otherwise have a right of audience before the court for reasons which apply to him or her as an individual. Thus a court could refuse to hear a person who was incompetent or irresponsible but should such a situation arise in relation to a solicitor's clerk, whether or not an employee, his or her principal may be called upon to give an explanation.

May 1991, updated February 1999

Choice of advocate – practice rule 16B – practice information

You should advise the client when it is appropriate to instruct counsel.

Practice rule 16B (choice of advocate), which appears at **21.04**, p.375 in the Guide, requires solicitors to consider and advise clients whether it is in their best interests for the solicitor's firm or some other advocate to provide any advocacy required. The rule lists some of the circumstances which would be relevant to the decision. Solicitors who propose to undertake advocacy should also have regard to the provisions of paragraph 4.1 of the code for advocacy (see Annex 21A at p.388 in the Guide). This requires solicitors not to accept a brief if:

▶ they lack the necessary experience;

▶ they will have inadequate time to prepare;

▶ the brief seeks to limit their authority;

▶ they would be unable to maintain professional independence;

▶ they have been responsible for actions that are in dispute; or

▶ there is a risk of a conflict or a breach of confidence.

In particular, solicitors, whether in private practice or employed, should note that where the fundamental interests, reputation or fortunes of a client are in issue in litigation, and the solicitor is for any reason likely to be regarded as intimately identified with the fortunes of the client in that litigation, the interests of the client are likely to be best served by the employment of another advocate who would clearly appear to the court to be objective.

There are two aspects which will be of particular concern to the client – which advocate to choose, and cost. Care should be taken that clients have and understand the information on which to base their decision. Where appropriate, the client will need to be aware of the relative cost of the advocacy being provided by the firm or by an outside advocate.

The scope of any discussion with the client, and the extent to which it should be recorded in writing, will depend on the circumstances. For example, in the magistrates' court advocacy often has to be arranged at short notice and the choice of advocate may in practice be limited. Where advocacy in the county court or in the higher courts is likely to last more than half a day, it would normally be appropriate for the discussion and decision to be recorded on file and in a letter to the client.

8th December 1993, updated January 1996

Annex 21I

Civil justice reforms – practice information

This Annex provides a brief overview of some of the main provisions and significant conduct implications of the civil justice reforms. Solicitors who practise civil litigation are strongly advised to acquaint themselves with the detailed provisions of the Civil Procedure Rules at the earliest opportunity. See the Lord Chancellor's Department's website, http://www.open.gov.uk/lcd for the rules.

1. Overriding objective – Part 1

The civil justice reforms, implemented in April 1999, herald a major change in litigation culture. The old *Rules of the Supreme Court* and the *County Court Rules* ('White Book' and 'Green Book') of civil court procedure have been replaced by one plain English rule book. Practice directions and revised court forms provide the detail for the rules and pre-action protocols have been introduced for some types of case to act as guides for good practice before proceedings are commenced. The new court rules, practice directions and protocols encourage a co-operative, less adversarial approach to dispute resolution.

The courts expect litigation to be started as a last resort after attempts have been made to settle the dispute by negotiations or other means, including alternative dispute resolution (ADR). The courts also expect parties, through their legal representatives, when appropriate, to have exchanged information (a 'cards on the table' approach): for claimants to provide to defendants detailed letters of claim (letters before action) to which defendants are expected to respond also in detail. The courts attach considerable importance to compliance with the new pre-action protocols for personal injury claims and clinical negligence disputes which set out codes of good practice and basic steps which should be followed in these types of case before proceedings are commenced. The courts have powers to penalise parties for issuing proceedings prematurely and for not complying with the spirit of the protocols.

When cases do go to court the overriding objective of the new rules is to enable the court to deal with cases justly. Rule 1.1(2) states that dealing justly with a case includes:

(a) ensuring that the parties are on an equal footing;

(b) saving expense;

(c) dealing with the case in ways which are proportionate:

    (i)   to the amount of money involved;

    (ii) to the importance of the case;

    (iii) to the complexity of the issues; and

    (iv) to the financial position of each party;

(d)   ensuring that it is dealt with expeditiously and fairly; and

(e)   allotting to it an appropriate share of the court's resources (whilst taking into account the need to allot resources to other cases).

The parties are required to help the court to further the overriding objective (rule 1.3). The court must further the overriding objective by actively managing cases (rule 1.4). This may include encouraging the parties to use an ADR procedure, fixing timetables and giving directions to ensure that the case proceeds quickly and efficiently.

Dealing with a case in ways which are proportionate is very important. Legal representatives are expected to consider carefully, with their clients, their whole approach to a case, particularly the amount of work that might be required to progress the case and take it to trial, if necessary, and the costs which might be incurred both by their own client and any other parties as a consequence of that work. The courts have the power to ask parties to tell the court, and other parties, the amount of costs which have been incurred to date, and to estimate costs which are likely to be incurred in the future, on specific steps or stages. Orders and directions made by the court will reflect the court's view of what is proportionate. Solicitors will need to explain this new power carefully to clients as it could have a significant impact on how clients view their case and instruct their solicitor to conduct it, and on their expectations.

The courts will be particularly concerned to 'level the playing field' where one party has significantly more resources than the other, and is willing, or can afford, to spend time and costs on a case out of proportion to what is in issue, or to what the other party can afford. This particular change in culture may have conduct implications. Although a solicitor's main duty will remain to do his or her best on behalf of the client, the courts will be less willing to allow to be pursued every point, technical or otherwise, that may be arguable on behalf of a client.

The court also has wide powers to take into account the conduct of the parties, including the conduct of their legal representatives, both pre-action and during the conduct of proceedings. The particular responsibility placed on the parties to help the court to further the overriding objective, is a development of the duty of solicitors to act as officers of the court.

2.   Court's case management powers – Part 3

One of the most significant changes of the Civil Procedure Rules is to strengthen the powers of the court to manage proceedings: some commentators describe it as shifting the responsibility for running and managing cases, once proceedings are issued, from the parties and their legal representatives to the court. Certainly, the court, through the procedural judges (in the High Court the Masters, and in the County Court the District Judges) are intended to be pro-active in their new case management function.

Rule 3.1(2) lists a number of powers which the courts may exercise when managing claims. The court may:

(a)   extend or shorten the time for compliance with any rule, practice direction or court order (even if an application for extension is made after the time for compliance has expired);

(b)   adjourn or bring forward a hearing;

(c)   require any party or a party's legal representative to attend the court;

(d)   hold a hearing by telephone or use any other method of direct oral communication;

(e) direct that part of any proceedings (such as a counterclaim) be dealt with as separate proceedings;

(f) exclude an issue from consideration;

(g) stay the whole or part of any proceedings either generally or until a specified date or event;

(h) consolidate proceedings;

(i) try two or more claims on the same occasion;

(j) direct a separate trial of any issue;

(k) decide the order in which issues are to be tried;

(l) dismiss or give a judgment on a claim after a decision on a preliminary issue;

(m) take any other step or make any other order for the purpose of managing the case and furthering the overriding objective.

21

The court may make an order of its own initiative (rule 3.3) and may also strike out a statement of case or part of a statement of case which, for example, discloses no reasonable grounds of complaint (rule 3.4).

Rules 3.7 to 3.9 set out the court's powers with regard to sanctions against parties and their legal representatives for non-compliance with the rules of court or specific court orders and directions. In general, sanctions will be spelt out in directions and orders, and will have effect unless the party in default applies for and obtains relief. Where parties require more time to comply with a rule, practice direction or court order, they will generally require the permission of the court and will need to apply before the specified time has expired. Rule 3.9 sets out the factors which the court will take into account in deciding whether to grant relief from a sanction. The types of sanctions which the court will have at its disposal will include striking out a party's case, or part of it, or ordering that the evidence which has not been served on time may not be relied upon, or imposing costs penalties, which might include payments of costs on the spot, or wasted costs. While automatic striking out of a claim for failure to set down on time in accordance with the previous County Court rules will no longer apply, there are new rules which provide for striking out of a claim for non-payment of court fees (rule 3.7).

Through its case management powers, the court will be seeking to level the playing field (see above) to minimise the opportunities for using procedural tactics to disadvantage the other party, particularly with regard to unwarranted delay or attempts to embark on 'excessive' steps (e.g. excessive disclosure of documents, or assembly of unnecessary witness and expert evidence).

Rule 3.8 states that time limits specified in rules, practice directions or a court order, may not be extended by agreement between the parties. The Law Society understands that this rule, applied strictly, could be counter-productive leading to unnecessary cost and time consuming applications to the court. In practice it will be acceptable for parties to agree to extend time, provided the 'milestone' dates (for example, the trial date) are not affected.

The new rules highlight the importance for solicitors of continuing to involve their client in the proceedings. Firstly, every statement of case and witness statement has to be endorsed by a statement of truth (see below); secondly, clients are to be encouraged to attend at case management conferences whenever practicable, particularly when key decisions are likely to be taken on the future conduct of the action; and thirdly, the cost rules specifically require solicitors to keep clients informed of costs incurred, including any adverse costs orders.

The new rules also give the court wider powers to look behind claims of litigation or legal professional privilege. While rules of court cannot supersede the well established common law principles in this area, the court will have specific new powers in the following respects:

► An expert's report must state the substance of all material instructions, whether written or oral, on the basis of which the report was written. The court will have the power in relation to such instructions to order disclosure or permit questioning in court, but only where there are reasonable grounds to consider that the statement of instructions given in the expert's report may be inaccurate or incomplete.

► In relation to the personal liability of legal representatives for costs (wasted costs orders, rule 48.7(3)), the court has the power to direct that privileged documents may be disclosed to the court and to the other party to the application for an order.

These provisions represent potentially significant changes to the established principle of solicitor/client privilege. Where the court orders disclosure of privileged documents, the solicitor will need to be particularly careful to take instructions from the client, and, where appropriate, to argue to the court, with reasons, why disclosure to the other party of documents or information should not be ordered.

3. Pre-action

Under the previous rules, the court had only limited powers prior to the issue of proceedings. These were mainly confined to powers to order pre-action disclosure of documents in personal injury claims and, under the court's inherent jurisdiction, to disallow the costs of issue of proceedings or assembly of evidence if the court concluded, in all the circumstances, that issuing proceedings was 'premature'. The new culture will encourage a climate of openness. Litigation should be viewed as a measure of last resort. Pre-action protocols have been developed for personal injury and clinical negligence disputes; these are annexed to the rules with a practice direction. Other protocols are being developed. The rules give the court specific powers to consider whether parties have complied with any relevant pre-action protocol when making case management orders, including with regard to costs.

4. Service of documents – Part 6

The rules provide that any document which is issued or prepared by the court will be served by the court, except where the appropriate party notifies the court in writing that he or she wishes to serve it, or the court so orders.

As service by the court may cause delay, solicitors who prefer to serve their own documents should make this clear to the court as early as possible.

5. How to start proceedings – the claim – Parts 7, 8 and 16

All proceedings are started when the claimant issues a claim form. Each form must:

(a)   contain a concise statement of the nature of the claim;

(b)   specify the remedy that the claimant seeks;

(c)   where the claimant is making a claim for money, contain a statement of value;

(d)   contain a statement of truth – see below; and

(e)   contain such other matters as may be set out in a practice direction.

6.   The statement of truth – Part 22

Either the claim form or any separate particulars of claim (and also defences, replies to statements of case and witness statements) must contain a 'statement of truth', i.e. a statement that the claimant, defendant, witness, etc., believes the facts stated in the document are true. If there is no statement of truth attached to a statement of case, the court has the power to order that it be struck out and, in the case of a witness statement, that it shall not be put in evidence. Proceedings for contempt of court may be brought against a party for any false statement of truth with dishonest intent. Rule 22.1(6) provides that the statement must be signed by the party or the legal representative. Practice direction 22 gives further guidance on statements of truth.

Generally, it will be preferable if clients sign statements of truth. Subject to **21.21** note 4 in the Guide (p.384), it may not be always appropriate for solicitors to do so. Solicitors have a duty to represent their client's case, but to do this they will normally have to accept that what their client states is true. Solicitors cannot cross-examine their own clients on the accuracy of every detail of the case. This would lead to serious conflicts of interest and thereby make it impossible to continue to represent clients. Solicitors must ensure that clients understand the importance of the statement of truth and the implications of signing it. If the solicitor is to sign on the client's behalf, the client's clear authority to do so must be obtained: this means that the client must see and approve the document in question, and understand that the solicitor is verifying that the client accepts the truth of its contents.

21

7.   Case management – Part 26

Each defended case will be allocated to one of three tracks:

(a)   the small claims track (claims for not more than £5,000, except in the case of claims for personal injury or claims by a tenant of residential premises and his or her landlord;

(b)   the fast track (claims with a value between £5,000 and £15,000); where the trial will not last more than one day and there will be only limited oral expert evidence; or

(c)   the multi-track (claims with a value over £15,000).

Case allocation to track will be decided by the District Judge or High Court Master based on the parties' completed allocation questionnaires, which the court will send out to all parties in an action after the defence is filed. Matters to which the court shall have regard in allocation are listed in rule 26.8. Completion of the allocation questionnaire will be a very important step (a milestone) in any action. The court will expect the parties to co-operate on the completion of the questionnaire as part of the new, less adversarial culture.

8.   Fast track – Part 28

When cases are allocated to the fast track, the court will give directions for the management of the case and set a timetable. The standard period between the giving of directions and the trial will be not more than 30 weeks. The trial date or period will either be specified in the notice of allocation or as soon as practicable after the date specified for filing a completed listing questionnaire. In the latter case, the courts will normally give the parties at least three weeks' notice of the date of trial.

9. Multi-track – Part 29

When a case is allocated to the multi-track, the court will either give directions for the management of the case and set a timetable for the steps to be taken, or fix a case management conference. Case management conferences will be very different from old style directions hearings. The court will expect those attending (usually the legal representative conducting the case and, where practicable, the client) to be thoroughly prepared, and to have:

▶ identified the key issues in the case, and which of these will need to progress to trial;

▶ considered, and continue to consider, the prospects of settlement (including by ADR);

▶ prepared an efficient timetable for the remaining stages of the action; and

▶ had regard to 'proportionality' (see above).

The court will give directions following the case management conference. In more complex cases, the court may arrange further case management conferences and/or a pre-trial review.

The court will fix the trial date, or the period in which the trial is to take place, as soon as practicable and, at the latest, when:

(a) each party has filed a completed listing questionnaire;

(b) the court has held a pre-trial review.

10. Disclosure and inspection of documents – Part 31

Under the new regime, a party is not required to give more than standard disclosure unless the court orders otherwise. Rule 31.6 defines standard disclosure as:

(a) all documents on which a party relies; and

(b) all documents which:

    (i) adversely affect his or her own case;

    (ii) adversely affect another party's case; or

    (iii) support another party's case; and

(c) all documents which he or she is required to disclose by any practice direction.

Standard disclosure only is likely to be the norm in the fast track; further or 'specific' disclosure may be ordered in some multi-track cases. Proportionality will be an important issue here.

When giving standard disclosure, a party will be required to make a reasonable search for documents falling within the definition. Rule 31.7(2) sets out the factors relevant to reasonableness. These include the number of documents, the nature and complexity of the proceedings, the ease and expense of retrieval and the likely significance of any document which may be found.

Disclosure of documents will usually be by list, as under the old rules, but the list must include a disclosure statement which sets out the extent of the search made and in which the party certifies that he or she understands the duty to disclose (rule 31.10(6)), and, in particular, if the search has been limited on the grounds of reasonableness or of cost, and if so, why and how.

A party's duty to disclose documents is limited to documents which are or have been in his or her control.

Under rule 31.16(1) the court may make an order, on application by a party, for disclosure before proceedings have started: this will no longer be limited only to personal injury claims. Under rule 31.17 the court may order disclosure if the person is not a party to potential or actual proceedings.

The new disclosure rules are designed to prevent cases being delayed and costs being increased by disclosure of irrelevant or unnecessary documents. In spite of the limited nature of the test of disclosure, solicitors are reminded of their duty under principle **21.01** in the Guide (p.374) not to mislead the court. The duties of search and the need to include a disclosure statement and certificate in the list of documents, will need to be explained to clients carefully as these are duties of the parties, not just of the legal representatives.

21

11. Experts and assessors – Part 35

It is the general duty of the court and the parties to restrict expert evidence to that which is reasonably required to resolve the proceedings (rule 35.1). Experts now have an overriding 'duty to the court' (rule 35.3), rather than to the party who instructs or pays them. They must set out in their reports a summary of the material on which the report is based, and the court has the power to order disclosure of the actual instructions, if there is some doubt as to their *bona fides*.

Rule 35.7 provides that where two or more parties wish to submit expert evidence on an issue, the court may direct that the evidence on that issue is given by one expert alone. In fast track cases, oral evidence from experts will only be allowed at trial with permission of the court – which will only be granted exceptionally.

The court also has the power to limit recoverable experts' fees.

Solicitors will need to take care to explain to their clients, and to experts when they are instructed, the courts' extended powers, and particularly to emphasise the expert's duty to the court, and the intention in the rules that parties co-operate much more than hitherto on the number, choice of and instructions to experts.

12. Settlement – Part 36

Part 36 contains rules about the new offers to settle, about payments into court and the costs consequences of these. Offers can be made by both claimants and defendants, including before proceedings are issued. However, where a defendant makes a Part 36 offer pre-proceedings, this should be followed by a payment into court once an action has started, if the defendant wants to secure the cost consequences provided in the rules (although the court does have a wide discretion to make costs orders in relation to offers).

Where a defendant's Part 36 offer/Part 36 payment is accepted, the claimant will generally be entitled to his or her costs of proceedings up to the date of giving notice of acceptance.

Where at trial a claimant fails to match a Part 36 payment, or fails to achieve a judgment which is more advantageous than that which was offered in the defendant's Part 36 offer, the court will usually order the claimant to pay any costs incurred by the defendant after the latest date on which the payment or offer could have been accepted without the permission of the court (unless it considers it unjust to do so).

Where, at trial, the claimant does better than he or she proposed in his or her own Part 36 offer which the defendant did not accept, the court may award the claimant extra damages, costs and interest at a rate not exceeding 10% above base rate for some or all of the period, starting at the latest date that the defendant could have accepted the offer without permission of the court, and/or award costs on an indemnity basis.

Offers to settle are a significant innovation, particularly for claimants. Solicitors will need to advise clients carefully of the implications of this new rule and to consider whether, and when, to make offers to settle.

February 1999

Chapter 22

Alternative dispute resolution

22

22.01   Provision of ADR services

Solicitors may offer ADR services as part of their practice.

1.   'ADR service' means a service where a solicitor acts as an independent neutral, e.g. mediator, conciliator or arbitrator.

2.   Solicitors offering ADR services as part of their practices will be covered by the Solicitors' Indemnity Fund up to the current limit of indemnity.

3.   Solicitors may also provide ADR services as a separate business. If so, they must have regard to the Solicitors' Separate Business Code 1994 (see Annex 3E, p.129). Solicitors who offer ADR services as a separate business will need to obtain separate indemnity cover on the commercial market.

4.   It is recommended that solicitors wishing to offer ADR services should undertake appropriate training and ensure that their skills are kept up to date.

22.02   Information to parties

A solicitor who provides ADR services must inform the parties to the dispute in writing, and the parties must agree, that the solicitor will be independent and impartial and will not advise either party.

22.03 Restrictions on acting for parties

A solicitor must not provide an ADR service in connection with a dispute in which he or she, or a member of his or her firm, has acted as a professional adviser to any party; nor, having provided an ADR service, may a solicitor or member of his or her firm act for any participant individually in relation to the dispute.

Principle **22.03** applies equally when a solicitor provides an ADR service through a separate business.

22.04 Codes of practice

The Society recommends that solicitors who offer ADR services comply with a code of practice.

1. The Society recommends that solicitors offering civil/commercial or family mediation as part of their practices comply with the Law Society's Code of Practice for Civil/Commercial Mediation, or the Law Society's Code of Practice for Family Mediation, as appropriate (see Annex 22A, p.419 or Annex 22B, p.428).

2. Many of the principles are the same in both codes. However, the codes also reflect essential differences between civil/commercial and family mediation. For example, the needs of children affected by the mediation form an important element in the Code of Practice for Family Mediation.

3. Solicitors offering mediation as part of their practices will still be subject to the rules and principles which govern solicitors' conduct generally. Solicitors offering mediation outside their practices should remember that they remain officers of the Court and members of the solicitors' profession. Disciplinary sanctions may be imposed if, for instance, a solicitor's behaviour tends to bring the profession into disrepute (see **1.08**, p.8).

4. Whilst the codes are not compulsory, the Society strongly recommends their use. If a complaint is made against a solicitor mediator, the Office for the Supervision of Solicitors are likely to see the code as evidence of good practice, and may require the solicitor to explain why he or she did not think it appropriate to follow the principles in the codes.

5. The Society will continue to monitor changes and developments in the practice of mediation and may revise the codes in the light of such changes.

6. If solicitors practising as mediators experience ethical difficulties which do not appear to be covered by the codes of practice, they should contact Professional Ethics (see p.xv for contact details).

Annex 22A

Law Society's Code of Practice for Civil/Commercial Mediation – practice information

This code is addressed to solicitors who practise as mediators in civil/commercial disputes.

INTRODUCTION

Principle **22.04** in the Guide (p.418) recommends that solicitors who offer alternative dispute resolution (ADR) services comply with a code of practice. The Law Society recommends that all solicitors offering civil/commercial mediation comply with this code.

This code is designed to deal with the fundamentals of civil/commercial mediation. It is not intended that it should cover every situation that may arise. The concept of not giving advice to the parties, individually or collectively, when acting as a mediator, permeates this entire code.

SECTION 1 – OBJECTIVES OF CIVIL/COMMERCIAL MEDIATION

Civil/commercial mediation is a process in which:

1.1   two or more parties in dispute

1.2   whether or not they are legally represented

1.3   and at any time, whether or not there are or have been legal proceedings

1.4   agree to the appointment of a neutral third party (the mediator)

1.5   who is impartial

1.6   who has no authority to make any decisions with regard to their issues

1.7   which may relate to all or any part of a dispute of a civil or commercial nature

1.8   but who helps them reach their own decisions

1.9   by negotiation

1.10 without adjudication.

Commentary

The code is aimed at those undertaking civil/commercial mediations on a commercial basis, although it may be observed equally by those undertaking civil/commercial mediations on a pro bono basis.

Whilst the mediation may deal, typically, with the whole of any dispute, the parties may, should they so choose, deal with only one aspect of a dispute, for example, liability or quantum.

Whilst the majority of mediations are undertaken by a sole mediator, there may be occasions where two or more mediators co-mediate the dispute. In those circumstances, the solicitor mediator should be aware that the co-mediator may need to comply with his or her own ethical rules and will need to obtain his or her own insurance cover.

The mediator must not give legal advice to the parties individually or collectively. The mediator may, however, provide legal information to the parties to assist them in understanding the principles of law applicable to their circumstances and the way in which those principles are generally applied.

In the context of the code, adjudication means the formal determination by a third party. It does not preclude the mediator, at his or her discretion and with the consent of the parties, from expressing an opinion or from providing some elements of non-binding evaluation in those models of mediation that are not purely facilitative but also evaluative. The mediator should not, however, advise parties in the sense of asserting what their rights are and recommending how those rights should be translated into settlement terms.

SECTION 2 – QUALIFICATIONS AND APPOINTMENT OF MEDIATOR

2.1 Every mediator must comply with the criteria and requirements for mediators stipulated from time to time by the Law Society, including those relating to training, consultancy, accreditation and regulation.

2.2 Save where appointed by or through the court, a mediator may only accept appointment if both or all parties to the mediation so request, or agree.

2.3 Whether a mediator is appointed by the parties or through the court or any other agency, he or she may only continue to act as such so long as both or all parties to the mediation wish him or her to do so. If any party does not wish to continue with the mediation, the mediator must discontinue the process as regards that party and may discontinue the process as regards all parties. Also, if the mediator considers that it would be inappropriate to continue the mediation, the mediator shall bring it to an end, and may, subject to the terms of the mediation agreement, decline to give reasons.

Commentary

This section should be read in conjunction with paragraph 4.1.

SECTION 3 – CONFLICTS OF INTEREST, CONFIDENTIAL INFORMATION AND THE IMPARTIALITY OF THE MEDIATOR

3.1   The impartiality of the mediator is a fundamental principle of mediation.

3.2   Impartiality means that:

    3.2.1   the mediator does not have any significant personal interest in the outcome of the mediation;

    3.2.2   the mediator will conduct the process fairly and even-handedly, and will not favour any party over another.

3.3   Save as set out in 3.2 above, a mediator with an insignificant personal interest in the outcome of the mediation may act if, and only if, full disclosure is made to all of the parties as soon as it is known, and they consent.

3.4   The mediator must not act, or, having started to do so, continue to act:

    3.4.1   in relation to issues on which he or she or a member of his or her firm has at any time acted for any party;

    3.4.2   if any circumstances exist which may constitute an actual or potential conflict of interest;

    3.4.3   if the mediator or a member of his or her firm has acted for any of the parties in issues not relating to the mediation, unless that has been disclosed to the parties as soon as it is known, and they consent.

3.5   Where a mediator has acted as such in relation to a dispute, neither he or she nor any member of his or her firm may act subsequently for any party in relation to the subject matter of the mediation.

Commentary

Whilst impartiality is fundamental to the role of the mediator, this does not mean that a mediator may never express a comment or view that one party may find more acceptable than another. However, the mediator must not allow his or her personal view of the fairness or otherwise of the substance of the negotiations between the parties to damage or impair his or her impartiality.

The mediator must appreciate that his or her involvement in the process is inevitably likely to affect the course of the negotiations between the parties. (His or her involvement is, of course, intended to assist that process so far as possible.) This would be the case whether the mediator intervenes directly or whether he or she deals with issues indirectly, for example, through questions. Consequently all mediator intervention needs to be conducted with sensitivity and care in order to maintain impartiality.

There may be circumstances where the mediator may have some personal interest in the outcome of the mediation (for example, he or she has a very small shareholding in a company which is a party to the mediation). In those circumstances, and where the mediator feels able to act impartially, he or she must disclose full details of his or her interest to the parties immediately, inviting them to decide whether or not the mediator should continue to act.

The mediator should decline to act if he or she feels he or she will be prejudiced (for example, he or she knows one of the parties socially), or in circumstances where either party may perceive there to be a prejudice.

It is important not only that the mediator should be neutral, but also that he or she should be perceived by the parties to be so. The mediator must therefore take particular care to avoid conflicts of interest, whether actual or potential, real or perceived.

Whilst a mediator may not undertake cases in respect of which his or her firm has already provided legal advice to one of the parties, the mediator would not be precluded from acting as such in respect of unrelated issues involving a party for whom his or her firm has previously acted, provided that, before undertaking the mediation, the mediator discloses this fact to the parties and the parties consent to the mediation.

*It is usual in mediation for the parties to agree that the mediator should treat as confidential information which he or she acquires during the course of private meetings; almost invariably such information will be relevant to the dispute and it is unlikely that it will give rise to a conflict situation as described in **15.02** and **15.03** in the Guide (see pp.314 and 316).*

However, if either:

▶ *the mediator acquires confidential information relevant to the dispute or to any of the parties involved in the mediation from another source (for example, from another client, partner, colleague or firm), whether before or during the mediation, or*

▶ *the mediator acquires confidential information relevant to another client of his or her firm, during the mediation,*

then, in either case, a conflict of interest as defined in Chapter 15 of the Guide would exist, necessitating the mediator's withdrawal from the mediation.

If the mediator is in any doubt on any possible conflict of interest or confidentiality point, the mediator should contact Professional Ethics for further advice (see p.xv for contact details).

SECTION 4 – MEDIATION PROCEDURES

4.1 The mediator must ensure that the parties agree the terms and conditions regulating the mediation before dealing with the substantive issues. This should be in a written agreement which should reflect the main principles of this code. Such agreement should also contain the terms of remuneration of the mediator.

4.2 The procedure for the conduct of the mediation is a matter for the decision of the mediator. Insofar as the mediator establishes an agenda of matters to be covered in the mediation, the mediator should be guided by the needs, wishes and priorities of the parties in doing so.

4.3 In establishing any procedures for the conduct of the mediation, the mediator must be guided by a commitment to procedural fairness and a high quality of process.

Commentary

This section should be read with section 5 and its commentary. The mediator is the manager of the process and should manage the mediation, at his or her discretion, with the object of meeting as best as possible the wishes of the parties.

The mediator and the parties should agree, as far as practicable, at the outset whether the mediator's role will be purely facilitative, or whether the mediator may at his or her discretion, provide an evaluative element based on his or her knowledge of the subject matter or legal issues involved.

The role of the mediator, whether facilitative or evaluative, may change during the course of the mediation by agreement of the parties.

SECTION 5 – THE DECISION-MAKING PROCESS

5.1   The primary aim of mediation is to help the parties to arrive at their own decisions regarding the disputed issues.

5.2   The parties should be helped to reach such resolution of such issues which they feel are appropriate to their particular circumstances. Such resolution may not necessarily be the same as that which may be arrived at in the event of adjudication by the court. That allows the parties to explore and agree upon a wider range of options for settlement than might otherwise be the case.

5.3   The mediator may meet the parties individually and/or together. Solicitors, barristers or other professional advisers acting for the individual parties may, but need not necessarily, participate in the mediation process if the parties so wish. Such solicitors and/or advisers may take part in discussions and meetings, with or without the parties, and in any other communication and representation, in such manner as the mediator may consider useful and appropriate.

5.4   Parties are free to consult with their individual professional advisers as the mediation progresses. The mediator may make suggestions to the parties as to the appropriateness of seeking further assistance from professional advisers such as lawyers, accountants, expert valuers or others.

5.5   The mediator must not seek to impose his or her preferred outcome on the parties.

5.6   The mediator shall be free to make management decisions with regard to the conduct of the mediation process.

5.7   The mediator may suggest possible solutions and help the parties to explore these, where he or she thinks that this would be helpful to them.

5.8   The mediator must recognise that the parties can reach decisions on any issue at any stage of a mediation.

5.9   Agreements reached in mediation fall into three categories:

    5.9.1   non-binding agreements

    5.9.2   binding agreements (which would be enforceable by a court)

    5.9.3   binding agreements enshrined in a court or arbitration order.

The mediator should ascertain how the parties wish their agreement to be treated. Where the parties do not wish to have a legally binding solution (for example, where they have resolved personal rather than legal issues), their wishes should be respected.

5.10 At the end of the mediation or at any interim stage, the mediator and/or the parties or their representatives may prepare a written memorandum or summary of any agreements reached by the parties, which may, where considered by the mediator to be appropriate, comprise draft heads of such agreements for formalisation by the legal advisers acting for the parties.

5.11 If the parties wish to consult their respective individual legal advisers before entering into any binding agreement, then any terms which they may provisionally propose as the basis for resolution will not be binding on them until they have each had an opportunity of taking advice from such advisers and have thereafter agreed, in writing, to be bound.

5.12 Mediation does not provide for the disclosure and inspection of documents in the same way or to the same extent as required by court rules. The parties may voluntarily agree to provide such documentation, or any lesser form of disclosure considered by them to be sufficient. This should be considered in advance of the mediation. The mediator may indicate any particular documents that he or she considers should be brought to the mediation.

5.13 The mediator may assist the parties, so far as appropriate and practicable, to identify what information and documents will help the resolution of any issue(s), and how best such information and documents may be obtained. However, the mediator has no obligation to make independent enquiries or undertake verification in relation to any information or documents sought or provided in the mediation.

5.14 If, in cases where one or more parties is unrepresented at the mediation and the parties are proposing a resolution which appears to the mediator to be unconscionable, having regard to the circumstances, then the mediator must inform the parties accordingly and may terminate the mediation and/or refer the parties to their legal advisers.

Commentary

The mediator is the manager of the process. It is important that, where possible, a flexible approach is adopted by the mediator. He or she may suggest the introduction into the process of professional, technical, and/or business advisers to the parties to assist in such a manner as agreed between the parties. It is for the parties to decide whether they wish to be represented in mediation, but for the mediator to decide how the process is managed.

Some mediation organisations suggest that, at the request of the parties and with his or her consent, the mediator may provide a non-binding written recommendation on terms of settlement. This is rarely used and then, usually, as a last resort at the end of the mediation. This would not be precluded by paragraph 5.5.

Whenever possible, the mediator should consider with the parties, in advance of the mediation, what documents should be made available and, where appropriate, how verification in relation to documents or information sought, should be obtained. It must be recognised, however, that there will be circumstances where this is not possible in advance of the meeting, in which circumstances, in the interests of fairness, consideration should be given to adjourning the mediation for further enquiries or for such verification to be obtained.

It is quite common and proper in the context of mediation for the parties to disclose information and documents on a confidential basis to the mediator only. This section should be read in conjunction with section 7 which deals with the confidentiality and privilege surrounding mediation.

Whilst the mediator must permit the parties, if they so wish, to adjourn a mediation to seek advice from their professional advisers once a resolution has been proposed and agreed in principle, caution should be exercised in recommending this, since this may have the effect of losing the momentum of the mediation and, in some cases, the resolution proposed.

The mediator is concerned with fairness of process. The mediator cannot be responsible for issues of justice and fairness of outcome; the parties must define their own 'fairness' of the substantive terms and criteria for agreeing terms. However, the mediator must be able to dissociate him or herself from the proposed resolutions in certain extreme circumstances, as indicated in paragraph 5.14. When deciding whether to terminate the mediation pursuant to paragraph 5.14, the mediator must consider all of the circumstances of the dispute and the mediation process itself. It is important to distinguish those who are represented at the mediation from those who are not; in the former situation, the mediator is entitled to rely on the fact that the party has reached a decision based on legal advice given to him or her by his or her legal representative and should not seek to look behind that decision; in the latter case, in extreme circumstances, the mediator must be able to distance him or herself from the resolution proposed. In those circumstances, the mediator may wish to suggest that the parties seek legal advice before proceeding further in the mediation.

22

SECTION 6 – DEALING WITH POWER IMBALANCES

6.1 The mediator should be alive to power imbalances existing between the parties. If such imbalances seem likely to cause the mediation process to become unfair or ineffective, the mediator must take reasonable steps to try to prevent this.

6.2 The mediator must seek, in particular, to prevent abusive or intimidating behaviour by any of the parties.

6.3 If the mediator believes that, because of power imbalances, the mediation would not be able to be fairly and effectively conducted, he or she may discuss this with the parties, recognising that the mediation may have to be brought to an end and/or the parties referred to their lawyers.

Commentary

Power imbalances will almost inevitably exist and will shift during the course of a mediation. The mediator cannot be responsible for redressing those imbalances. He or she must, however, seek to ensure that these do not cause the process to become ineffective as a result of the abuse of one party's stronger position. The likelihood of abuse occurring will diminish where the parties are legally represented in the mediation.

SECTION 7 – CONFIDENTIALITY AND PRIVILEGE

7.1 Before the mediation commences, the parties should agree in writing as to the provisions concerning confidentiality and privilege that will apply to the mediation process itself and any resultant mediation agreement, save as otherwise agreed in the mediation settlement agreement.

7.2 The mediator must maintain confidentiality in relation to all matters dealt with in the mediation. The mediator may disclose:

7.2.1 matters which the parties and the mediator agree may be disclosed;

7.2.2 matters which are already public;

7.2.3   matters which the mediator considers appropriate where he or she believes that the life or safety of any person is or may be at serious risk;

7.2.4   matters where the law imposes an overriding obligation of disclosure on the mediator.

In any such event the mediator should, where appropriate, try to agree with the party furnishing such information as to how disclosure shall be made.

7.3   Subject to paragraph 7.2 above, where the mediator meets the parties separately and obtains information from any party which is confidential to that party, the mediator must maintain the confidentiality of that information from all other parties, except to the extent that the mediator has been authorised to disclose any such information.

7.4   Mediators should note that the mediation privilege will not ordinarily apply in relation to communications indicating that any person is suffering or likely to suffer serious bodily harm, or where other public policy considerations prevail, or where for any other reason, the rules of evidence render privilege inapplicable.

7.5   The mediator should remind the parties that (unless the mediation agreement provides otherwise) the confidentiality and privilege attaching to the mediation process may not extend to the provisions of any settlement agreement which results. The mediator should suggest to the parties that they consider the extent to which they wish the terms of the resulting settlement to be disclosable – and to provide accordingly in the agreement itself.

Commentary

Prior to commencement of mediation, the mediator should obtain agreement from the parties that no party should be permitted to refer, in any proceedings that may subsequently take place, to any such privileged discussions and negotiations, or require the mediator to do so; nor should any party have access to any of the mediator's notes, or call any mediator as a witness in any proceedings, save where the parties agree that this is not appropriate.

The mediator should remind the parties that (unless the mediation agreement provides otherwise) the confidentiality and privilege attaching to the mediation process may not extend to the provisions of any settlement agreement which results. The mediator should suggest to the parties that they consider the extent to which they wish the terms of the resulting settlement to be disclosable, bearing in mind that they may have some overriding obligation of disclosure to a third party – and to provide accordingly in the agreement itself.

There are circumstances in which, even though the parties do not co-operate, there is an overriding duty of disclosure. In these circumstances general public policy prevails and the duty of disclosure would apply to all mediators, not merely solicitors. Mediators must have regard to the circumstances when confidentiality may be overridden, as set out in 16.02 in the Guide (see p.325). If in doubt, mediators should contact Professional Ethics (see p.xv for contact details).

Ordinarily, the mediator should suggest to the parties that they expressly agree that all discussions and negotiations during the mediation will be regarded as evidentially privileged and conducted on a 'without prejudice' basis.

SECTION 8 – PROFESSIONAL INDEMNITY COVER

8.1   All solicitor mediators must carry professional indemnity cover in respect of their acting as mediators.

    8.1.1   Solicitors who practise as mediators will be covered by the Solicitors' Indemnity Fund in respect of their acting as a mediator, provided they are doing so in their capacity as a member of their firm.

    8.1.2   If a solicitor is acting as a mediator as a separate activity outside his or her legal practice, separate indemnity insurance must be obtained.

Commentary

Solicitors who mediate outside their practices as members of mediation organisations may be covered by block insurance provided by those organisations. If not, they must make their own arrangements for appropriate cover.

*A solicitor practising as a mediator outside his or her legal practice must have regard to rule 5 of the Solicitors' Practice Rules 1990 and to the Solicitors' Separate Business Code 1994 (see **3.20**, p.89 and Annex 3E, p.129 in the Guide). Further guidance can be obtained by contacting Professional Ethics (see p.xv for contact details).*

22

SECTION 9 – PROMOTION OF MEDIATION

9.1   Solicitor mediators may promote their practice as such, but must always do so in a professional, truthful and dignified way. They may reflect their qualification as a mediator and their membership of any other relevant mediation organisation.

9.2   Solicitor mediators must comply with the Solicitors' Publicity Code 1990 (see Annex 11A, p.229 in the Guide).

April 1999

Annex 22B

Law Society's Code of Practice for Family Mediation – practice information

---

This code is addressed to solicitors who practise as mediators in family disputes.

INTRODUCTION

Principle **22.04** in the Guide (p.418) recommends that solicitors who offer alternative dispute resolution (ADR) services comply with a code of practice. The Law Society recommends that all solicitors offering family mediation within their practices comply with this code.

This code is designed to deal with the fundamentals of family mediation. It is not intended that it should cover every situation that may arise. The concept of not giving advice to the parties, individually or collectively, when acting as a mediator permeates this entire code.

SECTION 1 – OBJECTIVES OF FAMILY MEDIATION

Family mediation is a process in which:

1.1 a couple or any other family members

1.2 whether or not they are legally represented

1.3 and at any time, whether or not there are or have been legal proceedings

1.4 agree to the appointment of a neutral third party (the mediator)

1.5 who is impartial

1.6 who has no authority to make any decisions with regard to their issues

1.7 which may relate to separation, divorce, children's issues, property and financial questions or any other issues they may raise

1.8 but who helps them reach their own informed decisions

1.9 by negotiation

1.10 without adjudication.

Commentary

From time to time the dispute between a couple may involve a wider group of family members than just the couple. Family members may include step-parents, grandparents, aunts, uncles, children and even potential family members. Any of these may participate in the mediation with the agreement of the couple and the mediator, but with regard to involving children in the process, see the commentary to section 8.

The code is aimed at those undertaking family mediations on a commercial basis, although it may be observed equally by those undertaking family mediations on a pro bono *basis.*

Whilst the mediation may deal, typically, with the whole of any dispute, the parties may, should they so choose, deal with only one aspect of a dispute, for example, liability or quantum.

In one model of family mediation, two or more mediators co-mediate the dispute. In those circumstances, the solicitor mediator should be aware that the co-mediator may need to comply with his or her own ethical rules and will need to obtain his or her own insurance cover.

The mediator must not give legal advice to the parties individually or collectively. The mediator may, however, provide legal information to the parties to assist them in understanding the principles of law applicable to their circumstances, and the way in which those principles are generally applied.

In the context of this code, adjudication means the formal determination by a third party.

22

SECTION 2 – QUALIFICATIONS AND APPOINTMENT OF MEDIATOR

2.1 Every mediator must comply with the criteria and requirements for mediators stipulated from time to time by the Law Society, including those relating to training, consultancy, accreditation and regulation.

2.2 Save where appointed by or through the court, a mediator may only accept appointment if both or all parties to the mediation so request, or agree.

2.3 Whether a mediator is appointed by the parties or through the court or any other agency, he or she may only continue to act as such so long as both or all parties to the mediation wish him or her to do so. If any party does not wish to continue with the mediation, the mediator must discontinue the process. Also, if the mediator considers that it would be inappropriate to continue the mediation, the mediator shall bring it to an end, and may decline to give reasons.

Commentary

This section should be read in conjunction with paragraph 4.1.

SECTION 3 – CONFLICTS OF INTEREST, CONFIDENTIAL INFORMATION AND THE IMPARTIALITY OF THE MEDIATOR

3.1 The impartiality of the mediator is a fundamental principle of mediation.

3.2 Impartiality means that:

3.2.1   the mediator does not have any significant personal interest in the outcome of the mediation;

3.2.2   the mediator will conduct the process fairly and even-handedly, and will not favour any party over another.

3.3   Save as set out in 3.2 above, a mediator with an insignificant personal interest in the outcome of the mediation may act if, and only if, full disclosure is made to all of the parties as soon as it is known, and they consent.

3.4   The mediator must not act, or, having started to do so, continue to act:

3.4.1   in relation to issues on which he or she or a member of his or her firm has at any time acted for any party;

3.4.2   if any circumstances exist which may constitute an actual or potential conflict of interest;

3.4.3   if the mediator or a member of his or her firm has acted for any of the parties in issues not relating to the mediation, unless that has been disclosed to the parties as soon as it is known and they consent.

3.5   Where a mediator has acted as such in relation to a dispute, neither he or she nor any member of his or her firm may act subsequently for any party in relation to the subject matter of the mediation.

Commentary

Whilst impartiality is fundamental to the role of the mediator, this does not mean that a mediator may never express a comment or view that one party may find more acceptable than another. However, the mediator must not allow his or her personal view of the fairness or otherwise of the substance of the negotiations between the parties to damage or impair his or her impartiality.

The mediator must appreciate that his or her involvement in the process is inevitably likely to affect the course of the negotiations between the parties. (His or her involvement is, of course, intended to assist that process so far as possible.) This would be the case whether the mediator intervenes directly or whether he or she deals with issues indirectly, for example, through questions. Consequently all mediator intervention needs to be conducted with sensitivity and care in order to maintain impartiality.

There may be circumstances where the mediator may have some personal interest in the outcome of the mediation (for example, he or she has a very small shareholding in a company which is a party to the mediation). In those circumstances and where the mediator feels able to act impartially, he or she must disclose full details of his or her interest to the parties immediately, inviting them to decide whether or not the mediator should continue to act.

The mediator should decline to act if he or she feels he or she will be prejudiced (for example, he or she knows one of the parties socially), or in circumstances where either party may perceive there to be a prejudice.

It is important not only that the mediator should be neutral, but also that he or she should be perceived by the parties to be so. The mediator must therefore take particular care to avoid conflicts of interest, whether actual or potential, real or perceived.

Whilst a mediator may not undertake cases in respect of which his or her firm has already provided legal advice to one of the parties, the mediator would not be precluded from acting as such in respect of unrelated issues involving a party for whom his or her firm has previously acted, provided that, before undertaking the mediation, the mediator discloses this fact to the parties and the parties consent to the mediation.

It is usual in mediation for the parties to agree that the mediator should treat as confidential information which he or she acquires during the course of private meetings; almost invariably such information will be relevant to the dispute, and it is unlikely that it will give rise to a conflict situation as described in 15.02 and 15.03 in the Guide (pp.314 and 316).

However, if either:

▶   *the mediator acquires confidential information relevant to the dispute or to any of the parties involved in the mediation from another source (for example, from another client, partner, colleague or firm), whether before or during the mediation, or*

▶   *the mediator acquires confidential information relevant to another client of his or her firm, during the mediation,*

then, in either case, a conflict of interest as defined in Chapter 15 of the Guide would exist, necessitating the mediator's withdrawal from the mediation.

If the mediator is in any doubt on any possible conflict of interest or confidentiality point, the mediator should contact Professional Ethics for further advice (see p.xv for contact details).

SECTION 4 – MEDIATION PROCEDURES

4.1   The mediator must ensure that the parties agree the terms and conditions regulating the mediation before dealing with the substantive issues. This should ordinarily be in a written agreement which should reflect the main principles of this code. Such agreement should also contain the terms of remuneration of the mediator.

4.2   The procedure for the conduct of the mediation is a matter for the decision of the mediator. Insofar as the mediator establishes an agenda of matters to be covered in the mediation, the mediator should be guided by the needs, wishes and priorities of the parties in doing so.

4.3   In establishing any procedures for the conduct of the mediation, the mediator must be guided by a commitment to procedural fairness, the fostering of mutual respect between the parties and a high quality of process.

Commentary

This section should be read with section 5 and its commentary. The mediator is the manager of the process and should manage the mediation at his or her discretion, with the object of meeting as best as possible the wishes of the parties.

SECTION 5 – THE DECISION-MAKING PROCESS

5.1   The primary aim of family mediation is to help the parties to arrive at their own decisions regarding their issues, on an informed basis with an understanding, so far as reasonably practicable, of the implications and consequences of such decisions for themselves and any children concerned.

5.2 The parties may reach decisions on any issue at any stage of the mediation.

5.3 Subject to paragraph 5.4, decisions arrived at in family mediation should not be binding on the parties until they have had the opportunity to seek advice on those decisions from their own legal representatives.

5.4 The parties must be offered the opportunity to obtain legal advice before any decision can be turned into a binding agreement on any issue which appears to the mediator or to either party to be of significance to the position of one or both parties.

5.5 The mediator must not seek to impose his or her preferred outcome on the parties and should try to avoid becoming personally identified with any particular outcome.

5.6 The mediator shall, however, be free to make management decisions with regard to the conduct of the mediation process, and may suggest possible solutions and help the parties to explore these, where he or she thinks that this would be helpful to them.

5.7 The mediator should assist the parties, so far as appropriate and practicable, to identify what information and documents would help the resolution of any issue(s), and how best such information and documents may be obtained. However, the mediator has no obligation to make independent enquiries or undertake verification in relation to any information or documents sought or provided in the mediation. If necessary, consideration may be given in the mediation to the ways in which the parties may make such enquiries or obtain such verification.

5.8 Family mediation does not provide for the disclosure and discovery of documents in the same way or to the same extent as required by court rules. The mediator may indicate any particular documents that he or she considers each party should furnish.

5.9 Parties should be helped to reach such resolution of such issues which they feel are appropriate to their particular circumstances. Such resolutions may not necessarily be the same as those which may be arrived at in the event of an adjudication by the court.

5.10 The mediator should, if practicable, inform the parties if he or she considers that the resolutions which they are considering are likely to fall outside the parameters which a court might approve or order. In such circumstances the mediator should reaffirm the advisability of the parties each obtaining independent legal advice. If they nevertheless wish to proceed with such resolutions, they may do so. In these circumstances the mediation summary may identify any specific questions on which the mediator has indicated a need for independent legal advice. If, however, the parties are proposing a resolution which appears to the mediator to be unconscionable or fundamentally inappropriate, then the mediator should inform the parties accordingly and may terminate the mediation, and/or refer the parties to their legal advisers.

5.11 Parties may consult with their own solicitors as the mediation progresses, and shall be given the opportunity to do so before reaching any binding agreement on their substantive issues. Where appropriate, the mediator may assist the parties to consider the desirability of their jointly or individually seeking further assistance during the course of the mediation process from professional advisers such as lawyers, accountants, expert valuers or others, or from counsellors or therapists. The mediator may also assist the parties by providing relevant lists of names.

5.12 Mediation meetings are commonly conducted without lawyers present. However, solicitors or counsel acting for the individual parties may be invited to participate in the mediation process, and in any communications, in such manner as the mediator may consider useful and appropriate, and as the parties may agree.

Commentary

*The mediator is the manager of the process. The mediator should consult the parties on management decisions such as the ordering of issues and the agenda for each mediation session. The mediator must not relinquish control of the **process** to the parties.*

Family mediation does not provide for disclosure and discovery of documents and information in the same way, or to the same extent as is possible under existing court rules. However, mediators should explain to the parties why full and frank disclosure is essential to the mediation process, and at all stages should encourage the provision of full information and documentation. The mediator may indicate any particular documents or information that he or she considers each party should have. If either party declines to furnish any information and the mediator considers that the mediation cannot properly continue without it, the mediator must discuss this with the parties and may bring the mediation to an end.

Mediators cannot be responsible for issues of justice and fairness; the parties must define their own 'fairness' and criteria for agreeing terms, and the mediator must not try to influence them with his or her own ideas of fairness. However, the mediator must be able to dissociate him or herself from the proposed resolutions in certain extreme circumstances.

The decision to include solicitors for the individual parties should be taken by the parties with the help of the mediator, and not by the solicitors.

Mediators are likely to find that decisions can be made at any stage of the mediation. Early decisions may include, for example, interim arrangements for contact, the sale of items to raise cash, or holiday arrangements for children. Mediators should ensure that the parties do not arrive at decisions on some issues prematurely, if those decisions might prejudice either party in relation to an overall resolution.

Some decisions reached in mediation are unlikely to affect the long term rights and responsibilities of the parties, for example, decisions might be reached on interim contact arrangements, contact over an approaching holiday period, the sale of a non-material item or division of contents of the former matrimonial home with no real monetary value. In those circumstances, whilst parties should not be discouraged from seeking independent legal advice should they so choose, it would not be necessary for the mediator to offer them the opportunity to obtain such advice before those decisions are turned into binding agreements on those limited issues.

SECTION 6 – DEALING WITH POWER IMBALANCES

6.1 The mediator should be alive to the likelihood of power imbalances existing between the parties. These may relate to various different aspects including, for example, behaviour which is controlling, abusive or manipulative; finance; children and family; status; communication and other skills; possession of information; the withholding of co-operation; and many other kinds of power.

6.2   If power imbalances seem likely to cause the mediation process to become unfair or ineffective, the mediator must take appropriate steps to try to prevent this.

6.3   The mediator must ensure that the parties take part in mediation willingly and without fear of violence or harm. Additionally, the mediator must seek to prevent manipulative, threatening or intimidating behaviour by either party.

6.4   If the mediator believes that power imbalances cannot be redressed adequately and that in consequence the mediation will not be able to be fairly and effectively conducted, he or she may discuss this with the parties, but in any event must bring the mediation to an end as soon as practicable.

Commentary

Where power imbalances involve potential violence or harm, mediators must take particular care to establish whether mediation can take place at all, and if it can, under what circumstances and conditions.

Cases of potential violence and harm should be identified as soon as possible. The Family Law Act 1996 requires that this is undertaken in legally aided cases (see section 11 below); it is, however, to be regarded as good and required practice in all mediation matters, whether or not legally aided.

If mediation is to take place where a party is thought to be at any risk of harm by the other party, the mediator must take steps to try to ensure that both parties and the mediator are safe in the mediation. This should, for example, be addressed by appropriate arrangements for reception on arrival and for departure after the mediation, and by any other arrangements or conditions the mediator may consider suitable.

SECTION 7 – CONFIDENTIALITY AND PRIVILEGE

7.1   The mediator must maintain confidentiality in relation to all matters dealt with in the mediation. The mediator may disclose:

    7.1.1   matters which the parties and the mediator agree may be disclosed;

    7.1.2   matters which the mediator considers appropriate where he or she believes that any child or any other person affected by the mediation is suffering or likely to suffer significant harm (and in such case, the mediator should, so far as practicable and appropriate, discuss with the parties the way in which such disclosure is to take place); or

    7.1.3   matters where the law imposes an overriding obligation of disclosure on the mediator.

7.2   Any information or correspondence provided by any party should be shared openly with both and not withheld, except any address or telephone number and except as the parties may otherwise agree.

7.3   All information material to financial issues must be provided on an open basis, so that it can be referred to in court, either in support of an application made with the consent of the parties or in contested proceedings.

7.4   However, discussions about possible terms of settlement should be conducted on a 'without prejudice' basis; and in any event a mediation privilege should ordinarily be claimed for them, so that parties may explore their options freely.

7.5   The mediator must discuss arrangements about confidentiality with the parties before holding separate meetings or caucuses. It may be agreed that the mediator will either:

    7.5.1   report back to the parties as to the substance of the separate meetings; or

    7.5.2   maintain separate confidences: provided that if separate confidences are to be maintained, they must not include any material fact which would be open if discussed in a joint meeting.

7.6   The mediation privilege will not ordinarily apply in relation to communications indicating that a child or other person affected by the mediation is suffering, or likely to suffer, significant harm, or where other public policy considerations prevail, or where for any other reason the rules of evidence render privilege inapplicable.

Commentary

Before the mediation commences, the parties should agree in writing as to the provisions concerning confidentiality and privilege that will apply to the mediation. The principles are outlined in section 7, which the following commentary will amplify.

Confidentiality

The couple may expect a mediator to keep confidential all matters they have discussed in mediation. However, there are some circumstances when a mediator has a duty of disclosure which is greater than the duty to maintain confidentiality. Even without a code of practice or agreement between the parties, confidentiality might have to be broken where this is justified, as where public policy considerations prevail. Paragraph 7.1 of the code specifies circumstances in which a mediator would be expected to disclose matters arising in mediation; but this would not be a breach of confidentiality, nor would it be unexpected, since the parties would have been aware from their agreement to mediate of the mediator's duty in this regard.

In essence there are two main circumstances in which disclosure may take place:

1.   *Those involving children: the code and corresponding agreement to mediate make it clear that there may be disclosure where the mediator believes that any child is suffering, or likely to suffer, significant harm. This should be read with paragraph 8.2, which outlines the obligations of the mediator where he or she has this belief.*

    In some cases, the mediator will have the difficult task of assessing whether or not a party's right to confidentiality should prevail over the possible risk of harm to a child or other person. Solicitor mediators faced with difficulties may wish to contact Professional Ethics for further advice (see p.xv for contact details).

2.   *Other issues of public policy: these may involve similar principles to those outlined above, but relate to adults suffering, or likely to suffer, significant harm; or they may involve any other issues of public policy where public disclosure outweighs any duty of confidentiality to the parties.*

Privilege

Here again, two situations may be distinguished:

1.   *Where communications in mediation relate to children, there are two principles affecting the issue of privilege. On the one hand, a mediation privilege has been*

established by a line of cases relating to children's issues. On the other hand, that privilege will not ordinarily apply in relation to communications indicating that a child is suffering, or likely to suffer, significant harm.

2. *The mediation privilege afforded by the courts to children's issues has not yet been extended by the courts to other matters covered in the mediation. A general mediation privilege may exist or may become established, but this has not yet occurred in any reported case.*

Information furnished in mediation, material to financial issues, is treated as open, whereas information and communications relating to negotiations and attempts to reach a settlement are treated as privileged. This privilege should be asserted by requiring parties to deal with these matters on a 'without prejudice' basis; and it is also hoped that the mediation privilege established in children's cases will be confirmed by the courts as having been extended to other issues in mediation.

Even if privilege is established, there are some exceptions to the privileged nature of communications, as outlined in paragraph 7.6.

SECTION 8 – FAMILIES AND CHILDREN

8.1 Mediators shall have regard at all times to the provisions of Part I of the Family Law Act 1996.

8.2 In working with the parties, the mediator should also have regard to the needs and interests of the children of the family.

    8.2.1 When it appears to the mediator that a child is suffering, or is likely to suffer, significant harm, the mediator should consider with the parties what steps should be taken outside mediation to remedy the situation. But in exceptional circumstances where there is serious risk of harm to any person the mediator may decide not to inform the parties.

    8.2.2 Where it is necessary to protect the child from significant harm, the mediator must in any event contact an appropriate agency or take such steps outside the mediation as may be appropriate.

8.3 Occasionally children might be directly involved in mediation. The mediator should consider whether and when children may be directly involved in mediation. The mediator should not ordinarily invite children to be directly involved in the mediation unless specifically trained to do so, and alive to the issues such as confidentiality, and the dynamics inherent in doing so.

Commentary

Section 27(8) of the Family Law Act 1996 requires the mediator to have arrangements designed to ensure that the parties are encouraged to consider 'whether and to what extent each child could be given the opportunity to express his or her wishes and feelings in the mediation'.

The value of involving children directly in mediation has been widely discussed and debated, and this continues. Meanwhile the involvement of children directly in the mediation should only be undertaken with extreme caution and after careful consideration with parties as to the objectives of such involvement and the rules concerning confidentiality and other aspects. The needs, wishes and interests of children should generally be introduced and dealt with in the mediation through their parents.

It is important that any mediator considering involving children directly in mediation should undertake specific training covering these issues. Even then, the question remains as to the value of bringing children into the mediation room, and what children's perceptions and expectations might be of that. In consultation with mediation training providers, the Law Society's ADR Working Party is considering what constitutes appropriate training and what further guidance might be issued to assist mediators in this complex area. Such guidance will be published as soon as possible.

SECTION 9 – PROFESSIONAL INDEMNITY COVER

9.1   All solicitor mediators must carry professional indemnity cover in respect of their acting as mediators.

9.1.1   Solicitors who practise as mediators will be covered by the Solicitors' Indemnity Fund in respect of their acting as a mediator, provided they are doing so in their capacity as a member of their firm.

9.1.2   If a solicitor is acting as a mediator as a separate activity outside his or her legal practice, separate indemnity insurance must be obtained.

22

Commentary

Solicitors who mediate outside their practices as members of mediation organisations may be covered by block insurance provided by those organisations. If not, they must make their own arrangements for appropriate cover.

*A solicitor practising as a mediator outside his or her legal practice must have regard to rule 5 of the Solicitors' Practice Rules 1990 and to the Solicitors' Separate Business Code 1994 (see **3.20**, p.89 and Annex 3E, p.129 in the Guide). Further guidance can be obtained by contacting Professional Ethics (see p.xv for contact details).*

SECTION 10 – PROMOTION OF MEDIATION

10.1 Solicitor mediators may promote their practice as such, but must always do so in a professional, truthful and dignified way. They may reflect their qualification as a mediator and their membership of any other relevant mediation organisation.

10.2 Solicitor mediators must comply with the Law Society's Publicity Code (see Annex 11A, p.229 in the Guide).

SECTION 11 – FAMILY LAW ACT 1996, SECTION 27 (LEGAL AID ACT 1988, SECTION 13B)

Every mediator must have arrangements designed to ensure:

11.1 that parties participate in mediation only if willing and not influenced by fear of violence or other harm;

11.2 that cases where either party may be influenced by fear of violence or other harm are identified as soon as possible;

11.3 that the possibility of reconciliation is kept under review throughout mediation; and

11.4 that each party is informed about the availability of independent legal advice.

Commentary

This section should be read with section 6 and its commentary. As to keeping reconciliation under review, this may be inappropriate in many cases, but even in such cases, mediators should not ignore the possibility of reconciliation if it becomes appropriate.

April 1999

Chapter 23

Insolvency practice

23

23.01　Authorisation

To act as an insolvency practitioner within the meaning of the Insolvency Act 1986 a solicitor must, as an individual, be authorised by the Law Society unless he or she is directly authorised by the Department of Trade and Industry.

23.02　General requirements of conduct

Solicitor insolvency practitioners are bound by the practice rules, the Guide, the Insolvency Act 1986 and the rules and regulations made under it.

> See also Chapter 11 (p.222) on obtaining professional work and Chapter 15 (p.313) on conflicts of interest.

23.03　Independence

A solicitor insolvency practitioner may properly accept an appointment or act only if satisfied that his or her independence and objectivity will not be or appear to be compromised.

Before a solicitor insolvency practitioner (SIP) accepts or carries out the roles specified under **23.06** below, the SIP must not only be satisfied as to actual objectivity but must also be mindful of how his or her acceptance and conduct will be perceived by others.

23.04   Obtaining insolvency work

It is prohibited to pay or offer any commission, or furnish any valuable consideration, for the introduction of insolvency appointments.

Section 164 of the Insolvency Act 1986 (the Act) creates an offence of offering to a member or creditor of a company any valuable consideration with a view to securing nomination as a liquidator. See also paragraph 3 of the publicity code (Annex 11A at p.230) and section 2(3) of the introduction and referral code (Annex 11B at p.239).

23.05   Accepting appointments – conflict of interest

An SIP should not accept an appointment if to the SIP's knowledge this would result in a conflict of interest with clients of the firm unless acceptance is at the request of such clients or unless they are independently advised and consent.

The fact that the SIP or the firm acts for creditors of the insolvent is not in itself a conflict of interest unless there is likely to be a material dispute about the amount provable in the insolvency. If, having accepted appointment, a conflict is subsequently discovered, the SIP must instruct another firm of solicitors to act for him or her in relation to such conflict and ensure that the client with whom the conflict arises is independently advised. The SIP should resign his or her appointment on the ground of conflict of interest if actual personal knowledge prevents the SIP fulfilling the duties of office holder without breach of confidence. Imputed knowledge of other partners may be disregarded for this purpose in view of the public duties of an office holder to creditors.

23.06   Accepting appointments – professional independence

SIPs should consider their position before accepting appointments in the situations detailed below. In addition, where the SIP or his or her practice or a partner, consultant or senior employee of the practice has previously acted for an individual or company while solvent, the SIP should give careful consideration to the implications of acceptance of any insolvency role, and satisfy himself or herself that objectivity is unlikely to be compromised by a prospective conflict of interest or otherwise.

1.   Principle **23.06** would not prevent an SIP from accepting an appointment by the court, provided the court has been made aware of all the relevant circumstances.

2.   See also the statutory disqualification on acting as an insolvency practitioner in section 390 of the Act.

Material professional relationship

3.   A material professional relationship with a client arises where a practice or, subject to notes 21 and 22 below, a principal, director, consultant or senior employee of the practice, is carrying out, or has during the previous three years carried out, material professional work for that client. Material professional work would include the carrying out of one or more assignments, whether of a continuing nature or not, of such overall significance or in such circumstances that an SIP's objectivity in carrying out a subsequent insolvency appointment could be, or could reasonably be seen to be, prejudiced.

4.   A material professional relationship with a company or individual includes any material professional relationship with companies or entities controlled by that company or individual or under common control. A material professional relationship could also arise where a practice or person has carried out professional work for any director or shadow director of a company.

5.   Not all professional relationships are material professional relationships, particularly if they are with other members of the SIP's firm. SIPs should have regard to existing or previous relationships with firms with which they are, or have been, associated.

Personal relationships

6.   An SIP should have regard at all times to the requirement for independence and in particular rule 1 of the practice rules (see **1.01**, p.1) and should not accept an insolvency appointment in relation to an individual, firm or company where any personal connection with the individual, firm or company or with a director, former director or shadow director is such as to impair or reasonably appear to impair the SIP's objectivity. See also the definitions relating to persons 'connected' with a company in sections 249 and 435 of the Act.

7.   The Act and the Company Directors Disqualification Act 1986 impose specific statutory duties to report on the conduct of directors or shadow directors of an insolvent company.

Particular insolvency appointments

8. Where there has been a material professional relationship with a company which is now insolvent, an SIP should not accept appointment as liquidator, provisional liquidator, supervisor of a voluntary arrangement, administrator or administrative or other receiver. Where there has been a material professional relationship with an individual, an SIP should not accept appointment as supervisor of a voluntary arrangement or as trustee in bankruptcy, interim receiver and administrator of a bankrupt estate of a deceased person or as trustee under a deed registered under the Deeds of Arrangement Act 1914.

Appointment as liquidator

9. Where there has been a material professional relationship with a company which is solvent, an appointment as liquidator should not be accepted without consideration of the implications, and an SIP should satisfy himself or herself that the directors' declaration of solvency is likely to be substantiated.

Instruction by a creditor to investigate and report

10. A material professional relationship would not normally arise where the relationship is one which springs from the instruction of the practice by, or at the instigation of, a creditor or other party having an actual or potential financial interest in a company or business to investigate, monitor or advise on its affairs.

11. If the circumstances of the initial instruction of the practice are such as to prevent open discussion of the financial affairs of the company with the directors, an SIP and the other principals in the practice may be called upon to justify the propriety of any subsequent acceptance of an insolvency appointment.

Conversion of members' voluntary winding up into creditors' voluntary winding up

12. Where an SIP has accepted appointment as liquidator in a members' voluntary winding up but is obliged to summon a creditors' meeting under section 95 of the Act because it appears that the company will be unable to pay its debts in full within the period stated in the directors' declaration of solvency, the SIP's continuance as liquidator will depend on whether or not he or she believes that the company will eventually be able to pay its debts in full:

(a) If the company will not be able to pay its debts in full and the SIP has previously had a material professional relationship with the company, he or she should not accept nomination under the creditors' winding up.

(b) If the company will not be able to pay its debts in full but the SIP has had no such material professional relationship, he or she may accept nomination, subject to considering the implications (see **23.03**, p.439, **23.05**, p.440 and **23.06**).

(c) If the SIP believes that the company will eventually be able to pay its debts in full, he or she may accept nomination. However, if it should subsequently appear that this belief was mistaken, the SIP must then resign, but may accept re-appointment if he or she has had no previous material professional relationship with the company.

Insolvent liquidation following appointment as administrative or other receiver

13. Where an SIP or a principal, director, consultant or senior employee of the practice (subject to notes 21 and 22 below) is, or in the previous three years has been, administrative receiver of a company, or a receiver, under the Law of Property Act 1925 or otherwise, of any of its assets, the SIP should not accept appointment as liquidator in an insolvent liquidation, except where the previous appointment was made by the court. However, before a court-appointed receiver accepts subsequent appointment as liquidator, he or she should consider carefully whether his or her objectivity could be open to question. If so, the appointment should be refused.

Liquidation following appointment as supervisor of a voluntary arrangement or administrator

14. Where an SIP or a principal, director, consultant or senior employee of the practice, has been supervisor of a company's voluntary arrangement, the SIP may, if the considerations indicated in **23.03** (p.439), **23.05** (p.440) and **23.06** are satisfied, accept appointment as liquidator if so nominated by the creditors or appointed by the Secretary of State under section 137 of the Act. This applies also where an SIP was an administrator, but the SIP should not accept appointment without:

(a) the approval of a creditors' committee appointed under section 26 of the Act, or

(b) the approval of a meeting of creditors called either under the Act or informally, of which all known creditors have been given notice.

Bankruptcy following appointment as supervisor of individual voluntary arrangement

15. Where an SIP or a principal, director, consultant or senior employee of the practice, has been supervisor of a voluntary arrangement in relation to a debtor, the SIP may, provided the considerations indicated in **23.03** (p.439), **23.05** (p.440) and **23.06** are satisfied, accept appointment as trustee in bankruptcy of that debtor provided that the appointment is made by a general meeting of the creditors, by the court or by the Secretary of State under section 296 of the Act.

Administration following appointment as administrative receiver or other receiver

16. Where an SIP or a principal, director, consultant or senior employee of the practice (subject to notes 21 and 22 below) is, or in the previous three years has been, an administrative receiver or other receiver of a company or any of its assets, the SIP should not accept appointment as administrator of the company, unless the previous appointment was made by the court.

Supervision of a voluntary arrangement following appointment as administrative receiver

17. Where an SIP or a principal, director, consultant or senior employee of the practice (subject to notes 21 and 22 below) is, or in the previous three years has been, an administrative receiver of a company, the SIP should not accept appointment as supervisor of a voluntary arrangement in relation to that company.

Pension schemes of companies in liquidation, administration or receivership – appointment of 'independent trustee'

18. An SIP should not appoint a principal, director, consultant or senior employee of his or her practice, or any close connection of any of them or of the SIP, as 'independent trustee' of the pension scheme of a company of which he or she is the liquidator, administrator or administrative or other receiver. An SIP should be aware of the threat to objectivity if he or she were to engage in regular or reciprocal arrangements in relation to such appointments with another practice or organisation.

Group, associated and family-connected companies

19. Particular difficulties are likely to arise from the existence of inter-company transactions or guarantees in group, associated or 'family-connected'

company situations. Acceptance of an insolvency appointment in relation to more than one company in the group or association may raise issues of conflict of interest. Nevertheless, it may be impracticable for a series of different insolvency practitioners to act. An SIP should not accept multiple appointments in such situations unless he or she is satisfied that steps can be taken to minimise problems of conflict and that his or her overall integrity and objectivity are, and are seen to be, maintained.

Relationships between insolvent individuals and insolvent companies

20. Where an SIP or a principal, director, consultant or senior employee of the practice is acting as insolvency practitioner in relation to an individual, the SIP may be asked to accept an insolvency appointment in relation to a company of which the debtor is a major shareholder or creditor or where the company is a creditor of the debtor. If the SIP is to accept the new appointment, he or she must be able to show that the steps indicated in note 19 above can be taken; likewise the same applies if the company appointment precedes the individual appointment.

23

Transfer of principals and employees including practice merger

21. When practices merge, principals, directors, consultants and senior employees of the merged practice become subject to ethical constraints in relation to accepting new insolvency appointments to clients of either of the former practices. Existing appointments which are rendered in apparent breach of the guidance by such merger need not be determined automatically, provided that a review of the situation discloses no actual conflict or significant risk of a conflict, such as a potential need to sue a new colleague.

22. Where a principal, director, consultant or senior employee of a practice has, in any former practice, undertaken work on the affairs of a company or debtor in a capacity which is incompatible with an insolvency assignment of his or her new practice, he or she should not personally work or be employed on that assignment.

Relationship with a debenture holder

23. An SIP should, in general, decline to accept an insolvency appointment in relation to a company if the SIP or a principal, director, consultant or senior employee of the practice has a personal or close and distinct business connection with the debenture holder such as might impair or appear to impair the SIP's objectivity. A distinct connection of this kind would not normally be considered to exist between a solicitor and, for example, a clearing bank or major financial institution.

23.07   Gifts and acquisition of insolvents' assets

SIPs should decline any gift, benefit or favour which might influence or be seen by others as likely to influence them in the performance of their duties. In particular, SIPs holding any insolvency office must not themselves directly or indirectly acquire any assets of the insolvent or knowingly permit any principal, director, consultant or employee of their firm or any close relative of any of them directly or indirectly to do so.

> Where a contract for such an acquisition becomes known to the SIP, he or she should consider the propriety of accepting or continuing the appointment.

23.08   Legal services

SIPs may act as solicitors or instruct their own firms in relation to an insolvency, notwithstanding that they are office holders.

> However, under rules 4.128(3), 2.47(7) and 6.139(3) of the Insolvency Rules 1986 (S.I. 1986 no. 1925), SIPs and their firms will only be entitled to costs for the provision of legal services if such costs are authorised by the creditors or the court. An SIP should obtain appropriate authority from the creditors' committee or from the court for the SIP or the firm to undertake specific legal services and to be remunerated in accordance with the Solicitors' (Non-Contentious Business) Remuneration Order 1994 (see Annex 14D, p.296) or court order. Authority should be obtained before the services are rendered, except in an emergency where the services are clearly necessary and beneficial to creditors.

23.09   Solicitor creditors

If an SIP, or the SIP's firm, or a client of the firm, is a creditor of the person in relation to whom or which the SIP is an office holder, the SIP must not vote for or in relation to, or act as proxy for, or act as a solicitor in relation to, any such claim.

1. If the SIP is a sole office holder, the directions of the creditors' committee or the court must be sought in relation to such a claim.

2. If acting jointly, the other of the joint office holders must take all decisions regarding the claim; the SIP must not allow his or her firm to act in relation to such a claim in whatever capacity, but must instruct other advisers.

23.10   Joint appointments

An SIP who is invited to accept an insolvency appointment jointly with another practitioner should be guided by similar principles to those relating to insolvency appointments generally. Where an SIP is precluded from accepting an insolvency appointment as an individual, a joint appointment will not render the appointment acceptable.

An SIP may accept a joint appointment with a non-solicitor insolvency practitioner. They may receive a combined fee which may be apportioned between them. The solicitor could receive the joint fee in the first instance and then pass on the non-solicitor's fee without being in breach of practice rule 7 (see **3.03**, p.68).

23

Chapter 24

Wills, administration of estates, powers of attorney and mental capacity

---

24.01   Wills
24.02   Administration of estates
24.03   Powers of attorney
24.04   Mental capacity

Introductory note

The purpose of this chapter is to answer frequently asked questions posed by practitioners whose areas of work include wills, administration of estates, powers of attorney and mental capacity. It deals largely with best practice and does not seek to impose further conduct requirements on practitioners (i.e. over and above those detailed elsewhere in the Guide).

24.01   Wills

1. **Can I draft a will for the customer of a will-writing company?**

   Yes, but the introduction and referral code (see Annex 11B, p.238) will apply and the testator, not the introducer, will be the client. See also **11.07**, p.227 on freedom of choice of solicitor, **12.05**, p.246, on third party instructions and **12.06**, p.246, on who is my client?

2. **Can I draft a will on the basis of the testator's written instructions alone?**

   Yes, but you must consider carefully whether this is safe, bearing in mind the inherent dangers, e.g. lack of sufficient information, the difficulties in fully advising the client and ensuring capacity, and the possibility of fraud and undue influence.

3. **Can an unqualified member of staff be appointed executor?**

Yes, but in view of the principals' duty of supervision and their *prima facie* responsibility for the acts or omissions of staff, it may be appropriate to require unqualified staff to obtain the principals' consent to such an appointment and to deal with estate money through the firm's client account.

4. **Am I obliged to trace a former client who must be presumed to have died but whose will I am still holding?**

There is no obligation beyond writing to the client's last known address, but the will should not be destroyed. See Annex 12A, p.253.

5. **What considerations apply when drafting a will which benefits me, my family or a member of my firm?**

See **15.05**, p.318.

24.02   Administration of estates

1. **Who is my client?**

The personal representatives, but subject to their consent, you should nevertheless answer reasonable enquiries from beneficiaries reasonably promptly. Undue delay could lead to the finding of an inadequate professional service. Where a solicitor is a sole executor and is thus the client, the solicitor should when appropriate keep the beneficiaries informed about the progress of the matter and, as a matter of good practice, the solicitor/executor may wish to discuss costs with the beneficiaries.

2. **Can a beneficiary require me to obtain a remuneration certificate?**

Yes, but only in limited circumstances. See the Solicitors' (Non-Contentious Business) Remuneration Order 1994 (Annex 14D, p.296). Even where the beneficiary is not entitled to a remuneration certificate, if there is a dispute about costs, the solicitor may agree to obtaining a certificate, to prevent the beneficiary making a complaint to the Office for the Supervision of Solicitors.

3. **To whom do I owe the duty of confidentiality following the death of my client?**

Confidentiality passes to the personal representatives and can only be waived by them, but note that an administrator's power dates only from the issue of the grant of letters of administration.

4. **If requested, must I hand the deceased's files to the personal representatives?**

Yes, since they form part of the estate, but see Annex 12A, p.253 as regards ownership of documents. Bear in mind that where the deceased was

24

intestate, the administrator derives his or her powers from the grant of letters of administration. An executor's powers derive from the will, the grant of probate confirms the executor's authority as personal representative.

5. **Am I obliged to provide a copy of my file to a beneficiary where I and/or a member of my firm are the only personal representatives?**

No. However, it may be advisable to give copies of documents to the beneficiary to avoid a complaint being made to the Office for the Supervision of Solicitors.

6. **I drew up a will which is now in dispute. Can I disclose information concerning the making of the will other than to the personal representatives?**

Yes. To avoid unnecessary litigation, you should make a statement available concerning its execution to any person who is a party to probate proceedings or whom you believe has a reasonable claim under the will. If you are acting in the administration, you may need to consider the question of conflict.

7. **What if my clients' instructions will breach their duties as personal representatives?**

You are acting in the best interests of the estate as represented by the personal representatives. You should explain to them what their duties are at law and if the conflict is between their duty as personal representatives and their personal interests (e.g. as beneficiaries), the clients should be advised to seek independent advice as to their personal position. If the clients will not change their instructions, you must cease to act.

8. **What if the personal representatives cannot agree?**

You will need to explain to the personal representatives what their duties are at law and that it is incumbent upon them to agree upon their instructions. If there is a conflict between a personal representative's duty and his or her personal interests, he or she should be advised to seek independent advice as to his or her personal position. If agreement still cannot be reached, an application can be made to the court for directions. For the position regarding costs, see also *The Probate Practitioner's Handbook* (available from Marston Book Services, for contact details see p.xv).

9. **Must I comply with a request from the beneficiaries to renounce probate?**

No. You are however free to do so, although you should consider whether that would be in the best interests of the estate. No charge can be made for renouncing, although a charge can be made for work undertaken in doing so.

10. **Can I act as executor after I have retired?**

Yes, but bear in mind the restrictions imposed by sections 20–22 and 23–24 of the Solicitors Act 1974 (see Annex 2A at p.45). For more detailed guidance, see Annex 3G, p.136.

11. **Can I employ a firm of genealogists to trace a missing beneficiary?**

Yes, but genealogists usually charge a percentage of the beneficiary's entitlement, so you should first consider the size of the estate and the amount of the likely payment.

12. **Can I accept instructions from one or more personal representatives where another firm is already acting in the administration?**

Yes. It may be proper for more than one firm to be instructed, e.g. because of the complexity or the size of the estate, but normally it is incumbent upon the personal representatives jointly to agree upon the instruction of solicitors. If one of the personal representatives consults you because of animosity between the personal representatives or a personal conflict, it is likely that he or she personally will have to pay your costs and you should advise him or her of this. See *The Probate Practitioner's Handbook*.

13. **Can I be liable for my client's fraud or improper administration?**

Possibly. See Chapter 6 of *The Probate Practitioner's Handbook* for assistance, but bear in mind this is a rapidly changing area.

24

24.03   Powers of attorney

1. **Who is my client?**

Prima facie the donor, but there can be exceptions to this. If the donee requires advice on his or her personal position as donee, the solicitor will need to consider whether there is a conflict of interest. See Chapter 15, p.313. On authority to solicitors to act for patients or donors, see the Practice Direction of 9th August 1995 ([1995] *Gazette*, 11 October, 21), issued by the Master of the Court of Protection.

2. **Can I accept instructions from a donee to prepare a power of attorney?**

Yes, but you must take appropriate steps not only to confirm those instructions with the donor, as the donor is the client, but also to ensure that the donor has the necessary capacity. See **24.04** note 1, p.453 and **12.06**, p.246 on who is my client?

3. **Where does my duty of confidentiality lie?**

There is no confidentiality as between the donee and the donor (save as set out in question 4) since the donee is the donor's agent. Thus, the solicitor can at any stage, and should in cases of doubt, seek confirmation of instructions direct from the donor.

4. **Should I disclose the donor's will to the donee at the donee's request?**

    The answer to this question depends on the circumstances surrounding the request and some of the scenarios that can arise are set out below:

    (a) **Where the donor retains capacity and the power is unregistered:**

    In this case the donor's instructions must always be sought. This is because the donor's will is confidential to the donor and it cannot be disclosed to anyone without the donor's consent – see **16.01**, p.324.

    (b) **Where the power is registered and the solicitor is acting for the donor the position is as follows:**

    (i) If the donor retains testamentary capacity (different levels of capacity are required for different activities) then the donor's instructions must be sought.

    (ii) If the donor lacks testamentary capacity, solicitors are advised to seek advice from the Public Trust Office (see p.xv for contact details). The solicitor should indicate whether or not disclosure is in the best interests of the donor.

    (c) **Where the power is registered, but the solicitor holding the will is not currently acting for the donor:**

    If the donor retains testamentary capacity, the solicitor must ask the donee to obtain the donor's consent, or may wish to consider obtaining advice from the Public Trust Office.

    Although it may be in the donor's interests for there to be disclosure, in order to avoid the possibility of the donee acting against the donor's wishes in dealing with his or her property and affairs, there may be circumstances where it would not be in the donor's interests for disclosure to take place. When drafting an enduring power of attorney (EPA) it is advisable to take specific instructions about disclosure. If an EPA is a general one, without specific restriction, it is arguable that there is sufficient authority for the donee to have access to the will. Advice may be sought from Professional Ethics (for contact details see p.xv).

5. **Where I am appointed as attorney, are there any restrictions on how I act?**

    Yes. See **15.04** note 11, p.318.

6. **Do the Solicitors' Accounts Rules apply where I am the attorney?**

    Yes. For further information, see rule 11 and rule 13 notes (i) and (ix) of the Solicitors' Accounts Rules 1998 (Annex 28B at pp.693, 695 and 696).

7. **Can an unqualified member of staff be appointed as attorney?**

    Yes, but the same considerations will apply as in **24.01** note 3, p.449.

24.04 Mental capacity

1. **I am uncertain that my client has mental capacity. Can I act?**

   A solicitor cannot be retained by a client incapable of giving instructions. However, there is a legal presumption of capacity – and bear in mind that different levels of capacity are required for different activities. If in doubt, consider seeking an opinion from the client's doctor (with the client's consent), having first explained the relevant test of capacity. However, you should also make your own assessment and not rely solely upon the doctor's assessment. See also *Assessment of Mental Capacity – Guidance for Doctors and Lawyers* (available from Marston Book Services, for contact details see p.xv) and *Incapacitated Clients* by Phil Fennel, [1993] *Gazette*, 21 April, 27.

2. **What do I do if my client loses capacity in the course of the retainer?**

   The retainer will be determined by operation of law. However, you should contact, e.g. relatives, the Public Trust Office or the Official Solicitor, so that the relatives or the relevant agency can take reasonable steps to protect the client's interests (see p.xv for contact details).

3. **I am acting under instructions from the donee of an enduring power of attorney. Is my retainer terminated upon the donor becoming incapacitated?**

   No, but you would need to be satisfied that the power is then registered.

24

Chapter 25

Conveyancing

25.01 Practice rule 6 (avoiding conflicts of interest in conveyancing, property selling and mortgage related services)

(1) (General)

This rule sets out circumstances in which a solicitor may act for more than one party in conveyancing, property selling or mortgage related services, in connection with:

(i) the transfer of land for value at arm's length;

(ii) the grant or assignment of a lease, or some other interest in land, for value at arm's length; or

(iii) the grant of a mortgage of land.

The rule must be read in the light of the notes.

Notes

(i) "Solicitor" (except where the notes specify otherwise) means a solicitor, his or her practice, and any associated practice, and includes a SEAL; and

▶ *"associated practices" are practices with at least one principal in common;*

▶ *a "principal" is a sole practitioner, a partner in a practice (including a registered foreign lawyer partner), a director of a recognised body, a member of or beneficial owner of a share in a recognised body, or a recognised body; and*

▶ *a "SEAL" (Solicitors' Estate Agency Limited) means a recognised body which:*

(a) does not undertake conveyancing;

(b) is owned jointly by at least four participating practices which do not have any principals in common and none of which own a controlling majority of the shares; and

(c) is conducted from accommodation physically divided from, and clearly differentiated from that of any participating practice; and

a "participating practice" means a practice one or more of whose principals is a member of, or a beneficial owner of a share in, the SEAL.

(ii) "Property selling" means negotiating the sale for the seller.

(iii) "Mortgage related services" means advising on or arranging a mortgage, or providing mortgage related financial services, for a buyer; and

▶ *"seller" and "buyer" include lessor and lessee.*

(iv) Whether a transaction is "at arm's length" will depend on the relationship between the parties and the context of the transaction, and will not necessarily follow from the fact that a transaction is at market value, or is stated to be on arm's length terms.

A transaction would not usually be at arm's length, for example, if the parties are:

▶ *related by blood, adoption or marriage;*

▶ *the settlor of a trust and the trustees;*

▶ *the trustees of a trust and its beneficiary or the beneficiary's relative;*

▶ *personal representatives and a beneficiary;*

▶ *the trustees of separate trusts for the same family;*

▶ *a sole trader or partners and a limited company set up to enable the business to be incorporated;*

▶ *associated companies (i.e. where one is a holding company and the other is its subsidiary within the meaning of the Companies Act 1985, or both are subsidiaries of the same holding company); or*

▶ *a local authority and a related body within the meaning of paragraph 6(b) of the Employed Solicitors Code 1990.*

(v) "Mortgage" includes a remortgage.

(vi) Nothing in the rule allows a solicitor to act in breach of Rule 6A(5) (acting for seller and one of two prospective buyers), or any other rule or principle of professional conduct.

(2) (Solicitor acting for seller and buyer)

(a) A solicitor must not act for seller and buyer:

(i) without the written consent of both parties;

(ii) if a conflict of interest exists or arises; or

(iii) if the seller is selling or leasing as a builder or developer.

(b) Otherwise, a solicitor may act for seller and buyer, but only if:

(i) both parties are established clients; or

(ii) the consideration is £10,000 or less and the transaction is not the grant of a lease; or

(iii) there is no other qualified conveyancer in the area whom either the seller or the buyer could reasonably be expected to consult; or

      (iv) **seller and buyer are represented by two separate offices in different localities, and:**

          (A) **different solicitors, who normally work at each office, conduct or supervise the transaction for seller and buyer; and**

          (B) **no office of the practice (or an associated practice) referred either client to the office conducting his or her transaction; or**

      (v) **the only way in which the solicitor is acting for the buyer is in providing mortgage related services; or**

      (vi) **the only way in which the solicitor is acting for the seller is in providing property selling services through a SEAL.**

  (c) **When a solicitor's practice (including a SEAL) acts in the property selling for the seller and acts for the buyer, the following additional conditions must be met:**

      (i) **different persons must conduct the work for the seller and the work for the buyer; and if the persons conducting the work need supervision, they must be supervised by different solicitors; and**

      (ii) **the solicitor must inform the seller in writing, before accepting instructions to deal with the property selling, of any services which might be offered to a buyer, whether through the same practice or any practice associated with it; and**

      (iii) **the solicitor must explain to the buyer, before the buyer gives consent to the arrangement:**

          (A) **the implications of a conflict of interest arising; and**

          (B) **the solicitor's financial interest in the sale going through; and**

          (C) **if the solicitor proposes to provide mortgage related services to the buyer through a SEAL which is also acting for the seller, that the solicitor cannot advise the buyer on the merits of the purchase.**

25

Notes

(i) *If a builder or developer acquires a property in part exchange, and sells it on without development, he or she is not, for the purpose of this rule, selling "as a builder or developer".*

(ii) *The test of whether a person is an "established client" is an objective one; that is, whether a reasonable solicitor would regard the person as an established client.*

    ▶ *A seller or buyer who is instructing the solicitor for the first time is not an established client.*

▶ *A person related by blood, adoption or marriage to an established client counts as an established client.*

▶ *A person counts as an established client if selling or buying jointly with an established client.*

(iii) *The consideration will only count as £10,000 or less if the value of any property given in exchange or part exchange is taken into account.*

(iv) *Even where none of the other exceptions apply, a SEAL may act for the seller, and provide mortgage related services to the buyer; one of the participating practices may do the buyer's conveyancing, and another participating practice may do the seller's conveyancing.*

(v) *"Solicitor"*

▶ *in paragraph (2)(b)(iv)(A), means any individual solicitor conducting or supervising the matter; and*

▶ *in paragraph (2)(c)(i), means the individual solicitor supervising the transaction.*

(3) (Solicitor acting for lender and borrower)

[Note: Paragraph 3 of rule 6 comes into force on 1st October 1999. For the version of rule 6(3) which is in force prior to 1st October 1999, see Professional Standards Bulletin No. 18.]

(a) **A solicitor must not act for both lender and borrower on the grant of a mortgage of land:**

   (i) **if a conflict of interest exists or arises;**

   (ii) **on the grant of a private mortgage of land at arm's length;**

   (iii) **if, in the case of an institutional mortgage of property to be used as a private residence only, the lender's mortgage instructions extend beyond the limitations contained in paragraphs (3)(c) and (3)(e), or do not permit the use of the certificate of title required by paragraph (3)(d); or**

   (iv) **if, in the case of any other institutional mortgage, the lender's mortgage instructions extend beyond the limitations contained in paragraphs (3)(c) and (3)(e).**

(b) **A solicitor who proposes to act for both lender and borrower on the grant of an institutional mortgage of land, must first inform the lender in writing of the circumstances if:**

   (i) **the solicitor or a member of his or her immediate family is a borrower; or**

   (ii) **the solicitor proposes to act for seller, buyer and lender in the same transaction.**

(c) **A solicitor acting for both lender and borrower in an institutional mortgage may only accept or act upon instructions from the lender which are limited to the following matters:**

(i)   taking reasonable steps to check the identity of the borrower (and anyone else required to sign the mortgage deed or other document connected with the mortgage) by reference to a document or documents, such as a passport, precisely specified in writing by the lender;

following the guidance in the Law Society's "green card" warning on property fraud and "blue card" warning on money laundering;

checking that the seller's solicitors or licensed conveyancers (if unknown to the solicitor) appear in a current legal directory or hold practising certificates issued by their professional body;

and, in the case of a lender with no branch office within reasonable proximity of the borrower, carrying out the money laundering checks precisely specified in writing by the lender;

(ii)   making appropriate searches relating to the property in public registers (for example, local searches, commons registration searches, mining searches), and reporting any results specified by the lender or which the solicitor considers may adversely affect the lender; or effecting search insurance;

(iii)   making enquiries on legal matters relating to the property reasonably specified by the lender, and reporting the replies;

(iv)   reporting the purchase price stated in the transfer and on how the borrower says that the purchase money (other than the mortgage advance) is to be provided; and reporting if the solicitor will not have control over the payment of all the purchase money (other than a deposit paid to an estate agent or a reservation fee paid to a builder or developer);

(v)   reporting if the seller or the borrower (if the property is already owned by the borrower) has not owned or been the registered owner of the property for at least six months;

(vi)   if the lender does not arrange insurance, confirming receipt of satisfactory evidence that the buildings insurance is in place for at least the sum required by the lender and covers the risks specified by the lender; giving notice to the insurer of the lender's interest and requesting confirmation that the insurer will notify the lender if the policy is not renewed or is cancelled; and supplying particulars of the insurance and the last premium receipt to the lender;

(vii)   investigating title to the property and appurtenant rights; reporting any defects revealed, advising on the need for any consequential statutory declarations or indemnity insurance, and approving and effecting indemnity cover if

25

required by the lender; and reporting if the solicitor is aware of any rights needed for the use or enjoyment of the property over other land;

(viii)   reporting on any financial charges (for example, improvement or repair grants or Housing Act discounts) secured on the property revealed by the solicitor's searches and enquiries which will affect the property after completion of the mortgage;

(ix)   in the case of a leasehold property, confirming that the lease contains the terms stipulated by the lender and does not include any terms specified by the lender as unacceptable; obtaining a suitable deed of variation or indemnity insurance if the terms of the lease are unsatisfactory; enquiring of the seller or the borrower (if the property is already owned by the borrower) as to any known breaches of covenant by the landlord or any superior landlord and reporting any such breaches to the lender; reporting if the solicitor becomes aware of the landlord's absence or insolvency; making a company search and checking the last three years' published accounts of any management company with responsibilities under the lease; if the borrower is required to be a shareholder in the management company, obtaining the share certificate, a blank stock transfer form signed by the borrower and a copy of the memorandum and articles of association; obtaining any necessary consent to or prior approval of the assignment and mortgage; obtaining a clear receipt for the last payment of rent and service charge; and serving notice of the assignment and mortgage on the landlord;

(x)   if the property is subject to a letting, checking that the type of letting and its terms comply with the lender's requirements;

(xi)   making appropriate pre-completion searches, including a bankruptcy search against the borrower, any other person in whom the legal estate is invested and any guarantor;

(xii)   receiving, releasing and transmitting the mortgage advance, including asking for any final inspection needed and dealing with any retentions and cashbacks;

(xiii)   procuring execution of the mortgage deed and form of guarantee as appropriate by the persons whose identities have been checked in accordance with any requirements of the lender under paragraph (3)(c)(i) as those of the borrower, any other person in whom the legal estate is vested and any guarantor; obtaining their signatures to the forms of undertaking required by the lender in relation to the use, occupation or physical state of the property; and complying with the lender's requirements if any document is to be executed under a power of attorney;

(xiv) asking the borrower for confirmation that the information about occupants given in the mortgage instructions or offer is correct; obtaining consents in the form required by the lender from existing or prospective occupiers of the property aged 17 or over specified by the lender, or of whom the solicitor is aware;

(xv) advising the borrower on the terms of any document required by the lender to be signed by the borrower;

(xvi) advising any other person required to sign any document on the terms of that document or, if there is a conflict of interest between that person and the borrower or the lender, advising that person on the need for separate legal advice and arranging for him or her to see an independent conveyancer;

(xvii) obtaining the legal transfer of the property to the mortgagor;

(xviii) procuring the redemption of (A) existing mortgages on property the subject of any associated sale of which the solicitor is aware, and (B) any other mortgages secured against a property located in England or Wales made by an identified lender where an identified account number or numbers or a property address has been given by the lender;

(xix) ensuring the redemption or postponement of existing mortgages on the property, and registering the mortgage with the priority required by the lender;

(xx) making administrative arrangements in relation to any collateral security, such as an endowment policy, or in relation to any collateral warranty or guarantee relating to the physical condition of the property, such as NHBC documentation;

(xxi) registering the transfer and mortgage;

(xxii) giving legal advice on any matters reported on under this paragraph (3)(c), suggesting courses of action open to the lender, and complying with the lender's instructions on the action to be taken;

(xxiii) disclosing any relationship specified by the lender between the solicitor and borrower;

(xxiv) storing safely the title deeds and documents pending registration and delivery to or as directed by the lender;

(xxv) retaining the information contained in the solicitor's conveyancing file for at least six years from the date of the mortgage.

25

(d) **In addition, a solicitor acting for both lender and borrower in an institutional mortgage of property to be used as a private residence only:**

(i) **must use the certificate of title set out in the Appendix, or as substituted from time to time by the Council with the concurrence of the Master of the Rolls ("the approved certificate"); and**

(ii) **unless the lender has certified that its mortgage instructions are subject to the limitations contained in paragraphs (3)(c) and (3)(e), must notify the lender on receipt of instructions that the approved certificate will be used, and that the solicitor's duties to the lender are limited to the matters contained in the approved certificate.**

(See also note (iii) below.)

(e) **The terms of this rule will prevail in the event of any ambiguity in the lender's instructions, or discrepancy between the instructions and paragraph (3)(c) or the approved certificate.**

Anti-avoidance

(f) **A solicitor who is acting only for the borrower in an institutional mortgage of property must not accept or act upon any requirements by way of undertaking, warranty, guarantee or otherwise of the lender, the lender's solicitor or other agent which extend beyond the limitations contained in paragraph (3)(c).**

Notes

(i) *An "institutional mortgage" is a mortgage on standard terms, provided by an institutional lender in the normal course of its activities; and*

   ▶ *a "private mortgage" is any other mortgage.*

(ii) *A solicitor will not be in breach of paragraphs (3)(a)(iii)–(iv) or (c) if the lender has certified that its mortgage instructions and documents sent pursuant to those instructions are subject to the limitations set out in paragraphs (3)(c) and (e), and certifies any subsequent instructions and documents in the same way. If there is no certification, a solicitor acting in an exclusively residential transaction must notify the lender that the approved certificate of title will be used and that the solicitor's duties to the lender will be limited accordingly (see paragraph (3)(d)(ii)). In other types of transaction, the solicitor should draw the lender's attention to the provisions of paragraphs (3)(c) and (e) and state that he or she cannot act on any instructions which extend beyond the matters contained in paragraph (3)(c).*

(iii) *As an alternative to printing the approved certificate for each transaction, it is acceptable for a lender to use a short form certificate of title which incorporates the approved certificate by reference. The form must include in the following order:*

▶ *the title "Certificate of Title";*

▶ *the contents of the details box in the order set out in the approved certificate (use of two columns is acceptable) but with details not required shaded out or stated not to be required; and*

▶ *the wording "We, the conveyancers named above, give the Certificate of Title set out in the Appendix to Rule 6(3) of the Solicitors' Practice Rules 1990 as if the same were set out in full, subject to the limitations contained in it."*

Administrative details, such as a request for cheque, may follow the Certificate of Title.

(iv) *The approved certificate of title is only required for a transaction where the property is to be used as a private residence by the owner. The certificate need not, therefore, be used for "buy to let mortgages" on properties which are not intended for owner-occupation.*

(v) *"Solicitor" in paragraph (3)(b)(i) means any principal in the practice (or an associated practice), and any solicitor conducting or supervising the transaction, whether or not that solicitor is a principal; and*

▶ *"immediate family" means spouse, children, parents, brothers and sisters.*

"Solicitor" in sub-paragraphs (i)–(xxv) of paragraph (3)(c) means the practice instructed and any solicitor conducting or supervising the transaction.

(vi) *The lender must be informed of the circumstances, in accordance with paragraph (3)(b) so that the lender can decide whether or not to instruct the solicitor.*

(vii) *A lender's instructions (see paragraph (3)(c)(xxiii)) may require a wider disclosure of a solicitor's circumstances than paragraph (3)(b) requires; and a solicitor must assess whether the circumstances give rise to a conflict. For example, there will be a conflict between lender and borrower if the solicitor becomes involved in negotiations relating to the terms of the loan. A conflict might arise from the relationship a solicitor has with the borrower – for example, if the solicitor is the borrower's creditor or debtor or the borrower's business associate or co-habitant.*

25

APPENDIX

CERTIFICATE OF TITLE

Details Box

TO: (Lender)
Lender's Reference or Account No:
The Borrower:
Property:
Title Number:
Mortgage Advance:
Price stated in transfer:
Completion Date:
Conveyancer's Name & Address:
Conveyancer's Reference:
Conveyancer's bank, sort code and account number:
Date of instructions:

WE THE CONVEYANCERS NAMED ABOVE CERTIFY as follows:

(1) If so instructed, we have checked the identity of the Borrower (and anyone else required to sign the mortgage deed or other document connected with the mortgage) by reference to the document or documents precisely specified in writing by you.

(2) Except as otherwise disclosed to you in writing:

  (i) we have investigated the title to the Property, we are not aware of any other financial charges secured on the Property which will affect the Property after completion of the mortgage and, upon completion of the mortgage, both you and the mortgagor (whose identity has been checked in accordance with paragraph (1) above) will have a good and marketable title to the Property and to appurtenant rights free from prior mortgages or charges and from onerous encumbrances which title will be registered with absolute title;

  (ii) we have compared the extent of the Property shown on any plan provided by you against relevant plans in the title deeds and/or the description of the Property in any valuation which you have supplied to us, and in our opinion there are no material discrepancies;

  (iii) the assumptions stated by the valuer about the title (its tenure, easements, boundaries and restrictions on use) in any valuation which you have supplied to us are correct;

(iv) if the Property is leasehold the terms of the lease accord with your instructions, including any requirements you have for covenants by the Landlord and/or a management company and/or by a deed of mutual covenant for the insurance, repair and maintenance of the structure, exterior and common parts of any building of which the Property forms part, and we have or will obtain on or before completion a clear receipt for the last payment of rent and service charge;

(v) we have received satisfactory evidence that the buildings insurance is in place, or will be on completion, for the sum and in the terms required by you;

(vi) if the Property is to be purchased by the Borrower:

    (a) the contract for sale provides for vacant possession on completion;

    (b) the seller has owned or been the registered owner of the Property for not less than six months;

    (c) we are not acting on behalf of the seller;

(vii) we are in possession of: (A) either a local search or local search insurance and (B) such other searches or search insurance as are appropriate to the Property, the mortgagor and any guarantor, in each case in accordance with your instructions;

(viii) nothing has been revealed by our searches and enquiries which would prevent the Property being used by any occupant for residential purposes;

(ix) neither any principal nor any other solicitor in the practice giving this certificate nor any spouse, child, parent, brother or sister of such a person is interested in the Property (whether alone or jointly with any other) as mortgagor.

WE :

(a) undertake, prior to use of the mortgage advance, to obtain in the form required by you the execution of a mortgage and a guarantee as appropriate by the persons whose identities have been checked in accordance with paragraph (1) above as those of the Borrower, any other person in whom the legal estate is vested and any guarantor; and, if required by you:

    to obtain their signatures to the forms of undertaking required by you in relation to the use, occupation or physical state of the Property;

    to ask the Borrower for confirmation that the information about occupants given in your mortgage instructions or offer is correct; and

    to obtain consents in the form required by you from any existing or prospective occupier(s) aged 17 or over of the Property specified by you or of whom we are aware;

25

(b) have made or will make such Bankruptcy, Land Registry or Land Charges Searches as may be necessary to justify certificate no. (2)(i) above;

(c) will within the period of protection afforded by the searches referred to in paragraph (b) above:

(i) complete the mortgage;

(ii) arrange for stamping of the transfer if appropriate;

(iii) deliver to the Land Registry the documents necessary to register the mortgage in your favour and any relevant prior dealings;

(iv) effect any other registrations necessary to protect your interests as mortgagee;

(d) will despatch to you such deeds and documents relating to the Property as you require with a list of them in the form prescribed by you within ten working days of receipt by us of the Charge Certificate from the Land Registry;

(e) will not part with the mortgage advance (and will return it to you if required) if it shall come to our notice prior to completion that the Property will at completion be occupied in whole or in part otherwise than in accordance with your instructions;

(f) will not accept instructions, except with your consent in writing, to prepare any lease or tenancy agreement relating to the Property or any part of it prior to despatch of the Charge Certificate to you;

(g) will not use the mortgage advance until satisfied that, prior to or contemporaneously with the transfer of the Property to the mortgagor, there will be discharged (A) any existing mortgage on property the subject of an associated sale of which we are aware and (B) any other mortgages made by a lender identified by you secured against a property located in England or Wales where you have given either an account number or numbers or a property address;

(h) will notify you in writing if any matter comes to our attention before completion which would render the certificate given above untrue or inaccurate and, in those circumstances, will defer completion pending your authority to proceed and will return the mortgage advance to you if required;

(i) we confirm that we have complied, or will comply, with your instructions in all other respects to the extent that they do not extend beyond the limitations contained in paragraph (3)(c) of rule 6 of the Solicitors' Practice Rules 1990.

OUR duties to you are limited to the matters set out in this certificate and we accept no further liability or responsibility whatsoever. The payment by you to us (by whatever means) of the mortgage advance or any part of it

constitutes acceptance of this limitation and any assignment to you by the Borrower of any rights of action against us to which the Borrower may be entitled shall take effect subject to this limitation.

Signature Box

SIGNED on behalf of THE CONVEYANCERS	....
NAME of Authorised Signatory	....
QUALIFICATION of Authorised Signatory	....
DATE of Signature	....

Solicitors' Practice Rules 1990, rule 6

25.02   Avoiding conflicts – additional guidance

1.   Even in cases which fall within practice rule 6(2) (see p.456), a solicitor must not act for both the seller and a buyer where the seller is dealing with two or more prospective buyers (see practice rule 6A(5), p.472).

2.   A solicitor must not accept instructions to act for the buyer, where the seller is a builder who has stipulated that either the builder's or another solicitor must act for the buyer. This applies even if the buyer has been offered free conveyancing. To accept instructions in these circumstances would be a breach of practice rule 1 (see **1.01**, p.1) and, where the solicitor is acting for both parties, also a breach of practice rule 6 (a solicitor must not act for both parties where the seller is a builder or developer selling as such). Likewise, a solicitor must not act for the borrower where the mortgage offer is conditional on the solicitor acting for the borrower (see **11.07**, p.227).

3.   A solicitor might be instructed only by a lender or receive instructions from a lender on behalf of both lender and borrower. Where the solicitor is acting only for the lender he or she should ensure that no retainer arises by implication with the borrower. Practice rule 6 does not, in the absence of a conflict of interest, prohibit solicitors from acting for lender and borrower in an institutional mortgage, but see notes 6–9 below on the new requirements of rule 6(3).

25

4.   A conflict may arise through the unsuitability of a lender's mortgage package or scheme, when the general duty of a solicitor may require him or her to try to ensure that the borrower obtains independent financial advice. Much will depend on the level of sophistication, the vulnerability and the general understanding of the client as well as the complexity of the scheme. Where a solicitor's duties require him or her to advise a borrower client of the dangers of a lender's scheme, there would be a conflict of interest preventing the solicitor accepting instructions from the lender until that duty was discharged.

5.   A number of changes have been made to practice rule 6 in relation to the property selling provisions of rule 6(2). The Council issued the following statement on 5th March 1998:

> 'On 13th October 1997, as an interim measure to deregulate joint property selling practices, the 1996 version of rule 6 of the Solicitors' Practice Rules 1990 (avoiding conflicts of interest in conveyancing) was repealed, and replaced by a new rule 6 (avoiding conflicts of interest in conveyancing, property selling and mortgage related services).

> On 16th January 1998, as part of the general deregulation of property selling practices, this 1997 version of the rule was in turn repealed, and replaced by a new version under the same title.

> All existing waivers of these repealed versions of rule 6 granted during the period 1st June 1996 to 15th January 1998 are hereby extended, as waivers of the 1998 version of rule 6, until the earlier of:

> ► any expiry date in the existing waiver; or

> ► 31st March 2000.'

6.   The latest version of practice rule 6 was made on 29th April 1999. It made changes to rule 6(3), p.458, in an attempt to reduce the risk of conflict when a solicitor is acting for both the lender and the borrower in an institutional mortgage. These changes come into effect on 1st October 1999.

7.   The new rule 6(3) imposes two additional safeguards to reduce the risk of a conflict of interests arising:

   ► the lender's instructions must not extend beyond the limitations contained in paragraphs (c) and (e) (at p.458 and p.462). This applies to all types of transaction: residential, commercial or mixed;

   ► paragraph (d) (at p.462) requires the use of the approved certificate of title, set out in the appendix to rule 6(3) (at p.464), for exclusively residential transactions.

8.   It is envisaged that lenders will certify that their mortgage instructions do not extend beyond the limitations set out in rule 6(3) and, if that is the case, the solicitor need take no further action (see note (ii) to rule 6(3) at p.462).

If the instructions are not so certified, the combined effect of paragraph (d) and note (ii) to rule 6(3) requires the solicitor to take the following steps:

▶ in a residential transaction, notify the lender on receipt of instructions that the approved certificate of title will be used, and that the solicitor's duties to the lender are limited to the matters contained in the approved certificate;

▶ for other types of transaction, notify the lender that the solicitor cannot act on any instructions which extend beyond the matters contained in rule 6(3).

9. Paragraph (f) of rule 6(3) is an anti-avoidance provision. Its effect is that a solicitor who is acting for the borrower only must decline to accept, or act upon, any requirements of the lender's solicitor which extend beyond the matters contained in rule 6(3).

10. For the ownership of conveyancing documents, see **16.02** note 9 (p.326) and Annex 16C (p.341).

25.03   Conflict – solicitor providing bridging loan

A solicitor must not act where his or her own interests conflict with the interests of a client.

1. There is a conflict of interest where a solicitor in his or her personal capacity sells to, or buys from, or lends to or borrows from a client (see **15.04**, p.316).

2. A solicitor may wish to provide bridging finance to a client to cover a shortfall on completion. The solicitor should first consider whether the basis upon which the loan is to be made raises professional obligations to the client. Generally, where the solicitor stands to make no personal gain and where the terms of the facility are not unusually onerous, the client will not need to be separately represented in relation to the terms of the loan.

3. Independent advice may be required in other circumstances. For example, the solicitor who charges a commercial rate for the loan may stand to make a personal gain if the rate charged to the client is greater than the rate which the money would otherwise earn.

4. A solicitor may seek to secure the bridging loan by taking an equitable charge from the client. Provided the terms of the charge are usual this would not normally raise any issue of conflict. The solicitor should explain to the client the ramifications of granting this type of security and, where the charge contains unusual terms, the client should be advised to obtain separate independent advice.

5. A solicitor extending bridging finance where the loan does not exceed £25,000 should consider whether the provisions of the Consumer Credit Act 1974 apply.

25

25.04　Preparing contracts for other party's signature

A solicitor acting for the seller of property should not prepare a form of contract which he or she knows or ought to know will be placed before a prospective buyer for signature before that party has had a proper opportunity to obtain legal advice.

This is so even if the contract allows the buyer to rescind without penalty during a stated period. Although the buyer may consult a solicitor during that period, it could then be too late to negotiate any amendments to the contract if the buyer wished to proceed and, in practice, it may be impossible to make the necessary searches and enquiries of local authorities within that period.

25.05　Practice rule 6A (seller's solicitor dealing with more than one prospective buyer)

'(1) This rule applies to the conveyancing of freehold and leasehold property. The rule is to be interpreted in the light of the notes.

Notes

(i) *Rule 6A replaces the Council Direction of 6th October 1977 and principle and commentary 24.04 in the 1993 edition of "The Guide to the Professional Conduct of Solicitors" with effect from 1st March 1995. As was the case with the Council Direction, it applies to all conveyancing of land, whether the transaction is of a "commercial" or "domestic" nature.*

(ii) *The Council Direction did not and rule 6A does not set terms for a contract race. It lays down requirements which must be met when a solicitor is instructed to deal with more than one prospective buyer. The rule imposes no obligation on the seller's solicitor to exchange contracts with the first buyer to deliver a signed contract and deposit. It will be a matter of law whether or not the seller has entered into a contractual obligation to exchange with the buyer "first past the post", or whether the whole matter remains "subject to contract".*

(iii) *References to "solicitor" throughout the rule include a firm of solicitors, a multi-national partnership or a recognised body.*

(2) Where a seller instructs a solicitor to deal with more than one prospective buyer, the solicitor (with the client's consent) shall immediately disclose the seller's decision, if possible by telephone or fax, to the solicitor or other conveyancer acting for each prospective buyer or direct to the prospective buyer if acting in person. Such disclosure, if made by telephone, shall at once be confirmed by letter or fax. If the seller refuses to authorise disclosure, the solicitor shall immediately cease to act. Each prospective buyer must be notified each time a decision is taken to deal with any further prospective buyer.

Notes

(i) *It is the seller's decision to deal with more than one prospective buyer which must be notified. The seller's solicitor must not wait until contracts are actually submitted but must notify the appropriate parties immediately upon receiving instructions to deal with a prospective buyer (other than the first).*

(ii) *A solicitor will have been instructed to deal with a prospective buyer where the solicitor is asked to submit a draft contract or to provide any other documentation or information (e.g. a plan or a note of the Land Registry title number) in order to facilitate the conveyancing of the premises to the prospective buyer. The rule does not, however, cover activities normally performed by an estate agent, such as issuing particulars of sale, showing prospective buyers round the property, and negotiating the price.*

(iii) *The rule will apply where the contracts are to contain non-identical terms (e.g. where one contract is to include additional land). It will also apply where the contracts are to relate to different interests in the same property where the sale of one such interest would affect the sale of the other. For example, a party negotiating to take a lease of premises will be affected by another party negotiating to buy the freehold with vacant possession, since the sale of one precludes the sale of the other. On the other hand, the rule would not apply where the seller is proposing to grant a lease and to effect a simultaneous sale of the freehold reversion subject to that lease, since neither transaction precludes the other.*

(iv) *Where a prospective buyer has retained an unqualified conveyancer, solicitors are reminded to consult the Council guidance on dealing with unqualified conveyancers [see Annex 25A, p.482 in this edition of the Guide]. However, so far as rule 6A is concerned, the obligations in paragraph (2) will be met by disclosure either to the prospective buyer direct or to the unqualified conveyancer.*

(3) The obligations in paragraph (2) of this rule apply where a seller client, to the solicitor's knowledge, deals (whether directly or through another solicitor or other conveyancer) with another prospective buyer (or with that buyer's solicitor or other conveyancer).

Note

"Deals with another prospective buyer" should be interpreted in the light of note (ii) to paragraph (2).

(4) A solicitor shall not act for more than one of the prospective buyers.

Notes

(i) *"Prospective buyers" should be interpreted in the light of note (ii) to paragraph (2).*

(ii) *This part of the rule recognises the inevitable conflict of interest which makes it impossible for a solicitor to act for more than one of the prospective buyers.*

(5) A solicitor shall not act for both the seller and one of the prospective buyers, even in a case which would fall within rule 6(2) of these rules.

> *Notes*
>
> (i)   *"Prospective buyers" should be interpreted in the light of note (ii) to paragraph (2).*
>
> (ii) *Clearly a solicitor must not act for both where it is known at the time of taking instructions on behalf of the buyer that there is more than one prospective buyer. In addition, this part of the rule does not permit a solicitor to continue to act for both in a case falling within rule 6(2), where another prospective buyer is introduced during the course of the transaction because of the significant inherent conflict; the solicitor would find it impossible to reconcile the interests of both clients if, for example, it was in the seller's best interests to exchange with the other prospective buyer.*

(6) For the purposes of this rule a prospective buyer shall continue to be treated as such until either the prospective buyer or the seller gives written notice (either by letter or by fax) of withdrawal from the transaction, such notice to be between solicitors or other conveyancers save where such notice is given by or to a prospective buyer acting in person.

> *Notes*
>
> (i)   *Solicitors should take particular care where a contract has been submitted but nothing has been heard from the prospective buyer's solicitor for some time. If the seller decides to deal with another buyer, the rule must still be complied with unless the seller's solicitor has already given notice of withdrawal.*
>
> (ii) *Where a prospective buyer has retained an unqualified conveyancer, the provisions of paragraph (6) should be interpreted in the light of note (iv) to paragraph (2).*

(7) This rule does not apply to a proposed sale by auction or tender. The rule does, however, apply to require disclosure to a prospective buyer by private treaty of instructions to offer the property by auction or tender.'

Solicitors' Practice Rules 1990, rule 6A

25.06   Licensed conveyancers

A solicitor may normally deal with a licensed conveyancer as if the conveyancer were a solicitor, subject to the best interests of the solicitor's client.

1.   Licensed conveyancers are permitted to practise in partnership with other licensed conveyancers, or with other persons (although not with solicitors). Licensed conveyancers may also practise through the medium of a

'recognised body', i.e. a body corporate recognised by the Council for Licensed Conveyancers.

2. The identity of firms of licensed conveyancers can be checked in the *Directory of Solicitors and Barristers*. In cases of doubt contact the Council for Licensed Conveyancers – see p.xv for contact details.

3. Licensed conveyancers are subject to conduct and accounts rules similar to those which apply to solicitors. They are covered by compulsory indemnity insurance and contribute to a compensation fund. In dealings with licensed conveyancers, it should normally be possible to proceed as if the licensed conveyancer were a solicitor and bound by the same professional obligations. For example, if it is agreed to use the Law Society's code for exchange of contracts by telephone, it is understood that any failure to respect the code would expose the licensed conveyancer to disciplinary proceedings; this also applies to the Society's code for completion by post, and reliance on undertakings. Since licensed conveyancers may practise in partnership or association with others, it is important to ensure that the other party's representative is a licensed conveyancer, or a person working immediately under the supervision of a licensed conveyancer.

25.07 Unqualified conveyancers

If a solicitor discovers that the other party is represented by an unqualified conveyancer then, subject to the interests of his or her own client, the solicitor's proper course is to decline to communicate with the unqualified conveyancer.

1. A solicitor is not prohibited from dealing with an unqualified person, but see the Council guidance on dealing with unqualified conveyancers at Annex 25A, p.482. For guidance on dealing with licensed conveyancers see **25.06**, p.472.

2. Solicitors are asked to report to the Professional Adviser (see p.xv for contact details) whenever it appears that an unqualified conveyancer has acted in breach of the law.

25.08 General insurance

A solicitor who conducts general insurance business should do so only as independent intermediary and not as tied agent.

1. It is incompatible with the independence of the solicitor and the primacy of the solicitor's duty to the client to accept an accountability to an insurance company that could conflict with that duty to the client. Any tied agency would be inconsistent with the status of solicitors as independent intermediaries in the provision of financial services.

25

2.　Having the status of an independent intermediary does not prevent a solicitor having agency arrangements with whatever number of insurance companies the solicitor considers appropriate. Insurance companies make available to their intermediaries for signature declarations of status as either independent intermediary or company agent.

3.　The Council requires solicitors who act as intermediaries for general insurance business to do so only as independent intermediaries within the meaning of the relevant code of practice of the Association of British Insurers (ABI).

4.　The relevant code of practice and guidance on its requirements are available from the ABI – see p.xv for contact details. The cover given to solicitors by the Solicitors' Indemnity Fund satisfies the professional indemnity requirements of the code.

25.09　Mortgages and life policies

Solicitors should refer a client who is likely to need an endowment policy, or similar life insurance with an investment element, to an independent intermediary authorised to give investment advice.

1.　Where clients may need life insurance, solicitors should either act as independent intermediaries themselves, or introduce the client to another independent intermediary. The duty to give independent advice is not normally discharged by referring a client to an appointed representative, i.e. a tied agent. See also section 4 of the Solicitors' Introduction and Referral Code 1990 (Annex 11B at p.243).

2.　Although a mortgage of land is not an investment under the Financial Services Act 1986, solicitors who advise on or make arrangements in respect of mortgages where an endowment policy or pension policy is to be used as additional security may be caught by the Act. A mere referral to an independent intermediary is not caught by the Act, but solicitors should assess the client's needs and consider factors such as speed and reliability of administration, availability, interest rates and general terms. Referral to a mortgage provider who is a tied agent may result in the client not receiving independent investment advice. If the client's interests dictate a referral to a tied agent, the client should be informed that the agent can offer investment products from a single company only.

3.　Solicitors should be aware of the Financial Services Act status of persons to whom clients are referred, as many banks, building societies, estate agents and insurance agents are appointed representatives of particular insurance companies and are unable to offer independent advice.

4.　A client who is proposing to take out a company life policy or other financial product without independent advice may be referred to a solicitor by the life office, bank, building society or other tied agent. It is not a solicitor's duty to force clients to take independent advice, if they do not wish to do so. However, solicitors should be prepared to make enquiries of a client if the proposed policy seems unsuitable and, if appropriate, provide independent advice, or refer the client to an independent intermediary. The solicitor will need to consider and discuss with the client whether obtaining independent advice will involve additional cost or delay or prejudice the proposed purchase. See also section 2(6) of the Solicitors' Introduction and Referral Code 1990 (Annex 11B at p.239).

5. Similar considerations arise where the referral is by an independent financial adviser who has persuaded the client to enter into an obviously inappropriate scheme. Whilst a solicitor is not under a duty to re-advise, or to offer investment business advice as part of a conveyancing retainer, there may be a general duty in relation to the conveyancing retainer to give advice on the legal implications. See also **25.10** note 5, p.477.

6. All home income or equity release schemes, whereby homes are mortgaged to raise a capital sum for investment, carry an element of risk. Two home income plans sold to the elderly a few years ago have given rise to a number of claims against advisers, including solicitors. Reference may be made to *Using Your Home as Capital* by Cecil Hinton, published by Age Concern, for an account of these schemes – the 'investment bond income scheme' and the 'roll-up loan scheme'. So far as they can, solicitors should dissuade clients from entering into any scheme of this kind without expert and independent advice.

7. Rule 12 of the Solicitors' Practice Rules 1990 (see **27.21**, p.533) provides that solicitors shall not, in connection with investment business, be appointed representatives or operate any separate business which is an appointed representative, unless it is an appointed representative of an independent financial adviser. Solicitors' agency arrangements with building societies or other financial institutions which are tied agents, and the business transacted at the solicitor's agency office, must be confined to non-investment business. A solicitor operating a building society agency, etc., if asked about mortgages, should consider whether the customer needs independent advice.

8. The Society has a group licence covering credit brokerage by solicitors, limited to activities arising in the course of practice. Solicitors who arrange mortgages will be carrying on credit brokerage within the meaning of the Consumer Credit Act 1974.

9. Solicitors who advertise that they are able to arrange mortgages must comply with the Consumer Credit (Advertisements) Regulations 1989 (S.I. 1989 no. 1125). Such an advertisement, provided it contains no details of amounts due in repayment of the mortgage, will be an intermediate credit advertisement for the purpose of the regulations which provide that the following information must be contained in the advertisement:

(a) the name of the solicitors and a postal address or telephone number;

25

(b) a statement in the following form:

> 'Your home is at risk if you do not keep up repayments on a mortgage or other loan secured on it.'

This statement must be in capital letters and afforded no less prominence than the statement relating to the ability to arrange mortgages.

(c) the amount of any arrangement fee payable or a statement of its methods of calculation;

(d) a statement that individuals may obtain on request a quotation in writing about the terms on which the solicitors are prepared to do business, e.g. 'written details on request'.

10. Solicitors who act as mortgage intermediaries, i.e. who advise clients on which mortgage to apply for after reviewing a range of mortgage products, need to register with the Mortgage Code Register of Intermediaries, and to comply with the Mortgage Code. Note that although paragraph 11(2) of the code merely requires intermediaries to give details of mortgage arrangement fees over £250, rule 10 of the Solicitors' Practice Rules 1990 (see **14.13**, p.283) requires solicitors to account to clients for commission received of more than £20 unless the client has agreed otherwise. For the purpose of completing the registration form, firms may obtain their FSA number from Regulation and Information Services (see p.xv for contact details). The Law Society's group consumer credit licence number is G900001 and covers categories A, C, D and E. Firms wishing to register should contact the Mortgage Code Register of Intermediaries (see p.xv for contact details).

25.10   Contractual referrals for conveyancing

A solicitor must comply with section 3A of the Solicitors' Introduction and Referral Code 1990 when making an agreement for the introduction of clients under which the solicitor agrees with an introducer to be paid by the introducer to provide conveyancing services for the introducer's customers.

1. The normal solicitor/client relationship is unaffected by the fact that the introducer pays the solicitor for the conveyancing services. The work remains the professional responsibility of the solicitor.

2. An agreement under section 3A of the code (see Annex 11B at p.241) is not permitted with an introducer who is a seller (which can include a builder or developer) or a seller's agent if the conveyancing services are to be provided to the buyer.

3. Section 3A(8) of the code requires the introducer to give the client written details of the conveyancing service to be provided by the solicitor, the charge payable by the customer to the introducer, and any amount retained

by the introducer. Where the introducer is a lending institution and the solicitor will be doing the conveyancing for the lender, this must also be made clear, including details of any charge for that work.

4. Section 3A(9) of the code requires the solicitor to provide the client with written terms of business which must include certain specified matters. The section does not set out everything that should be included in terms of business and reference should also be made to practice rule 15 (see **13.01**, p.265).

5. Although normally the introducer's instructions will be limited to conveyancing services, the solicitor cannot disregard or exclude the general duty to act in the best interest of the client. While it is not part of a solicitor's general duty in conveyancing to re-advise the client on financial matters, it is a solicitor's responsibility to point out to the client any aspects of the transaction that are manifestly disadvantageous to the client.

6. If the client instructs the solicitor to carry out supplementary work not covered by the agreement, the solicitor should make it clear that the client and not the introducer will be liable for the additional costs.

25.11 Honouring professional undertakings

A solicitor who fails to honour the terms of a professional undertaking is *prima facie* guilty of professional misconduct.

1. See Chapter 18, p.351 on undertakings. An undertaking to redeem a mortgage means that the mortgage must be redeemed in the normal course of business. To delay doing so in order, for example, to arrange refinancing for a client would constitute a breach of the undertaking.

2. A reply to a requisition on title may amount to an undertaking. It is best to use the 'completion information and requisitions on title' forming part of the Law Society's TransAction scheme, which limits the undertaking to specific mortgages. Alternatively, see Annex 25B, p.487 for a form of undertaking recommended by the Society. A solicitor who is asked to reply to the old form of requisitions on title is advised to specify the mortgages which will be discharged. A solicitor who simply replies 'noted', 'confirmed', 'yes' or 'this will be done' to the general requisition concerning the discharge of mortgages on completion or the giving of an undertaking in lieu, without specifying which mortgages will be discharged, will have undertaken, in effect, to discharge all such mortgages if the matter proceeds to completion, whether or not the seller's solicitor, or the buyer's solicitor, was aware of the existence of any charge on the property.

3. Forms of undertakings agreed with banks are contained in Annex 25C, p.488. When sending redemption cheques through the post or document exchange, it is strongly recommended that the words 'account of ...' and the

25

account number be included after the payee's name (see rule 22, note (iv) of the Solicitors' Accounts Rules 1998, p.707).

4. In an undertaking to pay money out of the sale proceeds of a property, there is no implied term that the undertaking is intended to take effect only if the proceeds of sale actually come into the hands of the solicitor giving the undertaking. Accordingly, if this restriction is intended, it is crucial that a term to that effect is incorporated in the body of the undertaking itself; otherwise the solicitor giving the undertaking may have to satisfy the payment out of his or her own resources.

5. The Council of Mortgage Lenders (CML) has produced advice on mortgage redemption statements. It deals with the situation when a seller's solicitor is faced with the possibility of having insufficient funds to comply with an undertaking to discharge a mortgage on completion because the bank or building society supplied an incorrect redemption statement. CML take the view that where an incorrect redemption statement has been provided which is clearly due to an error by the lender or lack of clarification, it is unreasonable that a solicitor should be put in breach of undertaking. Lenders are therefore advised to seal the discharge (see Annex 25H, p.503).

6. The Law Society's formulae for exchanging contracts are contained in Annex 25D, p.492. Because professional undertakings form the basis of the formulae, solicitors are advised to consider carefully who is to be authorised to effect exchange of contracts in accordance with the formulae and ensure that the use of the procedure is restricted to those authorised. The formulae are recommended for use only between firms of solicitors and licensed conveyancers.

7. On exchange of contracts under formula B solicitors must comply with the undertaking which forms part of the formula that the contract (and if appropriate the deposit) will be sent to the other party's solicitor that day. If a solicitor knows that this will not be possible, the undertaking should be varied at the time of exchange. If it is not possible to send the deposit cheque, this should be made clear on exchange. Arrangements could be made for the deposit cheque to be sent direct to the seller's solicitor from another firm in the chain. This would mean either varying formula B or making use of formula C.

8. The Law Society's code for completion by post is at Annex 25E, p.496. The code embodies professional undertakings and is recommended for adoption only between solicitors, and between solicitors and licensed conveyancers.

9. The adoption of the National Conveyancing Protocol for domestic freehold or leasehold property has conduct implications. All solicitors engaged in domestic conveyancing should be aware of the Council statement which forms part of the Protocol. The following extract from the Council statement sets out those aspects relevant to professional conduct:

'4.   The Protocol is a form of "preferred practice" and its requirements should not be construed as undertakings. Nor are they intended to widen a solicitor's duty save as set out in the next paragraph. The Protocol must always be considered in the context of a solicitor's overriding duty to his or her own client's interests and where compliance with the Protocol would conflict with that duty, the client's wishes must always be paramount.

5.   A solicitor acting in domestic conveyancing transactions should inform the solicitor acting for the other party at the outset of a transaction, whether or not he or she is proposing to act in accordance with the Protocol in full or in part. If the solicitor is using the Protocol he or she should give notice to the solicitor acting for the other party if during the course of the transaction it becomes necessary to depart from Protocol procedures.

6.   A solicitor is, as a matter of professional conduct, under a duty to keep confidential client's business. The confidentiality continues until the client permits disclosure or waives the confidentiality. [*See* **16.02**, *p.325.*] With reference to paragraphs 4.5 and 5.3 of the National Protocol [supplying information to the other party], the disclosure of information about a client's position is strictly subject to obtaining that client's authority to disclose. In the absence of such authority, a solicitor is not deemed to be departing from the terms of the Protocol and, as such, is not required to give notice as set out in paragraph 5 of this Statement.'

For detailed guidance on the procedures to be adopted under the Protocol, refer to *The National Conveyancing Protocol* (third edition) available from Marston Book Services (see p.xv for contact details).

10. For detailed guidance on conveyancing practice, see *The Law Society's Conveyancing Handbook* available from Marston Book Services (see p.xv for contact details).

25.12   Property fraud

A solicitor must not act, or must cease to act further, where the instructions would involve the solicitor in a breach of the law or a breach of the principles of professional conduct, unless the client is prepared to change his or her instructions.

Annex 25G, p.501 contains the Society's 'green card' warning on property fraud. Annex 25F, p.500 contains guidance on a solicitor's duty in conduct when acting for a lender and borrower when there is some variation in the purchase price.

25.13   Money laundering

Conveyancing solicitors need to be aware of the legislation relating to money laundering.

1.   The purchase and sale of properties may be used as a method of laundering the proceeds of crime. A solicitor who knows or suspects that this may be happening will need to consider the provisions of the relevant legislation. An outline of the legislation and its conduct implications is given at **16.07**, p.333. A summary of the substantive law is at Annex 16B, p.337, and the Society's 'blue card' warning on money laundering is at Annex 16D, p.343.

2.   The Money Laundering Regulations 1993, which apply where certain services are provided by solicitors, are discussed more fully at **3.16**, p.84. The regulations are at Annex 3B, p.95.

3.   An information pack containing detailed guidance on the money laundering legislation may be obtained from Professional Ethics (see p.xv for contact details).

25.14   Lien over title deeds

It is not unprofessional for a solicitor to retain title deeds belonging to his or her client pending payment of professional costs owed by that client where the retention is a proper exercise of a solicitor's lien.

1.   Care should be taken to distinguish between a solicitor's lien and an unpaid seller's lien. For detailed commentary on the nature and effect of a solicitor's lien see *Cordery on Solicitors* and **12.14**, p.251.

2.   In relation to the unpaid seller's lien, reference should be made to an appropriate authority on the law of lien. Use of the Standard Conditions of Sale and the Law Society's code for completion by post will affect the seller's right to exercise a lien – see *The Law Society's Conveyancing Handbook* available from Marston Book Services (see p.xv for contact details).

25.15   Interest on stakeholder money

A solicitor must pay interest on money held in his or her capacity as stakeholder, in accordance with the Solicitors' Accounts Rules, to the person to whom the stake is paid.

1.   For the Solicitors' Accounts Rules 1998, see Annex 28B, p.684. For the application of the interest provisions, see rule 24 at p.709. For solicitors still operating under the Solicitors' Accounts Rules 1991, see Annex 28B at p.620 of the seventh edition of *The Guide to the Professional Conduct of Solicitors*.

2.   The operation of the interest provisions may be excluded by written
      agreement between the parties. It is not, however, normal practice for a
      stakeholder in conveyancing transactions to retain interest instead of paying
      it to the recipient of the stake (see rule 27(2), notes (ii)–(v) at p.712). For
      solicitors still operating under the Solicitors' Accounts Rules 1991, see
      Annex 28E at p.634 of the seventh edition of *The Guide to the Professional
      Conduct of Solicitors.*

25.16   Stamp duty and Land Registry fees

**Money paid to a solicitor for stamp duty or Land Registry fees must be paid
into client account and must remain there unless and until paid out.**

25.17   Refusal to complete for non-payment of costs

**Unless a solicitor has, at the outset of the retainer, required the client to
make a payment or payments on account of costs before completion of the
retainer, the solicitor should not refuse to complete a transaction for the
client if the sole reason for that refusal is that the client has not paid the
solicitor's costs.**

1.   See **14.01**, p.277 for further guidance. Principle **25.17** does not apply to the
      non-payment of disbursements. A solicitor may refuse to complete where
      disbursements which are necessary to enable completion to take place
      remain outstanding.

2.   A solicitor also acting for the client's mortgagee may refuse to complete in
      order to protect the interests of the mortgagee client. If completion does
      take place the solicitor should consider his or her duty to act in the best
      interests of the mortgagee client in relation to stamping and registration. It
      would normally be appropriate to take instructions from the mortgagee
      client prior to completion.

25

Annex 25A

Guidance – dealing with unqualified conveyancers

[See **25.06**, p.472 in the Guide for licensed conveyancers.]

Effect of section 22 of the Solicitors Act 1974

1.   Section 22 of the Solicitors Act 1974 (see Annex 2A at p.45 in the Guide) makes it an offence for an unqualified person to draw or prepare, *inter alia*, a contract for sale or a transfer, conveyance, lease or mortgage relating to land in expectation of fee, gain or reward. Qualified persons under this section are solicitors, barristers, notaries public, licensed conveyancers, some public officers and, for unregistered conveyancing, Scottish solicitors.

2.   It is inevitable that an unqualified person who undertakes a conveyancing transaction in the course of a conveyancing business will commit an offence under section 22, unless the drawing or preparation of the relevant documents is undertaken by a qualified person. In such circumstances, the unqualified conveyancer's client is likely, albeit unwittingly, to be guilty of aiding and abetting the offence. The solicitor acting for the other party could also be guilty of procuring the commission of an offence by inviting or urging the unqualified person to provide a draft contract or transfer or to progress the transaction.

3.   Solicitors should therefore refuse to have any dealings with any unqualified person carrying on a conveyancing business unless there is clear evidence that offences under section 22 will not be committed.

4.   It is recommended that, at the outset of any transaction, the solicitor should write to the unqualified conveyancer drawing attention to this guidance and saying that the solicitor cannot enter into any dealings with him or her unless there is clear evidence that no offences will be committed. An example of satisfactory evidence would be a letter from a qualified person confirming that he or she will prepare the relevant documents. The solicitor should also immediately report to his or her own client and explain why he or she cannot deal with the unqualified conveyancer unless clear evidence is forthcoming.

Draft letter to unqualified conveyancer

'We are instructed to act for the seller/buyer in connection with the above transaction and understand that you have been instructed by the buyer/seller. Please confirm that you are a solicitor or licensed conveyancer. If not, please state who will prepare the contract/conveyance/transfer for you; we need to receive written confirmation from a qualified person that he or she will personally settle the contract/conveyance/transfer.

As you know, it is an offence for an unqualified person to prepare a contract for sale or a transfer, conveyance or mortgage relating to land in expectation of fee, gain or reward.

We have been advised by the Law Society that we should not deal with an unqualified person carrying on a conveyancing business unless clear evidence is provided that offences under section 22 of the Solicitors Act 1974 will not be committed. The written confirmation referred to above, if explicit and unequivocal, could provide such evidence.

We regret that unless you are a solicitor or licensed conveyancer, we cannot deal with you until the evidence required above is provided.'

Draft letter to client of solicitor

'Thank you for your instructions relating to the above transactions. There is unfortunately a problem. The buyer/seller appears to have instructed an unqualified conveyancer to act for him/her and this could lead to the conveyancer, his/her client and myself being involved in the commission of criminal offences under the Solicitors Act 1974. The Law Society, my professional body, has advised solicitors not to deal with unqualified conveyancers because of the possibility of committing criminal offences.

I have therefore written to the firm acting for the buyer/seller asking for confirmation whether or not they are unqualified conveyancers and, if they are, whether they will be making arrangements to prevent the commission of such offences. If they cannot satisfy me about this, the buyer/seller will have to instruct a solicitor or licensed conveyancer, or deal with me direct.'

Further help

1.   Solicitors should first check with the Council for Licensed Conveyancers whether a person is a licensed conveyancer, since a licensed conveyancer can normally be dealt with as if a solicitor (see **25.06**, p.472 in the Guide).

2.   The Society can help practitioners dealing with unqualified conveyancers if the above guidance and the practice notes below do not cover the situation. Telephone calls and written requests for guidance should be made to the Practice Advice Service – for contact details see p.xv.

3.   The Professional Adviser (for contact details, see p.xv) has responsibility for investigating and prosecuting non-solicitors who appear to be in breach of the Solicitors Act 1974. Solicitors are asked to report (without submitting their files) any case where there is *prima facie* evidence of breaches of the Solicitors Act.

4.   For assistance in those cases where the solicitor has clear evidence that no offences under section 22 will be committed, there is set out below a series of practice notes relating to the problems which might arise in a transaction in which the other party is represented by an unqualified conveyancer. These practice notes give advice only and it is for solicitors to decide for themselves what steps should properly be taken in any particular situation.

25

PRACTICE NOTES

(applicable only where evidence is provided of compliance with section 22)

General

1.   Any undertaking which unqualified agents may offer in the course of a transaction is not enforceable in the same way as an undertaking given by a solicitor or licensed conveyancer. Solicitors should therefore never accept such undertakings.

2. Solicitors are under no duty to undertake agency work by way of completions by post on behalf of unqualified persons, or to attend to other formalities on behalf of third parties who are not clients, even where such third parties offer to pay the agent's charges.

3. The Council also suggests that in cases where a solicitor is dealing with an unqualified conveyancer, the solicitor should bear in mind the line of decisions starting with *Hedley Byrne* v. *Heller* [1964] A.C. 465, which extends the duty of care owed by a solicitor to persons who are not clients, but who rely and act on the solicitor's advice to his or her knowledge.

4. Solicitors must decide in each case whether special provisions should be incorporated in the draft contract to take account of the problems which arise by reason of the other party having no solicitor or licensed conveyancer, e.g. that the seller should attend personally at completion if represented by an unqualified agent. All such matters must be considered prior to exchange of contracts since contractual conditions cannot, of course, be imposed subsequently.

5. The protection provided by section 69 of the Law of Property Act 1925 only applies when a document containing a receipt for purchase money is handed over by a solicitor or licensed conveyancer or the seller himself or herself. Thus it should be considered whether the contract should provide either for the seller to attend personally at completion, or for an authority signed by the seller, for the purchase money to be paid to his or her agent, to be handed over on completion.

Acting for the seller: buyer not represented by a solicitor or licensed conveyancer

Completion

6. It is important to ensure that the deeds and keys are passed to the person entitled to receive them, i.e. the buyer. If an authority on behalf of the buyer is offered to the seller's solicitor, it is for the solicitor to decide whether or not to accept it, bearing in mind that no authority, however expressed, can be irrevocable. Again it is worth considering at the outset whether the point should be covered by express condition in the contract (see practice note 4 above).

Acting for the buyer: seller not represented by a solicitor or licensed conveyancer

Preliminary enquiries and requisitions on title

7. It may be prudent to require and ensure that replies to all preliminary enquiries and requisitions are signed by the seller.

Payment of deposit

8. Difficulties may arise in connection with payment of the deposit where there is no estate agent involved to whom the deposit may be paid as stakeholder in the ordinary way. The deposit may be paid direct to the seller, but this cannot be recommended since it is equivalent to parting with a portion of the purchase money in advance of investigation of the title and other matters.

9.   Some unqualified agents insist that the deposit be paid to them. The Council does not recommend this. If a solicitor is obliged to pay the deposit to unqualified agents, he or she should inform the client of the risks involved, and obtain specific instructions before proceeding.

10.   An alternative is for the deposit to be paid to the buyer's solicitor as stakeholder. The buyer's solicitor should insist on this where possible. If the seller will not agree to this, it may be possible to agree to place the deposit in a deposit account in the joint names of the buyer's solicitor and the seller, or in a deposit account in the seller's name, with the deposit receipt to be retained by the buyer's solicitor.

Payment of purchase money

11.   As referred to in practice note 5 above, the buyer's solicitor should ensure that all the purchase money, including any deposit, is paid either to the seller or to the seller's properly authorised agent.

Matters unresolved at completion

12.   Whilst it is unusual to leave any issues revealed by searches and other enquiries outstanding at completion, undertakings relating to their discharge or resolution may on occasions be given between solicitors or licensed conveyancers. Such undertakings should not be accepted from unqualified agents for the reason mentioned in practice note 1 above.

Power of attorney

13.   Unqualified agents sometimes obtain a power of attorney to enable themselves or their employees to conduct certain aspects of the transaction. It is clearly important to ensure that such powers are valid, properly granted, and effective for all relevant purposes.

Acting for the lender: borrower not represented by a solicitor or licensed conveyancer

14.   The lender's solicitor often finds himself or herself undertaking much of the work which a borrower's solicitor would do. Whilst the client's interests are paramount, the solicitor must ensure that he or she does not render the unqualified agent additional assistance in a way which might establish a solicitor/client relationship either with the unqualified conveyancer or with the borrower, or leave the solicitor open to a negligence claim either from the solicitor's lender client or from the borrower.

Advances

15.   As regards the drafting and preparation of the instrument of transfer by the borrower's representative, the lender's solicitor is not obliged to undertake work which would normally be done by the borrower's solicitor. Solicitors are reminded, however, that it is of paramount importance to their lender client that good title is conveyed to the borrower.

16. The importance of paying mortgage advances only to those properly entitled to receive them is a reason for insisting either that the borrower attends personally on completion, or that a signed authority from the borrower in favour of his or her agent is received on completion. Section 69 of the Law of Property Act 1925 is a relevant consideration in this context (see practice note 5 above).

Redemptions

17. On completion, cheques or drafts should be drawn in favour of solicitors or licensed conveyancers or their clients, and not endorsed over to some intermediate party. The deeds should normally be handed over to the borrower personally, unless he or she provides a valid authority for them to be handed to a third party.

18. Any issues of doubt or difficulty must be referred to the lender/client for detailed instructions. Where the lender is a building society and its solicitor considers that the totality of the work involved justifies a charge in excess of the building society's guideline fee, he or she should seek the approval of the lender/client, supported if necessary by a bill of costs containing sufficient detail of the work and the time spent on it.

16th March 1988, revised December 1995

Annex 25B

Guidance – recommended form of undertaking for discharge of building society mortgages

'In consideration of your today completing the purchase of .... WE HEREBY UNDERTAKE forthwith to pay over to the .... Building Society the money required to redeem the mortgage/legal charge dated .... and to forward the receipted mortgage/legal charge to you as soon as it is received by us from the Building Society.'

Annex 25C

Guidance – forms of undertaking agreed with banks

FORM No. 1

Undertaking by solicitor – deeds/land certificate loaned to solicitor for purpose of inspection only and return

[Date] ....

To .... Bank plc

I/We hereby acknowledge to have received on loan from you the title deeds and/or land certificate and documents relating to .... in accordance with the schedule hereto.

I/We undertake to hold them on your behalf and to return them to you on demand in the same condition in which they now are and without the property to which they relate or any interest therein being, to our knowledge, in any way charged, conveyed, assigned, leased, encumbered, disposed of or dealt with.

Signature ....

SCHEDULE

FORM No. 2

Undertaking by solicitor – deeds/land certificate handed to solicitor re sale or mortgage of property, or part of it, and to account to bank for net proceeds

[Date] ....

To .... Bank plc

I/We hereby acknowledge to have received from you the title deeds and/or land certificate and documents *together with a charge to the Bank [delete if no charge form has been taken]* relating to .... in accordance with the schedule hereto for the purpose of the sale/mortgage of this property.

I/We undertake to hold them on your behalf and to return them to you on demand in the same condition in which they now are, pending completion of such transaction. If the transaction is completed I/we undertake:

(a) to pay to you the amount of the purchase/mortgage money, not being less than £.......... gross subject only to the deduction therefrom of the deposit (if held by the estate agent(s)), the estate agents' commission and the legal costs and disbursements relating to the transaction, and

(b) if the title deeds and/or land certificate and documents also relate to other property in addition to that referred to above, to return same to you suitably endorsed or noted.

Signature ....

NOTE: *If there are likely to be any deductions from the purchase price other than those shown above, these must be specifically mentioned.*

SCHEDULE

FORM No. 3

Undertaking by solicitor – to send deeds/land certificate to bank on completion of a purchase, the bank and/or its customer having provided the purchase monies

[Date] ....

To .... Bank plc

If you provide facilities to my/our client .... for the purchase of the freehold/leasehold property *[description of property]*

I/We undertake:

(a) that any sums received from you or your customer for the purpose of this transaction will be applied solely for acquiring a good marketable title to such property and in paying any necessary deposit, legal costs and disbursements in connection with such purchase. The purchase price contemplated is £.......... gross and with apportionments and any necessary disbursements is not expected to exceed £.........., and

(b) after the property has been acquired by .... and all necessary stamping and registration has been completed, to send the title deeds and/or land certificate and documents to you and in the meantime to hold them to your order.

Signature ....

25

FORM No. 4 (BRIDGING FINANCE)

Undertaking by solicitor (with form of authority from client) to account to bank for net proceeds of sale of the existing property, the bank having provided funds in connection with the purchase of the new property

Authority from client(s)

[Date] ....

To .... *[name and address of solicitors]*

I/We hereby irrevocably authorise and request you to give an undertaking in the form set out below and accordingly to pay the net proceeds of sale after deduction of your costs to .... Bank plc .... Branch.

Signature of client(s)..

Undertaking

[Date] ....

To .... Bank plc

If you provide facilities to my/our client ....
for the purchase of the freehold/leasehold property (the new property)
.... *[description of property]*
pending the sale by my/our client of the freehold/leasehold property (the existing property)
.... *[description of property]*

I/we undertake:

1. That any sums received from you or your customer will be applied solely for the following purposes:

   (a)   in discharging the present mortgage(s) on the existing property *[delete if not applicable]*;

   (b)   in acquiring a good marketable title to the new property, subject to the mortgage mentioned below *[delete if not applicable]*;

   (c)   in paying any necessary deposit, legal fees, costs and disbursements in connection with the purchase.

The purchase price contemplated is £.......... gross.

I/We are informed that a sum of £......... is being advanced on mortgage by ....
[delete if not applicable]. The amount required from my/our client for the transaction including the deposit and together with costs, disbursements and apportionments is not expected to exceed £.......... .

2. To hold to your order when received by me/us the documents of title of the existing property pending completion of the sale (unless subject to any prior mortgage(s)) and of the new property (unless subject to any prior mortgage(s)).

3. To pay to you the net proceeds of sale of the existing property when received by me/us. The sale price contemplated is £.......... and the only deductions which will have to be made at present known to me/us are:

    (i)   the deposit (if not held by me/us),

    (ii) the estate agents' commission,

    (iii) the amount required to redeem any mortgages and charges, which so far as known to me/us at present do not exceed £..........,

    (iv) the legal fees, costs and disbursements relating to the transaction.

4. To advise you immediately of any subsequent claim by a third party upon the net proceeds of sale of which I/we have knowledge.

NOTES:

(1)   *If any deductions will have to be made from the net proceeds of sale other than those shown above, these must be specifically mentioned.*

(2)   *It would be convenient if this form of undertaking were presented in duplicate so that a copy could be retained by the solicitor.*

25

Annex 25D

Guidance – Law Society's formulae for exchanging contracts by telephone, fax or telex

Introduction

It is essential that an agreed memorandum of the details and of any variations of the formula used should be made at the time and retained in the file. This would be very important if any question on the exchange were raised subsequently. Agreed variations should also be confirmed in writing. The serious risks of exchanging contracts without a deposit, unless the full implications are explained to and accepted by the seller client, are demonstrated in *Morris* v. *Duke-Cohan & Co.* (1975) 119 S.J. 826.

As those persons involved in the exchange will bind their firms to the undertakings in the formula used, solicitors should carefully consider who is to be authorised to exchange contracts by telephone or telex and should ensure that the use of the procedure is restricted to them. Since professional undertakings form the basis of the formulae, they are only recommended for use between firms of solicitors and licensed conveyancers.

Law Society telephone/telex exchange – Formula A (1986)

(for use where one solicitor holds both signed parts of the contract):

A completion date of .... is agreed. The solicitor holding both parts of the contract confirms that he or she holds the part signed by his or her client(s), which is identical to the part he or she is also holding signed by the other solicitor's client(s) and will forthwith insert the agreed completion date in each part.

Solicitors mutually agree that exchange shall take place from that moment and the solicitor holding both parts confirms that, as of that moment, he or she holds the part signed by his or her client(s) to the order of the other. He or she undertakes that day by first class post, or where the other solicitor is a member of a document exchange (as to which the inclusion of a reference thereto in the solicitor's letterhead shall be conclusive evidence) by delivery to that or any other affiliated exchange, or by hand delivery direct to that solicitor's office, to send his or her signed part of the contract to the other solicitor, together, where he or she is the purchaser's solicitor, with a banker's draft or a solicitor's client account cheque for the deposit amounting to £..... .

Note:

1. A memorandum should be prepared, after use of the formula, recording:

    (a)   date and time of exchange;

    (b)   the formula used and exact wording of agreed variations;

(c)   the completion date;

(d)   the (balance) deposit to be paid;

(e)   the identities of those involved in any conversation.

Law Society telephone/telex exchange – Formula B (1986)

(for use where each solicitor holds his or her own client's signed part of the contract):

A completion date of .... is agreed. Each solicitor confirms to the other that he or she holds a part contract in the agreed form signed by the client(s) and will forthwith insert the agreed completion date.

Each solicitor undertakes to the other thenceforth to hold the signed part of the contract to the other's order, so that contracts are exchanged at that moment. Each solicitor further undertakes that day by first class post, or, where the other solicitor is a member of a document exchange (as to which the inclusion of a reference thereto in the solicitor's letterhead shall be conclusive evidence) by delivery to that or any other affiliated exchange, or by hand delivery direct to that solicitor's office, to send his or her signed part of the contract to the other together, in the case of a purchaser's solicitor, with a banker's draft or a solicitor's client account cheque for the deposit amounting to £..... .

Notes:

1.   A memorandum should be prepared, after use of the formula, recording:

    (a)   date and time of exchange;

    (b)   the formula used and exact wording of agreed variations;

    (c)   the completion date;

    (d)   the (balance) deposit to be paid;

    (e)   the identities of those involved in any conversation.

2.   Those who are going to effect the exchange must first confirm the details in order to ensure that both parts are identical. This means in particular, that if either part of the contract has been amended since it was originally prepared, the solicitor who holds a part contract with the amendments must disclose them, so that it can be confirmed that the other part is similarly amended.

9th July 1986, revised January 1996

Law Society telephone/fax/telex exchange – Formula C (1989)

Part I

The following is agreed:

Final time for exchange: pm

Completion date:

Deposit to be paid to:

Each solicitor confirms that he or she holds a part of the contract in the agreed form signed by his or her client, or, if there is more than one client, by all of them. Each solicitor undertakes to the other that:

(a)   he or she will continue to hold that part of the contract until the final time for exchange on the date the formula is used, and

(b)   if the vendor's solicitor so notifies the purchaser's solicitor by fax, telephone or telex (whichever was previously agreed) by that time, they will both comply with part II of the formula.

The purchaser's solicitor further undertakes that either he or she or some other named person in his or her office will be available up to the final time for exchange to activate part II of the formula on receipt of the telephone call, fax or telex from the vendor's solicitors.

Part II

Each solicitor undertakes to the other henceforth to hold the part of the contract in his or her possession to the other's order, so that contracts are exchanged at that moment, and to despatch it to the other on that day. The purchaser's solicitor further undertakes to the vendor's solicitor to despatch on that day, or to arrange for the despatch on that day of, a banker's draft or a solicitor's client account cheque for the full deposit specified in the agreed form of contract (divided as the vendor's solicitor may have specified) to the vendor's solicitor and/or to some other solicitor whom the vendor's solicitor nominates, to be held on formula C terms.

'To despatch' means to send by first class post, or, where the other solicitor is a member of a document exchange (as to which the inclusion of a reference thereto in the solicitor's letterhead is to be conclusive evidence) by delivery to that or any other affiliated exchange, or by hand delivery direct to the recipient solicitor's office. 'Formula C terms' means that the deposit is held as stakeholder, or as agent for the vendor with authority to part with it only for the purpose of passing it to another solicitor as deposit in a related property purchase transaction on these terms.

Notes:

1.   Two memoranda will be required when using formula C. One needs to record the use of part I, and a second needs to record the request of the vendor's solicitor to the purchaser's solicitor to activate part II.

2.   The first memorandum should record:

(a)   the date and time when it was agreed to use formula C;

(b)   the exact wording of any agreed variations;

(c)   the final time, later that day, for exchange;

(d)   the completion date;

(e)   the name of the solicitor to whom the deposit was to be paid, or details of amounts and names if it was to be split; and

(f)   the identities of those involved in any conversation.

3.   Formula C assumes the payment of a full contractual deposit (normally 10%).

4.   The contract term relating to the deposit must allow it to be passed on, with payment direct from payer to ultimate recipient, in the way in which the formula contemplates. The deposit must ultimately be held by a solicitor as stakeholder. Whilst some variation in the formula can be agreed this is a term of the formula which must *not* be varied, unless all the solicitors involved in the chain have agreed.

5.   If a buyer proposes to use a deposit guarantee policy, formula C will need substantial adaptation.

6.   It is essential prior to agreeing part I of formula C that those effecting the exchange ensure that both parts of the contract are identical.

7.   Using formula C involves a solicitor in giving a number of professional undertakings. These must be performed precisely. Any failure will be a serious breach of professional discipline. One of the undertakings may be to arrange that someone over whom the solicitor has no control will do something (i.e. to arrange for someone else to despatch the cheque or banker's draft in payment of the deposit). An undertaking is still binding even if it is to do something outside the solicitor's control (see **18.04**, p.353).

8.   Solicitors do not as a matter of law have an automatic authority to exchange contracts on a formula C basis, and should always ensure that they have the client's express authority to use formula C. A suggested form of authority is set out below. It should be adapted to cover any special circumstances:

I/We .... understand that my/our sale and purchase of .... are both part of a chain of linked property transactions, in which all parties want the security of contracts which become binding on the same day.

I/We agree that you should make arrangements with the other solicitors or licensed conveyancers involved to achieve this.

I/We understand that this involves each property-buyer offering, early on one day, to exchange contracts whenever, later that day, the seller so requests, and that the buyer's offer is on the basis that it cannot be withdrawn or varied during that day.

I/We agree that when I/we authorise you to exchange contracts, you may agree to exchange contracts on the above basis and give any necessary undertakings to the other parties involved in the chain and that my/our authority to you cannot be revoked throughout the day on which the offer to exchange contracts is made.

15th March 1989, revised January 1996

25

Annex 25E

Guidance – Law Society's code for completion by post

PREAMBLE

The code provides a procedure for postal completion which practising solicitors may adopt by reference. It may also be used by licensed conveyancers.

Before agreeing to adopt this code, a solicitor must be satisfied that doing so will not be contrary to the interests of the client (including any mortgagee client).

When adopted, the code applies without variation, unless agreed in writing in advance.

PROCEDURE

General

1. To adopt this code, all the solicitors must expressly agree, preferably in writing, to use it to complete a specific transaction.

2. On completion, the seller's solicitor acts as the buyer's solicitor's agent without any fee or disbursements.

Before completion

3. The seller's solicitor will specify in writing to the buyer's solicitor before completion the mortgages or charges secured on the property which, on or before completion, will be redeemed or discharged to the extent that they relate to the property.

4. The seller's solicitor *undertakes*:

    (i) to have the seller's authority to receive the purchase money on completion;

    and

    (ii) on completion to have the authority of the proprietor of each mortgage or charge specified under paragraph 3 to receive the sum intended to repay it,

    BUT

    if the seller's solicitor does not have all the necessary authorities then:

(iii)   to advise the buyer's solicitor no later than 4pm on the working day before the completion date that they do not have all the authorities or immediately if any is withdrawn later; and

(iv)   not to complete until he or she has the buyer's solicitor's instructions.

5.   Before the completion date, the buyer's solicitor will send the seller's solicitor instructions as to any of the following which apply:

(i)   documents to be examined and marked;

(ii)   memoranda to be endorsed;

(iii)   undertakings to be given;

(iv)   deeds, documents (including any relevant undertakings) and authorities relating to rents, deposits, keys, etc. to be sent to the buyer's solicitor following completion; and

(v)   other relevant matters.

In default of instructions, the seller's solicitor is under no duty to examine, mark or endorse any document.

6.   The buyer's solicitor will remit to the seller's solicitor the sum required to complete, as notified in writing on the seller's solicitor's completion statement or otherwise, or in default of notification as shown by the contract. If the funds are remitted by transfer between banks, the seller's solicitor will instruct the receiving bank to telephone to report immediately the funds have been received. Pending completion, the seller's solicitor will hold the funds to the buyer's solicitor's order.

7.   If by the agreed date and time for completion the seller's solicitor has not received the authorities specified in paragraph 4, instructions under paragraph 5 and the sum specified in paragraph 6, the seller's solicitor will forthwith notify the buyer's solicitor and request further instructions.

Completion

8.   The seller's solicitor will complete forthwith on receiving the sum specified in paragraph 6, or at a later time agreed with the buyer's solicitor.

9.   When completing, the seller's solicitor *undertakes*:

(i)   to comply with the instructions given under paragraph 5; and

(ii)   to redeem or obtain discharges for every mortgage or charge so far as it relates to the property specified under paragraph 3 which has not already been redeemed or discharged.

After completion

10.   The seller's solicitor *undertakes*:

(i)   immediately completion has taken place to hold to the buyer's solicitor's order every item referred to in (iv) of paragraph 5 and not to exercise a lien over any such item;

25

(ii)   as soon as possible after completion, and in any event on the same day,

     (a)   to confirm to the buyer's solicitor by telephone or fax that completion has taken place; and

     (b)   to send written confirmation and, at the risk of the buyer's solicitor, the items listed in (iv) of paragraph 5 to the buyer's solicitor by first class post or document exchange.

Supplementary

11.   The rights and obligations of the parties, under the contract or otherwise, are not affected by this code.

12.   (i)   References to the seller's solicitor and the buyer's solicitor apply as appropriate to solicitors acting for other parties who adopt the code.

     (ii)   When a licensed conveyancer adopts this code, references to a solicitor include a licensed conveyancer.

13.   A dispute or difference arising between solicitors who adopt this code (whether or not subject to any variation) relating directly to its application is to be referred to a single arbitrator agreed between the solicitors. If they do not agree on the appointment within one month, the President of the Law Society may appoint the arbitrator at the request of one of the solicitors.

NOTES TO THE CODE

1.   This code will apply to transactions where the code is adopted after 1st July 1998.

2.   The object of this code is to provide solicitors with a convenient means for completion on an agency basis when a representative of the buyer's solicitor is not attending at the office of the seller's solicitor.

3.   As with the Law Society's formulae for exchange of contracts by telephone and fax, the code embodies professional undertakings and is only recommended for adoption between solicitors and licensed conveyancers.

4.   Paragraph 2 of the code provides that the seller's solicitors will act as agents for the buyer's solicitors without fee or disbursements. The convenience of not having to make a specific appointment on the date of completion for the buyer's solicitors to attend to complete personally will offset the agency work that the seller's solicitor has to do and any postage payable in completing under the code. Most solicitors will from time to time act for both sellers and buyers. If a seller's solicitor does consider that charges and/or disbursements are necessary in a particular case this would represent a variation in the code and should be agreed in writing before the completion date.

5.   In view of the decision in *Edward Wong Finance Company Limited* v. *Johnson, Stokes and Master* [1984] A.C. 1296, clause 4(ii) of the code requires the seller's solicitors to undertake on completion to have authority of the proprietor of every mortgage or charge to be redeemed to receive the sum needed to repay such charge.

6.   Paragraph 11 of the code provides that nothing in the code shall override any rights and obligations of the parties under the contract or otherwise.

7.   The buyer's solicitor is to inform the seller's solicitor of the mortgages or charges which will be redeemed or discharged (see paragraph 3 above) and is to specify those for which an undertaking will be required on completion (paragraph 5(iii)). The information may be given in reply to requisitions on title. Such a reply may also amount to an undertaking.

8.   Care must be taken if there is a sale and sub-sale. The sub-seller's solicitor may not hold the title deeds nor be in a position to receive the funds required to discharge the seller's mortgage on the property. Enquiries should be made to ascertain if the monies or some part of the monies payable on completion should, with either the authority of the sub-seller or the sub-seller's solicitor, be sent direct to the seller's solicitor and not to the sub-seller's solicitor.

9.   Care must also be taken if there is a simultaneous resale and completion and enquiries should be made by the ultimate buyer's solicitor of the intermediate seller's solicitor as to the price being paid on that purchase. Having appointed the intermediate seller's solicitor as agent the buyer's solicitor is fixed with the knowledge of an agent even without having personal knowledge (see the Society's 'green card' warning on property fraud at Annex 25G, p.501).

10. If the seller's solicitor has to withdraw from using the code, the buyer's solicitor should be notified of this not later than 4pm on the working day prior to the completion date. If the seller's solicitor's authority to receive the monies is withdrawn later the buyer's solicitor must be notified immediately.

These notes refer only to some of the points in the code that practitioners may wish to consider before agreeing to adopt it. Any variation in the code must be agreed in writing before the completion date.

1984, revised 1998

25

Annex 25F

Guidance – mortgage fraud – variation in purchase price

This guidance deals with the solicitor's duty in conduct when acting for lender and borrower when there is some variation in the purchase price.

Professional Ethics (see p.xv for contact details) is frequently asked to advise on a solicitor's duty to the lender in conduct when there is some variation in the purchase price of a property of which the lender may be unaware. The Society has therefore prepared the following guidance (which is supported by the Council of Mortgage Lenders) on the professional conduct issues involved.

Solicitors acting contemporaneously for a buyer and a lender should consider their position very carefully if there is any change in the purchase price, or if the solicitors become aware of any other information which they would reasonably expect the lender to consider important in deciding whether, or on what terms, it would make the mortgage advance available. In such circumstances the solicitor's duty to act in the best interests of the lender would require him or her to pass on such information to the lender.

Solicitors have a duty of confidentiality to clients, but this does not affect their duty to act in the best interests of each client. Therefore any such information concerning variations to the purchase price should be forwarded to the lender with the consent of the buyer. If the buyer will not agree to the information being given to the lender, then there will be a conflict between the solicitor's duty of confidentiality to the buyer and the duty to act in the best interests of the lender. Solicitors must therefore cease acting for the lender and must consider carefully whether they are able to continue acting for the buyer, bearing in mind **15.02** note 1, p.314 in the Guide and also **12.02** note 1 referred to below.

Solicitors must not withhold information relevant to a transaction from any client. Where the client is a lender, this includes not only straightforward price reductions but may also include other allowances (e.g. for repairs, payment of costs, the inclusion of chattels in the price and incentives of the kind offered by builders such as free holidays and part-subsidisation of mortgage payments) which amount to a price reduction and which would affect the lender's decision to make the advance. Solicitors should not attempt to arbitrate on whether the price change is material but should notify the lender. It is recommended that solicitors advise their clients as soon as practicable that it would be regarded as fraud to misrepresent the purchase price and that a solicitor is under a duty to inform the lender of the true price being paid for a property.

Solicitors who are party to an attempt to deceive a lender may be exposing both the buyer and themselves to criminal prosecution and/or civil action and will be liable to be disciplined for having breached the principles of professional conduct (see **12.02** note 1, p.245 in the Guide). If a solicitor is aware that his or her client is attempting to perpetrate fraud in any form he or she must immediately cease acting for that client.

12th December 1990, updated February 1999

Annex 25G

'Green card' warning on property fraud – practice information

Could you be involved or implicated?

Could you be unwittingly assisting in a fraud? The general assumption is that if there has been a property fraud a solicitor *must* have been involved. Solicitors should therefore be vigilant to protect both their clients and themselves. Steps can be taken to minimise the risk of being involved or implicated in a fraud (see below).

Could you spot a property fraud?

The signs to watch for include the following (but this list is not exhaustive):

▶ **Fraudulent buyer or fictitious solicitors** – especially if the buyer is introduced to your practice by a third party (for example a broker or estate agent) who is not well known to you. Beware of clients whom you never meet and solicitors not known to you.

▶ **Unusual instructions** – for example a solicitor being instructed by the seller to remit the net proceeds of sale to anyone other than the seller.

▶ **Misrepresentation of the purchase price** – ensure that the true cash price actually to be paid is stated as the consideration in the contract and transfer and is identical to the price shown in the mortgage instructions and in the report on title to the lender.

▶ **A deposit or any part of purchase price paid direct** – a deposit or the difference between the mortgage advance and the price, paid direct, or said to be paid direct, to the seller.

▶ **Incomplete contract documentation** – contract documents not fully completed by the seller's representative, i.e. dates missing or the identity of the parties not fully described or financial details not fully stated.

▶ **Changes in the purchase price** – adjustments to the purchase price, particularly in high percentage mortgage cases, or allowances off the purchase price, for example, for works to be carried out.

▶ **Unusual transactions** – transactions which do not follow their normal course or the usual pattern of events:

(a) client with current mortgage on two or more properties

(b) client using alias

(c) client buying several properties from same person or two or more persons using same solicitor

(d) client reselling property at a substantial profit, for which no explanation has been provided.

25

What steps can I take to minimise the risk of fraud?

Be vigilant: if you have any doubts about a transaction, consider whether any of the following steps could be taken to minimise the risk of fraud:

► **Verify the identity and *bona fides* of your client and solicitors' firms you do not know** – meet the clients where possible and get to know them a little. Check that the solicitor's firm and office address appear in the *Directory of Solicitors and Barristers* or contact the Law Society's Regulation and Information Services (tel: 0870 606 2555).

► **Question unusual instructions** – if you receive unusual instructions from your client discuss them with your client fully.

► **Discuss with your client any aspects of the transaction which worry you** – if, for example, you have any suspicion that your client may have submitted a false mortgage application or references, or if the lender's valuation exceeds the actual price paid, discuss this with your client. If you believe that the client intends to proceed with a fraudulent application, you must refuse to continue to act for the buyer and the lender.

► **Check that the true price is shown in all documentation** – check that the actual price paid is stated in the contract, transfer and mortgage instructions. Where you are also acting for a lender, tell your client that you will have to cease acting unless the client permits you to report to the lender all allowances and incentives. See also the guidance printed in [1990] *Gazette*, 12 December, 16 [see Annex 25F, p.500 in the Guide].

► **Do not witness pre-signed documentation** – no document should be witnessed by a solicitor or his or her staff unless the person signing does so in the presence of the witness. If the document is pre-signed, ensure that it is re-signed in the presence of a witness.

► **Verify signatures** – consider whether signatures on all documents connected with a transaction should be examined and compared with signatures on any other available documentation.

► **Make a company search** – where a private company is the seller, or the seller has purchased from a private company in the recent past, and you suspect that the sale may not be on proper arm's length terms, you should make a search in the Companies Register to ascertain the names and addresses of the officers and shareholders, which can then be compared with the names of those connected with the transaction and the seller and buyer.

Remember that, even where investigations result in a solicitor ceasing to act for a client, the solicitor will still owe a duty of confidentiality which would prevent the solicitor passing on information to the lender. It is only where the solicitor is satisfied that there is a strong *prima facie* case that the client was using the solicitor to further a fraud or other criminal purpose that the duty of confidentiality would not apply.

Any failure to observe these signs and to take the appropriate steps may be used in court as evidence against you if you and your client are prosecuted, or if you are sued for negligence.

Further guidance can be obtained from the Law Society's Practice Advice Service (tel: 0870 606 2522).

March 1991, revised January 1996, updated February 1999

Annex 25H

Mortgage redemption statements – advice from the Council of Mortgage Lenders – practice information

Problems relating to mortgage redemption statements have caused difficulties for lenders and solicitors (this expression to include licensed conveyancers) for a number of years. In 1985 the Building Societies Association and the Law Society issued detailed advice to their respective members on this subject because of the difficulties which were apparent at that time.

The advice comprised paragraphs 9 to 13 of BSA circular No. 3155. Those paragraphs are now replaced by the new guidance set out hereunder. In recent months, the Council of Mortgage Lenders (CML) has received a number of enquiries in respect of redemption statements provided by lenders to solicitors acting for the lender (who will often also act for the seller). This guidance refers to some of the circumstances which can produce errors and problems, and the consequences which this can have for the solicitor in the conveyancing transaction. It also suggests certain practical measures designed to reduce problems in this area. Accordingly, it is of importance to all lenders and covers:

(a) the function and importance of solicitors' undertakings;

(b) the general principle that lenders should seal a discharge where a redemption statement was incorrect;

(c) ways in which lenders might overcome the difficulty caused when the borrower prematurely stops payments;

(d) similar proposals as to the problem of dishonoured cheques;

(e) suggestions for overcoming difficulties sometimes presented by multiple mortgage accounts;

(f) information to be provided to banks for inclusion in telegraphic transfers; and

(g) the importance of returning the sealed discharge promptly.

Terms of reference

This guidance applies to England and Wales; separate guidance for Scotland and Northern Ireland will follow, if necessary.

Redemption on sale

This guidance applies primarily to redemption of a mortgage on sale of the security and, consequently, the lender's/seller's solicitor is required to give an undertaking to the buyer's solicitor that the charge will be discharged.

Remortgages

It is appreciated that an undertaking will also be given on a remortgage and that, accordingly, the guidance should be interpreted as including this situation.

Simple redemption

Much of the guidance is inapplicable to a straightforward redemption (without sale or mortgage) as no undertaking is given. However, even in redemptions *per se*, solicitors and lenders will no doubt wish to provide accurate information and deal promptly with their respective responsibilities.

Solicitors' undertakings

The solicitor acting for the seller will need, on completion, to satisfy the buyer's solicitor that the mortgage on the property being sold has been or will be discharged. In theory the buyer's solicitor will wish to see the mortgage discharged before the purchase money is paid. However, where the monies to repay the mortgage are being provided wholly or partly by the proceeds of sale, then the mortgage cannot be paid off until after completion.

Most lenders will not seal the discharge (this expression to include sealing the vacating receipt on a mortgage deed or sealing of form DS1) until they receive the redemption money. This leaves the buyer's solicitor with a problem in that he or she has to be satisfied that the mortgage will be discharged and that he or she will obtain the receipted mortgage or Land Registry form DS1. This problem is solved by the use of the solicitor's undertaking.

On completion, the seller's/lender's solicitor will provide the buyer's solicitor with a written undertaking to redeem the mortgage(s) in a form recommended by the Law Society similar to that set out below:

> In consideration of your today completing the purchase of .... we hereby undertake forthwith to pay over to .... [the lender] the money required to redeem the mortgage/legal charge dated .... and to forward the receipted mortgage/legal charge/form DS1 to you as soon as it is received by us from .... [the lender].

Incorrect redemption statements

Before completion of sale, the lender's/seller's solicitor will obtain a redemption statement calculated to the date of redemption. He or she will sometimes request the daily figure for interest which will be added if completion is delayed. If the lender supplies an incorrect redemption statement, the solicitor is likely to forward insufficient money to redeem the mortgage. The lender might be unwilling to discharge the mortgage and, if the solicitor is not holding more funds on behalf of the borrower, the solicitor would be in breach of his or her undertaking.

Problem areas

Problems with redemption statements can arise for a number of reasons:

(a) a lender might simply make a mistake in calculating the redemption figure;

(b) difficulties could be caused by the cancellation of standing orders or direct debit payments or by borrowers' cheques being dishonoured; and

(c) there might be misunderstanding between a lender and the solicitor.

Some of the more common practical problems are outlined below.

Cancellation

A difficulty arises if the mortgage payments are made by standing order and, shortly before completion, the borrower stops the payments without notice to the lender. There will be a shortfall if the lender assumed, without making this assumption clear, that the next payment would be paid and made the redemption figure calculation accordingly. If this is the case, and the solicitor has acted in good faith and with no knowledge that a payment has been or is likely to be cancelled, the view of the CML is that the lender should seal the discharge. This is to avoid the solicitor being in breach of his or her undertaking to the buyer's solicitor. (The lender would then have to recoup the money from the borrower.)

This difficulty is less likely to arise where payments are made by direct debit because the lender is the originator of the debit and therefore has control over the raising of any future direct debits from the borrower's bank account. However, there is no guarantee that direct debits will be honoured and they may be returned on the ground of insufficient funds or that the customer has closed his or her account or instructed his or her bank to cancel the direct debit.

Some lenders overcome this problem by excluding any future payments due when calculating the redemption figure. In other words, they 'freeze' the account balance at the day of the redemption calculation. The disadvantages of this are that (if the payment has not been cancelled) the borrower has to pay a higher redemption figure and the lender has to make a refund to the borrower after redemption.

An alternative is for the lender on the redemption statement to make it clear to the solicitor that it is assumed that the next payment will be made and that, if it is not paid, the mortgage will not be discharged until the balance is received. This gives the solicitor an early chance to address his or her and his or her borrower client's mind to the situation and to ensure that sufficient monies will be available to redeem the mortgage. Indeed, this would also serve as a reminder to the solicitor to warn the borrower client of the importance of continuing the payments in the normal way up to completion.

Uncleared cheques

This is a very similar situation to that of standing orders and direct debits. The CML's view is that if the lender does not notify the solicitor that it is assumed that the borrower's cheque will clear then, provided that the solicitor acts in good faith and without knowledge that the cheque would be or is likely to be dishonoured, the lender should seal the discharge. Exceptions to this are if the lender:

25

(a) prepares the redemption statement on the assumption that the cheque will not clear and informs the solicitor of this, probably, in a note on the statement. This has the disadvantages described above; or

(b) notifies the solicitor that a cheque has been received and that, if it does not clear by the date of redemption, the mortgage will not be discharged until the balance is received.

Separate loan account

The lender may have more than one loan secured on the property. For example, in addition to the principal mortgage, there could be a secured personal loan which is a regulated agreement under the Consumer Credit Act 1974 and/or a further advance conducted on a separate account basis. In such cases, there will be more than one account number.

On a sale, as all mortgage accounts will be repaid, multiplicity of accounts should not present a problem unless the solicitor does not know and is unable to specify every account and has no notice or cause to query the matter and the lender fails to cross-check the matter internally.

However, it is possible, for example, on certain remortgages, that it is the intention of the borrower and the lender that not all mortgages will be discharged and replaced. If so, when requesting the redemption statement, the solicitor should make it clear to the lender which mortgages the borrower wishes to redeem. The solicitor should inform the lender of any mortgages of which he or she is aware which are outstanding with the lender but which are not being redeemed. The solicitor should also quote all relevant account numbers if known as far as possible and ensure that the redemption statement received from the lender includes all the mortgages which are intended to be redeemed.

The lender should have its own internal cross-checking system but it is vital that the solicitor (who will, after all, be acting for the lender in most cases) is as clear as possible about the mortgage account(s) being redeemed. It is suggested that the solicitor should if possible, and time permits, send a copy of that redemption statement to the borrower to check agreement on the amount shown as due to the lender. Solicitors should be encouraged to ask for a statement at the earliest possible date.

Telegraphic transfers

Lenders could request that solicitors adopt procedures to assist in the identification of telegraphic transfers. When mortgages are being redeemed the telegraphic transfer which a lender receives is often difficult to identify and to match to a particular account.

The administrative difficulties which are caused by the inability to identify the money would be overcome if solicitors provided to the bank the information to be included in the telegraphic transfer, i.e. the borrower's mortgage account number and the firm's name and address.

Delay

Lenders are sometimes criticised for delay in providing a form of discharge after redemption of the mortgage. It is recognised that most lenders can and do return the receipted mortgage or form DS1 promptly and that solicitors can apply for registration to protect priority. However, unless there is good reason for the delay, e.g. a solicitor sending the form to the wrong office of the lender, lenders will no doubt deal promptly with this important procedure.

It is suggested that lenders should aim to return the receipted mortgage or form DS1 within seven days, and if there is likely to be a delay beyond that period they should notify the seller's solicitor. This would enable the buyer's solicitor to lodge an application with the Land Registry pending receipt of receipted mortgage or sealed form DS1, although it is hoped that this would only be necessary in exceptional circumstances.

The CML view

Many of the difficulties described above would be reduced if, as a matter of course, solicitors gave lenders correct information about the borrower, the property, the account number(s), etc., and lenders, in turn, operated internal cross-checking systems and provided accurate and complete redemption statements showing clearly the last payment to be taken into account and, systems permitting, details of all the borrower's accounts relating to the property which represent mortgages to be discharged.

If the solicitor, relying on an incorrect redemption statement provided by the lender, sends insufficient money to redeem a mortgage, the lender should discharge the mortgage. (However, the lender might wish to make it clear that the release was not intended to discharge the borrower from his or her outstanding personal liability. This might prevent the borrower from successfully claiming estoppel against the lender.)

Such cases do not occur frequently; when they do, it is generally because of a clerical or administrative error on the part of the lender, such as by omitting one month's interest or an insurance premium, and the amount is usually small. Nevertheless, where it appears that there has been an error, the solicitor should immediately draw this to the lender's notice and should pursue his or her borrower client actively for any shortfall.

Very rare cases could arise where general guidance of this kind is inapplicable, for example, if there is such a major discrepancy in the redemption figure that the borrower, and, perhaps, his or her solicitor, could not reasonably have believed in the accuracy of the statement.

Conclusion

Where there is an incorrect redemption statement, which is clearly due to an error by the lender or lack of clarification, it is unreasonable that a solicitor should be put in breach of his or her undertaking. The undertaking given to the buyer's solicitor is a vital part of the conveyancing process. It is the CML's view, in such cases, that the lender should seal the discharge.

The Law Society and the Council for Licensed Conveyancers agree with the views expressed in these paragraphs. It is hoped that some of the practical measures referred to above will be implemented to avoid difficulties on redemption.

March 1992, updated February 1999

25

Chapter 26

Property selling

26.01   Solicitors selling property

Property selling as part of practice

1. Property selling is work which a solicitor may properly carry on in the course of his or her professional practice. Section 1(2)(a) of the Estate Agents Act 1979 exempts from that Act 'things done in the course of his profession by a practising solicitor or a person employed by him'. However, solicitors must comply with the Property Misdescriptions Act 1991 and regulations made under it. A solicitor's property selling work is covered by the Solicitors' Indemnity Rules, and the solicitor's earnings from property selling must be included in his or her gross fee returns.

2. If a solicitor sells property as part of his or her practice, the seller will be his or her client. The solicitor's relationship with and the work carried out

for the client will be subject to the same law and professional rules binding on solicitors in relation to their other work. (This contrasts with the situation where a solicitor sells property through a separate business – see **26.17**, p.520.)

3.   A solicitor may sell property either as an activity of his or her general practice or through a practice formed especially for that purpose, and either alone or with other firms of solicitors. If solicitors from two or more different practices form a partnership for the purpose of property selling, it will be a distinct practice for all purposes, including the indemnity rules, the accounts rules, the practice rules and conflict of interests.

Competence

4.   If a solicitor's firm does not have the resources, competence or experience to handle property of a particular value or character, the solicitor must, as in the case of any work which the solicitor does not feel competent to handle, decline instructions and advise the client to consult another property seller, possibly a specialist agent.

Incorporated practices

5.   A solicitor's property selling practice may be a company (recognised body). The guidance in this chapter applies equally to a recognised body and its directors, employees and shareholders. The rules vary slightly in relation to a 'SEAL' (see **26.02** below).

Fee sharing with estate agents

6.   Solicitors are prohibited from sharing fees, or practising in partnership, with estate agents. However, a solicitor may instruct an estate agent as sub-agent and pay the sub-agent on the basis of a proportion of the solicitor's fee, or accept instructions to act as the sub-agent of an estate agent. (See rule 7 of the practice rules at **3.03**, p.68.)

26

26.02   'SEALs'

1.   A 'SEAL' (Solicitors' Estate Agency Limited) is a special type of jointly owned solicitors' incorporated practice. Rule 6 of the practice rules (see **25.01**, p.455) defines a SEAL as a recognised body which:

(a)   does not undertake conveyancing;

(b)   is owned jointly by at least four participating practices which do not have any principals in common and none of which own a controlling majority of the shares; and

(c)   is conducted from accommodation physically divided from, and clearly differentiated from that of any participating practice.

A participating practice is defined as a practice one or more of whose principals is a member of, or a beneficial owner of a share in, the SEAL.

2. There can be advantages for conveyancing solicitors who undertake property selling through a SEAL rather than as an adjunct to their conveyancing practice (see **26.06** notes 8 and 14, pp.512 and 513).

26.03   Description of property selling work

1. The name of a solicitor's estate agency practice must comply with practice rule 11 at **3.04**, p.69.

2. Practice rule 11 also requires that the word 'solicitor(s)' or the words 'regulated by the Law Society' appear on the firm's letterhead.

3. A property selling practice or a property selling department may be described as 'solicitors and estate agents', 'estate agents', a 'property centre' or by any other suitable description. For appearance under 'Estate Agents' in a directory, see **26.07** note 6, p.514.

26.04   Staff

1. In property selling, a solicitor may employ staff experienced in estate agency. Rule 7(1) of the practice rules (see **3.03**, p.68) allows a solicitor to share fees with his or her *bona fide* employee, whether or not a solicitor. Thus, property selling negotiations may be paid on a commission basis.

2. Paragraph 7 of the publicity code (see Annex 11A at p.233) allows any member of staff to be named in publicity (including stationery), but the status of a staff member who is not a solicitor with a current practising certificate must be unambiguously stated.

26.05   Supervision

A solicitor may open a branch office with, for example, a street-level window purely for the purpose of property selling. A branch office must be staffed and supervised in accordance with practice rule 13 (supervision and management – see **3.08**, p.73). An application for a waiver will also be considered in the case of an office at which the only work carried out is property selling, surveying and mortgage related services. See also **26.14** notes 4–5, p.519 as regards a property display centre.

26.06   Conflict of interests

Connected persons

1. The requirements in notes 4 and 9–12 below are similar to those imposed on estate agents by the Estate Agents (Provision of Information)

Regulations 1991 (S.I. 1991 no. 859) and the Estate Agents (Undesirable Practices) (No. 2) Order 1991 (S.I. 1991 no. 1032).

2. Reference throughout **26.06** to a connected person includes:

    (a) any of the solicitor's family, meaning a spouse, former spouse, reputed spouse, brother, sister, uncle, aunt, nephew, niece, direct descendant, parent or other direct ancestor;

    (b) any employee of the solicitor and any family of an employee;

    (c) any partner in an associated practice as defined in rule 6 of the practice rules (i.e. where two or more practices have at least one common principal), any employee of that practice and any family of an employee;

    (d) any company of which the solicitor is a director or employee or in which the solicitor, either alone or with any other connected person or persons is entitled to exercise, or control the exercise of, one-third or more of the voting power at any general meeting;

    (e) any company of which any of the persons mentioned in (a), (b) and (c) above is a director or employee or in which any of them, either alone or with any other connected person or persons, is entitled to exercise, or control the exercise of, one-third or more of the voting power at any general meeting;

    (f) any other 'associate' of the solicitor as defined in section 32 of the Estate Agents Act 1979.

3. Reference throughout **26.06** to a solicitor's partners includes those with whom he or she carries on a joint property selling practice, and partners in an associated practice – see note 2(c) above and practice rule 6 at **25.01**, p.455 for the meaning of 'associated practice'.

Notification to client when connected person has interest in property

4. A solicitor must always place the client's interests first. In addition to the requirements of **15.04**, p.316, the solicitor should promptly inform the client in writing whenever the solicitor or, to his or her knowledge, any connected person has, or is seeking to acquire, a beneficial interest in the property or in the proceeds of sale of any interest in the property.

Avoiding conflicts of interest

5. A solicitor and his or her partners who act in the sale of a property may be faced with insuperable problems of conflict of interests. In accordance with the general principles of professional conduct, a solicitor must not act (nor continue to act) if a conflict of interests exists, arises or is likely to arise (see **15.01**, p.314).

6. The solicitor who or whose partners act in the sale of a property, even if not in the conveyancing, must not act also for the buyer in the negotiations.

Acting for the buyer

7. The solicitor who acts in the sale is always free to act for the seller in the conveyancing as well, or the seller may choose to instruct different solicitors. However, rule 6 of the practice rules generally prevents a solicitor from acting for both seller and buyer in conveyancing, property selling or mortgage related services, subject to certain important exceptions (see **25.01**, p.455 and note 14 below). Where these exceptions apply and the solicitor acts for both the buyer and the seller in the same transaction, rule 6 imposes specific conditions, including a full explanation of the position to both clients.

8. An effect of rule 6(2)(b)(v) and (vi) is to allow a SEAL to act for the seller, and provide mortgage related services to the buyer, whilst one of the participating practices in the SEAL does the buyer's conveyancing, and another participating practice does the seller's conveyancing.

Notification to client of sale instructions from prospective buyer

9. Apart from cases governed by rule 6, questions of conflict may arise where the solicitor and his or her partners act also for parties in related transactions. Where a prospective buyer has made an offer for a client's property, the solicitor must promptly inform the client in writing if, to the solicitor's knowledge, he or she or any connected person has also been instructed by the buyer to sell an interest in land, and that sale is necessary to enable the buyer to buy from the client or results from that prospective purchase.

Notification of offers to client

10. A solicitor must promptly send to the client written accurate details (other than those of a description which the client has indicated in writing he or she does not wish to receive) of any offer the solicitor has received from a prospective buyer in respect of an interest in the property.

Duties to buyers

11. In addition to the general requirements of **17.01**, p.346 (a solicitor must not use his or her position as a solicitor to take unfair advantage either for the solicitor or another person), a solicitor must promptly and in writing inform any person negotiating to acquire or dispose of any interest in the property whenever the solicitor or, to his or her knowledge, any connected person has a beneficial interest in the property or in the proceeds of sale of any interest in it. The solicitor should not enter into negotiations with a prospective buyer until that disclosure has been made.

12. A solicitor must not discriminate against a prospective buyer because he or she has not or is unlikely to instruct the solicitor to sell an interest in land, which sale is necessary to enable the buyer to buy from the solicitor's client or results from that prospective purchase.

13. A solicitor acting for a seller of property may need to contact the buyer direct but the communication should be restricted to the solicitor's estate agency function. Communications about legal matters should so far as possible be through the buyer's solicitor, and the buyer should not be led to believe that he or she is receiving legal advice from the seller's solicitor.

Mortgages for buyers

14. In order to facilitate the sale of properties, solicitors sometimes wish to assist buyers to obtain mortgages. Under the rule 6 exceptions, a solicitor or two associated practices may, in certain circumstances and subject to certain conditions, act for the seller in the sale of a property and for the buyer in respect of a mortgage. In particular:

   ► a solicitor may do the seller's conveyancing and property selling, whilst providing only mortgage related services to the buyer; or

   ► a SEAL may do the property selling for the seller and provide mortgage related services to the buyer, whilst two participating firms do the conveyancing for seller and buyer.

15. Even in cases to which the rule 6 exceptions do not apply, a solicitor may, acting as solicitor for the seller, arrange (in a particular case or as part of a scheme) with a building society or other financial institution that a mortgage will be available on a property (subject to the buyer's status). The solicitor may inform a prospective buyer of the availability of the mortgage but (unless one of the rule 6 exceptions applies) must make it clear in writing that the solicitor cannot advise or act for the prospective buyer in respect of the mortgage, that the mortgage may not be the only one available and that he or she should consult his or her own solicitor.

16. Where a solicitor wishes to advise on mortgages linked with a life policy, the solicitor must comply with the Financial Services Act 1986. It is likely that in order to give such advice the solicitor will require authorisation under that Act (see Chapter 27, p.522).

26.07 Publicity

1. A solicitor may publicise his or her property selling service or properties for sale, subject to the provisions of the Solicitors' Publicity Code 1990 (see Annex 11A, p.229). For the effect of the publicity code on the naming of staff in publicity, see **26.04** note 2, p.510.

2. Paragraph 3 of the publicity code at p.230, which contains the prohibition on unsolicited visits or unsolicited telephone calls, nevertheless permits an unsolicited visit or telephone call to publicise a specific commercial property or properties the solicitor has for sale or to let.

3. Paragraph 4 of the publicity code (at p.231) permits the naming or identification of a client in advertisements, with the client's written consent,

where the naming or identification is not likely to prejudice the client's interests. Subject to these provisions therefore, a solicitor may name a client in advertising property for sale or to let on that client's behalf.

4. In publicising properties for sale, solicitors must comply with the Property Misdescriptions Act 1991 and regulations made under it.

Composite fees

5. Where a solicitor publicises a composite fee for a package of property selling and conveyancing, paragraph 5(d) of the publicity code (at p.231) provides that he or she must be willing if required:

    (a) to quote separate fees for the individual services (which may total more than the composite fee); and

    (b) to carry out one service only on the basis of the separate fee.

    A solicitor is 'required' for this purpose if he or she has a clear indication that a prospective client may wish to give instructions in respect of only one service in the package.

Directories

6. An entry or advertisement of a solicitor who provides a property selling service may appear in a directory, such as the Yellow Pages, under the classification 'Estate Agents', provided that 'solicitor(s)' appears in a description of the practice appearing in the entry or advertisement itself. See paragraph 8 of the publicity code (at p.234).

Flag advertising

7. A reference may be made in publicity to the solicitor's membership of an organisation or association of solicitors, but if an advertisement does not name the solicitor's firm it must comply with paragraph 10 of the publicity code (at p.234).

Arranging mortgages

8. A solicitor may advertise the ability to arrange mortgages but will need to comply with relevant consumer credit regulations. See **25.09** notes 9 and 10 (pp.475 and 476) and also **26.06** note 16 (p.513).

26.08   Introductions and referrals

1. Rule 3 of the practice rules (see **11.04**, p.224) allows solicitors to enter into arrangements for the introduction and referral of clients to and from the solicitor's practice, subject to compliance with the Solicitors' Introduction and Referral Code 1990 (see Annex 11B, p.238). The code provides *inter alia* that a solicitor may not reward an introducer by the payment of commission or otherwise (see section 2(3) of the code).

Investment business and mortgages

2. Rule 12 of the practice rules (see **27.21**, p.533) places conditions on the ability of a solicitor to enter into arrangements for introductions and referrals in the field of investment business. In particular, a solicitor cannot act as an appointed representative, as defined in the Financial Services Act 1986, unless he or she is an appointed representative of an independent financial adviser.

3. In accepting or making referrals in the field of mortgages or investment business, solicitors must comply with **25.09**, p.474.

26.09 Remuneration

Statement as to remuneration

1. When accepting instructions to act in the sale of a property, a solicitor must give the client a written statement setting out their agreement as to the amount of the solicitor's fee or the method of its calculation, the circumstances in which it is to become payable, the amount of any disbursements to be charged separately (or the basis on which they will be calculated) and the circumstances in which they may be incurred, and as to the incidence of VAT. It should state the identity of the property, the interest to be sold and the price to be sought. This requirement is similar to that imposed on estate agents by the Estate Agents Act 1979 and enables the client to be clear as to the proposed basis of charging.

2. The statement should also deal with whether or not the solicitor is to have 'sole agency' or 'sole selling rights' and, if so, explain the intention and effect of those terms (or any similar terms used) in the following manner:

    (a) **Sole selling rights**

    'You will be liable to pay a fee to us, in addition to any other costs or charges agreed, in each of the following circumstances:

    ▶ if unconditional contracts for the sale of the property are exchanged in the period during which we have sole selling rights, even if the buyer was not found by us but by another agent or by any other person, including yourself; or

    ▶ if unconditional contracts for the sale of the property are exchanged after the expiry of the period during which we have sole selling rights but to a buyer who was introduced to you during that period or with whom we had negotiations about the property during that period.'

    (b) **Sole agency**

    'You will be liable to pay a fee to us, in addition to any other costs or charges agreed, if unconditional contracts for the sale of the property are exchanged at any time:

26

> ▶ with a buyer introduced by us with whom we had negotiations about the property in the period during which we have sole agency; or

> ▶ with a buyer introduced by another agent during the period of our sole agency.'

These requirements and those in notes 3–5 below are similar to the obligations imposed on estate agents by the Estate Agents (Provision of Information) Regulations 1991 (S.I. 1991 no. 859).

3. If reference is made to a 'ready, willing and able' buyer (or similar term), the statement should contain the following explanation:

> 'A buyer is a "ready, willing and able" buyer if he or she is prepared and is able to exchange unconditional contracts for the purchase of your property. You will be liable to pay a fee to us, in addition to any other costs or charges agreed, if such a buyer is introduced by us in accordance with your instructions and this must be paid even if you subsequently withdraw and unconditional contracts for sale are not exchanged, irrespective of your reasons.'

4. If, by reason of the provisions of the statement in which any of the terms referred to above appear, any of the prescribed explanations is in any way misleading, the content of the explanation should be altered so as accurately to describe the liability of the client to pay a fee in accordance with those provisions. Subject to this requirement, the prescribed explanations should be reproduced prominently, clearly and legibly without any material alterations or additions and should be given no less prominence than that given to any other information in the statement apart from the heading, practice names, names of the parties, numbers or lettering subsequently inserted.

5. The statement must be given at the time when communication commences between the solicitor and the client or as soon as is reasonably practicable thereafter, provided that this is before the client is committed to any liability towards the solicitor.

Commission – remuneration certificates and taxation

6. The Society does not make any recommendation about property selling commissions. Commission charged on property sales is, however, subject to the Society's remuneration certificate procedure, unless the client signs a non-contentious business agreement in accordance with section 57 of the Solicitors Act 1974 (see Annex 14A, p.284), and to taxation by the Court.

Commission from third party

7. Commission paid by a third party, e.g. by an insurance company where the client takes out an endowment policy, is distinct from the remuneration paid by the client to the solicitor in relation to the property transaction. The solicitor must deal with commission from a third party in accordance with

rule 10 of the practice rules (see **14.13**, p.283). An exception is where commission has been received for the referral of a prospective buyer who is merely browsing; rule 10 only comes into operation when a buyer expresses interest in a specific property.

Composite fees

8.   A solicitor may quote or publicise a composite fee for property selling and conveyancing but should be prepared to quote separate fees if asked. The separate fees may total more than the composite fee. **See 26.07** note 5, p.514.

26.10   Interest earned on preliminary deposits

A preliminary deposit is usually held on behalf of and is fully refundable to the buyer. The Solicitors' Accounts Rules apply only to interest arising on client and stakeholder money. However, as a matter of good practice, solicitors should consider, when refunding a preliminary deposit, whether it is appropriate to pay interest to the buyer. Regulation 7 of the Estate Agents (Accounts) Regulations 1981 (S.I. 1981 no. 1520) provides that estate agents must account to the buyer where the preliminary deposit exceeds £500, and the interest actually earned on it, or which could have been earned if it had been kept in a separate deposit account, is at least £10. In that case, the agent must account for all interest earned, or for the interest which could have been earned in a separate deposit account. Solicitors could follow these regulations themselves. Alternatively, they could refer to the Solicitors' Accounts Rules (see Annex 28B, p.684).

26.11   Practice rule 14 (structural surveys and formal valuations)

'**Solicitors may not provide structural surveys or formal valuations of property unless:**

(a)   **the work is carried out by a principal or employee who is a chartered surveyor or who holds another professional qualification approved by the Council; and**

(b)   **the appropriate contribution has been paid to the Solicitors' Indemnity Fund.**'

Solicitors' Practice Rules 1990, rule 14

26.12   Structural surveys and formal valuations – additional guidance

A solicitor may carry out structural surveys and formal valuations of property as part of his or her practice. Rule 44 of the Solicitors' Indemnity Rules 1998 (see Annex 29A at p.837) details the additional contribution payable and provides that any practice intending to undertake this work must immediately notify Solicitors Indemnity Fund Limited.

26

26.13   Joint property selling practice

1. For a joint property selling practice, see **26.01** note 3 (p.509).

2. Firms wishing to set up such a joint practice may wish to set it up as a SEAL because the participating firms in a SEAL will be less constrained under practice rule 6 (see **26.02**, p.509, and **26.06** notes 7 and 8, p.512).

26.14   Property display centre

1. As an alternative to setting up a SEAL or other form of joint property selling practice, a number of independent firms of solicitors (the participating firms) may join together to carry on a joint property display centre (PDC) to publicise properties in the sale of which an individual participating firm is instructed. In this way, the participating firms may avoid some of the constraints which arise under practice rule 6 in the case of a joint property selling practice.

2. A PDC which observes the requirements set out in note 3 below is regarded as an administrative extension of the practices of the participating firms. It is not regarded either as a department or branch office of all or any of the participating firms, or as a joint property selling practice. The address of a PDC should be notified to Regulation and Information Services (see p.xv for contact details) under section 84(1) of the Solicitors Act 1974 (see **2.09**, p.40) as a business address of all the participating firms. Although it may involve a partnership for administrative purposes between participating firms, a PDC is not a partnership for the purposes of carrying on a solicitors' practice.

Characteristics and functions of a PDC

3. (a) A PDC can have no clients; it may merely carry out certain activities on behalf of the participating firms. Only individual participating firms may be instructed in the sale of a property.

    (b) A PDC is a place where the principal activity carried on is the display and dissemination of information about properties which the individual participating firms have for sale.

    (c) No part of a solicitor's professional practice may be carried on at a PDC. In particular no negotiations may be conducted there; prospective buyers must be referred to the individual participating firm instructed in the sale of the property in question. Instructions to sell a property may only be accepted at offices of participating firms. To avoid problems with practice rule 6 (see **26.06**, p.510) the participating firms must operate totally independently so far as their professional business, including property selling, is concerned.

    (d) A PDC is inherently an administrative extension of the practices of the participating firms, not a separate entity.

(e)   The participating firms may wish to establish a joint service company to carry out support functions connected with the running of the PDC, e.g. hiring premises and equipment. The service company (as with a service company established by an individual firm of solicitors) cannot carry on any legal practice or have any dealings with the property selling or property buying public (see **3.19**, p.88).

(f)   Having regard to rule 1(b) and (c) of the practice rules (see **1.01**, p.1), a participating firm may not make it a condition that a prospective buyer instructs another participating firm in his or her conveyancing or any other matter.

Supervision and management

4.   As no part of a solicitor's practice is carried on at a PDC, rule 13 of the practice rules (supervision and management) does not apply. Note that the participating firms are nevertheless responsible for the activities of the PDC staff and have a duty to supervise them.

A single firm PDC

5.   A single firm of solicitors could establish its own PDC where no negotiations or any other part of the firm's practice was conducted. Rule 13 would not apply to such a PDC. The firm would nevertheless be responsible for the activities of its PDC staff and would have a duty to supervise them.

26.15   Joint property display centre – publicity

1.   Paragraph 10 of the Solicitors' Publicity Code 1990 governs 'flag advertising' (see Annex 11A at p.234). This term includes any advertising by a joint PDC which does not name the firm or firms whose services are being advertised.

2.   Any advertising under the logo of or in the name of a joint PDC, if it does not name the firm or firms whose services are being advertised, must include the word 'solicitor(s)' (see paragraph 10 of the publicity code at p.234) and the PDC's address (or some other address at which the names of all the participating firms are available). A name such as 'Solicitors' Property Centre' or 'Solicitors' Property Centre, Craxenford' (provided it is not misleading or inaccurate) may appear on the PDC premises, advertisements or stationery.

3.   On the PDC premises the PDC name must be accompanied by the names of the participating firms (either outside or visible from outside the premises) and the word 'solicitor(s)'. The PDC stationery must be used only in connection with activities which a PDC may properly undertake in accordance with **26.14** note 3, p.518. In particular it must not be used in connection with negotiations.

26

4.   For the reasons stated in **26.14** note 3, p.518, the name of a service
     company (e.g. 'Solicitors' Property Centre Ltd') should not appear on the
     PDC itself or in its advertisements or any stationery used for writing to the
     property buying and selling public.

5.   An individual participating firm advertising in its own name may refer to its
     membership of the PDC or include the PDC logo in its advertisements. The
     firm's stationery may include the PDC logo or refer to the firm's
     membership of the PDC. Notepaper used for a solicitor's professional
     business, including notepaper used in negotiating a sale of property, must
     include the name of the firm and not merely the name of the PDC.

6.   'For Sale' boards and particulars of properties for sale may, at the
     discretion of the participating firms, either be the boards and particulars of
     an individual participating firm or the boards and particulars of the PDC.
     Boards and particulars of the PDC must comply with notes 2–4 above. An
     individual participating firm may use the PDC name and/or logo on its
     boards or particulars in addition to the firm's own name.

26.16   Joint property display centre – referrals

In practice a prospective client may either first approach an individual
participating firm or the PDC itself. A joint PDC must not accept
instructions on behalf of participating firms. However, rule 3 of the practice
rules (see **11.04**, p.224) allows a PDC to refer prospective clients to the
participating firms. In the light of rule 1(b) of the practice rules (see **1.01**,
p.1) a prospective client should be asked to make his or her own choice
from amongst the participating firms. If he or she decides not to make a
choice, the method whereby a participating firm is selected for a referral is
a matter for the participating firms. Note, however, that if a member of the
PDC staff is asked for a recommendation (rather than for a referral), the
recommendation must only be given on the basis of a genuine belief that
the firm concerned should be recommended.

26.17   Selling property through a separate business

1.   Rule 5 of the practice rules and the Solicitors' Separate Business Code
     1994 (see **3.20**, p.89 and Annex 3E, p.129) permit a solicitor to conduct
     property selling through a separate business, subject to the provisions of
     section 5(2) of the code at p.132.

2.   A solicitor with a separate estate agency business may do conveyancing for
     its buyers, but only if:

     ▶   the estate agency is owned jointly with another practice or business;
         and

     ▶   the solicitor does not do the seller's conveyancing, or does the seller's
         conveyancing under one of the rule 6 exceptions; and

    ▶   the buyer and the seller give their written informed consent; and

    ▶   different individuals deal with the work for them.

3.   A solicitor with a separate estate agency business which provides mortgage related services to a buyer may, nevertheless, do conveyancing for the seller.

Chapter 27

Investment business

Introduction

27.01 Financial Services Act 1986 and future regulation

1. **The financial services regulatory regime is being restructured by the Government with the aim of establishing a single coherent system across the industry. The Financial Services Authority (FSA), which superseded the Securities and Investments Board (SIB) in October 1997, will become the single regulator in relation to the conduct of investment business across all financial markets, when the draft Financial Services and Markets Bill comes into force, which is expected in 2000. The Law Society will continue to regulate firms of solicitors until then. It is likely that a new definition of investment business will enable many firms to avoid the need for authorisation. Firms that do need authorisation under the new regime will be directly regulated by the FSA, as the Recognised Professional Bodies (of which the Law Society is one) will no longer have this role.**

2. Section 3 of the Financial Services Act 1986 (the Act) provides that no person shall carry on investment business unless authorised or exempted. Exempted persons include appointed representatives (tied agents), but rule 12 of the Solicitors' Practice Rules 1990 (see **27.21**, p.533) prohibits solicitors from being appointed representatives of life offices, independent networks or brokers. As solicitors are not exempted persons under the Act it is necessary for them to become authorised if they carry on any investment business as part of a business, as opposed to doing so in a purely personal capacity without remuneration. The definition of investment business is very wide and the majority of firms are likely to need to be authorised.

3. Investment business consists of two elements, an 'investment' and an 'activity constituting investment business'. Work done before 29th April 1988 (when the Act came into force) is not 'investment business'.

27.02 'Investments'

1. 'Investments' are defined in Part I of Schedule 1 to the Act (see Annex 27A, p.535) and include:

   ▶ stocks and shares, including gilt-edged stocks and deferred building society shares;

   ▶ units in collective investment schemes;

   ▶ long-term insurance contracts (for example life policies with an investment element and pensions).

2. The following are examples of financial products which are *not* 'investments' as defined by the Act:

▶ most building society share accounts;

▶ National Savings Certificates, Income Bonds and Premium Savings Bonds;

▶ bank or building society deposit or savings accounts;

▶ insurance policies taken out for pure protection, for example, buildings insurance;

▶ policies which pay benefits only on death or incapacity.

27.03 'Activities constituting investment business'

The activities that may constitute investment business (set out in Part II of Schedule 1 to the Act – see Annex 27A at p.539) are as follows:

▶ dealing in investments – this includes buying or selling shares as agent for a client, e.g. where the solicitor gives the instructions to a stockbroker;

▶ arranging deals in investments – this includes making arrangements for a client to buy a life policy in connection with a house purchase, or for a client to buy or sell unit trusts;

▶ custody of investments – this includes the safeguarding and administration of investments, for example, where the solicitor is holding share certificates and receiving dividends;

▶ managing investments – this has now been interpreted as applying only to discretionary management, which will occur, for example, if all trustees, executors or attorneys are in-house;

▶ investment advice – this includes giving advice on a particular investment, but not generic advice; for example, advice that a repayment mortgage is more appropriate than an endowment mortgage would not be caught;

▶ establishing, operating or winding up collective investment schemes;

▶ sending dematerialised instructions – this relates to paperless trading through CREST.

27.04 Authorisation

1. At present, authorisation under the Act may be obtained in three ways:

▶ through a recognised self-regulating organisation (SRO);

▶ through a recognised professional body (RPB); or

▶ directly from the Financial Services Authority (FSA).

2. As an RPB, the Law Society is able to authorise solicitors, multi-national partnerships and recognised bodies to conduct investment business, by issuing firms with investment business certificates, which will be either category 1 or category 2 certificates (see **27.05** below). Solicitors who are authorised by the Society must comply with the Solicitors' Investment Business Rules (SIBR) – see **27.12**, p.528 and Annex 27B, p.562. The majority of solicitors will obtain authorisation from the Society, but in certain cases, where a large proportion of a solicitor's work is investment business (in excess of the 35% limit set by the FSA – see **27.08**, p.527), it may be necessary for a firm to obtain authorisation through an SRO, such as the Personal Investment Authority (PIA) – see p.xv for contact details.

3. Paragraphs **27.05–27.19** apply to solicitors authorised by the Society to conduct investment business, but **27.20–27.22** (p.531) apply to all solicitors conducting investment business, whether authorised by the Society or by another regulator.

Requirements on solicitors authorised by the Society

27.05 Investment business certificates – application and renewal

1. Firms wishing to be authorised by the Society are required to apply for an investment business certificate. Initial application for a certificate must be made on the prescribed form which is available from Regulation and Information Services (see p.xv for contact details). Applications to renew certificates should be made by 31st October on the prescribed form, which will be sent automatically to all firms holding a current investment business certificate. The Society may, at its discretion, refuse to issue an investment business certificate or may issue one subject to conditions. The form requires general information about the firm, including whether the firm wishes to be authorised to conduct discrete or only non-discrete investment business.

2. Since 1st November 1995 there have been two categories of authorisation: category 1 for non-discrete investment business only, and category 2 for discrete investment business (DIB) (see **27.13**, p.528). Category 2 certificates will be issued only to firms employing a 'qualified person' (see **27.07**, p.526).

27.06 Fees

The fee for an investment business certificate consists of a fee per firm and a fee per partner. This latter fee is based on the number of principals (salaried or equity) within a firm. No refund will be made if a principal leaves the firm

27

during the certification year which runs from 1st November to 31st October, nor will any additional fee be levied for a new principal joining the firm during the year. The term 'principal' includes a sole practitioner, a solicitor or registered foreign lawyer who is a partner, and a solicitor or registered foreign lawyer who is a director or beneficial share-owner of a recognised body. No account will be taken of any partner who is a registered foreign lawyer practising mainly from an office or offices outside England and Wales, provided no investment business is conducted from that office in or into any part of the UK. Details of the fees are available from Regulation and Information Services (see p.xv for contact details).

27.07   Training and competence

1.   Under rules 4(4)(b) and 20 of the SIBR (Annex 27B at pp.566 and 580), firms of solicitors wishing to conduct DIB must hold a category 2 investment business certificate and have in post a 'qualified person' (a principal, director or employee) who is approved by the Society to conduct one or more of the three types of DIB:

   ▶   retail branded/packaged products (for example, life policies);

   ▶   securities/portfolio management; or

   ▶   corporate pensions and advanced schemes.

2.   Under rule 2(3) and (5) of the SIBR (Annex 27B at p.565), firms of solicitors cannot:

   ▶   advise on or effect contingent liability transactions;

   ▶   advise on or effect pension transfers or opt outs;

   ▶   manage ISAs;

   without permission from the Council.

3.   The Society has also issued good practice guidelines relating to the recruitment, supervision and training of non-solicitor financial advisers (see Annex 27O, p.673).

4.   The permission regime for solicitors who wish to manage ISAs was introduced in March 1999. The guidance note to rule 7 of the SIBR (Annex 27B at p.568) explains some of the conditions that will attach to the permssion. Inland Revenue approval will also be required. Further details are available from Professional Ethics or the Monitoring and Investigation Unit (see p.xv for contact details). Some firms may manage only the cash deposit component of an ISA. This activity does not fall within the definition of investment business, so neither the permission regime nor the general provisions of the SIBR will apply. However, the activity is governed by the general principles referred to in the Council statement on managed cash deposit ISAs (Annex 27N, p.671).

27.08   Scope of authorisation

1.   Solicitors authorised by the Society are prohibited from carrying out certain activities constituting investment business, as detailed in rule 2(1) of the SIBR (Annex 27B at p.564).

2.   It has been agreed with the FSA that the Society will not normally continue to authorise firms whose commission from investment business (excluding any amount paid or credited to the client) together with fee income from DIB (see **27.13**, p.528) exceeds 35% of the firm's total gross income from both investment business and non-investment business. This calculation is required in the prescribed form which may be obtained from Regulation and Information Services (see p.xv for contact details) and which requires detailed information about the commission retained by the firm and DIB fee income. Firms should maintain appropriate records throughout the year to enable them to complete the form as required by rules 4, 14 and, where appropriate, rule 26 of the SIBR at pp.565, 577 and 582. Firms that exceed the 35% limit will normally be required to seek authorisation elsewhere.

3.   Authorisation from the Society is given to the firm and covers the activities of all partners, employees and consultants of the firm. The certificate that is issued to a firm will cover only one partnership. Thus, if a firm has more than one office with different partnerships at each office, even though the practices have a common name, separate investment business certificates will be needed for each partnership. However, if one partnership has several offices which practise under different names, the certificate issued to the partnership will cover all the offices of that partnership if appropriate information is given on the notepaper. Further guidance is available from Professional Ethics (see p.xv for contact details).

27.09   Authorisation for non-UK offices

A firm's authorisation will extend to any overseas office provided that it is the same partnership. Where, for example, the Hong Kong office has a foreign lawyer as a partner who is not a partner in the London office, the Hong Kong office will not be covered by the authorisation. Firms carrying on investment business in the UK without a permanent place of business in the UK may be exempted from the need for certification by Part IV of Schedule 1 to the Act (see Annex 27A at p.555). The exemption does not apply if the investment activity results from an oral communication made to the client by the firm without express invitation. Thus, English solicitors practising outside the UK who discuss investment matters with clients in the UK are in danger of infringing the provisions of the Act unless their firms are authorised.

27

27.10   Notification

Chapter 3 of the SIBR (Annex 27B at p.570) contains the notification rules which require firms to notify Regulation and Information Services of certain events (see p.xv for contact details).

27.11 Monitoring

Under the Act, all SROs and RPBs are obliged to have adequate monitoring arrangements. The Society's Monitoring and Investigation Unit carries out periodic visits to firms to ensure compliance with the SIBR and other rules, principles and guidance governing the conduct of investment business by solicitors.

27.12 Investment Business Rules

1. Under the Act, the Society is obliged to have rules governing the conduct of investment business which provide adequate investor protection. The SIBR (Annex 27B, p.562) apply to all firms which hold an investment business certificate issued by the Society, either category 1 or category 2. Solicitors must also comply with SIB's Statement of Principle which together with guidance from the Society, is at Annex 27C, p.610. Principle 3 of SIB's Statement makes reference to codes of market practice; SIB (now the FSA) have endorsed the Takeover Code (guidance from the Society is at Annex 27K, p.665).

2. A step-by-step guide to the SIBR can be found in *Solicitors and Financial Services: a Compliance Handbook* by Peter Camp, which is available from Marston Book Services (see p.xv for contact details). Solicitors requiring advice on the SIBR may contact Professional Ethics (see p.xv for contact details).

27.13 Discrete investment business and non-discrete investment business

The SIBR distinguish between investment business that is discrete investment business (DIB) and that which (by way of exception) is non-discrete. DIB, which is defined in Chapter 4 of the SIBR (Annex 27B at p.571) is, in effect, mainstream investment business and most of the detailed rules of the SIBR will apply only to DIB. There are two main categories of exceptions that make investment business non-discrete:

▶ **Incidental exception** – where the investment business carried on is incidental to the main purpose of the retainer, for example:

    ▶ investment business that is incidental to the legal work involved in the takeover of a company; or

    ▶ the sale of shares that is incidental to the winding up of the estate of a deceased person.

Guidance on corporate finance activities appears at Annex 27I, p.659. However, the incidental exception is not available in relation to life policies, unit trusts or investment trust savings schemes, except for sales during the administration of estates. Thus, even though advice on an endowment policy may be incidental to a conveyancing transaction, the advice remains DIB.

▶ **Permitted third party exception** – where a permitted third party (PTP) is used by the solicitor to carry out investment business. The PTP may be an insurance broker or stockbroker, who is independent and authorised to conduct investment business. In such circumstances the PTP will be responsible for complying with the rules of his or her own SRO or RPB in respect of the particular client. However, the PTP exception will only be available where the firm complies with the specific requirements for using a PTP in rule 10(4) of the SIBR (see p.573).

27.14 Custody of investments

Solicitors providing custody services to a client must comply with rule 17 and appendix 8 of the SIBR (see Annex 27B at pp.579 and 605). Guidance on the custody rules is at Annex 27M, p.668. Solicitors requiring further guidance may contact Professional Ethics (see p.xv for contact details).

27.15 Product and commission disclosure

1. Solicitors conducting any investment business relating to a packaged product or pension fund withdrawal must also comply with appendix 7 of the SIBR (see Annex 27B at p.601).

2. Essentially, these rules require clients to be provided with:

    ▶ a 'key features document' which contains standard information regarding a packaged product or pension fund withdrawal;

    ▶ a 'reason why' letter regarding the suitability for the client of a transaction in a packaged product or pension fund withdrawal; and

    ▶ details of commission which may be receivable by a firm and/or by a PTP in respect of a transaction.

3. Detailed guidance on aspects of the rule is in Annex 27J, p.662. See also **27.20** note 5, p.531, and practice rule 10, see **14.13**, p.283.

27.16 Investment advertisements

Solicitors may issue their own investment advertisements or approve clients' investment advertisements for the purposes of section 57 of the Act. Rule 11 and appendices 1 and 6 of the SIBR (Annex 27B at pp.574, 592 and 597) set out the requirements for such issue or approval. The rule refers to the British Codes of Advertising and Sales Promotion (see Annex 27E, p.631) and to Part 7 of the Financial Services (Conduct of Business) Rules 1990 (Annex 27D, p.613).

27

27.17 Record keeping

1. Solicitors should establish systems within their offices that will enable them to comply with the record keeping requirements detailed in the SIBR. Such records must be made available for inspection by the Monitoring and Investigation Unit. As records are required to demonstrate compliance with the rules, they may be referred to by the client or the Office for the Supervision of Solicitors if any complaint is made about investment business.

2. In addition, the Money Laundering Regulations (see **3.16**, p.84 and Annex 3B, p.95) require all solicitors conducting investment business to verify their clients' identity, subject to certain exemptions, and to keep certain records.

3. Forms IB1, IB2 and IB3, which have been designed for the purpose of keeping some of the records required by the SIBR and the Money Laundering Regulations, are available from Marston Book Services (see p.xv for contact details).

27.18 Pension transfers and opt outs

1. Firms of solicitors who have advised or who currently advise clients about pension transfers and opt outs must comply with the relevant Council statement. Council statement A (Annex 27F, p.633) relating to future pension transfer work, was issued in July 1994, together with Council statement B (Annex 27G, p.642) which relates to past pension transfers. Council statement C (Annex 27G at p.647), issued in June 1995, requires firms to undertake a review of priority cases using the SIB's (now the FSA) specification. Council statement D (Annex 27G at p.653), issued in November 1998, requires firms to undertake phase 2 of the pension transfers and opt outs review in accordance with the FSA's model guidance. Copies of the FSA's specification document and model guidance may be obtained from Professional Ethics (see p.xv for contact details).

2. Guidance on preservation of pension records is at Annex 27H, p.658.

3. Firms wishing to conduct pension transfers and opt outs must apply for permission from the Council (see **27.07** note 2, p.526). Applications should be sent to the Monitoring and Investigation Unit (see p.xv for contact details).

27.19 Investment Services Directive

The Investment Services Directive (93/22/EEC) and the Capital Adequacy Directive (93/6/EEC) were implemented by the Investment Services Regulations 1995 (S.I. 1995 no. 3275). Most firms will not be affected by the directives or the regulations. However, firms conducting DIB will be affected unless they can bring themselves within the 'incidental' exemption referred to in the Investment Services Directive. Firms wishing to remain within this exemption must ensure that their investment services are not held out as a separate business. Further guidance on the directives may be found at Annex 27L, p.667.

Requirements on all solicitors

27.20   Conduct requirements on all solicitors

1.   The following requirements apply to all solicitors conducting investment business, whether authorised by the Society or by another regulator.

Publicity

2.   Solicitors conducting investment business must comply with the Solicitors' Publicity Code 1990 (see Annex 11A, p.229) and, if they are arranging mortgages and advertising this service, with the Consumer Credit (Advertisements) Regulations 1989 (see **25.09** note 9, p.475). Solicitors authorised by the Society to conduct investment business must also have regard to the advertisement provisions of the SIBR (see **27.16**, p.529 and Annex 27B, p.562).

Introductions and referrals

3.   Sections 2(6) and 4(2)–(3) of the Solicitors' Introduction and Referral Code 1990 (see Annex 11B at pp.239 and 243) relate to accepting and making referrals in the field of mortgages or investment business. It should also be noted that a solicitor must not reward an introducer by the payment of commission or otherwise (section 2(3)).

4.   In accordance with **25.09**, p.474, solicitors should ensure either that they refer clients needing investment advice to independent intermediaries or conduct DIB themselves. Where clients are referred by tied agents, solicitors should consider **25.09**, note 4 and, where appropriate, provide independent advice or refer the client to an independent intermediary.

Commissions

5.   Rule 10 of the Solicitors' Practice Rules 1990 (**14.13**, p.283) regarding a solicitor's duties in relation to any commission received of more than £20, is particularly relevant to investment business in view of the substantial commissions which are often received in relation to such business. For further guidance, see **14.14**, p.283 and Annex 14G, p.308. See also **27.15**, p.529.

27

Home income plans

6. Guidance on solicitors' duties in relation to home income plans is at **25.09** note 6, p.475.

General insurance

7. Solicitors involved in general insurance must also be independent intermediaries (see **25.08**, p.473).

Duty to Solicitors Indemnity Fund Ltd

8. All solicitors, including those authorised by a regulator other than the Society, are reminded in Council statement B (Annex 27G, p.642) on pension transfers and opt outs that they must comply with the Solicitors' Indemnity Rules in connection with any steps to be taken by way of rectification of past errors, including the duty to co-operate with SIF Ltd.

PIA members

9. Solicitors who are members of the PIA must ensure that any terms of business letter issued by them, pursuant to the rules of the PIA, comply with their obligations under rule 10 of the Solicitors' Practice Rules 1990 (**14.13**, p.283). Therefore, it has been agreed with the PIA that, where a firm of solicitors is a member of the PIA, the firm should substitute the following words for paragraph (4)(c), Section III, Table 4 of the PIA rules:

   '(c) a statement that as a firm of [solicitors] [solicitors and registered foreign lawyers] [registered foreign lawyers and solicitors] the Member is subject to rules made by the Law Society and that these rules require the Member to pay the customer or credit the customer with any commission which the Member receives unless, after the Member has told the customer the amount of the commission or, if the amount cannot be worked out, the basis of calculation of the commission, the customer agrees that the Member can keep it.'

Money laundering

10. All solicitors conducting investment business are required to observe the Money Laundering Regulations (see **27.17** note 2, p.530). See also **16.07**, p.333 for the conduct implications and Annex 16B, p.337 for a summary of the substantive law.

Separate businesses

11. Solicitors may have separate businesses providing investment business services. They must comply with the Solicitors' Separate Business Code 1994 (see **3.20–3.21**, p.89 and Annex 3E, p.129). Such a separate business will have to be authorised by a regulator other than the Society and must not be an appointed representative, unless an appointed representative of an independent financial adviser (see practice rule 12 at **27.21**, p.533).

27.21   Practice rule 12 (investment business)

'**(1) Without prejudice to the generality of the principles embodied in Rule 1 of these rules, solicitors shall not in connection with investment business:**

(a) **be appointed representatives; or**

(b) **have any arrangements with other persons under which the solicitors could be constrained to recommend to clients or effect for them (or refrain from doing so) transactions in some investments but not others, with some persons but not others, or through the agency of some persons but not others; or to introduce or refer clients or other persons with whom the solicitors deal to some persons but not others.**

(2) Solicitors shall not alone, or by or with others, control, actively participate in or operate any separate business which is an appointed representative, unless it is the appointed representative of an independent financial adviser.

(3) Where a solicitor, authorised to conduct investment business, is required by the rules of the relevant regulatory body to use a particular form of terms of business letter, the solicitor shall use a terms of business letter in a form which has been approved by the Council of the Law Society.

(4) This rule shall have effect in relation to the conduct of investment business within or into any part of the United Kingdom.

(5) In this rule "appointed representative", "investment" and "investment business" have the meanings assigned to them by the Financial Services Act 1986.'

Solicitors' Practice Rules 1990, rule 12

27.22   Practice rule 12 – additional guidance

27

Appointed representative

1. The rule applies specifically to investment business and prohibits a solicitor from being an appointed representative (i.e. a tied agent) or otherwise fettering his or her independence by entering into a restrictive arrangement. The rule also prevents a solicitor from setting up, operating, actively participating in or controlling any separate business which is an appointed representative, unless it is an appointed representative of an independent financial adviser. The rule would not prevent a solicitor from regularly introducing clients to a particular broker, provided that the solicitor had not entered into any arrangement which could constrain him or her to use that broker.

Building society agency arrangements

2.   Where solicitors have agency arrangements with, for example, building societies which are tied agents, the agency services must be confined to non-investment business; otherwise the solicitor-agent might be in breach of practice rule 12. This would apply equally whether the agency is conducted from the solicitor's general office or from an adjoining office which is used solely for the building society agency work.

Terms of business letter

3.   Practice rule 12(3) requires that where firms are authorised by other regulatory bodies and required to use a particular form of terms of business letter, that terms of business letter must be in a form approved by the Council of the Law Society. Guidance for solicitors who are members of the PIA is at **27.20** note 9, p.532. Solicitors who are authorised by the Law Society and are conducting discrete investment business will need to comply with rule 24 of the SIBR (see Annex 27B at p.582).

Annex 27A

Financial Services Act 1986

Schedule 1 – investments and investment business
(with consolidated amendments to 10th November 1997)

[Note: The "General Notes" are reproduced with the kind permission of the Financial Services Authority.]

PART I – INVESTMENTS

Shares etc.

1.   Shares and stock in the share capital of a company.

Note

In this paragraph "company" includes any body corporate and also any unincorporated body constituted under the law of a country or territory outside the United Kingdom but does not, except in relation to any shares of a class defined as deferred shares for the purposes of section 119 of the Building Societies Act 1986, include a building society incorporated under the law of, or of any part of, the United Kingdom, nor does it include an open-ended investment company or any body incorporated under the law of, or of any part of, the United Kingdom relating to industrial and provident societies or credit unions.

General note

By virtue of article 3 of the Financial Services Act 1986 (Investment Services) (Extension of Scope of Act) Order 1995, S.I. 1995 no. 3271, paragraph 1 shall have effect as if transferable shares in a body incorporated under the law of, or any part of, the United Kingdom relating to industrial and provident societies fell within that paragraph.

Debentures

2.   Debentures, including debenture stock, loan stock, bonds, certificates of deposit and other instruments creating or acknowledging indebtedness, not being instruments falling within paragraph 3 below.

Note

This paragraph shall not be construed as applying –

(a)   to any instrument acknowledging or creating indebtedness for, or for money borrowed to defray, the consideration payable under a contract for the supply of goods or services;

(b)   to a cheque or other bill of exchange, a banker's draft or a letter of credit; or

(c)   to a banknote, a statement showing a balance in a current, deposit or savings account or (by reason of any financial obligation contained in it) to a lease or other disposition of property, a heritable security or an insurance policy.

General note

By virtue of article 4 of the Financial Services Act 1986 (Investment Services) (Extension of Scope of Act) Order 1995, S.I. 1995 no. 3271, paragraph 2 shall have effect as if bills of exchange accepted by a banker fell within that paragraph.

Government and public securities

3.   Loan stock, bonds and other instruments creating or acknowledging indebtedness issued by or on behalf of a government, local authority or public authority.

Notes

(1)   In this paragraph "government, local authority or public authority" means –

    (a)   the government of the United Kingdom, of Northern Ireland, or of any country or territory outside the United Kingdom;

    (b)   a local authority in the United Kingdom or elsewhere;

    (c)   any international organisation the members of which include the United Kingdom or another member State.

(2)   The note to paragraph 2 above shall, so far as applicable, apply also to this paragraph.

(3)   This paragraph does not apply to any instrument creating or acknowledging indebtedness in respect of money received by the Director of Savings as deposits or otherwise in connection with the business of the National Savings Bank or in respect of money raised under the National Loans Act 1968 under the auspices of the Director of Savings or in respect of money treated as having been so raised by virtue of section 11(3) of the National Debt Act 1972.

General note

By virtue of section 2(1) of the European Economic Area Act 1993 "member State" in Note (1)(c) above means a state of the European Economic Area and a state of the European Union.

Instruments entitling to shares or securities

4.   Warrants or other instruments entitling the holder to subscribe for investments falling within paragraph 1, 2 or 3 above.

Notes

(1)   It is immaterial whether the investments are for the time being in existence or identifiable.

(2)   An investment falling within this paragraph shall not be regarded as falling within paragraph 7, 8 or 9 below.

Certificates representing securities

5.   Certificates or other instruments which confer –

    (a)   property rights in respect of any investment falling within paragraph 1, 2, 3 or 4 above;

    (b)   any right to acquire, dispose of, underwrite or convert an investment, being a right to which the holder would be entitled if he held any such investment to which the certificate or instrument relates; or

    (c)   a contractual right (other than an option) to acquire any such investment otherwise than by subscription.

Note

This paragraph does not apply to any instrument which confers rights in respect of two or more investments issued by different persons or in respect of two or more different investments falling within paragraph 3 above and issued by the same person.

Units in collective investment scheme

6.　Units in a collective investment scheme, including shares in or securities of an open-ended investment company.

Options

7.　Options to acquire or dispose of –

(a)　an investment falling within any other paragraph of this Part of this Schedule;

(b)　currency of the United Kingdom or of any other country or territory;

(c)　gold, palladium, platinum or silver; or

(d)　an option to acquire or dispose of an investment falling within this paragraph by virtue of (a), (b) or (c) above.

Futures

8.　Rights under a contract for the sale of a commodity or property of any other description under which delivery is to be made at a future date and at a price agreed upon when the contract is made.

Notes

(1)　This paragraph does not apply if the contract is made for commercial and not investment purposes.

(2)　A contract shall be regarded as made for investment purposes if it is made or traded on a recognised investment exchange or made otherwise than on a recognised investment exchange but expressed to be as traded on such an exchange or on the same terms as those on which an equivalent contract would be made on such an exchange.

(3)　A contract not falling within Note (2) above shall be regarded as made for commercial purposes if under the terms of the contract delivery is to be made within seven days.

(4)　The following are indications that any other contract is made for a commercial purpose and the absence of any of them is an indication that it is made for investment purposes –

(a)　either or each of the parties is a producer of the commodity or other property or uses it in his business;

(b)　the seller delivers or intends to deliver the property or the purchaser takes or intends to take delivery of it.

(5)　It is an indication that a contract is made for commercial purposes that the price, the lot, the delivery date or the other terms are determined by the parties for the purposes of the particular contract and not by reference to regularly published prices, to standard lots or delivery dates or to standard terms.

(6)　The following are also indications that a contract is made for investment purposes –

(a)　it is expressed to be as traded on a market or on an exchange;

(b)　performance of the contract is ensured by an investment exchange or a clearing house;

(c)　there are arrangements for the payment or provision of margin.

27

(7)　A price shall be taken to have been agreed upon when a contract is made –

(a)　notwithstanding that it is left to be determined by reference to the price at which a contract is to be entered into on a market or exchange or could be entered into at a time and place specified in the contract; or

(b)　in a case where the contract is expressed to be by reference to a standard lot and quality, notwithstanding that provision is made for a variation in the price to take account of any variation in quantity or quality on delivery.

Contracts for differences etc.

9.　Rights under a contract for differences or under any other contract the purpose or pretended purpose of which is to secure a profit or avoid a loss by reference to fluctuations in the value or price of property of any description or in an index or other factor designated for that purpose in the contract.

Notes

(1)　This paragraph does not apply where the parties intend that the profit is to be obtained or the loss avoided by taking delivery of any property to which the contract relates.

(2)　This paragraph does not apply to rights under any contract under which money is received by the Director of Savings as deposits or otherwise in connection with the business of the National Savings Bank or raised under the National Loans Act 1968 under the auspices of the Director of Savings or under which money raised is treated as having been so raised by virtue of section 11(3) of the National Debt Act 1972.

Long term insurance contracts

10.　Rights under a contract the effecting and carrying out of which constitutes long term business within the meaning of the Insurance Companies Act 1982.

Notes

(1)　This paragraph does not apply to rights under a contract of insurance if –

(a)　the benefits under the contract are payable only on death or in respect of incapacity due to injury, sickness or infirmity;

(b)　no benefits are payable under the contract on a death (other than a death due to accident) unless it occurs within ten years of the date on which the life of the person in question was first insured under the contract or before that person attains a specified age not exceeding seventy years;

(c)　the contract has no surrender value or the consideration consists of a single premium and the surrender value does not exceed that premium; and

(d)　the contract does not make provision for its conversion or extension in a manner that would result in its ceasing to comply with paragraphs (a), (b) and (c) above.

(2)　Where the provisions of a contract of insurance are such that the effecting and carrying out of the contract –

(a)　constitutes both long term business within the meaning of the Insurance Companies Act 1982 and general business within the meaning of that Act; or

(b)　by virtue of section 1(3) of that Act constitutes long term business notwithstanding the inclusion of subsidiary general business provisions, references in this paragraph to rights and benefits under the contract are references only to such rights and benefits as are attributable to the provisions of the contract relating to long term business.

(3)　This paragraph does not apply to rights under a re-insurance contract.

(4)　Rights falling within this paragraph shall not be regarded as falling within paragraph 9 above.

Rights and interests in investments

11. Rights to and interests in anything which is an investment falling within any other paragraph of this Part of this Schedule.

Notes

(1) This paragraph does not apply to interests under the trusts of an occupational pension scheme.

(2) This paragraph does not apply to rights or interests which are investments by virtue of any other paragraph of this Part of this Schedule.

PART II – ACTIVITIES CONSTITUTING INVESTMENT BUSINESS

Dealing in investments

12. Buying, selling, subscribing for or underwriting investments or offering or agreeing to do so, either as principal or as an agent.

Notes

(1) This paragraph does not apply to a person by reason of his accepting, or offering or agreeing to accept, whether as principal or as agent, an instrument creating or acknowledging indebtedness in respect of any loan, credit, guarantee or other similar financial accommodation or assurance which he or his principal has made, granted or provided or which he or his principal has offered or agreed to make, grant or provide.

(2) The references in (1) above to a person accepting, or offering or agreeing to accept, an instrument include references to a person becoming, or offering or agreeing to become, a party to an instrument otherwise than as a debtor or a surety.

Arranging deals in investments

13. Making, or offering or agreeing to make –

(a) arrangements with a view to another person buying, selling, subscribing for or underwriting a particular investment; or

(b) arrangements with a view to a person who participates in the arrangements buying, selling, subscribing for or underwriting investments.

Notes

(1) This paragraph does not apply to a person by reason of his making, or offering or agreeing to make, arrangements with a view to a transaction to which he will himself be a party as principal or which will be entered into by him as agent for one of the parties.

(2) The arrangements in (a) above are arrangements which bring about or would bring about the transaction in question.

(3) This paragraph does not apply to a person ("the relevant person") who is either a money-lending company within the meaning of section 338 of the Companies Act 1985 or a body corporate incorporated under the law of, or of any part of, the United Kingdom relating to building societies or a person whose ordinary business includes the making of loans or the giving of guarantees in connection with loans by reason of the relevant person making, or offering or agreeing to make, arrangements with a view to a person ("the authorised person") who is either authorised under section 22 or 23 of this Act or who is authorised under section 31 of this Act and carries on insurance business which is investment business selling an investment which falls within paragraph 10 above or, so far as relevant to that paragraph, paragraph 11 above if the arrangements are either –

27

(a) that the authorised person or a person on his behalf will introduce persons to whom the authorised person has sold or proposes to sell an investment of the kind described above, or will advise such persons to approach, the relevant person with a view to the relevant person lending money on the security of that investment; or

(b) that the authorised person gives an assurance to the relevant person as to the amount which will or may be received by the relevant person, should that person lend money to a person to whom the authorised person has sold or proposes to sell an investment of the kind described above, on the surrender or maturity of that investment if it is taken as security for the loan.

(4) This paragraph does not apply to a person by reason of his making, or offering or agreeing to make, arrangements with a view to a person accepting, whether as principal or as agent, an instrument creating or acknowledging indebtedness in respect of any loan, credit, guarantee or other similar financial accommodation or assurance which he or his principal has made, granted or provided or which he or his principal has offered or agreed to make, grant or provide.

(5) Arrangements do not fall within (b) above by reason of their having as their purpose the provision of finance to enable a person to buy, sell, subscribe for or underwrite investments.

(6) This paragraph does not apply to arrangements for the introduction of persons to another person if –

(a) the person to whom the introduction is made is an authorised or exempted person or is a person whose ordinary business involves him in engaging in activities which fall within this Part of this Schedule or would do apart from the provisions of Part III or Part IV and who is not unlawfully carrying on investment business in the United Kingdom; and

(b) the introduction is made with a view to the provision of independent advice or the independent exercise of discretion either –

(i) in relation to investments generally; or

(ii) in relation to any class of investments if the transaction or advice is or is to be with respect to an investment within that class.

(7) The references in (4) above to a person accepting an instrument include references to a person becoming a party to an instrument otherwise than as a debtor or a surety.

Custody of investments

13A. (1) Safeguarding and administering or arranging for the safeguarding and administration of assets belonging to another where –

(a) those assets consist of or include investments; or

(b) the arrangements for their safeguarding and administration are such that those assets may consist of or include investments and the arrangements have at any time been held out as being arrangements under which investments would be safeguarded and administered.

(2) Offering or agreeing to safeguard and administer, or to arrange for the safeguarding and administration of, assets belonging to another where the circumstances fall within sub-paragraph (1)(a) or (b) above.

Notes

(1) This paragraph does not apply to a person by reason of his safeguarding and administering assets, or offering or agreeing to do so, under arrangements –

(a) under which another person ("the primary custodian"), who is permitted to provide a service falling within this paragraph, undertakes to the person to whom the assets belong a responsibility in respect of the assets which is no less onerous than the responsibility which the primary custodian would undertake to that person if the primary custodian were safeguarding and administering the assets himself, and

(b) which are operated by the primary custodian in the course of carrying on in the United Kingdom investment business falling within this paragraph.

(2) None of the following activities constitutes the administration of assets –

(a) providing information as to the number of units or the value of any assets safeguarded;

(b) converting currency; and

(c) receiving documents relating to an investment solely for the purpose of onward transmission to, from or at the direction of the person to whom the investment belongs.

(3) For the purposes of this paragraph it is immaterial that the assets safeguarded and administered –

(a) constitute units of a security, title to which is recorded on the relevant register of securities as being held in uncertificated form; or

(b) may be transferred to another person, subject to a commitment by the person safeguarding and administering them, or arranging for their safeguarding and administration, that they will be replaced by equivalent assets at some future date or when so requested by the person to whom they belong.

(4) This paragraph does not apply to arrangements for the introduction of persons to another person if –

(a) the person to whom the introduction is made is permitted to provide a service falling within this paragraph; and

(b) the introduction is made with a view to the provision in the United Kingdom of a service falling within this paragraph or the making of arrangements operated in the United Kingdom for the provision of a service falling within this paragraph by a person who is not connected with the person by whom the introduction is made.

For the purposes of this Note, the person making the introduction shall be regarded as connected with the other person if he is either a body corporate in the same group as that other person or remunerated by that other person.

(5) For the purposes of Notes (1) and (4) above, a person is permitted to provide a service falling within this paragraph if –

(a) he is an authorised person who may provide that service –

(i) without contravening any rules that apply to him under section 48 of this Act; or

(ii) by virtue of his membership of a recognised self-regulating organisation or his certification by a recognised professional body; or

(b) he is an exempted person as respects any investment business which consists of or includes that service; or

(c) he is entitled to carry on investment business in the United Kingdom which consists of or includes that service pursuant either to regulation 5 of the Banking Coordination (Second Council Directive) Regulations 1992 or to regulation 5 of the Investment Services Regulations 1995.

27

Managing investments

14. Managing, or offering or agreeing to manage, assets belonging to another person if –

    (a) those assets consist of or include investments; or

    (b) the arrangements for their management are such that those assets may consist of or include investments at the discretion of the person managing or offering or agreeing to manage them and either they have at any time since the date of the coming into force of section 3 of this Act done so or the arrangements have at any time (whether before or after that date) been held out as arrangements under which they would do so.

Investment advice

15. Giving, or offering or agreeing to give, to persons in their capacity as investors or potential investors advice on the merits of their purchasing, selling, subscribing for or underwriting an investment, or exercising any right conferred by an investment to acquire, dispose of, underwrite or convert an investment.

Establishing etc. collective investment schemes

16. Establishing, operating or winding up a collective investment scheme, including acting as trustee of an authorised unit trust scheme or as depositary or sole director of an investment company with variable capital.

Sending dematerialised instructions etc.

16A. Sending on behalf of another person dematerialised instructions relating to an investment by means of –

    (a) a relevant system in respect of which an Operator is approved under the Uncertificated Securities Regulations 1995;

    (b) a computer-based system, established by the Bank of England and the London Stock Exchange, through the medium of which specified securities may be transferred or allotted without the need for an instrument in writing,

or offering or agreeing to do so, or causing on behalf of another person such instructions to be sent by such means or offering or agreeing to do so.

Notes

(1) This paragraph does not apply to a person by reason of his sending, or causing the sending of, instructions by means of a system falling within (a) above on behalf of –

    (a) a participating issuer or settlement bank acting in its capacity as such; or

    (b) an offeror making a takeover offer,

or by reason of his offering or agreeing to do so.

(1A) This paragraph does not apply to a person –

    (a) by reason of his sending, or causing the sending of, instructions by means of a system falling within (b) above on behalf of a settlement bank acting in its capacity as such, or by reason of his offering or agreeing to do so; or

    (b) by reason of any activity in which he engages, or in which he offers or agrees to engage, at a time when he is accredited by the Bank of England as a provider of a network for the purposes of a system falling within (b) above and which is a necessary part of the provision of such a network.

(2)   For the purposes of this paragraph a person shall be taken to cause, or to offer or agree to cause, the sending of a dematerialised instruction only if –

     (a)   in the case of a system falling within (a) above, he is a system-participant; and

     (b)   in the case of a system falling within (b) above, he is a person who, under an agreement with the Bank of England, is responsible for the operation of, and the maintenance of security over, a gateway.

(3)   In this paragraph –

"dematerialised instruction" –

     (a)   in relation to a system falling within (a) above, has the meaning given by regulation 3 of the Uncertificated Securities Regulations 1995, and

     (b)   in relation to a system falling within (b) above, means an instruction sent by means of a gateway;

"gateway", in relation to a system falling within (b) above, means computer hardware and software by means of which instructions are authenticated and encrypted for processing by the system;

"offeror" has the meaning given by section 428 of the Companies Act 1985;

"Operator", "participating issuer" and "relevant system" have the meaning given by regulation 3 of the Uncertificated Securities Regulations 1995;

"settlement bank" –

     (a)   in relation to a system falling witin (a) above, has the meaning given by regulation 3 of the Uncertificated Securities Regulations 1995, and

     (b)   in relation to a system falling within (b) above, means a person who has agreed to make payments in connection with the discharge of debts or liabilities arising from the transfer or allotment of specified securities made through the medium of that system;

"specified securities" has the meaning given by the Stock Transfer Act 1982;

"system-participant" has the meaning given by regulation 3 of the Uncertificated Securities Regulations 1995;

"takeover offer" has the meaning given by section 428 of the Companies Act 1985.

PART III – EXCLUDED ACTIVITIES

Dealings as principal

17.   (1)   Paragraph 12 above applies to a transaction which is or is to be entered into by a person as principal only if –

     (a)   he holds himself out as willing to enter into transactions of that kind at prices determined by him generally and continuously rather than in respect of each particular transaction; or

     (b)   he holds himself out as engaging in the business of buying investments with a view to selling them and those investments are or include investments of the kind to which the transaction relates; or

     (c)   he regularly solicits members of the public for the purpose of inducing them to enter as principals or agents into transactions to which that paragraph applies and the transaction is or is to be entered into as a result of his having solicited members of the public in that manner.

(2)   In sub-paragraph (1) above "buying" and "selling" means buying and selling by transactions to which paragraph 12 above applies and "members of the public", in relation to the person soliciting them ("the relevant person"), means any other persons except –

(a)   authorised persons, exempted persons, or persons holding a permission under paragraph 23 below;

(b)   members of the same group as the relevant person;

(c)   persons who are, or propose to become, participators with the relevant person in a joint enterprise;

(d)   any person who is solicited by the relevant person with a view to –

(i)   the acquisition by the relevant person of 20 per cent. or more of the voting shares in a body corporate (that is to say, shares carrying not less than that percentage of the voting rights attributable to share capital which are exercisable in all circumstances at any general meeting of the body); or

(ii)   if the relevant person (either alone or with other members of the same group as himself) holds 20 per cent. or more of the voting shares in a body corporate, the acquisition by him of further shares in the body or the disposal by him of shares in that body to the person solicited or to a member of the same group as that person; or

(iii) if the person solicited (either alone or with other members of the same group as himself) holds 20 per cent. or more of the voting shares in a body corporate, the disposal by the relevant person of further shares in that body to the person solicited or to a member of the same group as that person;

(e)   any person whose head office is outside the United Kingdom, who is solicited by an approach made or directed to him at a place outside the United Kingdom and whose ordinary business involves him in engaging in activities which fall within Part II of this Schedule or would do so apart from this Part or Part IV.

(3)   Sub-paragraph (1) above applies only –

(a)   if the investment to which the transaction relates or will relate falls within any of paragraphs 1 to 6 above or, so far as relevant to any of those paragraphs, paragraph 11 above; or

(b)   if the transaction is the assignment (or, in Scotland, the assignation) of an investment falling within paragraph 10 above or is the assignment (or, in Scotland, the assignation) of an investment falling within paragraph 11 above which confers rights to or interests in an investment falling within paragraph 10 above.

(4)   Paragraph 12 above does not apply to any transaction which relates or is to relate to an investment which falls within paragraph 10 above or, so far as relevant to that paragraph, paragraph 11 above nor does it apply to a transaction which relates or is to relate to an investment which falls within any of paragraphs 7 to 9 above or, so far as relevant to any of those paragraphs, paragraph 11 above being a transaction which, in either case, is or is to be entered into by a person as principal if he is not an authorised person and the transaction is or is to be entered into by him –

(a) with or through an authorised person, an exempted person or a person holding a permission under paragraph 23 below; or

(b) through an office outside the United Kingdom, maintained by a party to the transaction, and with or through a person whose head office is situated outside the United Kingdom and whose ordinary business is such as is mentioned in sub-paragraph (2)(e) above.

General notes

By virtue of regulation 55 of and sub-paragraph 44(1) of Schedule 9 to the Banking Coordination (Second Council Directive) Regulations 1992, S.I. 1992 no. 3218, paragraph 17 shall have effect as if any reference to authorised persons, or an authorised person, included a reference to European institutions, or a European institution, carrying on home-regulated investment business in the United Kingdom. By virtue of regulation 32 of and sub-paragraph 42(1) of Schedule 7 to the Investment Services Regulations 1995, S.I. 1995 no. 3275, paragraph 17 shall have effect as if any reference to authorised persons, or an authorised person, included a reference to European investment firms, or a European investment firm, carrying on home-regulated investment business in the United Kingdom. By virtue of article 2(1) of the Financial Services Act 1986 (Restriction of Scope of Act and Meaning of Collective Investment Scheme) Order 1996, S.I. 1996 no. 2996, nothing in paragraph 17 shall have the effect that the provision of any core investment service to third parties on a professional basis is excluded from the activities which fall within the paragraphs in Part II of Schedule 1 in any case in which the service is provided –

(a) by a UK investment firm; or

(b) by an investment firm which would be a UK investment firm if it was incorporated in or formed under the law of any part of the United Kingdom or, being an individual, had his head office in the United Kingdom.

Groups and joint enterprises

18. (1) Paragraph 12 above does not apply to any transaction which is or is to be entered into by a person as principal with another person if –

(a) they are bodies corporate in the same group; or

(b) they are, or propose to become, participators in a joint enterprise and the transaction is or is to be entered into for the purposes of, or in connection with, that enterprise.

(2) Paragraph 12 above does not apply to any transaction which is or is to be entered into by any person as agent for another person in the circumstances mentioned in sub-paragraph (1)(a) or (b) above if –

(a) where the investment falls within any of paragraphs 1 to 6 above or, so far as relevant to any of those paragraphs, paragraph 11 above, the agent does not –

(i) hold himself out (otherwise than to other bodies corporate in the same group or persons who are or propose to become participators with him in a joint enterprise) as engaging in the business of buying investments with a view to selling them and those investments are or include investments of the kind to which the transaction relates; or

(ii) regularly solicit members of the public for the purpose of inducing them to enter as principals or agents into transactions to which paragraph 12 above applies;

27

and the transaction is not or is not to be entered into as a result of his having solicited members of the public in that manner;

(b)   where the investment is not as mentioned in paragraph (a) above –

(i)   the agent enters into the transaction with or through an authorised person, an exempted person or a person holding a permission under paragraph 23 below; or

(ii)   the transaction is effected through an office outside the United Kingdom, maintained by a party to the transaction, and with or through a person whose head office is situated outside the United Kingdom and whose ordinary business involves him in engaging in activities which fall within Part II of this Schedule or would do so apart from this Part or Part IV.

(3)   Paragraph 13 above does not apply to arrangements which a person makes or offers or agrees to make if –

(a)   that person is a body corporate and the arrangements are with a view to another body corporate in the same group entering into a transaction of the kind mentioned in that paragraph; or

(b)   that person is or proposes to become a participator in a joint enterprise and the arrangements are with a view to another person who is or proposes to become a participator in the enterprise entering into such a transaction for the purposes of or in connection with that enterprise.

(3A) Paragraph 13A above does not apply to a service which a person provides or offers or agrees to provide or to arrangements which a person makes or offers or agrees to make for the provision of a service if –

(a)   that person is a body corporate and the service is or is to be provided to a body corporate in the same group and relates or will relate to assets which belong to that other body corporate; or

(b)   that person is or proposes to become a participator in a joint enterprise and the assets to which the service relates or will relate are or are to be held on behalf of another person who is or proposes to become a participator in the enterprise and are or are to be held for the purposes of or in connection with the enterprise.

(4)   Paragraph 14 above does not apply to a person by reason of his managing or offering or agreeing to manage the investments of another person if –

(a)   they are bodies corporate in the same group; or

(b)   they are, or propose to become, participators in a joint enterprise and the investments are or are to be managed for the purposes of, or in connection with, that enterprise.

(5)   Paragraph 15 above does not apply to advice given by a person to another person if –

(a)   they are bodies corporate in the same group; or

(b)   they are, or propose to become, participators in a joint enterprise and the advice is given for the purposes of, or in connection with, that enterprise.

(5A) Paragraph 16A does not apply to a body corporate by reason of its sending, or causing the sending of, dematerialised instructions relating to an investment or offering or agreeing to do so if –

    (a)   the person on whose behalf the instructions are, or are to be, sent or caused to be sent is a body corporate in the same group; and

    (b)   the investment to which the instructions relate, or will relate, is one in respect of which a body corporate in the same group is registered as the holder on the appropriate register of securities, or will be so registered as a result of the instructions.

(5B) In sub-paragraph (5A) "register of securities" –

    (a)   in relation to a system falling within paragraph 16A(a) above, has the meaning given by regulation 3 of the Uncertificated Securities Regulations 1995; and

    (b)   in relation to a system falling within paragraph 16A(b) above, means a register of holders of specified securities (within the meaning of the Stock Transfer Act 1982) which is kept by the Bank of England.

(6)   The definitions in paragraph 17(2) above shall apply also for the purposes of sub-paragraph (2)(a) above except that the relevant person referred to in paragraph 17(2)(d) shall be the person for whom the agent is acting.

General notes

By virtue of regulation 55 of and sub-paragraph 44(2) of Schedule 9 to the Banking Coordination (Second Council Directive) Regulations 1992, S.I. 1992 no. 3218, paragraph 18 shall have effect as if the reference in sub-paragraph (2) to an authorised person included a reference to a European institution carrying on home-regulated investment business in the United Kingdom. By virtue of regulation 32 of and sub-paragraph 42(2) of Schedule 7 to the Investment Services Regulations 1995, S.I. 1995 no. 3275, paragraph 18 shall have effect as if the reference in sub-paragraph 2 to an authorised person included a reference to a European investment firm carrying on home-regulated investment business in the United Kingdom. By virtue of article 2(1) of the Financial Services Act 1986 (Restriction of Scope of Act and Meaning of Collective Investment Scheme) Order 1996, S.I. 1996 no. 2996, nothing in paragraph 18 shall have the effect that the provision of any core investment service to third parties on a professional basis is excluded from the activities which fall within the paragraphs in Part II of Schedule 1 in any case in which the service is provided –

(a)   by a UK investment firm; or

(b)   by an investment firm which would be a UK investment firm if it was incorporated in or formed under the law of any part of the United Kingdom or, being an individual, had his head office in the United Kingdom.

Sale of goods and supply of services

19. (1)   Subject to sub-paragraph (9) below, this paragraph has effect where a person ("the supplier") sells or offers or agrees to sell goods to another person ("the customer") or supplies or offers or agrees to supply him with services and the supplier's main business is to supply goods or services and not to engage in activities falling within Part II of this Schedule.

    (2)   Paragraph 12 above does not apply to any transaction which is or is to be entered into by the supplier as principal if it is or is to be entered into by him with the customer for the purposes of or in connection with the sale or supply or a related sale or supply (that is to say, a sale or supply to the customer

otherwise than by the supplier but for or in connection with the same purpose as the first-mentioned sale or supply).

(3) Paragraph 12 above does not apply to any transaction which is or is to be entered into by the supplier as agent for the customer if it is or is to be entered into for the purposes of or in connection with the sale or supply or a related sale or supply and –

    (a) where the investment falls within any of paragraphs 1 to 6 above or, so far as relevant to any of those paragraphs, paragraph 11 above, the supplier does not –

        (i) hold himself out (otherwise than to the customer) as engaging in the business of buying investments with a view to selling them and those investments are or include investments of the kind to which the transaction relates; or

        (ii) regularly solicit members of the public for the purpose of inducing them to enter as principals or agents into transactions to which paragraph 12 above applies;

    and the transaction is not or is not to be entered into as a result of his having solicited members of the public in that manner;

    (b) where the investment is not as mentioned in paragraph (a) above, the supplier enters into the transaction –

        (i) with or through an authorised person, an exempted person or a person holding a permission under paragraph 23 below; or

        (ii) through an office outside the United Kingdom, maintained by a party to the transaction, and with or through a person whose head office is situated outside the United Kingdom and whose ordinary business involves him in engaging in activities which fall within Part II of this Schedule or would do so apart from this Part or Part IV.

(4) Paragraph 13 above does not apply to arrangements which the supplier makes or offers or agrees to make with a view to the customer entering into a transaction for the purposes of or in connection with the sale or supply or a related sale or supply.

(4A) Paragraph 13A above does not apply to a service which the supplier provides or offers or agrees to provide or to arrangements which the supplier makes or offers or agrees to make for the provision of a service where the assets to which the service relates or will relate are or are to be held for the purposes of or in connection with the sale or supply or a related sale or supply.

(5) Paragraph 14 above does not apply to the supplier by reason of his managing or offering or agreeing to manage the investments of the customer if they are or are to be managed for the purposes of or in connection with the sale or supply or a related sale or supply.

(6) Paragraph 15 above does not apply to advice given by the supplier to the customer for the purposes of or in connection with the sale or supply or a related sale or supply or to a person with whom the customer proposes to enter into a transaction for the purposes of or in connection with the sale or supply or a related sale or supply.

(7)   Where the supplier is a body corporate and a member of a group sub-paragraphs (2) to (6) above shall apply to any other member of the group as they apply to the supplier; and where the customer is a body corporate and a member of a group references in those sub-paragraphs to the customer include references to any other member of the group.

(8)   The definitions in paragraphs 17(2) above shall apply also for the purposes of sub-paragraph (3)(a) above.

(9)   This paragraph does not have effect where either –

(a)   the customer is an individual; or

(b)   the transaction in question is the purchase or sale of an investment which falls within paragraph 6 or 10 above or, so far as relevant to either of those paragraphs, paragraph 11 above; or

(c)   the investments which the supplier manages or offers or agrees to manage consist of investments falling within paragraph 6 or 10 above or, so far as relevant to either of those paragraphs, paragraph 11 above; or

(d)   the advice which the supplier gives is advice on an investment falling within paragraph 6 or 10 above or, so far as relevant to either of those paragraphs, paragraph 11 above.

General note

By virtue of article 2(1) of the Financial Services Act 1986 (Restriction of Scope of Act and Meaning of Collective Investment Scheme) Order 1996, S.I. 1996 no. 2996, nothing in paragraph 19 shall have the effect that the provision of any core investment service to third parties on a professional basis is excluded from the activities which fall within the paragraphs in Part II of Schedule 1 in any case in which the service is provided –

(a)   by a UK investment firm; or

(b)   by an investment firm which would be a UK investment firm if it was incorporated in or formed under the law of any part of the United Kingdom or, being an individual, had his head office in the United Kingdom.

Employees' share schemes

20.   (1)   Paragraphs 12, 13 and 13A above do not apply to anything done by a body corporate, a body corporate connected with it or a relevant trustee for the purpose of enabling or facilitating transactions in shares in or debentures of the first-mentioned body between or for the benefit of any of the persons mentioned in sub-paragraph (2) below or the holding of such shares or debentures by or for the benefit of any such persons.

(2)   The persons referred to in sub-paragraph (1) above are –

(a)   the bona fide employees or former employees of the body corporate or of another body corporate in the same group; or

(b)   the wives, husbands, widows, widowers, or children or step-children under the age of eighteen of such employees or former employees.

(3)   In this paragraph "a relevant trustee" means a person holding shares in or debentures of a body corporate as trustee in pursuance of arrangements made for the purpose mentioned in sub-paragraph (1) above by, or by a body corporate connected with, that body corporate.

(4) In this paragraph "shares" and "debentures" include any investment falling within paragraph 1 or 2 above and also include any investment falling within paragraph 4 or 5 above so far as relating to those paragraphs or any investment falling within paragraph 11 above so far as relating to paragraph 1, 2, 4 or 5.

(5) For the purposes of this paragraph a body corporate is connected with another body corporate if –

    (a) they are in the same group; or

    (b) one is entitled, either alone or with any other body corporate in the same group, to exercise or control the exercise of a majority of the voting rights attributable to the share capital which are exercisable in all circumstances at any general meeting of the other body corporate or of its holding company.

Sale of body corporate

21. (1) Paragraphs 12 and 13 above do not apply to the acquisition or disposal of, or to anything done for the purposes of the acquisition or disposal of, shares in a body corporate other than an open-ended investment company, and paragraph 15 above does not apply to advice given in connection with the acquisition or disposal of such shares, if –

    (a) the shares consist of or include shares carrying 75 per cent. or more of the voting rights attributable to share capital which are exercisable in all circumstances at any general meeting of the body corporate; or

    (b) the shares, together with any already held by the person acquiring them, carry not less than that percentage of those voting rights; and

    (c) in either case, the acquisition and disposal is, or is to be, between parties each of whom is a body corporate, a partnership, a single individual or a group of connected individuals.

(2) For the purposes of subsection (1)(c) above "a group of connected individuals", in relation to the party disposing of the shares, means persons each of whom is, or is a close relative of, a director or manager of the body corporate and, in relation to the party acquiring the shares, means persons each of whom is, or is a close relative of, a person who is to be a director or manager of the body corporate.

(3) In this paragraph "close relative" means a person's spouse, his children and step-children, his parents and step-parents, his brothers and sisters and his step-brothers and step-sisters.

General note

By virtue of article 2(1) of the Financial Services Act 1986 (Restriction of Scope of Act and Meaning of Collective Investment Scheme) Order 1996, S.I. 1996 no. 2996, nothing in paragraph 21 has the effect that the provision of any core investment service to third parties on a professional basis is excluded from the activities which fall within the paragraphs in Part II of Schedule 1 in any case in which the service is provided –

(a) by a UK investment firm; or

(b) by an investment firm which would be a UK investment firm if it was incorporated in or formed under the law of any part of the United Kingdom or, being an individual, had his head office in the United Kingdom.

Trustees and personal representatives

22. (1) Paragraph 12 above does not apply to a person by reason of his buying, selling or subscribing for an investment or offering or agreeing to do so if –

    (a) the investment is or, as the case may be, is to be held by him as bare trustee or, in Scotland, as nominee for another person;

    (b) he is acting on that person's instructions; and

    (c) he does not hold himself out as providing a service of buying and selling investments.

  (2) Paragraph 13 above does not apply to anything done by a person as trustee or personal representative with a view to –

    (a) a fellow trustee or personal representative and himself engaging in their capacity as such in an activity falling within paragraph 12 above; or

    (b) a beneficiary under the trust, will or intestacy engaging in any such activity,

unless that person is remunerated for what he does in addition to any remuneration he receives for discharging his duties as trustee or personal representative.

  (2A) Paragraph 13A above does not apply to anything done by a person as trustee or personal representative unless –

    (a) he holds himself out as providing a service falling within paragraph 13A above; or

    (b) he is remunerated for providing such a service in addition to any remuneration he receives for discharging his duties as trustee or personal representative.

  (3) Paragraph 14 above does not apply to anything done by a person as trustee or personal representative unless he holds himself out as offering investment management services or is remunerated for providing such services in addition to any remuneration he receives for discharging his duties as trustee or personal representative.

  (4) Paragraph 15 above does not apply to advice given by a person as trustee or personal representative to –

    (a) a fellow trustee or personal representative for the purposes of the trust or estate; or

    (b) a beneficiary under the trust, will or intestacy concerning his interest in the trust fund or estate,

unless that person is remunerated for doing so in addition to any remuneration he receives for discharging his duties as trustee or personal representative.

  (4A) Paragraph 16A does not apply to a person by reason of his sending, or causing the sending of, dematerialised instructions relating to an investment held by him as trustee or as personal representative, or by reason of his offering or agreeing to do so.

  (5) Sub-paragraph (1) above has effect to the exclusion of paragraph 17 above as respects any transaction in respect of which the conditions in sub-paragraph (1)(a) and (b) are satisfied.

Dealings in course of non-investment business

23. (1)   Paragraph 12 above does not apply to anything done by a person –

   (a)   as principal;

   (b)   if that person is a body corporate in a group, as agent for another member of the group; or

   (c)   as agent for a person who is or proposes to become a participator with him in a joint enterprise and for the purposes of or in connection with that enterprise, if it is done in accordance with the terms and conditions of a permission granted to him by the Secretary of State under this paragraph.

   (2)   Any application for permission under this paragraph shall be accompanied or supported by such information as the Secretary of State may require and shall not be regarded as duly made unless accompanied by the prescribed fee.

   (3)   The Secretary of State may grant a permission under this paragraph if it appears to him –

   (a)   that the applicant's main business, or if he is a member of a group the main business of the group, does not consist of activities for which a person is required to be authorised under this Act;

   (b)   that the applicant's business is likely to involve such activities which fall within paragraph 12 above; and

   (c)   that, having regard to the nature of the applicant's main business and, if he is a member of a group, the main business of the group taken as a whole, the manner in which, the persons with whom and the purposes for which the applicant proposes to engage in activities that would require him to be an authorised person and to any other relevant matters, it is inappropriate to require him to be subject to regulation as an authorised person.

   (4)   Any permission under this paragraph shall be granted by a notice in writing; and the Secretary of State may by a further notice in writing withdraw any such permission if for any reason it appears to him that it is not appropriate for it to continue in force.

   (5)   The Secretary of State may make regulations requiring persons holding permissions under the paragraph to furnish him with information for the purpose of enabling him to determine whether those permissions should continue in force; and such regulations may, in particular, require such persons –

   (a)   to give him notice forthwith of the occurrence of such events as are specified in the regulations and such information in respect of those events as is so specified;

   (b)   to furnish him at such times or in respect of such periods as are specified in the regulations with such information as is so specified.

   (6)   Section 61 of this Act shall have effect in relation to a contravention of any condition imposed by a permission under this paragraph as it has effect in relation to any such contravention as is mentioned in subsection (1)(a) of that section.

(7)　Section 104 of this Act shall apply to a person holding a permission under this paragraph as if he were authorised to carry on investment business as there mentioned; and sections 105 and 106 of this Act shall have effect as if anything done by him in accordance with such permission constituted the carrying on of investment business.

General note

By virtue of article 6(2) of the Financial Services Act 1986 (Investment Services) (Extension of Scope of Act) Order 1995, S.I. 1995 no. 3271, paragraph 23 shall have effect as if it precluded a permission being granted to any person who is an investment firm. The functions of the Secretary of State under this paragraph were transferred to the Securities and Investments Board Ltd by article 3 of the Financial Services Act 1986 (Delegation) Order 1987, S.I. 1987 no. 942.

Advice given or arrangements made in course of profession or non-investment business

24.　(1)　Paragraph 15 above does not apply to advice –

　　(a)　which is given in the course of the carrying on of any profession or of a business not otherwise constituting investment business; and

　　(b)　the giving of which is a necessary part of other advice or services given in the course of carrying on that profession or business.

　(2)　Paragraph 13 above does not apply to arrangements –

　　(a)　which are made in the course of the carrying on of any profession or of a business not otherwise constituting investment business; and

　　(b)　the making of which is a necessary part of other services provided in the course of carrying on that profession or business.

　(2A)　Paragraph 13A above does not apply to the provision of a service or to arrangements made for the provision of a service where –

　　(a)　the service is provided or the arrangements are made in the course of the carrying on of any profession or of a business not otherwise constituting investment business; and

　　(b)　the provision of the service or the making of the arrangements is a necessary part of other services provided in the course of carrying on that profession or business.

　(3)　Advice shall not be regarded as falling within sub-paragraph (1)(b) above, the making of arrangements shall not be regarded as falling within sub-paragraph (2)(b) above and the provision of a service or the arranging for the provision of a service shall not be regarded as falling within sub-paragraph (2A)(b) above if the giving of the advice, the making of the arrangements or the provision, or the arranging for the provision, of the service is remunerated separately from the other advice or services.

Custody of group pension funds by certain insurance companies

24A. (1)　Paragraph 13A above does not apply to anything done by a relevant insurance company in relation to the investments of any pension fund which is established solely for the benefit of the officers or employees and their dependants of that company or of any other body corporate in the same group as that company.

　(2)　In sub-paragraph (1) above "relevant insurance company" means an insurance company to which Part II of the Insurance Companies Act 1982 applies but to which section 22 of this Act does not apply.

27

Newspapers

25.   (1)   Paragraph 15 above does not apply to advice given in a newspaper, journal, magazine or other periodical publication if the principal purpose of the publication, taken as a whole and including any advertisements contained in it, is not to lead persons to invest in any particular investment.

     (2)   The Secretary of State may, on the application of the proprietor of any periodical publication, certify that it is of the nature described in sub-paragraph (1) above and revoke any such certificate if he considers that it is no longer justified.

     (3)   A certificate given under sub-paragraph (2) above and not revoked shall be conclusive evidence of the matters certified.

General note

The functions of the Secretary of State under this paragraph were transferred to the Securities and Investments Board Ltd by article 3 of the Financial Services Act 1986 (Delegation) Order 1987, S.I. 1987 no. 942.

Advice given in television, sound or teletext services

25A. (1)   Paragraph 15 above does not apply to any advice given in any programme included, or made for inclusion, in –

        (a)   any television broadcasting service or other television programme service (within the meaning of Part I of the Broadcasting Act 1990); or

        (b)   any sound broadcasting service or licensable sound programme service (within the meaning of Part III of that Act); or

        (c)   any teletext service.

    (2)   For the purposes of this paragraph, "programme", in relation to a service mentioned in sub-paragraph (1) above, includes an advertisement and any other item included in the service.

International securities self-regulating organisations

25B. (1)   An activity within paragraph 13 above engaged in for the purposes of carrying out the functions of a body or association which is approved under this paragraph as an international securities self-regulating organisation, whether by the organisation or by any person acting on its behalf, shall not constitute the carrying on of investment business in the United Kingdom for the purposes of Chapter II of Part I of this Act.

    (2)   In this paragraph –

"international securities business" means the business of buying, selling, subscribing for or underwriting investments (or offering or agreeing to do so, either as principal or agent) which fall within any of the paragraphs in Part I above other than paragraph 10 and, so far as relevant to paragraph 10, paragraph 11 and which, by their nature, and the manner in which the business is conducted, may be expected normally to be bought or dealt in by persons sufficiently expert to understand any risks involved, where either the transaction is international or each of the parties may be expected to be indifferent to the location of the other, and, for the purposes of this definition, the fact that the investments may ultimately be bought otherwise than in the course of international securities business by persons not so expert shall be disregarded; and "international securities self-regulating organisation" means a body corporate or unincorporated association which –

(a)   does not have its head office in the United Kingdom;

(b)   is not eligible for recognition under section 37 or section 39 of this Act on the ground that (whether or not it has applied, and whether or not it would be eligible on other grounds) it is unable to satisfy the requirements of section 40(2)(a) or (c) of this Act;

(c)   has a membership composed of persons falling within any of the following categories, that is to say, authorised persons, exempted persons, persons holding a permission under paragraph 23 above and persons whose head offices are outside the United Kingdom and whose ordinary business is such as is mentioned in paragraph 17(2)(e) above; and

(d)   which facilitates and regulates the activity of its members in the conduct of international securities business.

(3)   The Secretary of State may approve as an international securities self-regulating organisation any body or association appearing to him to fall within sub-paragraph (2) above if, having regard to such matters affecting international trade, overseas earnings and the balance of payments or otherwise as he considers relevant, it appears to him that to do so would be desirable and not result in any undue risk to investors.

(4)   Any approval under this paragraph shall be given by notice in writing; and the Secretary of State may by a further notice in writing withdraw any such approval if for any reason it appears to him that it is not appropriate for it to continue in force.

General note

The functions of the Secretary of State under this paragraph were transferred to the Treasury by article 2(1)(b) of the Transfer of Functions (Financial Services) Order, S.I. 1992 no. 1315.

PART IV – ADDITIONAL EXCLUSIONS FOR PERSONS WITHOUT PERMANENT PLACE OF BUSINESS IN UNITED KINGDOM

27

Transactions with or through authorised or exempted persons

26.   (1)   Paragraph 12 above does not apply to any transaction by a person not falling within section 1(3)(a) of this Act ("an overseas person") with or through –

(a)   an authorised person; or

(b)   an exempted person acting in the course of business in respect of which he is exempt.

(2)   Paragraph 13 above does not apply if –

(a)   the arrangements are made by an overseas person with, or the offer or agreement to make them is made by him to or with, an authorised person or an exempted person and, in the case of an exempted person, the arrangements are with a view to his entering into a transaction in respect of which he is exempt; or

(b)   the transactions with a view to which the arrangements are made are, as respects transactions in the United Kingdom, confined to transactions by authorised persons and transactions by exempted persons in respect of which they are exempt.

General note

By virtue of regulation 55 of and sub-paragraph 44(3) of Schedule 9 to the Banking Coordination (Second Council Directive) Regulations 1992, S.I. 1992 no. 3218, paragraph 26 shall have effect as if any reference to an authorised person, or authorised persons, included a reference to a European institution, or European institutions, carrying on home-regulated investment business in the United Kingdom. By virtue of regulation 32 of and sub-paragraph 42(3) of Schedule 7 to the Investment Services Regulations 1995, S.I. 1995 no. 3275, paragraph 26 shall have effect as if any reference to an authorised person, or authorised persons, included a reference to a European investment firm, or European investment firms, carrying on home-regulated investment business in the United Kingdom.

Unsolicited or legitimately solicited transactions etc. with or for other persons

27.   (1)   Paragraph 12 above does not apply to any transaction entered into by an overseas person as principal with, or as agent for, a person in the United Kingdom, paragraphs 13, 13A, 14 and 15 above do not apply to any offer made by an overseas person to or agreement made by him with a person in the United Kingdom and paragraph 15 above does not apply to any advice given by an overseas person to a person in the United Kingdom if the transaction, offer, agreement or advice is the result of –

(a)   an approach made to the overseas person by or on behalf of the person in the United Kingdom which either has not been in any way solicited by the overseas person or has been solicited by him in a way which has not contravened section 56 or 57 of this Act; or

(b)   an approach made by the overseas person which has not contravened either of those sections.

(2)   Where the transaction is entered into by the overseas person as agent for a person in the United Kingdom, sub-paragraph (1) above applies only if –

(a)   the other party is outside the United Kingdom; or

(b)   the other party is in the United Kingdom and the transaction is the result of such an approach by the other party as is mentioned in sub-paragraph (1)(a) above or of such an approach as is mentioned in sub-paragraph (1)(b) above.

(3)   Paragraph 16A does not apply to any offer made by an overseas person to or agreement made by him with a person in the United Kingdom if the offer or agreement is the result of –

(a)   an approach made to the overseas person by or on behalf of the person in the United Kingdom which either has not been in any way solicited by the overseas person, or has been solicited by him in a way which has not contravened section 56 or 57 of this Act; or

(b)   an approach made by the overseas person which has not contravened either of those sections.

PART V – INTERPRETATION

28. (1) In this Schedule –

    (a) "property" includes currency of the United Kingdom or any other country or territory;

    (b) references to an instrument include references to any record whether or not in the form of a document;

    (c) references to an offer include references to an invitation to treat;

    (d) references to buying and selling include references to any acquisition or disposal for valuable consideration.

  (2) In sub-paragraph (1)(d) above "disposal" includes –

    (a) in the case of an investment consisting of rights under a contract or other arrangements, assuming the corresponding liabilities under the contract or arrangements;

    (b) in the case of any other investment, issuing or creating the investment or granting the rights or interests of which it consists;

    (c) in the case of an investment consisting of rights under a contract, surrendering, assigning or converting those rights.

  (3) A company shall not by reason of issuing its own shares or share warrants, and a person shall not by reason of issuing his own debentures or debenture warrants, be regarded for the purposes of this Schedule as disposing of them or, by reason of anything done for the purpose of issuing them, be regarded as making arrangements with a view to a person subscribing for or otherwise acquiring them or underwriting them.

  (4) In sub-paragraph (3) above "company" has the same meaning as in paragraph 1 above, "shares" and "debentures" include any investments falling within paragraph 1 or 2 above and "share warrants" and "debenture warrants" means any investment which falls within paragraph 4 above and relates to shares in the company concerned or, as the case may be, to debentures issued by the person concerned.

29. For the purposes of this Schedule a transaction is entered into through a person if he enters into it as agent or arranges for it to be entered into by another person as principal or agent.

30. (1) For the purposes of this Schedule a group shall be treated as including any body corporate in which a member of the group holds a qualifying capital interest.

  (2) A qualifying capital interest means an interest in relevant shares of the body corporate which the member holds on a long-term basis for the purpose of securing a contribution to its own activities by the exercise of control or influence arising from that interest.

  (3) Relevant shares means shares comprised in the equity share capital of the body corporate of a class carrying rights to vote in all circumstances at general meetings of the body.

27

(4) A holding of 20 per cent. or more of the nominal value of the relevant shares of a body corporate shall be presumed to be a qualifying capital interest unless the contrary is shown.

(5) In this paragraph "equity share capital" has the same meaning as in the Companies Act 1985 and the Companies (Northern Ireland) Order 1986.

31. In this Schedule "a joint enterprise" means an enterprise into which two or more persons ("the participators") enter for commercial reasons related to a business or businesses (other than investment business) carried on by them; and where a participator is a body corporate and a member of a group each other member of the group shall also be regarded as a participator in the enterprise.

32. Where a person is an exempted person as respects only part of the investment business carried on by him anything done by him in carrying on that part shall be disregarded in determining whether any paragraph of Part III or IV of this Schedule applies to anything done by him in the course of business in respect of which he is not exempt.

33. In determining for the purposes of this Schedule whether anything constitutes an investment or the carrying on of investment business section 18 of the Gaming Act 1845, section 1 of the Gaming Act 1892, any corresponding provision in force in Northern Ireland and any rule of the law of Scotland whereby a contract by way of gaming or wagering is not legally enforceable shall be disregarded.

34. (1) For the purposes of this Schedule arrangements are not a collective investment scheme if –

    (a) the property to which the arrangements relate (other than cash awaiting investment) consists of shares;

    (b) they constitute a complying fund;

    (c) each participant is the owner of a part of the property to which the arrangements relate and, to the extent that his part of that property –

        (i) comprises relevant shares of a class which are admitted to the Official List of any member State or to dealings on a recognised investment exchange, he is entitled to withdraw it at any time after the end of the period of five years beginning with the date on which the shares in question were issued;

        (ii) comprises relevant shares which do not fall within sub-paragraph (i) above, he is entitled to withdraw it at any time after the end of the period of two years beginning with the date upon which the period referred to in sub-paragraph (i) above expired;

        (iii) comprises any other shares, he is entitled to withdraw it at any time after the end of the period of six months beginning with the date upon which the shares in question ceased to be relevant shares; and

        (iv) comprises cash which the operator has not agreed (conditionally or unconditionally) to apply in subscribing for shares, he is entitled to withdraw it at any time; and

    (d) the arrangements would meet the conditions described in section 75(5)(c) of this Act were it not for the fact that the operator is entitled to exercise all or any of the rights conferred by shares included in the property to which the arrangements relate.

(2)   For the purposes of this paragraph –

   (a)   "shares" means investments falling within paragraph 1 of this Schedule;

   (b)   shares shall be regarded as being relevant shares if and so long as they are shares in respect of which neither –

      (i)   a claim for relief made in accordance with section 306 of the Income and Corporation Taxes Act 1988 has been disallowed; nor

      (ii)   an assessment has been made pursuant to section 307 of that Act withdrawing or refusing relief by reason of the body corporate in which the shares are held having ceased to be a body corporate which is a qualifying company for the purposes of section 293 of that Act; and

   (c)   arrangements shall be regarded as constituting a complying fund if they provide that –

      (i)   the operator will, so far as practicable, make investments each of which, subject to each participant's individual circumstances, qualify for relief by virtue of Chapter III of Part VII of the Income and Corporation Taxes Act 1988; and

      (ii)   the minimum subscription to the arrangements made by each participant must be not less than £2,000.

General note

By virtue of section 2(1) of the European Economic Area Act 1993 "member State" in sub-paragraph (1)(c)(i) above means a state of the European Economic Area and a state of the European Union.

35.   For the purposes of this Schedule the following are not collective investment schemes –

   (a)   arrangements where the entire contribution of each participant is a deposit within the meaning of section 5 of the Banking Act 1987 or a sum of a kind described in subsection (3) of that section;

   (b)   arrangements under which the rights or interests of the participants are represented by the following –

      (i)   investments falling within paragraph 2 of this Schedule which are issued by a single body corporate which is not an open-ended investment company or which are issued by a single issuer which is not a body corporate and are guaranteed by the government of the United Kingdom, of Northern Ireland, or of any country or territory outside the United Kingdom; or

      (ii)   investments falling within sub-paragraph (i) above which are convertible into or exchangeable for investments falling within paragraph 1 of this Schedule provided that those latter investments are issued by the same person as issued the investments falling within sub-paragraph (i) above or are issued by a single other issuer; or

      (iii)   investments falling within paragraph 3 of this Schedule issued by the same government, local authority or public authority; or

      (iv)   investments falling within paragraph 4 of this Schedule which are issued otherwise than by an open-ended investment company and which confer

27

rights in respect of investments, issued by the same issuer, falling within paragraph 1 of this Schedule or within sub-paragraph (i), (ii) or (iii) above;

(c) arrangements which would fall within paragraph (b) above were it not for the fact that the rights or interests of a participant ("the counterparty") whose ordinary business involves him in engaging in activities which fall within Part II of this Schedule or would do so apart from Part III or IV are or include rights or interests under a swap arrangement, that is to say, an arrangement the purpose of which is to facilitate the making of payments to participants whether in a particular amount or currency or at a particular time or rate of interest or all or any combination of those things, being an arrangement under which –

(i) the counterparty is entitled to receive amounts (whether representing principal or interest) payable in respect of any property subject to the scheme or sums determined by reference to such amounts; and

(ii) the counterparty makes payments (whether or not of the same amount and whether or not in the same currency as those referred to in sub-paragraph (i) above) which are calculated in accordance with an agreed formula by reference to the amounts or sums referred to in sub-paragraph (i) above;

(d) arrangements under which the rights or interests of participants are rights to or interests in money held in a common account in circumstances in which the money so held is held on the understanding that an amount representing the contribution of each participant is to be applied either in making payments to him or in satisfaction of sums owed by him or in the acquisition of property or the provision of services for him;

(e) arrangements under which the rights and interests of participants are rights and interests in a fund which is a trust fund within the meaning of section 42(1) of the Landlord and Tenant Act 1987;

(f) arrangements where –

(i) each of the participants is a bona fide employee or former employee (or the wife, husband, widow, widower, or child (including, in Northern Ireland, adopted child) or step-child under the age of eighteen of such an employee or former employee) of any of the following bodies corporate, that is to say, The National Grid Company plc, Electricity Association Services Limited or any other body corporate in the same group as either of them being arrangements which are operated by any of those bodies corporate; and

(ii) the property to which the arrangements relate consists of shares or debentures (as defined in paragraph 20(4) above) in or of a body corporate which is an electricity successor company for the purposes of Part II of the Electricity Act 1989 or a body corporate which would be regarded as connected with such an electricity successor company for the purposes of paragraph 20 above,

and for the purposes of this paragraph references to former employees shall have the same meaning as in the Financial Services Act 1986 (Electricity Industry Exemptions) Order 1990.

36. (1)   For the purposes of this Schedule, arrangements are not a collective investment scheme if they are operated by a body corporate, a body corporate connected with it or a relevant trustee, for the purpose of enabling or facilitating transactions in shares in or debentures of the first-mentioned body between or for the benefit of any of the persons mentioned in sub-paragraph (2) below or the holding of such shares or debentures by or for the benefit of any such persons.

     (2)   The persons referred to in sub-paragraph (1) above are –

        (a)   the bona fide employees or former employees of the body corporate or of another body corporate in the same group; or

        (b)   the wives, husbands, widows, widowers, or children or step-children under the age of eighteen of such employees or former employees.

     (3)   In this paragraph, "a relevant trustee" means a person holding shares in or debentures of a body corporate as trustee in pursuance of arrangements mentioned in sub-paragraph (1) above which were made by, or by a body corporate connected with, that body corporate.

     (4)   In this paragraph "shares" and "debentures" include any investment falling within paragraph 1 or 2 above and also include any investment falling within paragraph 4 or 5 above so far as relating to those paragraphs or any investment falling within paragraph 11 above so far as relating to paragraphs 1, 2, 4 or 5.

     (5)   For the purposes of this paragraph a body corporate is connected with another body corporate if –

        (a)   they are in the same group; or

        (b)   one is entitled, either alone or with any other body corporate in the same group, to exercise or control the exercise of a majority of the voting rights attributable to the share capital which are exercisable in all circumstances at any general meeting of the other body corporate or its holding company.

37. For the purposes of this Schedule, arrangements are not a collective investment scheme if –

     (a)   the purpose of the arrangements is that participants should receive, by way of reward, payments or other benefits in respect of the introduction by any person of other persons who become participants;

     (b)   the arrangements are such that the payments or other benefits referred to in paragraph (a) above are to be wholly or mainly funded out of the contributions of other participants; and

     (c)   the only reason why the arrangements have either or both of the characteristics mentioned in section 75(3) of this Act is because, pending their being used to fund those payments or other benefits, contributions of participants are managed as a whole by or on behalf of the operator of the scheme.

27

Annex 27B

Solicitors' Investment Business Rules 1995

with consolidated amendments to 29th March 1999

Rules dated 20th December 1995 made by the Council of the Law Society with the concurrence of the Master of the Rolls under sections 31 and 32 of the Solicitors Act 1974, Schedule 15 paragraph 6 of the Financial Services Act 1986 and section 9 of the Administration of Justice Act 1985, regulating the English and Welsh practices of those firms of solicitors, multi-national partnerships and recognised bodies authorised by the Law Society in the conduct of investment business, and regulating the overseas practices of such persons in the conduct of investment business in or into any part of the United Kingdom.

CONTENTS

CHAPTER 1 – APPLICATION

CHAPTER 2 – CERTIFICATION RULES

CHAPTER 3 – NOTIFICATION RULES

CHAPTER 4 – DISCRETE INVESTMENT BUSINESS

CHAPTER 5 – CONDUCT OF BUSINESS RULES APPLICABLE TO ALL FIRMS

11. Advertisements

12. Unsolicited calls

13. Execution of transactions

14. Record of commissions

15. Compliance officer

16. Records

17. Custody of clients' assets

18. Special categories: EIS investments, packaged products and pension fund withdrawals

CHAPTER 6 – CONDUCT OF BUSINESS RULES APPLICABLE ONLY TO FIRMS UNDERTAKING DISCRETE INVESTMENT BUSINESS

19. Application

20. Qualified persons

21. Statement of authorisation

22. Know your client and investment advice

23. Contract notes

24. Client information and agreements

25. Managed portfolios

26. Bills of costs

27. Records

CHAPTER 7 – MONITORING

28. Inspection

CHAPTER 8 – MISCELLANEOUS

29. Reliance on others

30. Waivers

31. Service

CHAPTER 9 – INTERPRETATION

32–35   Interpretation

27

APPENDIX 1 – ADVERTISING (rule 11)

APPENDIX 2 – CLIENT INFORMATION AND AGREEMENTS (rule 24)

APPENDIX 3 – PERIODIC STATEMENTS (rule 25)

APPENDIX 4 – COSTS (rule 26)

APPENDIX 5 – SOLICITOR TRUSTEES (rules 9(3)(b)(i) and 9(4)(c))

APPENDIX 6 – ADDITIONAL RULES FOR ENTERPRISE INVESTMENT SCHEME INVESTMENTS (rule 18)

APPENDIX 7 – ADDITIONAL RULES FOR PACKAGED PRODUCTS AND PENSION FUND WITHDRAWALS (rule 18)

APPENDIX 8 – CUSTODY RULES (rule 17)

[Words in italics in these rules are defined in chapter 9 of the rules – see p.584.]

CHAPTER 1 – APPLICATION

1. COMMENCEMENT

(1) *These rules* shall come into operation on 1st June 1996, from which date they will replace the Solicitors' Investment Business Rules 1990.

(2) For the avoidance of doubt the provisions of the Solicitors' Investment Business Rules 1990 relating to the retention of records made or documents kept under those rules shall continue to apply, subject to any more stringent requirement under rule 27(3) where the records subsequently relate to an investment service performed after *these rules* come into force.

2. SCOPE OF AUTHORISATION

(1) Subject to any restrictions under *these rules* resulting from its category of *certificate*, a *firm* may carry on any activity constituting investment business **except:–**

    (a) market making in investments; or

    (b) buying, selling, subscribing for or underwriting investments as principal where the *firm* holds itself out as engaging in the business of buying such investments with a view to selling them; or

(c)   acting as a stabilising manager within the meaning of Part 10 of the Financial Services (Conduct of Business) Rules 1990; or

(d)   acting as the trustee or operator of a *regulated collective investment scheme*; or

(e)   entering into a *broker funds arrangement*.

(2)   The permission conferred by a *firm's certificate* shall extend to any activity carried out by an individual as a principal, *employee* or *officer* of the *firm*.

(3)   Subject as provided in sub-rule (4) a *firm* may not advise on or effect:–

(a)   *contingent liability transactions*, or

(b)   *pension transfers* or *opt-outs*

unless the Council has granted permission to the *firm* under rule 7.

(4)   Sub-rule (3)(a) above does not apply if the *activity is incidental* and sub-rule (3)(b) only applies where the activity is *discrete investment business* or where the *transaction* is effected on an *execution-only* basis.

(5)   A *firm* may not act as an *ISA manager* unless the Council has granted permission to the *firm* under rule 7.

Guidance note

The effect of sub-rule 4 is that firms may advise on or effect certain contingent liability transactions without Council permission. An example might be where the firm acts in relation to the sale or purchase of the shares in a company where the agreement involves the granting of options over shares; this activity is likely to be incidental and therefore not DIB. The definition of contingent liability transaction does not include the purchase of options.

3. APPLICATION

(1)   *These rules* shall apply to the conduct of investment business by a *firm* **except:–**

(a)   its *excepted insolvency activities*, or

(b)   investment business which is not *regulated business*.

Guidance note

Given the definition of regulated business, the application of these rules is likely to be confined to investment business carried on in or into any part of the UK.

(2)   Rule 28 shall apply to a *firm* which no longer holds a *certificate* but which has done so within 1 year preceding the requirement under rule 28(1) being made.

CHAPTER 2 – CERTIFICATION RULES

4. ISSUE OF CERTIFICATES

(1) Form of application and fee

Every application for a *certificate* shall be in such form and accompanied by such other information and such fee or fees as the Council may decide for the category sought.

(2) Issue of certificate

The Council may, following an application:–

(a)   issue a category 1 or 2 *certificate* as specified in sub-rule (4), or

(b)   refuse to issue a *certificate*, or

(c)   issue a *certificate* subject to conditions, or

(d)   request further information.

(3) Form of certificate

(a)   The *certificate* issued to a sole solicitor shall be in the name of the practice.

(b)   The *certificate* issued to a partnership:–

    (i)   shall be issued in the partnership name, and

    (ii)   shall authorise the carrying on of investment business in that name:–

        (A)   by the partnership to which that *certificate* is issued, or

        (B)   by any partnership which succeeds to that business, or

        (C)   by any person who succeeds to that business having previously carried it on in partnership.

(c)   If there is a dissolution of a partnership to which a *certificate* has been issued and more than one *firm* subsequently claims to be the successor to the business of the partnership, the *certificate* shall be treated as having been withdrawn 28 days after the dissolution.

(d)   If there is a merger of two or more *firms*, each of which holds a *certificate*, the *certificates* shall be treated as having merged and the separate *certificates* shall not subsequently be available in the event of a dissolution.

(e)   The *certificate* issued to a *recognised body* shall be issued in its name.

(4) Categories of certificate

Any *firm* is an *authorised person*, but:–

(a)   a *firm* holding a category 1 *certificate* may not conduct *discrete investment business*; and

(b)   a *firm* holding a category 2 *certificate* may conduct *discrete investment business* subject to rules 7 and 20.

(5) Renewal of certificate

By 31st October in each year or by such other date as the Council may decide:–

(a)   every *firm* wishing to continue to conduct investment business shall apply to the Society for the issue of a new *certificate* or

(b)   every *firm* no longer wishing to conduct investment business shall notify the Society that a new *certificate* is not required, notification being in such form and accompanied by such other information as the Council may decide.

(6) Liability

It shall be a condition of any *certificate* that neither the Society nor any of its officers or servants or agents nor any members of the Council or its committees shall be liable in damages or otherwise for anything done or omitted to be done in the discharge or purported discharge of its functions under *these rules*, unless the act or omission is shown to have been in bad faith.

5. CONTROL OF CERTIFICATES BY THE COUNCIL

(1) Withdrawing or suspending certificates or imposing conditions

The Council may suspend, withdraw, or impose conditions on, a *certificate* by giving written notice to the *firm* stating:–

(a) the reasons;

(b) the date on which the notice is to take effect;

(c) in the case of suspension, its duration or the circumstances in which the suspension will terminate.

(2) Automatic withdrawal of a certificate

A *certificate* shall be automatically withdrawn if:–

(a) a sole solicitor ceases to practise as such or to hold a practising certificate currently in force; or

(b) in the case of a partnership of solicitors and/or *recognised bodies* or a *multi-national partnership*, all the solicitors who are partners (if any) cease to hold practising certificates currently in force, and the recognition of all *recognised bodies* which are partners (if any) is revoked or expires; or

(c) in the case of a *recognised body*, its recognition is revoked or expires; or

(d) a *firm* ceases to be a *multi-national partnership* because it no longer has a solicitor as a member; or

(e) there has been a dissolution of a partnership without succession; or

(f) a new *certificate* is issued.

(3) Public notice

The Society may in respect of any *certificate* give public notice of any suspension or withdrawal or of the imposition of conditions.

6. APPEAL

(1) Where the Council have:–

(a) refused to issue a *certificate* or a *certificate* of the category sought; or

(b) issued a *certificate* subject to conditions; or

(c)   imposed conditions on a *certificate*; or

(d)   suspended or withdrawn a *certificate*;

the *firm* concerned may, after exhausting any internal appeal procedure, appeal to the Master of the Rolls within 1 month of being notified of the Council's final decision.

(2)   The Council have power to defer the operation of a decision pending the outcome of any appeal.

Guidance note

Any appeal is governed by the Master of the Rolls (Appeals and Applications) Regulations 1991 (as amended).

7.   APPROVALS AND PERMISSIONS

(1)   Approvals and permissions

The Council may, following an application:–

(a)   approve a person to conduct *discrete investment business* of any particular type (or types), or

(b)   grant permission to a *firm* to advise on or effect:–

  (i)   *contingent liability transactions*, or

  (ii)   *pension transfers* or *opt outs,* or

(c)   grant permission to a *firm* to act as an *ISA manager*,

subject to such conditions as the Council may decide.

(2)   Form of application

Every application for such approval or permission shall be made in such form and accompanied by such information as the Council may decide.

(3)   Withdrawing approval or permission or imposing conditions

The Council may suspend or withdraw, or impose conditions on, any approval or permission given under sub-rule (1) by giving written notice to the *qualified person* (in the case of approval) or to the *firm* (in the case of permission) stating:–

(a)   the reasons;

(b)   the date on which the notice is to take effect;

(c)   in the case of suspension, its duration or the circumstances in which the suspension will terminate.

Guidance note

The Council will only grant permission under rule 7(1)(c) if the firm fulfils the conditions of the Individual Savings Account Regulations 1998 and is seeking approval from the Commissioners of the Inland Revenue for the purposes of the Regulations as an account manager. Firms granted permission to act as an ISA manager will be required to confirm to the Law Society that the Commissioners of the

Inland Revenue have granted approval. Further, such firms will have to undertake to comply with the Adopted FIMBRA Rules of PIA applicable to such business as specified in Part II of Appendix A to Part 2 of the Financial Services (Conduct of Business) (ISAs) Rules 1999.

Individual Savings Accounts (ISAs) allow investors to invest in equity, insurance or cash components. An ISA may be a maxi ISA (where one manager looks after all the money invested) or a mini ISA (where the manager looks after only one component). Solicitors who, with the Council's permission, manage maxi ISAs will be involved in investment business as defined by the Financial Services Act 1986 and as such will be subject to these rules. Although cash is not an investment as defined by the Financial Services Act 1986, the management of cash with other investments will be regulated by the Act since management is defined in paragraph 14 of Schedule 1 as "Managing or offering or agreeing to manage assets belonging to another person if – (a) those assets consist of or include investments. . . ".

Solicitors who choose to be managers of a mini ISA looking after a client's cash deposit only will not be undertaking investment business. Consequently no permission will be required from the Council, although the Individual Savings Account Regulations 1998 require such solicitors to be approved by the Inland Revenue to act as ISA managers. However, solicitors are reminded that the provisions of the Solicitors' Accounts Rules will apply to the cash received and held by the firm and that the provisions of rule 1 of the Solicitors' Practice Rules 1990 will apply. Further, certain specified minimum information should be given to clients before solicitors enter into an agreement for a cash only mini ISA:

▶   if the ISA is stated as satisfying the CAT Standards (the Cost, Access and Terms Standards for ISAs prescribed from time to time by H.M. Treasury), a comparison of the account against the CAT Standards; or

▶   if the ISA is not stated as satisfying the CAT Standards, a statement making this clear, together with, if desired, any relevant information; and

▶   minimum amount to open an account;

▶   minimum yearly deposit;

▶   the interest rate earned, and if and how it might vary;

▶   the calculation of interest;

▶   how to make withdrawals and any limits;

▶   the amount of any commission or remuneration;

▶   details of the arrangements for application of the cooling-off period;

▶   the arrangements for handling complaints;

▶   that the favourable tax treatment may not be maintained;

▶   that the arrangements for managing the cash deposit of the ISA may not be covered in the scope of any consumer compensation scheme;

▶   where applicable, that the firm acts as agent in arranging the cash deposit, identifying the principal, and explaining that the principal has accepted responsibility for the activities of the firm in relation to the cash deposit;

▶   that a client in doubt whether an ISA is suitable should seek advice.

Solicitors should also note that rule 10 of the Solicitors' Practice Rules 1990 will apply to any commission received from managing a cash ISA. Further, although a solicitor's indemnity cover will normally include management of a client's cash ISA, it is possible that where the firm acts as agent in arranging the cash deposit, the principal will not be covered in the scope of any consumer compensation scheme. Therefore, the warning noted above should be given.

27

CHAPTER 3 – NOTIFICATION RULES

8. NOTIFICATION

(1) Notification 28 days in advance

(a) A *firm* shall notify the Society in writing not less than 28 days beforehand of a change in:–

   (i) its name; or

   (ii) the address of its principal office.

(b) Notification of a change in the name of a *firm* shall be accompanied by a request for an amendment to its *certificate* from a stated date to enable it to carry on investment business in the new name together with such fee as may be decided by the Council.

(2) Prior notification

A *firm* shall notify the Society in such form as the Council may decide before any investment business is conducted by, or under the supervision of, a partner or director who is a *registered foreign lawyer*.

(3) Immediate notification

A *firm* shall immediately notify the Society in writing of the occurrence of any of the following:–

(a) anyone has become or ceased to be a principal or director in the *firm*; or

(b) a *qualified person* has become or ceased to be a principal, *officer* or *employee* of the *firm*; or

(c) the appointment of a receiver, administrator, trustee or sequestrator of the assets of the *firm*; or

(d) the making of a composition or arrangement with creditors of the *firm*; or

(e) (where the *firm* is a partnership) an application or notice to dissolve the partnership; or

(f) the granting or refusal of any application for, or revocation of:–

   (i) authorisation to carry on investment, banking or insurance business in any country or territory outside the United Kingdom; or

   (ii) membership of any recognised self-regulating organisation or other recognised professional body under *the Act*; or

(g) the appointment by a regulatory authority of inspectors to investigate the affairs of the *firm* or the imposition by such an authority of any disciplinary measures on the *firm* in relation to its investment business; or

(h) the bringing of any action against the *firm* under sections 61 or 62 of *the Act*; or

(i) the conviction of any principal, *employee* or *officer* for any offence under legislation relating to investment or financial services, or involving fraud or dishonesty; or

(j) the presentation of a petition for a bankruptcy order or an award of sequestration or the making of a court order disqualifying a principal, *employee* or *officer* from serving as director of a company or from being concerned with the management of a company; or

(k) the presentation of a petition for its winding up or the winding up of any other *recognised body* which is an *officer*, subsidiary or holding company of the *firm*; or

(l) the happening of any event likely to give rise to suspension or withdrawal of the *certificate* or the imposition of conditions under *these rules*.

Guidance note

Sub-rule (3)(l) includes serious breaches of these rules, the Practice Rules, Accounts Rules, Council statements or other Law Society guidance. Regard must also be paid to Principle 10 of SIB's Statement of Principle which provides that a firm should deal with its regulator in an open and co-operative manner and keep the regulator promptly informed of anything concerning the firm which might reasonably be expected to be disclosed to it.

CHAPTER 4 – DISCRETE INVESTMENT BUSINESS

9. DEFINITION

Discrete investment business means the business of engaging in any of the following activities so far as they fall within Part II of Schedule 1 to *the Act* and are not excluded by Part III thereof:–

(1) dealing

(2) arranging

(3) discretionary management   as set out below

(4) advising

(5) establishing etc. collective investment schemes

27

(1) Dealing

Entering into a *transaction* or agreeing to do so either as principal or agent **except where**:–

(a) the *firm* acts as *disclosed agent* and the *transaction* is carried out with or through a *permitted third party*; or

(b) the *activity is incidental*; or

(c) the *transaction* is *execution-only*; or

(d) the dealing occurs as a result of an activity which is not *discrete investment business* because it falls within one of the exceptions contained in sub-rules (3)(b), (4)(c) or (5).

(2) Arranging

Making arrangements for a *client* to enter into a *transaction* **except where**:–

(a)   the *firm* acts as *disclosed agent* and the arrangements are carried out with or through a *permitted third party*; or

(b)   the arrangements are made in consequence of advice given by a *permitted third party* and the advice, if obtained by the firm, has been obtained by it acting as *disclosed agent*; or

(c)   the *transaction* is *execution-only*; or

(d)   the *activity is incidental*; **but this exception shall not apply to**:–

     (i)   the acquisition of a *packaged product*, or

     (ii)   the disposal of a *packaged product* unless the disposal is by or for a personal representative;

(e)   the arrangements are made as a result of an activity which is not *discrete investment business* because it falls within one of the exceptions contained in sub-rules (3)(b), (4)(c) or (5).

(3) Discretionary management

Managing or agreeing to manage assets on a discretionary basis:–

(a)   as a *discretionary portfolio manager*; or

(b)   where the *firm* or a partner, *employee* or *officer* of the *firm* is a trustee, donee of a power of attorney or receiver appointed by the Court of Protection, **except where**:–

     (i)   no remuneration is received for the discretionary management of investments in addition to any remuneration which may be received for acting as trustee, donee of a power of attorney or receiver; or

Guidance note

See appendix 5.

     (ii)   any decision to enter into a *transaction* is taken by or substantially in accordance with the advice of a *permitted third party* which advice, if obtained by the trustee, donee, receiver or *firm*, has been obtained after disclosure of the basis on which the individual or *firm* is acting.

(4) Advising

Recommending a *client* to enter into a *transaction* or to exercise a right conferred by an investment to acquire, dispose of, underwrite or convert an investment **except where**:–

(a)   such recommendation is in substance the advice of a *permitted third party* and, if obtained by the *firm*, has been obtained by it acting as disclosed agent; or

(b)   the *activity is incidental*; **but this exception shall not apply to**:–

     (i)   the acquisition of a *packaged product*, or

(ii)   the disposal of a *packaged product* unless the disposal is by or for a personal representative; or

(c)   the recommendation is made by a trustee to a co-trustee or attorney to a co-attorney, and no remuneration is received for this in addition to any remuneration which may be received for acting as trustee or attorney.

Guidance note

See appendix 5.

(5)   Establishing etc. collective investment schemes

Establishing, operating or winding-up an unregulated collective investment scheme **except where** the *activity is incidental*.

10.   SUPPLEMENTARY

For the purposes of *these rules:*–

(1)   no activity carried out by the *firm* or a partner, *employee* or *officer* of the *firm* as a personal representative of any deceased's estate shall be *discrete investment business*;

(2)   an *activity is incidental* if the *firm* carries it out while providing other services in the course of *carrying on the profession of a solicitor* (being services which do not themselves constitute *discrete investment business*) and such activity is subordinate to the main purpose for which those services are provided;

(3)   references to a *firm carrying on the profession of a solicitor* shall include references to:–

(a)   a *recognised body* providing professional services such as are provided by individuals practising as solicitors or by *multi-national partnerships*; and

(b)   a *multi-national partnership* providing professional services as such;

(4)   *permitted third party* means:–

(a)   an *authorised person*; or

(b)   a person exempted under *the Act* who, in engaging in the activity in question, is acting in the course of a business in respect of which that person is exempt; or

(c)   in relation to *overseas investments*, an *overseas professional*,

but in relation to *packaged products* does not include a *life office* or an operator of a *regulated collective investment scheme* or *investment trust savings scheme*, their appointed representative or member of their marketing group;

(5)   *disclosed agent* means disclosed agent for a named *client*;

(6)   in the case of any reference to the *firm* acting as *disclosed agent* where the *permitted third party* is:–

(a)   a member of the Investment Management Regulatory Organisation, the member must have agreed with or confirmed to the *firm* in writing that the *client* is or will be treated by the member as its customer, or

27

(b) a member of the Securities and Futures Authority, the member must have agreed with or confirmed to the *firm* in writing:–

(i) that the *client* is or will be treated by the member as its customer for the purposes of all the conduct of business rules of the Authority, or

(ii) if the agreement or confirmation was before 1st April 1992, that the *client* is or will be treated by the member as its customer.

Guidance note

1. Agreements or confirmations must be in writing and may cover all present and future clients, if this is expressly stated.

2. It is recommended that arrangements with permitted third parties who are not IMRO or SFA members should also be in writing.

3. If a firm is dealing with a broker on behalf of a named client and the broker agrees to treat the client as its customer, then (unless the broker has agreed to treat the client as a direct customer) the client is known as the 'indirect customer' of the broker according to terminology adopted by SIB and the SROs. This term may therefore be used as an alternative to 'customer' in (6) above.

CHAPTER 5 – CONDUCT OF BUSINESS RULES APPLICABLE TO ALL FIRMS

11. ADVERTISEMENTS

Guidance note

See also appendix 6 for EIS advertisements.

(1) Rules applying to both the issue and approval of advertisements

(a) Where a *firm issues* or approves an investment advertisement, it shall:–

(i) apply appropriate expertise, and

(ii) be able to show that it believes on reasonable grounds that the advertisement is fair and not misleading.

Guidance note

"Appropriate expertise" means that the firm should have knowledge and understanding of the type of matter covered by the advertisement.

(b) Where a *firm issues* or approves a *specific investment advertisement*, it shall ensure that the advertisement identifies it as issuer or approver and also states that it is regulated by the Society.

(c) A *firm* shall not *issue* or approve a *specific investment advertisement* which is calculated to lead directly or indirectly to an *overseas person* carrying on investment business:–

(i) which is not *regulated business*, and

(ii) with or for a *client* in the United Kingdom,

unless both the advertisement contains the *prescribed disclosure* and the *firm* has no reason to doubt that the *overseas person* will deal with investors in the United Kingdom in an honest and reliable way.

(d) A *firm* shall take reasonable steps to ensure that it does not *issue* or approve a *direct offer advertisement* for the sale of investments or the provision of *investment services* to anyone unless the advertisement gives information about the investments or *investment services*, the terms of the offer, and the risks involved, which is adequate and fair having regard to the UK or overseas regulatory protections which apply and the market to which the advertisement is directed.

(e) For the purposes of this rule, *issue* includes cause to be issued and reissue.

Guidance note

Although issue includes reissue, a limited exemption for the reissue of advertisements is provided by sub-rule (4)(b).

(2) Rules applying only to the issue of advertisements

(a) Any investment advertisement which a *firm issues* and to which the British Codes of Advertising and Sales Promotion applies shall also comply with appendix 1 part 1, but investment advertisements *issued* to *clients* need not repeat information which the *clients* have already been given in writing by the *firm*.

(b) Any advertisement which a *firm* issues in respect of a *PEP* operated by the *firm* shall also comply with appendix 1 part 2.

(c) A *firm* shall not *issue* a *direct offer advertisement* for the sale of investments or the provision of *investment services*, **except:–**

    (i) to a *client* for whom it believes on reasonable grounds that these are suitable; or

    (ii) where it constitutes any general offer or invitation to the holders of securities of any body corporate or any class of holder.

(d) The *issue* of any advertisement to which this sub-rule applies shall be authorised prior to its *issue* by a principal or *officer* designated for the purpose and a copy shall be kept for 6 years from the date of its *issue*.

(3) Rules applying only to the approval of advertisements

(a) (i) If a *firm* wishes to approve an investment advertisement, the provisions of Part 7 of the Financial Services (Conduct of Business) Rules 1990 shall have effect as if they applied to the *firm*.

    (ii) For the purposes of sub-rule (i), Rule 7.23 of Part 7 shall not apply:–

        (A) to any advertisement to the extent that it contains any general offer or invitation to the holders of securities of any body corporate or any class of holder; or

Guidance note

The purpose of this exception is to ensure that a firm is not prevented from approving an offer document which its company client might wish to circulate to shareholders of a company which the client wishes to take over.

        (B) to any advertisement for an *EIS scheme* which sets out the full *EIS scheme particulars* or an advertisement which contains a private offer of *EIS shares* and sets out a *statement of prescribed information*.

27

(b)　A *firm* shall not approve a *specific investment advertisement* if it relates to units in an unregulated collective investment scheme.

(c)　An investment advertisement may only be approved by a principal or *officer* designated for the purpose and a copy of the advertisement shall be kept for 6 years from the date of approval.

(4) Exemptions

Rule 11 shall not apply to:–

(a)　(i)　the *issue* of an investment advertisement outside the United Kingdom; or

    (ii)　the *issue* of an *exempt advertisement*; or

    (iii)　the *issue* or approval of a *DIE advertisement* or a *takeover advertisement*; or

(b)　the reissue of an investment advertisement which has been prepared and issued by another person and which the *firm* believes on reasonable grounds:–

    (i)　is an *exempt advertisement*, a *DIE advertisement* or a *takeover advertisement*; or

    (ii)　has already been issued or approved by an *authorised person* and is now being issued to a market for which it was intended at the time of its *issue* or approval by the *authorised person*;

but the exemption in this sub-rule (b) does not apply to *direct offer advertisements* under sub-rule (2)(c);

(c)　any advertisement issued by or on behalf of any body corporate for the purpose of giving financial or other information relating to it and/or the group of companies of which it forms part where the advertisement does not relate to an investment agreement to be entered into with that company or a member of that group and does not invite or advise those to whom the advertisement is directed to buy investments issued by that company from a person named in the advertisement.

Guidance note

The exemption contained in sub-rule (4)(c) ensures that, for example, approval of a company's press releases or summaries of a company's report and accounts will not be caught by rule 11.

12. UNSOLICITED CALLS

The restrictions imposed by section 56 of *the Act* do not apply if a *firm* complies with the Solicitors' Practice Rules 1990.

Guidance note

Although paragraph 3 of the Solicitors' Publicity Code 1990 provides that solicitors may publicise their practices by means (*inter alia*) of a telephone call to a current or former client, firms should bear in mind rule 1 of the Solicitors' Practice Rules. An unsolicited call should not be made in circumstances which may impair the good repute of the firm or of the profession, for example, where the client has not envisaged receiving unsolicited calls of the kind concerned.

13. EXECUTION OF TRANSACTIONS

Once a *firm* has agreed or decided in its discretion to effect a *transaction*, it shall do so as soon as possible, unless it reasonably believes that it is in the *client's* best interests not to do so.

Guidance note

1. Rule 1 of the Solicitors' Practice Rules emphasises a solicitor's duty to act in the best interests of the client. Accordingly, in cases where there is any doubt on the point, firms should ensure that transactions are effected on the best terms reasonably available.

2. Whether or not a firm is conducting discrete investment business, rules 1 and 15 of the Solicitors' Practice Rules provide that clients should be kept fully informed of transactions effected on their behalf, unless clients have indicated to the contrary. Firms conducting discrete investment business should also refer to rules 23 and 25 of these rules.

14. RECORD OF COMMISSIONS

A *firm* shall keep records of:–

(1) the total amount of commissions received which are attributable to investment business conducted by the *firm*, and

(2) the total amount of commissions in (1) above which are not paid or credited to *clients*.

Guidance note

The purpose of this rule is to ensure that a firm will be able to complete the application form for renewal of its investment business certificate – see the guidance note in appendix 4. Firms should bear in mind the duty to account to clients for commission, except as provided in rule 10 of the Solicitors' Practice Rules.

15. COMPLIANCE OFFICER

(1) A *firm* shall appoint a compliance officer who shall be responsible for ensuring that the *firm* has an adequate system in place to achieve compliance with *these rules*.

(2) The compliance officer shall be, in the case of:–

(a) a sole solicitor, that individual; or

(b) a partnership, a partner; or

(c) a *recognised body*, a director.

Guidance note

The compliance officer is the person primarily responsible for ensuring compliance with the rules relating to investment business, but all partners and directors retain ultimate responsibility.

27

16. RECORDS

(1) Application

This Rule shall apply to:–

(a)   the acquisition of a *packaged product*;

(b)   the disposal of a *packaged product* unless the disposal is by or for a personal representative; and

(c)   all investment business other than that referred to in sub-rules (a) and (b) **except where** the *activity is incidental*.

(2) Records of transactions

(a)   When a *firm* receives instructions from a *client* to effect a *transaction*, or makes a decision to effect a *transaction* in its discretion, it shall make a record of:–

     (i)   the name of the *client*;

     (ii)   the exact terms of the instructions or decision;

     (iii) in the case of instructions, the date and (except where received by letter or where they relate to a *life policy*) time when they were received.

Guidance note

1.   Where the instructions received relate to an 'execution-only' transaction, it is good practice to send the client written confirmation to the effect that the transaction is effected on an 'execution-only' basis and to keep a record of such confirmation. See also appendix 7, rule 3(2) which applies to long term commitments.

2.   The reference to a firm making a decision to effect a transaction in its discretion includes, for example, a decision by trustees all of whom are members of the firm, but does not include a decision by a solicitor trustee made jointly with lay co-trustees. However if, in this situation, instructions are subsequently given to the solicitor trustee's firm, the rule will apply by virtue of the firm receiving instructions from a client.

(b)   When a *firm* gives instructions to another person to effect a *transaction*, it shall make a record of:–

     (i)   the name of the *client*;

     (ii)   the exact terms of the instructions;

     (iii) the date and (except where given by letter or where they relate to a *life policy*) time when the instructions were given; and

     (iv) the name of the other person instructed.

Guidance note

References in sub-rules (2)(a)(ii) & (2)(b)(ii) to the exact terms of the instructions (or decision) mean the investment, the number of units and/or cash value and the nature of the transaction.

(3) Record of complaints

(a) A *firm* shall keep a record of complaints together with a record of the action taken in response to each complaint made by *clients*.

(b) This record shall be separate from the *client* files, but may refer to details kept in *client* files, which shall then be regarded as part of the record.

Guidance note

See also rule 15 of the Solicitors' Practice Rules. A firm's complaints handling procedure must, *inter alia*, ensure that clients are informed whom to approach in the event of any problem with the service provided.

(4) Retention of records

Each record made under this rule shall be kept for 6 years.

(5) General

(a) A record kept under *these rules* may be in any form, if it can be reproduced promptly in hard printed form.

(b) Subject to any duty of confidentiality or professional privilege, a *firm* shall allow a *client* (or the *client's* agent) on request during normal business hours to inspect any entry in a record kept by the *firm* under *these rules* of matters relating to the *client* and shall do so as soon as reasonably practicable but in any event within 7 days.

Guidance note

The other requirements for record keeping in this chapter are contained in rules 11(2)(d) & (3)(c), 14 and appendix 8, paragraph 7. In addition, firms are reminded of the obligation to keep records of relevant transactions under the Money Laundering Regulations 1993.

17. CUSTODY OF CLIENTS' ASSETS

(1) Where a *firm* provides *custody services* to a *client*, it shall comply with appendix 8.

(2) This rule shall not apply to the provision of *custody services* where the *firm* or a partner, *employee* or *officer* of the *firm* is a personal representative or a trustee (other than a bare trustee) provided that the *firm* is not separately remunerated for the *custody services*.

18. SPECIAL CATEGORIES: EIS INVESTMENTS, PACKAGED PRODUCTS AND PENSION FUND WITHDRAWALS

In addition to the requirements of chapters 5 and 6 of *these rules* a *firm* shall comply with:–

(1) appendix 6 in relation to *EIS* investments;

(2) appendix 7 in relation to *packaged products* and *pension fund withdrawals*.

CHAPTER 6 – CONDUCT OF BUSINESS RULES APPLICABLE ONLY TO FIRMS UNDERTAKING DISCRETE INVESTMENT BUSINESS

Guidance note

In this chapter there are a number of references to personal recommendations. A personal recommendation is one which is made to an individual client and not one, for example, which is made in a tip sheet or circular letter. These types of publications are governed by the rules on advertising (see rule 11).

19. APPLICATION

(1) The rules in this chapter shall apply only to the conduct of *discrete investment business*.

(2) Where the *firm* or a partner, *employee* or *officer* of the *firm* is a trustee (other than a bare trustee) or is acting as the donee of any *registered enduring power of attorney* or *trustee power of attorney* or is a receiver appointed by the Court of Protection, only the following rules in this chapter shall apply to the conduct of *discrete investment business* by him, her or it:–

20, 22(1)(a), (b) & (c) & (3)(b), 27 and appendix 7, part 2, rule 4(1).

(3) For the purposes of sub-rule (2), where such a partner, *employee* or *officer* decides to effect a *transaction*, but the consequent arrangements are made by another member of the *firm*, *these rules* shall apply to those arrangements as if the partner, *employee* or *officer* personally had made them.

20. QUALIFIED PERSONS

A *firm* shall not conduct any *discrete investment business* unless it is conducted by or under the direct supervision of a principal, *officer* or *employee* who is a *qualified person* for that type of *discrete investment business*, and whose identity has been notified to the Society in writing by the firm.

21. STATEMENT OF AUTHORISATION

In all its business letters, notices and other publications which relate to its *discrete investment business* a *firm* shall state that it is regulated by the Society in the conduct of investment business, or that it is authorised by the Society to conduct investment business.

22. KNOW YOUR CLIENT AND INVESTMENT ADVICE

(1) Suitability

(a) A *firm* shall not make a personal recommendation to, or effect a *transaction* for, a *client* unless the recommendation or *transaction* is suitable for the *client* having regard to the facts disclosed by the *client* and other relevant facts about the *client* of which the *firm* is, or reasonably should be, aware.

(b) But where, with the agreement of the *client*, a *firm* has pooled the *client's* funds with those of others with a view to taking common management decisions, the *transaction* must be suitable for the fund having regard to the stated investment objectives of the fund.

(c) A *firm* shall not make personal recommendations to, or exercise discretions for, a *client* which may result in *transactions* of unnecessary frequency or excessive size.

(2) Understanding of risk

A *firm* shall not make a personal recommendation to a *client*, or act as a *discretionary portfolio manager* for a *client*, unless it has taken reasonable steps to enable the *client* to understand the nature of the risks involved.

Guidance note

In appropriate circumstances, one way of complying with this rule would be to give similar warnings as are required in the case of advertisements, i.e. those warnings referred to in the British Codes of Advertising and Sales Promotion, Part 7 of the Financial Services (Conduct of Business) Rules 1990 and appendix 1 below (see rule 11(2)(a) or 11(3)(a)(i)). The warnings should be explained to the client and preferably confirmed in writing. Where the recommendation relates to an ISA the firm should ensure that the client receives information about the product which is adequate to enable the client to make an informed investment decision. This information must include whether the ISA is a mini or maxi ISA and the firm should explain the difference between the two. Further, if the ISA (or a component of the ISA) is stated as satisfying the CAT Standards (the Cost, Access and Terms Standards for ISAs prescribed from time to time by H.M. Treasury), the firm must explain the CAT Standards and warn the client that the CAT Standards do not necessarily mean that the investment is appropriate for the investor, or that there is any guarantee of investment performance. If the ISA is not stated as satisfying the CAT Standards, the firm must make this clear to the client.

(3) Exclusions

(a) Sub-rules (1) and (2) do not apply to an *investment service* performed for a partner or *officer* of the *firm* personally.

(b) For the purposes of sub-rules (1) and (2) a *firm* is not required to take into account or disclose facts known to it about the relevant investment if to do so would be a breach of duty to another person.

23. CONTRACT NOTES

(1) A *firm* which effects a *transaction* for a *client* (other than one relating to a *life policy*) shall ensure that there is sent to the *client* (or a person nominated by the *client*) as soon as possible a note containing the essential details of the *transaction*, unless these details are already known to the *client*.

Guidance note

An example of where the details would already be known to the client is a rights issue where the client has received the allotment letter.

(2) For the purposes of sub-rule (1), the person nominated by the *client* may not include the *firm* or any partner, *officer* or *employee* of the *firm*, unless the nomination is for that *client's* convenience and has been made by the *client* in writing.

(3) Where a *firm* is the plan manager of a *PEP*, it need not send a note under sub-rule (1) if the *client* is sent a statement in accordance with rule 25.

24. CLIENT INFORMATION AND AGREEMENTS

(1) A *firm* shall not begin to conduct *discrete investment business* for a *client* unless the *firm* has, at the same time or within the previous six months, supplied the *client* with the written information contained in appendix 2, part 1.

(2) If a *firm* acts as a *discretionary portfolio manager* it may only do so under a written agreement signed by the *client* in circumstances where the *firm* is satisfied that the *client* has had a proper opportunity to consider its terms.

(3) Sub-rule (2) shall not apply if the *client* is ordinarily resident outside the United Kingdom and the *firm* believes on reasonable grounds that the *client* does not wish to use such an agreement.

(4) An agreement made under sub-rule (2) shall include the matters set out in appendix 2 part 2 and the matters set out in appendix 2 part 3 if applicable.

Guidance note

Reference should also be made to rule 15 (client care) of the Solicitors' Practice Rules and the Written Professional Standards regarding information on costs for clients [now the Solicitors' Costs Information and Client Care Code]. These may be found in "Client Care – A Guide for Solicitors" published by the Society.

25. MANAGED PORTFOLIOS

Unless the *client* agrees otherwise in writing, a *firm* which acts as a *portfolio manager* shall send the *client* at suitable intervals a statement including the matters set out in appendix 3.

Guidance Note

Whilst an annual statement may be appropriate in some circumstances, for example, in relation to an advisory portfolio where contract notes are sent to the client, more frequent statements may be required e.g. in relation to a discretionary portfolio.

26. BILLS OF COSTS

(1) All bills of costs shall record separately the amount of costs attributable to *discrete investment business* (except where the *activity is incidental* or falls within rule 19(2)).

(2) Where a bill of costs requires a separate record under sub-rule (1), it shall be identified or recorded separately from other bills.

Guidance note

See appendix 4.

27. RECORDS

(1) A *firm* shall maintain a record in relation to each *client* of:–

(a) the facts referred to in rule 22(1)(a); and

(b) agreements referred to in rule 24(2).

(2) A *firm* shall maintain a record, separate from the *client* files, of the names of *clients* for whom *discrete investment business* is conducted.

(3) Each record maintained under this rule (whether the record was originally made under *these rules* or under any previous rules) shall be kept for 6 years from the performance of any *investment services* to which the record relates.

Guidance note

For other provisions regarding record keeping see rule 16(5) and appendix 7 rules 3(3) and 4(3).

CHAPTER 7 – MONITORING

28. INSPECTION

(1) In order to ascertain whether *these rules* or any other rule, Council statement or other guidance of the Society (insofar as it relates to the conduct of investment business) or statements of principle issued under section 47A(1) of *the Act* have been complied with, the Secretary of the Society, or such person as the Secretary may appoint, may require in writing any *firm* to produce, at a time and place notified, the accounting and other records of the *firm* relating to investment business and any other necessary documents for the inspection of any person appointed by the Secretary and to supply to such person any necessary information and explanations.

(2) If required so to do a *firm* shall produce such accounting and other records of the *firm* relating to investment business and any other necessary documents, information and explanations at the time and place fixed.

(3) For the purposes of this rule, if the requirement is sent by registered post or the recorded delivery service, it shall be treated as having been received by the *firm* within 48 hours (excluding Saturdays, Sundays and Bank Holidays) after the time of posting.

CHAPTER 8 – MISCELLANEOUS

29. RELIANCE ON OTHERS

(1) A *firm* shall be regarded as acting in conformity with *these rules* to the extent that:–

(a) the Society has issued and not withdrawn written guidance on compliance with them, and

(b) in reliance on the guidance, the *firm* believes on reasonable grounds that it is complying with the rules.

(2) Any communication required under *these rules* to be sent to a *client* may be sent to the order of the *client* if the recipient is independent of the *firm*.

27

30. WAIVERS

(1) In any particular case or cases the Council shall have power to waive in writing any of the provisions of *these rules*, but shall not do so unless it appears that:–

    (a) compliance with them would be unduly burdensome having regard to the benefit which compliance would confer on investors; and

    (b) the exercise of the power would not result in any undue risk to investors.

(2) The Council shall have power to revoke any waiver.

31. SERVICE

Except as otherwise provided in *these rules*, any notice, requirement or other document required or authorised by *these rules* may be served by leaving it at or sending it to the *firm's* principal practising address or registered office as last notified to the Society.

CHAPTER 9 – INTERPRETATION

32. In *these rules* unless the context otherwise requires:–

the Act means the Financial Services Act 1986;

activity is incidental has the meaning given in rule 10(2);

authorised insolvency practitioner means an individual who is qualified to act as an insolvency practitioner under the Insolvency Act 1986;

authorised person means:–

    (a) a person authorised under *the Act*;

    (b) a European institution carrying on home-regulated investment business in the United Kingdom; the terms "European institution" and "home-regulated investment business" shall have the meaning given by the Banking Coordination (Second Council Directive) Regulations 1992; and

    (c) a European investment firm carrying on home-regulated investment business in the United Kingdom; the terms "European investment firm" and "home-regulated investment business" shall have the meaning given by the Investment Services Regulations 1995;

Guidance note

For information concerning European institutions and home-regulated investment business which they carry on, reference should be made to the register kept by SIB.

broker funds arrangement means an arrangement between a *firm* and a *life office* (or operator of a *regulated collective investment scheme*) under which the *life office* (or operator of the *regulated collective investment scheme*) agrees to establish a separate fund whose composition may be determined by instructions from the *firm* and in which it is possible for more than one *client* to invest;

cancellation rights means any right to cancel an investment agreement (whether by terminating the agreement during the prescribed period after it has been made or by withdrawing the offer during the prescribed delayed-entry period) which is conferred by the *Cancellation Rules*;

Cancellation Rules means the Financial Services (Cancellation of Life Policies) Rules 1994 (as amended) and the Financial Services (Non-Life Cancellation) Rules 1997, as applicable, and any rules or regulations amending or replacing them;

carrying on the profession of a solicitor has the meaning given in rule 10(3);

certificate means a certificate (currently in force) issued under section 15 of *the Act*;

client, in relation to any *investment services* carried out by a *firm* for a trust or the estate of a deceased person, means the trustees or personal representatives in their capacity as such and not any person who is a beneficiary under the trust or interested in the estate;

contingent liability transaction means a transaction in which the *client* takes on actual or potential liabilities under options, futures or contracts for differences (other than payment of a premium on the purchase of an option or liabilities which would arise if the *client* exercises the option);

Guidance note

The definition does not cover the purchase of an option, or a transaction involving the closing out of any position in options, futures or contracts for differences.

custody services means safeguarding and administering or arranging for the safeguarding and administration of assets belonging to another person where those assets consist of or include investments, or may consist of or include investments, so far as those services fall within paragraph 13A of Schedule 1 to *the Act* and are not excluded by Part III thereof;

Guidance note

1.   A firm will not be providing custody services to a client if it merely holds an investment for safekeeping by, for example, holding a share certificate in its strong room, but does not administer the investment.

2.   "Administration" in this context includes (but the list is not exhaustive) any one of the following services:

   (a)   collecting and dealing with dividends and other income associated with the assets;

   (b)   carrying out corporate actions such as proxy voting (including exercising rights conferred by an investment on behalf of the beneficial owner);

   (c)   operating nominee accounts, including pooled accounts, which identify each client's assets in a ledger;

   (d)   settling transactions in investments;

   (e)   operating through depositaries, including dematerialised means of ownership;

   (f)   cash processing associated with clients' assets;

   (g)   maintaining accounts with clearing houses;

   (h)   appointing and operating through sub-custodians in other jurisdictions.

27

DIE advertisement means an advertisement:–

(a)   issued by a *designated investment exchange*; or

(b)   required or permitted to be published by the rules of a *designated investment exchange*;

defined benefits pension scheme means an *occupational pension scheme* where the benefits are calculated on the employee's pensionable earnings at or near the time of retirement or leaving the company or by reference to average earnings;

designated investment exchange means any investment exchange which is designated by the Securities and Investments Board;

direct offer advertisement means a *specific investment advertisement* which:–

(a)   contains:–

   (i)   an offer by the *firm* or another offeror to enter into an investment agreement with anyone who responds to the advertisement; or

   (ii)   an invitation to anyone to respond to the advertisement by making an offer to the *firm* or another offeree to enter into an investment agreement; and

(b)   specifies the manner or indicates a form in which any response is to be made (for example by providing a tear-off slip);

disclosed agent has the meaning given in rule 10(5);

discrete investment business has the meaning given in rule 9;

discretionary portfolio manager means a *portfolio manager* which has general authority to effect *transactions* at its discretion but, for the purposes of the definition of *discrete investment business* only, does not include the donee of a general power of attorney;

effecting a transaction for a *client* includes making arrangements for the *client* to enter into the *transaction* where the arrangements bring about the *transaction* in question;

EIS means the Enterprise Investment Scheme;

EIS fund means an arrangement which would be a collective investment scheme except that it constitutes a complying fund for the purposes of paragraph 34 of Schedule 1 to *the Act*;

EIS managed portfolio means a portfolio managed by a *discretionary portfolio manager* which is to be invested wholly or mainly in *EIS shares*;

EIS scheme means an arrangement which is an *EIS fund* or an *EIS managed portfolio*;

EIS scheme particulars means a document containing, so far as applicable, all the matters set out in appendix 6, rule 4, but where a *firm* is not the *scheme manager* of the relevant *EIS scheme* to which the *EIS scheme particulars* relate, means a document which the *firm* has reason to believe contains, so far as applicable, all such matters;

EIS share means a share in a company in relation to which the beneficial owner of the share may, subject to the individual circumstances, be qualified for relief by virtue of Chapter III of Part VII of the Income and Corporation Taxes Act 1988;

eligible custodian means:–

(a) a person authorised under *the Act* to provide *custody services* within paragraph 13A of Schedule 1;

(b) an E.C. credit institution whose authorisation includes the provision of *custody services*;

(c) a European Investment Firm whose authorisation includes the provision of *custody services*; or

(d) a body corporate which maintains its head office outside the UK and which the *firm* is satisfied is a person who:–

  (i) provides *custody services*; and

  (ii) in the provision of *custody services* is either regulated or supervised by a regulatory body or government agency, or is subject to independent and regular review by auditors with qualifications prescribed by law or by such a body or agency;

employee means an individual who is employed in connection with the *firm's* investment business under a contract of service or under a contract for services such that he or she is held out as an employee or consultant of the *firm*;

excepted insolvency activities means the activities of a principal, *employee* or *officer* of a *firm* acting in the capacity of an *authorised insolvency practitioner*;

execution-only (transaction) means a *transaction* which is effected by a *firm* for a *client* where the *firm* assumes on reasonable grounds that the *client* is not relying on the *firm* as to the merits or suitability of that *transaction*;

Guidance note

1. Whether a transaction is "execution-only" will depend on the existing relationship between the client and the firm and the circumstances surrounding that transaction. Generally, a transaction will be "execution-only" if the client instructs the firm to effect it without having received advice from the firm. Even though this is the case, however, the transaction may still not qualify as "execution-only" because, in view of the relationship, the client may reasonably expect the firm to indicate if the transaction is inappropriate. In any event, a firm may be negligent (and possibly in breach of Practice Rule 1) if it fails to advise on the appropriateness or otherwise.

2. A transaction will also be "execution-only" if the firm has advised the client that the transaction is unsuitable, but the client persists in wishing the transaction to be carried out. In those circumstances it is good practice for the firm to confirm in writing that its advice has not been accepted, and that the transaction is being effected on an "execution-only" basis. (See guidance note 1 to rule 16(2)(a).)

3. In some circumstances, there is a specific requirement to confirm in writing the "execution-only" nature of a transaction (appendix 7 paragraph 3(2).)

4. Effecting an "execution-only" transaction is not discrete investment business.

exempt advertisement means an investment advertisement which can lawfully be issued in the United Kingdom by a person who is not an *authorised person* without approval of its contents by an *authorised person*;

27

firm means a sole solicitor, employed solicitor, partnership of solicitors and/or *recognised bodies*, *multi-national partnership* or *recognised body* to which the Society has issued a *certificate*;

Guidance note

1.   The Society only issues certificates to employed solicitors in relation to the issue or approval of investment advertisements.

2.   The Society will not normally authorise firms where the 35% fee limit, detailed in appendix 4, is exceeded.

holding means shares, units and any other form of investment in a *scheme*;

individual pension contract means a *pension policy* or *pension contract* under which contributions are paid to:–

(a)   a personal pension scheme approved under section 630 of the Income and Corporation Taxes Act 1988, whose sole purpose is the provision of annuities or lump sums under arrangements made by individuals in accordance with the scheme;

(b)   a retirement benefits scheme approved under section 591(2)(g) of the Income and Corporation Taxes Act 1988, for the provision of relevant benefits by means of an annuity contract made with an insurance company of the employee's choice;

Individual Savings Account means an account which is a scheme of investment satisfying the conditions prescribed in the Individual Savings Account Regulations 1998 (S.I. 1998 no. 1870);

ISA means an *Individual Savings Account*;

ISA manager in relation to an *Individual Savings Account* means a person who fulfils the conditions of the Individual Savings Account Regulations 1998 and is approved by the Commissioners of the Inland Revenue for the purposes of the Regulations as an account manager;

investment services means any activities undertaken in the course of carrying on investment business;

investment trust means a closed-ended company which is listed in the United Kingdom or another member state and:–

(a)   is approved by the Inland Revenue under section 842 of the Income and Corporation Taxes Act 1988 (or, in the case of a newly formed company, has declared its intention to conduct its affairs so as to obtain approval); or

(b)   is resident in another member state and would qualify for approval if resident and listed in the United Kingdom;

investment trust savings scheme means a dedicated service for investment in the securities of one or more *investment trusts* within a particular marketing group (and references to an *investment trust savings scheme* include references to securities to be acquired through that scheme);

issue has the meaning given in rule 11(1)(e) for the purposes of rule 11 only;

key features document has the meaning given in appendix 7 rule 2(1);

LAUTRO means the Life Assurance and Unit Trust Regulatory Organisation;

life office means a person who carries on long term business within the meaning of section 1 of the Insurance Companies Act 1982;

life policy means an investment within paragraph 10 of Schedule 1 to *the Act* (long term insurance contracts) whether or not held within an *ISA*;

long term commitment means:–

(a) a regular premium *life policy* or an annuity; or

(b) any investment agreement necessarily involving the issue or purchase of an investment within (a) above;

multi-national partnership means a partnership whose members consist of one or more *registered foreign lawyers* and one or more solicitors;

occupational pension scheme means any scheme or arrangement which is comprised in one or more documents or agreements and which has, or is capable of having, effect in relation to one or more descriptions or categories of employment so as to provide benefits, in the form of pensions or otherwise, payable on termination of service, or on death or retirement, to or in respect of earners with qualifying service in an employment of any such description or category;

OEIC means a United Kingdom Open-Ended Investment Company, that is to say an investment company with variable capital as defined in the Open-Ended Investment Companies (Investment Companies with Variable Capital) Regulations 1996;

officer means a director or secretary of a *recognised body*;

opt out means a *transaction* resulting from a decision by an individual to opt out of or decline to join a final salary or money-purchase *occupational pension scheme* of which he or she is a current member, or which he or she is, or at the end of a waiting period will become, eligible to join, in favour of an *individual pension contract* or contracts;

overseas investments means investments issued by a person incorporated or established outside the United Kingdom which, in respect of the particular *transaction*, are not traded on a recognised investment exchange in the United Kingdom;

overseas person means a person who carries on investment business other than from a permanent place of business maintained by him or her in the United Kingdom;

overseas professional means a person:–

(a) whose ordinary business is carried on from a permanent place of business outside the United Kingdom and involves him or her in engaging in activities which fall within Part II of Schedule 1 to *the Act* or would do so apart from Parts III or IV of such schedule; and

(b) who the *firm* reasonably believes is suitable for performing the services in question;

own nominee means a corporate nominee which is a *recognised body* and is either controlled by the *firm* or whose directors are accustomed to act in accordance with the directions or instructions of the *firm*;

packaged product means a *life policy*, a unit or share in a *regulated collective investment scheme*, or an *investment trust savings scheme* whether or not held within an *ISA* or *PEP*;

27

pension contract means a right to benefits obtained by the making of contributions to an *occupational pension scheme* or to a personal pension scheme, where the contributions are paid to a *regulated collective investment scheme*;

pension fund management policy means a *life policy* the effecting or carrying out of which constitutes life insurance business by reason only that it is business falling within class VII of Schedule 1 to the Insurance Companies Act 1982;

pension fund withdrawals means in relation to a decision by a *client*, in respect of a personal pension scheme, to defer the purchase of an annuity and to take:–

(a) income withdrawals within the meaning of section 630 of the Income and Corporation Taxes Act 1988, as amended by section 58 and Schedule 11 of the Finance Act 1995, and any provisions amending or replacing it; or

(b) payments made under interim arrangements in accordance with section 28A of the Pension Schemes Act 1993, as inserted by section 143 of the Pensions Act 1995, and any provisions amending or replacing it;

pension policy means a right to benefits obtained by the making of contributions to an *occupational pension scheme* or to a personal pension scheme, where the contributions are paid to a *life office*;

pension transfer means a *transaction* resulting from a decision by an individual to transfer deferred benefits from a final salary *occupational pension scheme*, or from a money-purchase *occupational pension scheme*, in favour of an *individual pension contract* or contracts;

PEP means a personal equity plan within the Personal Equity Plan Regulations 1989;

permitted third party has the meaning given in rule 10(4);

PIA means the Personal Investment Authority Limited;

portfolio manager means a *firm* which undertakes to keep a *client's* portfolio of investments under review, unless the undertaking arises by reason of the *firm* or a partner, *employee* or *officer* of the *firm* being a trustee, personal representative, donee of any *registered enduring power of attorney* or *trustee power of attorney* or a receiver appointed by the Court of Protection;

prescribed disclosure means a written statement which must make clear:–

(a) that all or most of the protections provided by the United Kingdom regulatory system do not apply; and

(b) where the business is excluded from the Investors Compensation Scheme by its territorial scope (or would be so excluded if the person carrying it on were a participant *authorised person*), a statement that compensation under that scheme will not be available;

and which may also indicate the protections or compensation available under another system of regulation;

Guidance note

Territorial scope of Investors Compensation Scheme: business with overseas investments is excluded unless it is done directly with an office in the UK of a participant firm or an affiliated representative.

product provider means in relation to:–

(a) a *life policy*, the *life office* by which that policy is issued;

(b) units or shares in a r*egulated collective investment scheme*, the operator of that *scheme*;

(c) an *investment trust savings scheme*, the manager of that *scheme*;

qualified person, in relation to any particular type (or types) of *discrete investment business*, means an individual approved by the Council under rule 7(1) to conduct *discrete investment business* of that type (or types) which approval has not been suspended or withdrawn under rule 7(3);

recognised body means a body corporate recognised by the Council under the Solicitors' Incorporated Practice Rules 1988;

registered enduring power of attorney means a power of attorney which is registered by the Court under section 6 of the Enduring Powers of Attorney Act 1985;

registered foreign lawyer means a person whose name is on the register of foreign lawyers maintained by the Society under section 89 of the Courts and Legal Services Act 1990;

regulated business means investment business which is:–

(a) business carried on from a permanent place of business maintained by an *authorised person* (or its appointed representative) in the United Kingdom; or

(b) other business carried on with or for customers or *clients* in the United Kingdom, unless that business is:–

  (i)   business carried on from an office of an *authorised person* outside the United Kingdom which would not be treated as carried on in the United Kingdom if that office were a separate person; or

  (ii) business of an appointed representative of the *authorised person* which is not carried on in the United Kingdom;

regulated collective investment scheme means an authorised unit trust scheme or an overseas collective investment scheme recognised under sections 86, 87 or 88 of *the Act* or an *OEIC*;

scheme means:–

(a) a *regulated collective investment scheme*, whether or not held within an *ISA* or a *PEP*; or

(b) an *investment trust* where the relevant shares have been or are to be acquired through an *investment trust savings scheme*; or

(c) an *investment trust* where the relevant shares are to be held within an *ISA* or a *PEP* which promotes one or more specific *investment trusts*;

scheme manager means, in relation to an *EIS Fund* the operator of the fund and, in relation to an *EIS managed portfolio*, the manager;

SIB means the Securities and Investments Board Limited;

specific investment advertisement means an investment advertisement which identifies and promotes a particular investment or particular *investment services*;

27

statement of prescribed information means, in relation to an advertisement of *EIS shares*, all such information as a person such as the person or persons to whom the advertisement is addressed and that person's professional advisers would reasonably require and reasonably expect to find in the advertisement for the purpose of making an informed assessment of the assets and liabilities, financial position, profits and losses of the company issuing the shares and the rights attached to those shares;

takeover advertisement means an advertisement to which the *Takeover Code* applies (or would apply but for any exemption granted by the Panel on Takeovers and Mergers);

Takeover Code means the City Code on Takeovers and Mergers and the Rules Governing Substantial Acquisitions of Shares published by the Panel on Takeovers and Mergers;

these rules means the Solicitors' Investment Business Rules 1995 as amended from time to time;

title documents means a *client's* document of title, or a certificate evidencing a *client's* title to an investment (including a *life policy* or *pension contract*), or a record on a register of investments held in uncertificated form which is accepted as evidence of a *client's* title to that investment;

transaction means the purchase, sale, subscription or underwriting of a particular investment;

trustee power of attorney means a power of attorney entered into pursuant to section 25 of the Trustee Act 1925.

33. In *these rules* references to statutes, rules, codes or regulations, statements or principles etc. other than *these rules* include any modification or replacement thereof.

34. As the context requires, other words and expressions shall have the meanings assigned to them by the Interpretation Act 1978, *the Act* and the Solicitors Act 1974.

35. *These rules* are to be interpreted in the light of the guidance notes.

APPENDIX 1
ADVERTISING (rule 11)

Part 1 – General rules

1. If the advertisement contains any matter based on an assumed rate of taxation it shall state what that rate is.

2. The advertisement shall not describe any investment as being free of tax unless no tax is payable either by the investor in respect of the investment or by any fund of which the investment forms part or to which its value is linked.

3. If the advertisement relates to an investment where deductions for charges and expenses are loaded disproportionately onto the early years, the advertisement shall draw attention to that fact and state that, if the investor withdraws from the investment in the early years, he may not get back the amount he has invested.

4. Where the advertisement relates to an investment denominated in a foreign currency, the advertisement shall draw attention to the fact that changes in rates of exchange between currencies may cause the value of the investments to diminish or to increase.

5. If the advertisement contemplates the recipient entering into a *transaction* as a result of which the recipient may not only lose what he or she pays at the outset but may incur a liability to pay unspecified additional amounts later, it shall draw attention to both those facts.

Part 2 – Rules regarding PEPs operated by firm

1. Advertisement not to imply government approval

The advertisement shall not contain any matter that states or implies that the *PEP* has the approval of any government department. However, it may refer to any reliefs from taxation which may be available from time to time in respect of investment in *PEPs*.

2. Taxation

Any reference to reliefs from taxation:–

(a) shall state that the reliefs are those which currently apply; and

(b) shall contain a statement that the value of a relief from taxation depends upon the circumstances of the taxpayer.

APPENDIX 2
CLIENT INFORMATION AND AGREEMENTS (rule 24)

CLIENT INFORMATION

Part 1

27

Guidance note

This part contains a "checklist" of information which should be given to the client whether by way of a client agreement or terms of business or otherwise in writing. No form is prescribed. Where the firm acts as a discretionary portfolio manager, this information may be included in the client agreement if it has not already been provided to the client.

1. The fact that the *firm* is authorised/regulated in the conduct of investment business by the Law Society.

2. The *firm's* name, address and telephone number.

3. The name of the *qualified person* and of the person to whom any complaints about the services provided should be addressed.

4. Whether the service provided by the *firm* will include any review, or any regular review, of the *client's* investments and, if so, details of the frequency with which and the manner in which the *firm* will do so.

5. The method by which the *client* is to give instructions to the *firm*.

6. The basis on which the *firm* is to charge for its services.

7. The arrangements for handling money, including the income received on any investments held for *clients,* and the basis on which interest will be paid by the *firm*.

8. The arrangements for the safekeeping of documents of title and for the registration and identification of ownership of investments.

9. Where the services may relate to a *packaged product*, the following statement:–

"Those who advise on life assurance, pensions, or unit trust products are either independent advisers or representatives of one company.

We [name of the firm] as [solicitors] [solicitors and registered foreign lawyers] [registered foreign lawyers and solicitors] are independent. Because we are independent, if we act on your behalf in relation to life assurance, pensions or unit trust products, we can advise you on the products of different companies."

CLIENT AGREEMENT FOR A DISCRETIONARY MANAGED PORTFOLIO

Part 2 – Matters which must always be included

10. A statement:–

    (a) of the services to be provided;

    (b) of the *client's* investment objectives;

    (c) of any restrictions on the investments which may be acquired or that there are no restrictions.

Part 3 – Matters to be included if applicable

11. A statement:–

    (a) of any restrictions on the amount or the proportion of the *client's* funds which may be invested in any particular investment or category of investment;

    (b) that the *firm* may buy investments which may be difficult to realise;

    (c) that the *firm* may enter into *transactions*, either generally or subject to specific limitations, under which the *client* will incur obligations as an underwriter;

    (d) that the *firm* has authority to borrow money on the *client's* behalf, or enter into *transactions* which may mean that the *client* has to raise further funds; in this event, the maximum borrowing limit must be stated.

12. The dates when statements will be sent to the *client* under rule 25.

APPENDIX 3
PERIODIC STATEMENTS (rule 25)

1.   The date of the statement and the period covered.

2.   A list of assets at date of statement.

3.   Aggregate value of assets at date of transfer to the *firm* or at date of previous statement.

4.   Aggregate value of assets at date of statement.

5.   The basis of valuation.

6.   A list of assets lent to a third party at date of statement.

7.   Income received from each investment during the period, except if mandated to or on behalf of the *client*.

8.   Amount of interest payments made on borrowings during period.

9.   The following details of each *transaction* effected:–

      (a)   investment

      (b)   number of units

      (c)   sale or purchase

      (d)   price

10.   Details of *title documents* held by the *firm* or its *own nominee* at date of statement.

11.   *Firm's* fees during period.

Guidance note

With regard to item 9 above, if contract notes have already been sent to the client under rule 23, then it may be inappropriate to repeat the information in the periodic statements. Rule 25 allows the firm and a client to agree in writing, among other things, the contents of the statements.

APPENDIX 4
COSTS (rule 26)

Guidance note

The purpose of rule 26 is to ensure that a firm will be able to complete the application form for renewal of its certificate – see also rule 14. The form requires the following details from the firm's last financial year:–

1.   Aggregate gross commissions attributable to investment business conducted by the firm received from authorised persons and persons exempted under the Act.

2.   (i)   Aggregate gross commissions attributable to investment business conducted by the firm less amount thereof paid or credited to clients.

      (ii) Gross fee income for discrete investment business (unless the activity is incidental or falls within rule 19(2)).

3.   Total gross income (investment and non-investment business).

If the total of item 2 exceeds 35% of item 3, the Society will not normally be able to issue a certificate. Item 1 may be ignored for the purposes of the calculation.

Item 2(ii) (gross fee income) should not include any commissions. If commission is retained and used by way of set off against a bill, it counts as part payment of the bill. In that event the full amount of the bill relating to discrete investment business should be included.

Also, item 2(ii) should not include fees relating to an activity which is incidental or falls within rule 19(2). The exception relating to incidental activities might best be illustrated by an example. If a firm arranges an endowment policy in connection with a conveyancing transaction without the assistance of a broker, then although the arranging of the policy is "incidental" to the conveyancing, it remains discrete investment business by virtue of the definition of such business in rule 9 (unless the transaction is execution only). However, fees attributable to such arranging do not have to be included in item 2(ii) because the arranging is incidental. The effect of this is that in a conveyancing transaction, there need be no separate item on the bill in respect of the arranging of the endowment policy.

The position is similar in respect of rule 19(2). If a member of a firm is a trustee, then even though the work done includes discrete investment business, there is no need to attribute a separate fee to such work or to include any fee in item 2(ii).

APPENDIX 5
SOLICITOR TRUSTEES (rules 9(3)(b)(i) and 9(4)(c))

Guidance note

Discretionary management

1. In order to ascertain whether, in relation to trust funds, there will be discretionary management amounting to discrete investment business by the firm, three separate sets of circumstances may be considered:–

    (a) Outside trustees

    Where the firm is merely acting for outside trustees there will be no discretionary management by the firm unless the outside trustees have delegated their discretion to the firm.

    (b) Outside and in-house trustees jointly

    Where there are co-trustees inside and outside the firm there will be no discretionary management by the firm unless discretion has been delegated to the solicitor trustee or the firm.

    (c) In-house trustees

    There will be discretionary management where the sole trustee (or all the trustees) are in-house, but in such a case the "no additional remuneration" exception from discrete investment business in rule 9(3)(b)(i) will frequently apply.

"No additional remuneration" (rules 9(3)(b)(i) and 9(4)(c))

2. When solicitor trustees take decisions about investments, or advise their co-trustees – perhaps during an exchange of views regarding the trust investments following receipt of advice from a broker – they usually do so in their capacity as trustees. Although the trustees will be remunerated for those management and advisory services such remuneration will not usually be in addition to their normal remuneration as trustees, i.e. they will not usually receive extra remuneration for the discretionary management of investments or for their investment recommendations. The position is, however, likely to be different if the firm maintains and involves a specialist in-house investment department in which case the firm is likely to be conducting discrete investment business.

3. Remuneration includes retained commission.

APPENDIX 6
ADDITIONAL RULES RELATING TO ENTERPRISE
INVESTMENT SCHEME INVESTMENTS (rule 18)

1. ADVERTISEMENTS

(1) Rules applying to both the issue and approval of advertisements

(a) A *firm* shall not *issue* or approve a *specific investment advertisement* relating to an *EIS fund* unless the terms of the fund provide that not more than 27.5 per cent. of the subscriptions shall be invested in any one company.

(b) A *firm* shall not *issue* or approve any forecast, projection or illustration of the possible investment return on, or realisable value of, any *EIS* investment.

(2) Rules applying only to the issue of advertisements

A *firm* shall not issue a *direct offer advertisement* for *EIS shares*, or for an *EIS scheme* unless:–

(a) in the case of an *EIS scheme*, the advertisement sets out or is accompanied by the *EIS scheme particulars* and (if the *firm* is aware that the manager intends to invest subscriptions in *EIS shares* in a company in which the manager has a material interest) a copy of the prospectus or a *statement of prescribed information* relating to each such company, together with a statement that applications may only be made and accepted subject to the terms of the *EIS scheme particulars*;

(b) in the case of a private offer of *EIS shares*, the advertisement sets out or is accompanied by a *statement of prescribed information*;

(c) in the case of a public offer of *EIS shares*, the advertisement sets out or is accompanied by a prospectus relating to the shares.

2. PROVISION OF FUNDS FOR EIS INVESTMENT

A *firm* shall not lend money nor extend credit to assist any person to invest in an *EIS scheme* or to subscribe for *EIS shares*, nor arrange or be involved in arrangements for any third party to do so, unless the person concerned has sought to borrow money or obtain credit for that purpose without solicitation by the *firm*.

3. CLIENT AGREEMENTS AND PERIODIC STATEMENTS

(1) A *firm* which acts as the manager of an *EIS fund* shall comply with rule 24 (client agreements) and rule 25 (managed portfolios) in respect of each *client* which invests in the fund.

Guidance note

A firm which is the manager of an EIS managed portfolio will be a discretionary portfolio manager to which rules 24 and 25 apply in any event.

(2)   A *firm* which acts as the *scheme manager* of an *EIS scheme* must notify the *client* in writing of the *client's* right to withdraw from the arrangements during the seven days following the *firm's* receipt of the *client's* offer to enter into the arrangements, and provide the *client* with a tear-off slip or other form on which the *client* can communicate the *client's* withdrawal.

4.   EIS SCHEME PARTICULARS

EIS scheme particulars shall include:–

(1)   the following statements with particular prominence:–

   (a)   a statement that investment in unquoted shares carries higher risks than investment in quoted shares; and

   (b)   a statement to the effect that investments in unquoted shares may be difficult to realise, that there can be no certainty that market makers will be prepared to deal in them and, where the investment objectives of the scheme include investment in private companies, that restrictions may apply to the transfer of shares in such companies; and

   (c)   a statement that proper information for determining the current value of investments may not be available; and

   (d)   a statement to the effect that the recipient should before proceeding seek expert advice; and

   (e)   a statement that the *scheme manager* is regulated in the conduct of investment business by the Society, or that the *scheme manager* is authorised by the Society to conduct investment business;

(2)   the following statement:–

"The [firm] [fund manager] [scheme manager] [and its directors] [has] [have] taken all reasonable care to ensure that all facts stated in this document are true and accurate in all material respects and there are no other material facts the omission of which would make misleading any statement herein whether of fact or opinion. The [firm] [fund manager] [scheme manager] [and its directors] accept[s] responsibility accordingly;"

(3)   the name and business address of:–

   (a)   the *scheme manager*; and

   (b)   the promoter of the scheme (if any); and

   (c)   every person acting in a professional capacity in relation to the scheme; and

   (d)   every person likely to take part in any decision or recommendation relating to investment of moneys subscribed to the scheme;

(4)   the opening and closing dates for receipt of subscriptions;

(5)   the maximum and minimum sizes, if any, proposed for the scheme;

(6)   the maximum and minimum permitted individual subscription to the scheme;

(7)   a statement of the arrangements for the holding of subscription moneys pending investment;

(8) the arrangements for the return of subscription moneys should the scheme be over-subscribed or the moneys not accepted for other reasons;

(9) the arrangements for the return of subscription moneys remaining uninvested at the time when the final investment of the scheme has been made or the final date for investment has passed;

(10) any arrangements by virtue of which any preferential treatment will or may be given in relation to subscription to the scheme to particular persons or classes of persons subscribing to the scheme;

(11) the circumstances in which persons or particular classes of person are excluded from participation in the scheme or in any particular investment of scheme moneys;

(12) the manner in which shares in companies in which scheme moneys are to be invested are to be held on behalf of participants in the scheme and the manner in which, according to their subscriptions, interests in such shares are to be allocated to each participant;

(13) any arrangements for registering shares in the names of participants in the scheme at or after the end of the period during which shares must be held in order to obtain tax relief;

(14) any arrangements for the payment of dividends, if any, to participants in the scheme;

(15) the circumstances in which a person's participation in the scheme may be terminated;

(16) any arrangements for dealing with scheme moneys which become available as a result of a sale of scheme investments by the *scheme manager*;

(17) the *scheme manager's* powers and discretion in relation to the scheme, including, for example, the exercise of voting rights, the selection and the disposal of investments and syndication of the scheme with other sources of investment;

(18) the following information concerning charges and costs to be stated together in a part of the document dealing solely with that information:–

    (a) the amount or rate of the *scheme manager's* remuneration currently charged, whether that may be varied in any way in the future and, if so the maximum to which it may be increased, and

    (b) the same information as under sub-paragraph (a) but in relation to any other charges or costs made or arising in connection with the scheme;

(19) the commission rate payable to any intermediary in return for the introduction of participants to the scheme;

(20) whether the *scheme manager* remains free to subscribe for shares, or to hold options to do so, in companies in which the scheme is invested and, if so, an indication of the price or the formula by which a price is determined at which the *scheme manager* may subscribe and the maximum proportion of the ordinary share capital of those companies for which the *scheme manager* may subscribe or which may be the subject of options in the *scheme manager's* favour;

(21) whether the *scheme manager* proposes to establish another *EIS scheme* and, if so, whether or not arrangements exist to ensure that the *scheme manager* does not discriminate between one *EIS scheme* and another and, if such arrangements exist, what they are;

27

(22) a summary of the fiscal provisions concerning the *EIS*;

(23) a description of any arrangements there may be:–

    (a) for securing that any person who knowingly has a material interest in any decision or recommendation concerning the investment of subscriptions which is not subject to independent approval is excluded from participation in the making of that decision or recommendation, and

    (b) for securing independent approval of decisions and recommendations concerning the investment of subscriptions which may be made by persons who have a material interest in them,

    or, if no arrangements exist relating to any of the above matters, a statement to that effect;

(24) if the arrangements described in accordance with paragraph 23 do not cover any of the following interests:–

    (a) an interest of the *scheme manager* or of an associate of the *scheme manager* arising by way of remuneration in connection with the management or operation of the scheme or any other *EIS scheme*,

    (b) an interest arising from investment of subscriptions of the scheme or of any other *EIS scheme* of which the *scheme manager* of the scheme in question or the *scheme manager's* associate is also the *scheme manager*,

    (c) an interest of an authorised institution within the meaning of the Banking Act 1987 resulting from a loan made by such an institution,

    (d) an interest arising from the formation by the *scheme manager* or the *scheme manager's* associate of a company with a view to interests in that company being acquired on behalf of *EIS schemes* of which the *scheme manager* or the *scheme manager's* associate is the *scheme manager*,

    the fact that they do not cover that interest need not be disclosed if there be disclosed the fact that investment may be made despite the existence of such an interest and, in the case of (c), details of any arrangements made to avoid conflicts of interest or, if there be no such arrangements, that fact;

(25) if the *scheme manager* has any interest (whether direct or indirect) or duty the nature of which may place the *scheme manager* in conflict with the interests of participants in the scheme or any duty to those participants, particulars of that interest or duty;

(26) a statement at the head of any summary contained in the scheme particulars that the summary must be read subject to the full terms and conditions of the scheme as set out in the scheme particulars;

(27) a statement of any arrangements to enable participants in the scheme to notify the *scheme manager* of companies with which they are connected within the meaning of section 291 of the Income and Corporation Taxes Act 1988;

(28) a statement of the investment policies and objectives of the scheme including, for example, details of the status, nature, location and types of business activities of the companies in which it is intended the scheme should be invested;

(29) a statement of what periodic reports will be made to participants and how frequently those reports will be made in compliance with the requirements of the principal rules.

APPENDIX 7
ADDITIONAL RULES FOR PACKAGED PRODUCTS AND PENSION FUND WITHDRAWALS (rule 18)

PART 1 – CONDUCT OF BUSINESS RULES APPLICABLE TO ALL FIRMS

1. Commission disclosure

(1) In addition to complying with Rule 10 of the Solicitors' Practice Rules 1990, a *firm* shall comply with the following requirements in connection with any investment business relating to a *packaged product*.

(2) Where:–

(a) a *firm* or a *permitted third party* will receive commission in connection with a *transaction* arranged by the *firm*; or

(b) a *client* asks a *firm* to disclose the commission that would be payable in connection with a particular transaction if entered into through the *firm*; or

(c) a *firm* is providing a *client* with a *key features document* within rule 2 of this appendix about a *transaction* from which the *firm* or a *permitted third party* is expected to receive commission;

the *firm* shall disclose the total commission payable in connection with the *transaction*, including any commission payable to the *permitted third party*. If, as a result of a subsequent variation of the proposed *transaction*, the amount of the commission receivable is increased, this fact must be notified in writing to the *client*.

(3) The disclosure shall be made in cash terms, indicate the timing for payments, and distinguish between initial, renewal and level commission where appropriate. Disclosure shall be made in writing before the *client* signs any application or proposal to enter into the *transaction*, or, if relevant, before the *client* signs any authority to make *pension fund withdrawals*.

(4) For the purposes of this rule, commission shall be treated as payable in connection with a *transaction* even if the commission is payable in respect of another matter if the two matters are connected in any way, or if there is an arrangement to pay commission in relation to the two matters jointly.

(5) Where the *transaction* relates to a *life policy* which was issued on or after 1 January 1995, or where the *transaction* relates to a *scheme* and was entered into on or after 1 June 1997, the *firm* shall comply with the disclosure requirements of this rule in respect of any variation of a recommendation to or proposal made by the *client*, or any previous *transaction* into which the *client* has entered, in the following circumstances:–

(a) the variation would cause a fresh notice of the right to cancel to be deliverable; or

(b) the increase in the commission which would result from the variation is such that it would not be fair or reasonable not to disclose the increase (including any increased amount payable to a *permitted third party*) to the *client*;

and in either case the exemptions in sub-rule (6) do not apply.

(6)   Sub-rule 1(5) above does not apply in relation to a variation in the following circumstances:–

    (a)   the variation is effected on the *client's* own initiative and the *firm* or a *permitted third party* has not recommended the variation to the *client*; or

    (b)   (in the case of an appropriate personal pension wholly paid for by rebates recovered from the State Earnings Related Pension Scheme) the variation results solely from a subsequent change in salary or pensionable benefits.

2.   Key features document

(1)   For the purposes of this rule:–

    (a)   *Key features document* means a self-contained statement of the key features of a *packaged product* or *pension fund withdrawals* which must either:–

        (i)   be supplied as a *key features document* by a *product provider* regulated by *LAUTRO, PIA* or *SIB*; or

        (ii)   if the *product provider* concerned is not regulated by *LAUTRO, PIA* or *SIB*, comply with the adopted *LAUTRO* Rules which would have applied if the *product provider* had been a member of *PIA* issuing a *key features document*.

    (b)   Reference to a *life policy* does not include a *defined benefits pension scheme* or a *pension fund management policy*.

(2)   A *firm* shall provide the *client* with a *key features* document in the following circumstances:–

    (a)   before or when the *firm* makes a personal recommendation to a *client*:–

        (i)   to buy a *life policy*; or

        (ii)   to vary a *life policy* by increasing the premiums payable if that variation would cause a fresh notice of the right to cancel to be deliverable; or

        (iii)   which substantially modifies, in any material respect, an earlier recommendation made to the *client* (whether by the *firm* or another person) to buy or to vary a *life policy*; or

        (iv)   to modify, in any material respect, a proposal form already submitted (pursuant to an earlier recommendation by the *firm* or another person) to a *life office* to buy or to vary a *life policy*;

    except where the *life policy* was issued before 1st January 1995;

    (b)   before or when arrangements are made for the purchase of a *life policy* on an *execution-only* basis;

    (c)   before or when the *firm* makes a personal recommendation to a *client* to elect, or arranges an election, to make *pension fund withdrawals*; or

    (d)   before or when the *firm* makes a personal recommendation to a *client* to acquire a *holding* in a *scheme* or to change to a *holding* of different units or shares within a *scheme* but in the case of such an acquisition or change, a *firm* need not supply a *key features document*:–

(i) where the *firm* makes a personal recommendation to a *client* in circumstances in which the *qualified person* making the recommendation and the *client* are not physically in the same place at the same time and the *client* wishes to make the investment without delay;

(ii) where the change which is being recommended is from accumulation to income units, or vice versa, in a *scheme* for which the *client* has already received the key features;

(iii) in the case of an *execution-only transaction.*

(3) In circumstances within sub-rule 2(2)(d)(i) the *firm* must:–

(a) explain orally or in writing to the *client*, before the contract or change is made, the following main points from the *key features document*:–

(i) the name of the *scheme*;

(ii) its aims;

(iii) the relevant risk factors;

(iv) the charges which the *client* will or may bear or which will or may affect the value of the investment, and their effect;

(v) (if it is the case) that commission will be payable to your *firm*, or to a *permitted third party* and that the *client* is entitled to receive information about that commission; and

(b) enquire of the *client* whether or not he has been supplied with a *key features document* in relation to the *scheme* and, if it has not been supplied to the *client*:–

(i) send the *client* the *key features document*; and

(ii) record the reasons why it was not sent to the *client* before the contract or change was made, such record to be kept for 6 years.

(4) In circumstances within sub-rule 2(2)(d)(i) or (iii) above, the *firm* shall send the *key features document*, or cause it to be sent, to the *client* within 5 business days after the contract or change is made, and in any event no later than the contract note.

2A. Cancellation rights

(1) Before or when the *firm* makes a personal recommendation to a *client* to purchase a *packaged product*, the *firm* must advise the *client* whether *cancellation rights* apply and, if they do:–

(a) how long the cancellation period will be; and

(b) if it is the case, that upon cancellation the *client* may not recover the *client's* investment in full.

(2) Where a *firm* makes a personal recommendation to a *client* to buy a *life policy* which is a pension annuity, the *firm* must give the *client* notification of the right to cancel with the only or initial quotation.

3.   Packaged products and pension fund withdrawals

(1)   "Reason why" letter

Before or as soon as practicable after a *firm* makes a personal recommendation to a *client*:–

(a)   to buy a *life policy*; or

(b)   to vary the terms of an existing *life policy* by agreeing either:–

    (i)   that the *client* will from that time onwards pay regular premiums under the contract; or

    (ii)   that the *client* will pay an additional single premium; or

(c)   in respect of all or part of an existing *life policy*:–

    (i)   to sell, convert, cancel or surrender it; or

    (ii)   to suspend the payment of premiums on a permanent or temporary basis; or

(d)   to acquire a *holding* in a *scheme*; or

(e)   in respect of an existing *holding* in a *scheme*, to sell all or part of that *holding*; or

(f)   to elect to make *pension fund withdrawals*;

the *firm* must provide the *client* with a written explanation of the reasons why (on the basis of the facts about the *client* of which it is aware) it believes the recommendation to be suitable for the *client*.

(2)   Confirmation of execution-only business

If a *firm* arranges for a *client* on an *execution-only* basis any action which falls within rule 3(1)(a) to (f) above, the *firm* shall send the *client* written confirmation to the effect that:–

(a)   the *client* had not sought and was not given any advice from the *firm* in connection with that action; or

(b)   the *client* was given advice from the *firm* in connection with that action but nevertheless persisted in wishing the action to be effected;

and in either case the action is effected on the *client's* explicit instructions.

(3)   Records

A *firm* shall make a record in relation to each *client* of the written explanation and confirmation referred to in this rule, such record to be kept for 6 years from the performance of any *investment services* to which the record relates.

Guidance note

1.   A copy of the written explanation or confirmation will be a sufficient record for the purposes of this rule.

2.   For other provisions regarding record keeping see rules 16 and 27.

PART 2 – CONDUCT OF BUSINESS RULES APPLICABLE ONLY TO FIRMS UNDERTAKING DISCRETE INVESTMENT BUSINESS

4. Packaged products

(1) Standards of advice

    (a) A *firm* shall not make a personal recommendation to a *client* to buy a *packaged product*, or buy a *packaged product* for a *client* in the exercise of discretion, unless:–

        (i) it has taken reasonable steps to inform itself about *packaged products* which are generally available on the market, and

        (ii) it is not aware of another *packaged product* which would better meet the *client's* needs.

    (b) In assessing the merits of a *packaged product* to be held as the plan investment of a *PEP* or *ISA*, a *firm* shall take into account the characteristics (including charging arrangements) of the *PEP* or *ISA*, as well as those of the product.

(2) Provision of information

Before or when making a personal recommendation to a *client* to buy a *packaged product* or to elect to make *pension fund withdrawals*, a *firm* shall provide information about the product which is adequate to enable the *client* to make an informed investment decision.

(3) Records

A *firm* shall make a record in relation to each *client* of the steps referred to in sub-rule (1)(a)(i), such record to be kept for 6 years from the performance of any *investment services* to which the record relates.

Guidance note

For other provisions for record keeping see rules 16 and 27.

27

APPENDIX 8

CUSTODY RULES (rule 17)

1. TITLE TO CLIENTS' INVESTMENTS

(1) A *firm* shall ensure that evidence of title to a *client's* investments is maintained in such a way that those investments are separately identifiable from investments belonging to the *firm*, whether title to the *client's* investments passes by registration or delivery.

(2) Where a *client's* investments are registrable they must be properly registered in the *client's* name or, with the *client's* consent, in the name of a nominee.

(3)   For the purposes of paragraph 1(2) above, the nominee shall be the *firm's own nominee* unless the *client,* for the *client's* own convenience, instructs the *firm* in writing to register the *client's* investments in the name of another nominee.

Guidance note

Clients' investments would not be properly registered if they were registered in the same name as that used for investments belonging to the firm, its own nominee or a third party custodian unless they are held in a separate account designated solely for the use of clients' investments.

2.   SAFEKEEPING OF CLIENTS' ASSETS

(1)   A *firm* shall not release the *client's* investments (or assets), or *title documents*, into the control or possession of another person without the *client's* authority.

(2)   A *firm* shall not:–

(a)   use a *client's* investments for its own account;

(b)   pool (or commingle) the investments of different *clients* except where those *clients* have been notified of the implications for them and have given their clear and express consent in writing;

(c)   engage in stocklending of *clients'* pooled (or commingled) investments except where each of the *clients* whose investments are pooled (or commingled) has given clear and express consent in writing to their use for stocklending;

(d)   use for the account of one *client* the investments of any other *client* except pursuant to paragraph 2(2)(b) above or where both *clients* have given their clear and express consent in writing.

3.   SECURITY AND INTEGRITY OF CUSTODY ARRANGEMENTS

A *firm* shall have security arrangements, including appropriate systems and controls, which are adequate to safeguard *clients' title documents.*

Guidance note

1.   Arrangements including custody facilities and systems for the transfer of assets, must be appropriate to the value and risk of loss of the clients' assets.

2.   Data processing facilities and records relating to investments must be appropriately safeguarded.

4.   NOMINEES AND RESPONSIBILITIES IN RELATION TO CUSTODY SERVICES

(1)   Where a *firm* uses its *own nominee* to hold title to *clients'* investments, the *firm* shall:–

(a)   ensure that its *own nominee* acts, in relation to each *title document*, only in accordance with the *firm's* instructions; and

(b)   accept responsibility to its *clients* for the acts and omissions of its *own nominee.*

(2)   Where a *firm* provides *custody services*, it shall clarify in writing with its *clients* the *custody services* which are to be provided and the respective responsibilities of the *firm* and the *client* in relation to:–

(a)   arrangements for recording, registering and separately identifying title to the *client's* investments;

(b)   procedures for giving and receiving clear instructions;

(c)   provision of periodic statements or statements of *title documents*;

(d)   any liens or other security interest held by the *firm* over the *client's* investments;

(e)   the use of its *own nominee*, in accordance with paragraph 4(1);

(f)   losses of the *client's* investments; and

(g)   the appointment of sub-custodians, the review, as appropriate, of their performance and extent, if any, of the *firm's* responsibility for losses caused by their fraud, wilful default or negligence.

Guidance note

See exemption in paragraph 10 below.

(3)   A *firm* shall not disclaim responsibility for losses of investments due to fraud, wilful default or negligence arising from it or its *own nominee's* activities.

(4)   A *firm* shall (where appropriate) notify its *clients* that there may be different settlement, legal and regulatory requirements in overseas jurisdictions from those applying in the United Kingdom, together with different practices for the separate identification of *clients'* investments.

5.   APPOINTMENT OF A THIRD PARTY CUSTODIAN

(1)   A *firm* shall use due skill, care and diligence (including undertaking an appropriate risk assessment) in selecting and appointing a third party custodian.

(2)   A *firm* shall not appoint, or recommend to its *client,* a third party custodian who is not an *eligible custodian*, unless the *firm* has disclosed this fact to the *client*.

(3)   If a *firm* appoints a third party custodian:–

(a)   services shall be supplied under a written agreement between the *firm* and the custodian which covers, where relevant, the matters set out in paragraphs 4(2) and 4(3) of this appendix;

(b)   the *firm* shall require the custodian to:–

(i)   have appropriate arrangements for the safekeeping of *clients'* assets;

(ii)   distinguish, within its own records, the *firm's clients' title documents* from those of the *firm*;

(iii)   hold the *firm's* and the *firm's clients' title documents* separate from those of the custodian; and

(c)   the *firm* shall take reasonable steps to review the custodian's performance under the agreement.

27

(4) Where a *firm* appoints a third party custodian to hold *clients' title documents* overseas, the *firm* shall comply with paragraph 5(3) above, where it is reasonable to do so, unless the *client* agrees otherwise.

Guidance note

The firm's own nominee is not a third party custodian.

6. CLIENT APPOINTING ITS OWN CUSTODIAN

Where a *firm's client* appoints its own custodian, the *firm* shall agree in writing any necessary consequential arrangements (for example, for settlement) with the *client's* custodian.

7. RECORD OF TITLE DOCUMENTS

(1) The *firm* shall keep a record of all *title documents* held by the *firm* or its *own nominee* specifying:–

   (a)   the *client's* name;

   (b)   the nature, amount and, where appropriate, nominal value of the *title documents*;

   (c)   where the *title documents* are kept;

   (d)   the date on which each *title document* came into or left the custody of the *firm* or its *own nominee*; and

   (e)   whether the *title documents* have been lent or held as collateral.

(2) Where a *firm* appoints a third party custodian, the *firm* shall keep a record of the *clients'* investments which are subject to the arrangements.

(3) The records kept under this paragraph shall be separate from the *client* files and *title documents* and kept for at least 6 years from the date when the *firm*, its *own nominee* or the third party custodian ceases to hold such documents.

8. CHECKING TITLE DOCUMENTS

(1) A *firm* shall at least once a year reconcile its records, which are held under paragraph 7 above, with the *title documents* held by the *firm*, its *own nominee* or a third party custodian.

(2) Where any difference arises, the *firm* shall investigate the discrepancy and make good, or provide the equivalent for, any shortfall for which it is responsible as soon as reasonably practicable.

9. REPORTING TO CLIENTS

(1) A *firm* shall send the *client* a statement at least once a year, made up to a date not more than one month previously, specifying the *title documents* held for the *client* by the *firm* or its *own nominee* and identifying any which have been lent or which are held as collateral.

Guidance note

1. Where the firm provides the client with a periodic statement under rule 25 of these rules, it will not be necessary for the firm to send a separate statement of title documents held by the firm or its own nominee as the appropriate information will be contained in the periodic statement.

2. See exemption in paragraph 10 below.

(2) Where a *firm* has appointed a third party custodian, the *firm* shall ensure that the *client* receives a statement at least once a year of any *title documents* held for the *client* by the custodian.

10. EXEMPTION

(1) Paragraphs 4(2) and 9(1) above shall not apply where the *activity* is *incidental* or where the *firm* or a partner, *employee* or *officer* of the *firm* is acting as the donee of any *registered enduring power of attorney* or is a receiver appointed by the Court of Protection.

(2) Paragraph 9(1) above shall not apply where the *firm* or a partner, *employee* or *officer* of the *firm* is acting as the donee of a *trustee power of attorney*.

Guidance note

For the purposes of this paragraph the activity is the provision of custody services.

27

Annex 27C

SIB's Statement of Principle

This statement of principle was issued by SIB (now the Financial Services Authority (FSA)) on 15th March 1990 under section 47A of (and, in relation to friendly societies, paragraph 13A of Schedule 11 to) the Financial Services Act 1986.

Introduction

1. These principles are intended to form a universal statement of the standards expected. They apply directly to the conduct of investment business and financial standing of all authorised persons ("firms"), including members of recognised self-regulating organisations and firms certified by recognised professional bodies.

2. The principles are not exhaustive of the standards expected. Conformity with the principles does not absolve a failure to observe other requirements, while the observance of other requirements does not necessarily amount to conformity with the principles.

3. The principles do not give rise to actions for damages, but will be available for purposes of discipline and intervention.

4. Where the principles refer to customers, they should be taken to refer also to clients and to potential customers, and where they refer to a firm's regulator, they mean SIB [FSA], or a self-regulating organisation or professional body which regulates the firm.

5. Although the principles may be taken as expressing existing standards, they came into force formally, with additional sanctions resulting, on 30th April 1990.

The principles

Integrity

1. A firm should observe high standards of integrity and fair dealing.

Skill, care and diligence

2. A firm should act with due skill, care and diligence.

Market practice

3. A firm should observe high standards of market conduct. It should also, to the extent endorsed for the purpose of this principle, comply with any code or standard

as in force from time to time and as it applies to the firm either according to its terms or by rulings made under it.

Information about customers

4. A firm should seek from customers it advises or for whom it exercises discretion any information about their circumstances and investment objectives which might reasonably be expected to be relevant in enabling it to fulfil its responsibilities to them.

Information for customers

5. A firm should take reasonable steps to give a customer it advises, in a comprehensible and timely way, any information needed to enable him to make a balanced and informed decision. A firm should similarly be ready to provide a customer with a full and fair account of the fulfilment of its responsibilities to him.

Conflicts of interests

6. A firm should either avoid any conflict of interest arising or, where conflicts arise, should ensure fair treatment to all its customers by disclosure, internal rules of confidentiality, declining to act, or otherwise. A firm should not unfairly place its interests above those of its customers and, where a properly informed customer would reasonably expect that the firm would place his interests above its own, the firm should live up to that expectation.

Customer assets

7. Where a firm has control of, or is otherwise responsible for, assets belonging to a customer which it is required to safeguard, it should arrange proper protection for them, by way of segregation and identification of those assets or otherwise, in accordance with the responsibility it has accepted.

Financial resources

8. A firm should ensure that it maintains adequate financial resources to meet its investment business commitments and to withstand the risks to which its business is subject.

Internal organisation

9. A firm should organise and control its internal affairs in a responsible manner, keeping proper records, and where the firm employs staff or is responsible for the conduct of investment business by others, should have adequate arrangements to ensure that they are suitable, adequately trained and properly supervised and that it has well-defined compliance procedures.

27

Relations with regulators

10.   A firm should deal with its regulator in an open and co-operative manner and keep the regulator promptly informed of anything concerning the firm which might reasonably be expected to be disclosed to it.

Additional guidance issued by the Society

Under the Financial Services Act 1986, SIB [FSA] are empowered to issue 'statements of principle with respect to the conduct and financial standing expected of persons authorised to carry on investment business'.

The first of these statements of principle is set out above. The principles apply to all firms of solicitors which hold investment business certificates.

The following points should be noted:

▶   Solicitors are subject to the stringent requirements of rule 1 of the Solicitors' Practice Rules 1990 (**1.01**, p.1 in the Guide) and the general principles of professional conduct set out in the Guide; it seems unlikely that the principles promulgated by SIB [FSA] impose any greater duty on solicitors.

▶   Where the requirements of a particular principle are less onerous than the general standard of conduct expected of solicitors (e.g. in relation to principle 6 – conflicts of interest) then the higher standard of conduct will prevail.

▶   Principle 3 (market practice) is unlikely to be of significance to most solicitors. The reference to a 'code' is intended to relate to, e.g., the Takeover Code, which has been endorsed by SIB [FSA]. Further guidance is at Annex 27K, p.665 in the Guide.

▶   The combined effect of compliance with the Solicitors' Accounts Rules and the existence of the Solicitors' Indemnity Fund and the Solicitors' Compensation Fund will be sufficient to ensure compliance with principle 8 (financial resources).

2nd May 1990, updated February 1999

Financial Services (Conduct of Business) Rules 1990

Part 7 (advertisements)

(with consolidated amendments to 21st January 1999)

7.01 Application

(1) This Part of these rules applies to advertisements in respect of investment business other than:

    a. an advertisement which is excluded from paragraph (e) of section 48(2) of the Act by virtue of section 48(5) of the Act, and

    b. an advertisement which contains matter required or permitted to be published:

        (i) by or under any enactment, or

        (ia) by or under any provision of the law of a member State other than the United Kingdom corresponding to section 85 of the Act, or

        (ii) by an exchange which is:

            (A) a recognised investment exchange,

            (B) a designated investment exchange,

            (C) an approved exchange as defined by regulation 2(1) of the Public Offers of Securities Regulations 1995 (S.I. 1995/1537),

    and contains no other matter, and

    c. an advertisement announcing a public offer of securities for which a prospectus is or will be required under Part II of the Public Offers of Securities Regulations 1995 (S.I. 1995/1537), and

    d. an advertisement issued in such circumstances that it is unlikely that it will be communicated to persons who are neither business investors nor persons who carry on investment business.

Practice note

The Board considers that a person within sub-paragraph (d) who by way of business passes on an advertisement which he receives as such will be issuing an advertisement and so is subject to section 57 of the Act and, if a firm, this Part of these rules.

27

(2) Except where the context otherwise requires references in this Part of these rules to an advertisement are references to an advertisement to which this Part of these rules applies.

7.02   [Not used]

7.03   Issue of advertisements by a firm

A firm shall not issue an advertisement unless the requirements of this Part of these rules are complied with in relation to that advertisement.

7.04   Approval by a firm of advertisements issued by unauthorised persons

(1) [Not used]

(2) A firm shall not approve for the purposes of section 57 of the Act the contents of an investment advertisement to be issued or caused to be issued by a person who is not an authorised person unless the requirements of this rule are complied with in relation to that advertisement.

(3) In the case of an advertisement which relates to a collective investment scheme the requirements of this rule are that:

     a.   all the requirements of this Part of these rules are complied with in relation to the advertisement as if the unauthorised person were a firm, and

     b.   if the approval is required for the purpose of the advertisement's being issued by an overseas person, that person is the operator of a regulated collective investment scheme and the advertisement relates to units in that scheme.

(4) In the case of an advertisement which relates to a life policy the requirements of this rule are that:

     a.   all the requirements of rule 5.11 (if applicable) and of this Part of these rules are complied with in relation to the advertisement as if the unauthorised person were a firm, and,

     b.   if the life policy is to be issued by a life office which is an overseas person:

         (i)   that life office is one referred to in section 130(2)(c) or (d) of the Act, or

         (ii)   that life office is one referred to in section 130(3)(a) of the Act and the requirements of section 130(3) of the Act have been fulfilled.

(5) In the case of an advertisement which does not relate to a collective investment scheme or to a life policy and is an image advertisement or a short form advertisement, the requirements of this rule are that all the requirements of this Part of these rules are complied with in relation to the advertisement as if the unauthorised person were a firm.

(6) In the case of an advertisement which does not relate to a collective investment scheme or to a life policy and is not an image advertisement or a short form advertisement and is not an advertisement to which rule 7.23 applies, the requirements of this rule are:

a. if the approval is required for the purpose of the advertisement's being issued by an overseas person who is an associate of the firm in circumstances in which the advertisement is not likely to be received by anyone other than an established customer with whom the firm or the associate has a continuing relationship governed by a written agreement, that the firm has no reason to believe that any matter in the advertisement is inaccurate, unfair or misleading, or

b. if the approval is not required for the purpose and in the circumstances mentioned in sub-paragraph a.:

    (i) that all the requirements of this Part of these rules are complied with in relation to the advertisement as if the unauthorised person were a firm, and

    (ii) if the approval is required for the purpose of the advertisement's being issued by an overseas person:

        (A) that the firm carries on in the United Kingdom in compliance with rule 2.01 (business plan) investment business which relates to investments of the same description as the investment the subject of the advertisement, and

        (B) if the advertisement is a relevant publication within the meaning of Part 8 of these rules which will or may include recommendations to acquire investments which are not readily realisable, that the firm has reasonable grounds for believing that the issuer will not:

            (I) give or send that publication to any person in the United Kingdom, or

            (II) enter into any arrangement with any person in the United Kingdom or procure any such person to enter into any arrangement under which that person will be regularly given or sent issues of that publication, unless that person is a person whom the issuer believes, on the basis of such facts about his financial situation and competence in financial matters as may be expected to be relevant, to be a person for whom investments which are not readily realisable are suitable, and

        (C) that the firm has no reason to believe that the issuer of the advertisement will not treat responders to the advertisement honestly and fairly, and

        (D) that the advertisement contains warnings that rules and regulations made under the Act for the protection of investors do not apply to the issuer of the advertisement and that the Board's compensation scheme will not apply in relation to the investment the subject of the advertisement, and

        (E) except in the case of a tombstone, that the advertisement contains statements that the advertisement has been approved by the firm and that the firm is regulated in the conduct of its business by the Board.

27

7.04A Overseas insurers

(1) This rule applies in the case of an advertisement which relates to life policies which is issued at a time when the insurer who is to issue the life policies is not authorised to carry on long term business in the United Kingdom of the class to which the advertisement relates by or under section 3 or 4 of the Insurance Companies Act 1982 and is not otherwise permitted to carry on long term business of that class in the United Kingdom.

(2) A firm shall not issue an advertisement to which this rule applies unless the contents of the advertisement and the manner of its presentation are such that the advertisement would have complied with regulations 65 to 65C of the Insurance Companies Regulations 1981 (Statutory Instruments 1981 No. 1654) as amended by the Insurance Companies (Advertisements) (Amendment) (No. 2) Regulations 1983 (Statutory Instruments 1983 No. 396) as those regulations had effect on 20 September 1990 as if they applied to the advertisement but subject to the amendment that, in regulation 65B there be inserted at the beginning of sub-paragraph (f) of paragraph (3) the following:

'except in a case where the insurer is authorised to effect or carry out contracts of insurance to which the advertisement relates in any country or territory which is for the time being designated for the purposes of section 130 of the Financial Services Act 1986 by an order made by the Secretary of State and where any conditions imposed by the order designating the country or territory have been satisfied.'

7.05 Prominence of required statements

The significance of any statement or other matter required by these rules to be included in an advertisement shall not be disguised either through lack of prominence in relation to the other matter in the advertisement or by the inclusion of matter calculated to minimise the significance of the statement.

7.06 Approval

(1) A firm which issues an advertisement shall ensure that the advertisement is approved prior to its issue by an individual within the firm, or within a group of which the firm is a member, appointed for the purpose of this rule.

(2) A firm shall not approve the contents of an advertisement in pursuance of rules 7.03 or 7.04 except through the agency of an individual within the firm, or within a group of which the firm is a member, appointed for the purpose of this rule.

Practice note

In relation to a short form advertisement in the form of a screen price quotation service, the Board considers that an individual empowered by his firm to input its prices to the system might properly also be empowered to approve short form advertisements of that type.

7.07 Advertisements to be clear and not misleading

(1) The content of an advertisement and the manner of its presentation shall be such that the advertisement is not likely to be misunderstood by those to whom it is addressed including, if it be the case, persons who cannot be expected to have any special understanding of the matter in the advertisement.

(2) An advertisement shall not contain any statement, promise or forecast unless the firm issuing or approving the advertisement has taken all reasonable steps to satisfy itself that each such statement, promise or forecast is not misleading in the form or context in which it appears.

(3) An advertisement shall not contain any statement purporting to be a statement of fact which the firm issuing it does not reasonably believe at the time of issue, on the basis of evidence of which it has a record in its possession, to be true.

(4) An advertisement shall not contain any statement of fact which, although true when the advertisement is issued, the firm has reason to believe is likely to become untrue before the advertisement ceases to be current.

(5) An advertisement shall not state that any person is of any particular opinion unless the firm issuing or approving the advertisement has taken all reasonable steps to satisfy itself that the advertiser or other person, as the case may be, is of that opinion when the advertisement is issued.

(6) If the investment or service to which an advertisement relates is available in limited quantities, for a limited period or on special terms for a limited period the advertisement may say so but, if that is not the case, the advertisement shall not contain any statement or matter which implies that it is so.

7.08 Advertisements to be distinguished from other matter

(1) The terms of an advertisement and the manner of its presentation shall be such that it appears to be an advertisement issued with the object of promoting the investment, service or firm to which it relates.

(2) Where the medium in which the advertisement is carried contains or presents other matter, the advertisement shall be distinguished from that other matter so that what is an advertisement does not appear to be or to form part of a news item, report, bulletin, entertainment, instruction, story, drama, performance or other such means of communication.

Practice note

The Board takes the view that an advertisement on a hoarding at a football ground would not contravene this rule but that an advertisement forming part of a dialogue of a televised drama would do so.

7.09 Advertisements to identify the investments or services to which they relate

Except in the case of a short form advertisement or an image advertisement, the nature of the investment or the services to which an advertisement relates shall be clearly described.

7.10 Promotions to be genuine

An advertisement shall not be issued with the intention not of persuading persons who respond to the advertisement to pursue the subject matter of the advertisement but instead of persuading them to enter into an investment agreement, or use financial services, of a description not mentioned in the advertisement.

7.11   Disclosure of advertiser's capacity

An advertisement which invites those to whom it is addressed to enter into an investment agreement with a named person shall:

a.   disclose, by statement or by necessary implication, whether it is proposed that the named person will enter into the agreement as a principal on his own account or as an agent for another person, and

b.   if the named person is to enter into the agreement as an agent for another person and that person can be identified when the advertisement is issued, state the name of that other person.

7.12   Identity of regulators

(1)   An advertisement which is not a short form advertisement or an image advertisement shall state:

     a.   if the advertisement has been issued by a firm, that the person who has issued it is a person regulated by the Board, or

     b.   if the advertisement has not been issued by an authorised person but has been approved by a firm, that the advertisement has been approved by a person regulated by the Board.

(2)   Where an advertisement offers the product or the services of a person other than the firm which has issued or approved it, the advertisement shall state:

     a.   whether or not that other person is an authorised person, and

     b.   if he is an authorised person:

         (i)   the name of the body responsible for regulating his conduct of business, and

         (ii)   the fact that the body is so responsible or, if it be the case, that that person is a member of that body, and

         (iii)   if it be the case that that body regulates the conduct of that person on an interim basis only that that person has applied to that body:

     and any statement in an advertisement that that person has applied to a body responsible for regulating the conduct of that person's business shall be accompanied by the words "Not covered by The Investors' Compensation Scheme" and may be accompanied by a statement that that person is interim authorised.

(3)   An advertisement which is not an advertisement in respect of investment business shall not contain any matter referring to the Board.

7.13   Advertisements not to imply government approval

(1)   Subject to paragraphs (2) and (3) an advertisement shall not contain any matter which states or implies that the investment the subject of the advertisement or any matter in the advertisement has the approval of any Government department or of the Board.

(2)   This rule does not prohibit the issue of an advertisement which contains or advertises an offer for sale of investments owned by Her Majesty's Government.

(3)   Where the investment the subject of an advertisement is recognised by the Inland Revenue for the purpose of qualifying those who acquire the investment for any reliefs from taxation, the advertisement may refer to that recognition.

7.14   Synopses to be fair

An advertisement which states some only of the rights and obligations attaching to an investment or some only of the terms and conditions of an investment agreement shall:

a.   state sufficient of them to give a fair view of the nature of the investment or of the investment agreement, of the financial commitment undertaken by an investor in acquiring the investment or in entering into the agreement and of the risks involved, and

b.   state how a written statement of all of them can be obtained.

7.15   Commendations

An advertisement may include a quotation from a statement made by any person commending an investment or service if and only if:

a.   where that person is an employee or associate of the firm, that fact is disclosed in the advertisement, and

b.   the quotation is included with that person's consent, and

c.   the statement is relevant to the investment or service which is the subject of the advertisement, and

d.   where the whole of the statement is not quoted, what is quoted represents fairly the message contained in the whole of the statement, and

e.   the statement has not become inaccurate or misleading through the passage of time since it was made.

7.16   Comparison with other investments

(1)   An advertisement shall not compare or contrast:

    a.   an investment with an alternative application of an investor's funds, or

    b.   a service or a provider of a service or of an investment with an alternative service or provider,

unless the comparisons and contrasts are fair in relation to what is promoted and to the alternative having regard to what is not stated as well as to what is stated.

Practice note

The Board considers that it would be a breach of this rule:

a.   to omit a feature of possible comparison or contrast so as to exaggerate the significance of what is included, or

b.   to misrepresent or unfairly to criticise the alternative or the person who offers it.

(1A)   An advertisement of units in a regulated collective scheme shall not compare or contrast the performance or the likely performance of an investment in units of the scheme with an investment in a collective investment scheme which is not a regulated collective investment scheme.

27

(2)   Without prejudice to the generality of paragraph (1) if, in the case of an advertisement of units in a collective investment scheme or in a unit linked life policy, comparison is made between the performance of an investment in those units over a period of time with the performance of an alternative application of the investor's funds over the same period of time, the comparison shall be on an offer to bid basis, that is to say, on the basis of what it would have cost to acquire an amount of the investment and the alternative at the beginning of the period and what a disposal of that amount of the investment and the alternative would have realised at the end of the period, and the fact that that is the basis of the comparison shall be stated.

(3)   Without prejudice to the generality of paragraph (1) if, in the case of an advertisement of units in a collective investment scheme or in a unit linked life policy, comparison is made between the performance of an investment in those units over a period of time with the performance of an index over the same period of time, the comparison shall be on whatever basis is consistent with the basis on which the index is constructed, and the fact that that is the basis of the comparison shall be stated.

7.17   Life policies

(1)   The requirements of this Part of these rules apply to an advertisement relating to a life policy in addition to the requirements of rule 5.11 which rule applies in the case of an advertisement as it applies in the case of publications generally.

(2)   An advertisement relating to a life policy which gives particulars of any of the benefits payable under the policy shall state:

    a.   which of the benefits under the contract (if any) are of fixed amounts and what those amounts are, and

    b.   which of them (if any) are not of fixed amounts.

(3)   Such an advertisement may describe a benefit of a fixed amount or a minimum amount of a variable benefit as a 'guaranteed' amount but, if it does so and the advertisement refers to the participation of a third party and that third party will not stand as surety for the life office should the life office not meet its obligations, the advertisement shall not contain any matter which implies that the third party will so stand as surety.

Practice note

An example of a breach of this rule would be the following: an advertisement of a life policy, the benefits under which are linked to the performance of a fund held by a third party as trustee but not as a guarantor, states that certain benefits are 'guaranteed' without also stating that the trustee is not the guarantor of the obligations of the insurance company.

7.18   Taxation

(1)   An advertisement which refers to taxation shall contain a warning that the levels and bases of taxation can change.

(2)   An advertisement which contains any matter based on an assumed rate of taxation shall state what that rate is.

(3) An advertisement which refers to reliefs from taxation:

   a.   shall state that the reliefs are those which currently apply, and

   b.   shall contain a statement that the value of a relief from taxation depends upon the circumstances of the taxpayer.

(4) An advertisement which relates to an investment the income from which:

   a.   is payable out of a fund the income of which has already been taxed, and

   b.   is not or may not be subject to income tax in the hands of the investor,

   shall not describe the investment as one free from liability to income tax unless the fact that the income is payable out of a fund from which income tax has already been paid is stated with equal prominence.

(5) An advertisement which relates to an investment in whose case:

   a.   an investor will not be liable to taxation on realised capital gains in the investment, and

   b.   any realised capital gains of the assets of a fund to which the value of the investments is linked are subject to taxation,

   shall not describe the investment as one free from liability to capital gains taxation unless the fact that the value of the investment is linked to a fund which will be liable to taxation on realised capital gains in the assets of which it is comprised is stated with equal prominence.

(6) An advertisement which refers to reliefs from taxation shall distinguish between reliefs which apply directly to investors and those which apply to the issuer of the investment or to a fund in which the investor participates.

7.19   Cancellation rights

An advertisement may state (if it be the case) that an investor who enters into an investment agreement to which the advertisement relates will be given an opportunity to cancel the agreement but, if it does so, the advertisement shall state:

a.   the period during which the investor will have that right and the time when that period will begin, and

b.   (if it be the case) that the right to cancel is conferred by law, and

c.   if upon cancellation the investor will not recover his investment in full should the market have fallen since the investment was acquired:

   (i)   that fact, and

   (ii) if the advertisement is an advertisement of a higher volatility investment, notice that the shortfall in what he recovers should the market have fallen could be very high because of the possibility of sudden and large falls in the value of the units.

7.20   Past performance

An advertisement shall not contain information about the past performance of investments of any description unless:

a.   it is relevant to the performance of the investment the subject of the advertisement, and

b.   except where the source of the information is the advertiser itself, the source of the information is stated, and

bb. in the case of an advertisement of a higher volatility investment, information is given for the period of five years ending with the date on which the advertisement is approved for issue and beginning five years before that date or, if the fund came into existence less than five years before that date, beginning when the fund came into existence, and

c.   if the whole of the information is not set out:

   (i)   what is included is not unrepresentative, unfair or otherwise misleading, and

   (ii) the exclusion of what is excluded does not have the effect of exaggerating the success of performance over the period to which the information which is included relates, and

d.   if the information is presented in the form of a graph or chart, no part of the information is omitted so as to give a misleading impression of the rate at which variable quantities have changed, and

e.   in the case of an advertisement of units in a collective investment scheme or in a unit linked life policy, any comparison made between the value of an investment in those units at different times is on an offer to bid basis, that is to say, on the basis of what it would have cost to acquire an amount of the units at the earlier time and what a disposal of that amount of those units would have realised at the later time, and the fact that that is the basis of the comparison is stated, and

f.   the advertisement contains a warning that the past is not necessarily a guide to the future.

Practice note

The Board considers that a unit trust manager could commit a breach of this rule if it were to issue an advertisement which:

a.   advertised all or a number of its funds, and

b.   either:

   (i)   claimed notable successes for some of those funds without indicating that it was some only of those funds which had attained those levels of success, or

   (ii) chose to show only an unrepresentative few months of performance.

7.21   Indications of the scale of business activities

An advertisement shall not contain any statement indicating the scale of the activities or the extent of the resources of a person who carries on investment business, or of any group of which such a person is a member, so as to imply that the resources available to support performance of the firm's obligations are greater than they are.

Practice note

The Board would regard the following as breaches of this rule:

(1)   An advertisement which states the amount of the authorised share capital of a company but does not also state the amount of the issued share capital of that company.

(2)   An advertisement which states the amount of a company's issued share capital, but does not also state how much of that capital has been paid up.

(3)   An advertisement which states the amount of a company's total assets but does not also state the amount of the company's liabilities.

(4)   An advertisement which states the amount of a company's income or turnover but does not state the period to which that amount relates.

(5)   An advertisement which refers to a subsidiary in a group and which mentions the amount of the capital or of the assets of the group as a whole so as to imply that they are resources on which the subsidiary can draw when that is not the case.

(6)   An advertisement which states the amount of funds under a firm's management in such a way as to imply that those funds are assets of the firm.

7.22   Risk warnings

(1)   This rule applies to any advertisement which is not:

    a.   a short form advertisement, or

    b.   an image advertisement.

(2)   An advertisement to which this rule applies shall contain a statement or statements in accordance with this rule warning of the risks involved in acquiring or holding the investment the subject of the advertisement.

(3)   Where the advertisement relates to an investment in the case of which deductions for charges and expenses are not made uniformly throughout the life of the investment but are loaded disproportionately onto the early years, the advertisement shall draw attention to that fact and that accordingly, if the investor withdraws from the investment in the early years, he may not get back the amount he has invested.

(4)   Where the advertisement relates to an investment which can fluctuate in value in money terms, the statement shall draw attention to that fact and to the fact that the investor may not get back the whole of what he has invested and, where the advertisement is an advertisement of a higher volatility investment, the statement shall draw attention to the possibility of sudden and large falls in the value of the units and to the fact that the investor may lose the whole of his investment.

(5)   Where the advertisement offers an investment as likely to yield a high income or as suitable for an investor particularly seeking income from his investment, the statement shall draw attention to the fact that income from the investment may fluctuate in value in money terms.

(6)   Where the advertisement relates to an investment denominated in a currency other than that of the country in which the advertisement is issued, the advertisement shall draw attention to the fact that changes in rates of exchange between currencies may cause the value of the investment to diminish or to increase.

27

(7)   Where the advertisement relates to a with profits life policy, that statement shall draw attention to the fact that the return on the investment depends on what profits are made and on what decisions are made by the life office as to their distribution.

(8)   Where the advertisement contemplates the customer entering into a transaction the nature of which is such that the customer may not only lose what he pays at the outset but may incur a liability to pay unspecified additional amounts later, the statement shall draw attention to the fact that the investor may or, as the case may be, will have to pay more money later and that accordingly a transaction in that investment can lose the investor more than his first payment.

(9)   Where the advertisement relates to a margined transaction which is not a limited liability transaction and which will or may be effected otherwise than on a recognised or designated investment exchange and in a contract of a type traded thereon, the advertisement shall draw attention to the fact that the transaction is only suitable for a person who has experience in transactions of that description:

But this does not apply in the case of an advertisement which advertises the services of an execution-only dealer.

Practice note

This rule should be read in conjunction with rule 9.11(1)b.(iii) below.

(10)   Where the advertisement relates to an investment which is not readily realisable:

a.   if the investment is not traded on a recognised or designated investment exchange, the statement shall draw attention to the fact that there is no recognised market for the investment so that it may be difficult for the investor to sell the investment or for him to obtain reliable information about its value or the extent of the risks to which it is exposed, or

b.   if the investment is traded on a recognised or designated investment exchange but is dealt in so irregularly or infrequently:

(i)   that it cannot be certain that a price for that investment will be quoted at all times, or

(ii)   that it may be difficult to effect transactions at any price which may be quoted, and

the statement shall draw attention to that fact or those facts, as the case may be, and, if there are less than three market makers in that investment or the firm which has issued the advertisement is the only market maker in that investment, the statement shall draw attention to that or to those facts, as the case may be.

(11)   Where the advertisement relates to units:

a.   in a property fund, or

b.   in a constituent part of an umbrella fund which, if that part were a separate fund, would be a property fund, or

c.   in a fund of funds in the case of which one of the schemes to which it is dedicated is a property fund,

the statement shall draw attention:

(i)   to the fact that land and buildings may at times be difficult to sell so that there may be periods during which the operator will have the right to refuse to repurchase units offered to him for redemption, and

(ii)   to the fact that a valuation of land and buildings has to be the judgement of an individual valuer.

(12) Where the advertisement is of a life policy and refers to benefits under the policy which are measured by reference to the value of, to fluctuations in the value of or to income from land or any interest in land, the statement shall draw attention:

(i)   to the fact that the assets to which the benefits under the policy are linked may at times be difficult to sell so that there may be periods during which the life office will be unable to accept surrenders of the policy, and

(ii)   to the fact that a valuation of land and buildings has to be the judgement of an individual valuer.

(13) Where the advertisement relates to units in a regulated collective investment scheme, and at the time when the advertisement is prepared for issue, the property of the scheme consists, or there is an expectation that the property of the scheme may consist, as to more than 35% thereof in Government and other public securities issued by one issuer, the statement shall include reference to that fact or, as the case may be, to that expectation and shall identify that issuer.

7.22A   [Revoked]

7.23   General duty of disclosure in 'off-the-page' and 'off-the-screen' advertisements

(1) Subject to paragraph (1A) this rule applies to an advertisement containing:

a.   an offer to enter into an investment agreement with a person who responds to the advertisement, or

b.   an invitation to a person to respond to the advertisement by making an offer to enter into an investment agreement, and

in either case, specifying the manner in which that response is invited to be made.

(1A) This rule does not apply to an advertisement if:

a.   the investment agreement the subject of the advertisement is an agreement for the supply of a publication to which Part 8 of these rules applies, or

b.   the investment agreement the subject of the advertisement is an agreement for the acquisition or disposal of shares, debentures, warrants, options or other securities of a company or of an interest in the securities of a company and the advertisement contains:

(i)   all such information as investors and their professional advisers would reasonably require, and reasonably expect to find there, for the purpose of making an informed assessment of:

(A)   the assets and liabilities, financial position, profits and losses, and prospects of the issuer of the securities, and

(B)   the rights attaching to those securities, and

(ii)   no other matter.

(2)   An advertisement to which this rule applies may not be issued if the investment agreement the subject of the advertisement is an agreement for the provision of the

27

services of a portfolio manager or investor broker fund adviser or if it relates to an investment other than:

a.   a life policy, or

b.   units in a regulated collective investment scheme, or

c.   a type A or a type B PEP.

Note. *By rule 17.04 of these rules (as amended by the Financial Services (Conduct of Business) (Amendment No. 2) Rules 1994), rule 7.23(2) excludes a fourth category of investment.*

(3)   A firm shall not issue an advertisement to which this rule applies if the advertisement contains any matter likely to lead to the supposition that the investment agreement the subject of the advertisement is or is thought to be suitable for a particular individual who is the recipient of the advertisement.

Practice note

This rule constrains the issuer of personalised circulars to refrain from implying that he knows a recipient sufficiently well to be sure that the investment is suitable. The rule is not intended to constrain the content of letters to individuals whom the firm writing the letter does know.

(4)   A firm shall not issue an advertisement to which this rule applies unless the advertisement is contained in a printed document or is otherwise capable of being examined continuously for a reasonable period of time.

7.24   'Off-the-page' advertisements for life policies

A firm shall not issue an advertisement to which rule 7.23 applies which relates to a life policy unless the advertisement contains the information set out in, or required to be included in, a key features document prepared in accordance with the Adopted Lautro Rules as at 1 January 1999.

7.25   'Off-the-page' advertisements for schemes

A firm shall not issue an advertisement to which rule 7.23 applies in respect of regulated collective investment schemes whether or not held within a PEP, investment trusts where the relevant shares have been or are to be acquired through an investment trust savings scheme or an investment trust where the relevant shares are held with a PEP which promotes one or more specific investment trusts, unless the advertisement contains the information set out in, or required to be included in, a key features document prepared in accordance with the Adopted Lautro Rules as at 1 January 1999.

7.26   'Off-the-page' advertisements for type B PEPs

(1)   A firm shall not issue an advertisement to which rule 7.23 applies which relates to a type B PEP unless the terms of the type B PEP the subject of the advertisement do not give any authority to anyone to make unsolicited calls upon the investor.

(2)   The requirements of paragraph (1) are in addition to the requirements of Part 4 of these rules as to the contents of a customer agreement.

7.27 Restrictions on promotion of unregulated collective investment schemes

A firm shall not issue or cause to be issued an advertisement containing any matter which invites any person to become or offer to become a participant in a collective investment scheme which is not a regulated collective investment scheme or contains information calculated to lead directly or indirectly to any person becoming or offering to become a participant in such a scheme unless the issue of the advertisement does not contravene sub-section (1) of section 76 of the Act by virtue of sub-section (2), (3) or (4) of that section.

Practice note

In relation to an advertisement issued or caused to be issued by a firm, this rule merely restates what is already an obligation under section 76(1) of the Act, but the rule has effect, by virtue of section 58(1)(c) of the Act, in relation to advertisements issued or caused to be issued by a national of a member State other than the United Kingdom in the course of investment business lawfully carried on by him in such a State.

7.28 Advertisements by appointed representatives

(1) A firm which is a collective investment marketing firm shall ensure that an advertisement issued by an appointed representative of the firm (other than an image advertisement or a short form advertisement):

    a. does not contain any statement commending the principal or its services or products in such a way as to suggest or imply that the appointed representative was free to exercise independent judgement in deciding to make the commendation, and

    b. contains a prominent statement, no less prominent than any other statement describing the relationship between the advertiser and the firm which draws attention to:

        (i) the fact that the advertiser is an appointed representative of the firm, and

        (ii) the fact that the advertiser has entered into arrangements with the firm which preclude the advertiser from selling or recommending any products other than those of the firm, and

    c. if the advertisement relates to a product of the firm, is not cast in terms which suggest or imply that the product is that of the appointed representative and not that of the firm.

(2) A firm which is a collective investment marketing firm shall ensure that, in an advertisement issued by an appointed representative of the firm which relates to any activity of the appointed representative which is not investment business as well as to an activity of the appointed representative which is investment business, any claim made to independence in respect of the activity which is not investment business does not appear with such prominence relative to the matter in the advertisement which relates to investment business as to create a likelihood that a person reasonably attentive to the advertisement might suppose that the claim to independence applied to the activity of the appointed representative which is investment business.

27

(3)   A firm which is a collective investment marketing firm shall ensure that an advertisement issued by an appointed representative of the firm which is not an advertisement in respect of investment business does not contain any matter referring to the Board or to the fact that the advertiser is connected with a person who is regulated by the Board.

7.29   Advertisements not to disguise lack of independence

(1)   A firm which is not a collective investment marketing firm and which has an associate which is:

a.   a collective investment marketing firm, or

b.   an appointed representative of a collective investment marketing firm,

shall not issue an advertisement of the products or services of the firm in such manner or containing such matter as is likely to cause a reader of the advertisement in its context to suppose that the associate has the same independence as that of the firm.

(2)   A firm which is a collective investment marketing firm and which has an appointed representative which is an associate of a person who is not a collective investment marketing firm shall ensure that no advertisement of the products or services of the firm is issued by the appointed representative in such manner or containing such matter as is likely to cause a reader of the advertisement in its context to suppose that the firm has the same independence as that of the said person who is not a collective investment marketing firm.

(3)   A firm which is a collective investment marketing firm and which has an associate which is not a collective investment marketing firm shall not issue an advertisement of the products or services of the firm in such manner or containing such matter as is likely to cause a reader of the advertisement in its context to suppose that the firm has the same independence as that of the associate.

Practice note

The Board considers the following to be an example of a breach of this rule. The issue of an advertisement of the services of financial adviser X (the appointed representative of life office Y) in a brochure which advertises the services generally of firm Z (an independent financial adviser) without special mention of the status of X and so to give the impression that X has the same independence as Z. This would be particularly so if X and Z, being associates, have similar names.

7.30   Individual Savings Account advertisements

(1)   A firm must not issue an advertisement in respect of an ISA unless it complies with:

a.   the Adopted Lautro Rules of the PIA applicable to such advertisements as specified in Part I of Appendix A to Part I of these Rules in accordance with Rule 1.16(1).a; or

b.   the Adopted FIMBRA Rules of the PIA applicable to such advertisements as specified in Part II of Appendix A to Part I of these Rules in accordance with Rule 1.16(1).b; or

c.   the IMRO Rules as specified in Part I of Appendix A to Part III of these Rules in accordance with Rule 1.16(1).c.

Reproduced with the kind permission of the Financial Services Authority

Additional guidance issued by the Law Society

Updated April 1999

These rules, which were made by the Securities and Investments Board (SIB), now the Financial Services Authority (FSA), are referred to in rule 11(3)(a) of the Solicitors' Investment Business Rules 1995 (see Annex 27B at p.575 in the Guide).

Definitions

The following definitions are in SIB's (now the FSA's) Financial Services (Glossary and Interpretation) Rules and Regulations 1990:

Image advertisement: means an advertisement which does no more than:

a.   promote public awareness of the advertiser;

b.   describe the services it provides or the products it markets;

c.   commend the advertiser in general, but not any particular service it provides or product it markets; or

d.   offer to supply further information on request.

Short form advertisement: means an advertisement which contains the advertiser's name and in respect of investment business otherwise does no more than some or all of:

a.   display the advertiser's

address

telephone number

symbol or logogram;

b.   describe the advertiser's

business

fees charged;

c.   contain one or both of a statement that, or a symbol approved by the Board to show that, the advertiser (or the firm approving the advertisement) is regulated in the conduct of investment business by the Board;

d.   state, in relation to investments which the advertiser will or may buy or sell (or arrange to buy or sell)

their names

indicative prices

difference of prices from previous prices

their income and yields

their earnings (or price/earnings ratio);

e.   state, simply as a matter of fact, and not so as to imply any offer to deal, that the advertiser, alone or with others named, arranged the issue of or a transaction in a particular investment.

27

Transitional provision

The following is an extract from Part 17 of SIB's (now the FSA's) Financial Services (Conduct of Business) Rules 1990:

17.04

(1) In relation to an advertisement issued during the period in which this rule remains in force rule 7.23 shall have effect as if the following were added to paragraph (2):

'or

   (d) an investment (other than one mentioned in sub-paragraph (a), (b) or (c)) which could lawfully have been the subject of an advertisement of the same description as an advertisement to which this rule applies issued in the United Kingdom before 29 April 1988'

and rules 7.24 to 7.26 shall not apply to an advertisement the issue of which is, by virtue of rule 7.23(2)(d), excluded from the prohibition contained in this rule.

(2) Nothing in this rule applies to an advertisement relating to futures, options, contracts for differences or rights to any of them.

British Codes of Advertising and Sales Promotion

(relevant extracts – see the Solicitors' Investment Business Rules 1995, rule 11(2)(a))

Introduction

1.1 The Codes apply to:

a   advertisements in newspapers, magazines, brochures, leaflets, circulars, mailings, catalogues and other printed publications, facsimile transmissions, posters and aerial announcements

b   cinema and video commercials

c   advertisements in non-broadcast electronic media such as computer games

d   viewdata services

e   mailing lists except for business-to-business

f   sales promotions

g   advertisement promotions

h   advertisements and promotions covered by the Cigarette Code.

1.2 The Codes do not apply to:

a   broadcast commercials, which are the responsibility of the Independent Television Commission or the Radio Authority

b   the contents of premium rate telephone calls, which are the responsibility of the Independent Committee for the Supervision of Standards of Telephone Information Services

c   advertisements in foreign media

d   health-related claims in advertisements and promotions addressed only to the medical and allied professions

e   classified private advertisements

f   statutory, public, police and other official notices

g   works of art exhibited in public or private

27

h   private correspondence

i   oral communications, including telephone calls

j   press releases and other public relations material

k   the content of books and editorial communications

l   regular competitions such as crosswords

m   flyposting

n   packages, wrappers, labels and tickets unless they advertise a sales promotion or are visible in an advertisement

o   point of sale displays except for those covered by the Sales Promotion Code and the Cigarette Code.

Financial services and products

55.1 The rules that follow provide only general guidance. Advertisers, their agencies and the media must also comply with the numerous statutes that govern financial services and products including issuing advertisements, investment opportunities, credit facilities and the provision of financial information.

55.2 Offers of financial services and products should be set out in a way that allows them to be understood easily by the audience being addressed. Advertisers should ensure that they do not take advantage of people's inexperience or gullibility.

55.3 Advertisers asking for a commitment at a distance should make sure that their full address is given outside any response coupon or other mechanism.

55.4 Advertisements should indicate the nature of the contract being offered, any limitations, expenses, penalties and charges and the terms of withdrawal. Alternatively, where an advertisement is short or general in its content, free explanatory material giving full details of the offer should be readily available before a binding contract is entered into.

55.5 The basis used to calculate any rates of interest, forecasts or projections should be apparent immediately.

55.6 Advertisements should make clear that the value of investments is variable and, unless guaranteed, can go down as well as up. If the value of the investment is guaranteed details should be included in the advertisement.

55.7 Advertisements should specify that past performance or experience does not necessarily give a guide for the future. Any examples used should not be unrepresentative.

1st February 1995, reproduced with the kind permission of the Committee of Advertising Practice

Annex 27F

Guidance – future pension transfers and opt outs

---

*[**Note:** for additional requirements, see **27.07** note 2 (p.526 in the Guide).]*

COUNCIL STATEMENT – DOCUMENT A

INTRODUCTION

1. In March 1994 the Securities and Investments Board (SIB) issued a report entitled 'Pension Transfers and Opt Outs – Further Safeguards for Future Business'. This report sets out new standards for the conduct by firms of investment business involving advising clients on transfers and opt outs from occupational pension schemes into individual pension contracts. SIB have indicated that they expect the regulatory bodies to notify their members that they must comply with these standards and accordingly the Council is issuing this statement by way of guidance which has mandatory effect from 1st September 1994.

2. This guidance is not a compendious statement of 'best practice' in relation to pension transfers and opt outs; nor is it a comprehensive statement of all the applicable regulatory requirements relating to pension transfers and opt outs and it should be read in conjunction with those requirements. Firms should supply a copy of this guidance to an investor who requests it.

OPT OUTS: PROSPECTIVE INVESTORS WHO ARE CURRENT OR PROSPECTIVE MEMBERS OF OCCUPATIONAL PENSION SCHEMES

3. In this section 'opt out' refers to the situation where an individual withdraws from or decides not to join an occupational pension scheme and instead takes out a personal pension contract.

Defined benefit occupational pension schemes

4. The starting point for a firm considering the situation of an active member of a 'defined benefit' occupational pension scheme should be to assume that it would not be suitable to recommend opting out into a personal pension contract.

5. If an opt out is recommended, the onus is on the firm to demonstrate that, on the evidence available at the time, it appears *bona fide* to be in the investor's best interests. *An opt out is presumed to be adverse to the interests of the individual concerned unless the contrary can be affirmatively shown.*

6.   Any firm contemplating giving advice in favour of an opt out first needs to identify the specific rights and benefits available to the prospective investor under the occupational pension scheme and to consider carefully the effects on the investor's situation of their replacement by the very different benefits of a personal pension contract. An analysis will need to be carried out, by someone competent to do so, of the occupational pension scheme data compared with the available personal pension products. A number of factors relating to the occupational scheme will need to be taken into account including:

(i)   spouse's, dependants' and children's pensions;

(ii)   early retirement provision, including retirement in ill-health;

(iii) revaluation rates both in deferment and payment, and whether they are guaranteed or discretionary (and if discretionary, whether likely to continue);

(iv)   ancillary benefits (e.g. tax-free cash or lump-sum death benefit);

(v)   transfer club arrangements, if applicable;

(vi)   the investor's contribution/the employer's contribution;

(vii) benefits on leaving service.

7.   Additional factors, such as the following, will also need to be taken into account:

▶   whether or not the employer would contribute to the personal pension plan;

▶   whether or not eligibility for other benefits, such as permanent health insurance, is dependent on being a member of the occupational pension scheme;

▶   the financial security of the occupational scheme, by reference (for example) to the last actuarial statement issued under the Disclosure of Information Regulations or the most recent trustees' report and accounts;

▶   the charging structure of the prospective personal pension plan, and its impact on transfer values in the early years;

▶   finally, there will be a number of subjective factors which may be relevant in relation to the prospective investor's circumstances. These include:

  ▶   future career plans and earning prospects (including any reasonable likelihood of job progression making the prospective investor eligible for a better occupational scheme), and intended retirement date;

  ▶   attitude towards earnings-related compared with money-purchase benefits;

  ▶   attitude to financial risk and security;

  ▶   a possible wish to make pension arrangements separate from employment (e.g. because the prospective investor is on a short-term non-renewable employment contract or does not expect to stay in his current employment for more than a short period);

  ▶   any value the investor attaches to personal control;

  ▶   the investor's cash needs.

Where a transfer value may be taken in respect of all or part of the individual's benefit the factors set out in paragraphs 11–26 should also be taken into account.

Prospective investors who are changing employment

8.   If the prospective investor is changing – or has recently changed – employment, the considerations outlined above need to be considered in relation to any scheme operated by the new employer for which the prospective employee is eligible, or will become eligible in the foreseeable future.

'Money-purchase' occupational pension schemes

9.   The presumption against opting out extends to membership of money-purchase occupational pension schemes, and thus the guidance above should also be followed in situations where a prospective investor is an active or prospective member of such a scheme to the extent that the factors listed are relevant to such schemes (e.g. if membership of the scheme attracts an employer's contribution not otherwise payable or renders the individual eligible for ancillary benefits such as permanent health insurance). Another factor will be a comparison of the investment vehicle within the occupational scheme with any alternative vehicle under a personal pension.

Documentation and record-keeping

10.   Firms should ensure that any transactions involving an opt out are thoroughly documented and that those transactions can be identified by the firm. The records are to be kept indefinitely.

TRANSFERS: PROSPECTIVE INVESTORS WHO HAVE DEFERRED BENEFITS

Transfers from defined benefit occupational pension schemes

11.   The position is more finely balanced when a prospective investor currently has deferred benefits from a final salary occupational scheme (i.e. a defined benefit scheme) and is considering transferring these benefits to an individual pension contract (i.e. a personal pension or section 32 contract).

12.   Advice on whether to transfer deferred benefits must be preceded by a detailed consideration of the ceding scheme compared with the personal pension or section 32 contract, and of the personal circumstances and objectives of the investor. A factfind designed with pension transfers in mind will be needed. A properly established process is necessary to ensure the suitability of the advice provided.

13.   The process should include procedures:

   ▶   for gathering ceding scheme information (see paragraph 14 below);

   ▶   to assess prospective investor's attitude to risk and security; this is relevant not merely to the choice of contract or fund, but also (and more fundamentally) to the choice between an occupational pension scheme and an individual pension contract in the first place;

   ▶   to ascertain the prospective investor's career aspirations and desired retirement age and to consider what a realistic retirement age would be, having regard to the size of the transfer value and the extent to which it can be converted into a stream of income before state pension age;

27

▶ to ascertain whether the prospective investor's new employer (if any) has arrangements to accept transferred benefits;

▶ enabling the financial adviser to look at other pension options, if available;

▶ for carrying out an analysis of the yield required to match the benefits under the ceding scheme (see paragraph 17 below);

▶ for enabling the prospective investor to receive sufficient, clear information to make an informed investment decision based on a full understanding of the risks involved and a knowledge of what protection, rights, expectations and options they may be giving up (see paragraph 19 below).

The various steps in this process make it most unlikely that pension transfer business can be concluded on the basis of a single consultation.

14. The firm will need to obtain the following information as a minimum from the ceding scheme in respect of the investor:

   (i) spouse's, dependants' and children's pensions;

   (ii) early retirement provision, including retirement in ill-health;

   (iii) transfer value quote detailing:

      ▶ guaranteed period;

      ▶ pre/post April 1988 Guaranteed Minimum Pension/Excesses;

      ▶ revaluation rates both in deferment and payment, and whether they are guaranteed or discretionary (see paragraph 15 below);

      ▶ tax free cash arrangements;

   (iv) lump sum death benefits;

   (v) transfer club arrangements, if applicable;

   (vi) relevant earnings;

   (vii) period of service;

   (viii) scheme details (e.g. benefits, bridging pensions, guarantee periods, position pre/post Normal Retirement Date, history of discretionary increases);

   (ix) whether members' benefits have been equalised for service from 17th May 1990;

   (x) ill-health benefits.

15. To the extent that benefits are discretionary, consideration should be given to the likelihood of their continuation, and to how far they are reflected in the transfer value.

16. Consideration should also be given to the implications of the scheme's financial position (e.g. the significance of a deficit or surplus), and to whether the transfer value has been reduced because the scheme is underfunded.

17. A transfer value analysis must be undertaken or obtained. The purpose of this analysis is to put a value on the benefits offered by an occupational scheme and calculate what rate of investment return the individual pension arrangement under consideration will need in order to provide actuarially equivalent benefits. The analysis should be based on a proper consideration of all the relevant factors. It

should be documented and recorded before firm investment advice is offered to the prospective investor. A copy of the results of the transfer value analysis must be provided to the investor and the analysis should be discussed with him/her in simple clear language.

18. The analysis is usually done by a computerised system, although it is possible for it to be done otherwise. Computerised systems are held by pension providers and some independent financial advisers. While there is no bar to using a pension provider's system, care should be taken in interpreting the results in view of the pension provider's interest in the matter. In any event, it should not be left to the pension provider to obtain the relevant data about the investor and his or her occupational scheme benefits. Guidance on the standards to be applicable to the design and use of transfer value analysis systems will be issued by SIB in due course.

19. Relevant items of information for the prospective investor include:

   ▶ the different character of the risks associated with personal pension and defined benefit occupational pension provision;

   ▶ the impact of fluctuations in annuity rates on the size of the eventual pension;

   ▶ the impact of protected rights on the planned retirement date;

   ▶ changes to the tax-free cash;

   ▶ any reduction in immediate death benefits;

   ▶ the transfer value analysis including an indication of the rate of growth needed to ensure the investor is no worse off.

20. The use of a transfer value analysis does not preclude a conventional projection of future benefits under the new scheme. In this case, however, there is a danger that like may not be compared with like in terms of the structure of eventual benefits. Accordingly, any illustration of the possible future benefits of the individual pension contract should approximate as far as possible to the replication of the main forms of benefit offered by the occupational scheme (e.g. if applicable, escalation in payment at the occupational scheme's rate, and provision for a surviving spouse at a level corresponding to that offered by the occupational scheme). This does not preclude the supply of a non-matching illustration as well, where the investor is interested in changing the structure of the eventual benefits.

21. As well as ensuring that its advice to the prospective transferor is suitable, the firm should consider the position and interests of the prospective transferor's spouse and dependants.

Transfers from money-purchase occupational pension schemes

22. The general points set out in paragraphs 12 and 13 above also hold in relation to prospective transfers from money-purchase occupational schemes, save that there is no obligation to undertake a transfer value analysis.

23. In assessing the suitability of the prospective transfer and in explaining its financial implications to the prospective transferor, particular attention should be given to whether there is sufficient reason for the investor to incur early transfer penalties or a new set of front-end charges, if this will be an effect of the transfer.

24. Relevant items of information for the prospective investor include:

   ▶ how the transfer affects the investment risk;

   ▶ how the effect of charges or expenses differs between the schemes;

   ▶ changes to the tax-free cash;

   ▶ any reduction in immediate death benefits.

Conclusion on transfers of deferred benefits to personal pension arrangements

25. Firms will find it difficult to demonstrate compliance with the relevant rules if the process outlined above has not been completed and fully documented, including the collection of the relevant information from the ceding scheme and the prospective investor, and clear provision of the necessary information to the latter. The records are to be kept indefinitely.

26. The process will by no means point to all clients being confirmed as prospects for transfers into personal pension plans or section 32 contracts. It will confirm that many clients are better advised to remain in their occupational pension schemes and that some others should transfer to a new employer's scheme. Advice must be suitable at all times even where this means that no transfer into a personal pension plan or section 32 contract will be effected.

The 'reason why' letter

27. From 1st September 1994 firms responsible for advising an investor to make a pension transfer into a personal pension or section 32 contract or to opt out will be required to explain their recommendation in a 'reason why' letter to the investor.

28. The 'reason why' requirement is designed as underpinning to the suitability obligation. Accordingly the main purpose of the 'reason why' letter is to confirm the advice given to the client and *to explain why that advice is suitable*. That explanation should take explicit account of the alternative of remaining within the occupational scheme.

29. The 'reason why' letter should demonstrate a real link between the circumstances, objectives and risk profile of the investor, and the recommendation made to him or her by the firm. It should reiterate the tenor of the particular advice given and the main considerations which prompted that advice. It should not be a mechanistic recitation of stock motives applicable to any and every transaction.

30. The letter should ask the investor to get in touch with the firm if there is something which needs to be clarified, or if further information is needed, or if the letter does not accord with the investor's view of the position.

31. The letter may say that the firm has relied on information supplied by the investor and the occupational scheme, but beyond that it should not contain disclaimers or exclusion clauses.

32. In particular relation to opt outs, not only should the disadvantages be clearly set out, but there should also be an arithmetical analysis setting out the financial implications of leaving the occupational pension scheme.

33. Where a copy of the 'factfind' is given to the investor, the 'reason why' letter can take the form of a section in the factfind, provided that section is completed in a way that meets the criteria set out above.

34. Whatever its format, the 'reason why' letter should be supplied to the investor as soon as reasonably practicable after the recommendation has been made, and, in any event, in time for the start of the cooling-off period.

35. It is up to each firm to decide how to organise the preparation and despatch of such letters. The individual adviser could prepare and issue the letter or it could be sent out by some central agency within the firm. Whatever route is used, there should be such controls and systems in place as are necessary to ensure that the 'reason why' letter is consistent with the factfind, explains why the recommendation is suitable for the particular individual concerned, and is expressed in terms comprehensible to the average investor.

Investors who reject the advice of the firm

36. There will occasionally be investors who are advised by their firm against proceeding with a pension transfer or opt out but who, nevertheless, insist on going ahead with the transaction.

37. If the firm takes the view that it should proceed with the arrangement, then the following steps should be taken:

    (a) The investor should have the position fully explained to him/her, including the implications of his/her choice, and this advice should be confirmed in a letter.

    (b) The investor's decision to override the adviser's recommendation should also be credibly evidenced. Disclaimer forms and pre-printed letters using stock phrases should not be used since they cast doubt upon the genuineness of the process. A note from the client *in his or her own words* is best.

    (c) Firms will be expected to record the number of cases in which the investor overrides their advice and to investigate thoroughly those cases where there may be doubts about the credibility of the actions taken by the investor.

38. The Monitoring and Investigation Unit will pay particular attention to this area, looking for evidence of patterns developing and 'formula' selling.

Execution-only business

39. An 'execution-only' transaction is one where the client simply gives his order and does not rely on the firm to advise him or to exercise any judgment on his behalf about the merits of the transaction or its suitability for him.

40. Authentic execution-only pension transfers or opt outs are likely to be unusual where there has been personal contact or correspondence between the individual and the firm. The Monitoring and Investigation Unit will view purportedly execution-only transactions with lively scepticism, and a firm should consider its position carefully before classifying a transaction as execution-only. The execution-only status of a transaction must be credibly evidenced. The client's signature on a standard form is by no means conclusive in this regard. A note from the client *in his or her own words* is best.

27

Notification to the Society

41. The Council also require that in the circumstances set out below, notification is given to the Monitoring and Investigation Unit. A firm must notify the Unit:

    (i) of its intention to conduct transfer and opt out work;

    (ii) of its competence to conduct this work;

    (iii) if the proportion of this work it handles on an execution-only basis exceeds 1% of the total;

    (iv) if the proportion of this work transacted at the client's insistence in the face of a contrary recommendation exceeds 1% of the total;

    (v) if the firm proposes to handle this work without face to face contact with the client;

    (vi) of individual opt out transactions.

    The requirement relating to items (i) to (ii) will come into force on 1st November 1994 and the remaining items on 1st September 1994. Comments on certain of these items are set out below.

Item (ii) – competence

42. SIB take the view that all firms should be required to demonstrate that through some combination of individual expertise, on the one hand and organisational controls and checks, on the other, they are properly equipped to handle transfers and opt outs. The particular mix may vary according to the character of the firm. Accordingly:

    (a) Where a firm intends to rely on employees of ordinary competence and experience (defined by reference to the basic training and competence requirements currently being introduced by the regulators) for giving advice on transfers and opt outs, it should have in place (over and above its standard compliance arrangements) systems for double checking:

    ▶ procedural compliance by the firm's employee;

    ▶ correct application of the transfer analysis system;

    ▶ the substantive merits of the proposed transaction – i.e. does it in substance comply with the requirements of conduct for this type of business? This will require an appraisal of the whole factfind, not just of the data needed for a computerised transfer analysis. All transactions generated by advisers of ordinary competence and experience should be double checked, while the unit responsible for the checking should depend on staff whose expertise particularly qualifies them for this task.

    (b) Where a firm cannot operate a double checking system (e.g. because it is a small business), it should be able to demonstrate that the individuals responsible for handling pension transfer and opt out business have expertise which particularly qualifies them for this task (and not just the basic level of competence required of all investment advisers), or that an expert in another firm is appropriately consulted when such cases are handled. The same conditions will apply where a firm operates a double checking system, but dispenses with automatic double checking in relation to certain transactions.

The statement which has to be sent to the Society by 1st November must show how the firm meets the criteria set out in this paragraph.

Item (iii) – execution-only business

43. Notification is required if the proportion of transfer and opt out business a firm handles on an execution-only basis exceeds 1% of all pension transfers and opt outs, reckoned by number rather than value, transacted per quarter. Firms must therefore keep appropriate records to permit this calculation to be made each quarter and notification to the Monitoring and Investigation Unit, if applicable, must be made within one month at the end of each quarter.

Item (iv) – insistent client

44. Notification is required if the proportion of transfer and opt out transactions arranged at a client's insistence in the face of a contrary recommendation exceeds 1% of all pension transfers and opt outs, reckoned by number rather than value, transacted per quarter. Again, appropriate records must be maintained to enable the calculation to be done each quarter, following which notification must be made to the Monitoring and Investigation Unit, if applicable, within one month at the end of each quarter.

General

45. Notification of items (i) and (v) above must be given before the firm conducts the relevant work. In the case of item (vi), notification must be given within 14 days of the conclusion of the transaction.

28th July 1994, updated February 1999

27

Annex 27G

Guidance – past pension transfers and opt outs

COUNCIL STATEMENT – DOCUMENT B

INTRODUCTION

1. The Securities and Investments Board (SIB) [now the FSA] have recently issued guidance setting out what firms should start doing now in connection with past pension transfers and opt outs which they have arranged. This follows widespread concern that in a number of cases, inappropriate transfers or opt outs may have been arranged. SIB have indicated that they expect the regulatory bodies to notify their members that they must follow this guidance and accordingly the Council is issuing this statement which has mandatory effect.

2. Following further guidance by SIB, the Council will publish an overall set of standards and specifications for the reassessment of past business in this area. The present interim guidance indicates how firms can, and should, make progress from now on in a way that they can expect to be compatible with the requirements of the further statement.

3. The following are the general considerations underlying the details of the present interim guidance:

   ▶ Firms should prepare for a systematic reassessment of 'high priority' categories of case by taking steps now to *identify* the cases in those categories and by *collecting relevant data* on those cases.

   ▶ All identifiable *opt outs* are of high priority.

   ▶ With respect to *transfers*, the high priority categories (see paragraph 7 below) have been selected to reflect the regulators' judgement of where the likelihood of *immediate* or *imminent* harm is greatest.

   ▶ Where a firm becomes aware of a case of serious and immediate harm or risk of harm attributable to its poor advice or mis-selling, it should be prepared to take immediate steps to mitigate that harm or risk, for example by relieving present hardship where liability is not contested – subject always, of course, to the agreement of Solicitors Indemnity Fund Ltd (SIF). The firm must also consider its professional obligations as to advising the client to seek independent advice.

   ▶ Complaints should be progressed as far as possible.

4. This guidance deals only with first steps. Further categories of priority case may well be designated later. The regulators' intention is that the designation of further tranches of case for proactive review by firms should take account of any patterns of evidence that become apparent over the next few months. Experience gained from reassessing the initial tranche will also in due course be relevant to the scale and definition of later tranches. Different definitions may be found to be appropriate for different firms, depending on initial experience with them.

5. It should be noted that:

    ▶ the present interim guidance does not set out criteria for the systematic *reassessment* of individual cases in 'high priority' categories: its focus is on identifying them and piecing them together, thereby paving the way for reassessment;

    ▶ the designation of certain categories of case as being of 'high priority' in the present guidance can be expected to be consistent with the prioritisation in the further statement;

    ▶ it may not be possible for all firms to complete the process of identifying and piecing together high priority cases by the time of the further statement, but all firms should make a start and proceed as quickly as is reasonably practicable. A firm should not allow its overall progress to be dictated by the pace of its slowest cases. Subject to paragraph 9, it should aim to progress as far as possible. Where a firm has to cope with a large number of cases, it should ensure that at least a significant proportion of them are on a 'fast track'. Firms should make an appropriate allocation of resources to the project and should be prepared to demonstrate to their regulators that they are tackling it in an efficient, businesslike way.

6. The review of past business, both on paper and where appropriate in due course by direct contact with customers, will require the use of suitably qualified and trained staff. If they have not already done so, larger firms should take steps now to identify and train a nucleus of suitable staff to form the core of their resources for tackling the review.

TRANSFERS: IDENTIFICATION AND DATA-COLLECTION

7. The high priority categories are:

    (i)   those who have died;

    (ii) those who have started to draw their retirement benefits;

    (iii) women at or over 50 at the time of the transfer and men at or over 55 at that time.

    Firms should regard each category as equal priority.

8. The following cases should, however, be excluded:

    (i)   transfers into section 32 contracts effected before 29th April 1988;

    (ii) transfers imposed by occupational scheme trustees (e.g. on winding-up or bulk transfer);

    (iii) transfers out of pure defined contribution (wholly money-purchase) occupational schemes;

    (iv) transferors whose complaints or claims have already been settled (if the relevant correct data has already been collected).

9. The information which firms should aim to piece together for each case in the high priority categories is listed in Schedule 1. Firms should aim to have at least this information. However, in the absence of a client complaint, firms should not at this juncture solicit information from ceding schemes on individual transfer cases (except as indicated below). Ceding schemes may have to be approached for data on individual cases in due course, but it is important that this should be tackled in an orderly and efficient way. Accordingly it is envisaged that enquiries will be 'batched', with each firm grouping together the cases in respect of which it needs to approach a particular ceding scheme. It is also envisaged that enquiries will proceed on a 'missing information' basis, with firms requesting only the information which they lack in a given case, and with ceding schemes filling in the gaps in the firms' data. Firms should make ready for the approach to ceding schemes, but should not make that approach unless SIF requires it in a particular case.

10. Where a firm, with the agreement of SIF, has conceded liability for non-compliance, is prepared to arrange reinstatement, and has agreed this with the investor and the scheme, it may of course proceed.

OPT OUTS

11. Firms should regard *all* identifiable opt outs as being of high priority. An opt out is a decision by an individual, who is either (i) a current member of an occupational pension scheme (and who still has the job to which the pension scheme applies) or (ii) who is eligible, or at the end of a waiting period will become eligible, to join an occupational pension scheme, to leave or not to join that scheme in favour of a personal pension.

12. Action on opt outs (including cases where the policy concerned is now lapsed or paid up) should be as follows:

(A) Transactions known or believed to be opt outs

12.1 Firms should start now to reassess transactions *known* or *believed* to be opt outs, starting from the presumption that opt outs are non-compliant unless the contrary can be positively demonstrated.

12.2 Where, in the light of its reappraisal, the firm is not minded to accept liability for non-compliance, it should put the case on 'hold' until the further statement.

12.3 Where the firm does accept liability for non-compliance, it should proceed to the question of redress – subject always to the agreement of SIF.

12.4 Where reinstatement into the ceding scheme, both prospective and retrospective, so that the investor is effectively put into the position he/she would have been in had he/she never opted out in the first place, can be agreed with the scheme and the investor, it should be effected as soon as practicable. This is, of course, subject to SIF's agreement.

12.5 Where only prospective reinstatement can be agreed and effected, it may be undertaken with SIF's agreement provided it is done without prejudice to the investor's rights in respect of the opted-out period. The question of redress in respect of that period should then be put on 'hold' until the further statement, and the 'holding' position should be made clear to the investor.

12.6 Where any other form of remedy is in contemplation, the question of redress should be put on 'hold' until the further statement (except in cases of serious and immediate harm or risk of harm, where, subject to agreement with SIF, the firm should be prepared to take immediate interim steps to mitigate the problems), and again the 'holding' position should be made clear to the investor.

(B) Records of transactions from which actual or probable opt outs could be identified

12.7 Firms should start work, if they have not already done so, on identifying actual or probable opt outs.

12.8 Indicators which may make identification feasible include:

▶ records of personal pension contributors who are contracted out of SERPS but not in receipt of the incentive payment;

▶ records of cases where a single premium transfer payment into a personal pension has been followed by a series of regular premiums;

▶ the occupation of the investor (e.g. in the public service sector) at the time the factfind was taken.

12.9 If the firm has identified an individual representative who has recommended or arranged an opt out, it should look closely at all the other personal pension business generated by that individual.

12.10 Where a probable opt out is identified further enquiries should be made to determine whether it actually is or is not an opt out. In relation to all opt outs identified, (A) above should then be acted upon.

12.11 Insofar as a firm's records afford no real indication as to whether particular sales involved an opt out or not the firm can await the further statement, although it is open to it to institute a deeper search for opt outs if it wishes.

COMPLAINTS

13. Firms should initiate complaints investigation procedures in all cases of complaint and have regard to their obligation to notify SIF of any claims made or intimated against them.

14. Where having investigated, the firm is minded to reject the complaint, it should put the case on 'hold' until the further statement, keeping the investor informed of the position and having regard to the obligation to notify SIF as set out in paragraph 13.

15. Where the firm believes that there is a valid claim it should proceed to the question of redress – subject always to the agreement of SIF. Then, for *opt outs*, apply paragraphs 12.3–12.6.

16. For *transfers*, where reinstatement, so that the investor is effectively put in the position he/she would have been in had he/she never transferred, can be agreed with the scheme and the investor, it should be effected as soon as practicable. This is, of course, subject to SIF's agreement.

27

17. Where any other form of remedy is in contemplation, the question of redress should be put on 'hold' until the further statement (except in cases of serious and immediate harm or risk of harm, where, subject to agreement with SIF, the firm should be prepared to take immediate interim steps to mitigate the problem). Again the investor should be kept informed of the position.

GENERAL

18. Where firms notify SIF of any potential high priority cases which could result in claims, they must also inform the Monitoring and Investigation Unit at the same time.

SCHEDULE 1

Information to be gathered for each pension transfer undertaken

(1) Age.

(2) Sex.

(3) Now retired [present time].

(4) Desired/anticipated retirement age.

(5) Attitude to financial risk [this should be retained/collated if already recorded, but if it is not recorded the firm is not required to approach the investor to seek to reconstruct it at this juncture].

(6) Date of transfer.

(7) Product purchased: PPP/section 32 buyout.

(8) Did the option exist to stay in an existing employer's scheme?

(9) Did the option exist to join a new employer's scheme?

Transfer values

(10) Amount.

(11) Proportion earmarked for protected rights/GMP.

Ceding scheme

(12) Whether liquidated/in liquidation.

(13) Name of scheme administrator?

(14) Defined benefit or money purchase scheme or hybrid.

(15) Scheme retirement age.

(16) Death before retirement benefits.

(17) Rate of revaluation of pension before retirement (guaranteed/discretionary).

(18) Level of pension increase after retirement (guaranteed/discretionary).

(19) History of discretionary increases.

(20) Level of beneficiary's pension.

(21) Level of spouse's/dependants' pension.

(22) Early retirement option (including retirement on grounds of ill health).

(23) Maximum tax free cash.

(24) Bridging pension.

(25) Guarantee period.

(26) Discretionary benefits accounted for in transfer value.

Critical yield

(27) % rate of return required to match ceding scheme benefits if recorded.

(28) Where the critical yield is not recorded the general principle is that sufficient information should be gathered to enable it to be calculated.

GUIDANCE FOR FIRMS REGULATED BY OTHER REGULATORS

Firms of solicitors which are regulated for investment business by other regulators (e.g. PIA) should bear in mind that, in connection with rectification of past error (if any), they must comply with the Solicitors' Indemnity Rules. Any steps taken by way of rectification must be with the agreement of Solicitors Indemnity Fund Limited in order to avoid prejudicing their cover.

28th July 1994, updated February 1999

COUNCIL STATEMENT – DOCUMENT C

INTRODUCTION

1. Following widespread concern that in a number of cases inappropriate pension transfers and opt outs have been arranged, the Securities and Investments Board (SIB) [now the FSA] expects regulatory bodies to ensure that their authorised firms carry out a thorough review of past cases.

2. In July 1994, the Law Society issued a Council statement which required firms to start this review process pending the issue of further detailed requirements by SIB. The detailed documentation has now been issued by SIB in two parts:

   ► Review of Past Business Part I: Statement of Policy; and

   ► Review of Past Business Part II: Specification of Standards and Procedures.

   These documents are attached as Annexes 1 and 2 respectively of this Council statement.

3. The Council supports the action SIB has taken in promoting a review of past cases and arranging, where appropriate, for suitable redress to be provided for clients.

Substantial publicity has already been given to the potential adverse impact on financial services clients/customers of incorrect advice on pension transfer and opt out cases. The Council believes that, in accordance with the general principles enshrined in practice rule 1, and, in particular, the good repute of the solicitors' profession, firms should undertake such a review. The Council therefore requires firms to undertake the review of past cases using SIB's specification (Annex 2) as supplemented and modified by SIB's documents 'Simplifying the Pensions Review' (Annex 2A) to provide a consistent approach.

4.   The Council statement has effect from 7th June 1995.

THE REVIEW

5.   Firms are required to carry out a review of past cases of pensions transfers and pensions opt outs in accordance with the detailed specification document (Annex 2) as supplemented and modified by SIB's documents 'Simplifying the Pensions Review' (Annex 2A).

PENSION TRANSFERS

6.   The stages of review are:

▶   **Identifying priority cases (paragraphs 101 to 109).**

A schedule of priority cases and targets for the completion of the review is provided in paragraph 103.

▶   **Gathering information (paragraphs 201 to 242).**

Firms are required to take diligent steps to gather the facts necessary to judge whether or not the transaction was handled satisfactorily and to make an assessment of loss.

▶   **Compliance assessment (paragraphs 301 to 367).**

Redress will be necessary where an investor has suffered a loss as a result of transferring and that loss resulted from the transaction not complying with the relevant principles, rules and guidance in force at the time of the sale.

▶   **Loss assessment (paragraphs 401 to 423).**

If a transfer was non-compliant, the firm must test whether the investor has suffered a financial loss as a result of choosing to transfer.

▶   **Analysing the cause of the loss (paragraphs 501 to 508).**

Redress is needed if a loss has been suffered and the sale is non-compliant and the loss is caused by the sale being non-compliant.

▶   **Redress and settlement (paragraphs 601 to 618).**

If an investor has suffered loss because a case is non-compliant, redress is a way of compensating the investor for that loss. Several methods of redress are suggested but the normal methods should be regarded as reinstatement of the investor in the occupational scheme or augmentation of the personal pension.

PENSION OPT OUTS

7.   The stages of review are:

▶   **Identifying priority cases (paragraphs 701 to 712).**

A schedule of priority cases and targets for the completion of the review are provided in paragraph 706.

▶   **Gathering information (paragraphs 801 to 848).**

Firms are required to take diligent steps to gather the facts necessary to judge whether or not the opt out transaction was handled satisfactorily and to make an assessment of loss.

▶   **Compliance assessment (paragraphs 901 to 947).**

Redress will be necessary where an investor has suffered a loss as a result of opting out or transferring, and that loss resulted from the transaction not complying with the relevant principles, rules and guidance in force at the time of the sale.

▶   **Loss assessment (paragraphs 1001 to 1027).**

Firms are required to test whether the investor has suffered a financial loss because of the transaction.

▶   **Analysing the cause of the loss (paragraphs 1101 to 1109).**

Redress is needed if the advice, including the advice to opt out of the occupational scheme, did not meet the appropriate standards of compliance; and the sale is non-compliant; and the loss is caused by the sale being non-compliant.

▶   **Redress and settlement (paragraphs 1201 to 1221).**

Reinstatement or augmentation of the personal pension scheme should be regarded as the normal methods of redress. Reinstatement is the preferable form of redress, particularly where the individual concerned remains in the relevant employment.

REDRESS FOR CLIENTS

27

8.   Firms should, at the earliest opportunity, notify the Solicitors Indemnity Fund Limited (SIF) of potential claims arising from the review which they undertake in accordance with this Council statement.

9.   Where a firm identifies a case which is 'non-compliant' and the investor appears to have suffered a loss, the firm should consult with SIF as to how to proceed with action to provide redress.

APPROACH TO THE REVIEW BY FIRMS

10.   Firms should adopt a diligent and systematic approach to the review of cases and keep records to evidence the work undertaken, including reasons for reaching conclusions about cases which are considered to be either compliant or non-compliant. To assist this process, SIB have issued standard documentation which is provided as Annexes 3–5 of this Council statement.

MONITORING

11. Firms must make the records referred to above available for examination by the Monitoring Unit.

12. The Monitoring Unit on routine or specific visits will wish to examine these records and ascertain the progress which is being made by firms against the stated timetables. Firms are required also to provide to the Monitoring Unit on a periodic basis, to be determined, information on the progress which is being made in carrying out the review to enable the Law Society in turn to provide information on progress to SIB.

IDENTIFYING OPT OUTS AND NON-JOINERS

13. In its guidance, SIB recognised the difficulties firms would encounter in identifying reliably from existing records and files the priority cases of opt outs and non-joiners. SIB indicated that a model questionnaire would be made available along with guidance on its use.

14. The questionnaire is attached as Annex 3 and details are given below in respect of its use. The SIB guidance is precise and provides details of procedures for firms to follow and standards for them to attain in using the questionnaire to carry out the review of past pension transfers and opt outs.

POLICIES TO BE COVERED ('RELEVANT POLICIES')

15. The questionnaire must be sent to as many personal pension policy holders as need to be reached in order to identify priority cases. The policies to be covered are:

   ▶ those taken out between 29th April 1988 and 30th June 1988 in relation to retirement annuities,

   ▶ those taken out between 1st July 1988 and 31st August 1994 in relation to personal pensions.

   Policies taken out after 31st August 1994 should be included if the advice was provided before that date. Policies taken out on or after 29th April 1988 should be excluded if all the advice was provided before that date. Policies which have lapsed or been cancelled are not excluded.

RESPONSIBILITY FOR ADMINISTERING THE QUESTIONNAIRE

16. Primary responsibility for administering the questionnaire lies with the firm which arranged the acquisition of the personal pension policy. The firm should take responsibility for the transactions generated by its own representatives.

17. Firms should document in adequate detail the policy holders to whom questionnaires have been sent. Completed questionnaires should be returned to the firm which sent them out.

ANALYSIS OF COMPLETED QUESTIONNAIRES

18. In certain cases, a client's answer to some of the questions may conflict with the firm's own records. For example, the client may have indicated that his/her employer did not run an occupational pension scheme when it is clear from the firm's files or from other evidence that this is not the case.

19. Firms should assess the reliability of the client's answers fairly and with good faith. Any material conflict or inconsistency in answers, either within the questionnaire itself or with the firm's own records, should be investigated by the firm.

20. In particular, responses indicating that no advice was given should not be regarded as conclusive on that point, without further enquiry, unless the firm's own records positively support this position.

COMMUNICATION WITH CLIENTS

21. Firms will need to administer questionnaires in good time so as to allow an adequate period following receipt of a completed questionnaire to review the relevant cases in accordance with the target date set out in the specification of standards and procedures (Annex 2). Firms may adopt whatever method of communication they believe will enable them to achieve a high response rate, taking into account their client base and work force. This applies both in relation to the initial approach and any follow-up work.

22. Interviews with clients (whether face to face or via a telephone conversation) should follow the format of the model questionnaire. They should not be conducted by the person who gave the original advice other than in exceptional circumstances such as in very small firms where there is no economical alternative.

23. Firms adopting a telephone based approach may wish to write to clients first alerting them to the possibility of a telephone call. Adequately trained personnel should be used on this task who, it is suggested, should follow a set script. There should be no attempt to promote any service at the time of the initial contact or in the course of any follow-up activity.

24. There may be cases where the clients cannot be traced or fail to respond to the initial contact. Response rates can be increased materially by diligent follow-up work and accordingly the general principle is that firms should go to reasonable lengths to trace or make contact with such clients urging them to respond. Whilst it is not possible to give definitive guidance on what constitutes 'reasonable lengths' to follow up clients, action may involve a combination of communication by post, telephone or face to face interviews.

25. For firms adopting a postal approach, a model reminder letter is provided at Annex 5. Firms should normally allow at least two weeks between the initial mailing and sending out a reminder letter to allow clients adequate time to respond. A reminder letter should enclose another copy of the questionnaire and a pre-paid envelope.

26. The appropriate level of follow-up will also depend on the indications that emerge from the responses received. Where responses indicate an appreciable incidence of apparent opt outs, follow-up with non-respondents should be appropriately tenacious. Conversely, a good response rate coupled with a negligible incidence of

apparent opt outs may allow a firm to conclude, in consultation with the Law Society, that it has taken sufficient action.

27. If, after reasonable action has been taken to contact the client, there is still no response, the firm should send a final letter to the client's last known address stating what action (which may be 'no action') it intends to take if there is no response within 28 days of the date of that letter.

28. Primary responsibility for administering follow-up action on the questionnaire should rest with the firm which arranged the personal pension policy. That is, the firm should take responsibility for the transactions generated by its own representatives.

FORMAT OF QUESTIONNAIRE

29. Firms should use the questionnaire which is provided at Annex 3 and not include additional questions without prior consultation with the Law Society.

30. If a firm believes it can rely on its own records and files to complete a policy holder's personal details, questions 1 and 5 may be pre-completed. A firm may arrange for the client's authority to contact the occupational scheme to be in the form of a tear-off slip which could then be forwarded to the occupational scheme.

FORMAT OF COVERING LETTER

31. The model covering letter for firms writing to their clients is provided at Annex 4. Firms should not depart materially from the model letter or add paragraphs without prior consultation with the Law Society.

OVERALL PACKAGE

32. Where a postal approach is adopted, the overall package should comprise the following documents:

   ▶ covering letter, questionnaire and pre-paid envelope for reply.

   No other material should be included such as marketing or promotional material.

PRESENTATION OF DOCUMENTATION

33. The questionnaire, covering letter and envelope should be on the same quality paper as firms use when sending important documents.

34. A questionnaire printed on coloured paper is likely to elicit a higher response rate and accordingly firms may wish to consider printing the questionnaire on paper other than white to encourage clients to respond. Questions should be set out clearly on each page in a legible typeface.

35. The covering letter may be on the firm's normal letterhead and may include the firm's logo. No marketing logo should be printed on the envelope but this may carry the firm's logo when it is normal practice for this to appear.

HELPLINES

36. Firms wishing to set up their own helplines to assist clients to complete the questionnaire may do so. Firms may also wish to advise clients of the availability of the PIA Investors' Helpline (tel. 0171 417 7001 or 020 7417 7001).

NOTE

37. In Annex 2, paragraph 348 (page 24) reference is made to 'relevant rules'. These rules, for firms authorised by the Law Society, are the Solicitors' Investment Business Rules 1988 (the relevant provisions of which were effective from 29th April 1988) and the Solicitors' Investment Business Rules 1990.

Annex 1 – Review of Past Business Part I: Statement of Policy

Annex 2 – Review of Past Business Part II: Specification of Standards and Procedures

Annex 2A – Simplifying the Pensions Review: Parts 1, 2 and schedules

Annex 3 – Model questionnaire

Annex 4 – Model covering letter

Annex 5 – Model reminder letter

[The annexes are not reproduced here but are available from Professional Ethics, see p.xv for contact details.]

7th June 1995, amended 11th December 1996

COUNCIL STATEMENT – DOCUMENT D

INTRODUCTION

1. In August and October 1998, the Financial Services Authority (FSA) and the Personal Investment Authority (PIA) issued guidance on standards and procedures for phase 2 of the pension transfers and opt outs review. The detailed documentation has been issued in three parts:

   ▶ Pension transfers and opt outs review phase 2: Policy Statement;

   ▶ Pension transfers and opt outs review phase 2: Model Guidance;

   ▶ Pension transfers and opt outs review phase 2: Model Guidance, Further Information.

   These documents are attached as Annexes 1 to 3 respectively of this Council statement.

2.   The first phase of the pension transfers and opt outs review required firms to concentrate their resources on 'priority' cases. Phase 2 relates to the remaining transfer and opt out cases which fall outside those designated as priority cases under phase 1. It requires firms to identify such cases and to invite investors to request reviews of their cases.

3.   The Council supports the action that the FSA has taken in relation to phase 2 of the pension transfers and opt outs review. The Council believes that in accordance with the general principles enshrined in practice rule 1, and in particular, the good repute of the solicitors' profession, firms should undertake phase 2 of the pension transfers and opt outs review. The Council therefore requires firms to comply with the FSA's Model Guidance (Annex 2) and Model Guidance, Further Information (Annex 3) together with any additional guidance issued under this Council statement.

4.   The Council statement has effect from 16th October 1998.

SCOPE OF PHASE 2

5.   Phase 2 covers any pension transfer and opt out/non-joiner business transacted between 29th April 1988 and 30th June 1994 that does not fall within the priority categories defined by the Securities and Investments Board (SIB) in previous regulatory guidance (see Council statement – Document C (as amended)), and in respect of which a client has not by the effective date of the Model Guidance already requested a review. Copies of Council statement – Document C (as amended) are available from the Pensions Review Team of the Monitoring and Investigation Unit [see p.xv for contact details]. Phase 2 also covers any clients who fall within the priority categories and who, having not previously responded to communications from the firm, now die, retire or decide to request a review.

6.   The position within phase 2 of opt outs and non-joiners who took out rebate-only personal pensions (and have either never made any contributions of their own or did not start making such contributions until after 30th June 1994) will be the subject of further guidance to be issued by the FSA in the Autumn. Rebate-only personal pension policies are personal pension policies into which the only contributions are National Insurance contribution rebates and contracting out incentives paid by the Department of Social Security. Firms should comply also with this further guidance when it is issued.

[In the remainder of this Council statement, references to paragraphs are to be read as references to paragraphs in the Model Guidance (Annex 2).]

CASE IDENTIFICATION

7.   Firms should identify cases for review under phase 2 by adopting either of the approaches set out in the Model Guidance (Annex 2).

8.   The *direct invitation* approach (paragraphs 8–32) requires firms to:

▶   **inform** clients about the review process and about factors relevant to their situation;

▶   **invite** them to put their case forward for review; and

▶   **ask** clients, at the same time as putting their case forward for review, to provide certain information which firms may require to complete a loss assessment in accordance with Council statement – Document C (as amended).

9. The procedure for transfer cases is set out in paragraph 13.

10. The procedure for opt outs and non-joiners is set out in paragraphs 15–19.

11. No mailing to clients is required for either transfer and opt out/non-joiner cases in the circumstances set out in paragraphs 14 and 20 respectively. These are cases where the firm can identify reliably from its own records that there is no need to include them in phase 2.

12. Non-respondents should be dealt with in accordance with paragraphs 21–23. Following the initial mailing, one reminder letter should be sent (with a full set of materials) in the form specified in Annex A or B of the Model Guidance. In addition, the letter should be accompanied by a form that clients can return if they wish to indicate that they do not want a review.

13. The 'alternative' approach (paragraphs 33–35) is the same as that required by Council statement – Document C (as amended). This approach may be adopted by firms wishing to start phase 2 before 4th January 1999.

FORMAT OF MATERIAL SENT TO CLIENTS

14. Firms should use the materials specified in the Model Guidance, in the format(s) specified in paragraphs 24–32. Firms should not alter the materials other than where the exceptions set out in paragraph 31 apply or following prior consultation with the Law Society.

HELPLINES

15. Firms should provide clients who have been sent phase 2 material with a telephone number, operated by appropriately trained staff, to deal with clients' questions (see paragraphs 41 and 42).

TARGET DATES

16. Firms should comply with the timing and target dates set out in paragraphs 44–51, which include the following:

    ▶ Firms should send phase 2 material, including reminder letters where necessary, to clients in the period 4th January 1999 to 31st March 1999. Any follow-up work arising before 31st March 1999 should also have been dealt with promptly.

    ▶ Where the 'alternative' approach to identification is adopted, firms may begin to contact clients before 4th January 1999, but all necessary pension review forms and reminder letters should be issued by 31st March 1999 and any follow-up work dealt with promptly.

    ▶ Firms should complete assessments of death and retirement cases no later than six months from the date of their notification or request.

    ▶ Targets will be set for later stages of the review by reference to the proportion of potentially reviewable phase 2 cases (i.e. clients have either been made an offer of redress or informed that no redress is due).

27

WORK ALREADY DONE

17. Subject to paragraphs 56 and 57, firms may apply the provisions of paragraphs 54 and 55 in relation to work already done under the pensions review. Where phase 2 cases are being reviewed in accordance with Council statement – Document C (as amended), firms need not apply to the Law Society for credit for this work, but must be able to demonstrate that they have applied the priority review standards to all cases.

REVIEW OF CASES

18. Cases where a client has requested a review, either with or without having first received the phase 2 material, should be reviewed as normal, i.e. in accordance with Council statement – Document C (as amended). This includes requests from clients with rebate-only policies.

19. Other cases which fall to be reviewed either as a result of the 'alternative' approach to identification or as a result of death or retirement before 30th June 1999 (see **Cut-off dates** below) should also be reviewed as normal.

SOLICITORS' INDEMNITY FUND

20. Firms should, at the earliest opportunity, notify Solicitors Indemnity Fund Limited (SIF) of potential claims arising from the review which they undertake in accordance with this Council statement.

21. Where a firm identifies a case which is 'non-compliant' and as a result the client appears to have suffered a loss, the firm should consult with SIF as to how to proceed with action to provide redress.

CUT-OFF DATES (PHASE 1 AND PHASE 2)

22. The death or retirement of a client **after 30th June 1999** will no longer lead to an automatic requirement to review that client's case (provided that the guidance has been properly complied with), but firms will be expected to deal sympathetically with any request for review.

23. The FSA will in due course announce a second cut-off date or dates, after which firms will no longer be required to review cases simply in response to a request from a client.

RECORD KEEPING

24. Firms should document clearly the processes they have used to ensure that all phase 2 cases have been identified and mailed, including records of which clients replied to the different phase 2 mailings and which did not.

25. Firms should maintain records of each case, showing progress to date.

26. Firms will be required to submit returns to the Law Society at quarterly intervals, summarising the progress made.

PROJECT PLANS

27. All firms will need to prepare and maintain 'up-to-date' project plans (paragraphs 69–71).

28. To assist with the setting of target dates for later stages of the phase 2 review, all firms will be asked to submit a form based on their project plan indicating when they anticipate reaching certain stages of the phase 2 review.

MONITORING

29. Firms must make the records referred to above available for examination by the Monitoring and Investigation Unit (MIU). MIU officers, on routine or specific visits, will wish to examine these records and ascertain the progress which is being made by firms against the target dates.

GUIDANCE

30. Further guidance on the Council statement may be obtained from the Pensions Review Team of the Monitoring and Investigation Unit or Professional Ethics [see p.xv for contact details].

Annex 1 Pension transfers and opt outs review phase 2: Policy Statement

Annex 2 Pension transfers and opt outs review phase 2: Model Guidance

Annex 3 Pension transfers and opt outs review phase 2: Model Guidance, Further Information

[The Annexes are not reproduced here but are available from Professional Ethics; see p.xv for contact details.]

16th October 1998

27

Annex 27H

Guidance – preservation of pension records

This guidance relates to the preservation of records of transactions involving personal pensions and 'section 32' buy out contracts by firms conducting discrete investment business (DIB).

The Society has issued this guidance because:

▶ on 8th December 1993 SIB [now the Financial Services Authority (FSA)] announced that it was co-ordinating a review of transactions where members of occupational pension schemes have opted out of such a scheme in favour of a personal pension or have effected a transfer payment from such a scheme into a personal pension or a 'section 32' buy out contract;

▶ any opt out or transfer arranged on or after 29th April 1988 is liable to fall within the coverage of the review;

▶ the statement of 8th December 1993 also anticipated further activity in connection with appropriate personal pensions and contracting out of SERPS;

▶ by virtue of their age, some of the records in question are no longer (or may shortly no longer be) subject to the detailed record-keeping requirements of the Solicitors' Investment Business Rules.

Accordingly the Society advises firms conducting DIB that they should *take steps to secure the preservation, in accessible form, of their records of any personal pension or 'section 32' transaction arranged on or after 29th April 1988*, including records of enquiries into the personal and financial circumstances of clients and of the recommendations made. In due course the Society will indicate the circumstances under which the records in question may properly be disposed of.

The Society and SIB [FSA] take the view that, from March 1994 onwards, the disposal or loss of records which relate (or may relate) to these transactions is unlikely to be compatible with the observance of principle 9 of SIB's Statement of Principle (which requires a firm to organise and control its internal affairs in a responsible manner, keeping proper records) or of principle 10 (which requires a firm to deal with its regulator in an open and co-operative manner) – see Annex 27C, p.610 in the Guide.

2nd March 1994, updated February 1999

Annex 27I

Guidance – corporate finance activities

1. Introduction

1.1 The Society has received a number of inquiries as to how the Solicitors' Investment Business Rules (SIBR) apply to so-called 'corporate finance activities'. The commonest inquiry relates to the situation where a firm advises a client who is a principal shareholder and director of a family company which is to be sold to a third party. The first concern is whether the firm can become involved in the negotiation of the deal without engaging in discrete investment business (DIB). The second is whether it can express views directly or indirectly to the client about the adequacy of the price or other business or financial aspects of the deal without engaging in DIB.

1.2 The answers to these inquiries depend not only on the terms of the SIBR but upon those of the Financial Services Act. There are three distinct questions:

► Is the firm's activity capable of constituting investment business under the Financial Services Act? This depends on whether it falls within Part II of Schedule 1 (see Annex 27A at p.539 in the Guide).

► If so, is the activity exempted from the statutory definition of investment business as falling within one of the 'excluded activities' in Part III of Schedule 1 at p.543 in the Guide?

► If the activity is capable of being investment business under the Act and is not excluded from the definition, then is it DIB for the purposes of the SIBR (see Chapter 4, Annex 27B at p.571 in the Guide)? In the context of corporate finance activities, this will depend on whether the activity is 'incidental'. If it is 'incidental' then it is not DIB.

1.3 It is the Council's view (which has been confirmed by leading counsel) that firms engaged in this sort of work will frequently be carrying on investment business. However, except in unusual situations, they will not be carrying on DIB. Accordingly, Chapter 6 of the SIBR (conduct of business rules applicable only to firms undertaking DIB) is unlikely to apply to such activities.

2. The position under the Act

2.1 It is not every involvement in a deal or every kind of advice about it which is affected by the Act. The application of the Act depends on the exact nature of the services provided. However, a firm which itself negotiates the deal or gives advice not only about the legal aspects but about the business or other financial considerations, will frequently be carrying on an activity within Part II of Schedule 1 to the Act. The relevant

27

headings are 'arranging deals in investments' (paragraph 13), at p.539 in the Guide and 'investment advice' (paragraph 15) at p.542 in the Guide. In these cases the question whether the Act applies therefore depends upon the ambit of its exceptions.

The exemption for sales of companies

2.2 There is an exemption in paragraph 21 of Schedule 1 to the Act (at p.550 in the Guide) which may be applicable. Under that exemption paragraphs 12, 13 and 15 of Schedule 1 do not apply to the sale or purchase of any company (other than an open-ended investment company) where the shares being sold carry 75% or more of the voting rights or where those shares, together with shares already held by the purchaser, carry not less than that percentage. However, it is a condition of the exemption that both the sellers and the buyers fall into one of the following categories:

► a body corporate,

► a partnership,

► a single individual, or

► a group of connected individuals (as defined).

It is not necessary that the sellers should fall into the same category as the buyers. However, all the sellers must fall into one category and all the buyers must fall into one category. Thus the sale of a typical family company to a corporate buyer will qualify for exemption only if the sellers are 'a group of connected individuals'. This will often not be the case.

The exemption for 'necessary' activities

2.3 Paragraph 24 of Schedule 1 (at p.553 in the Guide) contains an exemption applicable to arranging deals and investment advice. The exemption arises only if the activity in question constitutes 'arranging deals' or giving 'investment advice' as those activities are defined in Part II: see paragraph 2.1 above. The activity is exempted if the arranging is done or the advice is given in the course of carrying on a profession not otherwise constituting investment business and is a *necessary* part of the other advice or services given in the course of carrying on that profession. The operation of the exemption will depend upon the particular facts of each case. The variety of possible facts and the uncertain ambit of the exemption mean that it would be unwise for any solicitor who engages in corporate finance activities to place undue reliance upon it. It is the view of the Council (and of leading counsel) that 'arranging deals' and giving 'investment advice' in the course of such activities is unlikely to be a 'necessary' part of other advice or services given by a solicitor in the course of his or her profession. The reason is that in almost every case the solicitor will be instructed because he or she is a provider of legal services. In very many cases it will be convenient for the firm also to undertake negotiation and investment advice, and instructions to do so will accordingly be given either expressly or by implication. But although convenient, it will not be 'necessary' (in the sense meant by the Act) for the firm to perform these activities even if such instructions are given and accepted. This is because the firm can provide the legal services for which it is primarily retained and which constitute the essence of a solicitor's profession without doing so.

2.4 It is an additional condition of the exemption for 'necessary' activities that the activity in question should not be remunerated separately from other activities. Separate remuneration in such circumstances would be unusual. This condition is therefore unlikely to cause a problem.

3. The position under the SIBR

3.1 Many firms may find themselves in the position where the arrangements made or advice given by them do not fall within one of the statutory exemptions in all respects, or where it is unclear whether they do. This does not mean that the work which is carried out will necessarily be DIB for the purposes of the SIBR. The reason is that the exclusion of an activity from DIB depends not upon its being a 'necessary' part of the professional activities for which the solicitor is primarily employed, but upon its being 'incidental' to them, which is a wider test.

3.2 The SIBR provide that an activity is 'incidental' if the firm carries it out while providing other services in the course of carrying on the profession of a solicitor (being services which do not themselves constitute DIB) and such activity is subordinate to the main purpose for which those services are provided. To decide what is 'incidental' it is therefore necessary to decide what is the main purpose of the other services provided and whether the other services are themselves DIB.

3.3 In the view of the Council (and of leading counsel) the main purpose for which a solicitor's services are provided is to make available to the client the solicitor's knowledge of the law and his or her expertise in activities (such as drafting or dealing with regulatory or other quasi-legal bodies) for which a specifically legal expertise is required. A client will normally choose a solicitor (as opposed to some other professional person) for that reason. The negotiation of the deal may be particularly important to the client. The client's choice of a *particular* solicitor may well be influenced by the fact that that solicitor possesses other skills also, such as a special expertise in negotiation. Nevertheless, in the great majority of cases, it is the legal qualification of the solicitor which has led to his or her employment. The solicitor's other skills are desirable but subordinate.

3.4 When the SIBR were being drafted some suggested that where a firm was involved in arranging a deal or was instructed, *inter alia*, to negotiate its terms, the 'incidental' exemption would not apply because, in effect, the main purpose of the services provided by the solicitor was 'arranging deals in investments', the solicitor's legal advice being incidental to that activity rather than the other way round. As a result, it was suggested, the arranging or advising function could not be regarded as subordinate to an activity which did not constitute DIB. The Council's view (which leading counsel has confirmed) is that for the reasons given above this is not correct.

3.5 As regards advice on the price or other business or financial aspects of the deal, the answer is similar. If the solicitor gives that advice in the course of his or her services as a solicitor, the exemption should apply.

3.6 It is therefore the Council's view that in most cases the 'incidental' exemption will apply to corporate finance activities where those activities are not exempted by Schedule 1 of the Act. Inevitably, some cases will arise where neither exemption applies or where there is some doubt. However, these are likely to be unusual cases such as, for example, where the firm acts as a merger broker for a fee.

31st January 1990, updated February 1999

27

Annex 27J

Guidance – product and commission disclosure

1. Introduction

Rules relating to product and commission disclosure are contained in appendix 7 of the Solicitors' Investment Business Rules 1995 (SIBR) (see Annex 27B at p.601 in the Guide). These rules apply to solicitors conducting 'discrete investment business' (DIB) and to solicitors conducting non-DIB by using a permitted third party (PTP). Guidance on the rules appears below.

2. 'Key features' document – UK-regulated product providers

UK-regulated product providers need to produce a 'key features document' providing, in a standard format, a general summary of the product, and including information on surrender values, the effects of charges and expenses and the commissions (or equivalent) which may be paid to independent financial advisers or the product provider's sales force in relation to the transaction. The key features document, which has to be specific to the particular transaction proposed for the client, must be provided to the investor no later than when the transaction is recommended.

Where the firm is using a PTP and the firm itself is not conducting DIB in relation to the transaction, the PTP is responsible for providing the key features document and, if this is sent to the firm, the firm should promptly forward it to the client.

Where a firm is conducting DIB by recommending a client to purchase a packaged product or to elect to make pension fund withdrawals, it will be the responsibility of the firm to ensure that the key features document is provided to the client. The firm should obtain the key features document from the product provider, and forward it to the client (see rule 2(2) of appendix 7 of the SIBR at p.602 in the Guide).

3. 'Key features' information – non-UK-regulated life offices

In some cases life policies issued by overseas life offices which are not UK-regulated can be marketed to UK investors. If a firm recommends such a life policy, then it will be the firm's responsibility to ensure that the client receives the same information as would have been included in a 'key features document' issued by a UK-regulated life office. The relevant information, which needs to be provided in writing to the client, is as follows:

(i) the name of the life office;

(ii) whether it is incorporated or unincorporated;

(iii) that its head office is in the UK or, if it is elsewhere, the name of the member state of the EU or other state in which it is situated; and, if a policy contract is to be made with an agency or branch of the life office, the name of the state in which the agency or branch is situated;

(iv) the address of the head office and, where appropriate, the agency or branch in question;

(v) definition of each benefit and each option under the policy;

(vi) the term of the contract;

(vii) how the contract may be terminated;

(viii) how the premiums are payable and for how long a period or periods;

(ix) how bonuses are calculated and distributed;

(x) an indication of surrender and paid-up values, and the extent to which they are guaranteed;

(xi) information on the premiums for each benefit, both main benefits and supplementary benefits where appropriate;

(xii) where the policy is unit-linked, a definition of the units to which the benefits are linked and an indication of the nature of the underlying assets;

(xiii) the arrangements for application of the cooling-off period;

(xiv) general information on the tax arrangements applicable to the type of policy in question;

(xv) the applicable arrangements for handling complaints about policies by policy holders, lives assured or beneficiaries under the contract, including, where appropriate, a statement that there is a complaints body, without prejudice to the right to take legal proceedings; and

(xvi) the law that is, or will be, applicable to the contract.

If the life policy will never have any surrender value, this fact must be stated in the information provided, instead of giving details of the surrender values.

4. Client-specific information

Whilst, generally, the 'key features' information must be provided on a client-specific basis, this is not the case where the policy is a single premium life policy and the terms of the recommended contract do not depend upon any personal circumstances of the client. Nor does the information need to be client-specific if the premiums payable are expected to be £120 a year or less, or the policy is a master policy underlying an occupational pension scheme, where the client is the trustee of the scheme.

5. 'Reason why' letter

Where the firm gives certain recommendations in relation to life policies, regulated collective investment schemes or pension fund withdrawals, it must supply the client with a written explanation of why the firm believes the transaction to be suitable (rule 3(1), appendix 7 of the SIBR at p.604 in the Guide). This 'reason why' letter must be provided before or as soon as practicable after the recommendation is given.

If the firm is arranging for a client on an execution-only basis, any action which falls within rule 3(1)(a) to (f), no 'reason why' letter is required, but instead the firm must confirm in writing that it has not advised on the transaction (or that the client was given advice but nevertheless persisted in wishing the transaction to be effected), and that the transaction was arranged on the client's explicit instructions (rule 3(2) of appendix 7 of the SIBR at p.604 in the Guide).

6. Commission disclosure

Rule 10 of the Solicitors' Practice Rules 1990 (see **14.13**, p.283 in the Guide) requires the firm to account to the client for any commission it receives in excess of £20 unless the client has consented to the firm retaining it. Nothing in the rules relating to product and commission disclosure detracts in any way from practice rule 10.

Rule 1 of appendix 7 of the SIBR (at p.601 in the Guide) requires the firm to disclose to the client, in advance of the transaction, the total commission which may be receivable in respect of that transaction by the firm and any PTP which the firm has used in connection with the transaction.

7. Records

The relevant record keeping requirements are set out in rule 3(3) of appendix 7 of the SIBR at p.604 in the Guide.

30th November 1994, revised February 1999

Annex 27K

Guidance – SIB's endorsement of Takeover Code

The Securities and Investments Board's Statement of Principle requires a firm authorised to conduct investment business to comply with any code or standard endorsed by SIB (now the FSA) to the extent of that endorsement. SIB endorsed the Takeover Code in 1995. This means that it applies to authorised firms in the same way as any other rules or regulations governing the conduct of investment business.

However, the terms of the endorsement contain an exception relating to professional bodies. The exception is designed to recognise the supremacy of professional rules, particularly relating to the confidentiality and privilege that attaches to legal advice. In the case of solicitors, the terms of the endorsement are designed to ensure that a client who might be in breach of the Takeover Code would not be denied legal representation by virtue of any 'cold shouldering' that might otherwise be required by the code.

Disciplinary action in respect of any alleged breach of the Takeover Code by a firm of solicitors, insofar as the code was applicable to that firm, will only be considered at the specific request of the Takeover Panel.

The terms of the endorsement in relation to recognised professional bodies are as follows:

'A firm which is certified by a recognised professional body, or which is a member of a recognised self-regulating organisation but is also regulated by a recognised professional body in relation to the firm's professional practice generally, should comply with the Takeover Code (insofar as it would, by its terms, apply to such a firm) unless the firm would thereby be in breach of any rule or principle of, or any requirement of a published guidance note relating to, professional conduct applying generally to members of the profession regulated by that body.'

The Society has issued guidance on the endorsement by the SIB of the Takeover Code in the following terms:

'The Takeover Code does not apply to the activities of legal advisers acting as such. Occasionally however a solicitor may provide other services in connection with a takeover, similar to those provided by merchant banks. If the client insists on a course of action which is contrary to the code, the solicitor may not continue to provide such other services in connection with the takeover.

While it is the duty of a solicitor to act in the best interests of a client, the duty cannot override the provisions of the code so as to require the solicitor to provide such other services in breach of the code. A breach of the code would be a breach of the provision of practice rule 1 that prohibits a solicitor from doing anything that would compromise or impair the good repute of the solicitor or the solicitors'

27

profession. If a client instructs a solicitor, it is an implied term of the retainer that the solicitor must not be required to participate in any activity which would breach regulations or codes of conduct applying to the solicitor.'

15th March 1995, revised February 1999

Annex 27L

Guidance – Investment Services Directive

The Investment Services Directive (93/22/EEC) and Capital Adequacy Directive (93/6/EEC), which were implemented in the UK on 31st December 1995, were the subject of a note in [1993] *Gazette,* 15 September, 37.

Advising on or arranging the purchase of life policies are not activities covered by the Investment Services Directive (ISD). The ISD also states that 'persons providing an investment service where that service is provided in an incidental manner in the course of a professional activity' will not be subject to the Directive.

A common understanding as to the interpretation to be placed on the 'incidental' exemption has been reached by the Society, the SIB (now the FSA) and the Treasury, and is set out below.

The scope of the exemption cannot be precisely defined; ultimately, it would be for the European Court of Justice to determine this matter. Clearly, the reference to providing a service in an incidental manner means that the service cannot be a major part of the practice of a firm of solicitors. In any event, since the Society cannot normally certify firms whose discrete investment business amounts to more than 35% of their total business, this restriction is somewhat academic. However, the test in this case is not the same as for the 35% limit; nor is it the same as for the 'incidental' exception in the Solicitors' Investment Business Rules, because it depends on a qualitative judgement about the way in which the services are provided.

One measure of a firm's position against the test could be whether the investment service is held out as a separate service on a sufficiently large scale. Because the test is a qualitative one, the impression that the firm conveys as to the manner in which the investment services are provided is important. The manner in which a firm advertises its investment services is clearly a critical point in forming the crucial judgement about whether the provision of investment services is run as a separate business within the overall practice, or whether they are services which the firm provides incidentally as part of its general practice. It is the latter case which will be exempt under the ISD.

Firms must, therefore, be aware of the overall effect of their advertising, particularly if this is done in specialist investment publications. Or, to put it another way, if firms wish to remain within the exemption, they must take care that, on balance, their advertising does not have the effect of holding out the investment services as a separate business.

It has been decided that the Society will not be able to authorise firms who fall outside the exemption for services covered by the ISD, if indeed there are any such firms. Therefore, it will be necessary for such firms to seek authorisation from an SRO, at least in respect of services covered by the ISD.

7th September 1994, revised February 1999

Annex 27M

Guidance – custody of investments – common questions

Amendments to the Solicitors' Investment Business Rules 1995 (SIBR) regarding the custody of investments came into force on 31st March 1998. Appendix 8 to the rules (see Annex 27B at p.605 in the Guide) contains the main requirements. Guidance was contained in [1998] *Gazette,* 11 February, and further guidance is set out below.

1. Why has the Law Society introduced new rules?

The Law Society, in common with all other financial services regulators, had to integrate the Securities and Investments Board's (SIB) 'Standards for the custody of customers' investments' into the Solicitors' Investment Business Rules 1995. Therefore, similar requirements apply to all authorised firms, e.g. stockbrokers, and not only solicitors. The Financial Services Act 1986 was extended on 1st June 1997 to cover the new investment activity of 'custody of investments'.

2. What are 'title documents'?

'Title documents' are documents or evidence (either certificated or uncertificated) of title to an *investment,* e.g. share or unit trust certificates, life policies, pension contracts and dematerialised investments. Therefore, the term 'title documents' does not include wills, leases, miscellaneous documents or deeds.

3. What are 'custody services'?

'Custody services' essentially means safeguarding **and** administering investments; so that a firm which is merely holding investments for safekeeping will not be caught by the new rules. However, a firm which is holding a share certificate for safe custody and collecting and dealing with dividends is likely to be undertaking custody business. Brief guidance is contained in the new rules themselves, but the SIB's custody guidance is available free from Professional Ethics (see p.xv for contact details).

4. Is there an exemption for solicitor/personal representatives or solicitor/trustees?

Yes, rule 17(2) of the SIBR (at p.579 in the Guide) makes it clear that the new rule does not apply to the provision of custody services where the firm or a partner, employee or officer of the firm is a personal representative or a trustee (other than a bare trustee), provided that the firm is not separately remunerated for the custody services. The exemption applies to mixed trusts as well as controlled trusts.

5. How is our probate department affected?

The new rules will apply where the firm is acting for personal representatives or trustees. However, generally speaking in probate work, the custody services will be incidental to the winding up of the estate and the exemption in paragraph 10(1) of appendix 8 of the SIBR (see p.609 in the Guide) will be available (see rule 10(2) of the SIBR (p.573 in the Guide) for the definition of 'activity is incidental').

Paragraph 10(1) (see p.609 in the Guide) makes it clear that the requirement to clarify in writing the responsibilities and the need to report to the client will not apply where the 'activity is incidental' or where the firm or a partner, employee or officer of the firm is acting as the donee of any registered enduring power of attorney or as a receiver appointed by the Court of Protection. Similarly, paragraph 9(1) (the need to report to clients) (see p.608 in the Guide) will not apply where the firm or a partner, employee or officer of the firm is acting as the donee of a trustee power of attorney.

6. What information do I need to record under paragraph 7, appendix 8 of the SIBR?

You will have to record the client's name and the details of the investment, for example, that the firm holds a share certificate for 500 Marks and Spencer ordinary £1 shares. You will have to record where the title documents are kept, e.g. in the fireproof safe at the principal office. You will have to record the date on which each title document came into the custody of the firm although, in the case of documents already held on 31st March 1998, it will be sufficient to make a record to that effect. You will also have to record the date on which the document left the custody of the firm and whether the title documents have been lent or held as collateral.

7. How often must we check that we are still holding the title documents?

You will need to reconcile your records at least once a year with the title documents held by the firm, its own nominee or a third party custodian. If there is a discrepancy, the firm must investigate it and make good any shortfall for which it is responsible or provide the equivalent for any shortfall as soon as is reasonably practicable.

8. How often must I report to clients?

At least once a year, you must send the client a statement setting out the details of the title documents held for that client as set out in paragraph 9, appendix 8 of the SIBR (see p.608 in the Guide). It is not necessary in that statement to give the information required by paragraph 7 (see p.608 in the Guide), e.g. the date on which each title document came into or left the custody of the firm. However, firms may give more information than required by the rules if they so choose.

9. Our firm uses a firm of stockbrokers; how do these rules apply?

If you are providing custody services either by safeguarding and administering, or arranging for the safeguarding and administration of assets, then the rules will apply to you.

If you then appoint a broker as a third party custodian, you will need to comply with paragraph 5, appendix 8 of the SIBR (see p.607 in the Guide). Many firms will have

27

already received agreements from brokers setting out their services because the brokers are complying with their own custody rules which are very similar to our rules. The third party custodian's agreement will need to cover, where relevant, the matters set out in paragraphs 4(2) and 4(3), appendix 8 of the SIBR (see p.607 in the Guide).

This will, for example, include clarification in writing in relation to liens and other security. Lien is ultimately a matter of law and firms will need to consider whether the broker's paragraph clarifying the position as to lien merely reflects the existing common law provision, or whether it performs some other function.

Further guidance on the new custody rules may be obtained from the Professional Ethics Division (see p.xv for contact details).

Gazette, 25th March 1998

Annex 27N

Guidance – Council statement on managed cash deposit ISAs

Individual Savings Accounts (ISAs) are the new form of tax efficient savings product, which will come into effect from 6th April 1999. These products allow investors to invest in equity, insurance or cash components within a tax efficient wrapper. An ISA may be a maxi ISA (where one manager looks after all the money invested) or a mini ISA (where the manager looks after only one component).

Solicitors who wish to manage ISAs which include equity or insurance components will require the Council's permission under the Solicitors' Investment Business Rules 1995 (as amended). Solicitors who manage maxi ISAs, or who manage mini ISAs which consist of an equity or insurance component, will be involved in investment business as defined by the Financial Services Act 1986 and, as such, will be subject to the Solicitors' Investment Business Rules.

Although cash is not an investment as defined by the Financial Services Act 1986, the management of cash with other investments within an ISA will be regulated by the Act since management is defined in paragraph 14 of Schedule 1 as 'Managing or offering or agreeing to manage assets belonging to another person if – (a) those assets consist of or include investments …'.

Solicitors who choose to be managers of a mini ISA looking after a client's cash deposit only will not be undertaking investment business. Consequently no permission will be required from the Council, although the Individual Savings Account Regulations 1998 require such solicitors to be approved by the Inland Revenue to act as ISA managers. However, solicitors are reminded that the provisions of the Solicitors' Accounts Rules will apply to the cash received and held by the firm and that the provisions of rule 1 of the Solicitors' Practice Rules 1990 will apply. Further, certain specified minimum information should be given to clients before solicitors enter into an agreement for a cash only mini ISA:

(a) if the ISA is stated as satisfying the CAT Standards (the Cost, Access and Term standards for ISAs prescribed from time to time by H.M. Treasury), a comparison of the account against the CAT Standards; or

(b) if the ISA is not stated as satisfying the CAT Standards, a statement making this clear, together with, if desired, any relevant information; and:

  (i) minimum amount to open an account;

  (ii) minimum yearly deposit;

  (iii) the interest rate earned, and if and how it might vary;

27

(iv)   the calculation of interest;

(v)   how to make withdrawals and any limits;

(vi)   the amount of any commission or remuneration;

(vii) details of the arrangements for application of the cooling-off period;

(viii) the arrangements for handling complaints;

(ix)   that the favourable tax treatment may not be maintained;

(x)   that the arrangements for managing the cash deposit of the ISA may not be covered in the scope of any consumer compensation scheme;

(xi)   where applicable, that the firm acts as agent in arranging the cash deposit, identifying the principal, and explaining that the principal has accepted responsibility for the activities of the firm in relation to the cash deposit;

(xii) that a client in doubt whether an ISA is suitable should seek advice.

Solicitors should also note that rule 10 of the Solicitors' Practice Rules 1990 will apply to any commission received from managing a cash ISA. Further, although a solicitor's indemnity cover will normally include management of a client's cash ISA, it is possible that where the firm acts as agent in arranging the cash deposit, the principal will not be covered in the scope of any consumer compensation scheme. Therefore, the warning noted above should be given.

March 1999

Good practice guidelines – investment business – recruitment and supervision of employees – practice information

Introduction

These guidelines are issued as part of the Society's training and competence scheme, which has been put in place following the SIB's (now the FSA) recommendations. They represent a statement of good practice which each firm should interpret and put into action as appropriate to their structure and their investment business policy.

They are particularly relevant to firms which employ non-solicitor financial services specialists. Compliance problems have been found at some firms as a result of a lack of suitable experience of some staff and the absence of effective supervision. Non-compliance has resulted in disciplinary action being taken by the Society against partners or sole principals.

Recruitment

Firms should implement SIB's recommendations which are:

'[Recruitment practices] must be sufficiently thorough as to enable the firm to have reasonable grounds for being satisfied that an individual is capable of acting, with whatever training and supervision may be appropriate, with the necessary degree of competence and integrity. Proper reference checks, with follow-up enquiries where necessary, especially where there are gaps in employment, are essential. Records of these references and checks should be maintained and made available to the regulatory body both as proof that recruitment procedures were sufficiently diligent, and to be available in the event of difficulties within a firm which may be traceable to a particular individual.'

Policy

The firm will need to make a policy decision as to whether it wishes to offer advice on one or more of the three types of discrete investment business (DIB):

▶ retail branded/packaged products (e.g. life policies with an investment element);

▶ securities/portfolio management;

▶ corporate pensions and advanced schemes.

A category 2 investment business certificate is required to conduct DIB and such a certificate will only be issued to firms with a 'qualified person' in post. That individual must have been approved by the Society to conduct one or more of the above types of DIB.

Any DIB must be conducted by or under the direct supervision of a 'qualified person' for that type of DIB and whose identity has been notified to Regulation and Information Services (see p.xv for contact details).

Approval as a 'qualified person' may be obtained by attaining the relevant Law Society qualification or by holding an accredited qualification. An information pack about the Society's training and competence scheme is available from the Monitoring and Investigation Unit or Professional Ethics (see p.xv for contact details).

Procedures

Firms will usually advertise the post, indicating the profile of the applicant and what type(s) of investment expertise (e.g. retail branded/packaged products) is required.

If there has been a direct approach from an individual, the firm may still wish to advertise the post.

Written references should be obtained and checks regarding authorisation under the Financial Services Act should be made with the relevant/previous employer. Enquiries should be made of the last employer by telephone and further checks are likely to be necessary where there are, for example, indications of poor performance.

When interviewing, firms should consider whether the applicant understands the basic principles underlying a solicitors' practice, in particular the requirements of practice rule 1 (see **1.01**, p.1 in the Guide) including the need to act in the client's best interests.

Firms may wish to use consultants to assist in establishing the extent of the applicant's abilities, especially where the firm is lacking financial services expertise.

The contract of employment should reflect the job description and the standard of work expected.

Supervision and training

Firms should implement SIB's recommendations, which are:

> '[Supervision arrangements] must be sufficient to ensure that individuals are not acting beyond their competence or without integrity. In some cases, for example new recruits, supervision should be personal, i.e. accompanying the recruit and providing on-the-spot training. In other cases, the supervision should include quality checking of the activities of the individual; the track record on persistency of business produced from a particular individual; complaints experienced in respect of an individual; and so on.'

Supervision

As a matter of conduct, solicitors are 'responsible for exercising proper supervision over both admitted and unadmitted staff' (see **3.07**, p.72 in the Guide). Practice rule 13 also governs supervision and management of offices (see **3.08**, p.73). The employee should have clear lines of reporting and accountability to a partner – preferably the compliance partner.

It is a matter of judgement as to how much supervision should be given to an employee, but in the initial stages of employment, the employee is likely to need a substantial amount of personal supervision.

The firm must ensure on-going supervision, for example by the supervisor attending interviews with clients and examining investment business files.

Solicitors should ensure that the employee has good communication skills, in particular, clients should be addressed clearly and provided with explanations in terms which they can understand.

It should be clear from the files that compliance systems are being adhered to and that relevant information about the client (know your client/factfind) is obtained and recorded.

There should also be evidence on the file of the reasons why the particular investment decision was made and that the decision appears to be suitable for the client. The file should also be properly structured and maintained to the highest professional standards and demonstrate that the employee has communicated effectively and clearly with the client.

Whilst solicitors should already be fully aware of the necessity for maintaining adequate files and the method by which this is achieved, some non-solicitors, particularly those from a sales oriented background, may need training on the proper management of client files.

Although the employee may have a level of expertise beyond that of the supervisor, the supervisor must be able to supervise effectively, for example by routinely asking the employee to explain the rationale behind particular investment decisions.

Training

All non-solicitor 'qualified persons' will need to attend the one day course on professional conduct, the Solicitor's Accounts Rules and the Solicitors' Investment Business Rules (SIBR), the aim of which is to ensure that they understand the specific requirements of conduct and regulation affecting a solicitor's practice.

The firm should also provide detailed training on the above matters, in particular the SIBR and the other rules and principles of conduct which impact directly on investment business. As the financial services field is changing rapidly, it is also important that managers and employees keep up to date with investment products and changes in the rules. Firms should also give tuition on the office systems, including compliance and accounting procedures, and provide induction manuals and other reference materials.

All 'qualified persons', solicitors and non-solicitors, are required to undertake 50 hours per year continuing professional development (CPD). Guidance notes on CPD relating to DIB are available from Legal Education (see p.xv for contact details).

The manager should ensure that there is an adequate supply of up-to-date reference material and be aware of suitable courses and seminars.

27

Remuneration, incentives and disciplinary procedures

Firms should implement SIB's recommendations, which are:

> 'Thorough supervision and quality checking will provide their own incentives for individuals to seek to keep within the bounds of competence and integrity. But there needs also to be a certainty that appropriate action will follow where shortcomings are perceived. In many cases that appropriate action may be education or re-training or other assistance to the well-intentioned but misguided. But in other cases, stronger action would be called for and firms must not allow their commercial self-interest in the profitability of business to stand in the way of the correct selling of that business, and the regulator must ensure that it does not.'

Remuneration

As the means of remuneration may have a bearing on the manner in which the employee approaches his or her work, it is recommended that employees are rewarded fully or mainly by salary. Where an employee's remuneration is linked to the income generated by the individual for the firm, there is a risk that his or her investment recommendations will be influenced by rewards such as commissions.

It is particularly important that the provisions of practice rule 10 (see **14.13**, p.283 in the Guide) are fully understood; in particular the need to obtain the client's informed consent to the retention of commission by the firm.

If an incentive element in remuneration is considered to be appropriate, the firm should find an alternative to retained commission, such as a performance bonus. However, firms should consider practice rule 7 (fee sharing) (**3.03**, p.68 in the Guide) which provides that whilst a solicitor may share his or her professional fees with a *bona fide* employee, that provision shall not permit, under the cloak of employment, a partnership which would otherwise be prohibited.

Disciplinary procedures

The firm should have established procedures for dealing with disciplinary issues arising from the performance and conduct of all its staff. These procedures should be linked with contracts of employment.

Conclusions

Financial services work can be lucrative but, if undertaken by the wrong type of employee without suitable training and supervision, it can be the source of considerable problems for the firm. The employment of a specialist may appear for some firms to be the logical solution for undertaking financial services work when the partners or sole principal have insufficient expertise.

The full benefits from financial services work cannot be realised without the active involvement of the management of the firm to ensure that employees continue to operate with the proper level of expertise and in a manner which is consistent with the conduct expected of solicitors and their staff.

July 1992, revised February 1999

PART VI – FINANCIAL REGULATIONS

Chapter 28

Accounts

28.01   Operation of the accounts rules

Until 1st May 2000, solicitors can operate under either the Solicitors' Accounts Rules 1998 (see Annex 28B, p.684) or under the Solicitors' Accounts Rules 1991, the Solicitors' Accounts (Legal Aid Temporary Provision) Rule 1992 and the Accountant's Report Rules 1991 (see **28.03**). Transitional arrangements for the delivery of accountants' reports are set out at Annex 28C (p.771).

28.02   The 1998 rules

The Solicitors' Accounts Rules 1998 (see Annex 28B, p.684) came into effect on 22nd July 1998. Solicitors must implement them on or before 1st May 2000. The 1998 rules consolidate all rules and guidance relating to

28

solicitors' accounts, including the requirements for an accountant's report. The consolidation of rules and guidance means that this chapter is relatively short, as the 1998 rules contain all the guidance previously set out in Chapter 28 in the seventh edition of the Guide. The 1998 rules start with a list of contents (p.684) and conclude with an index (p.748).

28.03   Continued use of the 1991 rules

Those solicitors who continue to use the Solicitors' Accounts Rules 1991, the Solicitors' Accounts (Legal Aid Temporary Provision) Rule 1992 and the Accountant's Report Rules 1991 (which they may use up to and including 30th April 2000) will need to refer to Chapter 28 of the seventh edition of the Guide and subsequent *Professional Standards Bulletins*.

28.04   New provisions in the 1998 rules

The 1998 rules include the following substantive changes:

▶ a limited application of the rules to liquidators, trustees in bankruptcy, Court of Protection receivers and trustees of occupational pension schemes (rule 9, p.691);

▶ a limited application of the rules to joint accounts (rule 10, p.692);

▶ a limited application of the rules to clients' own accounts (rule 11, p.693);

▶ a relaxation of the rule on unpaid professional disbursements to allow them to be placed temporarily in an office account (rule 19(1)(b), p.702);

▶ a requirement to transfer billed costs out of client account within 14 days (rule 19(3), p.702);

▶ a consolidation of the requirements relating to legal aid costs (rule 21, p.704);

▶ a £20 *de minimis* figure for the payment of interest, as well as the table of interest (rule 24, p.709);

▶ controlled trust money to be treated substantially in the same way as client money (rules 8 and 15, pp.691 and 698) except for the payment of interest (rule 24, p.709), and reconciliations for passbook operated accounts (rule 32(7), p.716).

28.05   Accounts of an overseas practice

Solicitors who practise outside England and Wales continue to be bound by the Solicitors' Overseas Practice Rules 1990, rules 12–16 (see Annex 9A at p.185) in respect of their accounts, accountant's reports and investigation of accounts. These rules embody the general principles of the accounts rules, but are less detailed and less onerous in their requirements. The Law Society sends out the form of accountant's report for overseas practices directly to solicitors.

28.06   Controlled trust accounts of an overseas practice

1.   The Solicitors' Overseas Practice Rules 1990 include a requirement for reporting accountants to make a test check of controlled trust accounts. This applies to trusts where a solicitor is controlled trustee (see rule 20(d) and (f)–(g), Annex 9A at p.190), or where a recognised body is controlled trustee (see rule 20(e)–(f)), or where, in respect of an overseas incorporated practice, a solicitor is treated as holding money subject to a controlled trust by virtue of rule 9(4) at p.184. Rule 9(4) provides that the solicitor shareowners and directors in an overseas corporate practice in which solicitors own a controlling majority of the shares will be treated as holding money subject to a controlled trust, where the corporate practice itself holds that money as sole trustee or co-trustee with an officer or employee. The test check provisions will thus apply to trust money held by individual solicitors themselves or by their incorporated practices.

2.   Money held by a hived-off overseas trust company, i.e. a company not forming part of a solicitors' practice and not regulated by the Society as a solicitors' practice, falls outside the scope of the accountant's report. However, the following notes will apply to an overseas trust company operated as an overseas corporate practice in accordance with rule 9(1) of the overseas practice rules (at p.183), as well as to trusts where a solicitor himself or herself is a controlled trustee:

(a)   The accountant is required to make a test check of only a limited number of accounts and files relating to controlled trusts. The number and selection of controlled trust accounts included in the examination is left to the discretion of the reporting accountant. The fact that an accountant (not necessarily the reporting accountant) is already engaged in the management of a particular trust may well be relevant to the reporting accountant's decision whether or not to do test checks in respect of that particular trust, especially if annual accounts are prepared by the trust's accountant.

(b)   There is no question of the reporting accountant having to check that the investments made in respect of the trust are appropriate. Accountants may find it useful to refer to the series of checks contained in rule 4(1)(B) of the Accountant's Report Rules 1991 (see Annex 28D at p.628 of *The Guide to the Professional Conduct of Solicitors 1996* (seventh edition)) and rule 42 of the Solicitors' Accounts Rules 1998 (see Annex 28B at p.725). The overseas practice

28

rules require solicitors practising overseas either to keep a central register of controlled trusts or to keep the accounts relating to controlled trusts together centrally.

(c) The solicitor's duty to keep separate accounting records for each controlled trust will in many cases be discharged by simply retaining bank statements, etc., provided that the narrative is sufficient to understand the various movements on the account. However, in the case of a trust which is particularly complex or is likely to be protracted, formal records should be kept.

(d) The reporting accountant should select what he or she considers to be a suitable sample of controlled trust accounts and it may then be appropriate to make a correspondingly reduced number of checks in respect of the client and other accounts. However, where trust work forms all or the major part of the business of a practice, the scale of work carried out by the reporting accountant will be on a par with that undertaken for a firm carrying out a similar amount of client account business.

(e) Where a trust company which is operated as an overseas corporate practice holds shares in investment companies established for individual clients, the reporting accountant is simply required to check the book-keeping system and accounting entries relating to the operations of the trust company itself, including its purchase of shares in individual investment companies. The operation of the investment companies themselves falls outside the scope of the accountant's report.

28.07 Waivers for overseas practices

If local law or local conditions make it difficult or impossible for a solicitor to comply with the Solicitors' Overseas Practice Rules 1990, application may be made to Professional Ethics (see p.xv for contact details) for a waiver under rule 19 (see Annex 9A at p.190).

Solicitors Act 1974

sections 34 and 85 (accountants' reports and bank accounts)

(with consolidated amendments to May 1995)

---

34. Accountants' reports

(1)   Every solicitor shall once in each period of twelve months ending with 31st October, unless the Council are satisfied that it is unnecessary for him to do so, deliver to the Society, whether by post or otherwise, a report signed by an accountant (in this section referred to as an 'accountant's report') and containing such information as may be prescribed by rules made by the Council under this section.

(2)   An accountant's report shall be delivered to the Society not more than six months (or such other period as may be prescribed by rules made under this section) after the end of the accounting period for the purposes of that report.

(3)   Subject to any rules made under this section, the accounting period for the purposes of an accountant's report –

    (a)   shall begin at the expiry of the last preceding accounting period for which an accountant's report has been delivered;

    (b)   shall cover not less than twelve months; and

    (c)   where possible, consistently with the preceding provisions of this section, shall correspond to a period or consecutive periods for which the accounts of the solicitor or his firm are ordinarily made up.

(4)   The Council shall make rules to give effect to the provisions of this section, and those rules shall prescribe –

    (a)   the qualification to be held by an accountant by whom an accountant's report is given;

    (b)   the information to be contained in an accountant's report;

    (c)   the nature and extent of the examination to be made by an accountant of the books and accounts of a solicitor or his firm and of any other relevant documents with a view to the signing of an accountant's report;

    (d)   the form of an accountant's report; and

    (e)   the evidence, if any, which shall satisfy the Council that the delivery of an accountant's report is unnecessary and the cases in which such evidence is or is not required.

28

(5)   Rules under this section may include provision –

(a)   permitting in such special circumstances as may be defined by the rules a different accounting period from that specified in subsection (3); and

(b)   regulating any matters of procedure or matters incidental, ancillary or supplemental to the provisions of this section.

(5A)   Without prejudice to the generality of subsection (5)(b), rules under this section may make provision requiring a solicitor in advance of delivering an accountant's report to notify the Society of the period which is to be the accounting period for the purposes of that report in accordance with the preceding provisions of this section.

(6)   If any solicitor fails to comply with the provisions of this section or of any rules made under it, a complaint in respect of that failure may be made to the Tribunal by or on behalf of the Society.

(7)   A certificate under the hand of the Secretary of the Society shall, until the contrary is proved, be evidence that a solicitor has or, as the case may be, has not delivered to the Society an accountant's report or supplied any evidence required under this section or any rules made under it.

(8)   Where a solicitor is exempt from rules under section 32 –

(a)   nothing in this section shall apply to him unless he takes out a practising certificate;

(b)   an accountant's report shall in no case deal with books, accounts or documents kept by him in the course of employment by virtue of which he is exempt from those rules; and

(c)   no examination shall be made of any such books, accounts and documents under any rules made under this section.

[NOTES

1.   For a similar provision in relation to registered foreign lawyers see paragraph 8 of Schedule 14 to the Courts and Legal Services Act 1990.

2.   By virtue of section 89(3) of the Courts and Legal Services Act 1990 the power to make rules under section 34 is also exercisable in relation to registered foreign lawyers.

3.   For the application of section 34 to a recognised body (i.e. an incorporated practice recognised under section 9 of the Administration of Justice Act 1985) see paragraph 5 of Schedule 2 to the Administration of Justice Act 1985.

4.   By virtue of section 9(2)(f) of the Administration of Justice Act 1985 rules made under section 34 may be made to have effect in relation to a recognised body.]

85.   Bank accounts

Where a solicitor keeps an account with a bank or a building society in pursuance of rules under section 32 –

(a)   the bank or society shall not incur any liability, or be under any obligation to make any inquiry, or be deemed to have any knowledge of any right of any person to any money paid or credited to the account, which it would not incur or be under or be deemed to have in the case of an account kept by or person entitled absolutely to all the money paid or credited to it; and

(b) the bank or society shall not have any recourse or right against money standing to the credit of the account, in respect of any liability of the solicitor to the bank or society, other than a liability in connection with the account.

[NOTES

1.   For the application of section 85 to a recognised body see paragraph 31 of Schedule 2 to the Administration of Justice Act 1985.

2.   Section 85 is extended to client accounts of multi-national partnerships by the Registered Foreign Lawyers Order 1991 (S.I. 1991 no. 2831).]

Annex 28B

Solicitors' Accounts Rules 1998

[For Index to the accounts rules, see p.748.]

Made by: *the Council of the Law Society with the concurrence, where requisite, of the Master of the Rolls;*

date: *22nd July 1998;*

authority: *sections 32 and 34 of the Solicitors Act 1974, section 9 of the Administration of Justice Act 1985 and Schedule 15 paragraph 6 of the Financial Services Act 1986;*

replacing: *the Solicitors' Accounts Rules 1991, the Solicitors' Accounts (Legal Aid Temporary Provision) Rule 1992 and the Accountant's Report Rules 1991;*

regulating: *the accounts of solicitors, registered foreign lawyers and recognised bodies in respect of their English and Welsh practices.*

CONTENTS:

INDEX
For the definition of words in italics see rule 2 – Interpretation.

28

PART A – GENERAL

Rule 1 – Principles

The following principles must be observed. A *solicitor* must:

(a) comply with the requirements of practice rule 1 as to the *solicitor's* integrity, the duty to act in the *client's* best interests, and the good repute of the *solicitor* and the profession;

(b) keep other people's money separate from money belonging to the *solicitor* or the practice;

(c) keep other people's money safely in a *bank* or *building society* account identifiable as a *client account* (except when the rules specifically provide otherwise);

(d) use each *client's* money for that *client's* matters only;

(e) use *controlled trust money* for the purposes of that *trust* only;

(f) establish and maintain proper accounting systems, and proper internal controls over those systems, to ensure compliance with the rules;

(g) keep proper accounting records to show accurately the position with regard to the money held for each *client* and each *controlled trust*;

(h) account for interest on other people's money in accordance with the rules;

(i) co-operate with the *Society* in checking compliance with the rules; and

(j) deliver annual accountant's reports as required by the rules.

Rule 2 – Interpretation

(1) The rules are to be interpreted in the light of the notes.

(2) In the rules, unless the context otherwise requires:

    (a) "accounting period" has the meaning given in rule 36;

    (b) "agreed fee" has the meaning given in rule 19(5);

    (c) "bank" means an institution authorised under the Banking Act 1987 (which includes a European authorised institution), the Post Office in the exercise of its powers to provide banking services, or the Bank of England;

    (d) "building society" means a building society within the meaning of the Building Societies Act 1986;

    (e) "client" means the person for whom a *solicitor* acts;

    (f) "client account" has the meaning given in rule 14(2);

    (g) "client money" has the meaning given in rule 13;

    (h) a "controlled trust" arises when:

        (i) a *solicitor* is the sole trustee of a *trust*, or co-*trustee* only with one or more of his or her partners or employees;

(ii) a *solicitor* who is a director or employee of a *recognised body* is the sole *trustee* of a *trust*, or co-*trustee* only with one or more of the *recognised body's* other officers or employees or with the *recognised body* itself;

(iii) a *registered foreign lawyer* who is a partner in a *multi-national partnership* is, by virtue of being a partner in that partnership, the sole *trustee* of a *trust*, or co-*trustee* only with one or more of the other partners or employees of that partnership;

(iv) a *registered foreign lawyer* who is the director of a *recognised body* is, by virtue of practising as a director of the *recognised body*, the sole *trustee* of a *trust*, or co-*trustee* only with one or more of the *recognised body's* other officers or employees or with the *recognised body* itself; or

(v) a *recognised body* is the sole *trustee* of a *trust*, or co-*trustee* only with one or more of the *recognised body's* officers, employees or partners;

and "controlled trustee" means a *trustee* of a *controlled trust*; (see also paragraph (y) below on the meaning of "trustee" and "trust");

(i) "controlled trust money" has the meaning given in rule 13;

(j) "costs" means a *solicitor's* fees and *disbursements*;

(k) "disbursement" means any sum spent or to be spent by a *solicitor* on behalf of the *client* or *controlled trust* (including any VAT element);

(l) "fees" of a *solicitor* means the *solicitor's* own charges or profit costs (including any VAT element);

(m) "general client account" has the meaning given in rule 14(5)(b);

(n) "mixed payment" has the meaning given in rule 20(1);

(o) "multi-national partnership" means a partnership comprising one or more *solicitors* and one or more *registered foreign lawyers*;

(p) "office account" means an account of the *solicitor* or the practice for holding *office money*, or other means of holding *office money* (for example, the office cash box);

(q) "office money" has the meaning given in rule 13;

(r) "principal" means:

(i) a sole practitioner;

(ii) a partner or a person held out as a partner (including a "salaried" or "associate" partner);

(iii) the principal *solicitor* (or any one of the principal *solicitors*) in an in-house practice (for example, in a law centre or in commerce and industry);

(s) "professional disbursement" means the fees of counsel or other lawyer, or of a professional or other agent or expert instructed by the *solicitor*;

(t) "recognised body" means a company recognised by the *Society* under section 9 of the Administration of Justice Act 1985;

(u) "registered foreign lawyer" means a person registered by the *Society* under section 89 of the Courts and Legal Services Act 1990;

28

(v)   "separate designated client account" has the meaning given in rule 14(5)(a);

(w)   "Society" means the Law Society of England and Wales;

(x)   "solicitor" means a solicitor of the Supreme Court of England and Wales; and for the purposes of these rules also includes: a solicitors' partnership; a *registered foreign lawyer* practising as a member of a *multi-national partnership* or as the director of a *recognised body*; a *multi-national partnership*; a *recognised body*; a partnership of *recognised bodies*; and a partnership of solicitors and *recognised bodies*;

(y)   "trustee" includes a personal representative (i.e. an executor or an administrator), and "trust" includes the duties of a personal representative; and

(z)   "without delay" means, in normal circumstances, either on the day of receipt or on the next working day.

Notes

(i)   Although many of the rules are expressed as applying to an individual solicitor, the effect of the definition of "solicitor" in rule 2(2)(x) is that the rules apply equally to all those who carry on a practice and to the practice itself. See also rule 4(1)(a) (persons governed by the rules) and rule 5 (persons exempt from the rules).

(ii)   A client account must be at a bank or building society's branch in England and Wales – see rule 14(4).

(iii) For the full definition of a "European authorised institution" (rule 2(2)(c)), see the Banking Coordination (Second Council Directive) Regulations 1992 (S.I. 1992 no. 3218).

(iv)   The definition of a controlled trust (rule 2(2)(h)), which derives from statute, gives rise to some anomalies. For example, a partner, assistant solicitor or consultant acting as sole trustee will be a controlled trustee. Two or more partners acting as trustees will be controlled trustees, but two or more assistant solicitors or consultants acting as trustees fall outside the definition. In the latter case, if the matter is dealt with through the firm, the partners will hold any money as client money.

(v)   The fees of interpreters, translators, process servers, surveyors, estate agents, etc., instructed by the solicitor are professional disbursements (see rule 2(2)(s)). Travel agents' charges are not professional disbursements.

(vi)   The general definition of "office account" is wide (see rule 2(2)(p)). However, rule 19(1)(b) (receipt and transfer of costs) and rule 21(1)(b) (payments from the Legal Aid Board) specify that certain money is to be placed in an office account at a bank or building society.

(vii) An index is attached to the rules but it does not form part of the rules. For the status of the flowchart (Appendix 1) and the chart dealing with special situations (Appendix 2), see note (xiii) to rule 13.

Rule 3 – Geographical scope

The rules apply to practice carried on from an office in England and Wales.

Note

Practice carried on from an office outside England and Wales is governed by the Solicitors' Overseas Practice Rules.

Rule 4 – Persons governed by the rules

(1)   The rules apply to:

(a)   *solicitors* who are:

(i)   sole practitioners;

(ii)   partners in a practice, or held out as partners (including "salaried" and "associate" partners);

(iii)   assistants, associates, consultants or locums in a private practice;

(iv)   employed as in-house *solicitors* (for example, in a law centre or in commerce and industry); or

(v)   directors of *recognised bodies*;

(b)   *registered foreign lawyers* who are:

(i)   partners in a *multi-national partnership*, or held out as partners (including "salaried" and "associate" partners); or

(ii)   directors of *recognised bodies*; and

(c)   *recognised bodies*.

(2)   Part F of the rules (accountants' reports) also applies to reporting accountants.

Notes

(i)   In practical terms, the rules also bind anyone else working in a practice, such as cashiers and non-solicitor fee-earners. Non-compliance by any member of staff will lead to the principals being in breach of the rules – see rule 6. Misconduct by an employee can also lead to an order of the Solicitors Disciplinary Tribunal under section 43 of the Solicitors Act 1974 imposing restrictions on his or her employment.

(ii)   Solicitors who have held or received client money or controlled trust money, but no longer do so, whether or not they continue in practice, continue to be bound by some of the rules – for instance:

►   rule 7 (duty to remedy breaches);

►   rule 19(2), and note (xi) to rule 19, rule 32(8) to (15) and rule 33 (retention of records);

►   rule 34 (production of records);

►   Part F (accountants' reports), and in particular rule 35(1) and rule 36(5) (delivery of final report), and rule 38(2) and rule 46 (retention of records).

(iii)   The rules do not cover a solicitor's trusteeships carried on in a purely personal capacity outside any legal practice. It will normally be clear from the terms of the appointment whether the solicitor is being appointed trustee in a purely personal capacity or in his or her professional capacity. If a solicitor is charging for the work, it is clearly being done as solicitor. Use of professional stationery may also indicate that the work is being done in a professional capacity.

(iv)   A solicitor who wishes to retire from private practice must make a decision about any professional trusteeship. There are three possibilities:

(a)   continue to act as a professional trustee (as evidenced by, for instance, charging for work done, or by continuing to use the title "solicitor" in connection with the trust). In this case, the solicitor must continue to hold a practising certificate, and money subject to the trust must continue to be dealt with in accordance with the rules;

28

(b) continue to act as trustee, but in a purely personal capacity. In this case, the solicitor must stop charging for the work, and must not be held out as a solicitor (unless this is qualified by words such as "non-practising" or "retired") in connection with the trust;

(c) cease to be a trustee.

Rule 5 – Persons exempt from the rules

The rules do not apply to:

(a) a *solicitor* when practising as an employee of:

    (i) a local authority;

    (ii) statutory undertakers;

    (iii) a body whose accounts are audited by the Comptroller and Auditor General;

    (iv) the Duchy of Lancaster;

    (v) the Duchy of Cornwall; or

    (vi) the Church Commissioners; or

(b) a *solicitor* who practises as the Solicitor of the City of London; or

(c) a *solicitor* when carrying out the functions of:

    (i) a coroner or other judicial office; or

    (ii) a sheriff or under-sheriff.

Notes

(i) "Statutory undertakers" means:

    (a) any persons authorised by any enactment to carry on any railway, light railway, tramway, road transport, water transport, canal, inland navigation, dock, harbour, pier or lighthouse undertaking or any undertaking for the supply of hydraulic power; and

    (b) any licence holder within the meaning of the Electricity Act 1989, any public gas supplier, any water or sewerage undertaker, the Environment Agency, any public telecommunications operator, the Post Office, the Civil Aviation Authority and any relevant airport operator within the meaning of Part V of the Airports Act 1986.

(ii) "Local authority" means any of those bodies which are listed in section 270 of the Local Government Act 1972 or in section 21(1) of the Local Government and Housing Act 1989.

Rule 6 – Principals' responsibility for compliance

All the *principals* in a practice must ensure compliance with the rules by the *principals* themselves and by everyone else working in the practice. This duty also extends to the directors of a *recognised body*, and to the *recognised body* itself.

Rule 7 – Duty to remedy breaches

(1) Any breach of the rules must be remedied promptly upon discovery. This includes the replacement of any money improperly withheld or withdrawn from a *client account*.

(2) In a private practice, the duty to remedy breaches rests not only on the person causing the breach, but also on all the *principals* in the practice. This duty extends to replacing missing *client money* or *controlled trust money* from the *principals'* own resources, even if the money has been misappropriated by an employee or fellow *principal*, and whether or not a claim is subsequently made on the Solicitors' Indemnity or Compensation Funds.

Note

For payment of interest when money should have been held in a client account but was not, see rule 24(2).

Rule 8 – Controlled trustees

A *solicitor* who in the course of practice acts as a *controlled trustee* must treat the *controlled trust money* as if it were *client money*, except when the rules provide to the contrary.

Note

The following are examples of controlled trust money being treated differently from client money:

► rule 18 (controlled trust money withheld from a client account) – special provisions for controlled trusts, in place of rules 16 and 17 (which apply to client money);

► rule 19(2), and note (xi) to rule 9 – original bill etc., to be kept on file, in addition to central record or file of copy bills;

► rule 23, note (v) and rule 32, note (ii)(d) – controlled trustees may delegate to an outside manager the day to day keeping of accounts of the business or property portfolio of an estate or trust;

► rule 24(7), and note (x) to rule 24 – interest;

► rule 32(7) – quarterly reconciliations.

Rule 9 – Liquidators, trustees in bankruptcy, Court of Protection receivers and trustees of occupational pension schemes

(1) A *solicitor* who in the course of practice acts as

► a liquidator,

► a trustee in bankruptcy,

► a Court of Protection receiver, or

► a trustee of an occupational pension scheme which is subject to section 47(1)(a) of the Pensions Act 1995 (appointment of an auditor) **and** section 49(1) (separate bank account) **and** regulations under section 49(2)(b) (books and records),

must comply with:

(a) the appropriate statutory rules or regulations;

(b) the principles set out in rule 1; and

28

(c)   the requirements of paragraphs (2) to (4) below;

and will then be deemed to have satisfactorily complied with the Solicitors' Accounts Rules.

(2)   In respect of any records kept under the appropriate statutory rules, there must also be compliance with:

(a)   rule 32(8) – bills and notifications of costs;

(b)   rule 32(9)(c) – retention of records;

(c)   rule 32(12) – centrally kept records;

(d)   rule 34 – production of records; and

(e)   rule 42(1)(l) – reporting accountant to check compliance.

(3)   If a liquidator or trustee in bankruptcy uses any of the practice's *client accounts* for holding money pending transfer to the Insolvency Services Account or to a local bank account authorised by the Secretary of State, he or she must comply with the Solicitors' Accounts Rules in all respects whilst the money is held in the *client account*.

(4)   If the appropriate statutory rules or regulations do not govern the holding or receipt of *client money* in a particular situation (for example, money below a certain limit), the *solicitor* must comply with the Solicitors' Accounts Rules in all respects in relation to that money.

Notes

(i)   The Insolvency Regulations 1986 (S.I. 1986 no. 994) regulate liquidators and trustees in bankruptcy.

(ii)   The Court of Protection Rules 1994 (S.I. 1994 no. 3046) regulate Court of Protection receivers.

(iii)   Money held or received by solicitor liquidators, trustees in bankruptcy and Court of Protection receivers is client money but, because of the statutory rules and rule 9(1), it will not normally be kept in a client account. If for any reason it is held in a client account, the Solicitors' Accounts Rules apply to that money for the time it is so held (see rule 9(3) and (4)).

(iv)   Money held or received by solicitor trustees of occupational pension schemes is either client money or controlled trust money but, because of the statutory rules and rule 9(1), it will not normally be kept in a client account. If for any reason it is held in a client account, the Solicitors' Accounts Rules apply to that money for the time it is so held (see rule 9(4)).

Rule 10 – Joint accounts

(1)   If a *solicitor* acting in a *client's* matter holds or receives money jointly with the *client*, another *solicitors'* practice or another third party, the rules in general do not apply, but the following must be complied with:

(a)   rule 32(8) – bills and notifications of costs;

(b)   rule 32(9)(b)(ii) – retention of statements and passbooks;

(c)   rule 32(13) – centrally kept records;

(d)   rule 34 – production of records; and

(e)   rule 42(1)(m) – reporting accountant to check compliance.

Operation of the joint account by the solicitor only

(2)   If the joint account is operated only by the *solicitor*, the *solicitor* must ensure that he or she receives the statements from the *bank, building society* or other financial institution, and has possession of any passbooks.

Shared operation of the joint account

(3)   If the *solicitor* shares the operation of the joint account with the *client*, another *solicitor's* practice or another third party, the *solicitor* must:

(a)   ensure that he or she receives the statements or duplicate statements from the *bank, building society* or other financial institution and retains them in accordance with rule 32(9)(b)(ii); and

(b)   ensure that he or she either has possession of any passbooks, or takes copies of the passbook entries before handing any passbook to the other signatory, and retains them in accordance with rule 32(9)(b)(ii).

Operation of the joint account by the other account holder

(4)   If the joint account is operated solely by the other account holder, the *solicitor* must ensure that he or she receives the statements or duplicate statements from the *bank, building society* or other financial institution and retains them in accordance with rule 32(9)(b)(ii).

Note

Although a joint account is not a client account, money held in a joint account is client money.

Rule 11 – Operation of a client's own account

(1)   If a *solicitor* in the course of practice operates a *client's* own account as signatory (for example, as donee under a power of attorney), the rules in general do not apply, but the following must be complied with:

(a)   rule 33(1) to (3) – accounting records for clients' own accounts;

(b)   rule 34 – production of records; and

(c)   rule 42(1)(n) – reporting accountant to check compliance.

Operation by the solicitor only

(2)   If the account is operated by the *solicitor* only, the *solicitor* must ensure that he or she receives the statements from the *bank, building society* or other financial institution, and has possession of any passbooks.

Shared operation of the account

(3)   If the *solicitor* shares the operation of the account with the *client* or a co-attorney outside the *solicitor's* practice, the *solicitor* must:

28

(a)   ensure that he or she receives the statements or duplicate statements from the *bank, building society* or other financial institution and retains them in accordance with rule 33(1) to (3); and

(b)   ensure that he or she either has possession of any passbooks, or takes copies of the passbook entries before handing any passbook to the *client* or co-attorney, and retains them in accordance with rule 33(1) to (3).

Operation of the account for a limited purpose

(4)   If the *solicitor* is given authority (whether as attorney or otherwise) to operate the account for a limited purpose only, such as the taking up of a share rights issue during the *client's* temporary absence, the *solicitor* need not receive statements or possess passbooks, provided that he or she retains details of all cheques drawn or paid in, and retains copies of all passbook entries, relating to the transaction, and retains them in accordance with rule 33(1) and (2).

Application

(5)   This rule applies only to *solicitors* in private practice.

Notes

(i)   Money held in a client's own account (under a power of attorney or otherwise) is not "client money" for the purpose of the rules because it is not "held or received" by the solicitor. If the solicitor closes the account and receives the closing balance, this becomes client money and must be paid into a client account, unless the client instructs to the contrary in accordance with rule 16(1)(a).

(ii)   A solicitor who merely pays money into a client's own account, or helps the client to complete forms in relation to such an account, is not "operating" the account.

(iii)   A solicitor executor who operates the deceased's account (whether before or after the grant of probate) will be subject to the limited requirements of rule 11. If the account is subsequently transferred into the solicitor's name, or a new account is opened in the solicitor's name, the solicitor will have "held or received" controlled trust money (or client money) and is then subject to all the rules.

(iv)   The rules do not cover money held or received by a solicitor attorney acting in a purely personal capacity outside any legal practice. If a solicitor is charging for the work, it is clearly being done in the course of legal practice. See rule 4, note (iv) for the choices which can be made on retirement from private practice.

(v)   "A client's own account" covers all accounts in a client's own name, whether opened by the client himself or herself, or by the solicitor on the client's instructions under rule 16(1)(b).

(vi)   "A client's own account" also includes an account opened in the name of a person designated by the client under rule 16(1)(b).

(vii)   Solicitors should also remember the requirements of rule 32(8) – bills and notifications of costs.

(viii)   For payment of interest, see rule 24, note (iii).

Rule 12 – Solicitor's rights not affected

Nothing in these rules deprives a *solicitor* of any recourse or right, whether by way of lien, set off, counterclaim, charge or otherwise, against money standing to the credit of a *client account*.

Rule 13 – Categories of money

All money held or received in the course of practice falls into one of the following categories:

(a)   "client money" – money held or received for a *client,* and all other money which is not *controlled trust money* or *office money*;

(b)   "controlled trust money" – money held or received for a *controlled trust*; or

(c)   "office money" – money which belongs to the *solicitor* or the practice.

Notes

(i)   "Client money" includes money held or received:

(a)   as agent, bailee, stakeholder, or as the donee of a power of attorney, or as a liquidator, trustee in bankruptcy or Court of Protection receiver;

(b)   for payment of unpaid professional disbursements (for definition of "professional disbursement" see rule 2(2)(s));

(c)   for payment of stamp duty, Land Registry registration fees, telegraphic transfer fees and court fees; this is not office money because the solicitor has not incurred an obligation to the Inland Revenue, the Land Registry, the bank or the court to pay the duty or fee (contrast with note (xi)(c)(C) below); (on the other hand, if the solicitor has already paid the duty or fee out of his or her own resources, or has received the service on credit, payment subsequently received from the client will be office money – see note (xi)(c)(B) below);

(d)   as a payment on account of costs generally;

(e)   as commission paid in respect of a solicitor's client, unless the client has given the solicitor prior authority to retain it in accordance with practice rule 10, or unless it falls within the £20 de minimis figure specified in that rule.

(ii)   A solicitor to whom a cheque or draft is made out, and who in the course of practice endorses it over to a client or employer, has received client money. Even if no other client money is held or received, the solicitor will be subject to some provisions of the rules, e.g.:

▶   rule 7 (duty to remedy breaches);

▶   rule 32 (accounting records for client money);

▶   rule 34 (production of records);

▶   rule 35 (delivery of accountants' reports).

(iii)   Money held by solicitors who are trustees of occupational pension schemes will either be client money or controlled trust money, according to the circumstances.

(iv)   Money held jointly with another person outside the practice (for example, with a lay trustee, or with another firm of solicitors) is client money subject to a limited application of the rules – see rule 10.

(v)   Money held to the sender's order is client money.

(a)   If money is accepted on such terms, it must be held in a client account.

(b)   However, a cheque or draft sent to a solicitor on terms that the cheque or draft (as opposed to the money) is held to the sender's order must not be presented for payment without the sender's consent.

(c)   The recipient is always subject to a professional obligation to return the money, or the cheque or draft, to the sender on demand.

(vi)   An advance to a client from the solicitor which is paid into a client account under rule 15(2)(b) becomes client money. For interest, see rule 24(3)(e).

28

(vii) Money subject to a trust will be either:

    (a) controlled trust money (basically if members of the practice are the only trustees, but see the detailed definition of "controlled trust" in rule 2(2)(h)); or

    (b) client money (if the trust is not a controlled trust; typically the solicitor will be co-trustee with a lay person, or is acting for lay trustees).

(viii) If the Office for the Supervision of Solicitors (OSS) intervenes in a practice, money from the practice is held or received by the OSS's intervention agent subject to a trust under Schedule 1 paragraph 7(1) of the Solicitors Act 1974, and is therefore controlled trust money. The same provision requires the agent to pay the money into a client account.

(ix) A solicitor who, as the donee of a power of attorney, operates the donor's own account is subject to a limited application of these rules – see rule 11. Money kept in the donor's own account is not "client money", because it is not "held or received" by the solicitor.

(x) Money held or received by a solicitor in the course of his or her employment when practising in one of the capacities listed in rule 5 (persons exempt from the rules) is not "client money" for the purpose of the rules, because the rules do not apply at all.

(xi) Office money includes:

    (a) money held or received in connection with running the practice; for example, PAYE, or VAT on the firm's fees;

    (b) interest on general client accounts; the bank or building society should be instructed to credit such interest to the office account – but see also rule 15(2)(d), and note (vi) to rule 15 for interest on controlled trust money; and

    (c) payments received in respect of:

        (A) fees due to the practice against a bill or written notification of costs incurred, which has been given or sent in accordance with rule 19(2);

        (B) disbursements already paid by the practice (for definition of "disbursement" see rule 2(2)(k));

        (C) disbursements incurred but not yet paid by the practice, but excluding unpaid professional disbursements (for definition of "professional disbursement" see rule 2(2)(s), and note (v) to rule 2);

        (D) money paid for or towards an agreed fee – see rule 19(5); and

    (d) money held in a client account and earmarked for costs under rule 19(3) (transfer of costs from client account to office account).

(xii) A solicitor cannot be his or her own client for the purpose of the rules, so that if a practice conducts a personal or office transaction – for instance, conveyancing – for a principal (or for a number of principals), money held or received on behalf of the principal(s) is office money. However, other circumstances may mean that the money is client money, for example:

    (a) If the practice also acts for a lender, money held or received on behalf of the lender is client money.

    (b) If the practice acts for a principal and, for example, his or her spouse jointly (assuming the spouse is not a partner in the practice), money received on their joint behalf is client money.

    (c) If the practice acts for an assistant solicitor, consultant or non-solicitor employee (or, in the case of a recognised body, a director), he or she is regarded as a client of the practice, and money received for him or her is client money – even if he or she conducts the matter personally.

(xiii) For a flowchart summarising the effect of the rules, see Appendix 1. For more details of the treatment of different types of money, see the chart "Special situations – what applies" at Appendix 2. These two appendices are included to help solicitors and their staff find their way about the rules. Unlike the notes, they are not intended to affect the meaning of the rules.

PART B – CLIENT MONEY, CONTROLLED TRUST MONEY AND OPERATION OF A CLIENT ACCOUNT

Rule 14 – Client accounts

(1) A *solicitor* who holds or receives *client money* and/or *controlled trust money* must keep one or more *client accounts* (unless all the *client money* and *controlled trust money* is always dealt with outside any *client account* in accordance with rule 9, rule 10 or rules 16 to 18).

(2) A "client account" is an account of a practice kept at a *bank* or *building society* for holding *client money* and/or *controlled trust money*, in accordance with the requirements of this part of the rules.

(3) The *client account(s)* of:

(a) a sole practitioner must be either in the *solicitor's* own name or in the practice name;

(b) a partnership must be in the firm name;

(c) a *recognised body* must be in the company name;

(d) in-house *solicitors* must be in the name of the current *principal solicitor* or *solicitors*;

(e) executors or *trustees* who are *controlled trustees* must be either in the name of the firm or in the name of the *controlled trustee(s)*;

and the name of the account must also include the word "client".

(4) A *client account* must be:

(a) a *bank* account at a branch (or a *bank's* head office) in England and Wales; or

(b) a *building society* deposit (not share) account at a branch (or a society's head office) in England and Wales.

(5) There are two types of *client account*:

(a) a "separate designated client account", which is a deposit account for money relating to a single *client*, or a current or deposit account for money held for a single *controlled trust*; and which includes in its title, in addition to the requirements of rule 14(3) above, a reference to the identity of the *client* or *controlled trust*; and

(b) a "general client account", which is any other *client account*.

28

Notes

(i) For the client accounts of a recognised body owned by a solicitor's partnership, see rule 31.

(ii) In the case of in-house solicitors, any client account should be in the names of all solicitors held out on the notepaper as principals. The names of other solicitor employees may also be included if so desired. Any solicitor whose name is included will be subject to the full Compensation Fund contribution and his or her name will have to be included on the accountant's report.

(iii) "Bank" and "building society" are defined in rule 2(2)(c) and (d) respectively.

(iv)   A practice may have any number of separate designated client accounts and general client accounts.

(v)   The word "client" must appear in full; an abbreviation is not acceptable.

(vi)   Compliance with rule 14(1) to (4) ensures that clients, as well as the bank or building society, have the protection afforded by section 85 of the Solicitors Act 1974.

(vii)   Money held in a client account must be immediately available, even at the sacrifice of interest, unless the client otherwise instructs, or the circumstances clearly indicate otherwise.

Rule 15 – Use of a client account

(1)   *Client money* and *controlled trust money* must *without delay* be paid into a *client account*, and must be held in a *client account*, except when the rules provide to the contrary (see rules 16 to 18).

(2)   Only *client money* or *controlled trust money* may be paid into or held in a *client account*, except:

(a)   an amount of the *solicitor's* own money required to open or maintain the account;

(b)   an advance from the *solicitor* to fund a payment on behalf of a *client* or *controlled trust* in excess of funds held for that *client* or *controlled trust*; the sum becomes *client money* or *controlled trust money* on payment into the account (for interest on *client money*, see rule 24(3)(e); for interest on *controlled trust money*, see rule 24(7) and note (x) to rule 24);

(c)   money to replace any sum which for any reason has been drawn from the account in breach of rule 22; the replacement money becomes *client money* or *controlled trust money* on payment into the account; and

(d)   a sum in lieu of interest which is paid into a *client account* for the purpose of complying with rule 24(2) as an alternative to paying it to the client direct (for interest on *controlled trust money*, see note (vi) below);

and except when the rules provide to the contrary (see note (iv) below).

Notes

(i)   See rule 13 and notes for the definition and examples of client money and controlled trust money.

(ii)   "Without delay" is defined in rule 2(2)(z).

(iii)   Exceptions to rule 15(1) (client money and controlled trust money must be paid into a client account) can be found in:

▶   rule 9 – liquidators, trustees in bankruptcy, Court of Protection receivers and trustees of occupational pension schemes;

▶   rule 10 – joint accounts;

▶   rule 16 – client's instructions;

▶   rules 17 and 18:

– cash paid straight to client, beneficiary or third party;

– cheque endorsed to client, beneficiary or third party;

– money withheld from client account on the Society's authority;

– controlled trust money paid into an account which is not a client account;

► rule 19(1)(b) – receipt and transfer of costs;

► rule 21(1) – payments by the Legal Aid Board.

(iv) Rule 15(2)(a) to (d) provides for exceptions to the principle that only client money and controlled trust money may be paid into a client account. Additional exceptions can be found in:

► rule 19(1)(c) – receipt and transfer of costs;

► rule 20(2)(b) – receipt of mixed payments.

(v) Only a nominal sum will be required to open or maintain an account. In practice, banks will usually open (and, if instructed, keep open) accounts with nil balances.

(vi) Rule 15 allows controlled trust money to be mixed with client money in a general client account. However, the general law requires a solicitor to act in the best interests of a controlled trust and not to benefit from it. The interest rules in Part C do not apply to controlled trust money. A solicitor's legal duty means that the solicitor must obtain the best reasonably obtainable rate of interest, and must account to the relevant controlled trust for all the interest earned, whether the controlled trust money is held in a separate designated client account or in a general client account. To ensure that all interest is accounted for, one option might be to set up a general client account just for controlled trust money. When controlled trust money is held in a general client account, interest will be credited to the office account in the normal way, but all interest must be promptly allocated to each controlled trust – either by transfer to the general client account, or to separate designated client account(s) for the particular trust(s), or by payment to each trust in some other way.

Solicitors should also consider whether they have received any indirect benefit from controlled trust money at the expense of the controlled trust(s). For example, the bank might charge a reduced overdraft rate by reference to the total funds (including controlled trust money) held, in return for paying a lower rate of interest on those funds.   In this type of case, the law may require the solicitor to do more than simply account for any interest earned.

(vii) If controlled trust money is invested in the purchase of assets other than money – such as stocks or shares – it ceases to be controlled trust money, because it is no longer money held by the solicitor. If the investment is subsequently sold, the money received is, again, controlled trust money. The records kept under rule 32 must include entries to show the purchase or sale of investments.

(viii) Some schemes proposed by banks would aggregate the sums held in a number of client accounts in order to maximise the interest payable. It is not acceptable to aggregate money held in separate designated client accounts with money held in general client accounts (see note (i) to rule 24).

(ix) Solicitors may need to exercise caution if asked to provide banking facilities through a client account. There are criminal sanctions against assisting money launderers.

Rule 16 – Client money withheld from client account on client's instructions

28

(1) *Client money* may be:

(a) held by the *solicitor* outside a *client account* by, for example, retaining it in the *solicitor's* safe in the form of cash, or placing it in an account in the *solicitor's* name which is not a *client account*, such as a *building society* share account or an account outside England and Wales; or

(b) paid into an account at a *bank, building society* or other financial institution opened in the name of the *client* or of a person designated by the *client*;

but only if the *client* instructs the *solicitor* to that effect for the *client's* own convenience, and only if the instructions are given in writing, or are given by other means and confirmed by the *solicitor* to the client in writing.

(2)   It is improper to seek blanket agreements, through standard terms of business or otherwise, to hold *client money* outside a *client account*.

Notes

(i)   For advance payments from the Legal Aid Board, withheld from a client account on the Board's instructions, see rule 21(1)(a).

(ii)   If a client instructs the solicitor to hold part only of a payment in accordance with rule 16(1)(a) or (b), the entire payment must first be placed in a client account. The relevant part can then be transferred out and dealt with in accordance with the client's instructions.

(iii)   Money withheld from a client account under rule 16(1)(a) remains client money, and the record-keeping provisions of rule 32 must be complied with.

(iv)   Once money has been paid into an account set up under rule 16(1)(b), it ceases to be client money. Until that time, the money is client money and a record must therefore be kept of the solicitor's receipt of the money, and its payment into the account in the name of the client or designated person, in accordance with rule 32. If the solicitor can operate the account, the solicitor must comply with rule 11 (operating a client's own account) and rule 33 (accounting records for clients' own accounts). In the absence of instructions to the contrary, any money withdrawn must be paid into a client account – see rule 15(1).

(v)   Clients' instructions under rule 16(1) must be kept for at least six years – see rule 32(9)(d).

(vi)   A payment on account of costs received from a person who is funding all or part of the solicitor's fees may be withheld from a client account on the instructions of that person given in accordance with rule 16(1) and (2).

(vii)   For payment of interest, see rule 24(6) and notes (ii) and (iii) to rule 24.

Rule 17 – Other client money withheld from a client account

The following categories of *client money* may be withheld from a *client account*:

(a)   cash received and *without delay* paid in cash in the ordinary course of business to the *client* or, on the *client's* behalf, to a third party;

(b)   a cheque or draft received and endorsed over in the ordinary course of business to the *client* or, on the *client's* behalf, to a third party;

(c)   money withheld from a *client account* on instructions under rule 16;

(d)   unpaid *professional disbursements* included in a payment of *costs* dealt with under rule 19(1)(b);

(e)   unpaid *professional disbursements* included in a payment of costs from the Legal Aid Board (see rule 21); and

(f)   money withheld from a *client account* on the written authorisation of the *Society*. The *Society* may impose a condition that the *solicitor* pay the money to a charity which gives an indemnity against any legitimate claim subsequently made for the sum received.

Notes

(i)   "Without delay" is defined in rule 2(2)(z).

(ii)   If money is withheld from a client account under rule 17(a) or (b), rule 32 requires records to be kept of the receipt of the money and the payment out.

(iii)   It makes no difference, for the purpose of the rules, whether an endorsement is effected by signature in the normal way or by some other arrangement with the bank.

(iv)   The circumstances in which authorisation would be given under rule 17(f) must be extremely rare. Applications for authorisation should be made to the Professional Ethics Division [see p.xv for contact details].

Rule 18 – Controlled trust money withheld from a client account

The following categories of *controlled trust money* may be withheld from a *client account*:

(a)   cash received and *without delay* paid in cash in the execution of the *trust* to a beneficiary or third party;

(b)   a cheque or draft received and *without delay* endorsed over in the execution of the *trust* to a beneficiary or third party;

(c)   money which, in accordance with the trustee's powers, is paid into or retained in an account of the *trustee* which is not a *client account* (for example, a *building society* share account or an account outside England and Wales), or properly retained in cash in the performance of the *trustee's* duties;

(d)   money withheld from a *client account* on the written authorisation of the *Society*. The *Society* may impose a condition that the *solicitor* pay the money to a charity which gives an indemnity against any legitimate claim subsequently made for the sum received.

Notes

(i)   "Without delay" is defined in rule 2(2)(z).

(ii)   If money is withheld from a client account under rule 18(a) or (b), rule 32 requires records to be kept of the receipt of the money and the payment out – see also rule 15, note (vii). If money is withheld from a client account under rule 18(c), rule 32 requires a record to be kept of the receipt of the money.

(iii)   It makes no difference, for the purpose of the rules, whether an endorsement is effected by signature in the normal way or by some other arrangement with the bank.

(iv)   The circumstances in which authorisation would be given under rule 18(d) must be extremely rare. Applications for authorisation should be made to the Professional Ethics Division [see p.xv for contact details].

Rule 19 – Receipt and transfer of costs

(1)   A *solicitor* who receives money paid in full or part settlement of the *solicitor's* bill (or other notification of *costs*) **must follow one of the following four options:**

(a)   **determine the composition of the payment *without delay*, and deal with the money accordingly:**

(i)   if the sum comprises *office money* only, it must be placed in an *office account*;

(ii)   if the sum comprises only *client money* (for example an unpaid *professional disbursement* – see rule 2(2)(s), and note (v) to rule 2), the entire sum must be placed in a *client account*;

    (iii) if the sum includes both *office money* and *client money* (such as unpaid *professional disbursements*; purchase money; or payments in advance for court fees, stamp duty, Land Registry registration fees or telegraphic transfer fees), the solicitor must follow rule 20 (receipt of mixed payments); **or**

(b)   **ascertain that the payment comprises only *office money*, and/or *client money* in the form of *professional disbursements* incurred but not yet paid, and deal with the payment as follows:**

    (i)   place the entire sum in an *office account* at a *bank* or *building society* branch (or head office) in England and Wales; and

    (ii) by the end of the second working day following receipt, either pay any unpaid *professional disbursement*, or transfer a sum for its settlement to a *client account*; **or**

(c)   **pay the entire sum into a *client account* (regardless of its composition), and transfer any *office money* out of the *client account* within 14 days of receipt; or**

(d)   **on receipt of *costs* from the Legal Aid Board, follow the option in rule 21(1)(b).**

(2)   A *solicitor* who properly requires payment of his or her fees from money held for the *client* or *controlled trust* in a *client account* must first give or send a bill of *costs*, or other written notification of the *costs* incurred, to the *client* or the paying party.

(3)   Once the *solicitor* has complied with paragraph (2) above, the money earmarked for costs becomes *office money* and must be transferred out of the *client account* within 14 days.

(4)   A payment on account of *costs* generally is *client money*, and must be held in a *client account* until the *solicitor* has complied with paragraph (2) above. (For an exception in the case of legal aid payments, see rule 21(1)(a).)

(5)   A payment for an *agreed fee* must be paid into an *office account*. An "agreed fee" is one that is fixed – not a *fee* that can be varied upwards, nor a *fee* that is dependent on the transaction being completed. An *agreed fee* must be evidenced in writing.

Notes

(i)   For the definition and further examples of office and client money, see rule 13 and notes.

(ii)   Money received for paid disbursements is office money.

    ▶ Money received for unpaid professional disbursements is client money.

    ▶ Money received for other unpaid disbursements for which the solicitor has incurred a liability to the payee (for example, travel agents' charges, taxi fares, courier charges or Land Registry search fees, payable on credit) is office money.

    ▶ Money received for disbursements anticipated but not yet incurred is a payment on account, and is therefore client money.

(iii) The option in rule 19(1)(a) allows a solicitor to place all payments in the correct account in the first instance. The option in rule 19(1)(b) allows the prompt banking into an office account of an invoice payment when the only uncertainty is whether or not the payment includes some client money in the form of unpaid professional disbursements. The option in rule 19(1)(c) allows the prompt banking into a client account of any invoice payment in advance of determining whether the payment is a mixture of office and client money (of whatever description) or is only office money.

(iv)   A solicitor who is not in a position to comply with the requirements of rule 19(1)(b) cannot take advantage of that option.

(v)   The option in rule 19(1)(b) cannot be used if the money received includes a payment on account – for example, a payment for a professional disbursement anticipated but not yet incurred.

(vi)   In order to be able to use the option in rule 19(1)(b) for electronic payments or other direct transfers from clients, a solicitor may choose to establish a system whereby clients are given an office account number for payment of costs. The system must be capable of ensuring that, when invoices are sent to the client, no request is made for any client money, with the sole exception of money for professional disbursements already incurred but not yet paid.

(vii)   Rule 19(1)(c) allows clients to be given a single account number for making direct payments by electronic or other means – under this option, it has to be a client account.

(viii)   A solicitor will not be in breach of rule 19 as a result of a misdirected electronic payment or other direct transfer, provided:

(A)   appropriate systems are in place to ensure compliance;

(B)   appropriate instructions were given to the client;

(C)   the client's mistake is remedied promptly upon discovery; and

(D)   appropriate steps are taken to avoid future errors by the client.

(ix)   "Properly" in rule 19(2) implies that the work has actually been done, whether at the end of the matter or at an interim stage, and that the solicitor is entitled to appropriate the money for costs.

(x)   Costs transferred out of a client account in accordance with rule 19(2) and (3) must be specific sums relating to the bill or other written notification of costs, and covered by the amount held for the particular client or controlled trust. Round sum withdrawals on account of costs will be a breach of the rules.

(xi)   In the case of a controlled trust, the paying party will be the controlled trustee(s) themselves. The solicitor must keep the original bill or notification of costs on the file, in addition to complying with rule 32(8) (central record or file of copy bills, etc.).

(xii)   Undrawn costs must not remain in a client account as a "cushion" against any future errors which could result in a shortage on that account, and cannot be regarded as available to set off against any general shortage on client account.

(xiii)   The rules do not require a bill of costs for an agreed fee, although a solicitor's VAT position may mean that in practice a bill is needed. If there is no bill, the written evidence of the agreement must be filed as a written notification of costs under rule 32(8)(b).

Rule 20 – Receipt of mixed payments

(1)   A "mixed payment" is one which includes *client money* or *controlled trust money* as well as *office money*.

(2)   A *mixed payment* must either:

(a)   be split between a *client account* and *office account* as appropriate; or

(b)   be placed *without delay* in a *client account*.

(3)   If the entire payment is placed in a *client account*, all *office money* must be transferred out of the *client account* within 14 days of receipt.

(4)   See rule 19(1)(b) and (c) for additional ways of dealing with (among other things) *mixed payments* received in response to a bill or other notification of costs.

28

(5)   See rule 21(1)(b) for (among other things) *mixed payments* received from the Legal Aid Board.

Note

"Without delay" is defined in rule 2(2)(z).

Rule 21 – Treatment of payments to legal aid practitioners

Payments from the Legal Aid Board

(1)   Two special dispensations apply to payments from the Legal Aid Board:

    (a)   An advance payment in anticipation of work to be carried out, although *client money*, may be placed in an *office account*, provided the Board instructs in writing that this may be done.

    (b)   A payment for *costs* (interim and/or final) may be paid into an *office account* at a *bank* or *building society* branch (or head office) in England and Wales, regardless of whether it consists wholly of *office money*, or is mixed with *client money* in the form of:

        (i)   advance payments for *fees* or *disbursements*; or

        (ii)   money for unpaid *professional disbursements*;

    provided all money for payment of *disbursements* is transferred to a *client account* (or the *disbursements* paid) within 14 days of receipt.

Payments from a third party

(2)   If the Legal Aid Board has paid any costs to a *solicitor* or a previously nominated *solicitor* in a matter ("green form" *costs,* advance payments or interim *costs*), or has paid *professional disbursements* direct, and *costs* are subsequently settled by a third party:

    (a)   The entire third party payment must be paid into a *client account*.

    (b)   A sum representing the payments made by the Board must be retained in the *client account*.

    (c)   Any balance belonging to the *solicitor* must be transferred to an *office account* within 14 days of the *solicitor* sending a report to the Board containing details of the third party payment.

    (d)   The sum retained in the *client account* as representing payments made by the Board must be:

        (i)   **either** recorded in the individual *client's* ledger account, and identified as the Board's money;

        (ii)   **or** recorded in a ledger account in the Board's name, and identified by reference to the *client* or matter;

    and kept in the *client account* until notification from the Board that it has recouped an equivalent sum from subsequent legal aid payments due to the *solicitor*. The retained sum must be transferred to an *office account* within 14 days of notification.

Notes

(i)   This rule deals with matters which specifically affect legal aid practitioners. It should not be read in isolation from the remainder of the rules which apply to all solicitors, including legal aid practitioners.

(ii)   Franchised firms can apply for advance payments on the issue of a certificate. The Legal Aid Board has issued instructions that these payments may be placed in office account.

(iii)   Rule 21(1)(b) deals with the specific problems of legal aid practitioners by allowing mixed or indeterminate payments (or even a payment consisting entirely of unpaid professional disbursements) to be paid into an office account, which for the purpose of rule 21(1)(b) must be an account at a bank or building society. However, it is always open to the solicitor to comply with rule 19(1)(a) to (c), which are the options for all solicitors for the receipt of costs.

(iv)   Solicitors are required by the Legal Aid Board to report promptly to the Legal Aid Board on receipt of costs from a third party. It is advisable to keep a copy of the report on the file as proof of compliance with the Board's requirements, as well as to demonstrate compliance with the rule.

(v)   A third party payment may also include unpaid professional disbursements or outstanding costs of the client's previous solicitor. This part of the payment is client money and must be kept in a client account until the solicitor pays the professional disbursement or outstanding costs.

Rule 22 – Withdrawals from a client account

(1)   *Client money* may only be withdrawn from a *client account* when it is:

(a)   properly required for a payment to or on behalf of the *client* (or other person on whose behalf the money is being held);

(b)   properly required for payment of a *disbursement* on behalf of the *client*;

(c)   properly required in full or partial reimbursement of money spent by the *solicitor* on behalf of the *client*;

(d)   transferred to another *client account*;

(e)   withdrawn on the *client's* instructions, provided the instructions are for the *client's* convenience and are given in writing, or are given by other means and confirmed by the *solicitor* to the *client* in writing;

(f)   a refund to the *solicitor* of an advance no longer required to fund a payment on behalf of a *client* (see rule 15(2)(b));

(g)   money which has been paid into the account in breach of the rules (for example, money paid into the wrong *separate designated client account*) – see paragraph (4) below; or

(h)   money not covered by (a) to (g) above, withdrawn from the account on the written authorisation of the *Society*. The *Society* may impose a condition that the *solicitor* pay the money to a charity which gives an indemnity against any legitimate claim subsequently made for the sum received.

(2)   *Controlled trust money* may only be withdrawn from a *client account* when it is:

(a)   properly required for a payment in the execution of the particular *trust*, including the purchase of an investment (other than money) in accordance with the *trustee's* powers;

28

    (b)   properly required for payment of a *disbursement* for the particular *trust*;

    (c)   properly required in full or partial reimbursement of money spent by the *solicitor* on behalf of the particular *trust*;

    (d)   transferred to another *client account*;

    (e)   transferred to an account other than a *client account* (such as a *building society* share account or an account outside England and Wales), but only if the *trustee's* powers permit, or to be properly retained in cash in the performance of the *trustee's* duties;

    (f)   a refund to the *solicitor* of an advance no longer required to fund a payment on behalf of a *controlled trust* (see rule 15(2)(b));

    (g)   money which has been paid into the account in breach of the rules (for example, money paid into the wrong *separate designated client account*) – see paragraph (4) below; or

    (h)   money not covered by (a) to (g) above, withdrawn from the account on the written authorisation of the *Society*. The *Society* may impose a condition that the *solicitor* pay the money to a charity which gives an indemnity against any legitimate claim subsequently made for the sum received.

(3)   *Office money* may only be withdrawn from a *client account* when it is:

    (a)   money properly paid into the account to open or maintain it under rule 15(2)(a);

    (b)   properly required for payment of the *solicitor's costs* under rule 19(2) and (3);

    (c)   the whole or part of a payment into a *client account* under rule 19(1)(c);

    (d)   part of a mixed payment placed in a *client account* under rule 20(2)(b); or

    (e)   money which has been paid into a *client account* in breach of the rules (for example, interest wrongly credited to a *general client account*) – see paragraph (4) below.

(4)   Money which has been paid into a *client account* in breach of the rules must be withdrawn from the *client account* promptly upon discovery.

(5)   Money withdrawn in relation to a particular *client* or *controlled trust* from a *general client account* must not exceed the money held on behalf of that *client* or *controlled trust* in all the *solicitor's general client accounts* (except as provided in paragraph (6) below).

(6)   A *solicitor* may make a payment in respect of a particular *client* or *controlled trust* out of a *general client account*, even if no money (or insufficient money) is held for that *client* or *controlled trust* in the *solicitor's general client account(s)*, provided:

    (a)   sufficient money is held for that *client* or *controlled trust* in a *separate designated client account*; and

    (b)   the appropriate transfer from the *separate designated client account* to a *general client account* is made immediately.

(7)   Money held for a *client* or *controlled trust* in a *separate designated client account* must not be used for payments for another *client* or *controlled trust*.

(8) A *client account* must not be overdrawn, except in the following circumstances:

    (a) A *separate designated client account* for a *controlled trust* can be overdrawn if the *controlled trustee* makes payments on behalf of the *trust* (for example, inheritance tax) before realising sufficient assets to cover the payments.

    (b) If a sole practitioner dies and his or her *client accounts* are frozen, the *solicitor*-manager can operate *client accounts* which are overdrawn to the extent of the money held in the frozen accounts.

Notes

Withdrawals in favour of solicitor, and for payment of disbursements

(i) Disbursements to be paid direct from a client account, or already paid out of the solicitor's own money, can be withdrawn under rule 22(1)(b) or (c) (or rule 22(2)(b) or (c)) in advance of preparing a bill of costs. Money to be withdrawn from a client account for the payment of costs (fees and disbursements) under rule 19(2) and (3) becomes office money and is dealt with under rule 22(3)(b).

(ii) Money is "spent" under rule 22(1)(c) (or rule 22(2)(c)) at the time when the solicitor despatches a cheque, unless the cheque is to be held to the solicitor's order. Money is also regarded as "spent" by the use of a credit account, so that, for example, search fees, taxi fares and courier charges incurred in this way may be transferred to the solicitor's office account.

(iii) See rule 23(3) for the way in which a withdrawal from a client account in favour of the solicitor must be effected.

Cheques payable to banks, building societies, etc.

(iv) In order to protect clients' funds (or controlled trust funds) against misappropriation when cheques are made payable to banks, building societies or other large institutions, it is strongly recommended that solicitors add the name and number of the account after the payee's name.

Drawing against uncleared cheques

(v) A solicitor should use discretion in drawing against a cheque received from or on behalf of a client before it has been cleared. If the cheque is not met, other clients' money will have been used to make the payment in breach of the rules. See rule 7 (duty to remedy breaches). A solicitor may be able to avoid a breach of the rules by instructing the bank or building society to charge all unpaid credits to the solicitor's office or personal account.

Non-receipt of telegraphic transfer

(vi) If a solicitor acting for a client withdraws money from a general client account on the strength of information that a telegraphic transfer is on its way, but the telegraphic transfer does not arrive, the solicitor will have used other clients' money in breach of the rules. See also rule 7 (duty to remedy breaches).

28

Withdrawals on instructions

(vii) One of the reasons why a client might authorise a withdrawal under rule 22(1)(e) might be to have the money transferred to a type of account other than a client account. If so, the requirements of rule 16 must be complied with.

Withdrawals on the Society's authorisation

(viii) Applications for authorisation under rule 22(1)(h) or 22(2)(h) should be made to the Professional Ethics Division [for contact details see p.xv], who can advise on the criteria which must normally be met for authorisation to be given.

(ix) After a practice has been wound up, banks sometimes discover unclaimed balances in an old client account. This money remains subject to rule 22 and rule 23. An application can be made to the Society under rule 22(1)(h) or 22(2)(h).

Rule 23 – Method of and authority for withdrawals from client account

(1) A withdrawal from a *client account* may be made only after a specific authority in respect of that withdrawal has been signed by at least one of the following:

(a) a *solicitor* who holds a current practising certificate;

(b) a Fellow of the Institute of Legal Executives of at least three years standing who is employed by such a *solicitor*;

(c) in the case of an office dealing solely with conveyancing, a licensed conveyancer who is employed by such a *solicitor*; or

(d) a *registered foreign lawyer* who is a partner in the practice or, in the case of a *recognised body*, a director.

(2) There is no need to comply with paragraph (1) above when transferring money from one *general client account* to another *general client account* at the same *bank* or *building society*.

(3) A withdrawal from a *client account* in favour of the *solicitor* or the practice must be either by way of a cheque to the *solicitor* or practice, or by way of a transfer to the *office account* or to the *solicitor's* personal account. The withdrawal must not be made in cash.

Notes

(i) Instructions to the bank or building society to withdraw money from a client account (rule 23(1)) may be given over the telephone, provided a specific authority has been signed in accordance with this rule before the instructions are given. If a solicitor decides to take advantage of this arrangement, it is of paramount importance that the scheme has appropriate inbuilt safeguards, such as passwords, to give the greatest protection possible for client money (or controlled trust money). Suitable safeguards will also be needed for practices which operate a CHAPS terminal.

(ii) In the case of a withdrawal by cheque, the specific authority (rule 23(1)) is usually a signature on the cheque itself. Signing a blank cheque is not a specific authority.

(iii) A withdrawal from a client account by way of a private loan from one client to another can only be made if the provisions of rule 30(2) are complied with.

(iv) It is advisable that a withdrawal for payment to or on behalf of a client (or on behalf of a controlled trust) be made by way of a crossed cheque whenever possible.

(v) Controlled trustees who instruct an outside manager to run, or continue to run, on a day-to-day basis, the business or property portfolio of an estate or trust will not need to comply with rule 23(1), provided all cheques are retained in accordance with rule 32(10). (See also rule 32, note (ii)(d).)

(vi) Where the sum due to the client is sufficiently large, the solicitor should consider whether it should not appropriately be transferred to the client by direct bank transfer. For doing this, the solicitor would be entitled to make a modest administrative charge in addition to any charge made by the bank in connection with the transfer.

PART C – INTEREST

Rule 24 – When interest must be paid

(1) When a *solicitor* holds money in a *separate designated client account* for a *client*, or for a person funding all or part of the *solicitor's fees*, the *solicitor* must account to the *client* or that person for all interest earned on the account.

(2) When a *solicitor* holds money in a *general client account* for a *client*, or for a person funding all or part of the *solicitor's fees* (or if money should have been held for a *client* or such other person in a *client account* but was not), the *solicitor* must account to the *client* or that person for a sum in lieu of interest calculated in accordance with rule 25.

(3) A *solicitor* is not required to pay a sum in lieu of interest under paragraph (2) above:

  (a) if the amount calculated is £20 or less;

  (b) (i) if the *solicitor* holds a sum of money not exceeding the amount shown in the left hand column below for a time not exceeding the period indicated in the right hand column:

Amount	Time
£1,000	8 weeks
£2,000	4 weeks
£10,000	2 weeks
£20,000	1 week

  (ii) if the *solicitor* holds a sum of money exceeding £20,000 for one week or less, unless it is fair and reasonable to account for a sum in lieu of interest having regard to all the circumstances;

  (c) on money held for the payment of counsel's fees, once counsel has requested a delay in settlement;

  (d) on money held for the Legal Aid Board;

  (e) on an advance from the *solicitor* under rule 15(2)(b) to fund a payment on behalf of the *client* in excess of funds held for that *client*; or

  (f) if there is an agreement to contract out of the provisions of this rule under rule 27.

(4) If sums of money are held intermittently during the course of acting, and the sum in lieu of interest calculated under rule 25 for any period is £20 or less, a sum in lieu of interest should still be paid if it is fair and reasonable in the circumstances to aggregate the sums in respect of the individual periods.

(5) If money is held for a continuous period, and for part of that period it is held in a *separate designated client account*, the sum in lieu of interest for the rest of the period when the money was held in a *general client account* may as a result be £20 or less. A sum in lieu of interest should, however, be paid if it is fair and reasonable in the circumstances to do so.

(6) (a) If a *solicitor* holds money for a *client* (or person funding all or part of the *solicitor's fees*) in an account opened on the instructions of the *client* (or that person) under rule 16(1)(a), the *solicitor* must account to the *client* (or that person) for all interest earned on the account.

28

(b)   If a *solicitor* has failed to comply with instructions to open an account under rule 16(1)(a), the *solicitor* must account to the *client* (or the person funding all or part of the *solicitor's fees*) for a sum in lieu of any net loss of interest suffered by the *client* (or that person) as a result.

(7)   This rule does not apply to *controlled trust money*.

Notes

Requirement to pay interest

(i)   The whole of the interest earned on a separate designated client account must be credited to the account. However, the obligation to pay a sum in lieu of interest for amounts held in a general client account is subject to the de minimis provisions in rule 24(3)(a) and (b). Section 33(3) of the Solicitors Act 1974 permits solicitors to retain any interest earned on client money held in a general client account over and above that which they have to pay under these rules. (See also note (viii) to rule 15 on aggregation of accounts.)

(ii)   There is no requirement to pay a sum in lieu of interest on money held on instructions under rule 16(1)(a) in a manner which attracts no interest.

(iii)   Accounts opened in the client's name under rule 16(1)(b) (whether operated by the solicitor or not) are not subject to rule 24, as the money is not held by the solicitor. All interest earned belongs to the client. The same applies to any account in the client's own name operated by the solicitor as signatory under rule 11.

(iv)   Money subject to a trust which is not a controlled trust is client money (see rule 13, note (vii)), and rule 24 therefore applies to it.

De minimis provisions (rule 24(3)(a) and (b))

(v)   The sum in lieu of interest is calculated over the whole period for which money is held (see rule 25(2)); if this sum is £20 or less, the solicitor need not account to the client. If sums of money are held in relation to separate matters for the same client, it is normally appropriate to treat the money relating to the different matters separately, so that, if any of the sums calculated is £20 or less, no sum in lieu of interest is payable. There will, however, be cases when the matters are so closely related that they ought to be considered together – for example, when a solicitor is acting for a client in connection with numerous debt collection matters.

Administrative charges

(vi)   It is not improper to charge a reasonable fee for the handling of client money when the service provided is out of the ordinary.

Unpresented cheques

(vii)   A client may fail to present a cheque to his or her bank for payment. Whether or not it is reasonable to recalculate the amount due will depend on all the circumstances of the case. A reasonable charge may be made for any extra work carried out if the solicitor is legally entitled to make such a charge.

Liquidators, trustees in bankruptcy, Court of Protection receivers and trustees of occupational pension schemes

(viii)   Under rule 9, Part C of the rules does not normally apply to solicitors who are liquidators, etc. Solicitors must comply with the appropriate statutory rules and regulations, and rules 9(3) and (4) as appropriate.

Joint accounts

(ix)   Under rule 10, Part C of the rules does not apply to joint accounts. If a solicitor holds money jointly with a client, interest earned on the account will be for the benefit of the client unless otherwise agreed. If money is held jointly with another solicitors' practice, the allocation of interest earned will depend on the agreement reached.

Requirements for controlled trust money (rule 24(7))

(x)   Part C does not apply to controlled trust money. Under the general law, trustees of a controlled trust must account for all interest earned. For the treatment of interest on controlled trust money in a general client account, see rule 13, note (xi)(b), rule 15(2)(d) and note (vi) to rule 15. (See also note (viii) to rule 15 on aggregation of accounts.)

Rule 25 – Amount of interest

(1)   *Solicitors* must aim to obtain a reasonable rate of interest on money held in a *separate designated client account*, and must account for a fair sum in lieu of interest on money held in a *general client account* (or on money which should have been held in a *client account* but was not). The sum in lieu of interest need not necessarily reflect the highest rate of interest obtainable but it is not acceptable to look only at the lowest rate of interest obtainable.

(2)   **The sum in lieu of interest** for money held in a *general client account* (or on money which should have been held in a *client account* but was not) **must be calculated:**

▶   **on the balance or balances held over the whole period for which cleared funds are held**

▶   **at a rate not less than (whichever is the higher of) the following:**

(i)   the rate of interest payable on a *separate designated client account* for the amount or amounts held, or

(ii)   the rate of interest payable on the relevant amount or amounts if placed on deposit on similar terms by a member of the business community

▶   **at the *bank* or *building society* where the money is held.**

(3)   If the money, or part of it, is held successively or concurrently in accounts at different *banks* or *building societies*, the relevant *bank* or *building society* for the purpose of paragraph (2) will be whichever of those *banks* or *building societies* offered the best rate on the date when the money was first held.

(4)   If, contrary to the rules, the money is not held in a *client account*, the relevant *bank* or *building society* for the purpose of paragraph (2) will be a clearing bank or *building society* nominated by the *client* (or other person on whose behalf *client money* is held).

28

Notes

(i)   The sum in lieu of interest has to be calculated over the whole period for which money is held – see rule 25(2). The solicitor will usually account to the client at the conclusion of the client's matter, but might in some cases consider it appropriate to account to the client at intervals throughout.

(ii)   When looking at the period over which the sum in lieu of interest must be calculated, it will usually be unnecessary to check on actual clearance dates. When money is received by cheque and paid out by cheque, the normal clearance periods will usually cancel each other out, so that it will be satisfactory to look at the period between the dates when the incoming cheque is banked and the outgoing cheque is drawn.

(iii)   Different considerations apply when payments in and out are not both made by cheque. So, for example, the relevant periods would normally be:

- ▶ from the date when a solicitor receives incoming money in cash until the date when the outgoing cheque is sent;

- ▶ from the date when an incoming telegraphic transfer begins to earn interest until the date when the outgoing cheque is sent;

- ▶ from the date when an incoming cheque or banker's draft is or would normally be cleared until the date when the outgoing telegraphic transfer is made or banker's draft is obtained.

(iv)   The sum in lieu of interest is calculated by reference to the rates paid by the appropriate bank or building society (see rule 25(2) to (4)). Solicitors will therefore follow the practice of that bank or building society in determining how often interest is compounded over the period for which the cleared funds are held.

(v)   Money held in a client account must be immediately available, even at the sacrifice of interest, unless the client otherwise instructs, or the circumstances clearly indicate otherwise. The need for access can be taken into account in assessing the appropriate rate for calculating the sum to be paid in lieu of interest, or in assessing whether a reasonable rate of interest has been obtained for a separate designated client account.

Rule 26 – Interest on stakeholder money

When a *solicitor* holds money as stakeholder, the *solicitor* must pay interest, or a sum in lieu of interest, on the basis set out in rule 24 to the person to whom the stake is paid.

Note

For contracting out of this provision, see rule 27(2) and the notes to rule 27.

Rule 27 – Contracting out

(1)   In appropriate circumstances a *client* and his or her *solicitor* may by a written agreement come to a different arrangement as to the matters dealt with in rule 24 (payment of interest).

(2)   A *solicitor* acting as stakeholder may, by a written agreement with his or her own *client* and the other party to the transaction, come to a different arrangement as to the matters dealt with in rule 24.

Notes

(i)   Solicitors should act fairly towards their clients and provide sufficient information to enable them to give informed consent if it is felt appropriate to depart from the interest provisions. Whether it is appropriate to contract out depends on all the circumstances, for example, the size of the sum involved or the nature or status or bargaining position of the client. It might, for instance, be appropriate to contract out by standard terms of business if the client is a substantial commercial entity and the interest involved is modest in relation to the size of the transaction. The larger the sum of interest involved, the more there would be an onus on the solicitor to show that a client who had accepted a contracting out provision was properly informed and had been treated fairly. Contracting out is never appropriate if it is against the client's interests.

(ii)   In principle, a solicitor-stakeholder is entitled to make a reasonable charge to the client for acting as stakeholder in the client's matter.

(iii)   Alternatively, it may be appropriate to include a special provision in the contract that the solicitor-stakeholder retains the interest on the deposit to cover his or her charges for acting as stakeholder. This is only acceptable if it will provide a fair and reasonable payment for the work and risk involved in holding a stake. The contract could stipulate a maximum charge, with any interest earned above that figure being paid to the recipient of the stake.

(iv)   Any right to charge the client, or to stipulate for a charge which may fall on the client, would be excluded by, for instance, a prior agreement with the client for a fixed fee for the client's matter, or for an estimated fee which cannot be varied upwards in the absence of special circumstances. It is therefore not normal practice for a stakeholder in conveyancing transactions to receive a separate payment for holding the stake.

(v)   A solicitor-stakeholder who seeks an agreement to exclude the operation of rule 26 should be particularly careful not to take unfair advantage either of the client, or of the other party if unrepresented.

Rule 28 – Interest certificates

Without prejudice to any other remedy:

(a)   any *client*, including one of joint *clients,* or a person funding all or part of a *solicitor's fees*, may apply to the *Society* for a certificate as to whether or not interest, or a sum in lieu of interest, should have been paid and, if so, the amount; and

(b)   if the *Society* certifies that interest, or a sum in lieu of interest, should have been paid, the *solicitor* must pay the certified sum.

Notes

(i)   Applications for an interest certificate should be made to the Office for the Supervision of Solicitors (OSS). It is advisable for the client (or other person) to try to resolve the matter with the solicitor before approaching the OSS.

(ii)   If appropriate, the OSS will require the solicitor to obtain an interest calculation from the relevant bank or building society.

PART D – ACCOUNTING SYSTEMS AND RECORDS

Rule 29 – Guidelines for accounting procedures and systems

The Council of the Law Society, with the concurrence of the Master of the Rolls, may from time to time publish guidelines for accounting procedures and systems to assist *solicitors* to comply with Parts A to D of the rules, and *solicitors* may be required to justify any departure from the guidelines.

28

Notes

(i)   The current guidelines appear at Appendix 3.

(ii)   The reporting accountant does not carry out a detailed check for compliance, but has a duty to report on any substantial departures from the guidelines discovered whilst carrying out work in preparation of his or her report (see rules 43 and 44(e)).

Rule 30 – Restrictions on transfers between clients

(1)   A paper transfer of money held in a *general client account* from the ledger of one *client* to the ledger of another *client* may only be made if:

   (a)   it would have been permissible to withdraw that sum from the account under rule 22(1); and

   (b)   it would have been permissible to pay that sum into the account under rule 15;

(but there is no requirement in the case of a paper transfer for the written authority of a solicitor, etc., under rule 23(1)).

(2)   No sum in respect of a private loan from one *client* to another can be paid out of funds held for the lender either:

   (a)   by a payment from one *client account* to another;

   (b)   by a paper transfer from the ledger of the lender to that of the borrower; or

   (c)   to the borrower directly,

except with the prior written authority of both clients.

Notes

(i)   "Private loan" means a loan other than one provided by an institution which provides loans on standard terms in the normal course of its activities – rule 30(2) does not apply to loans made by an institutional lender. See also practice rule 6, which prohibits a solicitor from acting for both lender and borrower in a private mortgage at arm's length.

(ii)   If the loan is to be made by (or to) joint clients, the consent of each client must be obtained.

Rule 31 – Recognised bodies

(1)   If a *solicitors'* partnership owns a *recognised body*, the partnership and the *recognised body* must not operate shared *client accounts*, but may:

   (a)   use one set of accounting records for money held, received or paid by the partnership and the *recognised body*; and/or

   (b)   deliver a single accountant's report for both the partnership and the *recognised body*.

(2)   If a *recognised body* as nominee receives a dividend cheque made out to the *recognised body*, and forwards the cheque, either endorsed or subject to equivalent instructions, to the share-owner's *bank* or *building society*, etc., the *recognised body* will have received (and paid) *controlled trust money*. One way of complying with rule 32 (accounting records) is to keep a copy of the letter to the share-owner's *bank* or *building society*, etc., on the file, and, in accordance with rule 32(14), to keep another copy in a central book of such letters. (See also rule 32(9)(f) (retention of records for six years).)

Notes

(i)   Rule 31(1) applies equally to a recognised body owned by a sole practitioner, or by a multi-national partnership, or indeed by another recognised body.

(ii)   If a recognised body holds or receives money as executor, trustee or nominee, it is a controlled trustee.

Rule 32 – Accounting records for client accounts, etc.

Accounting records which must be kept

(1)   A *solicitor* must at all times keep accounting records properly written up to show the *solicitor's* dealings with:

(a)   *client money* received, held or paid by the *solicitor*; including *client money* held outside a *client account* under rule 16(1)(a);

(b)   *controlled trust money* received, held or paid by the *solicitor*; including *controlled trust money* held under rule 18(c) in accordance with the *trustee's* powers in an account which is not a *client account*; and

(c)   any *office money* relating to any *client* matter, or to any *controlled trust* matter.

(2)   All dealings with *client money* (whether for a *client* or other person), and with any *controlled trust money*, must be appropriately recorded:

(a)   in a client cash account or in a record of sums transferred from one client ledger account to another; and

(b)   on the client side of a separate client ledger account for each *client* (or other person, or *controlled trust*).

No other entries may be made in these records.

(3)   If s*eparate designated client accounts* are used:

(a)   a combined cash account must be kept in order to show the total amount held in *separate designated client accounts*; and

(b)   a record of the amount held for each *client* (or other person, or *controlled trust*) must be made either in a deposit column of a client ledger account, or on the client side of a client ledger account kept specifically for a *separate designated client account*, for each *client* (or other person, or *controlled trust*).

(4)   All dealings with *office money* relating to any *client* matter, or to any *controlled trust* matter, must be appropriately recorded in an office cash account and on the office side of the appropriate client ledger account.

Current balance

(5)   The current balance on each client ledger account must always be shown, or be readily ascertainable, from the records kept in accordance with paragraphs (2) and (3) above.

Acting for both lender and borrower

(6)   When acting for both lender and borrower on a mortgage advance, separate client ledger accounts for both *clients* need not be opened, provided that:

(a)   the funds belonging to each *client* are clearly identifiable; and

(b)   the lender is an institutional lender which provides mortgages on standard terms in the normal course of its activities.

28

Reconciliations

(7)   The *solicitor* must, at least once every fourteen weeks for *controlled trust money* held in passbook-operated *separate designated client accounts*, and at least once every five weeks in all other cases:

   (a)   compare the balance on the client cash account(s) with the balances shown on the statements and passbooks (after allowing for all unpresented items) of all *general client accounts* and *separate designated client accounts*, and of any account which is not a *client account* but in which the *solicitor* holds *client money* under rule 16(1)(a) (or *controlled trust money* under rule 18(c)), and any *client money* (or *controlled trust money*) held by the *solicitor* in cash; and

   (b)   as at the same date prepare a listing of all the balances shown by the client ledger accounts of the liabilities to *clients* (and other persons, and *controlled trusts*) and compare the total of those balances with the balance on the client cash account; and also

   (c)   prepare a reconciliation statement; this statement must show the cause of the difference, if any, shown by each of the above comparisons.

Bills and notifications of costs

(8)   The *solicitor* must keep readily accessible a central record or file of copies of:

   (a)   all bills given or sent by the *solicitor*; and

   (b)   all other written notifications of *costs* given or sent by the *solicitor*;

in both cases distinguishing between *fees, disbursements* not yet paid at the date of the bill, and paid *disbursements*.

Retention of records

(9)   The *solicitor* must retain for at least six years from the date of the last entry:

   (a)   all documents or other records required by paragraphs (1) to (8) above;

   (b)   all statements and passbooks, as printed and issued by the *bank, building society* or other financial institution, and/or all duplicate statements and copies of passbook entries permitted in lieu of the originals by rule 10(3) or (4), for:

      (i)   any *general client account* or *separate designated client account*;

      (ii)   any joint account held under rule 10;

      (iii)   any account which is not a *client account* but in which the *solicitor* holds *client money* under rule 16(1)(a);

      (iv)   any account which is not a *client account* but in which *controlled trust money* is held under rule 18(c); and

      (v)   any *office account* maintained in relation to the practice;

   (c)   any records kept under rule 9 (liquidators, trustees in bankruptcy, Court of Protection receivers and trustees of occupational pension schemes) including, as printed or otherwise issued, any statements, passbooks and other accounting records originating outside the *solicitor's* office;

(d)   any written instructions to withhold *client money* from a *client account* (or a copy of the *solicitor's* confirmation of oral instructions) in accordance with rule 16;

(e)   any central registers kept under paragraphs (11) to (13) below; and

(f)   any copy letters kept centrally under rule 31(2) (dividend cheques endorsed over by recognised body).

(10) The *solicitor* must retain for at least two years:

(a)   all paid cheques, unless there is a written arrangement with the *bank, building society* or other financial institution that it will retain the cheques on the *solicitor's* behalf for that period; and

(b)   originals or copies of all other authorities for the withdrawal of money from a *client account*.

Centrally kept records for certain accounts, etc.

(11) Statements and passbooks for *client money* or *controlled trust money* held outside a *client account* under rule 16(1)(a) or rule 18(c) must be kept together centrally, or the *solicitor* must maintain a central register of these accounts.

(12) Any records kept under rule 9 (liquidators, trustees in bankruptcy, Court of Protection receivers and trustees of occupational pension schemes) must be kept together centrally, or the *solicitor* must maintain a central register of the appointments.

(13) The statements, passbooks, duplicate statements and copies of passbook entries relating to any joint account held under rule 10 must be kept together centrally, or the *solicitor* must maintain a central register of all joint accounts.

(14) If a *recognised body* as nominee follows the option in rule 31(2) (keeping instruction letters for dividend payments), a central book must be kept of all instruction letters to the share-owner's *bank* or *building society*, etc.

Computerisation

(15) Records required by this rule may be kept on a computerised system, apart from the following documents, which must be retained as printed or otherwise issued:

(a)   original statements and passbooks retained under paragraph (9)(b) above;

(b)   original statements, passbooks and other accounting records retained under paragraph (9)(c) above; and

(c)   original cheques and copy authorities retained under paragraph (10) above.

There is no obligation to keep a hard copy of computerised records. However, if no hard copy is kept, the information recorded must be capable of being reproduced reasonably quickly in printed form for at least six years.

Suspense ledger accounts

(16) Suspense client ledger accounts may be used only when the *solicitor* can justify their use; for instance, for temporary use on receipt of an unidentified payment, if time is needed to establish the nature of the payment or the identity of the *client*.

28

Notes

(i)   It is strongly recommended that accounting records are written up at least weekly, even in the smallest practice, and daily in the case of larger firms.

(ii)   Rule 32(1) to (6) (general record-keeping requirements) and rule 32(7) (reconciliations) do not apply to:

(a)   solicitor liquidators, trustees in bankruptcy, Court of Protection receivers and trustees of occupational pension schemes operating in accordance with statutory rules or regulations under rule 9(1)(a);

(b)   joint accounts operated under rule 10;

(c)   a client's own account operated under rule 11; the record-keeping requirements for this type of account are set out in rule 33;

(d)   controlled trustees who instruct an outside manager to run, or continue to run, on a day-to-day basis, the business or property portfolio of an estate or trust, provided the manager keeps and retains appropriate accounting records, which are available for inspection by the Society in accordance with rule 34. (See also note (v) to rule 23.)

(iii)   When a cheque or draft is received on behalf of a client and is endorsed over, not passing through a client account, it must be recorded in the books of account as a receipt and payment on behalf of the client. The same applies to cash received and not deposited in a client account but paid out to or on behalf of a client. A cheque made payable to a client, which is forwarded to the client by the solicitor, is not client money and falls outside the rules, although it is advisable to record the action taken.

(iv)   For the purpose of rule 32, money which has been paid into a client account under rule 19(1)(c) (receipt of costs), or under rule 20(2)(b) (mixed money), and for the time being remains in a client account, is to be treated as client money; it should be recorded on the client side of the client ledger account, but must be appropriately identified.

(v)   For the purpose of rule 32, money which has been paid into an office account under rule 19(1)(b) (receipt of costs), or under rule 21(1)(b) (payments from the Legal Aid Board), and for the time being remains in an office account without breaching the rules, is to be treated as office money; it should be recorded on the office side of the client ledger account (for the individual client or for the Legal Aid Board), but must be appropriately identified.

(vi)   Some accounting systems do not retain a record of past daily balances. This does not put the solicitor in breach of rule 32(5).

(vii)   "Clearly identifiable" in rule 32(6) means that by looking at the ledger account the nature and owner of the mortgage advance are unambiguously stated. For example, if a mortgage advance of £100,000 is received from the ABC Building Society, the entry should be recorded as "£100,000, mortgage advance, ABC Building Society". It is not enough to state that the money was received from the ABC Building Society without specifying the nature of the payment, or vice versa.

(viii)   Although the solicitor does not open a separate ledger account for the lender, the mortgage advance credited to that account belongs to the lender, not to the borrower, until completion takes place. Improper removal of these mortgage funds from a client account would be a breach of rule 22.

(ix)   Reconciliations should be carried out as they fall due, and in any event no later than the due date for the next reconciliation. In the case of a separate designated client account operated with a passbook, there is no need to ask the bank, building society or other financial institution for confirmation of the balance held. In the case of other separate designated client accounts, the solicitor should either obtain statements at least monthly, or should obtain written confirmation of the balance direct from the bank, building society or other financial institution. There is no requirement to check that interest has been credited since the last statement, or the last entry in the passbook.

(x)   In making the comparisons under rule 32(7)(a) and (b), some solicitors use credits of one client against debits of another when checking total client liabilities. This is improper because it fails to show up the shortage.

(xi)   The effect of rule 32(9)(b) is that the solicitor must ensure that the bank issues hard copy statements. Statements sent from the bank to its solicitor customer by means of electronic mail, even if capable of being printed off as hard copies, will not suffice.

(xii)   Rule 32(9)(d) – retention of client's instructions to withhold money from a client account – does not require records to be kept centrally; however this may be prudent, to avoid losing the instructions if the file is passed to the client.

(xiii)   A solicitor who holds client money (or controlled trust money) in a currency other than sterling should hold that money in a separate account for the appropriate currency. Separate books of account should be kept for that currency.

Rule 33 – Accounting records for clients' own accounts

(1)   When a *solicitor* operates a *client's* own account as signatory under rule 11, the *solicitor* must retain, for at least six years from the date of the last entry, the statements or passbooks as printed and issued by the *bank, building society* or other financial institution, and/or the duplicate statements, copies of passbook entries and cheque details permitted in lieu of the originals by rule 11(3) or (4); and any central register kept under paragraph (2) below.

(2)   The *solicitor* must either keep these records together centrally, or maintain a central register of the accounts operated under rule 11.

(3)   If, when the *solicitor* ceases to operate the account, the *client* requests the original statements or passbooks, the *solicitor* must take photocopies and keep them in lieu of the originals.

(4)   This rule applies only to *solicitors* in private practice.

Note

Solicitors should remember the requirements of rule 32(8) (central record of bills, etc.).

PART E – MONITORING AND INVESTIGATION BY THE SOCIETY

Rule 34 – Production of records

(1)   Any *solicitor* must at the time and place fixed by the *Society* produce to any person appointed by the *Society* any records, papers, *client* and *controlled trust* matter files, financial accounts and other documents, and any other information, necessary to enable preparation of a report on compliance with the rules.

(2)   A requirement for production under paragraph (1) above must be in writing, and left at or sent by registered post or recorded delivery to the most recent address held by the *Society's* Regulation and Information Services department, or delivered by the *Society's* appointee. If sent through the post, receipt will be deemed 48 hours (excluding Saturdays, Sundays and Bank Holidays) after posting.

(3)   Material kept electronically must be produced in the form required by the *Society's* appointee.

28

(4)   The *Society's* appointee is entitled to seek verification from *clients* and staff, and from the *banks, building societies* and other financial institutions used by the *solicitor*. The *solicitor* must, if necessary, provide written permission for the information to be given.

(5)   The *Society's* appointee is not entitled to take original documents away but must be provided with photocopies on request.

(6)   A *solicitor* must be prepared to explain and justify any departures from the guidelines for accounting procedures and systems published by the *Society* (see rule 29).

(7)   Any report made by the *Society's* appointee may, if appropriate, be sent to the Crown Prosecution Service or the Serious Fraud Office and/or used in proceedings before the Solicitors Disciplinary Tribunal. The report may also be sent to any of the accountancy bodies set out in rule 37(1)(a) and/or taken into account by the *Society* in relation to a possible disqualification of a reporting accountant under rule 37(3).

Notes

(i)   "Solicitor" in rule 34 (as elsewhere in the rules) includes any person to whom the rules apply – see rule 2(2)(x), rule 4 and note (ii) to rule 4.

(ii)   The Society's powers override any confidence or privilege between solicitor and client.

(iii)   The Society's monitoring and investigation powers are exercised by the Monitoring and Investigation Unit of the Office for the Supervision of Solicitors.

(iv)   Reasons are never given for a visit by the Monitoring and Investigation Unit, so as:

(a)   to safeguard the Society's sources of information; and

(b)   not to alert a defaulting principal or employee to conceal or compound his or her misappropriations.

Some visits are made at random.

PART F – ACCOUNTANTS' REPORTS

Rule 35 – Delivery of accountants' reports

(1)   A *solicitor, registered foreign lawyer* or *recognised body* who or which has, at any time during an *accounting period*, held or received *client money* or *controlled trust money*, or operated a *client's* own account as signatory, must deliver to the *Society* an accountant's report for that *accounting period* within six months of the end of the *accounting period*.

(2)   A *recognised body* which has not, at any time during an *accounting period*, held or received *client money* or *controlled trust money*, or operated a *client's* own account as signatory, must deliver to the *Society* a declaration to that effect within six months of the end of the *accounting period*. The declaration must be signed by one of its directors.

Notes

(i)   Section 34 of the Solicitors Act 1974 requires every solicitor to deliver an accountant's report once in every twelve months ending 31st October, unless the Society is satisfied that this is unnecessary. This provision is applied to recognised bodies by the Administration of Justice Act 1985, Schedule 2, paragraph 5(1). The Courts and Legal Services Act 1990, Schedule 14, paragraph 8(1) imposes the same duty on registered foreign lawyers. In general, the Society is satisfied that no report is necessary when the rules do not require a report to be delivered, but this is without prejudice to the Society's overriding discretion. In addition, a condition imposed on a solicitor's practising certificate under section 12(4)(b) of the Solicitors Act 1974 may require the solicitor to deliver accountant's reports at more frequent intervals.

(ii) A solicitor who practises only in one or more of the ways set out in rule 5 is exempt from the rules, and therefore does not have to deliver an accountant's report.

(iii) The requirement for a registered foreign lawyer to deliver an accountant's report applies only to a registered foreign lawyer practising as a partner in a multi-national partnership.

(iv) The form of report is dealt with in rule 47.

(v) When client money is held or received by a practice, the principals in the practice (including those held out as principals) will have held or received client money. A salaried partner whose name is included in the list of partners on a firm's letterhead, even if the name appears under a separate heading of "salaried partners" or "associate partners", has been held out as a principal. In the case of an incorporated practice, it is the company (i.e. the recognised body) which will have held or received client money.

(vi) Assistant solicitors and consultants do not normally hold client money. An assistant solicitor or consultant might be a signatory for a firm's client account, but this does not constitute holding or receiving client money. If a client or third party hands cash to an assistant solicitor or consultant, the principals (rather than the assistant solicitor or consultant) are regarded as having received and held the money.

(vii) If, exceptionally, an assistant solicitor or consultant has a client account (for example, as a controlled trustee), or operates a client's own account as signatory, the assistant solicitor or consultant will have to deliver an accountant's report. The assistant solicitor or consultant can be included in the report of the practice, but must ensure that his or her name is added, and an explanation given.

(viii) A solicitor to whom a cheque or draft is made out, and who in the course of practice endorses it over to a client or employer, has received (and paid) client money. That solicitor will have to deliver an accountant's report, even if no other client money has been held or received.

(ix) When only a small number of transactions is undertaken or a small volume of client money is handled in an accounting period, a waiver of the obligation to deliver a report may sometimes be granted. Applications should be made to Regulation and Information Services [for contact details see p.xv].

(x) If a solicitors' partnership owns a recognised body, the partnership and the company may deliver a single accountant's report (see rule 31(1)(b)).

Rule 36 – Accounting periods

The norm

28

(1) An "accounting period" means the period for which the accounts of the *solicitor* are ordinarily made up, except that it must:

(a) begin at the end of the previous *accounting period*; and

(b) cover twelve months.

Paragraphs (2) to (5) below set out exceptions.

First and resumed reports

(2)   For a *solicitor* who is under a duty to deliver his or her first report, the *accounting period* must begin on the date when the *solicitor* first held or received *client money* or *controlled trust money* (or operated a *client's* own account as signatory), and may cover less than twelve months.

(3)   For a *solicitor* who is under a duty to deliver his or her first report after a break, the *accounting period* must begin on the date when the *solicitor* for the first time after the break held or received *client money* or *controlled trust money* (or operated a *client's* own account as signatory), and may cover less than twelve months.

Change of accounting period

(4)   If a practice changes the period for which its accounts are made up (for example, on a merger, or simply for convenience), the *accounting period* immediately preceding the change may be shorter than twelve months, or longer than twelve months up to a maximum of 18 months.

Final reports

(5)   A *solicitor* who for any reason stops holding or receiving *client money* or *controlled trust money* (and operating any *client's* own account as signatory) must deliver a final report. The *accounting period* must end on the date upon which the *solicitor* stopped holding or receiving *client money* or *controlled trust money* (and operating any *client's* own account as signatory), and may cover less than twelve months.

Notes

(i)   In the case of solicitors joining or leaving a continuing partnership, any accountant's report for the practice as a whole will show the names and dates of the principals joining or leaving. For a solicitor who did not previously hold or receive client money, etc., and has become a principal in the firm, the report for the practice will represent, from the date of joining, the solicitor's first report for the purpose of rule 36(2). For a solicitor who was a principal in the firm and, on leaving, stops holding or receiving client money, etc., the report for the practice will represent, up to the date of leaving, the solicitor's final report for the purpose of rule 36(5) above.

(ii)   When a partnership splits up, it is usually appropriate for the books to be made up as at the date of dissolution, and for an accountant's report to be delivered within six months of that date. If, however, the old partnership continues to hold or receive client money, etc., in connection with outstanding matters, accountant's reports will continue to be required for those matters; the books should then be made up on completion of the last of those matters and a report delivered within six months of that date. The same would be true for a sole practitioner winding up matters on retirement.

(iii)   When a practice is being wound up, the solicitor may be left with money which is unattributable, or belongs to a client who cannot be traced. It may be appropriate to apply to the Society for authority to withdraw this money from the solicitor's client account – see rule 22(1)(h), rule 22(2)(h), and note (viii) to rule 22.

Rule 37 – Qualifications for making a report

(1)   A report must be prepared and signed by an accountant

(a)   who is a member of:

(i)   the Institute of Chartered Accountants in England and Wales;

(ii)   the Institute of Chartered Accountants of Scotland;

(iii)   the Association of Chartered Certified Accountants;

(iv)   the Institute of Chartered Accountants in Ireland; or

(v)   the Association of Authorised Public Accountants; **and**

(b)   who is also:

(i)   an individual who is a registered auditor within the terms of section 35(1)(a) of the Companies Act 1989; or

(ii)   an employee of such an individual; or

(iii)   a partner in or employee of a partnership which is a registered auditor within the terms of section 35(1)(a) of the Companies Act 1989; or

(iv)   a director or employee of a company which is a registered auditor within the terms of section 35(1)(a) of the Companies Act 1989.

(2)   An accountant is not qualified to make a report if:

(a)   at any time between the beginning of the *accounting period* to which the report relates, and the completion of the report:

(i)   he or she was a partner, employee or officer in the practice to which the report relates; or

(ii)   he or she was employed by the same non-solicitor employer as the *solicitor* for whom the report is being made; or

(b)   he or she has been disqualified under paragraph (3) below and notice of disqualification has been given under paragraph (4) (and has not subsequently been withdrawn).

(3)   The *Society* may disqualify an accountant from making any accountant's report if:

(a)   the accountant has been found guilty by his or her professional body of professional misconduct or discreditable conduct; or

(b)   the *Society* is satisfied that a *solicitor* has not complied with the rules in respect of matters which the accountant has negligently failed to specify in a report.

In coming to a decision, the *Society* will take into account any representations made by the accountant or his or her professional body.

(4)   Written notice of disqualification must be left at or sent by registered post or recorded delivery to the address of the accountant shown on an accountant's report or in the records of the accountant's professional body. If sent through the post, receipt will be deemed 48 hours (excluding Saturdays, Sundays and Bank Holidays) after posting.

28

(5) An accountant's disqualification may be notified to any *solicitor* likely to be affected and may be printed in the Law Society's Gazette or other publication.

Note

It is not a breach of the rules for a solicitor to retain an outside accountant to write up the books of account and to instruct the same accountant to prepare the accountant's report. However, the accountant will have to disclose these circumstances in the report – see the form of report in Appendix 5.

Rule 38 – Reporting accountant's rights and duties – letter of engagement

(1) The *solicitor* must ensure that the reporting accountant's rights and duties are stated in a letter of engagement incorporating the following terms:

"In accordance with rule 38 of the Solicitors' Accounts Rules 1998, you are instructed as follows:

(i) that you may, and are encouraged to, report directly to the Law Society without prior reference to me/this firm/this company should you, during the course of carrying out work in preparation of the accountant's report, discover evidence of theft or fraud affecting client money, controlled trust money, or money in a client's own account operated by a solicitor (or registered foreign lawyer, or recognised body) as signatory; or information which is likely to be of material significance in determining whether any solicitor (or registered foreign lawyer, or recognised body) is a fit and proper person to hold client money or controlled trust money, or to operate a client's own account as signatory;

(ii) to report directly to the Law Society should your appointment be terminated following the issue of, or indication of intention to issue, a qualified accountant's report, or following the raising of concerns prior to the preparation of an accountant's report;

(iii) to deliver to me/this firm/this company with your report the completed checklist required by rule 46 of the Solicitors' Accounts Rules 1998; to retain for at least three years from the date of signature a copy of the completed checklist; and to produce the copy to the Law Society on request;

(iv) to retain these terms of engagement for at least three years after the termination of the retainer and to produce them to the Law Society on request; and

(v) following any direct report made to the Law Society under (i) or (ii) above, to provide to the Law Society on request any further relevant information in your possession or in the possession of your firm.

To the extent necessary to enable you to comply with (i) to (v) above, I/we waive my/the firm's/the company's right of confidentiality. This waiver extends to any report made, document produced or information disclosed to the Law Society in good faith pursuant to these instructions, even though it may subsequently transpire that you were mistaken in your belief that there was cause for concern."

(2) The letter of engagement and a copy must be signed by the *solicitor* (or by a partner or director) and by the accountant. The *solicitor* must keep the copy of the signed letter of engagement for at least three years after the termination of the retainer and produce it to the *Society* on request.

Notes

(i)   Any direct report by the accountant to the Society under rule 38(1)(i) or (ii) should be made to the Office for the Supervision of Solicitors.

(ii)   Rule 38(1) envisages that the specified terms are incorporated in a letter from the solicitor to the accountant. Instead, the specified terms may be included in a letter from the accountant to the solicitor setting out the terms of the engagement. If so, the text must be adapted appropriately. The letter must be signed in duplicate by both parties – the solicitor will keep the original, and the accountant the copy.

Rule 39 – Change of accountant

On instructing an accountancy practice to replace that previously instructed to produce accountant's reports, the *solicitor* must immediately notify the *Society* of the change and provide the name and business address of the new accountancy practice.

Rule 40 – Place of examination

Unless there are exceptional circumstances, the place of examination of a *solicitor's* accounting records, files and other relevant documents must be the *solicitor's* office and not the office of the accountant. This does not prevent an initial electronic transmission of data to the accountant for examination at the accountant's office with a view to reducing the time which needs to be spent at the solicitor's office.

Rule 41 – Provision of details of bank accounts etc.

The accountant must request, and the *solicitor* must provide, details of all accounts kept or operated by the *solicitor* in connection with the *solicitor's* practice at any *bank*, *building society* or other financial institution at any time during the *accounting period* to which the report relates. This includes *client accounts, office accounts,* accounts which are not *client accounts* but which contain *client money* or *controlled trust money*, and *clients'* own accounts operated by the *solicitor* as signatory.

Rule 42 – Test procedures

(1)   The accountant must examine the accounting records (including statements and passbooks), *client* and *controlled trust* matter files selected by the accountant as and when appropriate, and other relevant documents of the *solicitor*, and make the following checks and tests:

    (a)   confirm that the accounting system in every office of the *solicitor* complies with:

        ► rule 32 – accounting records for client accounts, etc.;

        ► rule 33 – accounting records for clients' own accounts;

        ► (for all *solicitors* authorised by the *Society* to conduct investment business) rule 14 of the Solicitors' Investment Business Rules 1995 – record of commissions;

        ► (for those *solicitors* authorised by the *Society* to conduct discrete investment business) rule 26 of the Solicitors' Investment Business Rules 1995 – bills of costs;

    and is so designed that:

28

(i) an appropriate client ledger account is kept for each *client* (or other person for whom *client money* is received, held or paid) and each *controlled trust*;

(ii) the client ledger accounts show separately from other information details of all *client money* and *controlled trust money* received, held or paid on account of each *client* (or other person for whom *client money* is received, held or paid) and each *controlled trust*; and

(iii) transactions relating to *client money, controlled trust money* and any other money dealt with through a *client account* are recorded in the accounting records in a way which distinguishes them from transactions relating to any other money received, held or paid by the *solicitor*;

(b) make test checks of postings to the client ledger accounts from records of receipts and payments of *client money* and *controlled trust money*, and make test checks of the casts of these accounts and records;

(c) compare a sample of payments into and from the *client accounts* as shown in *bank* and *building society* statements or passbooks with the *solicitor's* records of receipts and payments of *client money* and *controlled trust money*;

(d) test check the system of recording *costs* and of making transfers in respect of *costs* from the *client accounts*;

(e) make a test examination of a selection of documents requested from the *solicitor* in order to confirm:

(i) that the financial transactions (including those giving rise to transfers from one client ledger account to another) evidenced by such documents comply with Parts A and B of the rules, rule 30 (restrictions on transfers between clients) and rule 31 (recognised bodies); and

(ii) that the entries in the accounting records reflect those transactions in a manner complying with rule 32;

(f) subject to paragraph (2) below, extract (or check extractions of) balances on the client ledger accounts during the *accounting period* under review at not fewer than two dates selected by the accountant (one of which may be the last day of the *accounting period*), and at each date:

(i) compare the total shown by the client ledger accounts of the liabilities to the *clients* (or other persons for whom *client money* is held) and *controlled trusts* with the cash account balance; and

(ii) reconcile that cash account balance with the balances held in the *client accounts*, and accounts which are not *client accounts* but in which *client money* or *controlled trust money* is held, as confirmed direct to the accountant by the relevant *banks, building societies* and other financial institutions;

(g) confirm that reconciliation statements have been made and kept in accordance with rule 32(7) and (9)(a);

(h) make a test examination of the client ledger accounts to see whether payments from the *client account* have been made on any individual account in excess of money held on behalf of that *client* (or other person for whom *client money* is held) or *controlled trust*;

(i) check the office ledgers, office cash accounts and the statements provided by the *bank, building society* or other financial institution for any *office account* maintained by the *solicitor* in connection with the practice, to see whether any *client money* or *controlled trust money* has been improperly paid into an *office account* or, if properly paid into an *office account* under rule 19(1)(b) or rule 21(1), has been kept there in breach of the rules;

(j) check the accounting records kept under rule 32(9)(d) and (11) for *client money* held outside a *client account* to ascertain what transactions have been effected in respect of this money and to confirm that the *client* has given appropriate instructions under rule 16(1)(a);

(k) make a test examination of the client ledger accounts to see whether rule 32(6) (accounting records when acting for both lender and borrower) has been complied with;

(l) for liquidators, trustees in bankruptcy, Court of Protection receivers and trustees of occupational pension schemes, check that records are being kept in accordance with rule 32(8), (9)(c) and (12), and cross-check transactions with *client* or *controlled trust* matter files when appropriate;

(m) check that statements and passbooks and/or duplicate statements and copies of passbook entries are being kept in accordance with rule 32(9)(b)(ii) and (13) (record-keeping requirements for joint accounts), and cross-check transactions with *client* matter files when appropriate;

(n) check that statements and passbooks and/or duplicate statements, copies of passbook entries and cheque details are being kept in accordance with rule 33 (record-keeping requirements for clients' own accounts), and cross-check transactions with *client* matter files when appropriate;

(o) check that interest earned on *separate designated client accounts*, and in accounts opened on *clients'* instructions under rule 16(1)(a), is credited in accordance with rule 24(1) and (6)(a), and note (i) to rule 24; and

(p) ask for any information and explanations required as a result of making the above checks and tests.

Extracting balances

(2) For the purposes of paragraph (1)(f) above, if a *solicitor* uses a computerised or mechanised system of accounting which automatically produces an extraction of all client ledger balances, the accountant need not check all client ledger balances extracted on the list produced by the computer or machine against the individual records of client ledger accounts, provided the accountant:

(a) confirms that a satisfactory system of control is in operation and the accounting records are in balance;

(b) carries out a test check of the extraction against the individual records; and

(c) states in the report that he or she has relied on this exception.

28

Notes

(i)   The rules do not require a complete audit of the solicitor's accounts nor do they require the preparation of a profit and loss account or balance sheet.

(ii)   In making the comparisons under rule 42(1)(f), some accountants improperly use credits of one client against debits of another when checking total client liabilities, thus failing to disclose a shortage. A debit balance on a client account when no funds are held for that client results in a shortage which must be disclosed as a result of the comparison.

(iii)   The main purpose of confirming balances direct with banks, etc., under rule 42(1)(f)(ii) is to ensure that the solicitor's records accurately reflect the sums held at the bank. The accountant is not expected to conduct an active search for undisclosed accounts.

Rule 43 – Departures from guidelines for accounting procedures and systems

The accountant should be aware of the Council's guidelines for accounting procedures and systems (see rule 29), and must note in the accountant's report any substantial departures from the guidelines discovered whilst carrying out work in preparation of the report. (See also rule 44(e).)

Rule 44 – Matters outside the accountant's remit

The accountant is not required:

(a)   to extend his or her enquiries beyond the information contained in the documents produced, supplemented by any information and explanations given by the *solicitor*;

(b)   to enquire into the stocks, shares, other securities or documents of title held by the *solicitor* on behalf of the *solicitor's clients*;

(c)   to consider whether the accounting records of the *solicitor* have been properly written up at any time other than the time at which his or her examination of the accounting records takes place;

(d)   to check compliance with the provisions in rule 24(2) to (5) and (6)(b) on payment of sums in lieu of interest; or

(e)   to make a detailed check on compliance with the guidelines for accounting procedures and systems (see rules 29 and 43).

Rule 45 – Privileged documents

A *solicitor,* acting on a *client's* instructions, always has the right on the grounds of privilege as between *solicitor* and *client* to decline to produce any document requested by the accountant for the purposes of his or her examination. In these circumstances, the accountant must qualify the report and set out the circumstances.

Rule 46 – Completion of checklist

The accountant should exercise his or her professional judgment in adopting a suitable "audit" programme, but must also complete and sign a checklist in the form published from time to time by the Council of the Law Society. The *solicitor* must obtain the completed checklist, retain it for at least three years from the date of signature and produce it to the *Society* on request.

Notes

(i)   The current checklist appears at Appendix 4. It is issued by the Society to solicitors at the appropriate time for completion by their reporting accountants.

(ii)   The letter of engagement required by rule 38 imposes a duty on the accountant to hand the completed checklist to the solicitor, to keep a copy for three years and to produce the copy to the Society on request.

Rule 47 – Form of accountant's report

The accountant must complete and sign his or her report in the form published from time to time by the Council of the Law Society.

Notes

(i)   The current form of accountant's report appears at Appendix 5.

(ii)   The form of report is prepared and issued by the Society to solicitors at the appropriate time for completion by their reporting accountants. Separate reports can be delivered for each principal in a partnership but most firms deliver one report in the name of all the principals. For assistant solicitors and consultants, see rule 35, notes (vi) and (vii).

(iii)   Although it may be agreed that the accountant send the report direct to the Society, the responsibility for delivery is that of the solicitor. The form of report requires the accountant to confirm that either a copy of the report has been sent to each of the solicitors (and registered foreign lawyers) to whom the report relates, or a copy of the report has been sent to a named partner on behalf of all the partners in the firm. A similar confirmation is required for a report which relates to a recognised body.

(iv)   A reporting accountant is not required to report on trivial breaches due to clerical errors or mistakes in book-keeping, provided that they have been rectified on discovery and the accountant is satisfied that no client suffered any loss as a result.

(v)   In many practices, clerical and book-keeping errors will arise. In the majority of cases these may be classified by the reporting accountant as trivial breaches. However, a "trivial breach" cannot be precisely defined. The amount involved, the nature of the breach, whether the breach is deliberate or accidental, how often the same breach has occurred, and the time outstanding before correction (especially the replacement of any shortage) are all factors which should be considered by the accountant before deciding whether a breach is trivial.

(vi)   The Society receives a number of reports which are qualified only by reference to trivial breaches, but which show a significant difference between liabilities to clients and client money held in client and other accounts. An explanation for this difference, from either the accountant or the solicitor, must be given.

(vii)   Accountants' reports should be sent to Regulation and Information Services [for contact details see p.xv].

(viii)   For direct reporting by the accountant to the Society in cases of concern, see rule 38 and note (i) to that rule.

28

Rule 48 – Practices with two or more places of business

If a practice has two or more offices:

(a)   separate reports may be delivered in respect of the different offices; and

(b)   separate *accounting periods* may be adopted for different offices, provided that:

(i) separate reports are delivered;

(ii) every office is covered by a report delivered within six months of the end of its *accounting period*; and

(iii) there are no gaps between the *accounting periods* covered by successive reports for any particular office or offices.

Rule 49 – Waivers

The *Society* may waive in writing in any particular case or cases any of the provisions of Part F of the rules, and may revoke any waiver.

Note

Applications for waivers should be made to Regulation and Information Services [for contact details see p.xv]. In appropriate cases, solicitors may be granted a waiver of the obligation to deliver an accountant's report (see rule 35, and note (ix) to that rule). The circumstances in which a waiver of any other provision of Part F would be given must be extremely rare.

PART G – COMMENCEMENT

Rule 50 – Commencement

(1) These rules must be implemented not later than 1st May 2000; until a practice implements these rules, it must continue to operate the Solicitors' Accounts Rules 1991.

(2) Practices opting to implement these rules before 1st May 2000 must implement them in their entirety, and not selectively.

(3) Part F of the rules (accountants' reports) will apply to:

(a) reports covering any period of time after 30th April 2000; and also

(b) reports covering any earlier period of time for which a practice has opted to operate these rules.

(4) The Accountant's Report Rules 1991 will continue to apply to:

(a) reports covering any period of time before 22nd July 1998; and also

(b) reports covering any period of time after 21st July 1998 and before 1st May 2000 during which a practice continued to operate the Solicitors' Accounts Rules 1991.

(5) If a practice operated the Solicitors' Accounts Rules 1991 for part of an *accounting period*, and these rules for the rest of the *accounting period*, the practice may, in respect of that *accounting period* ("the transitional accounting period") either:

(a) deliver a single accountant's report covering the whole of the transitional accounting period, made partly under the Accountant's Report Rules 1991 and partly under Part F of these rules, as appropriate; or

(b) deliver a separate accountant's report for each part of the transitional accounting period, one under the Accountant's Report Rules 1991 and the other under Part F of these rules; or

(c)   deliver a report under the Accountant's Report Rules 1991 to cover that part of the transitional accounting period during which the practice operated the Solicitors' Accounts Rules 1991; and subsequently a report under Part F of these rules to cover the remaining part of the transitional accounting period plus the whole of the next *accounting period*; or

(d)   deliver a report under the Accountant's Report Rules 1991 to cover the last complete *accounting period* during which the practice operated the Solicitors' Accounts Rules 1991 plus that part of the transitional accounting period during which the practice continued to operate those rules; and subsequently a report under Part F of these rules to cover the remaining part of the transitional accounting period.

28

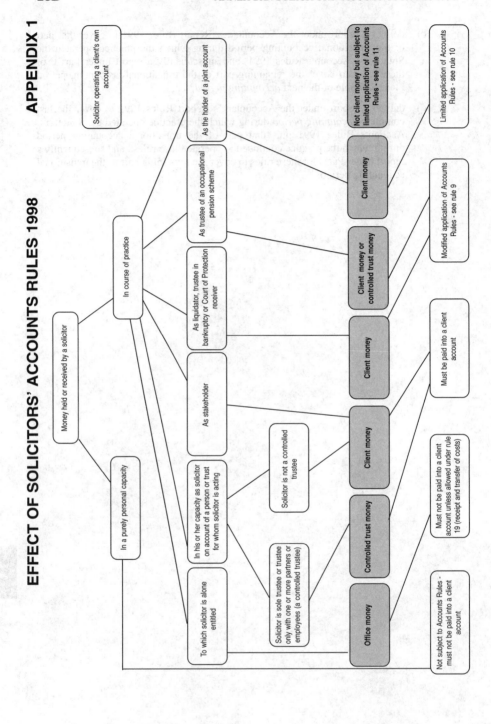

APPENDIX 1

EFFECT OF SOLICITORS' ACCOUNTS RULES 1998

APPENDIX 2

SPECIAL SITUATIONS – WHAT APPLIES

	Is it client money?	Subject to reconciliations?	Keep books?	Retain statements?	Subject to Accountant's Report?	Produce records to Law Society?	Deposit Interest?	Retain records generally?	Central records?	Subject to reporting accountant's comparisons?
1 Controlled trust money in client a/c – r.15(1)	No	Yes – r.32(7)	Yes – r.32(1) and (2)	Yes – r.32(9)	Yes – r.42 – same as for client money	Yes – r.34	All interest goes to trust	Yes – r.32(9)	Bills – r.32(8)	Yes – r.42(1)(f) – same as for client money
2 Controlled trust money held outside a client account – r.18	No	Yes – r.32(7)	Yes – r.32(1) and (2)	Yes – r.32(9)	Yes – r.42 – same as for client money	Yes – r.34	All interest goes to trust	Yes – r.32(9)	Bills – r.32(8)	Yes – r.42(1)(f) – same as for client money
3 R.16(1)(a) a/cs in solicitor's name (not client a/c)	Yes	Yes	Yes – r.32(1)(a) and 32(2)	Yes – r.32(9)	Yes	Yes	Yes – r.24	Yes – r.32(9)	Statements or register – r.32(11), bills – r.32(8)	Yes – r.42(1)(f)
4 R.16(1)(b) a/cs in name of client – not operated by solicitor	No	No	No-record solicitor's receipt and payment only	No	No	No	No – all interest earned for client – r.24, note (iii)	No – except record of solicitor's receipt and payment	Bills – r.32(8)	No
5 R.16(1)(b) a/cs in name of client – operated by solicitor	No	No	No-record solicitor's receipt and payment only	Yes – r.33	No	No	No – all interest earned for client – r.24, note (iii)	No – except record of solicitor's receipt and payment		No
6 Liquidators, trustees in bankruptcy and Court of Protection receivers	Yes – r.9	No – r.9	Modified-statutory records – r.9	Yes – r.9 and r.32(9)(c)	Limited – r.42(1)(l)	Yes – r.9	No – r.9 – comply with statutory rules	Yes – modified r.32(9)(c)	Statements – r.33, Bills r.32(8)	No – r.9
7 Trustees of occupational pension schemes	Will be either client money or controlled trust money	No – r.9	Modified – statutory records – r.9	Yes – r.9 and r.32(9)(c)	Limited – r.42(1)(l)	Yes – r.9	No – r.9 – comply with statutory rules	Yes – modified r.32(9)(c)	Yes – r.32(12) Bills r.32(8)	No – r.9
8 Joint accounts – r.10	Yes – r.10	No – r.10	No – r.10	Yes – r.10 and 32(9)(b)(ii)	Limited – r.42(1)(m)	Yes – r.10	No. For joint a/c with client, all interest to client(r.24, note (x)); for joint a/c with sol. depends on agreement	No – r.10	Statements – r.32(13) Bills – r.32(8)	No – r.10
9 Solicitor acting under power of attorney	Yes	Yes	Yes	Yes	Yes	Yes	Yes	Yes	Bills – r.32(8)	Yes
10 Solicitor operates client's own a/c e.g. under power of attorney – r.11	No	No	No	Yes – r.33	Limited – r.42(1)(n)	Yes – r.11	No – all interest earned for client (r.24, note (iii))	No – r.11	Statements – r.33, Bills – r.32(8)	No
11 Exempt solicitors under r.5	No	No	No	No	No	No	No	No	No	No

28

APPENDIX 3

LAW SOCIETY GUIDELINES
ACCOUNTING PROCEDURES AND SYSTEMS

1. Introduction

1.1 These guidelines, published under rule 29 of the Solicitors' Accounts Rules 1998, are intended to be a benchmark or broad statement of good practice requirements which should be present in an effective regime for the proper control of client money and controlled trust money. They should therefore be of positive assistance to firms in establishing or reviewing appropriate procedures and systems. They do not override, or detract from the need to comply fully with, the accounts rules.

1.2 It should be noted that these guidelines apply equally to client money and to controlled trust money.

1.3 References to partners or firms in the guidelines are intended to include sole practitioners, recognised bodies and their directors.

2. General

2.1 Compliance with the accounts rules is the equal responsibility of all partners in a firm. They should establish policies and systems to ensure that the firm complies fully with the rules. Responsibility for day-to-day supervision may be delegated to one or more partners to enable effective control to be exercised. Delegation of total responsibility to a cashier or book-keeper is not acceptable.

2.2 The firm should hold a copy of the current version of the Solicitors' Accounts Rules. The person who maintains the books of account must have a full knowledge of the requirements of the rules and the accounting requirements of solicitors' firms.

2.3 Proper books of account should be maintained on the double-entry principle. They should be legible, up to date and contain narratives with the entries which identify and/or provide adequate information about the transaction. Entries should be made in chronological order and the current balance should be shown on client ledger accounts, or be readily ascertainable, in accordance with rule 32(5).

2.4 Ledger accounts for clients, other persons or controlled trusts should include the name of the client or other person or controlled trust and contain a heading which provides a description of the matter or transaction.

2.5 Separate designated client accounts should be brought within the ambit of the systems and procedures for the control of client money and controlled trust money – including reconciliations (see 5.4 below).

2.6 Manual systems for recording client money and controlled trust money are capable of complying with these guidelines and there is no requirement on firms to adopt computerised systems. A computer system, with suitable support procedures will, however, usually provide an efficient means of producing the accounts and associated control information.

2.7   If a computer system is introduced care must be taken to ensure:

(1)   that balances transferred from the old books of account are reconciled with the opening balances held on the new system before day-to-day operation commences;

(2)   that the new system operates correctly before the old system is abandoned. This may require a period of parallel running of the old and new systems and the satisfactory reconciliation of the two sets of records before the old system ceases.

2.8   The firm should ensure that office account entries in relation to each client or controlled trust matter are maintained up to date as well as the client account entries. Credit balances on office account in respect of client or controlled trust matters should be fully investigated.

2.9   The firm should operate a system to identify promptly situations which may require the payment of deposit interest to clients.

3.   Receipt of client money and controlled trust money

3.1   The firm should have procedures for identifying client money and controlled trust money, including cash, when received in the firm, and for promptly recording the receipt of the money either in the books of account or a register for later posting to the client cash book and ledger accounts. The procedures should cover money received through the post, electronically or direct by fee earners or other personnel. They should also cover the safekeeping of money prior to payment to bank.

3.2   The firm should have a system which ensures that client money and controlled trust money is paid promptly into a client account.

3.3   The firm should have a system for identifying money which should not be in a client account and for transferring it without delay.

3.4   The firm should determine a policy and operate a system for dealing with money which is a mixture of office money and client money (or controlled trust money), in compliance with rules 19–21.

4.   Payments from client account

4.1   The firm should have clear procedures for ensuring that all withdrawals from client accounts are properly authorised. In particular, suitable persons, consistent with rule 23(1), should be named for the following purposes:

(1)   authorisation of internal payment vouchers;

(2)   signing client account cheques;

(3)   authorising telegraphic or electronic transfers.

No other personnel should be allowed to authorise or sign the documents.

4.2   Persons nominated for the purpose of authorising internal payment vouchers should, for each payment, ensure there is supporting evidence showing clearly the reason for the payment, and the date of it. Similarly, persons signing cheques and authorising transfers should ensure there is a suitable voucher or other supporting evidence to support the payment.

28

4.3   The firm should have a system for checking the balances on client ledger accounts to ensure no debit balances occur. Where payments are to be made other than out of cleared funds, clear policies and procedures must be in place to ensure that adequate risk assessment is applied.

> *N.B. If incoming payments are ultimately dishonoured, a debit balance will arise, in breach of the rules, and full replacement of the shortfall will be required under rule 7. See also rule 22, notes (v) and (vi).*

4.4   The firm should establish systems for the transfer of costs from client account to office account in accordance with rule 19(2) and (3). Normally transfers should be made only on the basis of rendering a bill or written notification. The payment from the client account should be by way of a cheque or transfer in favour of the firm or sole principal – see rule 23(3)).

4.5   The firm should establish policies and operate systems to control and record accurately any transfers between clients of the firm. Where these arise as a result of loans between clients, the written authority of both the lender and borrower must be obtained in accordance with rule 30(2).

5.   Overall control of client accounts

5.1   The firm should maintain control of all its bank and building society accounts opened for the purpose of holding client money and controlled trust money. In the case of a joint account, a suitable degree of control should be exercised.

5.2   Central records or central registers must be kept in respect of:

(1)   accounts held for client money, or controlled trust money, which are not client accounts (rules 16(1)(a), 18(c) and 32(11));

(2)   practice as a liquidator, trustee in bankruptcy, Court of Protection receiver or trustee of an occupational pension scheme (rules 9 and 32(12));

(3)   joint accounts (rules 10 and 32(13));

(4)   dividend payments received by a recognised body as nominee (rules 31(2) and 32(14)); and

(5)   clients' own accounts (rules 11, 16(1)(b) and 33(2)).

5.3   In addition, there should be a master list of all:

▶   general client accounts;

▶   separate designated client accounts;

▶   accounts held in respect of 5.2 above; and

▶   office accounts.

The master list should show the current status of each account; e.g. currently in operation or closed with date of closure.

5.4   The firm should operate a system to ensure that accurate reconciliations of the client accounts, whether comprising client and/or controlled trust money, are carried out at least every five weeks or, in the case of passbook-operated separate designated client accounts for controlled trust money, every 14 weeks. In particular it should ensure that:

(1)   a full list of client ledger balances is produced. Any debit balances should be listed, fully investigated and rectified immediately. The total of any debit balances cannot be "netted off" against the total of credit balances;

(2)   a full list of unpresented cheques is produced;

(3)   a list of outstanding lodgments is produced;

(4)   formal statements are produced reconciling the client account cash book balances, aggregate client ledger balances and the client bank accounts. All unresolved differences must be investigated and, where appropriate, corrective action taken;

(5)   a partner checks the reconciliation statement and any corrective action, and ensures that enquiries are made into any unusual or apparently unsatisfactory items or still unresolved matters.

5.5   Where a computerised system is used, the firm should have clear policies, systems and procedures to control access to client accounts by determining the personnel who should have "write to" and "read only" access. Passwords should be held confidentially by designated personnel and changed regularly to maintain security. Access to the system should not unreasonably be restricted to a single person nor should more people than necessary be given access.

5.6   The firm should establish policies and systems for the retention of the accounting records to ensure:

▶   books of account, reconciliations, bills, bank statements and passbooks are kept for at least six years;

▶   paid cheques and other authorities for the withdrawal of money from a client account are kept for at least two years;

▶   other vouchers and internal expenditure authorisation documents relating directly to entries in the client account books are kept for at least two years.

5.7   The firm should ensure that unused client account cheques are stored securely to prevent unauthorised access. Blank cheques should not be pre-signed. Any cancelled cheques should be retained.

28

REPORTING ACCOUNTANT'S CHECKLIST

APPENDIX 4

SOLICITORS' ACCOUNTS RULES 1998

The following items have been tested to satisfy the examination requirements under rules 41 - 43, with the results as indicated. Where the position has been found to be unsatisfactory as a result of these tests, further details have been reported in section 6 of this checklist or reported by separate appendix.

THE LAW SOCIETY

Name of practice	

Results of test checks:

1. For all client money and controlled trust money	Satisfactory (Tick the appropriate column)		If 'no' should breaches be noted in the accountant's report		Cross references to audit file documentation
(a) Book-keeping system for every office:	Yes	No	Yes	No	
(i) The accounting records satisfactorily distinguish client money and controlled trust money from all other money dealt with by the firm.					
(ii) A separate ledger account is maintained for each client and controlled trust (excepting section (l) below) and the particulars of all client money and controlled trust money received, held or paid on account of each client and controlled trust, including funds held on separate designated deposits, or elsewhere, are recorded.					
(iii) The client ledgers for clients and controlled trusts show a current balance at all times, or the current balance is readily ascertainable.					
(iv) A record of all bills of costs and written notifications has been maintained, which distinguishes profit costs from disbursements, either in the form of a central record or a file of copies of such bills.					
(b) Postings to ledger accounts and casts:	Yes	No	Yes	No	
(i) Postings to ledger accounts for clients and controlled trusts from records of receipts and payments are correct.					
(ii) Casts of ledger accounts for clients and controlled trusts and receipts and payments records are correct.					
(iii) Postings have been recorded in chronological sequence with the date being that of the initiation of the transaction.					
(c) Receipts and payments of client money and controlled trust money:	Yes	No	Yes	No	
(i) Sample receipts and payments of client money and controlled trust money as shown in bank and building society statements have been compared with the solicitor's records of receipts and payments of client money and controlled trust money, and are correct.					
(ii) Sample paid cheques have been obtained and details agreed to receipts and payment records.					
(d) System of recording costs and making transfers:	Yes	No	Yes	No	
(i) The firm's system of recording costs has been ascertained and is suitable.					
(ii) Costs have been drawn only where required for or towards payment of the firm's costs where there has been sent to the client a bill of costs or other written notification of the amount of the costs.					
(e) Examination of documents for verification of transactions and entries in accounting records:	Yes	No	Yes	No	
(i) Make a test examination of a number of client and controlled trust files.					

1. For all client money and controlled trust money (cont.)	Satisfactory (Tick the appropriate column)		If 'no' should breaches be noted in the accountant's report		Cross references to audit file documentation
(e) Examination of documents for verification of transactions and entries in accounting records (cont.):	Yes	No	Yes	No	
(ii) All client and controlled trust files requested for examination were made available.					
(iii) The financial transactions as detailed on client and controlled trust files and other documentation (including transfers from one ledger account to another) were valid and appropriately authorised in accordance with Parts A and B of the Solicitors' Accounts Rules 1998 (SAR).					
(iv) The financial transactions evidenced by documents on the client and controlled trust files were correctly recorded in the books of account in a manner complying with Part D SAR.					
(f) Extraction of client ledger balances for clients and controlled trusts:	Yes	No	Yes	No	
(i) The extraction of client ledger balances for clients and controlled trusts has been checked for no fewer than two separate dates in the period subject to this report.					
(ii) The total liabilities to clients and controlled trusts as shown by such ledger accounts has been compared to the cash account balance(s) at each of the separate dates selected in (f)(i) above and agreed.					
(iii) The cash account balance(s) at each of the dates selected has/have been reconciled to the balance(s) in client bank account and elsewhere as confirmed directly by the relevant banks and building societies.					
(g) Reconciliations:	Yes	No	Yes	No	
(i) During the accounting year under review, reconciliations have been carried out at least every five weeks or, in the case of passbook-operated separate designated client accounts for controlled trust money, every fourteen weeks.					
(ii) Each reconciliation is in the form of a statement set out in a logical format which is likely to reveal any discrepancies.					
(iii) Reconciliation statements have been retained.					
(iv) On entries in an appropriate sample of reconciliation statements:	Yes	No	Yes	No	
(A) All accounts containing client money and controlled trust money have been included.					
(B) All ledger account balances for clients and controlled trusts as at the reconciliation date have been listed and totalled.					
(C) No debit balances on ledger accounts for clients and controlled trusts have been included in the total.					
(D) The cash account balance(s) for clients and controlled trusts is/are correctly calculated by the accurate and up to date recording of transactions.					
(E) The client bank account totals for clients and controlled trusts are complete and correct being calculated by:					
the closing balance *plus* an accurate and complete list of outstanding lodgments *less* an accurate and complete list of unpresented cheques.					

28

1. For all client money and controlled trust money (cont.)	Satisfactory (Tick the appropriate column)		If 'no' should breaches be noted in the accountant's report		Cross references to audit file documentation
(g) Reconciliations (cont.):	Yes	No	Yes	No	
(v) Each reconciliation selected under paragraph (iv) above has been achieved by the comparison and agreement *without adjusting or balancing entries* of:					
total of ledger balances for clients and controlled trusts;					
total of cash account balances for clients and controlled trusts;					
total of client bank accounts.					
(vi) In the event of debit balances existing on ledger accounts for clients and controlled trusts, the firm has investigated promptly and corrected the position satisfactorily.					
(vii) In the event of the reconciliations selected under paragraph (iv) above not being in agreement, the differences have been investigated and corrected promptly.					
(h) Payments of client money and controlled trust money:	Yes	No	Yes	No	
Make a test examination of the ledger accounts for clients and controlled trusts in order to ascertain whether payments have been made on any individual account in excess of money held on behalf of that client or controlled trust.					
(i) Office accounts - client money and controlled trust money:	Yes	No	Yes	No	
(i) Check such office ledger and cash account and bank and building society statements as the solicitor maintains with a view to ascertaining whether any client money or controlled trust money has not been paid into a client account.					
(ii) Investigate office ledger credit balances and ensure that such balances do not include client money or controlled trust money incorrectly held in office account.					
(j) Client money and controlled trust money not held in client account:	Yes	No	Yes	No	
(i) Have sums not held on client account been identified?					
(ii) Has the reason for holding such sums outside client account been established?					
(iii) Has a written client agreement been made if appropriate?					
(iv) Are central records or a central register kept for client money held outside client account on the client's instructions?					
(k) Rule 30 - inter-client transfers	Yes	No	Yes	No	
Make test checks of inter-client transfers to ensure that rule 30 has been complied with.					
(l) Rule 32 (6) - acting for borrower and lender	Yes	No	Yes	No	
Make a test examination of the client ledger accounts in order to ascertain whether rule 32(6) SAR has been complied with, where the firm acts for both borrower and lender in a conveyancing transaction.					
(m) Rule 32(14) - recognised bodies:	Yes	No	Yes	No	
Is a central book of dividend instruction letters kept?					
(n) Information and explanations:	Yes	No	Yes	No	
All information and explanations required have been received and satisfactorily cleared.					

2.	Liquidators, trustees in bankruptcy, Court of Protection receivers and trustees of occupational pension schemes (rule 9)	Satisfactory (Tick the appropriate column)		If 'no' should breaches be noted in the accountant's report		Cross references to audit file documentation
		Yes	No	Yes	No	
(a)	A record of all bills of costs and written notifications has been maintained which distinguishes profit costs from disbursements, either in the form of a central record or a file of copies of such bills or notifications.					
(b)	Records kept under rule 9 including any statements, passbooks and other accounting records originating outside the solicitor's office have been retained.					
(c)	Records kept under rule 9 are kept together centrally, or a central register is kept of the appointments.					

3.	Joint accounts (rule 10)	Satisfactory (Tick the appropriate column)		If 'no' should breaches be noted in the accountant's report		Cross references to audit file documentation
		Yes	No	Yes	No	
(a)	A record of all bills of costs and written notifications has been maintained which distinguishes profit costs from disbursements, either in the form of a central record or a file of copies of such bills or notifications.					
(b)	Statements and passbooks and/or duplicate statements or copies of passbook entries have been retained.					
(c)	Statements, passbooks, duplicate statements and copies of passbook entries are kept together centrally, or a central register of all joint accounts is kept.					

4.	Clients' own accounts (rule 11)	Satisfactory (Tick the appropriate column)		If 'no' should breaches be noted in the accountant's report		Cross references to audit file documentation
		Yes	No	Yes	No	
(a)	Statements and passbooks and/or duplicate statements, copies of passbook entries and cheque details have been retained.					
(b)	Statements and passbooks and/or duplicate statements, copies of passbook entries and cheque details are kept together centrally, or a central register of clients' own accounts is kept.					

5.	Law Society guidelines - accounting procedures and systems			
		Yes	No	
	Discovery of substantial departures from the guidelines?			*If "yes" please give details below.*

28

6. Please give further details of unsatisfactory items below. *(Please attach additional schedules as required)*

Signature

Date

Reporting Accountant

Print name

Appendix 5   Form AR 1

Accountant's Report Form (Year 2000)

THE LAW SOCIETY

Every solicitor, registered foreign lawyer and recognised body who holds or receives client money or controlled trust money, or who operates a client's own account as signatory, must produce annually a report by an accountant qualified under rule 37 of the Solicitors' Accounts Rules 1998 to the effect that the solicitor, etc, has complied with Parts A and B, rule 24(1) of Part C, and Part D of the rules.

- The report must be delivered once during each practice year (i.e. between 1st November and the following 31st October).
- When a solicitor retires from practice (or for any reason stops holding or receiving client money or controlled trust money, or operating any client's own account as signatory), he or she is obliged to deliver a report covering the period up to the date on which the solicitor ceased to hold client money or controlled trust money, or to operate any client's own account as signatory.
- An accountant's report is required from a solicitor who has been held out as a partner in a practice which has held or received client money or controlled trust money. Therefore, any solicitor whose name is included in the list of partners on the firm's letterhead, even if the name appears under a separate heading of 'salaried partner' or 'associate partner', should be included in this report.

1   Firm details. *Please complete the name of the solicitors' firm, multi-national partnership, recognised body or in-house practice for which this report is being submitted.*

Firm		Law Society reference number	
Report Period		to	

The Law Society reference number. *This is the firm's Law Society reference number. The firm should be able to provide this for you. However, if the number is not known, this box can be left blank.*

2   Firm's name(s) and address(es) covered by this report. *The name(s) under which the office(s) practise.* **Address(es)** *All address(es) at which the solicitor(s)/recognised body/multi-national partnership practise(s) must be covered by an accountant's report or reports. Please list on a separate sheet all other offices not covered by this report, with reasons.*

1 Address (main office)

2 Other office

Postcode

Postcode

Name of firm if different from that in Section 1

Name of firm if different from that in Section 1

3 Other office

4 Other office

Postcode

Postcode

Name of firm if different from that in Section 1

Name of firm if different from that in Section 1

28

3 Solicitors and registered foreign lawyers covered by this report. *For a recognised body, complete the names of directors and any other solicitor(s) or registered foreign lawyer(s) who have held or received client money or controlled trust money, or who have operated any client's own account as signatory.* **Report period.** *This is the period of the report which covers each individual. This only needs to be completed if it is different from the firm's accounting period.* **Quote date ceased to hold client money, etc.** *This needs to be completed if the solicitor/registered foreign lawyer has ceased to hold client money and/or controlled trust money, and to operate any client's own account as signatory.*

Surname	Forename(s)	Law Society Reference No.	Status	Report period From:	To:	If appropriate, quote date if ceased to hold client money, etc

4 Comparison dates.

The results of the comparisons required under rule 42(1)(f) of the Solicitors' Accounts Rules 1998, at the dates selected by me/us were:

(a)   at _____   *(insert date 1)*

    (i)   Liabilities to clients and controlled trusts (and other persons for whom client money is held) as shown by ledger accounts for client and controlled trust matters

    (ii)   Cash held in client account, and client money and controlled trust money held in any account other than a client account, after allowances for lodgments cleared after date and for outstanding cheques

    (iii)   Difference between (i) and (ii) (if any)

(b)   at _____   *(insert date 2)*

    (i)   Liabilities to clients and controlled trusts (and other persons for whom client money is held) as shown by ledger accounts for client and controlled trust matters

    (ii)   Cash held in client account, and client money and controlled trust money held in any account other than a client account, after allowances for lodgments cleared after date and for outstanding cheques

    (iii)   Difference between (i) and (ii) (if any)

Note: *The figure to be shown in 4(a)(i) and 4(b)(i) above is the total of credit balances, without adjustment for debit balances (unless capable of proper set off being in respect of the same client), or for receipts and payments not capable of allocation to individual ledger accounts.*

5   Qualified report.

Have you found it necessary to make this report "Qualified"?   No [ ]   If 'No' proceed to Section 6

    Yes [ ]   If 'Yes' please complete relevant boxes

(a) Please indicate in the space provided any matters (other than trivial breaches) in respect of which it appears to you that the solicitors(s)/registered foreign lawyer(s)/recognised body(ies) has/have not complied with the provisions of Parts A and B, rule 24(1) of Part C, and Part D of the Solicitors' Accounts Rules 1998 and, where he/she/it is/they are authorised in the conduct of investment business by the Law Society, rules 14 and 26 of the Solicitors' Investment Business Rules 1995 *(continue on an additional sheet if necessary)*:

(b) Please indicate in the space provided any matters in respect of which you have been unable to satisfy yourself and the reasons for that inability, e.g. because a client's file is not available *(continue on an additional sheet if necessary)*:

28

6 Accountant details.

Name		Reference Number	
		Law Society use only	
Professional body		Firm name	
Firm Address			

Note: *The reporting accountant must be qualified in accordance with rule 37 of the Solicitors' Accounts Rules 1998.*

7 Declaration. In compliance with section 34 of the Solicitors Act 1974, section 9 of the Administration of Justice Act 1985, schedule 14, paragraph 8(1) of the Courts and Legal Services Act 1990, schedule 15, paragraph 6 of the Financial Services Act 1986, and Part F of the Solicitors' Accounts Rules 1998, I/we have examined to the extent required by rule 42 of those rules, the accounting records, files and other documents produced to me/us in respect of the above practice(s) of the above named solicitor(s)/RFL(s)/recognised body(ies).

In so far as an opinion can be based on this limited examination I am/we are satisfied that during the above - mentioned period he/she/the body has/they have complied with the provisions of:

(a) Parts A and B, rule 24(1) of Part C, and Part D of the Solicitors' Accounts Rules 1998 and

(b) where he/she/the body is/they are authorised in the conduct of investment business by the Law Society, rules 14 and 26 of the Solicitors' Investment Business Rules 1995

except so far as concerns:

(i) certain trivial breaches due to clerical errors or mistakes in book-keeping, all of which were rectified on discovery and none of which, I am/we are satisfied, resulted in any loss to any client; and/or

(ii) any matters detailed in section 5 of this report.

I/we have*/have not relied on the exception contained in rule 42(2) of the Solicitors' Accounts Rules 1998 *(*delete as appropriate)*

Rule 42(2) of the Solicitors' Accounts Rules 1998 states: *"For the purposes of paragraph (1)(f) above [extraction of balances] if a solicitor uses a computerised or mechanised system of accounting which automatically produces an extraction of all client ledger balances, the accountant need not check all client ledger balances extracted on the list produced by the computer or machine against the individual records of client ledger accounts, provided the accountant:*

(a) confirms that a satisfactory system of control is in operation and the accounting records are in balance;

(b) carries out a test check of the extraction against the individual records; and

(c) specifies in the report that he or she has relied on this exception."

In carrying out work in preparation of this report, I/we have discovered the following substantial departures from the Law Society's current Guidelines for Accounting Procedures and Systems *(continue on an additional sheet if necessary)*:

7 Declaration (continued).

Please tick the "yes" or "no" box for the following items (i) to (v) to show whether, so far as you are aware, the relevant statement applies in respect of yourself or any principal, director or employee of your accountancy practice.
Give details if appropriate.

	Yes	No
(i) Any of the parties mentioned above is related to any solicitor to whom this report relates.		
(ii) Any of the parties mentioned above normally maintained, on a regular basis, the accounting records to which this report relates.		
(iii) Any of the parties mentioned above, or the practice, places substantial reliance for referral of clients on the solicitor(s) to whom this report relates.		
(iv) Any of the parties mentioned above, or the practice, is a client or former client of the solicitor(s) to whom this report relates.		
(v) There are other circumstances which might affect my independence in preparing this report.		

* The information is intended to help the Law Society to identify circumstances which might make it difficult to give an independent report. Answering "yes" to any part of this section does not disqualify the accountant from making the report.
* Information within the accountant's personal knowledge should always be disclosed. Detailed investigations are not necessary but reasonable enquiries should be made of those directly involved in the work.

I/we have completed and signed the Law Society checklist and retained a copy. The original checklist
has been sent to _____ *(sole principal, partner, director)*

I/we confirm that a copy of this report has been sent to *(*delete as appropriate)*

(a) * Each of the solicitors and/or RFL(s) to whom this report relates; or

(b) * The following partner of the firm, on behalf of all the partners in the firm:
_____

(c) * Each of the directors of the recognised body to which this report relates; or

(d) * The following officer of the recognised body, on behalf of the recognised body:
_____

The form should then be signed and dated. The report can be signed in the name of the firm of accountants of which the accountant is a partner or employee. Particulars of the individual accountant signing the report must be given in section 6.

Date	
Signature	
Name *(block capitals)*	

28

INDEX TO THE SOLICITORS' ACCOUNTS RULES 1998

This index does not form part of the rules.

References are to the numbers of the rules. An 'n' after the rule number refers to one of the notes appended to that rule. References to the appendices are prefaced by 'app.'.

Accountancy bodies, 34(7), 37

Accountants

disqualification, 37(3)–(5)
governed by the rules, 4(2)
independence of, app.5 (para. 7)
letter of engagement, 38
qualification, 37(1)–(2)
rights and duties, 38
same accountant, writing up accounting records and preparing accountant's report,
    37n
termination to be reported, 38(1)(ii)

Accountant's examination of accounting records, 42, app.4

Accountants' reports, 1(j)

application of Accountant's Report Rules 1991, 50(4)
checklist, 46, app.4
checks required, 42
checks not required, 42n(i), 44
commencement of Part F of the rules, 50(3)
confidentiality, 38(1)
delivery, 35, 38(1)(iii), 47n(iii)
    assistant solicitor, 35n(vi)–(vii)
    consultant, 35n(vi)–(vii)
explanations for discrepancies, 47n(vi)
form required, 47, app.5
joint accounts, 10(1)(e)
netting off debits and credits not allowed, 42n(ii)
privilege, 45
qualifications of accountant, 37
recognised bodies, 31(1)(b)
transitional accounting period, 50(5)
trivial breaches, 47n(iv)–(vi)
unnecessary, 35n(i)–(iii), 35n(vi)
waivers, 35n(ix), 49

Accountant's Report Rules 1991, application, 50(4)

Accounting periods

changes, 36(4)
final report, 36(5)
first report, 36(2)
meaning, 36(1)
resumed reports, 36(3)
transitional, 50(5)

28

Assistant solicitors

> accountant's reports, 35n(vi)–(vii)
> application of rules to, 4(1)(a)(iii)
> practice acts for, 13n(xii)(c)

Associate partners

> accountant's reports, 35n(v)
> application of rules to, 4(1)(a)(ii)
> as "principal", 2(2)(r)(ii)

Associate, application of rules to, 4(1)(a)(iii)

Association of Authorised Public Accountants, 37(1)(a)

Association of Chartered Certified Accountants, 37(1)(a)

Availability, money held in client accounts, 14n(vii), 25n(v)

Bailees, client money, 13n(i)(a)

Balance sheets, 42n(i)

Balances *see* Current balances; Daily balances; Reporting Accountants – extraction of balances

Bank, meaning, 2(2)(c)

Bank accounts

> for client accounts, 14(2), 14(4)
> provision of details to reporting accountant, 41

Bank balances, confirmation direct to reporting accountant, 42(1)(f)(ii), 42n(iii)

Bank statements, retention, 32(9)(b)–(c), 32n(xi), 32(15)

Banker's draft *see* Drafts

Banks, safeguards, withdrawal from client account, 23n(i)

Bill of costs

> accounting records, 32(8)
> fees, 19(2)
> investment business, 42(1)(a)
> receipt of costs from client, 19(1)
> transfer of costs from client account, 19(3)

Blank cheques, 23n(ii), app.3 (para. 5.7)

Blanket agreements, to hold client money outside client account, 16(2)

Books of account *see* Accounting records

Breaches of rules

> duty to remedy, 7, 22(4), 22n(v)–(vi)
> improper removal of mortgage funds, 32n(viii)
> trivial, accountant's report, 47n(iv)–(vi)

Building society, meaning, 2(2)(d)

Building society accounts

> for client accounts, 14(2), 14(4)
> provision of details to reporting accountant, 41
> *see also* Share accounts

28

28

28

28

28

Liquidators

client money, 13n(i)(a), app.1, app.2
compliance with rules, 9, 24n(viii)
record-keeping, 32(9)(c), 32n(ii)(a)
register of appointments, 32(12)
retention of accounting records, 32(9)(c)
test procedures, 42(1)(l)
use of client accounts, 9(3)

Loan *see* Private loans

Local authority, meaning, 5n(ii)

Location, client accounts, 14(4)

Location of examination, books of account, 34(1), 40

Locum, application of rules to, 4(1)(a)(iii)

Manual accounting system, app.3 (para. 2.6)

Mechanised accounting systems

test procedures, 42(2)
see also Computerised accounting systems

Misconduct, employees, 4n(i)

Mistakes, accounts, 47n(iv)–(v)

Mixed money, treated as client money, 32n(iv)

Mixed payments

legal aid practitioners, 21(1)(b), 21n(iii)
meaning, 20(1)
receipt and transfer, 20(2)–(5)
receipt from Legal Aid Board, 20(5)

Money

held for stamp duty, 13n(i)(c)
held in client accounts
    aggregation, 15n(viii)
    availability, 14n(vii), 25n(v)
held in personal capacity, app.1
held or received by solicitor, app.1
held to sender's order, 13n(v)
not held in client accounts, interest, 24(2), 24(6), 25
paid in accordance with trust, 18(c)
paid into client accounts, 15
subject to a trust, 13n(vii), 24n(iv)
transfers between general client accounts, 23(2)
withdrawn from client account, on Society's authority, 22(1)(h), 22(2)(h),
    22n(viii)–(ix)
withheld from client account, on Society's authority, 17(f), 17n(iv), 18(d), 18n(iv)

Money laundering, 15n(ix)

Money not held by solicitor, 11,16(1)(b), 24n(iii)

28

28

Profit and loss account, 42n(i)

Properly, meaning, 19n(ix)

Public posts held by solicitors, exemption from rules, 5(c)

Qualification and disqualification, accountants, 37

Random visits, monitoring of compliance, 34n(iv)

Rate of interest, 25

Reasons, monitoring of compliance, 34n(iv)

Receipt and transfer, mixed payments, 20

Receipt of costs, 19

Receipts from Legal Aid Board, 21

Receipt from third parties, in legal aid cases, 21(2)

Receivers, Court of Protection
    central keeping of accounting records, 32(12)
    client money, 13n(i)(a)
    compliance with rules, 9, 24n(viii)
    record-keeping, 32(9)(c), 32(12), 32n(ii)(a)
    register of appointments, 32(12)
    retention of accounting records, 32(9)(c)
    test procedures, 42(1)(l)

Recognised bodies
    accountant's reports, 31(1)(b)
    accounting systems, 31
    central book of instruction letters, 32(14)
    delivery of accountant's reports, 35
    dividend cheques received, 31(2), 32(9)(f), 32(14)
    governed by rules, 4(1)(c)
    holding money as executor, trustee or nominee, 31(2), 31n(ii), 32(14)
    meaning, 2(2)(t)
    owned by partnerships, accountant's reports, 35n(x)
    record keeping, 31, 32(9)(f), 32(14)
    shared client accounts, 31(1)
    trustees of controlled trusts, 2(2)(h)(ii), 2(2)(h)(iv)–(v)

Recognised body, owning recognised body, 31n(i)

Reconciliation
    accounting records, 32(7), 32n(ix)–(x)
    netting off of debits and credits not allowed, 32n(x)
    partner to check, app.3 (para. 5.4(5))
    passbook-operated accounts for controlled trust money, 32(7)
    test procedures, 42(1)(f) and (g)

Record of commissions, test procedures, 42(1)(a)

Record keeping, joint accounts, 10, 32(9)(b)(ii), 32(13)

Refund of solicitor's advance, 22(1)(f), 22(2)(f)

28

Sole practitioner
>   death of, 22(8)(b)
>   name of client account, 14(3)(a)
>   owning recognised body, 31n(i)
>   retirement, accounting period, 36n(ii)
>   unattributable money in client account, 36n(iii)

Solicitor
>   acting for self, 13n(xii)
>   meaning, 2(2)(x)

Solicitors, governed by rules, 4(1)(a)

Solicitors' Accounts Rules 1998
>   commencement, 50
>   flowchart of effects, app.1
>   geographical scope, 3
>   persons exempt, 5, app.2
>   persons governed, 4
>   special situations, chart, app.2

Solicitors' Compensation Fund, contributions, in-house solicitors, 14n(ii)

Solicitors Disciplinary Tribunal
>   misconduct by employee of a solicitor, 4n(i)
>   report by Monitoring and Investigation Unit used in proceedings, 34(7)

Solicitor's rights, against money in client account, 12

Special situations chart, app.2

Spent, meaning, 22n(ii)

Stakeholder
>   administrative charges, 27n(ii)–(iv)
>   contracting out of interest rules, 27(2), 27n(ii)–(v)
>   holding client money, 13n(i)(a), app.1
>   interest, 26

Stamp duty
>   client money, 13n(i)(c)
>   included with payment of costs, 19(1)(a)(iii)

Standard terms of business
>   client money held outside client account, 16(2)
>   contracting out by, 27n(i)

Statutory rules
>   accounting records, 9, 32(9)(c), 32(12), 32(15)(b), 32n(ii)(a)
>   interest, 24n(viii)

Statutory undertakers
>   exempt from rules, 5(a)(ii)
>   meaning, 5n(i)

Stocks, checks not required in accountant's reports, 44(b)

Successive accounts, amount of interest, 25(3)

28

28

Annex 28C

Guidance – transitional arrangements for the delivery of accountants' reports

The new accounts rules

The Solicitors' Accounts Rules 1998 ('the new rules' – for full text see Annex 28B, p.684) received the concurrence of the Master of the Rolls on 22nd July 1998. The new rules will eventually replace the Solicitors' Accounts Rules 1991 and the Solicitors' Accounts (Legal Aid Temporary Provision) Rule 1992 'the old rules' – see Annexes 28B and 28C in the 1996 edition of the Guide). Commencement provisions are contained in rule 50 of the new rules.

All firms must implement the new rules by 1st May 2000, but firms are free to implement the new rules before that date. When a firm introduces the new rules, they must be implemented in their entirety. However, a firm which has separate accounting systems or different accounting periods for two different offices could implement the new rules on different dates for each office.

The majority of firms' accounting periods end on 30th April, and many of these firms may wish to implement the new rules either on 1st May 1999 or on 1st May 2000.

Accountants' reports and checklists

The Accountant's Report Rules 1991 ('the Accountant's Report Rules' – see Annex 28D in the 1996 edition of the Guide) will in due course be replaced by Part F of the new rules. Transitional arrangements for accountants' reports are to be found in rule 50 of the new rules.

Accountants' reports covering a period when a practice was operating the old rules:

> ▶ will be prepared in accordance with the Accountant's Report Rules;

> ▶ will relate to compliance with the old rules;

> ▶ from 1st September 1998, will also note departures from the guidelines published under the Accountant's Report Rules (see Bulletin 16);

> ▶ from 1st September 1998, will involve completion of the checklist produced under the Accountant's Report Rules – this will be a version as amended by the Council in June 1998 (see Bulletin 18, p.102 which amends the checklist in Bulletin 16, p.44); and

28

▶   will be submitted on the form approved under the Accountant's Report Rules ('the old form') – from 1st September 1998 this will be the amended form embodying changes in the role of the reporting accountant (as in the form in Bulletin 17).

Accountants' reports covering a period when a practice was operating the new rules:

▶   will be prepared in accordance with Part F of the new rules;

▶   will relate to compliance with the new rules;

▶   will also report on departures from the guidelines published under the new rules (see Appendix 3 to the rules, Annex 28B at p.734);

▶   will involve completion of the checklist published under Part F of the new rules ('the new checklist' – as in Appendix 4 to the rules, see Annex 28B at p.738); and

▶   will be submitted on the form published under Part F of the new rules ('the new form' – as in Appendix 5 to the rules, see Annex 28B at p.743).

For the procedure where a firm wishes to deliver a single report to cover an accounting period when the firm operated the old rules for part of the accounting period and the new rules for the remainder:

▶   see option (a) below.

Implementation at beginning of accounting period

If a firm implements the new rules to coincide with the start of its accounting period, the position is simple. The firm will deliver an accountant's report on the old form to cover the last accounting period when the firm was operating the old rules. The firm will subsequently deliver an accountant's report on the new form to cover the first accounting period under the new rules.

When reporting on the firm's last accounting period under the old rules, the reporting accountant should endorse at the top of the form: **'Last report under the Solicitors' Accounts Rules 1991'**.

> Example: The firm implements the new rules on 1st May 2000, and its accounting period runs from **1st May to 30th April**. The last report on the old form will cover the 12 months 1st May 1999 to 30th April 2000, to be delivered by 30th October 2000. The first report on the new form will cover the 12 months 1st May 2000 to 30th April 2001, to be delivered by 30th October 2001.

Implementation part way through an accounting period

If a firm introduces the new rules part way through an accounting period, the firm has four options. The accounting period during which the firm introduces the new rules is called 'the transitional accounting period'.

Option (a)

The firm delivers an accountant's report covering the whole of the transitional accounting period. The reporting accountant will need to complete the new form. However, the reporting accountant will need to check compliance with the old rules (not the new rules) for that part of the transitional accounting period when the firm was operating under the old rules, and compliance with the new rules for the remainder.

If the transitional accounting period ends on or before 30th April 2000, the firm will need to ask the Law Society to send **the new form** (instead of the old form) in time for preparation of the accountant's report on the transitional accounting period.

In relation to that part of the transitional accounting period when the firm was operating under the old rules, the reporting accountant should endorse at the top of the new form: **'For the period .... to .... this report relates to compliance with the Solicitors' Accounts Rules 1991'**.

The reporting accountant has to make the appropriate comparisons for at least two dates during the transitional accounting period. It will be for the accountant to select the number and dates of the comparisons. The accountant may consider it appropriate to do two comparisons only.

The accountant may choose one comparison date in the period when the firm was operating the old rules (and will carry out that comparison in accordance with the Accountant's Report Rules), and a second comparison date in the period when the firm was operating the new rules (and will carry out that comparison in accordance with Part F of the new rules). Alternatively, both dates could be in the period when the firm was operating the new rules. Indeed, both dates could be in the earlier period, but this may be unlikely, given the standard procedure, validated by the rules, of selecting the last day of the accounting period as one of the comparison dates.

The reporting accountant will complete the new checklist. In relation to that part of the transitional accounting period when the firm was operating under the old rules, the accountant should endorse at the top of the new checklist: **'Any checks made in respect of the period .... to .... relate to compliance with the Solicitors' Accounts Rules 1991'**.

> Example: The firm implements the new rules on 1st May 2000, part way through its accounting period, which runs from **1st September** to **31st August**. The firm delivers an accountant's report on the new form covering the whole 12-month period 1st September 1999 to 31st August 2000, to be delivered by 28th February 2001. The form is endorsed: 'For the period 1st September 1999 to 30th April 2000 this report relates to compliance with the Solicitors' Accounts Rules 1991.' The accountant completes the new checklist, which is endorsed: 'Any checks made in respect of the period 1st September 1999 to 30th April 2000 relate to compliance with the Solicitors' Accounts Rules 1991.'

Option (b)

The firm decides that it will deliver two separate 'short' accountant's reports for the transitional accounting period, one made on the old form to cover the period when the firm was operating the old rules, and one made on the new form to cover the period when the firm was operating the new rules. The first report will have to be delivered six months after the end of the period to which it relates. The second report will have to be delivered six months after the end of the transitional accounting period. The reporting accountant will have to select at least two comparison dates for the first report, **plus** at least two comparison dates for the second report.

The firm will need to ask the Law Society to send **an accountant's report form** (the old form) in time for preparation of the accountant's report on the first part of the transitional accounting period.

The reporting accountant should endorse at the top of the first report: **'Short report under rule 50(5)(b) for the period .... to ...., being the 1st part of the transitional**

accounting period'. The second report should be endorsed: **'Short report for the period .... to ...., being the 2nd part of the transitional accounting period'**.

Example: The firm implements the new rules on 1st May 2000, part way through its accounting period, which runs from **1st September** to **31st August**. The first report (on the old form) will cover the eight-month period 1st September 1999 to 30th April 2000, to be delivered by 30th October 2000. The second report (on the new form) will cover the four-month period 1st May 2000 to 31st August 2000, to be delivered by 28th February 2001.

Option (c)

The firm decides that it will deliver a 'short' accountant's report, followed by an extended report. The 'short' report (on the old form) covers the first part of the transitional accounting period, when the firm was operating the old rules. Its subsequent accountant's report (on the new form) covers the rest of the transitional accounting period, when the firm was operating the new rules, **plus** the whole of the next accounting period.

The firm will need to ask the Law Society to send **an accountant's report form** (the old form) in time for preparation of the accountant's report on the first part of the transitional accounting period.

For the 'short' report, covering the first part of the transitional accounting period, the reporting accountant will have to select at least two comparison dates. For the extended report, covering the second part of the transitional accounting period plus the whole of the next accounting period, the rules contain no requirement that more than two comparison dates be selected, although that lies within the discretion of the accountant.

The reporting accountant should endorse at the top of the 'short' report: **'Short report under rule 50(5)(c) for the period .... to ...., being the 1st part of the transitional accounting period'**. The extended report should be endorsed: **'Extended report for the period .... to ...., including the 2nd part of the transitional accounting period'**.

Example: The firm implements the new rules on 1st May 2000, part way through its accounting period, which runs from **1st September** to **31st August**. The 'short' report (on the old form) will cover the eight-month period 1st September 1999 to 30th April 2000, to be delivered by 30th October 2000. The extended report (on the new form) will cover the 16-month period 1st May 2000 to 31st August 2001, to be delivered by 28th February 2002.

Option (d)

The firm delivers an extended accountant's report (on the old form) for the last complete accounting period when the firm operated the old rules, **plus** the first part of the transitional accounting period, when the firm was continuing to operate the old rules. The firm subsequently delivers a report (on the new form) to cover the remainder of the transitional accounting period, when the firm was operating the new rules.

The firm will need to ask the Law Society **not to send** an accountant's report form at the normal time for a report on the last complete accounting period when the firm operated the old rules. The firm will also need to specify their **implementation date** for the new rules.

For the extended report, covering the last complete accounting period under the old rules plus the first part of the transitional accounting period, the rules contain no requirement that more than two comparison dates be selected, although that lies within the discretion of the accountant. For the 'short' report, covering the remainder of the transitional accounting period, the reporting accountant will have to select at least two comparison dates.

The reporting accountant should endorse at the top of the extended report: '**Extended report for the period .... to ...., including the 1st part of the transitional accounting period**'. The 'short' report should be endorsed: '**Short report for the period .... to ...., being the 2nd part of the transitional accounting period**'.

Example: The firm implements the new rules on 1st May 2000, part way through its accounting period, which runs from **1st September** to **31st August**. The extended report (on the old form) will cover the 20-month period 1st September 1998 to 30th April 2000, to be delivered by 30th October 2000. The 'short' report (on the new form) will cover the four-month period 1st May 2000 to 31st August 2000, to be delivered by 28th February 2001.

July 1998, updated February 1999

28

Annex 28D

Tax on bank and building society interest – practice information

Since April 1996, savings income received by an individual, the estate of a deceased person or an interest in possession trust has been taxable at the lower rate (20%), unless in the case of an individual his or her total income makes him or her liable to higher rate tax, rather than the basic rate of tax (section 73 of the Finance Act 1996 inserting a new section 1A into the Income and Corporation Taxes Act 1988). This is relevant to the tax treatment of bank and building society interest received by solicitors.

The Solicitors' Accounts Rules 1998, Part C

Under this part of the rules ('the interest provisions'), a solicitor who is required to account for interest to a client may do so by either of two methods. He or she may:

(a)   account to the client for the interest earned on the client's money in a separate designated client account; or

(b)   pay to the client a sum in lieu of interest when the money is held in a general client account.

These two procedures are referred to as Method A and Method B respectively.

Deduction of tax at source

The tax deduction at source rules apply, broadly, to separate designated client accounts, e.g. accounts held for individuals who are ordinarily resident in the U.K.

Interest on general client accounts, whether with a bank or a building society, is paid gross.

When opening any separate designated client account the solicitor must provide the necessary information for the bank or building society to decide whether or not deduction of tax at source is appropriate.

Tax treatment of interest – Method A

Method A applies to separate designated client accounts. Where tax is deducted at source by the bank or building society interest will be received by the solicitor net, and he or she will simply pass it on to the client net – no tax deduction certificate is required. Interest from separate designated client accounts is taxable as savings income. The client, when making his or her tax return, will declare the interest as having been received under deduction of tax, and will only be liable to be assessed in relation to higher rate tax in respect of it (since he or she will have a tax credit for the lower rate of tax). If the client is for any reason not liable to income tax, he or she can recover any tax deducted from the interest. In those circumstances the solicitor must, on being required by the client, obtain a certificate of deduction of tax from the bank or building society and deliver this to the client. The client's position is, therefore, for practical purposes, the same as that which arises where he or she receives interest from a building society or bank on a deposit of his or her own.

Where the client is not liable to tax or is not ordinarily resident (NOR) in the U.K. the bank or building society will pay the interest gross provided that it holds the relevant declaration. Declarations of non-ordinary residence can be completed by either the solicitor or the client but declarations of non-liability by U.K. residents will normally be completed by the client. However, in view of the difficulty of obtaining complete information about an overseas client, solicitors may feel that it is more appropriate for the client concerned to make the declaration, especially since it contains an undertaking to notify the bank or building society should circumstances change.

Where the tax deduction at source rules do not apply, the solicitor will receive interest from the bank or building society gross and may account to the client for it gross, even if the client is non-resident. The client will be assessed on the gross receipt (but a non-resident client may, by concession, not be assessed) and (unless the solicitor has been acting as the client's agent for tax purposes – see below under 'Solicitors as agents') the solicitor himself or herself will not be assessed in respect of the interest.

Tax treatment of interest – Method B

Where Method B is used, deduction of tax at source does not apply to the solicitor's general client account at either a bank or building society, and interest is therefore paid to the solicitor gross. When making a payment to the client of a sum in lieu of interest under the interest provisions, the solicitor should make the payment gross even if the client is not ordinarily resident. The Revenue's view is that such payments may be treated as within Case III of Schedule D, so that the lower rate of tax on savings income may apply where appropriate. The client will be assessed to income tax on his or her receipt, but a non-resident may, by concession, not be assessed.

Wherever payments are made by solicitors to clients under Method B they can, in practice, be set off against the solicitor's Case III assessment on gross interest received on general client account deposits; if the payments exceed the interest received, a Case II deduction can be claimed for the excess.

Stake money

Since 1st June 1992, stake money has been included in the definition of 'client money'. Interest will be payable to the person to whom the stake is paid using either Method A or B above. But there will still be circumstances in which payment is not possible until a later tax year. Where this situation looks likely to arise, e.g. if the stake is held pending the outcome of litigation, the deposit would normally be placed in a general client account until it is established to whom the stake is to be paid. Because, in the meantime, interest will be included in the solicitor's Case III assessment, it is again important to make provision for the tax liability to be met out of the interest as it arises.

Tax treatment of interest – money paid into court

The position of money paid into court is covered by the Supreme Court Funds Rules as amended. Where any order for payment out of money paid into court is made, the order should provide for the disposal of any interest accrued to the date of the judgement or order, and for interest accruing thereafter up to the date the money is paid out in accordance with the order. In the absence of such provision, interest accruing between the date of the payment into court, and its acceptance or the judgement or order for payment out, goes to the party who made the payment in, and interest from the date of the judgement or order follows the capital payment.

Where interest is paid to a party to proceedings in respect of money held in court, it should be paid to the client gross, even if he or she is non-resident. The client will normally be assessable under Case III, but the solicitor will not, unless exceptionally he or she is assessable as the client's agent.

Solicitors as agents

Where a solicitor acts for tax purposes as agent for a non-resident client, the solicitor will remain liable to be assessed on behalf of the client in relation to interest earned in a separate designated client account, where Method A is used, unless he or she is an agent without management or control of the interest, in which case, under Extra Statutory Concession B13, no assessment will be made on him or her. Where the solicitor is assessable, the charge may, if appropriate, be to higher rate tax, so the solicitor will need to retain tax at the client's marginal rate of income tax from interest received gross from a bank or building society before remitting it to the client. This is the case even though the account would not be subject to deduction of tax at source since the client would have completed a declaration of non-liability due to his or her non-residence. No question of the solicitor being taxed as an agent will arise where the interest in question has been earned in a general client account, or on stake money, but it could very exceptionally do so in relation to money held in court.

Determination of whether a solicitor has management or control for the purposes of the extra statutory concession will depend on the nature of the solicitor's relationship with the client. Under the Finance Act 1995, a person not resident in the U.K. is assessable and chargeable to income tax in the name of an agent if the agent has management or control of the interest. Acting as a solicitor in giving advice or in conducting a transaction on the client's instructions will not of itself give management or control nor usually would the holding of a power of attorney on behalf of the client for a specific purpose, e.g. concluding a specified purchase or sale. If a client had no fixed place of business in the U.K., and his or her solicitor had, and habitually exercised, an authority to conclude contracts on behalf of the client, this would give rise to the client having a permanent establishment in the U.K., and accordingly the client would be taxable. In essence, the solicitor would be deemed to have management and control if he or she were effectively carrying on the client's business in the U.K., rather than merely acting as a solicitor, even regularly. Therefore, in order for the agency principle to apply, the solicitor/client relationship would normally have to go beyond a solicitor's usual representative capacity. It should be noted that where interest arises in connection with the receipt of rents on behalf of the non-resident, the solicitor would be chargeable as agent in relation to the rent.

For a more detailed analysis of when solicitors can be taxed as agents, see [1991] *Gazette,* 1 May, 15 (article by John Avery Jones).

If a solicitor is assessable on behalf of the client, he or she has a general right to reimbursement, out of the client's money coming into his or her hands, for any tax for which the client is liable and in respect of which the solicitor has been charged. For the exercise of this right see the Finance Act 1995.

Trusts

Deduction of tax at source may apply depending upon the type of trust and where the investment is held. But it can only apply where money is held in a separate designated client account. The income of trusts where none of the beneficiaries is ordinarily resident in the U.K. will not be subject to deduction of tax at source, even if a separate designated client account is used, provided that the appropriate declaration has been made.

Administration of estates

Interest on money held for U.K. resident personal representatives will, if placed in a separate designated client account, be subject to deduction of tax at source unless a declaration is made by the solicitor or the personal representatives that the deceased was not resident in the U.K. immediately before his death.

AIDE-MEMOIRE OF NORMAL SITUATIONS

Type of account	Payment of interest by bank or building society	Consequences
A Designated – where subject to tax deduction	Net	Pay net to client, who gets basic rate tax credit. No further tax deductions for residents (unless solicitor is assessable as an agent).
B Designated – where paid gross (client money generally)	Gross	Pay gross to client who is assessable on payment as gross income. No deduction of tax for non-residents (unless the solicitor is assessable as agent).
C Bank and building society general client account – always paid gross (client money generally and stake money)	Gross	Pay gross to client who in turn is assessable on payment as gross income; in practice solicitor assessed on interest after setting-off this payment. No deduction of tax for non-residents.

4th March 1992, revised February 1999

28

Treatment of VAT on counsel's fees – practice information

The 1991 accounts rules provided that unpaid counsel's fees should be paid into and kept in client account, rather than in office account as was possible under the previous rules. The 1998 rules allow unpaid counsel's fees to be held temporarily in office account for a short period before payment or transfer to client account.

This has raised the question of how the solicitor should deal with the VAT element on such fees.

Unpaid counsel's fees paid into and kept in client account

The position with regard to VAT on counsel's fees paid into and kept in client account is that by concession of the Customs and Excise, solicitors may either:

> **Method (i)**
>
> treat the fee as their own expense (and thus reclaim the VAT element as input tax);
>
> or
>
> **Method (ii)**
>
> cross out their name on the receipted fee note and replace it with the name of the client. In this case the supply is deemed to be made direct to the client (who can reclaim the VAT if registered) and no VAT record need be kept in the solicitor's books.

If method (i) is used, when the solicitor delivers his own bill of costs, the value of the supply for VAT purposes is the value of his or her own costs, plus the tax exclusive value of counsel's fees. Thus in this case the solicitor is charging output tax on a higher level of supply.

The following examples show the effect of the two methods:

Assume solicitor's profit costs as £1,200 plus £210 VAT and the bill includes unpaid counsel's fees of £800, plus £140 VAT:

> **Method (i)**
>
> The £140 VAT on counsel's fee note is treated as the solicitor's input tax and can be reclaimed from Customs and Excise. When the solicitor's bill is delivered it must show:

Value of supply:	
Costs	1,200.00
Counsel's fees	800.00
	£2,000.00
VAT	350.00
	£2,350.00

When the £2,350 is received, the effect of the accounts rules is that the cheque must either be split, sending the office element (£1,200 costs and £350 VAT) to office account and counsel's fees to client account (£800), or alternatively the entire sum of £2,350 must be paid into client account.

Because counsel's fee is being treated for VAT purposes as an expense of the solicitor and the VAT element is being reclaimed by the solicitor, payment, when it is made, must be from office account (so that the appropriate entry can be made in the Customs and Excise ledger account). At that stage the sum held in client account can be transferred.

Method (ii)

The solicitor will simply deliver a bill showing no book-keeping entries for the counsel's fees and VAT. It will simply show:

Profit costs	1,200.00
VAT	210.00
	£1,410.00
Counsel's fees	
(including VAT)	940.00
	£2,350.00

The effect of the accounts rules is that the cheque must either be split as to £1,410 office account and £940 client account, or alternatively the entire sum of £2,350 must be paid into client account. In this case, when counsel is paid payment can be made from either client or office account (with a subsequent transfer to office account from client account).

Placing and holding unpaid counsel's fees temporarily in office account

Solicitors who use the new option, under the 1998 Accounts Rules, of placing unpaid counsel's fees initially in office account, would be unable to treat the supply as being made direct to the client. The office account should not, therefore, be used for unpaid counsel's fees if the intention is to take advantage of the concessionary treatment and treat the supply as being made direct to the client.

For further details of the concessionary treatment, see *The Law Society's VAT Guide* published 1996 and available from Marston Book Services – see p.xv for contact details.

September 1992, revised February 1999

28

Chapter 29

Professional indemnity

29.01   Cover provided by the Solicitors' Indemnity Fund

'The following persons, namely

(a) solicitors, former solicitors, registered foreign lawyers practising in partnership with solicitors, and persons formerly practising as registered foreign lawyers in partnership with solicitors;

(b) employees and former employees of the above;

(c) recognised bodies and former recognised bodies; and

(d) officers and employees and former officers and employees of recognised bodies and former recognised bodies,

shall be provided with indemnity out of the Fund against loss arising from claims in respect of civil liability incurred in Private practice in their aforesaid capacities or former capacities in the manner set out in Rule 15 and in the circumstances, to the extent and subject to the conditions set out in Part II of these Rules and not otherwise.'

Solicitors' Indemnity Rules 1998, rule 9

1. All references in this chapter to rules are references to the Solicitors' Indemnity Rules 1998 (see Annex 29A, p.793) unless otherwise stated.

Exemptions

2. Solicitors who provide services as solicitors solely in all or any of the following ways are exempted from the obligations to provide information and make contributions to the Solicitors' Indemnity Fund ('the Fund') and will not be provided with indemnity out of the Fund – rule 32 (at p.819):

   (a) conducting professional business for personal friends, relatives, companies wholly owned by the solicitor's family or registered charities without remuneration; provided that the client for whom the solicitor acts is notified of the indemnity position in writing;

   (b) administering oaths or taking affidavits.

3. Solicitors who provide services as solicitors without remuneration to persons or bodies other than those referred to in rule 32 will be subject to the indemnity rules and therefore must:

   (a) carry out the work as part of an existing practice; or

   (b) set up a new practice and make an appropriate contribution to the Fund; or

   (c) obtain a waiver of their obligations from the Society.

Overseas cover

4. The indemnity rules do not apply to a private practice carried on from an office outside England and Wales by:

   (a) a sole practitioner with no office in England and Wales;

   (b) a firm of solicitors, if the same partnership has no office in England and Wales;

   (c) a multi-national partnership with 25% or less registered foreign lawyer principals, if the same partnership has no office in England and Wales;

   (d) a multi-national partnership with more than 25% registered foreign lawyer principals, whether or not the same partnership also has an office in England and Wales;

   (e) a recognised body with more than 25% registered foreign lawyer principals (for the definition of 'principal' see rule 12.19(b) at p.799);

   (f) a firm of solicitors and other lawyers practising solely outside England and Wales;

   (g) an incorporated legal practice carried on wholly outside England and Wales;

   (h) an assistant solicitor employed by lawyers of a jurisdiction other than England and Wales.

29

However, in all such cases, every solicitor who is a partner or a director in that practice, and every solicitor who works as an assistant at that office outside England and Wales, must have the indemnity cover required by rule 17(1) of the Solicitors' Overseas Practice Rules 1990 – see Annex 9A (at p.189).

5.   The overseas offices of a partnership or recognised body, of which more than 25% of the principals are registered foreign lawyers, are deemed to be practices separate from the practice in England and Wales and, as such, are outside the cover provided by the Fund.

6.   Cover is given by the Fund to the overseas offices of a partnership or a recognised body with 25% or less registered foreign lawyer principals, provided that the overseas offices and the offices in England and Wales belong to the same practice. This means that the principals must be common to all offices of the practice and all fees must accrue to the common partnership and be returned in the annual gross fees certificate.

7.   The indemnity rules allow that, if a principal or a limited number of principals represent all principals in a practice on a local basis, this shall not, of itself, cause the overseas office to be treated as a separate office and therefore be outside cover, provided that any fees or other income arising from that office accrue to the practice as a whole.

Recognised body

8.   The indemnity rules allow that if only some of the principals in a practice beneficially own all the shares in a recognised body, this shall not, of itself, cause the recognised body to be treated as a separate practice requiring its own cover, provided that any fees or other income arising out of the recognised body accrue to the practice.

Scope of cover

9.   The indemnity provided by the Fund is against all civil liability incurred in connection with the practice of a solicitor, subject to the exclusion of certain specific items such as wrongful dismissal, trading debts and death and bodily injury. The cover is wide-ranging. As well as negligence cover it also includes defamation, the giving of undertakings and loss arising from damage to or destruction of documents. The cover even extends to a solicitor director where the solicitor's appointment arises in the course of his or her practice, provided that any fees received are paid into the partnership account for distribution under the partnership agreement. It is sometimes difficult to determine in advance of an actual claim whether a solicitor director is acting in the course of his or her practice, but in most cases common sense will indicate whether or not cover will be given by the Fund, or whether resort should be had to some other form of indemnity cover.

10. All members of the practice are covered. 'Member' of a practice is defined in rule 12.9 as meaning any principal (which includes any person held out as such); any recognised body which is a partner or held out to be a partner in the practice and any officer of the recognised body; any person employed in connection with the practice (including any trainee solicitor); any solicitor who is a consultant to or associate in the practice; any foreign lawyer who is a consultant or associate in the practice; and any solicitor or foreign lawyer who is working in the practice as an agent or *locum tenens* and the estate and/or personal representatives of any such persons. Cover is, however, limited to those in private practice and does not extend to those employed elsewhere, e.g. in commerce, industry, local government or law centres.

11. Cover is provided on an each and every claim basis. This means that cover up to the current indemnity limit is available for every valid claim, subject to the payment by the practice of the appropriate deductible (otherwise called an excess). All claims against the practice arising from the same act or omission should be regarded as one claim. This does not mean, however, that where a practice uses a standard form document on a number of different occasions or loss is occasioned by theft from a general client account (where a number of different clients are affected), the losses will be aggregated and treated as one claim. In such cases, each loss will be treated as a separate claim with not only a separate indemnity limit but also a separate deductible.

12. Cover is given for loss arising from fraud or dishonesty of an employee or a fellow principal. The Fund does not cover the fraud or dishonesty of a sole practitioner nor of a partnership where all partners are party to the fraud or dishonesty. Such matters are for the consideration of the Compensation Fund (see **30.08**, p.847). Furthermore, the cover does not extend to the partnership assets, so it follows that loss of office money is not covered.

Amount of cover

13. The indemnity limit for the indemnity period 1st September 1998 to 31st August 1999 is £1 million for each and every claim (including claimants' costs), a figure which has prevailed since 1st September 1989. For cases where there is also a Compensation Fund claim, see **30.08**, p.847.

Deductibles

14. The standard deductible provided by the rules is calculated by reference to the number of liable principals at the date of the negligent act and the average gross fees of practices with the same number of principals as set out in table I in the rules (see p.811). Each of these deductibles is subject to a minimum figure of £3,000 and a maximum of £150,000. Upon payment of an additional contribution to the Fund, practices can remove or reduce their deductible.

29

15. Each liable principal is responsible for his or her proportion of the deductible (e.g. if there are three liable principals, each is liable for one third of the deductible) and SIF will collect the due proportion from each liable principal. Where any liable principals are still practising together in the same practice at the date of notification of the claim, each will be jointly and severally liable for the sum of all the due proportions of the liable principals in that practice. Where a principal ceases to be a principal in all the practices for whatever reason, that person will not be liable to pay any part of the deductible in respect of any claim only if the date of notification is after the date the person ceases to be a principal. Such a principal's due proportion is waived by the Fund.

16. Further protection is given by the limit on the aggregate amount that a practice will be required to pay out in respect of claims falling within any one indemnity period (the 'aggregate' limit). Currently the limit is three times the deductible of the practice. Thus when a practice has contributed the figure of three times its deductible in settling claims falling within one indemnity period, the Fund will meet all further claims within that indemnity period without seeking further contribution from the practice, subject always to the indemnity limit in force. Upon payment of an additional contribution, a practice can reduce its aggregate limit to one or two times its deductible, or remove it entirely.

17. In addition to any standard deductible that might be applicable, the rules provide that claims arising from certain specified failures will attract a penalty deductible of 50% of the unamended deductible for the claim, as shown in table I (see p.811), provided that such a failure occurred on or after 1st September 1996. The relevant claims (see rule 23.2) are those arising from a failure to:

    (a) commence proceedings within the time permitted under sections 2, 5 or 11 of the Limitation Act 1980;

    (b) commence proceedings within the time permitted under section 111 of the Employment Rights Act 1996;

    (c) serve High Court proceedings within the time permitted under Order 6 Rule 8 of the Rules of the Supreme Court 1965 (or County Court proceedings within the time permitted under Order 7 Rule 20 of the County Court Rules 1981);

    (d) request the proper officer to fix a day for a hearing as required under Order 17 Rule 11 of the County Court Rules 1981;

    (e) serve a notice or issue an application within the periods permitted under Part II of the Landlord and Tenant Act 1954;

    (f) register at Companies House a charge against the assets of a company within the time permitted by section 395 of the Companies Act 1985;

    (g) apply to register a protected transaction within the priority period afforded under the Land Registration (Official Searches) Rules 1993 (S.I. 1993 no. 3276);

(h)   execute a deed of variation within the two years permitted under section 142(1) of the Inheritance Tax Act 1984 and/or to give written notice to the Inland Revenue within the six months permitted under section 142(2).

18.   Amounts payable by a practice in respect of any one indemnity period are subject to an aggregate limit. Currently, the aggregate penalty deductible limit is three times the penalty deductible for the practice as shown in table II in the rules (see p.812) by reference to the number of principals in the practice. The penalty deductible aggregate is separate from, but works in the same way as, the standard deductible aggregate.

29.02   Obligation to provide information – gross fees certificate

'In respect of each Indemnity Period commencing on or after 1st September 1998 each Principal shall by or on the preceding 31st October deliver to Solicitors Indemnity Fund Limited a Certificate in respect of each Practice (except a New Practice or an Overseas Practice) in which he or she is or was at any time during the year ending on the preceding 31st October a Principal.'

Solicitors' Indemnity Rules 1998, rule 27.2

1.   The certificate must be in the approved form.

2.   A practice which is required to deliver a certificate and which fails to do so will be treated as a practice in default and will therefore be subject to the default contribution and the default deductible.

3.   The information contained in the certificate will be taken into account in calculating any contribution due on the following 1st September.

29.03   Obligation to provide information – notice of succession

Rule 27.1 of the Solicitors' Indemnity Rules 1998 requires that the principals in a successor practice (other than a Case I successor practice) shall within 28 days of the succession deliver to Solicitors Indemnity Fund Limited a notice of succession.

29

1.   For rule 27.1 see Annex 29A at p.815. For the definition of a successor practice and Case I successor practice see rule 12.24 (p.800).

2.   The notice of succession must be in the approved form.

3. The information contained in the notice of succession will be taken into account in calculating the contribution due up to the succession and that due from any successor practice for the balance of the indemnity year.

29.04 Obligation to provide practice information

'A solicitor or registered foreign lawyer shall forthwith give to Solicitors Indemnity Fund Limited notice in writing of:

(a) the address of any New Practice which he commences or in which he becomes a Principal and the date of such commencement or becoming a Principal;

(b) the name and address of any Practice in which he becomes a Principal and the date of becoming such Principal;

(c) any change in the place or places of business of any other Practice of which he is or becomes a Principal;

(d) any cessation of any Practice in which he was before such cessation a Principal;

(e) in the case of a solicitor or registered foreign lawyer who is a Principal in a Practice which is carried on by a recognised body alone, or in which a recognised body is or is held out to be a partner, any expiry or revocation of the recognition of such recognised body under the Solicitors' Incorporated Practice Rules in force from time to time, or any revocation of recognition of such recognised body under the Administration of Justice Act 1985 schedule 2.'

Solicitors' Indemnity Rules 1998, rule 26

29.05 Obligation to provide information – Year 2000 Compliance Questionnaire

'In respect of the Indemnity Period commencing on 1st September 1998 a solicitor or registered foreign lawyer who is or becomes a Principal in a Practice (other than through a Case I succession) shall by or on a date to be determined by the Council or within 28 days of the commencement of the Practice, which ever is the later, deliver to the Solicitors Indemnity Fund Limited a Year 2000 Compliance Questionnaire fully and accurately completed in respect of such a Practice.'

Solicitors' Indemnity Rules 1998, rule 27.4

1. For the definition of Year 2000 Compliant/Compliance see rule 12.26 (p.801).

2. The Year 2000 Compliance Questionnaire must be in the approved form.

3. A practice which is required to deliver a Year 2000 Questionnaire and which fails to do so will be treated as a practice in questionnaire default and will therefore be subject to the additional contribution of 10% of the practice's annual indemnity contribution, subject to a minimum of £3,000 (see rule 43, p.837).

29.06   Obligation to make contributions

'**Each Principal shall make or cause to be made Initial and Supplementary Contributions in relation to each Indemnity Period as herein provided in respect of:**

(a) **each Separate Practice in which he is a Principal on 1st September;**

(b) **each Separate New Practice commencing during and in which he becomes a Principal during the Indemnity Period;**

(c) **each Separate Successor Practice commencing during and in which he becomes a Principal during the Indemnity Period.**'

Solicitors' Indemnity Rules 1998, rule 31.1

1. The initial contribution is made up of two parts:

   ▶ the initial annual contribution calculated in accordance with rule 39; and

   ▶ the initial shortfall contribution calculated in accordance with rule 40.

2. The basic annual contribution for practices is 10.12% of gross fees. Practices with gross fees of more than £250,000 are subject to a tapering factor as set out in rule 39.3(a) (see Annex 29A at p.823).

3. The minimum basic annual contribution before risk banding and claims loading is £500 per practice for the 1998/99 indemnity period.

4. The basic annual contribution is then subject to adjustment in accordance with rule 39.3(b) and table III (see pp.823 and 824) to take account of risk banding and in accordance with rule 42 to take account of claims history. There is an additional contribution payable by practices which undertake structural surveys and formal valuations of property.

5. The basic shortfall contribution is assessed in accordance with rule 40 and table IV of the rules. It may then be adjusted in accordance with rules 41 and 44 to take account of low risk work, structural surveys and formal valuations of property. The resulting figure is then subject to claims discount in accordance with rule 42. See Annex 29A at p.826 *et seq.*

6. The minimum shortfall contribution before claims discount is £100 per practice for the 1998/99 indemnity period.

29

7. Where a practice fails to deliver a certificate or notice of succession in accordance with the rules, it is treated as a practice in default and is subject to the default initial contribution. For the indemnity period 1998/99, the rate is £15,000 per principal in respect of the annual contribution and £5,000 per principal in respect of the shortfall contribution.

8. The initial contributions before claims adjustment in respect of a new practice are an annual contribution of £500 per practice and a shortfall contribution of £100 per practice for the 1998/99 indemnity period. These contributions are subject to apportionment for new practices which commence part way through the indemnity period.

9. All contributions are subject to VAT.

10. A practice (other than a practice in default or a successor practice to a practice in default) may pay in full on or before 1st November or by ten monthly instalments by direct debit commencing 1st November. Where a practice opts to pay by instalments, its contribution will be subject to a 4% charge.

11. It is important to note that all solicitors and registered foreign lawyers who are principals in a practice on 1st September (the beginning of the indemnity period), or become principals in a new practice (see rule 12.11 at p.797) which commences during the indemnity period, remain jointly and severally liable to pay the full contribution due in respect of the practice. If, during the indemnity period, they leave the practice, or if the practice is the subject of a split, dissolution, merger or acquisition, they remain liable to pay a proportion of the contribution. If they become a principal in a successor practice during an indemnity period then they become liable to pay the contribution for that successor practice for the balance of the indemnity period. No apportionment will apply to contributions in respect of any practice which succeeds in whole or any part to a new practice, a successor practice falling within Case I (see rule 12.24 at p.800) or a practice ceasing as a result of a Case I succession.

29.07 Incorporated practices

A recognised body with limited liability must take out top-up insurance over and above the indemnity limit of £1 million provided by the Fund. The additional cover required is for a further £500,000 in respect of each and every claim or a further £2 million per annum on an aggregate basis.

1. A company is exempt from this provision if it can show that it is wholly owned by an unincorporated solicitors' practice and can act only as agent for that practice.

2. A recognised body with unlimited liability is not subject to this requirement.

3.   The indemnity rules apply to recognised bodies (incorporated practices) as they do to any other private practice.

4.   When the same principals in number and identity carry on practice under more than one name or style, there is only one practice for the purpose of the indemnity rules. Therefore, if the beneficial owners of shares in a recognised body are the same in number and identity as the principals in a partnership, then for the purpose of the indemnity rules the two are treated as one and the same practice.

5.   An incorporated legal practice carried on wholly outside England and Wales is outside the scope of the indemnity rules (see **29.01** note 4, p.783).

29.08   Claims handling – obligation to notify claims

If a client or third party makes a claim against a solicitor which is likely to exceed £500 (or gives notice of an intention to make such a claim) and the claim is one in respect of which indemnity is provided by the Fund, the solicitor must as soon as is practicable notify Solicitors Indemnity Fund Limited and co-operate with them or their agents in order to enable such a claim to be dealt with in the appropriate manner.

1.   Although there is no obligation to give notice of circumstances that could give rise to a claim, such notice may be given to Solicitors Indemnity Fund Limited (SIF) – rule 19.2 (Annex 29A at p.805). Notification of circumstances enables consideration to be given to possible remedial action before the claim actually develops.

2.   If a practice has an existing deductible amendment (i.e. has made an extra contribution to reduce its deductible) and circumstances are discovered which might give rise to a claim, then to obtain the benefit of such deductible amendment the circumstances should be notified within the indemnity period.

3.   Notification of a claim or potential claim does not of itself give rise to claims loading or an increase in the cost of amending a practice's deductible in subsequent years, unless and until the claim has been paid or SIF has placed a reserve on the claim.

4.   If a practice has taken out top-up insurance (i.e. for cover over and above the £1 million indemnity limit), then the onus of notifying circumstances or claims to top-up insurers rests with the practice, although details as to any such insurance affected should be supplied to SIF when completing the necessary report form.

5.   A practice or any successor practice, or any member thereof, should not admit liability for or settle any claim for which indemnity is provided, or incur any costs or expenses in connection therewith, without the prior consent of SIF. If a breach of this or any other provision of the indemnity

29

rules results in prejudice to the Fund, the solicitor may be required to reimburse the difference between the sum payable out of the Fund in respect of the claim and the sum which would have been payable in the absence of that prejudice (see rule 19.11 at p.807).

29.09   Independent advice for clients

If a client makes a claim against a solicitor or notifies an intention to do so, or if the solicitor discovers an act or omission which would justify such a claim, the solicitor is under a duty to inform the client that independent advice should be sought.

1. In cases where a client is not aware of the circumstance but the solicitor discovers an act or omission which would justify a claim, the Council recommends that the solicitor should in addition:

    (a)   inform SIF;

    (b)   seek the approval of SIF regarding the terms of any further communication to the client;

    (c)   confirm any oral communication in writing.

2. If the client refuses to seek independent advice, the solicitor should decline to continue to act unless satisfied that there is no conflict of interest. See also **15.04**, p.316.

3. In cases where the client or third party seeks independent advice and the solicitor is asked to make papers available to the new solicitor who is instructed, it is strongly recommended that the original solicitor keeps copies of these documents for reference.

29.10   Claims handling – rights of SIF

Solicitors Indemnity Fund Limited has the right to take over the conduct of the defence or settlement of claims.

SIF will not require any legal proceedings to be contested unless so advised by leading counsel – see rule 19.6 (Annex 29A at p.806).

Solicitors' Indemnity (Enactment) Rules 1998 and Solicitors' Indemnity Rules 1998

SOLICITORS' INDEMNITY (ENACTMENT) RULES 1998

Rules made under section 37 of the Solicitors Act 1974 and section 9 of the Administration of Justice Act 1985 with the concurrence of the Master of the Rolls on the 21st day of July, 1998.

1. The Solicitors' Indemnity Rules 1987 as amended from time to time shall be further amended with effect from 1st September 1998 and shall continue in force thereafter in the form annexed hereto in which form they may be known as the Solicitors' Indemnity Rules 1998.

2. The Solicitors' Indemnity (Incorporated Practice) Rules 1991 as amended from time to time shall continue in force only in respect of the Indemnity Periods commencing on 1st September 1991 and 1st September 1992.

3. The contributions payable in respect of the Indemnity Periods commencing prior to 1st September 1996 shall remain unaltered.

4. In respect of any Indemnity Periods commencing on or after 1st September 1996 the Society shall retain the power under Rule 35 of the Solicitors' Indemnity Rules 1996 to determine Supplementary Contributions in respect of any such period.

5. The indemnity available in respect of the Indemnity Periods commencing prior to 1st September 1998 shall remain unaltered.

ANNEX

SOLICITORS' INDEMNITY RULES 1998

Rules made under section 37 of the Solicitors Act 1974 and section 9 of the Administration of Justice Act 1985 by the Council of the Law Society with the concurrence of the Master of the Rolls on the 4th day of May 1987, as amended subsequently, regulating indemnity provision in respect of the practices of solicitors, recognised bodies and registered foreign lawyers carried on wholly or in part in England and Wales.

29

PART I – GENERAL PROVISIONS AND DEFINITIONS

1. CITATION

The Rules may be cited as the Solicitors' Indemnity Rules 1998.

2. ESTABLISHMENT AND MAINTENANCE OF FUND

The Society is hereby authorised to establish and maintain a Fund (hereinafter called "the Fund") in accordance with the provisions of these Rules.

3. PURPOSE OF THE FUND

The purpose of the Fund is to provide indemnity against loss as mentioned in section 37 of the Solicitors Act 1974 as extended by section 9 of the Administration of Justice Act 1985 and section 89 of the Courts and Legal Services Act 1990 in the circumstances, to the extent and subject to the conditions and exclusions specified by the Solicitors' Indemnity Rules 1987 as the same have been and are in force and amended and applied from time to time and by any future Rules continuing, amending, adding to, applying or re-enacting such or other Rules to provide such indemnity in respect of annual Indemnity Periods commencing on 1st September in each year (starting in 1987) unless and until otherwise determined by future Rules.

4. INDEMNITY PERIODS BEFORE 1ST SEPTEMBER 1987

The Master Policies taken out and maintained and the certificates issued by the Society pursuant to the Solicitors' Indemnity Rules 1975 to 1986 shall continue to provide cover subject to and in accordance with their terms in respect of their respective periods up to and including 31st August 1987. They shall not provide cover in respect of any subsequent period.

5. APPLICATION OF THE RULES

These Rules shall apply to a Practice carried on by:

(a)   a sole solicitor or a partnership of solicitors;

(b)   a multi-national partnership;

(c)   a recognised body; and

(d)   a recognised body in partnership with one or more solicitors and/or one or more other recognised bodies.

6. CONTRIBUTIONS

The Fund shall be established and maintained by payments (hereinafter called "Contributions") which shall be made or caused to be made by solicitors, recognised bodies and registered foreign lawyers in respect of each Indemnity Period in accordance with Part IV of these Rules.

7. CONTINUITY OF FUND

Notwithstanding the power (if the Society so determines) to levy Supplementary Contributions in respect of any Indemnity Period, the Society may maintain the Fund as a single continuous Fund, and any deficiency in respect of one Indemnity Period may be met in whole or part from Contributions in respect of another Period or Periods and any balance in respect of one Period may be applied to the benefit of any other Period or Periods.

8. MANAGEMENT AND ADMINISTRATION

The Fund shall be held, managed and administered in accordance with Part V of these Rules by Solicitors Indemnity Fund Limited, a company set up by the Society for this purpose, or by such other person or persons (including the Society itself) as the Society may hereafter designate for such purpose, in place of Solicitors Indemnity Fund Limited. References in these Rules to Solicitors Indemnity Fund Limited shall include any such other person or persons.

9. SCOPE OF INDEMNITY

The following persons, namely

(a) solicitors, former solicitors, registered foreign lawyers practising in partnership with solicitors, and persons formerly practising as registered foreign lawyers in partnership with solicitors;

(b) employees and former employees of the above;

(c) recognised bodies and former recognised bodies; and

(d) officers and employees and former officers and employees of recognised bodies and former recognised bodies,

shall be provided with indemnity out of the Fund against loss arising from claims in respect of civil liability incurred in Private practice in their aforesaid capacities or former capacities in the manner set out in Rule 15 and in the circumstances, to the extent and subject to the conditions and exclusions set out in Part II of these Rules and not otherwise.

10. WAIVERS

The Society shall have power in any case or class of cases to waive in writing prospectively or retrospectively any obligation on any solicitor, recognised body or registered foreign lawyer under these Rules and to amend or revoke any such waiver.

11. TERMINATION OF THE FUND

29

Following the expiry of the last Indemnity Period in respect of which the Fund shall provide indemnity as aforesaid, the Fund shall continue to be held, managed and administered by Solicitors Indemnity Fund Limited for so long as and to the extent that the Society, in the light of the reports made to it by Solicitors Indemnity Fund Limited, may consider necessary or appropriate for the purpose of providing indemnity in respect of any claim(s) made or intimated during any Indemnity Period and/or during or subsequent to any Indemnity Period arising out of circumstances notified during any

Indemnity Period as circumstances which might give rise to such claim(s). As and when the Society no longer considers it necessary or appropriate that all or any part of the Fund should be so held, managed and administered, the Society may require all or any part of the Fund not so required to be released to the Society which shall apply the same if and to the extent the Society considers it practicable for the purpose of providing indemnity in any other way permitted by section 37(2) of the Solicitors Act 1974 and otherwise for the overall benefit of the solicitors' profession in such manner as it may decide.

12. DEFINITIONS

For the purposes of these Rules:

12.1   A "Certificate" means in respect of each Indemnity Period a certificate required to be delivered in respect of a Practice under Rule 27.

12.2   A "Continuing Practice" means:

(a) for the purposes of calculating any Contribution due in respect of the Indemnity Period commencing on 1st September 1998, a Practice

    (i)   which commenced prior to 1st October 1997 and which was required to deliver a Certificate by 31st October 1997;

    (ii) in which the number and identity of the Principals has not changed since 31st October 1997 or, if a Certificate was duly delivered, from that of the Practice to which such Certificate related;

    (iii) which has not since 31st October 1997 succeeded to the whole or any part of any Previous Practice; and

    (iv) which is not an Existing New Practice as defined by Rule 12.4(a);

(b) for the purposes of the Certificate required to be delivered by 31st October 1998 under Rule 27, a Practice

    (i)   which commenced prior to 1st October 1998 and which was required to deliver a Certificate by 31st October 1998;

    (ii) in which the number and identity of the Principals has not changed since 31st October 1998 or, if a Certificate was duly delivered, from that of the Practice to which such Certificate related;

    (iii) which has not since 31st October 1998 succeeded to the whole or any part of any Previous Practice; and

    (iv) which is not an Existing New Practice as defined by Rule 12.4(b).

12.3   (a) "Default Initial Annual Contribution" bears the meaning ascribed in Rule 39.4.2 and Rule 39.6.2.

    (b) "Default Initial Shortfall Contribution" bears the meaning ascribed in Rule 40.4.2 and Rule 40.6.2.

12.4   An "Existing New Practice" is:

(a) for the purposes of calculating any Contribution due in respect of the Indemnity Period commencing on 1st September 1998, a Practice which has commenced since 30th September 1996 and before 1st September 1997, and which has not succeeded to the whole or any part of any Previous Practice (other than a New Practice);

(b) for the purposes of the Certificate required to be delivered by 31st October 1998 under Rule 27, a Practice which has commenced since 30th September 1997 and before 1st September 1998, and which has not succeeded to the whole or any part of any Previous Practice (other than a New Practice).

12.5 "Foreign lawyer" and "registered foreign lawyer" have the meanings assigned to them by section 89 of the Courts and Legal Services Act 1990.

12.6 The "Gross Fees" of a Practice include all professional fees, remuneration, retained commission and income of any sort whatsoever of the Practice including notarial fees where a solicitor notary operates a notarial practice in conjunction with a solicitor's practice but excluding only:

(a) interest;

(b) the reimbursement of disbursements;

(c) any amount charged in respect of Value Added Tax;

(d) remuneration derived from any office excluded from the definition of Private practice by virtue of Rule 12.15(3)(c);

(e) dividends;

(f) rents received by a Practice;

(g) income and capital profits from reserved funds established or other investments made by a Practice;

(h) bad debts accepted as written off by either the Inland Revenue or Customs and Excise.

12.7 "Indemnity Period" means the period of one year commencing on 1st September in any calendar year (starting in 1987) unless and until otherwise determined by future Rules; and the "Relevant Indemnity Period" in relation to contributions or indemnity means that Indemnity Period in respect of which such contributions are payable or such indemnity is to be provided in accordance with these Rules.

12.8 "Master Policies" and "Master Policy Certificates" means the policies and certificates referred to in Rule 4 and "Master Policy Insurers" means the insurers thereunder.

12.9 "Member" of a practice means any principal therein; any officer thereof in the case of a recognised body; any recognised body which is a partner or held out to be a partner therein and any officer of such recognised body; any person employed in connection therewith (including any trainee solicitor); any solicitor who is a consultant to or associate in the practice; any foreign lawyer who is a consultant or associate in the practice; and any solicitor or foreign lawyer who is working in the practice as an agent or locum tenens, whether he or she is so working under a contract of service or contract for services; and the estate and/or personal representative(s) of any such persons.

12.10 A "multi-national partnership" means a partnership whose members consist of one or more registered foreign lawyers and one or more solicitors.

12.11 A "New Practice" means:

(a) for the purposes of calculating any Contribution due in respect of the Indemnity Period commencing on 1st September 1998, a Practice which has commenced on or since 1st September 1997, and which has not succeeded to the whole or any part of any Previous Practice (other than another New Practice);

29

(b) for the purpose of the Certificate required to be delivered by 31st October 1998 under Rule 27, a Practice which has commenced on or since 1st September 1998 and which has not succeeded to the whole or any part of any Previous Practice (other than another New Practice).

12.12 A "Notice of Succession" means a notice under Rule 27 and "succeed" and "succession" includes any taking over of the whole or any part of any Previous Practice whether as a result of any merger, acquisition, split or cession of any practice(s) or of any retirement or addition of principals.

12.13 "Overseas" means outside England and Wales.

12.14 An "Overseas Practice" means a Practice carried on wholly from an overseas office or offices, including a Practice deemed to be a Separate Practice by virtue of Rule 12.21(b).

12.15 (1) "Practice" means a practice to the extent that it carries on Private practice providing professional services as a solicitor or solicitors or as a multi-national partnership and shall include the business or practice carried on by a recognised body in the providing of professional services such as are provided by individuals practising in Private practice as solicitors or by multi-national partnerships, whether such Practice is carried on by the recognised body alone or in partnership either with a solicitor or solicitors or with another recognised body.

(2) "Private practice" shall be deemed to include:

(a) the acceptance and performance of obligations as trustees;

(b) notarial practice where a solicitor notary operates such notarial practice in conjunction with a solicitor's practice, whether or not the notarial fees accrue to the benefit of the solicitor's practice.

(3) "Private practice" does not include:

(a) practice to the extent that any fees or other income accruing do not accrue to the benefit of the Practice carrying on such practice (except as provided by paragraph (2)(b) above);

(b) practice by a solicitor in the course of his or her employment with an employer other than a solicitor or recognised body or multi-national partnership; in which connection and for the avoidance of doubt:

(i) any such solicitor does not carry on Private practice when he or she acts in the course of his or her employment for persons other than his or her employer;

(ii) any such solicitor does not carry on Private practice merely because he or she uses in the course of his or her employment a style of stationery or description which appears to hold him or her out as a principal or solicitor in Private practice;

(iii) any practice carried on by such a solicitor outside the course of his or her employment will constitute Private practice;

(c) discharging the functions of the following offices:

(i) judicial office;

(ii) Under Sheriffs;

      (iii) members and clerks of such tribunals, committees, panels and boards as the Council may from time to time designate but including those subject to the Tribunals and Inquiries Act 1992, the Monopolies and Mergers Commission, Legal Aid Area Committees and Parole Boards;

      (iv) Justices' Clerks;

      (v) Superintendent Registrars and Deputy Superintendent Registrars of Births, Marriages and Deaths and Registrars of Local Crematoria;

      (vi) such other offices as the Council may from time to time designate.

12.16 (a) A "Practice in Default" is a Practice which is either in Certificate Default, Succession Default or Questionnaire Default.

      (b) A "Practice in Certificate Default" is any Practice which is required to deliver a Certificate by or on the preceding 31st October or within 28 days of any succession and in respect of which no Certificate has been so delivered.

      (c) A "Practice in Succession Default" is any Practice required to deliver a Notice of Succession within 28 days of any succession during the Relevant Indemnity Period and in respect of which no Notice of Succession has been so delivered.

      (d) A "Practice in Questionnaire Default", in respect of the Indemnity Period commencing on 1st September 1998, is any Practice which is required to deliver a Year 2000 Compliance Questionnaire by or on a date determined by the Council or within 28 days of the commencement of the Practice, whichever is the later, under Rule 27.4 and in respect of which no such Questionnaire has been so delivered in accordance with that Rule.

12.17 The "preceding 30th September" and "preceding 31st October" mean the 30th September and 31st October respectively preceding the commencement on 1st September of the Relevant Indemnity Period.

12.18 "Previous Practice" means any practice which shall have ceased to exist as such (for whatever reason, including by reason of (a) any death, retirement or addition of principals or (b) any split or cession of the whole or part of its practice to another without any change of principals).

12.19 "Principal" means:

      (a) a solicitor who is a partner or sole practitioner, or a registered foreign lawyer who is a partner, and includes any solicitor or registered foreign lawyer held out as a principal; and

      (b) additionally in relation to a Practice carried on by a recognised body alone, or a Practice in which a recognised body is or is held out to be a partner:

         (i) a solicitor or registered foreign lawyer who beneficially owns the whole or any part of a share in such recognised body; or

         (ii) a solicitor or registered foreign lawyer who is the ultimate beneficial owner of the whole or any part of a share in such recognised body through the medium of some other recognised body or bodies.

29

12.20   A "recognised body" means a body corporate for the time being recognised under section 9 of the Administration of Justice Act 1985.

12.21   (a)   A "Separate Practice" means a Practice in which the number and identity of the Principals is not the same as the number and identity of the Principals in any other Practice. When the same Principals in number and identity carry on practice under more than one name or style, there is only one Practice.

      (b)   In the case of a partnership or recognised body of which more than 25% of the Principals are registered foreign lawyers, any overseas offices shall be deemed to form a Separate Practice from the offices in England and Wales.

      (c)   In the case of an Overseas office of a Practice, the fact that a Principal or a limited number of Principals represent all the Principals in the Practice on a local basis shall not of itself cause that Overseas office to be a Separate Practice provided that any fee or other income arising out of that office accrues to the benefit of the Practice.

      (d)   In the case of a recognised body the fact that all of the shares in the recognised body are beneficially owned by only some of the Principals in another Practice, shall not, of itself, cause such a recognised body to be a Separate Practice provided that any fee or other income arising out of the recognised body accrues to the benefit of that other Practice.

12.22   "The Society" and "the Council" have the meanings assigned to them by the Solicitors Act 1974.

12.23   A "solicitor" means a person who has been admitted as a solicitor of the Supreme Court of England and Wales and whose name is on the roll kept by the Society under section 6 of the Solicitors Act 1974.

12.24   A "Successor Practice" means:

      (i)   for the purposes of calculating any Contribution due in respect of the Indemnity Period commencing on 1st September 1998, a Practice which is not a New Practice and which after 30th September 1997 succeeds (whether in consequence of any change in Principals or not) to the whole or any part of any Previous Practice, for value or otherwise, in any of the following cases, or in any other case of succession not specified thereby:

Case (I):

A Practice which would be a Continuing Practice but for the retirement therefrom of one or more Principal(s) or the addition of one or more new Principal(s).

Case (II):

A Practice which would be a New Practice but for its acquisition of the whole or part of another Practice commencing prior to or on 30th September 1997 and being required to deliver a Certificate by or on 31st October 1997.

Case (III):

A Practice commencing prior to or on 30th September 1997 and required to deliver a Certificate by or on 31st October 1997 which succeeds to the whole or part of a New Practice.

Case (IV):

A Practice resulting from the merger between the whole or part of two or more Previous Practices, or the acquisition by one of the whole or part of one or more other Previous Practices, such Previous Practices having commenced prior to or on 30th September 1997 and being required to deliver a Certificate by or on 31st October 1997.

Case (V):

A Practice remaining after a Previous Practice splits or cedes part of its Practice to another Practice or to a firm of foreign lawyers;

(ii) for the purposes of the Certificate required to be delivered by a Practice under Rules 27.2 and 27.3, a Practice which is not a New Practice and which after the preceding 30th September succeeds (whether in consequence of any change in Principals or not) to the whole or any part of any Previous Practice, for value or otherwise, in any of the following cases, or in any other case of succession not specified thereby:

Case (I):

A Practice which would be a Continuing Practice but for the retirement therefrom of one or more Principal(s) or the addition of one or more new Principal(s).

Case (II):

A Practice which would be a New Practice but for its acquisition of the whole or part of another Practice commencing prior to or on the preceding 30th September and being required to deliver a Certificate by or on the preceding 31st October.

Case (III):

A Practice commencing prior to or on the preceding 30th September and required to deliver a Certificate by or on the preceding 31st October which succeeds to the whole or part of a New Practice.

Case (IV):

A Practice resulting from the merger between the whole or part of two or more Previous Practices, or the acquisition by one of the whole or part of one or more other Previous Practices, such Previous Practices having commenced prior to or on the preceding 30th September and being required to deliver a Certificate by or on the preceding 31st October.

Case (V):

A Practice remaining after a Previous Practice splits or cedes part of its Practice to another Practice or to a firm of foreign lawyers.

12.25 "Usual Basis of Accounting" means the basis of accounting used by a Practice, being a generally accepted basis of accounting for solicitors and applied to the Practice consistently from year to year.

12.26 (a) "Year 2000 Compliant" and "Year 2000 Compliance" mean that neither performance nor functionality of the Computer System is affected by dates prior to, during and after the year 2000. In particular:

29

    (i)   no value for current date will cause any interruption in operation of the Computer System;

    (ii)   date-based functionality must behave consistently for dates prior to, during and after year 2000;

    (iii) in all interfaces and data storage, the century in any date must be specified either explicitly or by unambiguous algorithms or inferencing rules;

    (iv) year 2000 must be recognised as a leap year.

(b)   "Computer System" shall mean all or any part or combination of any of the following: any computer, data processing equipment or media, storage and retrieval or communication system, network, protocol, storage device, micro chip, integrated circuit, real-time clock system or similar device or any computer software (including but not limited to application software, operating systems, run time environments or compilers), hardware, firmware or micro code.

PART II – INDEMNITY COVER

13. INDEMNITY

Upon receipt of the Initial Contribution due and any Value Added Tax payable thereon in accordance with these Rules, the Practice and each Member thereof, shall become entitled to be provided with indemnity out of the Fund in the manner, to the extent and subject to the conditions and exclusions set out in these Rules against:

(a)   all loss (including liability for third party claimants' costs) incurred by the Practice or any Member thereof at any time arising directly from:

    (i)   any claim(s) first made or intimated against the Practice or any Member thereof during the Indemnity Period in respect of any description of civil liability whatsoever which may have been incurred in Private practice by the Practice or by a Member as a Member of such Practice or (in the case of a Principal in the Practice) by such Principal as a Principal in any Previous Practice;

    (ii)   any claim in respect of any such description of civil liability as aforesaid made or intimated against the Practice or any Member thereof whether during or subsequent to the Indemnity Period arising out of circumstances notified to Solicitors Indemnity Fund Limited during the Indemnity Period as circumstances which might give rise to such a claim; and

(b)   all costs and expenses incurred with the consent of Solicitors Indemnity Fund Limited (such consent not to be unreasonably withheld) in the defence or settlement or compromise of any such claim as aforesaid.

14. EXCLUSIONS FROM COVER

14.1   The Fund shall not afford any indemnity in respect of any loss arising out of any claim:

(a) for death, bodily injury, physical loss or physical damage to property of any kind whatsoever (other than property in the care, custody and control of the Practice or Member thereof in connection with its, his or her Private practice for which it, he or she is responsible, not being property occupied or used by it, him or her for the purposes of the Practice);

(b) for any alleged breach or other relief in respect of any partnership or partnership agreement between the Principals in the Practice or between any Principal therein and any other person as Principals in any Previous Practice;

(c) for wrongful dismissal or termination of articles of clerkship or training contract or any other alleged breach or any other relief by either party in respect of any contract of employment by the Practice or any Member thereof; and/or for wrongful termination or any other alleged breach or any other relief by either party in respect of any contract for supply to or use by the Practice or any Member thereof of services and/or materials and/or equipment and/or other goods;

(d) for the payment of a trading debt incurred by the Practice or any Member thereof;

(e) in respect of any undertaking given by any Principal or by a recognised body or on his, her or its behalf (whether in his, her or its own name or in the name of the Practice) to any person in connection with the provision of finance, property, assistance or other advantage whatsoever to or for the benefit of such Principal or any other Principal or of his or her or any other Principal's spouse or children or of such recognised body or of any business, firm, company, enterprise, association or venture owned or controlled by him, her or it or any other Principal or in a beneficial capacity whether alone or in concert with others, EXCEPT to the extent that the person seeking indemnity shall establish that he, she or it was unaware that the undertaking was or was likely to be connected with the provision of any such finance, property, assistance or other advantage;

(f) in respect of any dishonest or fraudulent act or omission, but nothing in this exclusion shall prevent any particular Member of the Practice who is not concerned in such dishonesty or fraud being indemnified in accordance with these Rules in respect of any loss arising out of any claim in respect of any dishonest or fraudulent act or omission by any other such Member;

(g) in respect of any liability incurred in connection with an Overseas Practice. In relation to a partnership or recognised body having any overseas offices deemed by Rule 12.21(b) to form a Separate Practice, a liability shall be deemed to have been incurred in connection with the office where or from which the major part of the work out of which the loss arose in respect of which indemnity is sought was being done. In the event of doubt as to which (if any) office satisfies this requirement, the liability shall be deemed to have been incurred in connection with the office to which the person who accepted the initial instructions was most closely connected;

(h) in respect of any liability incurred in connection with a Practice in relation to which the obligation to pay Contribution under the Rules has been exempted under Rule 32 or, unless otherwise provided by the terms of the waiver, waived by the Council under Rule 10 (or in each case under any corresponding earlier Rule);

29

(i)   arising out of any circumstances or occurrences which have been notified under the Master Policy or any certificate issued under the Master Policy or any other insurance existing prior to 1st September 1987;

(j)   in respect of any adjustment by way of claims loading which may at any future date or in respect of any future period be made by reference to any claim or claims first made or intimated during any Indemnity Period;

(k)   in respect of any liability incurred by any person in his, her or its capacity as a shareholder or beneficial owner of a share in a recognised body notwithstanding the definition of Principal in Rule 12.19;

(l)   in respect of any act or omission on the part of any Principal whilst acting on behalf of any Practice or any Member thereof in connection with any matter affecting the business of the Practice provided that at the time of such act or omission such Principal was a Principal in such Practice;

(m)   where a Practice or any Member thereof is entitled to indemnity under any insurance except in respect of any amount greater than the amount which would have been payable under such insurance in the absence of the indemnity provided by the Fund.

14.2   For the avoidance of doubt, any claim or claims by any Member or former Member of any Practice or any Previous Practice against any Member or former Member of any such Practice for the payment of the whole or any part of the deductible paid or due in respect of a claim already notified or made under these Rules or any previous Rules is not a loss arising within the meaning of Rule 13 and shall in no event be recoverable hereunder.

15.   MANNER OF INDEMNITY

15.1   Such indemnity shall be provided, according to the decision of Solicitors Indemnity Fund Limited as set out in Rule 15.2, in any one or any combination of the following ways:

(a)   by payment, in or towards satisfaction of the claim and/or claimant's costs and expenses, to or to the order of the claimant making the claim;

(b)   by payment, in respect of the claim and/or claimant's costs and expenses and/or costs and expenses incurred in respect of the defence or settlement or compromise of the claim, to or to the order of the person against whom the claim is made;

(c)   by payment, in or towards discharge of costs and expenses incurred in respect of the defence or settlement or compromise of the claim, to or to the order of the legal advisers, adjusters or other persons by whom or in respect of whose services such costs and expenses were incurred.

15.2   Solicitors Indemnity Fund Limited shall in any particular case, and notwithstanding the insolvency or bankruptcy of any person for whom indemnity is provided, have the sole and absolute right to decide in which way or combination of ways indemnity is provided.

16.   SOURCE OF INDEMNITY

16.1   Such indemnity shall be provided and any claim thereto shall lie and be made exclusively out of and against the Fund.

16.2   Solicitors Indemnity Fund Limited shall have no obligation to provide indemnity save to the extent that the same can be provided out of the Fund.

16.3   In no circumstances shall any claim to indemnity lie or be made against the Society or the Council.

16.4   Save as provided in Rule 11, the Fund shall be available exclusively for the purpose specified in Rule 3.

16.5   In no circumstances shall the Fund or any part thereof be available or be treated by any person as available (whether by virtue of any claim, attachment, execution or proceeding or otherwise howsoever) for or in connection with any other purpose.

17.   MAXIMUM LIABILITY OF THE FUND

17.1   The liability of the Fund as stated in Rule 13(a) shall in no event exceed in respect of each such claim the Indemnity Limit for the Relevant Indemnity Period.

17.2   All claims arising from the same act or omission (whether or not made or intimated or arising out of circumstances notified during the same Indemnity Period and whether or not involving the same or any number of different Practices and/or Members of such Practices) shall be regarded as one claim.

17.3   If a payment exceeding the Indemnity Limit is made to dispose of any such claim (or, in circumstances within Rule 17.2, claims) for loss (including claimants' costs) such as stated in Rule 13(a), then any liability of the Fund for costs and expenses under Rule 13(b) shall be limited to such proportion of such costs and expenses as the Indemnity Limit bears to the amount of the payment so made.

18.   INDEMNITY LIMIT

The Indemnity Limit shall be £1,000,000 each and every claim (including claimants' costs).

19.   CONDITIONS

19.1   The Practice and each Member thereof shall procure that notice to Solicitors Indemnity Fund Limited shall be given in writing as soon as practicable of:

(a)   any claim(s) the subject of Rule 13 made or intimated during the Relevant Indemnity Period against it, him or her including any claim for or likely to be for more than £500 which but for Rules 21 to 23 would have fallen within the scope of indemnity afforded by these Rules;

(b)   the receipt by it, him or her of notice of any intention to make any such claim(s).

19.2   The Practice and any Member thereof may also give notice in writing to Solicitors Indemnity Fund Limited of any circumstances of which it, he or she shall become aware which may (whether during or after the Relevant Indemnity Period) give rise to any such claim(s).

29

19.3   If notice is given to Solicitors Indemnity Fund Limited under Rule 19.1(b) or 19.2, any claim subsequently made (whether during or after the Relevant Indemnity Period) pursuant to such an intention to claim or arising from circumstances so notified shall be deemed to have been made at the date when such notice was given.

19.4   The Practice and each Member thereof shall not admit liability for, or settle, any claim falling within Rule 13 or incur any costs or expenses in connection therewith without the prior consent of Solicitors Indemnity Fund Limited (such consent not to be unreasonably withheld).

19.5   Subject to Rule 19.6:

(a)   the Practice and each Member thereof shall procure that Solicitors Indemnity Fund Limited shall be entitled at the Fund's own expense at any time to take over the conduct in the name of the Practice or Member of the defence or settlement of any such claim, including any claim in respect of which the Practice or Member may become entitled to partial indemnity under any insurance with any insurers and any claim which but for Rules 21 to 23 would have fallen within the scope of the indemnity afforded by these Rules; and

(b)   Solicitors Indemnity Fund Limited may after taking over the defence or settlement of any such claim conduct the same as it may in its absolute discretion think fit notwithstanding any dispute or difference, whether or not referred to arbitration under Rule 20, which may exist or arise between it and the Practice or Member.

19.6   No Practice or Member thereof shall be required to contest any legal proceedings unless a Queen's Counsel (to be mutually agreed upon or failing agreement to be appointed by the President of the Society for the time being) shall advise that such proceedings should be contested.

19.7   Without prejudice to Rules 19.4, 19.5 and 19.6, the Practice and each Member thereof shall keep Solicitors Indemnity Fund Limited informed in writing at all times, whether or not Solicitors Indemnity Fund Limited shall specifically so request, as to the development and handling of any claim, intimated claim, notice or circumstances the subject of or arising subsequent to any notice given to Solicitors Indemnity Fund Limited under Rule 19.1 or 19.2; and shall consult and co-operate with Solicitors Indemnity Fund Limited in relation thereto as Solicitors Indemnity Fund Limited may request whether or not Solicitors Indemnity Fund Limited shall take over the conduct thereof.

19.8   The Fund waives any rights of subrogation against any Member of the Practice save where those rights arise in connection with

(a)   a dishonest or criminal act by that Member; or

(b)   the provision of indemnity under the exception to Rule 14.1(e); or

(c)   a claim to indemnity in circumstances where that Member has received a net benefit to which he or she was not entitled as a consequence of another Member being provided with indemnity out of the Fund;

and save as otherwise expressly provided in these Rules.

19.9   If the Practice or any Member thereof shall prefer any claim to indemnity out of the Fund knowing the same to be false or fraudulent as regards amount or otherwise, it, he or she shall forfeit any claim to any such indemnity in respect of any claim or future claim against the Practice or Member to which the false or fraudulent claim to indemnity out of the Fund may have related or relate.

19.10 Where there has been a failure to pay any instalment of any Contribution due or any Value Added Tax payable in accordance with these Rules and a claim has been made or intimated against the Practice or any Member thereof in respect of which such Practice or Member would otherwise have been entitled to be provided with indemnity, Solicitors Indemnity Fund Limited shall provide such indemnity by payment (up to the Indemnity Limit) in or towards satisfying, or enabling the Practice or Member concerned to satisfy, the claim and claimants' costs and such Practice shall thereafter upon request reimburse to Solicitors Indemnity Fund Limited on behalf of the Fund the whole or such part as Solicitors Indemnity Fund Limited may request of any payment so made and of any costs and expenses incurred in its defence, settlement or compromise, and each Principal therein shall be jointly and severally responsible to Solicitors Indemnity Fund Limited for such reimbursement accordingly. Provided always that Solicitors Indemnity Fund Limited shall require such reimbursement only to the extent of (a) any increase which in its opinion may have occurred in the total payable out of the Fund (including costs and expenses) as a result of such failure, together with (b) such amount as may be necessary to satisfy any unpaid Contribution and Value Added Tax and interest thereon at the rate of 4% above Barclays Bank base rate with quarterly rests or at such other rate as the Society may from time to time publish in the Law Society's Gazette.

19.11 Where non-compliance with any provision of these Rules by any Practice or any Member thereof claiming to be entitled to indemnity out of the Fund has resulted in prejudice to the handling or settlement of any claim in respect of which such Practice or Member is entitled to indemnity hereunder, such Practice or Member shall reimburse to Solicitors Indemnity Fund Limited on behalf of the Fund the difference between the sum payable out of the Fund in respect of that claim and the sum which would have been payable in the absence of such prejudice. Provided always that it shall be a condition precedent of the right of the Fund to such reimbursement that it shall first have provided full indemnity for such Practice or Member by payment (up to the Indemnity Limit) in or towards satisfying, or enabling such Practice or Member to satisfy, the claim and claimants' costs in accordance with the terms hereof.

19.12 In respect of any loss arising from any claim or claims as described by Rule 13(a) arising out of any dishonest or fraudulent act or omission of any Member of the Practice, the Fund shall nonetheless be available to afford indemnity in accordance with these Rules to the Practice and any Member thereof, other than and excluding in each case the particular Member concerned in such dishonesty or fraud. Provided always that at the request of Solicitors Indemnity Fund Limited, the Practice or Member being indemnified shall:

(a) take or procure to be taken at the Fund's expense all reasonable steps to obtain reimbursement for the benefit of the Fund from or from the personal representatives of any such Member concerned in such dishonesty or fraud, and

(b) procure that any reimbursement so obtained together with any monies which but for such fraud or dishonesty would be due to such Member concerned in such dishonesty or fraud shall be paid to the Fund up to but not exceeding

29

the amounts paid by the Fund in respect of such claim together with any expenditure reasonably incurred by the Fund in obtaining such reimbursement.

19.13 In the event of indemnity being afforded under the exception to Rule 14.1(e), the Practice or Member being indemnified shall take or procure to be taken at the Fund's expense all reasonable steps to obtain reimbursement for the benefit of the Fund from any person to whom any benefit arising from the giving of any undertaking accrues in the circumstances set out in Rule 14.1(e). Provided always that such reimbursement shall not exceed:

(a) the amount paid by the Fund by way of indemnity together with any expenditure reasonably incurred by the Fund in obtaining such reimbursement, or

(b) the amount of any benefit accruing to such person,

whichever is the lesser.

19.14 In respect of any claim to indemnity including any claim which but for Rules 21 to 23 would have fallen within the scope of the indemnity afforded by these Rules, Solicitors Indemnity Fund Limited may appoint solicitors (hereinafter Panel Solicitors) to act on its behalf and on behalf of the Practice or any Member thereof, and Panel Solicitors shall:

(a) act at the sole direction of the Fund for any purpose falling within the scope of these Rules, including acting on the Court record for the Practice or any Member thereof, and

(b) disclose to Solicitors Indemnity Fund Limited as required any statement or information given to or which becomes known to Panel Solicitors in the course of so acting, and such disclosure shall be treated as having been made directly to Solicitors Indemnity Fund Limited by the Practice or Member.

19.15 (a) Every Practice and each Principal therein shall take all reasonable steps and precautions and exercise all due diligence to ensure that any Computer System, wherever situated and whether or not the property of the Practice, which is used, operated or directly or indirectly relied upon by the Practice or any Member thereof is Year 2000 Compliant.

(b) In respect of each and every matter on which it is retained every Practice and each Principal therein shall consider the potential or actual relevance of the Year 2000 Compliance (or lack of it) of any Computer System of any party in any way connected with the said matter (whether or not that party has itself retained the Practice) and shall either provide such advice (if any) as is appropriate in the light of the nature and scope of the Practice's retainer or recommend that such advice (if any) as is appropriate in the light of the nature and scope of the Practice's retainer be sought from a third party.

(c) Where a claim has been made or intimated against a Practice or any Member thereof as a direct or indirect consequence of:

(i) any matter which constitutes or arises from a failure on the part of the Practice to comply with sub-paragraph (a) and/or (b) above and/or

(ii) the actual, alleged or possible lack of Year 2000 Compliance of any Computer System or the actual, alleged or possible failure of any party (whether or not they are the claimant(s)) to ensure the Year 2000 Compliance of any Computer System

the Fund shall nonetheless afford indemnity in accordance with and subject to these Rules to the Practice and any Member thereof. Solicitors Indemnity Fund Limited shall provide such indemnity by payment (up to the Indemnity Limit) in or towards satisfying, or enabling the Practice or Member concerned to satisfy, the claim and claimants' costs and such Practice shall thereafter upon request reimburse to Solicitors Indemnity Fund Limited on behalf of the Fund the whole or such part as Solicitors Indemnity Fund Limited in its discretion (having regard to the extent of the attempts by the Practice (whether before or after 1st September 1998) before the act or omission giving rise or allegedly giving rise to the claim to comply with sub-paragraph (a) and/or (b) above and to avert or minimise any claims of the type to which this sub-paragraph (c) refers, including steps taken by the Practice by way of education and training on Year 2000 Compliance issues) may request of any payment so made and of any costs and expenses incurred in its defence, settlement or compromise and each Principal therein shall be jointly and severally responsible to Solicitors Indemnity Fund Limited for such reimbursement accordingly.

20. ARBITRATION

Any dispute or difference concerning any claim or the quantum of any claim to be provided with indemnity in accordance with these Rules shall be referred to the sole arbitrament, which shall be final and binding, of a person to be appointed on the application of either party in default of agreement by the President of the Society for the time being. Any such arbitration shall take place and be conducted between, on the one hand, the person for whom indemnity is provided, the party to the dispute or difference and, on the other hand, Solicitors Indemnity Fund Limited for and in respect of the Fund.

21. DEDUCTIBLES

21.1   For the purposes of these Rules:

   (a)   the "Deductible" means in respect of any claim the sum calculated by reference to the total number of Relevant Principals and shall be the amount set out in Table I which corresponds to a Practice with the same number of Principals as there are Relevant Principals;

   (b)   a "Relevant Principal" means a Principal or former Principal who is liable for the claim by virtue of having been a Principal in the Practice which was concerned with the matters giving rise to the claim at the date when such matters occurred;

   (c)   "Due Proportion of the Deductible" means a sum equal to the amount of the Deductible divided by the number of Relevant Principals except where the number of Relevant Principals exceeds fifty when it means a sum equal to the amount of the Deductible divided by the number of Relevant Principals still in practice as Principals at the Date of Notification (provided such number still exceeds fifty);

   (d)   the "Date of Notification" means either the date of receipt by Solicitors Indemnity Fund Limited of the first of any notices given under either Rule 19.1 or 19.2, or the date of receipt by Solicitors Indemnity Fund Limited of

29

any claim or intimation of claim in respect of which there is or may be an entitlement to indemnity out of the Fund, whichever is the earlier. Provided however that if in either case such date is subsequent to the Relevant Indemnity Period, the Date of Notification shall be deemed to be the date any claim was first made or intimated against the Practice or any Member thereof;

(e) the "Aggregate Deductible" is the amount set out in Table II corresponding to the number of Principals in the Practice as at 1st September 1998 or, where applicable, the date of commencement given in any notice required to be delivered under either Rule 26 or 27 during the Relevant Indemnity Period.

21.2 Each and every claim shall be subject to a Deductible in respect of which the Fund shall not afford indemnity under Rule 13(a).

21.3 Each Relevant Principal shall be liable for a Due Proportion of the Deductible PROVIDED THAT:

(a) In the case of any Relevant Principal practising in the same Practice as any other Relevant Principal(s) at the Date of Notification such Relevant Principal shall be jointly and severally liable for such sum as is equal to the total sum of the Due Proportions of the Deductible payable by all Relevant Principals in that Practice.

(b) Solicitors Indemnity Fund Limited shall disregard the Due Proportion(s) of the Deductible payable by:

(i) any insolvent or bankrupt Relevant Principal;

(ii) any Relevant Principal in a Practice where the total sum of Deductible payments in respect of claims to which the Relevant Indemnity Period applies is equal to that Practice's Aggregate Deductible;

(iii) any Relevant Principal in a Practice to the extent that such Practice has reduced its Deductible liability under Rule 22.1;

(iv) any Relevant Principal who as at the Date of Notification has ceased to be a Principal in any Practice and who does not become a Principal in any Practice within 12 months of that date;

PROVIDED ALWAYS THAT where the number of Relevant Principals exceeds fifty, the definition in Rule 21.1(c) shall apply and (i) and (iv) above shall not apply unless the number of Principals in practice as Principals at the Date of Notification is fifty or less.

(c) Solicitors Indemnity Fund Limited may pay, or include in any payment made, out of the Fund in respect of any claim, the whole or any part of any Deductible applicable thereto, and in that event the Deductible or any Due Proportion of the Deductible shall be reimbursed forthwith to the Fund by the appropriate Relevant Principal(s) in accordance with Rule 21.3(a).

21.4 Every Practice shall have an Aggregate Deductible.

22. REDUCING THE DEDUCTIBLE OR AGGREGATE DEDUCTIBLE

22.1 In respect of any claim not yet made or intimated and not arising from circumstances already known to the Practice or any Member thereof or notified to Solicitors Indemnity Fund Limited:

(a) the Deductible applicable to the Practice in accordance with Table I may be reduced to 50% or to nil (such reduction also having the effect of reducing the Aggregate Deductible applicable to the Practice in accordance with Table II to 50% or to nil);

(b) the Aggregate Deductible applicable to the Practice in accordance with Table II may be reduced as follows:

(i) to one third or two thirds;

(ii) to one third or two thirds, of any aggregate calculated in accordance with Rule 22.1(a);

in each case upon payment by the Practice to the Fund of an additional Contribution in an amount calculated on a scale approved by the Society from time to time taking into account the claims record of such Practice and of any other Practice(s) in which any Principal therein was previously a Member.

| TABLE I | | | |
| Deductible (Rule 21.1(a)) | | | |
Number of Principals in Practice	Amount per Practice (£)	Number of Principals in Practice	Amount per Practice (£)
1	3,000	27	74,250
2	3,000	28	77,000
3	4,500	29	79,750
4	6,000	30	82,500
5	7,500	31	93,000
6	10,500	32	96,000
7	12,250	33	99,000
8	14,000	34	102,000
9	18,000	35	105,000
10	20,000	36	108,000
11	22,000	37	111,000
12	24,000	38	114,000
13	26,000	39	117,000
14	28,000	40	120,000
15	30,000	41	123,000
16	32,000	42	126,000
17	36,000	43	129,000
18	40,000	44	132,000
19	44,000	45	135,000
20	48,000	46	138,000
21	52,000	47	141,000
22	56,000	48	144,000
23	60,000	49	147,000
24	64,000	50	150,000
25	68,000	Over 50	150,000
26	71,500		

29

TABLE II Aggregate Deductible (Rule 21.1(e))			
Number of Principals in Practice	Amount per Practice (£)	Number of Principals in Practice	Amount per Practice (£)
1	9,000	27	222,750
2	9,000	28	231,000
3	13,500	29	239,250
4	18,000	30	247,500
5	22,500	31	279,000
6	31,500	32	288,000
7	36,750	33	297,000
8	42,000	34	306,000
9	54,000	35	315,000
10	60,000	36	324,000
11	66,000	37	333,000
12	72,000	38	342,000
13	78,000	39	351,000
14	84,000	40	360,000
15	90,000	41	369,000
16	96,000	42	378,000
17	108,000	43	387,000
18	120,000	44	396,000
19	132,000	45	405,000
20	144,000	46	414,000
21	156,000	47	423,000
22	168,000	48	432,000
23	180,000	49	441,000
24	192,000	50	450,000
25	204,000	Over 50	450,000
26	214,500		

22.2   Without prejudice to Rule 22.1, where a claim arises out of circumstances known to the Practice or any Member thereof but not notified prior to the Relevant Indemnity Period and an amendment to the Deductible or Aggregate Deductible was in force during the Indemnity Period when such knowledge was acquired, Solicitors Indemnity Fund Limited may apply the benefit of any Deductible or Aggregate Deductible amendment effected for the Relevant Indemnity Period under Rule 22.1 to any such claim, but shall not be required to do so in any circumstances.

23.   PENALTY DEDUCTIBLES

23.1   For the purposes of these Rules:

(a)   the "Penalty Deductible" means in respect of any claim arising out of the circumstances referred to in Rule 23.2 such sum as is equal to 50% of the amount set out in Table I which corresponds to a Practice with the same number of Principals as there are Relevant Principals;

(b) "Due Proportion of the Penalty Deductible" means a sum equal to the amount of the Penalty Deductible divided by the number of Relevant Principals except where the number of Relevant Principals exceeds fifty when it means a sum equal to the amount of the Penalty Deductible divided by the number of Relevant Principals still in practice as Principals at the Date of Notification (provided such number still exceeds fifty);

(c) the "Aggregate Penalty Deductible" is the sum equivalent to 50% of the amount set out in Table II corresponding to the number of Principals in the Practice as at 1st September 1998 or, where applicable, the date of commencement given in any notice required to be delivered under either Rule 26 or 27 during the Relevant Indemnity Period.

23.2 Each and every claim arising from a failure to:

(a) commence proceedings within the time permitted under sections 2, 5 or 11 of the Limitation Act 1980;

(b) commence proceedings within the time permitted under section 111 of the Employment Rights Act 1996;

(c) serve High Court proceedings within the time permitted under Order 6 Rule 8 of the Rules of the Supreme Court 1965 (or County Court proceedings within the time permitted under Order 7 Rule 20 of the County Court Rules 1981);

(d) request the proper officer to fix a day for a hearing as required under Order 17 Rule 11 of the County Court Rules 1981;

(e) serve a notice or issue an application within the periods permitted under Part II of the Landlord and Tenant Act 1954;

(f) register at Companies House a charge against the assets of a company within the time permitted by section 395 of the Companies Act 1985;

(g) apply to register a protected transaction within the priority period afforded under the Land Registration (Official Searches) Rules 1993;

(h) execute a Deed of Variation within the two years permitted under section 142(1) of the Inheritance Tax Act 1984 and/or to give written notice to the Inland Revenue within the six months permitted under section 142(2);

shall in addition to any Deductible applicable be subject to a Penalty Deductible in respect of which the Fund shall not afford indemnity under Rule 13(a) PROVIDED THAT such failure occurred on or after 1st September 1996.

23.3 Each Relevant Principal shall be liable for a Due Proportion of the Penalty Deductible PROVIDED THAT:

(a) In the case of any Relevant Principal practising in the same Practice as any other Relevant Principal(s) at the Date of Notification such Relevant Principal shall be jointly and severally liable for such sum as is equal to the total sum of the Due Proportions of the Penalty Deductible payable by all Relevant Principals in that Practice.

(b) Solicitors Indemnity Fund Limited shall disregard the Due Proportion(s) of the Penalty Deductible payable by:

(i) any insolvent or bankrupt Relevant Principal;

29

(ii) any Relevant Principal in a Practice where the total sum of Penalty Deductible payments in respect of claims to which the Relevant Indemnity Period applies is equal to that Practice's Aggregate Penalty Deductible;

(iii) any Relevant Principal who as at the Date of Notification has ceased to be a Principal in any Practice and who does not become a Principal in any Practice within 12 months of that date;

PROVIDED ALWAYS THAT where the number of Relevant Principals exceeds fifty, the definition in Rule 23.1(b) shall apply and (i) and (iii) above shall not apply unless the number of Principals in practice as Principals at the Date of Notification is fifty or less.

(c) Solicitors Indemnity Fund Limited may pay, or include in any payment made, out of the Fund in respect of any claim, the whole or any part of any Penalty Deductible applicable thereto, and in that event the Penalty Deductible or any Due Proportion of the Penalty Deductible shall be reimbursed forthwith to the Fund by the appropriate Relevant Principal(s) in accordance with Rule 23.3(a).

23.4 Every Practice shall have an Aggregate Penalty Deductible.

24. INTEREST ON OVERDUE DEDUCTIBLE PAYMENTS

Solicitors Indemnity Fund Limited may at any time give in respect of any Practice notice that any reimbursement to the Fund of the whole or any part of any Deductible or Penalty Deductible payment made by Solicitors Indemnity Fund Limited on behalf of the Practice shall, unless paid in full within such further period as Solicitors Indemnity Fund Limited may stipulate, carry interest on any outstanding balance from time to time at 4% above Barclays Bank base rate with quarterly rests or at such other rate as the Society may from time to time determine and publish in the Law Society's Gazette. Any such interest shall be calculated from the date(s) when such balance was payable or from such later date(s) as Solicitors Indemnity Fund Limited may direct.

25. COVER FOR MEMBERS OF PREVIOUS PRACTICES

Any Member of any Previous Practice who

(a) shall during any period of insurance or Indemnity Period have been either:

(i) an Assured as a result of the issue of a certificate under one or more of the Master Policies, or

(ii) a person entitled to be indemnified by virtue of the issue of a receipt under the Solicitors' Indemnity Rules 1987–1990 or a payment of Contribution and Value Added Tax thereon as stated in any subsequent Rules, and who

(b) is not, at the time during the Relevant Indemnity Period when a claim is first made or intimated against him or her or when circumstances which might give rise to such a claim are first notified by him or her to Solicitors Indemnity Fund Limited, either

(i) a person entitled to be indemnified as aforesaid, or

    (ii)   a person who would be entitled to be indemnified but for the failure (whether by him or her or any other person) to pay Initial Contribution due in accordance with these Rules, or

    (iii) a former Principal in a Previous Practice in respect of which any other Principal at the date when the matters giving rise to the claim occurred is entitled to indemnity under Rule 13(a)

shall, nevertheless, be entitled to indemnity out of the Fund in respect of any such claim first made or intimated or arising out of any such circumstances notified to the extent and subject to the conditions and exclusions (including specifically, for the avoidance of any doubt, that in Rule 14.1(h)) set out in these Rules, mutatis mutandis. For this purpose references in these Rules to the Practice and any Member thereof shall, where appropriate, be read as referring to the Previous Practice and the Members thereof.

PART III – OBLIGATION TO PROVIDE INFORMATION

26.   NOTICE OF PRACTICE INFORMATION

A solicitor or registered foreign lawyer shall forthwith give to Solicitors Indemnity Fund Limited notice in writing of:

(a)   the address of any New Practice which he or she commences or in which he or she becomes a Principal and the date of such commencement or becoming a Principal;

(b)   the name and address of any Practice in which he or she becomes a Principal and the date of becoming such Principal;

(c)   any change in the place or places of business of any other Practice in which he or she is or becomes a Principal;

(d)   any cessation of any Practice in which he or she was before such cessation a Principal;

(e)   in the case of a solicitor or registered foreign lawyer who is a Principal in a Practice which is carried on by a recognised body alone, or in which a recognised body is or is held out to be a partner, any expiry or revocation of the recognition of such recognised body under the Solicitors' Incorporated Practice Rules in force from time to time, or any revocation of recognition of such recognised body under the Administration of Justice Act 1985 schedule 2.

27.   NOTICE OF SUCCESSION, CERTIFICATE AND YEAR 2000 COMPLIANCE QUESTIONNAIRE

27.1   A solicitor or registered foreign lawyer who is or becomes a Principal in a practice which succeeds by succession (other than a Case I succession) to any Previous Practice shall within 28 days of such succession deliver to Solicitors Indemnity Fund Limited a Notice of Succession.

27.2   In respect of each Indemnity Period commencing on or after 1st September 1998 each Principal shall by or on the preceding 31st October deliver to Solicitors Indemnity Fund Limited a Certificate in respect of each Practice (except a New Practice or an Overseas Practice) in which he or she is or was at any time during the year ending on the preceding 31st October a Principal.

29

27.3   In respect of each Indemnity Period commencing on or after 1st September 1998 a solicitor or registered foreign lawyer who is or becomes a Principal in a Practice which succeeds by succession (other than a Case I succession) to any Previous Practice in the period between the preceding 31st October and the commencement of the Relevant Indemnity Period shall within 28 days of the succession deliver to Solicitors Indemnity Fund Limited a Certificate in respect of such Successor Practice.

27.4   In respect of the Indemnity Period commencing on 1st September 1998 each solicitor or registered foreign lawyer who is or becomes a Principal in a Practice (other than through a Case I succession) shall by or on a date to be determined by the Council or within 28 days of the commencement of the Practice, whichever is the later, deliver to Solicitors Indemnity Fund Limited a Year 2000 Compliance Questionnaire fully and accurately completed in respect of each such Practice.

28.   FORM OF NOTICE OF SUCCESSION, CERTIFICATE AND YEAR 2000 COMPLIANCE QUESTIONNAIRE

28.1   A Certificate required under Rule 27.2 or Rule 27.3 and a Notice of Succession required under Rule 27.1 shall be in the forms set out in the Schedule hereto or such other forms as may from time to time be approved by the Council and shall

(a)   state with reasonable accuracy the Gross Fees of the Practice to which it relates calculated in accordance with the Usual Basis of Accounting of the Practice in respect of an accounting period which complies with the requirements of Rule 28.3 or Rule 28.4;

(b)   contain the other information required by the forms;

(c)   contain the declaration required by the forms.

28.2   A Year 2000 Compliance Questionnaire required under Rule 27.4 shall be in such form as may from time to time be approved by the Council and shall contain the information and the declaration required by the form.

28.3   An accounting period in respect of a Practice other than an Existing New Practice complies with the requirements of this Rule if:

(a)   it is of twelve months' duration or of such duration as the Council may in any case or class of cases determine;

(b)   it ends not earlier than 30th September 12 months prior to the preceding 30th September nor later than the preceding 30th September; and

(c)   it begins on the day after the end of the accounting period to which the last previous Certificate (if any) or the last previous Notice of Succession, whichever is the later, delivered in respect of the Practice related except where the last previous Certificate was delivered in respect of an Existing New Practice in which case the accounting period shall begin on the same day as that given in the previous Certificate.

28.4   An accounting period in respect of an Existing New Practice complies with the requirements of this Rule if it begins on the day when the Practice commenced and ends on the preceding 30th September.

28.5   In respect of any Practice which has succeeded to any Previous Practice the Certificate and any Notice of Succession shall state or include

    (a)   the Gross Fees of any such Previous Practice merged in or wholly acquired or succeeded to by the Practice;

    (b)   where the Practice has acquired or succeeded to a part, but not the whole, of a Previous Practice, a due proportion corresponding to the part so acquired or succeeded to of the Gross Fees of that Previous Practice;

for as much of the relevant accounting period as elapsed before such succession.

28.6   In respect of an Existing New Practice the Gross Fees stated in the Certificate and any Notice of Succession shall be grossed up to produce a notional Gross Fees figure for a 12 month period deemed to have commenced on the date of commencement of the Practice and for the purposes of Rules 38, 39 and 40 "the Gross Fees disclosed in the Certificate" and "the Gross Fees disclosed in the Notice of Succession" shall be taken to be the grossed up notional Gross Fees figure.

29. INVESTIGATORY POWERS

29.1   In order to ascertain whether full and accurate information has been provided in accordance with these Rules and to obtain such information so far as it may not have been, Solicitors Indemnity Fund Limited or the Society may appoint any person whom it thinks fit and may require any solicitor or Practice or any registered foreign lawyer who is or was a Principal to produce to any person so appointed at such times and places as he or she may request all such accounting and other records and documents, and to supply him or her in relation thereto with such information and explanations, as he or she may from time to time request.

29.2   Any solicitor, Practice or registered foreign lawyer to whom any requirement under Rule 29.1 is made by Solicitors Indemnity Fund Limited or the Society shall comply therewith and with such requests as may be made by the person appointed.

29.3   Any person appointed under Rule 29.1 may make to the Society and to Solicitors Indemnity Fund Limited such report or reports as may be requested or as he or she may think fit.

29.4   Any such requirement under Rule 29.1 shall be made in writing and may be sent or delivered by Solicitors Indemnity Fund Limited or the Society to the solicitor, Practice or registered foreign lawyer, or to such person as is mentioned in Rule 30.3, at any place specified as the principal practising address or registered office of the Practice as stated in the latest Certificate, Notice of Succession or other notice delivered under these Rules (where such a Certificate or notice has been delivered).

29.5   Any such requirement sent by registered post or recorded delivery to any such place so specified shall be deemed to have been received by the solicitor, Practice or registered foreign lawyer, or by such person as is mentioned in Rule 30.3, within 48 hours (excluding Saturdays, Sundays and Bank Holidays) after the time of posting.

29

30. GENERAL

30.1 A solicitor or registered foreign lawyer shall not be required to deliver or give such a Certificate, Year 2000 Compliance Questionnaire, Notice of Succession or other notice in respect of a Practice in relation to which another Principal therein, or such person as is mentioned in Rule 30.3, delivers or gives such a Certificate, Year 2000 Compliance Questionnaire, Notice of Succession or other notice as the case may be containing all of the information required in accordance with this Part of the Rules. In such case the Certificate, Year 2000 Compliance Questionnaire, Notice of Succession or other notice delivered or given by that other Principal or other person shall be deemed to be a Certificate, Year 2000 Compliance Questionnaire, Notice of Succession or other notice delivered or given by such solicitor or registered foreign lawyer and any declaration thereto signed by that other Principal or other person shall be deemed to be a declaration signed by such solicitor or registered foreign lawyer.

30.2 The obligation to supply information under this Part of the Rules shall not apply to a solicitor whose obligation to pay Contribution has been exempted under Rule 32.

30.3 In relation to a Practice carried on by a recognised body alone, or a Practice in which a recognised body is or is held out to be a partner, any obligation to provide any form of information under this Part of the Rules shall in addition rest upon any officer of such recognised body and upon the recognised body.

SCHEDULE
(Rule 28.1)

CERTIFICATE

[This form is sent out by Solicitors Indemnity Fund Limited and is not reproduced here.]

NOTICE OF SUCCESSION

[This form is sent out by Solicitors Indemnity Fund Limited and is not reproduced here.]

PART IV – CONTRIBUTIONS

31. OBLIGATION TO MAKE CONTRIBUTIONS

31.1 Each Principal shall make or cause to be made Initial and Supplementary Contributions in relation to each Indemnity Period as herein provided in respect of:

(a) each Separate Practice in which he or she is a Principal on 1st September;

(b) each Separate New Practice commencing during and in which he or she becomes a Principal during the Indemnity Period;

(c) each Separate Successor Practice commencing during and in which he or she becomes a Principal during the Indemnity Period.

31.2   In relation to a Practice carried on by a recognised body alone, or a Practice in which a recognised body is or is held out to be a partner, the obligation to make or cause to be made Initial and Supplementary Contributions under this Rule shall in addition rest upon the recognised body.

32.   EXEMPTIONS

Solicitors who would otherwise be required to comply with these Rules but who provide services as solicitors in all or any of the following ways and none other shall be exempted from any obligation to make Contributions under these Rules and shall not be indemnified against professional indemnity risks by the Fund:

(a)   conduct professional business for personal friends, relatives, companies wholly owned by the solicitor's family or registered charities without remuneration; PROVIDED THAT it is a condition of this exemption that every person or body for whom the solicitor acts shall be notified beforehand that the solicitor is not indemnified against professional indemnity risks by the Fund and, if such be the case, that he or she is not insured against professional indemnity risks or, if he or she is so insured to what extent and in what amount. Any such notification required by this proviso must if given orally immediately be confirmed in writing;

(b)   administer oaths or take affidavits.

33.   CONTRIBUTIONS – WHEN DUE AND PAYABLE

33.1   Subject to Rules 34 and 35, the Initial Contribution calculated under this Part of the Rules, any additional Contribution payable under Rule 22.1 and any additional charge payable under Rule 45 (together in each case with Value Added Tax) shall be due in full on the first day of the Indemnity Period or on the date of the commencement of the Practice whichever is the later but shall be payable as follows:

(a)   **Continuing Practice, Existing New Practice, New Practice and Successor Practice in existence prior to the start of the Relevant Indemnity Period and not in Certificate Default**

In respect of a Separate Practice falling within Rule 31.1(a), other than a Practice in Certificate Default, either

(i)   in ten consecutive monthly instalments by direct debit on the first day of each month commencing on 1st November during the Indemnity Period; or

(ii)   in full on or before the first day of the Indemnity Period;

(b)   **Continuing Practice, Existing New Practice and Successor Practice in existence prior to the start of the Relevant Indemnity Period and in Certificate Default**

In respect of a Separate Practice falling within Rule 31.1(a) which is a Practice in Certificate Default, either

(i)   in ten consecutive monthly instalments by direct debit on the first day of each month commencing on 1st November during the Indemnity Period; or

(ii)   in full on or before the first day of the Indemnity Period;

29

(c) **New Practices commencing after the start of the Relevant Indemnity Period**

In respect of a Separate New Practice falling within Rule 31.1(b) either

(i) in consecutive monthly instalments by direct debit on the first day of each month commencing on the first day of the month immediately after the date of its commencement or on 1st November during the Indemnity Period whichever is the later date and concluding on 1st August during the Indemnity Period; or

(ii) in full on or before the date of its commencement;

(d) **Successor Practices commencing after the start of the Relevant Indemnity Period and not in Succession Default**

In respect of a Separate Successor Practice falling within Rule 31.1(c) either

(i) in consecutive monthly instalments by direct debit on the first day of each month commencing on the first day of the month immediately after the date of the succession or on 1st November during the Indemnity Period whichever is the later date and concluding on 1st August during the Indemnity Period; or

(ii) in full on or before the date of the succession;

(e) **Successor Practices commencing after the start of the Relevant Indemnity Period and in Succession Default**

In respect of a Separate Successor Practice falling within Rule 31.1(c) which is a Practice in Succession Default, either

(i) in consecutive monthly instalments by direct debit on the first day of each month commencing on the first day of the month immediately after the date of the succession or on 1st November during the Indemnity Period whichever is the later date and concluding on 1st August during the Indemnity Period; or

(ii) in full on or before the first day of its commencement; or

(f) **All Practices**

In such other manner deemed acceptable by Solicitors Indemnity Fund Limited.

33.2 If either

(a) a Practice in existence on 1st September in the Relevant Indemnity Period shall fail to provide Solicitors Indemnity Fund Limited by that date with a valid direct debit to pay such instalments in accordance with these Rules; or

(b) a Practice commencing during the Relevant Indemnity Period shall fail to provide Solicitors Indemnity Fund Limited not later than 28 days after the commencement of the Practice with a valid direct debit to pay such instalments in accordance with these Rules; or

(c) any Practice shall fail to pay any such instalment within seven days of it having become payable;

then the whole of its Contribution or, as the case may be, of any remaining instalments for the Relevant Indemnity Period and the additional charge payable under Rule 45 shall become payable forthwith.

34. APPORTIONMENT OF CONTRIBUTION

34.1 Subject to Rules 34.4 and 34.5, in respect of any Practice which ceases after 1st September in the Relevant Indemnity Period

(a) the Initial Contribution calculated under these Rules, any additional Contribution payable under Rule 22.1 and any additional charge payable under Rule 45 (together in each case with Value Added Tax) shall be apportioned from 1st September in the Relevant Indemnity Period or the date of commencement of the Practice whichever is the later to the date of cessation inclusive and the sum so determined shall be due in accordance with Rule 33;

(b) any amount remaining outstanding immediately after the cessation, if any, shall be payable in full within 28 days of cessation;

(c) any amount overpaid, if any, shall be refundable in full within 28 days of the cessation.

34.2 Subject to Rules 34.3, 34.4 and 34.5 in respect of any Practice which commences after 1st September in the Relevant Indemnity Period, the Initial Contribution calculated under these Rules, any additional Contribution payable under Rule 22.1, and any additional charge payable under Rule 45 (together in each case with Value Added Tax) shall be apportioned from the date of commencement to 31st August in the Relevant Indemnity Period and the sum so determined shall be due and payable in accordance with Rule 33.

34.3 Subject to Rule 34.5 in respect of any Practice which reduces its Deductible Proportion or aggregate under Rule 22.1 on a date after 1st September in the Relevant Indemnity Period, any additional contribution payable under Rule 22.1 and any additional charge payable under Rule 45 (together in each case with Value Added Tax) shall be apportioned from that date to 31st August in the Relevant Indemnity Period and the sum so determined shall be due and payable in accordance with Rule 33.

34.4 In respect of any Practice which has reduced its Deductible Proportion or aggregate under Rule 22.1 and which has or should have in the Relevant Indemnity Period notified Solicitors Indemnity Fund Limited of a claim or receipt of any notice of intention to make a claim under Rule 19.1, no apportionment under Rule 34.1 will apply to the additional contribution payable under Rule 22.1 save where any Successor Practice to such Practice reduces its Deductible Proportion or aggregate immediately following the period in respect of which the apportionment is made.

34.5 No apportionment of contribution will apply to contributions due and payable in respect of a Successor Practice falling within Case I and a Practice ceasing as a result of a Case I succession.

35. INACCURACY IN CALCULATION OF CONTRIBUTION

29

35.1 Solicitors Indemnity Fund Limited may at any time give to any Practice written notice correcting any inaccuracy in the calculation of any Initial Contribution, whether attributable to Solicitors Indemnity Fund Limited or to any failure to provide information or inaccuracy in information provided under Part III, or howsoever occurring; and any reimbursement or any payment of additional

Contribution hereby required shall be made forthwith upon, respectively, issue or receipt of such a notice, together with any Value Added Tax applicable and (in the case of any additional Contribution payable upon correction of an inaccuracy in calculation attributable to failure to provide information or to inaccuracy in information provided under Part III) interest at a rate of 4% above Barclays Bank base rate with quarterly rests or at such other rate as the Society may from time to time determine and publish in the Law Society's Gazette.

35.2   Solicitors Indemnity Fund Limited will recalculate any claims adjustment under Rule 42 applicable to a Practice consequent upon:

(a)   a reduction in the Practice's Claims Pool calculated under Rule 42 in relation to the Indemnity Period commencing on 1st September 1998 by virtue of a reassessment as at the last Friday in June 1999 of the Indemnity Sums in respect of those claims included in the Practice's Claims Pool;

(b)   a recovery being made;

but in neither case will Solicitors Indemnity Fund Limited be liable to pay interest on the amount of any refund resulting from such recalculation.

36.   SUPPLEMENTARY CONTRIBUTIONS

Supplementary Contributions (if any) shall be made if and as the Society may at any time or times during or after the expiry of the Indemnity Period determine and in making any such determination the Society shall have complete liberty to decide whether or not all or any part of any losses or potential losses it takes into account shall consist of losses or potential losses arising from claims made or intimated or circumstances notified in the same or any previous Indemnity Period.

37.   INTEREST ON OVERDUE CONTRIBUTION

Solicitors Indemnity Fund Limited may at any time give in respect of any Practice notice that any Initial and/or Supplementary Contributions payable in respect of that Practice shall, unless paid in full within such further period as Solicitors Indemnity Fund Limited may stipulate, carry interest on any outstanding balance from time to time at 4% above Barclays Bank base rate with quarterly rests or at such other rate as the Society may from time to time determine and publish in the Law Society's Gazette. Any such interest shall be calculated from the date(s) when such balance was payable or from such later date(s) as Solicitors Indemnity Fund Limited may direct.

38.   CALCULATION OF INITIAL CONTRIBUTION

38.1   The Initial Contribution

The Initial Contribution in respect of each Practice shall be the total of:

(i)   the Initial Annual Contribution calculated in accordance with Rule 39; and

(ii)   the Initial Shortfall Contribution calculated in accordance with Rule 40.

38.2   Overseas Principals

In the calculation under this Rule and Rules 39 to 42 (inclusive) of the Initial Contribution due in respect of a Practice having any overseas offices deemed by Rule

12.21(b) to form a Separate Practice, those Principals who, as at the date of the relevant Certificate or Notice of Succession, are practising mainly from an overseas office or offices shall not be taken into account.

39. CALCULATION OF INITIAL ANNUAL CONTRIBUTION

39.1 New Practice in existence prior to the start of the Relevant Indemnity Period

The Initial Annual Contribution in respect of a New Practice in existence prior to the start of the Relevant Indemnity Period shall be £500 subject to any claims adjustment or additional contribution where appropriate under Rules 42 and 44.

39.2 New Practice commencing after the start of the Relevant Indemnity Period

The Initial Annual Contribution in respect of a New Practice commencing after the start of the Relevant Period shall be £500 subject to any claims adjustment or additional contribution where appropriate under Rules 42 and 44 apportioned from the date of commencement of the Practice to the end of the Relevant Indemnity Period in accordance with Rule 34.

39.3 All other Practices in existence prior to the start of the Relevant Indemnity Period and not in Certificate Default

Where a Certificate was duly delivered under Rule 27 (or, in the case of a Case I succession, where no Certificate was required), the Initial Annual Contribution in respect of a Continuing Practice, an Existing New Practice and a Successor Practice shall be calculated as follows

(a) by taking the Gross Fees disclosed in the Certificate (or, in the case of a Case I succession, the Certificate duly delivered by the Previous Practice) and

   (i) if the Gross Fees are less than or equal to £250,000 applying to the Gross Fees the standard rate of 10.12% to produce the unadjusted base annual contribution; or

   (ii) if the Gross Fees are more than £250,000 applying to the Gross Fees the standard rate of 10.12% multiplied by the "Tapering Factor" applicable to the Practice to produce the unadjusted base annual contribution.

   (iii) A Practice's "Tapering Factor" is determined by the following equation:

   "Tapering Factor" $= 93.6112 \times$ (Gross Fees of the Practice)$^{-0.3652}$

   (iv) In no case shall the unadjusted base annual contribution be less than £500.

(b) The unadjusted base annual contribution shall be subject to risk banding by applying against the appropriate proportions of the unadjusted base annual contribution (in accordance with the breakdown of the fees of the Practice by work type as disclosed in the Certificate) the appropriate risk factor in accordance with Table III to produce the total risk banded annual contribution.

(c) The total risk banded annual contribution shall be subject to claims adjustment where appropriate in accordance with Rule 42.

(d) The Initial Annual Contribution due shall be that resulting from the calculation specified in (a), (b) and (c) together with any additional sum payable under Rule 44.

29

TABLE III		
	Category of Work	**Risk Factor**
1	Criminal Law Work	0.04
2	Debt Collection	0.04
3	Children Work	0.04
4	Mental Health Tribunal Work	0.04
5	Welfare Work	0.04
6	Immigration Work	0.04
7	Offices and Appointments	0.04
8	Arbitration Work	0.04
9	Adjudication Work	0.04
10	Mediation Work	0.04
11	Administering Oaths	0.04
12	Employment Work (non-litigious)	0.04
13	Property Selling and Valuation Work	0.04
14	Parliamentary Agency	0.04
15	Agency Advocacy Work	0.04
16	Residential Conveyancing Work	2.02
17	Commercial Conveyancing Work	2.29
18	Landlord and Tenant Work	0.74
19	Town and Country Planning	0.25
20	Trust and Probate Work	0.46
21	Matrimonial Work	0.17
22	Personal Injury Work	1.20
23	Debt Collection Work (other)	0.68
24	Financial Advice and Services	1.00
25	Commercial Work	0.52
26	Defendant Litigious Work for Insurers	0.55
27	Litigious Work (other)	0.55
28	Non-Litigious Work (other)	0.30

39.4 **All Practices in existence prior to the start of the Relevant Indemnity Period and in Certificate Default**

39.4.1 Where no Certificate was delivered under Rule 27 (save where, in the case of a Case I succession, the Previous Practice has delivered a Certificate under Rule 27), a Continuing Practice, an Existing New Practice and a Successor Practice shall be treated as a Practice in Certificate Default and the Default Initial Annual Contribution shall be as follows:

39.4.2 The Initial Annual Contribution in respect of any Practice in Certificate Default ("the Default Initial Annual Contribution") consists of the sum of £15,000 multiplied by the number of Principals in such Practice at the commencement of the Relevant Indemnity Period subject to any loading (but not any discount) and additional contribution where appropriate in accordance with Rules 42 and 44.

39.4.3 Where there is delivered in respect of any Practice in Certificate Default a Certificate which (apart from its lateness) complies with the requirements of Part III, an assessment will be made taking account of such Certificate of the Initial Annual Contribution which would have been due under Rule 39.3 in respect of any Practice in respect of which there became due as a Practice in Certificate Default a Default Initial Annual Contribution. Such Practice shall then

(a) be entitled to a rebate of any difference in its favour between the Initial Annual Contribution actually paid and the Final Annual Contribution shown by such assessment, but any such rebate shall be paid without interest and not earlier than 15 months after 1st September on which the Relevant Indemnity Period began or, in the case of a Successor Practice, not earlier than 15 months after the date of commencement of the Practice; or

(b) forthwith pay any balance shown to be payable together, if Solicitors Indemnity Fund Limited shall so require in writing, with interest on any outstanding balance from time to time at the rate of 4% above Barclays Bank base rate with quarterly rests or such other rate, for such period and with such rests as the Society may from time to time determine and publish in the Law Society's Gazette.

39.5 Successor Practice commencing after the start of the Relevant Indemnity Period and not in Succession Default

Where a Notice of Succession is duly delivered consequent upon a succession during the Relevant Indemnity Period, the Initial Annual Contribution in respect of a Successor Practice shall be calculated as follows

(a) by taking the Gross Fees disclosed in the Notice of Succession and

(i) if the Gross Fees are less than or equal to £250,000 applying to the Gross Fees the standard rate of 10.12% to produce the unadjusted base annual contribution; or

(ii) if the Gross Fees are more than £250,000 applying to the Gross Fees the standard rate of 10.12% multiplied by the "Tapering Factor" applicable to the Practice to produce the unadjusted base annual contribution.

(iii) A Practice's "Tapering Factor" is determined by the following equation:

"Tapering Factor" $= 93.6112 \times (\text{Gross Fees of the Practice})^{-0.3652}$

(iv) In no case shall the unadjusted base annual contribution be less than £500.

(b) The unadjusted base annual contribution shall be subject to risk banding by applying against the appropriate proportions of the unadjusted base annual contribution (in accordance with the breakdown of the fees of the Practice by work type as disclosed in the Notice of Succession) the appropriate risk factor in accordance with Table III to produce the total risk banded annual contribution.

(c) The total risk banded annual contribution shall be subject to claims adjustment where appropriate in accordance with Rule 42.

(d) The Initial Annual Contribution due shall be that resulting from the calculation specified in (a), (b) and (c) together with any additional sum payable under Rule 44 apportioned from the date of commencement of the Practice to the end of the Relevant Indemnity Period in accordance with Rule 34.

29

39.6 **Successor Practice commencing after the start of the Relevant Indemnity Period and in Succession Default**

39.6.1 Where no Notice of Succession is delivered within 28 days of the commencement of practice, a Successor Practice which commenced after the start of the Relevant Indemnity Period shall be treated as a Practice in Succession Default.

39.6.2 The Initial Annual Contribution in respect of any Practice in Succession Default ("the Default Initial Annual Contribution") consists of the sum of £15,000 multiplied by the number of Principals in such Practice at the date of commencement of such Practice subject to any loading (but not any discount) and additional contribution where appropriate in accordance with Rules 42 and 44.

39.6.3 Where subsequent to the commencement of the Practice there is delivered in respect of any Practice in Succession Default a Notice of Succession which (apart from its lateness) complies with the requirements of Part III, an assessment will be made taking account of such Notice of Succession of the Initial Annual Contribution which would have been due under Rule 39.5 in respect of any Practice in respect of which there became due as a Practice in Succession Default a Default Initial Annual Contribution. Such Practice shall then

(a) be entitled to a rebate of any difference in its favour. The rebate shall be paid without interest and not earlier than 15 months after 1st September on which the Relevant Indemnity Period began or, in the case of a Successor Practice not earlier than 15 months after the date of commencement of the Practice; or

(b) forthwith pay any balance shown to be payable together, if Solicitors Indemnity Fund Limited shall so require in writing, with interest on any outstanding balance from time to time at the rate of 4% above Barclays Bank base rate and with quarterly rests or such other rate, for such period and with such rests as the Society may from time to time determine and publish in the Law Society's Gazette.

40. CALCULATION OF INITIAL SHORTFALL CONTRIBUTION

40.1 **New Practice in existence prior to the start of the Relevant Indemnity Period**

The Initial Shortfall Contribution in respect of a New Practice in existence prior to the start of the Relevant Indemnity Period shall be £100 subject to any claims adjustment where appropriate under Rule 42.

40.2 **New Practice commencing after the start of the Relevant Indemnity Period**

The Initial Shortfall Contribution in respect of a New Practice commencing after the start of the Relevant Period shall be £100 subject to any claims adjustment where appropriate under Rule 42 apportioned from the date of commencement of the Practice to the end of the Relevant Indemnity Period in accordance with Rule 34.

40.3 **All other Practices in existence prior to the start of the Relevant Indemnity Period and not in Certificate Default**

Where a Certificate was duly delivered under Rule 27 (or, in the case of a Case I succession, where no Certificate was required), the Initial Shortfall Contribution in respect of a Continuing Practice, an Existing New Practice and a Successor Practice shall be calculated as follows

(a)   by taking the Gross Fees disclosed in the Certificate (or, in the case of a Case I succession, the Certificate duly delivered by the Previous Practice) and applying to those fees the percentages in respect of the relevant bands in accordance with Table IV to produce the unadjusted base shortfall contribution which in no case shall be less than £100;

(b)   the proportion of the sum so arrived at equivalent to the proportion undertaken of work regarded as low risk work in accordance with Rule 41.1 shall be subject to a discount of 80% where appropriate;

(c)   the sum arrived at after taking into account any discount in respect of low risk work shall also be subject to claims adjustment where appropriate in accordance with Rule 42;

(d)   the Initial Shortfall Contribution due shall be that resulting from the calculation specified in (a), (b) and (c).

TABLE IV		
Gross Fees		% of Gross Fees
Over £	Up to £	
	70,000	2.94
70,000	250,000	2.28
250,000	500,000	1.99
500,000	750,000	1.60
750,000	1,500,000	1.22
1,500,000	2,500,000	1.05
2,500,000	5,000,000	0.64
5,000,000	15,000,000	0.57
15,000,000	60,000,000	0.41
60,000,000	100,000,000	0.32
100,000,000	125,000,000	0.25
125,000,000	150,000,000	0.22
150,000,000		0.17

40.4   All Practices in existence prior to the start of the Relevant Indemnity Period and in Certificate Default

40.4.1   Where no Certificate was delivered under Rule 27 (save where, in the case of a Case I succession, the Previous Practice has delivered a Certificate under Rule 27), a Continuing Practice, an Existing New Practice and a Successor Practice shall be treated as a Practice in Certificate Default and the Default Initial Contribution shall be as follows:

40.4.2   The Initial Contribution in respect of any Practice in Certificate Default ("the Default Initial Shortfall Contribution") consists of the sum of £5,000 multiplied by the number of Principals in such Practice at the commencement of the Relevant Indemnity Period but excluding any claims adjustment under Rule 42.

40.4.3   Where there is delivered in respect of any Practice in Certificate Default a Certificate which (apart from its lateness) complies with the requirements of Part

29

III, an assessment will be made taking account of such Certificate of the Initial Shortfall Contribution which would have been due under Rule 40.3 in respect of any Practice in respect of which there became due as a Practice in Certificate Default a Default Initial Shortfall Contribution. Such Practice shall then

(a) be entitled to a rebate of any difference in its favour between the Initial Shortfall Contribution actually paid and the Final Shortfall Contribution shown by such assessment, but any such rebate shall be paid without interest and not earlier than 15 months after 1st September on which the Relevant Indemnity Period began or, in the case of a Successor Practice, not earlier than 15 months after the date of commencement of the Practice; or

(b) forthwith pay any balance shown to be payable together, if Solicitors Indemnity Fund Limited shall so require in writing, with interest on any outstanding balance from time to time at the rate of 4% above Barclays Bank base rate with quarterly rests or such other rate, for such period and with such rests as the Society may from time to time determine and publish in the Law Society's Gazette.

40.5 Successor Practice commencing after the start of the Relevant Indemnity Period and not in Succession Default

Where a Notice of Succession is duly delivered consequent upon a succession during the Relevant Indemnity Period, the Initial Shortfall Contribution in respect of a Successor Practice shall be calculated as follows

(a) by taking the Gross Fees disclosed in the Notice of Succession and applying to those fees the percentages in respect of the relevant bands in accordance with Table IV to produce the unadjusted base shortfall contribution which in no case shall be less than £100;

(b) the proportion of the sum so arrived at equivalent to the proportion undertaken of work regarded as low risk work in accordance with Rule 41.1 shall be subject to a discount of 80% where appropriate;

(c) the sum arrived at after taking into account any discount in respect of low risk work shall also be subject to claims adjustment where appropriate in accordance with Rule 42;

(d) the Initial Shortfall Contribution due shall be that resulting from the calculation specified in (a), (b) and (c).

40.6 Successor Practice commencing after the start of the Relevant Indemnity Period and in Succession Default

40.6.1 Where no Notice of Succession is delivered within 28 days of the commencement of practice, a Successor Practice which commenced after the start of the Relevant Indemnity Period shall be treated as a Practice in Succession Default.

40.6.2 The Initial Shortfall Contribution in respect of any Practice in Succession Default ("the Default Initial Shortfall Contribution") consists of the sum of £5,000 multiplied by the number of Principals in such Practice at the date of commencement of such Practice but excluding any claims adjustment under Rule 42.

40.6.3   Where subsequent to the commencement of the Practice there is delivered in respect of any Practice in Succession Default a Notice of Succession which (apart from its lateness) complies with the requirements of Part III, an assessment will be made taking account of such Notice of Succession of the Initial Shortfall Contribution which would have been due under Rule 40.5 in respect of any Practice in respect of which there became due as a Practice in Succession Default a Default Initial Shortfall Contribution. Such Practice shall then

(a)   be entitled to a rebate of any difference in its favour. The rebate shall be paid without interest and not earlier than 15 months after 1st September on which the Relevant Indemnity Period began or, in the case of a Successor Practice not earlier than 15 months after the date of commencement of the Practice; or

(b)   forthwith pay any balance shown to be payable together, if Solicitors Indemnity Fund Limited shall so require in writing, with interest on any outstanding balance from time to time at the rate of 4% above Barclays Bank base rate and with quarterly rests or such other rate, for such period and with such rests as the Society may from time to time determine and publish in the Law Society's Gazette.

41.   CATEGORIES OF WORK

41.1   Low Risk Work

Subject to any future determination by the Society, the following categories of work as referred to in Table III shall each be regarded as low risk work and shall be used for the purposes of calculating the Initial Shortfall Contribution under Rule 40 and, together with the other categories set out in Rule 41.2, the Initial Annual Contribution under Rule 39 in respect of any Practice where appropriate:

(1)   **criminal law work;**

(2)   **debt collection** defined as the collection of judgment debts of not more than £7,500 or debts without dispute as to liability of not more than £7,500, and the collection of rents not exceeding £7,500 per property per annum;

(3)   **children work** defined as applications made in relation to family proceedings as defined by section 8(3) of the Children Act 1989 and including Parts III and V of the Children Act 1989;

(4)   **mental health tribunal work** defined as representation of patients detained under the Mental Health Act 1983 at hearings of the Mental Health Review Tribunal;

(5)   **welfare work** defined as advice and assistance about assessment of a client's entitlement to welfare benefits and for verifying an assessment by the Department of Social Security or other benefit granting bodies such as Local Authorities;

(6)   **immigration work** defined as advice and assistance on UK immigration and nationality law, including preparation for and representation before Immigration Adjudicators, Special Adjudicators, and any Tribunals or Courts up to but not including the Divisional Court, the Court of Justice of the European Union or the Commission on Human Rights of the Council of Europe;

29

(7)   discharging the functions of the following **offices and appointments:** –

   (i)   Clerk to any of the following:

   City Livery Company, Dean and Chapter, Drainage Board, Local Council, Charity or School Governing Body;

   (ii)   Diocesan Registrar, Archdeacon's Registrar or Provincial Registrar of the Provinces of the Church of England, but in each case only in respect of work covered by an Ecclesiastical Fees Order;

   (iii)   Company Secretary;

(8)   **arbitration work** defined as any work done in the discharge or the purported discharge of the functions of an arbitrator in relation to an arbitration to which the Arbitration Acts 1950–1996 apply;

(9)   **adjudication work** defined as acting as a neutral third party engaged by disputing parties to provide a non-judicial resolution of their dispute which is, subject to the terms of any contract between the disputing parties, binding upon them, but excluding arbitration work;

(10)   **mediation work** defined as acting as a neutral third party engaged by disputing parties to assist them to resolve their dispute by negotiated agreement without resort to adjudication;

(11)   **administering oaths and taking affidavits;**

(12)   **employment work** defined as all non-litigious work which excludes tribunal work in connection with employment, termination, dismissal, redundancy, discrimination at work and pension rights affected thereby;

(13)   **property selling and valuation work** defined as property selling whether or not through an estate agency and informal valuations undertaken by the practice;

(14)   **parliamentary agency** defined as all work done in the promotion of or opposition to primary or subordinate legislation;

(15)   **agency advocacy work** defined as all civil advocacy work, including attendance at a Court or Tribunal for the purpose of such advocacy, done on behalf of another indemnified practice but excluding any work done as a solicitor working as an agent or locum tenens in another practice.

41.2   Other Categories of Work

41.2.1   For the purposes of this Rule "conveyancing work" includes all work relating to the purchase, sale, transfer or mortgage of any freehold or leasehold interest in land including the creation, renewal or termination of any leasehold interest and also work done in connection with right to buy legislation.

41.2.2   Subject to any future determination by the Society, the following additional categories of work referred to in Table III shall be used for the purposes of calculating the Initial Annual Contribution under Rule 39 in respect of any Practice where appropriate:

   (16)   **residential conveyancing work** defined as work done in connection with an individual property used exclusively as a single private dwelling house including mortgage related work where the client is not, in any way, dealing with the property as part of a business;

(17) **commercial conveyancing work** defined as all non-residential conveyancing work;

(18) **landlord and tenant work** defined as litigious work relating to the creation, termination or renewal of any leasehold interest or tenancy be it commercial or residential, and any other dispute between landlord and tenant;

(19) **town and country planning** includes compulsory purchase, listed buildings and conservation areas work;

(20) **trust and probate work** includes the creation and administration of estates and trusts, statutory or otherwise, wills, enduring powers of attorney and deeds of family arrangement;

(21) **matrimonial work** includes all aspects of financial settlement but excluding work within category (3) children work and excluding work within category (16) residential conveyancing work;

(22) **personal injury work** includes medical negligence work;

(23) **debt collection work (other)** defined as debt collection not within category (2) debt collection;

(24) **financial advice and services** defined as all work done in respect of discrete investment business as defined by the Solicitors Investment Business Rules 1995;

(25) **commercial work** includes all company work;

(26) **defendant litigious work for insurers** defined as litigious work done on behalf of any person, firm, company or other body acting as a defendant insurer;

(27) **litigious work (other)** defined as all litigious work not included in any of the specific categories (1) to (26) above;

(28) **non-litigious work (other)** is all non-litigious work not included in any of the specific categories (1) to (26) above.

42. CLAIMS ADJUSTMENT

42.1 For the purposes of these Rules:

(a) The "Relevant Period" is the five year period ending on 31st August 1996.

(b) A "Discounted Probable Maximum Loss Reserve" is the maximum amount which in the judgement of the Fund is yet to be paid by the Fund in respect of a claim, discounted by 25%.

(c) An "Indemnity Sum" is any payment made by the Fund and any Discounted Probable Maximum Loss Reserve set by the Fund, in respect of, arising out of or in any way in connection with, any claim other than:

(i) any payments and reserves in respect of the costs of defending or investigating any such claim or the circumstances giving rise to it;

(ii) any reserve in respect of the claimant's costs in making any claim; and

(iii) any payments which would not have been made but for the payment of additional contribution to reduce the Deductible Proportion and/or the aggregate.

29

(d) A "Loading Claim" is any claim which was notified to the Fund during the Relevant Period in respect of which an Indemnity Sum has been incurred.

(e) The "Originating Practice" is the Practice or Previous Practice in which the act or omission giving rising to the Loading Claim occurred.

(f) The "Originating Principals" are the Principals in the Originating Practice at the date of the act or omission giving rise to the Loading Claim.

(g) A "Principal Claim Portion" is the result of dividing the Indemnity Sums incurred in respect of a Loading Claim as at the last Friday in June 1998 by the number of Originating Principals and shall attach and apply to each Originating Principal in his or her capacity as a Principal in all Practices in which he or she is a Principal.

(h) A "Principal Contribution Portion" is the result of dividing the indemnity contribution payable by a Practice or Previous Practice, other than any additional contribution payable to reduce the Deductible Proportion and/or the aggregate, by the number of Principals in the Practice at the commencement of each Indemnity Period within the Relevant Period, or in respect of a Practice or Previous Practice commencing during an Indemnity Period, the number of Principals in the Practice as at the date of commencement and shall attach to each such Principal in his or her capacity as a Principal in all Practices in which he or she is a Principal.

(i) The "Claims Pool" is the sum of the Principal Claims Portions of the Principals in a Practice.

(j) The "Contribution Pool" is the sum of the Principal Contribution Portions of the Principals in a Practice.

(k) The "Claims Ratio" is the value obtained by dividing the Claims Pool by the Contribution Pool.

(l) The "Claims Loading Factor" is the number "one" in respect of each Loading Claim.

(m) The "Principal Loading Factor" is the result of dividing the Claims Loading Factor by the number of Originating Principals and shall attach and apply to each Originating Principal in his or her capacity as a Principal in all Practices in which he or she is a Principal.

(n) The "Practice Loading Factor" is the sum of the Principal Loading Factors of the Principals in a Practice.

42.2 The calculation of the Initial Annual Contribution in respect of any Separate Practice carried out in accordance with Rule 39 shall, where appropriate, include a claims adjustment in a percentage equal to that shown opposite the claims ratio in Table V and the calculation of the Initial Shortfall Contribution in respect of any Separate Practice carried out in accordance with Rule 40 shall, where appropriate, include a claims adjustment in a percentage equal to that shown opposite the claims ratio in Table VI, save only that:

(a) a loading shall not apply to any Practice which has a Contribution Pool of nil;

(b) the amount of loading payable in any year by any Practice shall not exceed 9% of the Claims Pool for the Relevant Indemnity Period; and

(c) a discount shall not apply unless at least one Principal in the Practice shall have been credited with a Principal Contribution Portion in respect of at least three Indemnity Periods within the Relevant Period.

TABLE V (Rule 42.2)					
Claims Ratio					**Adjustment %**
	0.00				− 65
Exceeding	0.00	but not exceeding		0.02	− 60
"	0.02	"	"	0.04	− 55
"	0.04	"	"	0.06	− 50
"	0.06	"	"	0.08	− 45
"	0.08	"	"	0.10	− 40
"	0.10	"	"	0.12	− 38
"	0.12	"	"	0.14	− 36
"	0.14	"	"	0.16	− 34
"	0.16	"	"	0.18	− 32
"	0.18	"	"	0.20	− 30
"	0.20	"	"	0.24	− 28
"	0.24	"	"	0.28	− 26
"	0.28	"	"	0.32	− 24
"	0.32	"	"	0.36	− 22
"	0.36	"	"	0.40	− 20
"	0.40	"	"	0.44	− 18
"	0.44	"	"	0.49	− 16
"	0.49	"	"	0.54	− 14
"	0.54	"	"	0.59	− 12
"	0.59	"	"	0.64	− 10
"	0.64	"	"	0.69	− 8
"	0.69	"	"	0.74	− 6
"	0.74	"	"	0.79	− 4
"	0.79	"	"	0.80	− 2
"	0.80	"	"	1.20	0
"	1.20	"	"	1.24	1
"	1.24	"	"	1.28	2
"	1.28	"	"	1.32	3
"	1.32	"	"	1.36	4
"	1.36	"	"	1.40	5

etc., with the adjustment increasing by 1% in respect of each Claims Ratio increase of 0.04 up to:

Exceeding	4.80	but not exceeding		4.84	91
"	4.84	"	"	4.88	92
"	4.88	"	"	4.92	93
"	4.92	"	"	4.96	94
"	4.96	"	"	5	95
Exceeding	5				100

29

42.3   The amount of any claims loading shall be reduced by 25% if the Practice Loading Factor applicable to the Practice does not exceed that shown in Table VII and by 50% if it does not exceed that set out in Table VIII for a Practice with the same number of Principals as that which is subject to the loading.

TABLE VI (Rule 42.2)						
Claims Ratio						**Adjustment %**
	0.00					− 30
Exceeding	0.00	but	not	exceeding	0.02	− 29
"	0.02	"	"	"	0.04	− 28
"	0.04	"	"	"	0.06	− 27
"	0.06	"	"	"	0.08	− 26
"	0.08	"	"	"	0.10	− 25
"	0.10	"	"	"	0.12	− 24
"	0.12	"	"	"	0.14	− 23
"	0.14	"	"	"	0.16	− 22
"	0.16	"	"	"	0.18	− 21
"	0.18	"	"	"	0.20	− 20
"	0.20	"	"	"	0.24	− 19
"	0.24	"	"	"	0.28	− 18
"	0.28	"	"	"	0.32	− 17
"	0.32	"	"	"	0.36	− 16
"	0.36	"	"	"	0.40	− 15
"	0.40	"	"	"	0.44	− 14
"	0.44	"	"	"	0.49	− 13
"	0.49	"	"	"	0.54	− 12
"	0.54	"	"	"	0.59	− 11
"	0.59	"	"	"	0.64	− 10
"	0.64	"	"	"	0.69	− 9
"	0.69	"	"	"	0.74	− 8
"	0.74		"	"	0.79	− 7
"	0.79	"	"	"	0.85	− 6
"	0.85	"	"	"	0.91	− 5
"	0.91	"	"	"	0.97	− 4
"	0.97	"	"	"	1.04	− 3
"	1.04	"	"	"	1.12	− 2
"	1.12	"	"	"	1.20	− 1
Exceeding	1.20					0

TABLE VII (Rule 42.3)

Number of Principals	Practice Loading Factor	Number of Principals	Practice Loading Factor	Number of Principals	Practice Loading Factor	Number of Principals	Practice Loading Factor	Number of Principals	Practice Loading Factor	Number of Principals	Practice Loading Factor	Number of Principals	Practice Loading Factor
1	1.93	51	11.90	101	16.28	151	20.65	201	25.03	251	29.40	301	33.78
2	2.80	52	11.99	102	16.36	152	20.74	202	25.11	252	29.49	302	33.86
3	3.50	53	12.08	103	16.45	153	20.83	203	25.20	253	29.58	303	33.95
4	3.94	54	12.16	104	16.54	154	20.91	204	25.29	254	29.66	304	34.04
5	4.38	55	12.25	105	16.63	155	21.00	205	25.38	255	29.75	305	34.13
6	5.25	56	12.34	106	16.71	156	21.09	206	25.46	256	29.84	306	34.21
7	5.43	57	12.43	107	16.80	157	21.18	207	25.55	257	29.93	307	34.30
8	5.60	58	12.51	108	16.89	158	21.26	208	25.64	258	30.01	308	34.39
9	5.78	59	12.60	109	16.98	159	21.35	209	25.73	259	30.10	309	34.48
10	5.95	60	12.69	110	17.06	160	21.44	210	25.81	260	30.19	310	34.56
11	6.13	61	12.78	111	17.15	161	21.53	211	25.90	261	30.28	311	34.65
12	6.30	62	12.86	112	17.24	162	21.61	212	25.99	262	30.36	312	34.74
13	6.48	63	12.95	113	17.33	163	21.70	213	26.08	263	30.45	313	34.83
14	6.65	64	13.04	114	17.41	164	21.79	214	26.16	264	30.54	314	34.91
15	6.83	65	13.13	115	17.50	165	21.88	215	26.25	265	30.63	315	35.00
16	7.00	66	13.21	116	17.59	166	21.96	216	26.34	266	30.71	316	35.09
17	7.21	67	13.30	117	17.68	167	22.05	217	26.43	267	30.80	317	35.18
18	7.44	68	13.39	118	17.76	168	22.14	218	26.51	268	30.89	318	35.26
19	7.65	69	13.48	119	17.85	169	22.23	219	26.60	269	30.98	319	35.35
20	7.88	70	13.56	120	17.94	170	22.31	220	26.69	270	31.06	320	35.44
21	8.05	71	13.65	121	18.03	171	22.40	221	26.78	271	31.15	321	35.53
22	8.23	72	13.74	122	18.11	172	22.49	222	26.86	272	31.24	322	35.61
23	8.40	73	13.83	123	18.20	173	22.58	223	26.95	273	31.33	323	35.70
24	8.58	74	13.91	124	18.29	174	22.66	224	27.04	274	31.41	324	35.79
25	8.75	75	14.00	125	18.38	175	22.75	225	27.13	275	31.50	325	35.88
26	8.93	76	14.09	126	18.46	176	22.84	226	27.21	276	31.59	326	35.96
27	9.10	77	14.18	127	18.55	177	22.93	227	27.30	277	31.68	327	36.05
28	9.28	78	14.26	128	18.64	178	23.01	228	27.39	278	31.76	328	36.14
29	9.45	79	14.35	129	18.73	179	23.10	229	27.48	279	31.85	329	36.23
30	9.63	80	14.44	130	18.81	180	23.19	230	27.56	280	31.94	330	36.31
31	9.80	81	14.53	131	18.90	181	23.28	231	27.65	281	32.03	331	36.40
32	9.98	82	14.61	132	18.99	182	23.36	232	27.74	282	32.11	332	36.49
33	10.15	83	14.70	133	19.08	183	23.45	233	27.83	283	32.20	333	36.58
34	10.33	84	14.79	134	19.16	184	23.54	234	27.91	284	32.29	334	36.66
35	10.50	85	14.88	135	19.25	185	23.63	235	28.00	285	32.38	335	36.75
36	10.59	86	14.96	136	19.34	186	23.71	236	28.09	286	32.46	336	36.84
37	10.68	87	15.05	137	19.43	187	23.80	237	28.18	287	32.55	337	36.93
38	10.76	88	15.14	138	19.51	188	23.89	238	28.26	288	32.64	338	37.01
39	10.85	89	15.23	139	19.60	189	23.98	239	28.35	289	32.73	339	37.10
40	10.94	90	15.31	140	19.69	190	24.06	240	28.44	290	32.81	340	37.19
41	11.03	91	15.40	141	19.78	191	24.15	241	28.53	291	32.90	341	37.28
42	11.11	92	15.49	142	19.86	192	24.24	242	28.61	292	32.99	342	37.36
43	11.20	93	15.58	143	19.95	193	24.33	243	28.70	293	33.08	343	37.45
44	11.29	94	15.66	144	20.04	194	24.41	244	28.79	294	33.16	344	37.54
45	11.38	95	15.75	145	20.13	195	24.50	245	28.88	295	33.25	345	37.63
46	11.46	96	15.84	146	20.21	196	24.59	246	28.96	296	33.34	346	37.71
47	11.55	97	15.93	147	20.30	197	24.68	247	29.05	297	33.43	347	37.80
48	11.64	98	16.01	148	20.39	198	24.76	248	29.14	298	33.51	348	37.89
49	11.73	99	16.10	149	20.48	199	24.85	249	29.23	299	33.60	349	37.98
50	11.81	100	16.19	150	20.56	200	24.94	250	29.31	300	33.69	350	38.06

29

TABLE VIII (Rule 42.3)

Number of Principals	Practice Loading Factor	Number of Principals	Practice Loading Factor	Number of Principals	Practice Loading Factor	Number of Principals	Practice Loading Factor	Number of Principals	Practice Loading Factor	Number of Principals	Practice Loading Factor	Number of Principals	Practice Loading Factor
1	1.44	51	8.92	101	12.21	151	15.48	201	18.77	251	22.05	301	25.33
2	2.10	52	8.99	102	12.27	152	15.55	202	18.83	252	22.11	302	25.39
3	2.62	53	9.06	103	12.33	153	15.62	203	18.90	253	22.18	303	25.46
4	2.95	54	9.12	104	12.40	154	15.68	204	18.96	254	22.24	304	25.52
5	3.28	55	9.18	105	12.47	155	15.75	205	19.03	255	22.31	305	25.59
6	3.93	56	9.25	106	12.53	156	15.81	206	19.09	256	22.38	306	25.65
7	4.07	57	9.32	107	12.60	157	15.88	207	19.16	257	22.44	307	25.72
8	4.20	58	9.38	108	12.66	158	15.94	208	19.23	258	22.50	308	25.79
9	4.33	59	9.45	109	12.73	159	16.01	209	19.29	259	22.57	309	25.85
10	4.46	60	9.51	110	12.79	160	16.08	210	19.35	260	22.64	310	25.92
11	4.59	61	9.58	111	12.86	161	16.14	211	19.42	261	22.71	311	25.98
12	4.72	62	9.64	112	12.93	162	16.20	212	19.49	262	22.77	312	26.05
13	4.86	63	9.71	113	12.99	163	16.27	213	19.56	263	22.83	313	26.11
14	4.98	64	9.78	114	13.05	164	16.34	214	19.62	264	22.90	314	26.18
15	5.12	65	9.84	115	13.12	165	16.41	215	19.68	265	22.97	315	26.25
16	5.25	66	9.90	116	13.19	166	16.47	216	19.75	266	23.03	316	26.31
17	5.40	67	9.97	117	13.26	167	16.53	217	19.82	267	23.10	317	26.38
18	5.58	68	10.04	118	13.32	168	16.60	218	19.88	268	23.16	318	26.44
19	5.73	69	10.11	119	13.38	169	16.67	219	19.95	269	23.23	319	26.51
20	5.91	70	10.17	120	13.45	170	16.73	220	20.01	270	23.29	320	26.57
21	6.03	71	10.23	121	13.52	171	16.80	221	20.08	271	23.36	321	26.64
22	6.17	72	10.30	122	13.58	172	16.86	222	20.14	272	23.43	322	26.70
23	6.30	73	10.37	123	13.65	173	16.93	223	20.21	273	23.49	323	26.77
24	6.43	74	10.43	124	13.71	174	16.99	224	20.28	274	23.55	324	26.84
25	6.56	75	10.50	125	13.78	175	17.06	225	20.34	275	23.62	325	26.90
26	6.69	76	10.56	126	13.84	176	17.13	226	20.40	276	23.69	326	26.97
27	6.82	77	10.63	127	13.91	177	17.19	227	20.47	277	23.76	327	27.03
28	6.96	78	10.69	128	13.98	178	17.25	228	20.54	278	23.82	328	27.10
29	7.08	79	10.76	129	14.04	179	17.32	229	20.61	279	23.88	329	27.16
30	7.22	80	10.83	130	14.10	180	17.39	230	20.67	280	23.95	330	27.23
31	7.35	81	10.89	131	14.17	181	17.46	231	20.73	281	24.02	331	27.30
32	7.48	82	10.95	132	14.24	182	17.52	232	20.80	282	24.08	332	27.36
33	7.61	83	11.02	133	14.31	183	17.58	233	20.87	283	24.15	333	27.43
34	7.74	84	11.09	134	14.37	184	17.65	234	20.93	284	24.21	334	27.49
35	7.87	85	11.16	135	14.43	185	17.72	235	21.00	285	24.28	335	27.56
36	7.94	86	11.22	136	14.50	186	17.78	236	21.06	286	24.34	336	27.62
37	8.01	87	11.28	137	14.57	187	17.85	237	21.13	287	24.41	337	27.69
38	8.07	88	11.35	138	14.63	188	17.91	238	21.19	288	24.48	338	27.75
39	8.13	89	11.42	139	14.70	189	17.98	239	21.26	289	24.54	339	27.82
40	8.20	90	11.48	140	14.76	190	18.04	240	21.33	290	24.60	340	27.89
41	8.27	91	11.55	141	14.83	191	18.11	241	21.39	291	24.67	341	27.95
42	8.33	92	11.61	142	14.89	192	18.18	242	21.45	292	24.74	342	28.02
43	8.40	93	11.68	143	14.96	193	18.24	243	21.52	293	24.81	343	28.08
44	8.46	94	11.74	144	15.03	194	18.30	244	21.59	294	24.87	344	28.15
45	8.53	95	11.81	145	15.09	195	18.37	245	21.66	295	24.93	345	28.21
46	8.59	96	11.88	146	15.15	196	18.44	246	21.72	296	25.00	346	28.28
47	8.66	97	11.94	147	15.22	197	18.51	247	21.78	297	25.07	347	28.35
48	8.73	98	12.00	148	15.29	198	18.57	248	21.85	298	25.13	348	28.41
49	8.79	99	12.07	149	15.36	199	18.63	249	21.92	299	25.20	349	28.48
50	8.85	100	12.14	150	15.42	200	18.70	250	21.98	300	25.26	350	28.54

43. QUESTIONNAIRE DEFAULT CONTRIBUTION

43.1 Where a Year 2000 Compliance Questionnaire is required to be delivered under Rule 27.4 and has not been so delivered (save where, in the case of a Case I succession, the Previous Practice has delivered a Year 2000 Compliance Questionnaire under Rule 27.4), a Practice shall be treated as a Practice in Questionnaire Default and an additional Contribution shall become due and payable in full 28 days after written notice requiring payment of the same shall have been issued to the Practice by Solicitors Indemnity Fund Limited, save that where a Practice has opted to pay the Initial Contribution in monthly instalments by direct debit under Rule 33 Solicitors Indemnity Fund Limited may collect such additional Contribution in a similar manner.

43.2 The additional Contribution payable by a Practice in Questionnaire Default shall be the greater of £3,000 or an amount equivalent to 10% of the Initial Annual Contribution in respect of the Practice calculated in accordance with Rule 39, apportioned in a similar manner to that set out in Rule 34 but with reference to the "date to be determined by the Council" under Rule 27.4 rather than "1st September in the Relevant Indemnity Period".

43.3 Any additional Contribution due under this Rule may be payable in such other manner deemed acceptable to Solicitors Indemnity Fund Limited.

44. STRUCTURAL SURVEYS AND FORMAL VALUATIONS OF PROPERTY

(a) In addition to any Contributions otherwise provided for by these Rules, any Practice or Successor Practice providing structural surveys and/or formal valuations of property shall immediately pay an additional Contribution of £1,000 per Practice per Indemnity Period or a due proportion of that sum in respect of a Practice which provides such services for only part of the Relevant Indemnity Period.

(b) Any such Practice or Successor Practice shall notify Solicitors Indemnity Fund Limited immediately of the following:

   (i) its intention to provide structural surveys and/or formal valuations of property, and

   (ii) the number, names and qualifications of all individuals who will undertake such work within the Practice and the like information in respect of any changes or additions which may occur during the Indemnity Period.

45. PAYMENT BY INSTALMENTS – ADDITIONAL CHARGE

Any Contribution provided for by these Rules in respect of any Practice which is to be paid in instalments by direct debit, shall be subject to a charge of 4%.

46. VALUE ADDED TAX

Value Added Tax, to the extent chargeable on any relevant supply which takes or may be treated as taking place under or by virtue of these Rules, will be charged and payable in addition to and at the same time as the Contributions payable hereunder.

29

47. DECISIONS BY THE SOCIETY

For the purpose of determining the amount of any Contribution required by these Rules the Society's decision shall be final and binding on all affected on any question arising as to:

(a)   the part of any Practice merged, acquired or succeeded to;

(b)   the due proportion of any Gross Fees or Default Initial Contribution;

(c)   the number of Principals in any Practice at any date;

(d)   the information and position (including the date) in accordance with which any adjustment of Initial Contribution (if any) is assessed under Rules 39, 40, 43 and 44;

(e)   the categories of work and the risk factors (if any) which such categories may attract and the categories which are to be regarded as low risk work;

(f)   the calculation and/or the amount of any claims adjustment under Rule 42;

(g)   the Initial Contribution payable in any case of succession;

(h)   the calculation and/or amount of any Supplementary Contributions;

(i)   the Gross Fees to be attributed to the offices in England and Wales of a partnership or recognised body whose overseas offices are deemed to form a Separate Practice by virtue of Rule 12.21(b).

PART V – MANAGEMENT AND ADMINISTRATION OF THE FUND

48. POWERS OF THE SOCIETY

Solicitors Indemnity Fund Limited shall hold, and have full power to manage and administer, the Fund, subject only to:

(a)   such directions, conditions and/or requirements as the Society may from time to time issue to or impose upon it expressly pursuant to this provision, and/or

(b)   such further detailed arrangements as the Society may from time to time agree with it.

49. POWERS OF SOLICITORS INDEMNITY FUND LIMITED

Without limiting the generality of Rule 48, the management and administration of the Fund shall include power:

(a)   to collect and recover Contributions due to the Fund in accordance with these Rules;

(b)   to deposit or invest in such manner as Solicitors Indemnity Fund Limited may determine all or any part of the Fund, including any interest, dividends, profits, gains or other assets accruing to or acquired by the Fund;

(c)   to arrange such insurances as Solicitors Indemnity Fund Limited may determine in respect of the Fund and/or its assets and/or the Fund's liability under these Rules to afford indemnity in respect of claims and costs and expenses; and to handle all aspects of any such insurances, including the payment of premiums thereon out of the Fund and the making and recovery of claims thereunder;

(d) to receive, investigate and handle claims to indemnity and other notices prescribed to be given to Solicitors Indemnity Fund Limited by these Rules, including settlement and compromise and making of ex gratia payments out of the Fund in respect thereof and conduct of any dispute or difference referred to arbitration under Rule 20;

(e) to receive, investigate and handle any claim made or intimated against any person in respect of which they are or may be entitled to be provided with indemnity out of the Fund (whether or not a claim to indemnity hereunder has been made) and/or in respect of which the conduct is by these Rules assigned to Solicitors Indemnity Fund Limited, including settlement and compromise and making of ex gratia payments and conduct of any proceedings arising in respect of such claim;

(f) to claim and recover reimbursement in respect of any sums paid by way of indemnity in any circumstances in which such reimbursement may under these Rules be claimed;

(g) to exercise any right of subrogation save where such rights are waived in accordance with these Rules;

(h) to maintain full and proper records and statistics (which subject to Rule 50, shall at all reasonable times be available on request to the Society for inspection and copying) as to the Fund and all aspects of its management and administration;

(i) to make to and review with the Council of the Society annually and at any other time that the Council may require, written and (if the Council so requires) oral reports as to the Fund and, subject to Rule 50, its management and administration, including *inter alia* recommendations as to the Contributions which are or may be required in respect of past, present and/or future Indemnity Periods and the circumstances in which, extent to which and conditions and exclusions subject to which indemnity should in any future Indemnity Period be afforded out of the Fund;

(j) to engage the assistance of any third party in respect of all or any aspect(s) of the management and administration of the Fund;

(k) to delegate to any third party all or any aspect(s) of the management and administration of the Fund;

(l) to institute and/or conduct such proceedings as it may consider necessary or appropriate for the due management and administration of the Fund in its own name or (subject to prior consent of the Society) in the name of the Society;

(m) to disburse and/or reimburse out of the Fund all administrative and legal and other costs, overheads, fees and other expenses and liabilities incurred in respect of the Fund, including without prejudice to the generality of the foregoing any such costs, overheads, fees and other expenses and liabilities incurred by the Society in respect of the establishment or maintenance, or the management, administration or protection, of the Fund;

(n) to disburse and/or reimburse out of the Fund payments for any educational, charitable or other useful purpose which in its opinion is likely directly or indirectly to lead to the reduction or prevention of claims on the Fund or otherwise to further the purpose or interests of the Fund;

29

(o) to disburse and/or reimburse out of the Fund the costs, fees and expenses of the handling after 31st August 1987 of claims and potential claims against Assureds notified under the Master Policies and Master Policy Certificates;

(p) to effect out of the Fund or by arrangement with third parties the funding pending reimbursement by Master Policy Insurers of such claims and potential claims and to bear out of the Fund the costs, fees and expenses incurred thereby.

50. USE OF INFORMATION

50.1 Without prejudice to the Society's power under Rule 8 to designate itself as the person responsible for holding, managing and administering the Fund, information and documents obtained by Solicitors Indemnity Fund Limited about any particular Practice or Member thereof in the course of investigating and handling any claim made or intimated or any circumstances notified as mentioned in Rule 13, may be utilised by Solicitors Indemnity Fund Limited for the purpose of preparation of general records, statistics, reports and recommendations (not identifying the particular Practice or Member) for or to the Society.

50.2 Such information and documents shall not otherwise be disclosed or available to the Society without the prior consent of the Practice (or any Subsequent or Successor Practice thereto) or Member concerned, except:

(a) where Solicitors Indemnity Fund Limited or the Society shall have reason to suspect dishonesty on the part of any Practice, Previous, Subsequent or Successor Practice or any Member or former Member thereof;

(b) where Solicitors Indemnity Fund Limited considers that there has been any non-compliance with Rule 19.7.

50.3 Any information and documents held by Solicitors Indemnity Fund Limited about a particular Practice or Member thereof may be disclosed or available to the Society without the prior consent of the Practice (or any Subsequent or Successor Practice thereto) or Member concerned where the Society has been requested by any Practice, Subsequent or Successor Practice or Member thereof to grant, amend or revoke any waiver under Rule 10 or to make a determination under Rule 47.

50.4 Solicitors Indemnity Fund Limited may give to the Society at any time and in such manner as it may determine information (whether or not obtained in the course of investigating and handling any claim made or intimated or any circumstances notified as mentioned in Rule 13) as to

(a) the failure to provide information in respect of any Practice as required by Part III or any material omission or inaccuracy in such information;

(b) the payment or non-payment in respect of any Practice of any Contribution or Value Added Tax due and payable in accordance with these Rules;

together with a copy of any relevant Certificate, Notice of Succession or other notice under Part III and of any notice calculating or specifying any Contribution due or payable.

50.5 Solicitors Indemnity Fund Limited may pass to the Society the name of any Practice (including any Subsequent, Successor or Previous Practice) or any

Member or former Member thereof in circumstances where Solicitors Indemnity Fund Limited has cause for concern having regard to:

(i) the nature, incidence or value of paid and/or reserved claims in respect of any such Practice or Member; or

(ii) the existence of circumstances which are considered by the Fund to create an increased risk of claims occurring in respect of that Practice or Member; or

(iii) failure on the part of a Practice or Member thereof to comply with their obligations under these Rules;

and for the purposes of paragraphs (ii) and (iii) above Solicitors Indemnity Fund Limited shall have the power to determine criteria which would indicate the likelihood of an increased risk of claims occurring and to specify those obligations in respect of which a failure to comply could form the basis for Solicitors Indemnity Fund Limited to pass on information.

50.6　　In the exercise of the powers set out in Rule 50.5 Solicitors Indemnity Fund Limited may give details to the Society of the reasons for the decision to pass the name of the Practice or Member thereof to the Society including, in appropriate cases, releasing documentary information provided that no such documentary information will be released which could breach the general duty of confidentiality owed by a Practice or Member thereof to a client or former client.

29

PART VII – COMPLAINTS AND DISCIPLINE

Chapter 30

Office for the Supervision of Solicitors

30.01 Role of the OSS

The Office for the Supervision of Solicitors (OSS) – formerly the Solicitors Complaints Bureau, is the Law Society's independent complaints handling arm. It also deals with a number of related regulatory matters. The powers of the OSS derive from statute and the Society's Charter. They are delegated by the Council under section 79 of the Solicitors Act 1974 to the Compliance and Supervision Committee and to the senior staff of the OSS. The committee similarly delegates powers to various sub-committees.

30.02 Investigation of complaints

1. The OSS investigates and takes action on complaints and concerns about:
    ▶ professional misconduct; and
    ▶ inadequate professional services.

Professional misconduct

2. Generally, complaints of misconduct are investigated through correspondence. The investigation may be concluded by an Assistant Director of the OSS. If this is not possible or appropriate a formal decision will be made by the Compliance and Supervision Committee.

3. The Compliance and Supervision Committee issued, in [1998] *Gazette*, 18 March, the following statement on the standard of proof to be used when investigating matters:

    'The correct standard of proof to apply is the flexible civil standard taking account of the gravity of the allegations, the potential consequences and the context of the particular case. Serious allegations against solicitors involving elements such as alleged dishonesty, or deceit, or matters of a similar nature must be proved to a level which admits no reasonable doubt, whilst less serious allegations need to be proved on the balance of probabilities. The committee when setting out decisions, will make it clear how it has applied the standard of proof in the circumstances.

    Where the committee decides to refer a matter to the Solicitors Disciplinary Tribunal it needs to be satisfied that there is a *prima facie* case against the solicitor and that the Tribunal is the appropriate forum for the determination of that case.'

Inadequate professional services (IPS)

4. In IPS cases the OSS will first establish whether the complaint has been dealt with by the firm. If not, the OSS will require the complainant to refer it to the firm under the complaints procedure which a solicitor must establish under practice rule 15 (see **13.01**, p.265).

5. If the matter cannot be resolved speedily by the firm, the OSS will attempt to conciliate it. If this procedure fails, a formal decision will be made.

6. Failure by the firm to attempt to resolve a complaint under practice rule 15 may result in additional compensation being awarded, if a formal decision has to be made (see **30.04** note 4(b), p.845).

Complaints from third parties

7. The OSS can investigate complaints alleging professional misconduct from persons, including solicitors, who are not clients of the solicitor complained of, provided the complaint raises a *prima facie* issue of professional misconduct. However, investigation may show that the action to which the complainant refers was taken properly by the solicitor in the best interests of his or her own client.

8. In some circumstances the OSS can deal with IPS complaints from third parties (e.g. residuary beneficiaries).

9. For solicitors' general obligations to third parties, see Chapter 17, p.346.

30

30.03 Obstruction of complaints and agreements to settle

Professional misconduct

1. It is unbefitting conduct for a solicitor to seek to preclude his or her client or former client from reporting the solicitor's conduct to the OSS.

2. A solicitor must not accept instructions which involve any agreement whereby the OSS is precluded from investigating the conduct of a solicitor or a solicitor's clerk.

3. A solicitor must not demand or accept payment for refraining from reporting an alleged breach of professional conduct to the OSS.

4. Complaints to the Society or the OSS about the professional conduct of solicitors are protected by qualified privilege. It is improper for a solicitor to issue defamation proceedings in respect of material contained in a complaint made to the Society or the OSS, unless the solicitor is prepared to allege malice. If it comes to the attention of the OSS that any solicitor has acted in this way, it will be treated as *prima facie* evidence of professional misconduct and dealt with accordingly.

5. A solicitor must not victimise or bring improper pressure to bear on complainants or would-be complainants.

Inadequate professional services

6. Where a client is separately represented in reaching a settlement involving IPS, it is not professional misconduct to propose an agreement concerning IPS that is in full and final settlement. The client should be advised that this does not prevent him or her from making an IPS complaint to the OSS, but that the OSS will take into account the terms of the agreement when deciding whether to initiate an investigation.

7. It is not improper for a solicitor for either party to a dispute about the standard of service to accept instructions to offer a settlement on similar terms.

30.04 Powers of the OSS

1. A solicitor is obliged to deal promptly and substantively with correspondence from the OSS. Failure to answer commonly results in disciplinary proceedings and failure to give a sufficient and satisfactory explanation of the solicitor's conduct may make the solicitor subject to sections 12 and 13A of the Solicitors Act 1974 by virtue of section 12(1)(e) – see Annex 2A at p.43. For the effect of sections 12 and 13A, see note 4(d)–(e) below.

2.   The OSS has the power to direct a solicitor to produce a file irrespective of the client's consent (see section 44B of the Solicitors Act 1974). No advance notice is required.

3.   Failure to comply with a decision of the Compliance and Supervision Committee (or one of its sub-committees) or one made by staff of the OSS under delegated powers can in itself amount to professional misconduct and commonly results in a referral to the Solicitors Disciplinary Tribunal.

4.   The powers of the OSS in respect of professional misconduct and IPS include the following:

(a)   to reprimand the solicitor for professional misconduct;

(b)   on a finding of inadequate professional services (see section 37A of and Schedule 1A to the Solicitors Act 1974):

(i)   to disallow all or part of the solicitor's costs;

(ii)   to direct the solicitor to rectify an error at his or her expense;

(iii) to direct the solicitor to pay compensation to the client up to a limit of £1,000;

(iv) to direct the solicitor to take at his or her expense such other action in the interests of the client as the OSS may specify;

(c)   to require a solicitor to pay interest under rule 24 of the Solicitors' Accounts Rules 1998 (see Annex 28B at p.709);

(d)   to refuse a practising certificate or issue a conditional certificate, under section 12 of the Solicitors Act 1974 (see Annex 2A, p.42);

(e)   to impose conditions on a solicitor's current practising certificate under section 13A of the Solicitors Act 1974;

(f)   to suspend, withdraw or impose conditions on an investment business certificate (see rule 5 of the Solicitors' Investment Business Rules 1995 – Annex 27B at p.567);

(g)   to recover money and papers for the client or his or her new solicitor on a complaint of undue delay (see Schedule 1, paragraph 3 of the Solicitors Act 1974 – Annex 30A at p.851);

(h)   to order an inspection of accounts under rule 34 of the Solicitors' Accounts Rules 1998 (see Annex 28B at p.719) or rule 15 of the Solicitors' Overseas Practice Rules 1990 (see Annex 9A at p.187);

(i)   to disqualify an accountant from giving an accountant's report under rule 37(3) of the Solicitors' Accounts Rules 1998 (see Annex 28B at p.723);

(j)   to intervene in a solicitor's practice under Schedule 1 to the Solicitors Act 1974 (see Annex 30A, p.850);

(k)   to institute disciplinary proceedings before the Solicitors Disciplinary Tribunal (see Chapter 31, p.856).

30

30.05 Interventions

The Compliance and Supervision Committee can exercise the powers contained in Schedule 1 to the Solicitors Act 1974 (see Annex 30A, p.850) to intervene in a solicitor's practice. These powers are often exercised by the Chairman under delegated powers, because of the urgency of the case. Examples of the circumstances in which these powers may be exercised are:

(a) where there is reason to suspect dishonesty on the part of a solicitor or a member of his or her staff or the personal representative of a deceased solicitor;

(b) where there is failure to comply with the Solicitors' Accounts Rules;

(c) where a solicitor is practising uncertificated; and

(d) where a sole practitioner is incapacitated by, for example, illness, accident or age.

30.06 Solicitor's bankruptcy

1. When a solicitor is adjudged bankrupt, his or her practising certificate is automatically suspended by virtue of section 15(1) of the Solicitors Act 1974. Bankruptcy also triggers the operation of section 12 of the Act (see section 12(1)(h)–(i) in Annex 2A at p.43), and is a ground for possible intervention (see Schedule 1, paragraph 1(1)(d) in Annex 30A, p.850).

2. A solicitor who has been, or is about to be, adjudged bankrupt can apply to the OSS for the reinstatement of his or her practising certificate. Applications are normally determined by the Compliance and Supervision Committee (or an appropriate sub-committee). If a certificate is restored it will usually be issued subject to a condition – see Annex 3H, p.141, for further information.

30.07 Remuneration certificates

1. Remuneration certificates are issued under the Solicitors' (Non-Contentious Business) Remuneration Order 1994 (see **14.08**, p.280 and Annex 14D, p.296). In a non-contentious matter, a client or 'other entitled' person (a residuary beneficiary immediately entitled to a share of the estate where the only personal representatives are solicitors) may require a solicitor to obtain a remuneration certificate in respect of a bill where the profit costs are not more than £50,000. Solicitors should apply to the Remuneration Certificates Section at the OSS (for contact details see p.xv). A remuneration certificate states what would be a fair and reasonable charge, which then becomes the amount payable. This does not affect the right to taxation of the bill. The client must normally pay half of the profit costs, all the VAT, and any disbursements before an application can proceed.

2.   Failure to apply for a certificate, if requested, is professional misconduct and may also give rise to a finding of IPS and to an award of compensation.

30.08   Compensation Fund

Obligation to contribute to the Fund

1.   The Society maintains the Solicitors' Compensation Fund pursuant to section 36 of and Schedule 2 to the Solicitors Act 1974. The Fund is administered by the OSS. For the obligation to contribute to the Fund see:

▶   **2.04** notes 5–6, p.36 (solicitors);

▶   **3.17** note 14, p.87 (recognised bodies); and

▶   **8.02** note 4, p.175 (registered foreign lawyers).

Information pack

2.   Application forms and an information pack, which includes the Solicitors' Compensation Fund Rules 1995 and other information on making claims, may be obtained from the Compensation Fund Section at the OSS (for contact details see p.xv).

The purpose of the Fund

3.   The Fund is used to enable the Society:

(a)   to make grants to those who have suffered loss by reason of the dishonesty of a solicitor, or an employee in connection with a solicitor's practice, or in connection with a trust of which a solicitor is a trustee. Grants may also be made in the event of hardship suffered as a result of a solicitor failing to account for monies due. For details see section 36(2)–(3) of the Solicitors Act 1974;

(b)   to make grants in similar circumstances arising from the practice of a recognised body. For details see paragraph 6(2)–(3) of Schedule 2 to the Administration of Justice Act 1985;

(c)   to make grants in similar circumstances arising from the practice of a registered foreign lawyer as a member of a multi-national partnership. For details see paragraph 6 of Schedule 14 to the Courts and Legal Services Act 1990 and rule 4 of the Solicitors' Compensation Fund Rules 1995.

4.   The Fund is a discretionary fund. Decisions are made by senior staff and the Compliance and Supervision Committee. There is a wide discretion to make payments, but the main purpose of the Fund is to replace money that a practitioner has misappropriated within the course of practice. Personal or

30

trading debts are not usually covered. For more details as to the circumstances in which grants will normally be paid, see the Schedule to the Solicitors' Compensation Fund Rules 1995.

5. The Fund is a fund of last resort. Thus, no grant will be made where an applicant is otherwise indemnified against loss, for example by an insurance policy; nor where the loss is capable of being made good by recourse to any other person.

6. Losses arising from the dishonesty of a partner or an employee will normally be recoverable from the Solicitors' Indemnity Fund (see **29.01** note 12, p.785). A grant may, however, be made out of the Compensation Fund in respect of such part of an applicant's claim which lies within the firm's 'deductible' (excess) if the partners are unable to meet this from their own resources.

7. The Compensation Fund does not generally underwrite a solicitor's undertaking. A grant may, however, be made if the committee is satisfied that the claim arises out of an undertaking given with dishonest intent by a solicitor in the course of his or her practice.

8. Counsel and professional or other agents are entitled to apply for a grant out of the Fund if it can be established that the solicitor concerned had been put in funds by the client to pay counsel or the agent, or had received a sufficient sum on account of costs generally out of which the fees could have been paid, and that the solicitor misappropriated or otherwise failed to account for the funds.

9. If a grant is authorised, a further discretionary payment is normally made in respect of interest and the reasonable legal costs incurred by the applicant (see rules 9–10 of the Solicitors' Compensation Fund Rules 1995).

10. In most cases the committee will refuse to make a grant which would result in a total of more than £1,000,000 (inclusive of costs and interest) being paid from the Fund, or from the Fund and the Indemnity Fund together, in respect of any individual matter – see rule 11 of, and paragraph 15 to the Schedule to the Solicitors' Compensation Fund Rules 1995.

11. The committee expects an applicant to show utmost good faith in any application, and any grant may be reduced or refused in the light of evidence of bad faith.

30.09 Legal Services Ombudsman

1. The Legal Services Ombudsman (LSO) is appointed by the Lord Chancellor under section 21 of the Courts and Legal Services Act 1990 with a primary function of assessing the adequacy of complaints handling procedures of the Law Society and other legal professions. It is generally exercised by investigating referrals by individuals who complain and by providing remedies where appropriate.

2. The LSO's main powers in relation to solicitors are to recommend that the OSS reconsider the complaint and/or that the OSS or practitioner complained of should pay compensation to the complainant. There is no limit to the compensation which may be recommended.

3. The LSO's recommendations are not enforceable at law. If the OSS or the practitioner concerned does not comply with a recommendation, the LSO can require them to publicise failure to comply and the reasons for it at their own expense. If they do not, the LSO may recover the cost.

4. Most investigations are confined to the handling of complaints by professional bodies and do not extend to the merits. They can usually be dealt with by reference to the OSS file on the complaint. The LSO may, however, extend investigations to the merits and may require any person to furnish such information or documents as the LSO considers relevant to the investigation. The LSO also has powers of the High Court to require attendance and examination of witnesses.

5. The LSO may investigate any allegation properly made in writing which must normally be done within three months of the date on which the OSS told the complainant of its decision. The LSO may, however, accept allegations outside that time limit if there are special reasons.

6. The LSO has no jurisdiction to investigate allegations made by practitioners about the way in which the OSS has handled complaints about them.

30

Solicitors Act 1974

Schedule 1 (intervention in solicitor's practice)

(with consolidated amendments to May 1995)

Part I – Circumstances in which Society may intervene

1. (1)   Subject to sub-paragraph (2), the powers conferred by Part II of this Schedule shall be exercisable where –

   (a)   the Council have reason to suspect dishonesty on the part of –

      (i)   a solicitor, or

      (ii)   an employee of a solicitor, or

      (iii) the personal representatives of a deceased solicitor,

      in connection with that solicitor's practice or in connection with any trust of which that solicitor is or formerly was a trustee;

   (b)   the Council consider that there has been undue delay on the part of the personal representatives of a deceased solicitor who immediately before his death was practising as a sole solicitor in connection with that solicitor's practice or in connection with any controlled trust;

   (c)   the Council are satisfied that a solicitor has failed to comply with rules made by virtue of section 32 or 37(2)(c);

   (d)   a solicitor has been adjudged bankrupt or has made a composition or arrangement with his creditors;

   (e)   a solicitor has been committed to prison in any civil or criminal proceedings;

   (ee) the Council are satisfied that a sole solicitor is incapacitated by illness or accident to such an extent as to be unable to attend to his practice;

   (f)   the powers conferred by section 104 of the Mental Health Act 1959 or section 98 of the Mental Health Act 1983 (emergency powers) or section 105 of the said Act of 1959 or section 99 of the said Act of 1983 (appointment of receiver) have been exercised in respect of a solicitor;

   (g)   the name of a solicitor has been removed from or struck off the roll or a solicitor has been suspended from practice;

   (h)   the Council are satisfied that a sole solicitor has abandoned his practice;

(i)   the Council are satisfied that a sole solicitor is incapacitated by age to such an extent as to be unable to attend to his practice;

(j)   any power conferred by this Schedule has been exercised in relation to a sole solicitor by virtue of sub-paragraph (1)(a) and he has acted as a sole solicitor within the period of eighteen months beginning with the date on which it was so exercised;

(k)   the Council are satisfied that a person has acted as a solicitor at a time when he did not have a practising certificate which was in force;

(l)   the Council are satisfied that a solicitor has failed to comply with any condition, subject to which his practising certificate was granted or otherwise has effect, to the effect that he may act as a solicitor only –

    (i)   in employment which is approved by the Society in connection with the imposition of that condition;

    (ii)   as a member of a partnership which is so approved;

    (iii)   as an officer of a body recognised by the Council of the Law Society under section 9 of the Administration of Justice Act 1985 and so approved; or

    (iv)   in any specified combination of those ways.

(2)   The powers conferred by Part II of this Schedule shall only be exercisable under sub-paragraph (1)(c) if the Society has given the solicitor notice in writing that the Council are satisfied that he has failed to comply with rules specified in the notice and also (at the same or any later time) notice that the powers conferred by Part II of this Schedule are accordingly exercisable in his case.

2.   On the death of a sole solicitor paragraphs 6 to 8 shall apply to the client accounts of his practice.

3.   The powers conferred by Part II of this Schedule shall also be exercisable, subject to paragraphs 5(4) and 10(3), where –

(a)   a complaint is made to the Society that there has been undue delay on the part of a solicitor in connection with any matter in which the solicitor or his firm was instructed on behalf of a client or with any controlled trust; and

(b)   the Society by notice in writing invites the solicitor to give an explanation within a period of not less than 8 days specified in the notice; and

(c)   the solicitor fails within that period to give an explanation which the Council regard as satisfactory; and

(d)   the Society gives notice of the failure to the solicitor and (at the same or any later time) notice that the powers conferred by Part II of this Schedule are accordingly exercisable.

4.   (1)   Where the powers conferred by Part II of this Schedule are exercisable in relation to a solicitor, they shall continue to be exercisable after his death or after his name has been removed from or struck off the roll.

(2)   The references to the solicitor or his firm in paragraphs 5(1), 6(2) and (3), 8, 9(1) and (5) and 10(1) include, in any case where the solicitor has died, references to his personal representatives.

30

Part II – Powers exercisable on intervention

Money

5. (1) The High Court, on the application of the Society, may order that no payment shall be made without the leave of the court by any person (whether or not named in the order) of any money held by him (in whatever manner and whether it was received before or after the making of the order) on behalf of the solicitor or his firm.

(2) No order under this paragraph shall take effect in relation to any person to whom it applies unless the Society has served a copy of the order on him (whether or not he is named in it) and, in the case of a bank or other financial institution, has indicated at which of its branches the Society believes that the money to which the order relates is held.

(3) A person shall not be treated as having disobeyed an order under this paragraph by making a payment of money if he satisfies the court that he exercised due diligence to ascertain whether it was money to which the order related but nevertheless failed to ascertain that the order related to it.

(4) This paragraph does not apply where the powers conferred by this Part of this Schedule are exercisable by virtue of paragraph 3.

6. (1) Without prejudice to paragraph 5, if the Council pass a resolution to the effect that any sums of money to which this paragraph applies, and the right to recover or receive them, shall vest in the Society, all such sums shall vest accordingly (whether they were received by the person holding them before or after the Council's resolution) and shall be held by the Society on trust to exercise in relation to them the powers conferred by this Part of this Schedule and subject thereto upon trust for the persons beneficially entitled to them.

(2) This paragraph applies –

    (a) where the powers conferred by this paragraph are exercisable by virtue of paragraph 1, to all sums of money held by or on behalf of the solicitor or his firm in connection with his practice or with any trust of which he is or formerly was a trustee;

    (b) where they are exercisable by virtue of paragraph 2, to all sums of money in any client account; and

    (c) where they are exercisable by virtue of paragraph 3, to all sums of money held by or on behalf of the solicitor or his firm in connection with the trust or other matter to which the complaint relates.

(3) The Society shall serve on the solicitor or his firm and on any other person having possession of sums of money to which this paragraph applies a certified copy of the Council's resolution and a notice prohibiting the payment out of any such sums of money.

(4) Within 8 days of the service of a notice under sub-paragraph (3), the person on whom it was served, on giving not less than 48 hours' notice in writing to the Society and (if the notice gives the name of the solicitor instructed by the Society) to that solicitor, may apply to the High Court for an order directing the Society to withdraw the notice.

(5) If the court makes such an order, it shall have power also to make such other order with respect to the matter as it may think fit.

(6)   If any person on whom a notice has been served under sub-paragraph (3) pays out sums of money at a time when such payment is prohibited by the notice, he shall be guilty of an offence and liable on summary conviction to a fine not exceeding level 3 on the standard scale.

7.   (1)   If the Society takes possession of any sum of money to which paragraph 6 applies, the Society shall pay it into a special account in the name of the Society or of a person nominated on behalf of the Society, or into a client account of a solicitor nominated on behalf of the Society, and any such person or solicitor shall hold that sum on trust to permit the Society to exercise in relation to it the powers conferred by this Part of this Schedule and subject thereto on trust for the persons beneficially entitled to it.

(2)   A bank or other financial institution at which a special account is kept shall be under no obligation to ascertain whether it is being dealt with properly.

8.   Without prejudice to paragraphs 5 to 7, if the High Court is satisfied, on an application by the Society, that there is reason to suspect that any person holds money on behalf of the solicitor or his firm, the court may require that person to give the Society information as to any such money and the accounts in which it is held.

Documents

9.   (1)   The Society may give notice to the solicitor or his firm requiring the production or delivery to any person appointed by the Society at a time and place to be fixed by the Society –

(a)   where the powers conferred by this Part of this Schedule are exercisable by virtue of paragraph 1, of all documents in the possession of the solicitor or his firm in connection with his practice or with any controlled trust; and

(b)   where they are exercisable by virtue of paragraph 3, of all documents in the possession of the solicitor or his firm in connection with the trust or other matters to which the complaint relates (whether or not they relate also to other matters).

(2)   The person appointed by the Society may take possession of any such documents on behalf of the Society.

(3)   Except in a case where an application has been made to the High Court under sub-paragraph (4), if any person having possession of any such documents refuses, neglects or otherwise fails to comply with a requirement under sub-paragraph (1), he shall be guilty of an offence and liable on summary conviction to a fine not exceeding level 3 on the standard scale.

(4)   The High Court, on the application of the Society, may order a person required to produce or deliver documents under sub-paragraph (1) to produce or deliver them to any person appointed by the Society at such time and place as may be specified in the order, and authorise him to take possession of them on behalf of the Society.

(5)   If on an application by the Society the High Court is satisfied that there is reason to suspect that documents in relation to which the powers conferred by sub-paragraph (1) are exercisable have come into the possession of some person other than the solicitor or his firm, the court may order that person to produce or deliver the documents to any person appointed by the Society at such time and place as may be specified in the order and authorise him to take possession of them on behalf of the Society.

30

(6)   On making an order under this paragraph, or at any later time, the court, on the application of the Society, may authorise a person appointed by the Society to enter any premises (using such force as is reasonably necessary) to search for and take possession of any documents to which the order relates.

(7)   The Society, on taking possession of any documents under this paragraph, shall serve upon the solicitor or personal representatives and upon any other person from whom they were received on the Society's behalf or from whose premises they were taken a notice that possession has been taken on the date specified in the notice.

(8)   Subject to sub-paragraph (9) a person upon whom a notice under sub-paragraph (7) is served, on giving not less than 48 hours' notice to the Society and (if the notice gives the name of the solicitor instructed by the Society) to that solicitor, may apply to the High Court for an order directing the Society to deliver the documents to such person as the applicant may require.

(9)   A notice under sub-paragraph (8) shall be given within 8 days of the service of the Society's notice under sub-paragraph (7).

(10)   Without prejudice to the foregoing provisions of this Schedule, the Society may apply to the High Court for an order as to the disposal or destruction of any documents in its possession by virtue of this paragraph or paragraph 10.

(11)   On an application under sub-paragraph (8) or (10), the Court may make such order as it thinks fit.

(12)   Except so far as its right to do so may be restricted by an order on an application under sub-paragraph (8) or (10), the Society may take copies of or extracts from any documents in its possession by virtue of this paragraph or paragraph 10 and require any person to whom it is proposed that such documents shall be delivered, as a condition precedent to delivery, to give a reasonable undertaking to supply copies or extracts to the Society.

Mail

10.   (1)   The High Court, on the application of the Society, may from time to time order that for such time not exceeding 18 months as the court thinks fit postal packets (as defined by section 87(1) of the Post Office Act 1953) addressed to the solicitor or his firm at any place or places mentioned in the order shall be directed to the Society or any person appointed by the Society at any other address there mentioned; and the Society, or that person on its behalf, may take possession of any such packets received at that address.

(2)   Where such an order is made the Society shall pay to the Post Office the like charges (if any), as would have been payable for the re-direction of the packets by virtue of any scheme made under section 28 of the Post Office Act 1969, if the addressee had permanently ceased to occupy the premises to which they were addressed and had applied to the Post Office to redirect them to him at the address mentioned in the order.

(3)   This paragraph does not apply where the powers conferred by this Part of this Schedule are exercisable by virtue of paragraph 3.

Trusts

11.   (1)   If the solicitor or his personal representative is a trustee of a controlled trust, the Society may apply to the High Court for an order for the appointment of a new trustee in substitution for him.

(2)   The Trustee Act 1925 shall have effect in relation to an appointment of a new trustee under this paragraph as it has effect in relation to an appointment under section 41 of that Act.

General

12.   The powers in relation to sums of money and documents conferred by this Part of this Schedule shall be exercisable notwithstanding any lien on them or right to their possession.

13.   Subject to any order for the payment of costs that may be made on an application to the court under this Schedule, any costs incurred by the Society for the purposes of this Schedule, including, without prejudice to the generality of this paragraph, the costs of any person exercising powers under this Part of this Schedule on behalf of the Society, shall be paid by the solicitor or his personal representatives and shall be recoverable from him or them as a debt owing to the Society.

14.   Where an offence under this Schedule committed by a body corporate is proved to have been committed with the consent or connivance of, or to be attributable to any neglect on the part of, any director, manager, secretary or other similar officer of the body corporate or any person who was purporting to act in any such capacity, he, as well as the body corporate, shall be guilty of that offence and shall be liable to be proceeded against and punished accordingly.

15.   Any application to the High Court under this Schedule may be disposed of in chambers.

16.   The Society may do all things which are reasonably necessary for the purpose of facilitating the exercise of its powers under this Schedule.

[NOTES

1.   As regards the exercise of the intervention powers in relation to a registered foreign lawyer and the practice of a multi-national partnership see paragraph 5 of Schedule 14 to the Courts and Legal Services Act 1990.

2.   As regards the exercise of the intervention powers in relation to a recognised body (i.e. an incorporated practice recognised under section 9 of the Administration of Justice Act 1985) see paragraphs 32–35 of Schedule 2 to the Administration of Justice Act 1985.]

30

Chapter 31

The Solicitors Disciplinary Tribunal

31.01 The Tribunal

1. The Solicitors Disciplinary Tribunal is independent of the Society and is established under section 46 of the Solicitors Act 1974. Its members are appointed by the Master of the Rolls and are either solicitors of not less than ten years' standing or lay members who must be neither solicitors nor barristers. For the purpose of hearing and determining applications, the Tribunal sits in divisions of three, comprising two solicitor members and one lay member.

2. The Tribunal, with the concurrence of the Master of the Rolls, makes rules governing its procedure and practice. The current rules are the Solicitors (Disciplinary Proceedings) Rules 1994 (S.I. 1994 no. 288).

3. The principal function of the Tribunal is to hear and determine applications in respect of solicitors relating to allegations of unbefitting conduct or breaches of the rules of professional conduct. The Tribunal also has jurisdiction in respect of registered foreign lawyers, recognised bodies (incorporated practices), solicitors' clerks and former clerks, and former solicitors.

4.   Disciplinary proceedings before the Tribunal are dealt with in sections 43–44, 46–48 and 54–55 of the Solicitors Act 1974, paragraphs 16–21 of Schedule 2 to the Administration of Justice Act 1985 and paragraphs 15–16 of Schedule 14 to the Courts and Legal Services Act 1990.

31.02   Applications to the Tribunal

1.   The vast majority of applications to the Tribunal are made by the Office for the Supervision of Solicitors (OSS) on behalf of the Society but, except in those instances under the Act where applications are limited to the Society alone, it is open to anyone to make an application to the Tribunal without recourse to the Society.

2.   Applications are lodged with the clerk to the Tribunal and the Tribunal's first duty is to determine whether there is a *prima facie* case for the respondent to answer. The Tribunal will hold a pre-listing meeting when the Tribunal endeavours to ascertain whether or not allegations are admitted, the probable length of the hearing and dates when the parties are not available. At this meeting a hearing date is allocated.

31.03   The hearing

1.   The Tribunal normally hears applications in public. Parties may be represented or may appear in person, and may call witnesses. Evidence before the Tribunal is given on oath and it has power to accept affidavit evidence.

2.   In the event of any party failing to appear at the hearing, the Tribunal may dispose of the case in the party's absence.

31.04   Findings and orders

The Tribunal's order is pronounced immediately after the hearing, when a written copy is handed to the parties. It is usually filed with the Law Society the same day. Written findings are produced in general some four to six weeks after the hearing. They are also filed with the Society.

31.05   Powers of the Tribunal

The Tribunal's powers in relation to solicitors are defined by section 47 of the Solicitors Act 1974. The Tribunal may *inter alia*:

   (a)   strike a solicitor off the roll;

   (b)   suspend a solicitor from practice indefinitely or for a specified period;

31

(c)   fine a solicitor up to £5,000 for every allegation proved;

(d)   exclude a solicitor from legal aid work permanently or for a specified period;

(e)   in the case of a former solicitor whose name has been voluntarily removed from the roll, prohibit his or her restoration to the roll except by further order of the Tribunal;

(f)   order any party to pay costs or a contribution towards costs.

31.06   Registered foreign lawyers

In the case of registered foreign lawyers, the Tribunal's powers are set out in Schedule 14, paragraph 15 to the Courts and Legal Services Act 1990. A registered foreign lawyer may be struck off the register, suspended or fined.

31.07   Recognised bodies

The Tribunal's powers in respect of recognised bodies (incorporated practices) are set out in Schedule 2, paragraph 18 to the Administration of Justice Act 1985. The Tribunal may revoke a body's recognition or impose a fine.

31.08   Solicitors' clerks

1.   Section 43 of the Solicitors Act 1974 (see Annex 3A at p.93) empowers the Society to make an application to the Tribunal for an order controlling the employment of a person who is or was a clerk to a solicitor and:

(a)   has been convicted of a criminal offence which discloses such dishonesty that, in the opinion of the Society, it would be undesirable for that person to be employed by a solicitor in connection with his or her practice, or

(b)   in the opinion of the Society, has occasioned or been a party to, with or without the connivance of the solicitor to whom he or she is or was a clerk, an act or default in relation to the solicitor's practice, which involved conduct on the part of the clerk of such a nature that, in the opinion of the Society, it would be undesirable for him or her to be employed by a solicitor in connection with his or her practice.

2.   A solicitor who employs, or formerly employed, a clerk who has been convicted of dishonesty, or who has committed an act or default in relation to the solicitor's practice justifying an application to the Tribunal, is under a professional duty to report these circumstances to the OSS.

3.   Where a section 43 order is made in respect of a clerk or former clerk to a solicitor, the Tribunal may order payment of the costs of such application

to be made by the clerk, or by his or her employer or former employer if joined as a party to the application.

4.   The effect of a section 43 order is to vest in the Society the control of any employment of the clerk in connection with a solicitor's practice. Any solicitor wishing to employ the clerk must first obtain the written consent of the Society. The Compliance and Supervision Committee consider applications for such consent and it is their practice to seek the view of the appropriate local law society and former employers.

5.   When a solicitor employed in local government or in commerce or industry seeks to engage a clerk who is subject to a section 43 order, the consent of the Society is required.

6.   Section 44 of the Solicitors Act 1974 provides that a clerk who acts in contravention of a section 43 order is guilty of an offence. Any solicitor who knowingly contravenes the provisions of such an order, or the conditions imposed by the Society when application is made to employ a clerk to whom it applies, may be the subject of complaint to the Tribunal at the instance of the Society.

31.09   Applications for restoration to the roll

1.   The Tribunal has jurisdiction to restore to the roll a former solicitor who has been struck off the roll, or in respect of whom a direction has been made under section 47(2)(g) of the Solicitors Act 1974 (see **31.05** note (e), p.858).

2.   It is very difficult to establish a case for restoration, and applications are granted only rarely. The principles applied by the Tribunal when considering applications for restoration come from:

   ▶   the established practice of the Tribunal;

   ▶   decisions of the Master of the Rolls on appeals from the Tribunal (all unreported but summarised below); and

   ▶   the decision in *Bolton* v. *The Law Society* 1 W.L.R. 512; [1994] 2 All E.R. 486.

   In the case of *Bolton*, the Court of Appeal held:

   'Only infrequently, particularly in recent years, has [the Tribunal] been willing to order the restoration to the roll of a solicitor against whom serious dishonesty had been established, even after a passage of years, and even where the solicitor has made every effort to re-establish himself and redeem his reputation.'

   And also:

   'The second purpose [of the Tribunal's orders] is the most fundamental of all: to maintain the reputation of the solicitors'

31

profession as one in which every member, of whatever standing, may be trusted to the ends of the earth. To maintain this reputation and sustain public confidence in the integrity of the profession it is often necessary that those guilty of serious lapses are not only expelled but denied re-admission.... A profession's most valuable asset is its collective reputation and the confidence which it inspires.

Because orders made by the Tribunal are not primarily punitive, it follows that the considerations which would ordinarily weigh in mitigation of punishment have less effect on the exercise of this jurisdiction than on the ordinary run of sentences imposed in criminal cases. It often happens that a solicitor appearing before the Tribunal can adduce a wealth of glowing tributes from his professional brethren. He can often show that for him and his family the consequences of striking off or suspension would be little short of tragic. Often he will say, convincingly, that he has learned his lesson and will not offend again. On applying for restoration after striking off, all these points may be made, and the former solicitor may also be able to point to real efforts made to re-establish himself and redeem his reputation. All these matters are relevant and should be considered. *But none of them touches the essential issue, which is the need to maintain among members of the public a well-founded confidence that any solicitor whom they instruct will be a person of unquestionable integrity, probity and trustworthiness... The reputation of the profession is more important than the fortunes of any individual member. Membership of a profession brings many benefits, but that is part of the price.'* [Emphasis added]

3.   The following additional principles emerge from decisions of the Tribunal and successive Masters of the Rolls:

(a)   An application for restoration is not to be regarded as an appeal against the decision to strike off.

(b)   The successful applicant must satisfy the Tribunal not only that he or she is personally fit to be admitted (a matter demonstrated by rehabilitation, support from the profession and, for example, a willing solicitor employer), but much more importantly 'apparent fitness' that he or she is fit, *in the eyes of a member of the public*, to be re-admitted as a solicitor.

(c)   The applicant must satisfy the Tribunal that the public would consider that any profession would be proud to have the applicant as a member, and that public confidence in the profession, as a whole, would not be damaged by the successful application. In the light of the comments made by the Court of Appeal in *Bolton* it is extremely unlikely that any solicitor struck off for dishonesty would be able to satisfy this test.

(d)   As restoration to the roll is an exceptional course, it is necessary to demonstrate that the original offences occurred in exceptional circumstances (this is not to be confused with exceptional rehabilitation).

(e) Account will be taken of any continuing loss to the profession, either by the Compensation Fund or the Indemnity Fund, by reason of the applicant's defaults, and the extent to which the applicant has repaid those debts.

(f) As the Tribunal makes orders for suspension from practice for up to five years, any application, however meritorious, will be almost bound to be regarded as premature if it is made within six years of the order for striking off. Most applications are not made until at least ten years have passed.

4. A summary of the unreported decisions of the Master of the Rolls from which many of the above principles are drawn can be found in the current edition of *Cordery on Solicitors*.

31.10   Appeals

1. Appeals from the Tribunal lie to the High Court or to the Master of the Rolls, as provided by section 49 of the Solicitors Act 1974.

2. The rules relating to appeals are in Order 106 of the Rules of the Supreme Court, and in the Master of the Rolls (Appeals and Applications) Regulations 1991 (see Annex 2D, p.55).

31.11   Disciplinary role of the Court

1. The Supreme Court – i.e. the High Court, the Crown Court and the Court of Appeal – has inherent jurisdiction over solicitors as officers of the Court. See section 50 of the Solicitors Act 1974.

2. Sections 51–55 of the Act deal with disciplinary proceedings before the High Court and the Court of Appeal.

3. In addition, the Solicitors Act 1974 and other statutes give the courts a number of specific functions and powers in relation to the regulation and discipline of solicitors.

31

Index

Notes: **All references are to pages**
An index to the accounts rules is at pp.748–770
A list of contact details is at p.xv

Index

An index to the accounts rules is at pp.748–770
A list of contact details is at p.xv

An index to the accounts rules is at pp.748–770
A list of contact details is at p.xv

Index

An index to the accounts rules is at pp.748–770
A list of contact details is at p.xv

An index to the accounts rules is at pp.748–770
A list of contact details is at p.xv

Index

An index to the accounts rules is at pp.748–770
A list of contact details is at p.xv

An index to the accounts rules is at pp.748–770
A list of contact details is at p.xv

Index

An index to the accounts rules is at pp.748–770
A list of contact details is at p.xv

An index to the accounts rules is at pp.748–770
A list of contact details is at p.xv

Index

An index to the accounts rules is at pp.748–770
A list of contact details is at p.xv

THE GUIDE TO THE PROFESSIONAL CONDUCT OF SOLICITORS 1999

An index to the accounts rules is at pp.748–770
A list of contact details is at p.xv

An index to the accounts rules is at pp.748–770
A list of contact details is at p.xv

An index to the accounts rules is at pp.748–770
A list of contact details is at p.xv

An index to the accounts rules is at pp.748–770
A list of contact details is at p.xv

An index to the accounts rules is at pp.748–770
A list of contact details is at p.xv

An index to the accounts rules is at pp.748–770
A list of contact details is at p.xv

An index to the accounts rules is at pp.748–770
A list of contact details is at p.xv

Index

An index to the accounts rules is at pp.748–770
A list of contact details is at p.xv

An index to the accounts rules is at pp.748–770
A list of contact details is at p.xv

Index

An index to the accounts rules is at pp.748–770
A list of contact details is at p.xv

An index to the accounts rules is at pp.748–770
A list of contact details is at p.xv

An index to the accounts rules is at pp.748–770
A list of contact details is at p.xv

An index to the accounts rules is at pp.748–770
A list of contact details is at p.xv

Index

An index to the accounts rules is at pp.748–770
A list of contact details is at p.xv

An index to the accounts rules is at pp.748–770
A list of contact details is at p.xv

Index

An index to the accounts rules is at pp.748–770
A list of contact details is at p.xv

An index to the accounts rules is at pp.748–770
A list of contact details is at p.xv

An index to the accounts rules is at pp.748–770
A list of contact details is at p.xv

Index

An index to the accounts rules is at pp.748–770
A list of contact details is at p.xv

An index to the accounts rules is at pp.748–770
A list of contact details is at p.xv